PREFATORY ADVERTISEMENT.

THOSE who have traced the progress of modern surgery to its true source will not fail to have discerned, in the principles which Hunter established, the germs of almost all the improvements which have been since introduced. Like a wise master-builder, he laid the foundation of the profession upon so broad a basis that it has withstood the attacks of adversaries and the versatility of public opinion not only uninjured, but with fresh accession of fame to himself, and (with few exceptions,) the most complete verification of his opinions. The strict inductive method of reasoning which he pursued, upon physiological subjects, led the way to juster modes of investigation; the zeal which he evinced stimulated many ardent followers in the path which he had opened, and the principles which he inculcated became the fruitful source of an infinity of practical applications, which were capable of being worked out by inferior minds. Thus the fame of Hunter, after a lapse of nearly half a century, is rather augmented than diminished by each succeeding year: the country which gave him birth is justly proud of his name; and those who have shown the deepest insight into the principles of their profession, and made the greatest improvements in the practice of it, have ever been most forward in celebrating his merits.

But it is unnecessary to enlarge further on the celebrity of this distinguished philosopher, of whom it has been truly said, that " he was the greatest man in the combined character of physiologist and surgeon that the whole annals of medicine can furnish *." For a more full account of the character of Hunter's genius, and the peculiarities of his works, the Editor begs leave to refer the reader to the ensuing memoir, in which the language of indiscriminate panegyric, so freely employed by his preceding biographers, has given place to the voice of truth. His merits have been weighed in a just balance, and the less favourable parts of his character, as a man and as a philosopher, pointed out without disguise.

The reconstruction and enlargement of the Hunterian Museum, together with the publication of well-digested catalogues of its contents, seem well calculated to extend the fame of its founder, as well as to fix it on a more rational foundation. To the Editor these circumstances have appeared to afford a favourable occasion for the re-publication of Mr. Hunter's writings, considering that as all his labours were directed to the elucidation of the laws of life, they can only be advantageously studied in their totality. Those,·

* Lawrence.

Merry Christmas 2012
to My dear friend
Pompous.

Given with fondest wishes from

Alison

x

The Works Of John Hunter V1: With Notes

John Hunter

THE

W O R K S

OF

JOHN HUNTER, F.R.S.

WITH

N O T E S.

EDITED BY

JAMES F. PALMER,

SENIOR SURGEON TO THE ST. GEORGE'S AND ST. JAMES'S DISPENSARY; FELLOW
OF THE ROYAL MEDICAL AND CHIRURGICAL SOCIETY OF LONDON, ETC.

IN FOUR VOLUMES,

ILLUSTRATED BY A VOLUME OF PLATES, IN QUARTO.

VOL. I.

LONDON:

PUBLISHED BY

LONGMAN, REES, ORME, BROWN, GREEN, AND LONGMAN,

PATERNOSTER-ROW.

1835.

PRINTED BY RICHARD TAYLOR,
RED LION COURT, FLEET STREET.

JOHN HUNTER.

TO

THE GOVERNORS AND MEDICAL OFFICERS
OF St. GEORGE'S HOSPITAL

THE FOLLOWING EDITION

OF THE

COLLECTED WORKS OF JOHN HUNTER

IS RESPECTFULLY INSCRIBED

BY THEIR OBEDIENT

AND OBLIGED SERVANT,

J. F. PALMER.

London, September 1835.

therefore, who have familiarized themselves with his style and mode of thought, as displayed in his writings, possess the best clue to his museum ; as, on the other hand, those who have made themselves well acquainted with the contents of his museum, possess the best guide in the perusal of his works. The two may be regarded as forming necessary parts of that general undertaking in which the author was engaged ; his writings forming the text to his museum,—his museum the appropriate illustration of his writings.

It cannot but be a subject of deep regret to all those who have the interests of science or of their profession at heart, that no one should have undertaken to collect these writings before. Dispersed through scattered volumes of the Transactions of the Royal and other learned Societies, many of his most valuable papers have been unknown or neglected, or at least have been inaccessible to the great bulk of the profession ; while of those which have been published separately, some are nearly out of print and scarcely to be obtained, others are extremely incorrect, and the greater number are excluded from general circulation in consequence of their expensive form or inconvenient bulk. To remove these disadvantages, by presenting to the profession a cheap and correct edition of the author's *whole works,* has been one of the principal objects of the present edition.

It was considered that the utility of the work would be greatly promoted by an incorporation of the most important results of modern discoveries, in the form of foot notes; and in the prosecution of this part of his scheme the Editor has to acknowledge the able assistance of several distinguished friends, whose particular acquaintance with the subjects which they have respectively undertaken is well known to the public. As far as possible brevity has been consulted, and it is scarcely necessary to add, that each gentleman is alone responsible for the opinions contained in his own notes.

The illustrations to this edition (comprehending 348 figures, in 61 plates,) embrace the whole of those which accompanied the original publications, and, with the exception of those on the teeth, and two or three others, (which have been newly executed by Mr. Basire,) are impressions from the original plates, which have been re-touched, by the permission of the Council of the Royal College of Surgeons, wherever it was found necessary, from the Hunterian drawings and preparations. To these have been added several others, together with the celebrated engraving of Hunter by Sharp, after Sir Joshua Reynolds, and a medallion head taken from the author's bust in the Royal College of Surgeons, by Flaxman.

For the ability to render the work thus complete, the Editor is indebted to the learned Council of the Royal Society, to whom he is obliged for the use of the splendid engravings attached to Mr. Hunter's papers in the Philosophical Transactions, as well as to Sir Benjamin Brodie, for his prompt and liberal assistance in procuring him this permission. The Editor has particular satisfaction in expressing, in the most public manner, his grateful acknowledgements to both these parties.

The superiority of the present edition above all the preceding will appear from the following particulars :—

1. It embraces the *whole* of Mr. Hunter's published works.
2. It contains a full and collated copy of his Surgical and Croonian Lectures.
3. It is preceded by a new life of the author, containing original anecdotes, a critical disquisition concerning the character and writings of the author, and a summary exposition of his Museum ; to which has also been added Mr. Hunter's correspondence with Dr. Jenner and Sir Joseph Banks.
4. It is illustrated by the whole of the original engravings, to which several others have been added.
5. The whole work is accompanied by illustrative notes, with the purpose of supplying such deficiencies as the progress of science has rendered necessary.
6. The text has been corrected, the punctuation rectified, and the modern synonyms introduced. Obscurities (so far as they have appeared to depend on improprieties of expression,) have been obviated, and a copious index has been added to the whole.
7. The work has been printed in a clear and legible type, at the same time that the size and price of the Edition, and the manner of its publication, have been accommodated to the convenience of purchasers.

Having thus stated the design and object of the undertaking, it is hoped that the reader will not be disappointed in his expectations. The writer is well aware that the works of so great a master deserve a much more learned and critical Editor than he can pretend to be.　He begs, however, that it may be borne in mind, that so far as he is concerned, the work is not designed for those who have completed, but for those who are commencing their profession, and if he has failed in the execution of his task, he at least will have the satisfaction of having attempted a good work, which ought, in his opinion, to have been long since finished by a more able hand.

J. F. PALMER.

London, 38, Golden Square, September 1835.

CONTENTS OF VOL. I.

THE LIFE

OF

JOHN HUNTER, F.R.S.

BY

DREWRY OTTLEY.

LIFE OF JOHN HUNTER, F.R.S.

CONTENTS.

b

CHAPTER IV.

CHAPTER V.

CHAPTER VI.

CHAPTER VII.

INTRODUCTION TO THE LIFE.

BESIDES several brief memoirs of John Hunter which have appeared in various works of general biography, his life has already been written at considerable length by three different authors. Neither of these publications, however, furnishes us with more than a very imperfect account of his character, either as a private individual or as a Natural Philosopher.

The memoir by Sir Everard Home, prefixed to the work on Inflammation, is a scanty outline, almost wholly devoid of those characteristic anecdotes which form so essential a part of biography, and which his near connexion with Mr. Hunter would have enabled him to introduce; whilst nearly a third part of the whole is occupied with a detailed account of his various illnesses. The memoirs by Dr. Adams, and Mr. Jesse Foot, stand in singular contrast to each other, the former displaying everywhere marks of indiscriminate and unbounded partiality towards Mr. Hunter, the latter of bitter hostility, leading to the most flagrant misrepresentations of facts.

It appeared, therefore, if not necessary, at least ap-

propriate and desirable, to prefix to this new and re-
vised edition of his writings, a full and impartial account of this eminent man.

It is known to most of those who have kindly furnished information for this work, that Mr. Palmer did
at first intend himself to have undertaken the office of
Mr. Hunter's biographer; and he feels that some apology is due to those from whom he received communications under this supposition, for transferring the
task to another.

A want of sufficient time to execute the task was the
chief, if not the only reason, for his declining to
fulfil his intention; and it was only when satisfied that
such was the fact that I consented to engage in an
undertaking which I should gladly have seen continued
in more able hands.

In fulfilling the charge with which I have been entrusted, I have endeavoured to avail myself of all the
information respecting Mr. Hunter to be found in preceding publications; nor have I scrupled to adopt the
opinions of others regarding him where I thought
them correct.

In addition to the materials gathered from these
sources, I have been enabled to enrich this memoir
with the whole of the letters written by Mr. Hunter to
Dr. Jenner, during a friendship of more than twenty
years' duration. The originals of these, many of which
have already appeared in Dr. Baron's Life of Jenner,
were liberally communicated to Mr. Palmer by Robert
Fitzhardinge Jenner, Esq., of Berkeley.

The letters of Hunter to Sir Joseph Banks, as well as the interesting correspondence between the latter and Lord Auckland, respecting the Museum, were obtained through the kind intervention of Dawson Turner, Esq., of Yarmouth, to whom were entrusted the whole of Sir Joseph Banks's papers, by his executor, Sir Edward Knatchbull.

During the time that Mr. Palmer contemplated writing this life himself, he was at the pains to gather as much general information, and as many authentic anecdotes as possible, respecting the subject of this memoir, from his surviving friends and pupils. Of these anecdotes, many of which are highly characteristic, I have introduced by far the greater number; some which I have inserted may be thought so trivial as scarcely to have merited notice, but I have preferred rather to risk having this laid to my charge than to omit anything that might serve to illustrate Hunter's real character.

It will be seen from what I have said that my duty has been greatly lightened by having the already accumulated materials placed at my disposal; in addition to this I have to acknowledge the receipt of many valuable suggestions from my friend Mr. Palmer, respecting the various parts of the work,—suggestions from which I have rarely dissented, but which have often made me regret that circumstances prevented his being able himself to carry them into execution. How far I may have satisfactorily accomplished what I have undertaken, is not for me to judge. I will not pretend to indifference respecting the judgment that others may come to on the point; on the contrary, it would afford me much satisfaction to feel that my time had not been uselessly employed, but that I had succeeded in furnishing, what has been hitherto a desideratum in medical literature, a full and faithful account of the life of John Hunter.

DREWRY OTTLEY.

Exeter, March 3rd, 1835.

Sir

I beg leave to solicit your votes and interest for Mr Br Bailie my Nephew to succeed to an approaching vacancy of pay &c.

Your Most Obed Or Servant

John Hunter

THE LIFE

OF

JOHN HUNTER, F.R.S.

CHAPTER I.

1728 to 1751.

Mr. Hunter's birth and family ;—his early habits.—Dr. Wm. Hunter's rise to fame ;—his difficulties at the outset of life.—Mr. Hunter's arrival in London ;—his rapid acquisition of anatomical knowledge ;—becomes a pupil of Cheselden.—Cheselden's mode of operating for stone ;—his character and death.—Mr. Hunter's employments at this period ;—the advantages which he derives from his brother's society.

JOHN HUNTER was born at Long Calderwood, a small estate belonging to his family, situated about eight miles from Glasgow, in the parish of Kilbride East, Lanarkshire. His father, who appears to have been a small farmer living on his own estate, was descended from the ancient family of Hunter of Hunterston, a part of which property they had received from Robert the Second. His mother, whose maiden name was Paul, was the daughter of a respectable citizen of Glasgow, who held the office of Treasurer of that place. John, the youngest of ten children, was born in the year 1728, but on what day is not exactly known : the parish register states the 13th of February to have been his birthday, but he himself used to date it on the day following, and it is on the 14th, consequently, that his anniversary is celebrated at the College of Surgeons. We have no means of knowing whether either of his parents displayed any remarkable degree of talent, but it is certain that their offspring, both in the first and second generation, included an unusual number of persons eminent for their intellectual superiority*. Besides William, of whom mention will often be made in the course of these memoirs, another brother, James, the eldest of the family, possessed considerable abilities. He was intended for the Law, and completed his studies with a view to practising as a writer to the Signet in Edinburgh ; but on visiting London in his twenty-seventh year, he became so enamoured of the pursuits in which he found his brother William engaged, that he determined on devoting himself thenceforward to Physic. He immediately began the study of anatomy, and pursued it with such zeal and diligence, as speedily to attain considerable proficiency ; added to this he was possessed of peculiarly engaging manners, and displayed talents which, in Dr. Hunter's opinion, could not have failed to place him in the highest rank as a professional man in London. He was, however, attacked with a spitting of blood, which obliged him to relinquish his pursuits and return to his native place ; but the change proved of no avail, his complaint increased, and in no long time proved fatal.

* Mr. Wardrop, in his interesting life of Dr. Baillie, observes, that " the extent of talent united in his family and connexions was remarkable. He was not only the son of an able Professor, and nephew of the two Hunters, but his sister, Miss Joanna Baillie, has attained the most elevated rank in literature. Mrs. Baillie's sister was married to the late Sir Richard Croft, a man whose name is endeared in the recollection of many, as well for his manly and upright heart as for his professional celebrity : and Mr. Denman, who has distinguished himself so much at the bar, (now Lord Chief Justice,) was Dr. Baillie's brother-in-law." Of this tendency of genius to display itself in various members of the same family, many remarkable examples might be adduced from ancient as well as modern history.

One of the daughters, Dorothea, was married to Dr. James Baillie, Professor of Divinity in the University of Glasgow, and gave birth to the late Dr. Baillie, author of the 'Morbid Anatomy', and for many years the first physician in London; and to Mrs. Joanna Baillie, the highly gifted authoress of the Dramas on the Passions.

Agnes, another daughter, married Mr. Buchanan, a cabinet-maker at Glasgow. The other children all died young. Hunter's father died in 1738, at the age of 78, and John was thus left, at ten years of age, to the care of a fond, and apparently over-indulgent mother: the consequence was, that being in a great measure master of his own actions, and having little taste for books, he preferred engaging in country sports, to studying those elementary branches of knowledge which are best acquired in youth, and the want of which, as in the case before us, is sure to be severely felt in after-life.

When Hunter was about seventeen, he went to stay for a time at the house of his brother-in-law, Mr. Buchanan, under the hope of being able to assist in freeing him from the pecuniary difficulties into which his convivial habits and inattention to business had led him. It is probable that whilst here, Hunter, who prided himself on his manual dexterity, assisted his brother-in-law in his workshop, and that hence originated the statement made by Foot, that he had served as a millwright or a carpenter. His efforts, however, proved unavailing to accomplish the object of his visit, and Mr. Buchanan soon after resigned his business, and earned a scanty livelihood as a teacher of music, and clerk to an Episcopalian chapel in Glasgow.

During this time Wm. Hunter was rapidly pursuing his way to fame and fortune. After receiving a classical education at Glasgow University, and studying medicine for three years as a pupil of Cullen, who was at that time practising at Hamilton, he resorted to Edinburgh, where he spent a winter attending the schools of anatomy and medicine, and finally settled in London in 1741.

He was immediately engaged by Dr. Douglas to assist him in making preparations for a work on the bones, and also to take charge of the education of his son. With these views, accordingly, he became an inmate of the family; but on the death of Douglas, in the following year, he turned his thoughts to lecturing on anatomy, and immediately set about making preparations on a large scale for the purpose.

In 1745 a fair opening for his exertions offered, on the resignation of Wm. Sharpe, who had for several years past given a course of lectures on surgery, which he had undertaken at the express request of a number of naval surgeons. To this class Wm. Hunter succeeded, and after a time altered the plan of the lectures so as to render his course much more of an anatomical.than of a surgical nature *.

Previously to this time, Wm. Hunter's means had been very limited, for though the family property had fallen to him at his brother James's death, yet as his mother continued, with his permission, to reside on the estate, the surplus accruing to him could have been but small. In proof of this, Mr. Watson, formerly surgeon to the Westminster Hospital, and one of Wm. Hunter's earliest pupils,

---

* It was customary for the lecturers of that day to treat in one course on a number of subjects, sufficient to furnish matter for three or four distinct courses according to our present system; and the meagre amount of information afforded to their hearers may be judged of by the following facts, mentioned by Mr. Chevalier in his Hunterian Oration. Mr. Bromfield, who was surgeon to St. George's and a lecturer of considerable note, comprised anatomy and surgery in a course of thirty-six lectures. Dr. Nicholls, at whose school Wm. Hunter studied, professed to teach anatomy, physiology, and the general principles of pathology and midwifery in thirty-nine, and Mr. Nourse of St. Bartholomew's embraced "totam rem anatomicam" in twenty-three lectures.

used to relate, that as they were walking home together after the introductory lecture, the latter, who carried a bag containing seventy guineas, which he had received for entrance fees, remarked, that this was a larger sum than he had ever before been possessed of. Linnæus gives a similar account of his own slender beginnings where he says, "Exivi patriâ, triginti sex nummis aureis dives;" and it is related by Sir James Earle, that at Pott's death, a small box was found among his papers, containing a few pieces of money, not amounting to five pounds, being the whole which he ever received from the wreck of his father's fortune. Such anecdotes may serve to encourage those who, at the outset of their journey through life, chance to have their purses but slenderly furnished : numbers more might be found by a reference to the lives of eminent men in all professions, many of whom, though they have afterwards reaped a bountiful share of the favours of Fortune, were doubtless obliged, on their first starting in life, to have recourse to shifts quite as curious as those of Johnson's Irish friend, who in describing how a man may live respectably in London on thirty pounds a year, allots ten for the expenses of clothes, and provides that all visits are to be paid on *clean shirt days*.

Wm. Hunter had many difficulties to overcome in establishing his anatomical school ; he was the first surgeon, unconnected with an hospital, who had lectured on anatomy*, and no one had attempted it on a scale at all equal

* It was not until 1745 that the alliance between barbers and surgeons was happily dissolved : before this time, any surgeon dissecting a body out of their Hall was liable to a fine of ten pounds. Amongst other privileges, they possessed the right of claiming annually the bodies of four executed felons, which probably led Dr. Caius to choose the Barber-Surgeons' Hall, to deliver his anatomical lectures in, soon after their incorporation in 1540. From this time to the dissolution of the company, their readers of anatomy were, with very few exceptions, chosen from the College of Physicians, to whom, with the excep-

to what he proposed : his predecessors had been accustomed to employ but one subject for demonstrating all parts of the body, excepting the bones and arteries, which were described on preparations ; and the nerves, for exhibiting which a fœtus was usually employed. Practical dissection was unknown to the great bulk of the profession. Added to all this, a far greater horror of anatomical pursuits existed in the public mind at that time than at the present.

William Hunter's address and perseverance at length triumphed over all these difficulties, and he succeeded in forming an establishment, which, in consequence of the superior advantages it afforded, and the unrivalled talent of its founder as a lecturer, for a long time maintained its rank as by far the first anatomical school in London.

John Hunter was now in his twentieth year, when the fame of his brother's success made him desirous of entering into the same profession. He accordingly wrote to his brother, requesting to be allowed to join him in London, and offering his services as an assistant in the dissecting-room. The reply was favourable, and contained a kind invitation to visit London. He lost no time in complying with this, but set out on horseback in September, in company with Mr. Hamilton, a friend of the family, and arrived at his brother's house about a fortnight before the commencement of the autumnal course of lectures. No long

tion of Cowper and Cheselden, is due the merit of supporting the fame of this country in anatomical pursuits, from the time of Caius to that of the Hunters. In the list of physicians who successively taught anatomy in England, we find the names of Caius, Harvey, Glisson, Mead, Willis, Lower, Wm. Hunter, and last, though not least, of Matthew Baillie. With Dr. Baillie ended the race of Physician-Anatomists, with the exception of Dr. Wilson, who lectures at the present day. This resignation of the professor's chair of anatomy on the part of the physicians, arose not however from any lack of able men to fill it, but from a conviction that the surgeons were now fully capable of instructing their own pupils, and with more practical effect.

time elapsed before John's skill was put to the trial in preparing for the lecture a dissection of the muscles of the arm. It is probable that Wm. Hunter had not as yet formed a very high estimate of the talents of his hitherto idle brother, and little foresaw that he was ere long to eclipse his preceptor: he was, however, so well pleased with his pupil's first essay, that he soon after entrusted him with the preparation of a similar part, of which the blood-vessels were injected. In this the young student again succeeded so well as to obtain much praise for his dexterity from his brother, who foretold that he would soon become a good anatomist, and promised that he should never want employment. From this time, therefore, we may consider Hunter as engaged in the dissecting-room, under the instruction of his brother's assistant, Mr. Symonds, where he pursued his studies with such zeal and diligence that by the next season he was able to take the charge of directing the pupils in their dissections ;—thus, by his rapid progress, showing what may be effected by great diligence, and adding another to the examples furnished by Cheselden, Haller, Albinus, Baillie, Abernethy, and a host of others, that the surest foundation for future professional eminence is an early and extensive knowledge of anatomy.

The summer after he arrived in town, Wm. Hunter obtained permission for his brother to attend at the Chelsea Hospital, under Cheselden, of whom, as Hunter's first master in surgery, and as the most celebrated surgeon of his day, no apology will be necessary for introducing a short account. This admirable surgeon was now more than sixty years of age, and had retired in great part from the toils of a profession in which he had been engaged during nearly forty years, and in which he had attained the highest rank. As a surgeon, Cheselden may be said to have enjoyed the same repute, both in England and on the Continent, which his contemporary and friend Dr. Mead had acquired as a physician.   He was educated at St. Thomas's Hospital, under Mr. Ferne, a very able man, and studied anatomy under the celebrated Cowper.   At twenty-two he became a lecturer on surgery and anatomy, and in the following year was elected a member of the Royal Society, to whose Transactions he contributed several papers, the most remarkable of which contained the description of the operation by which he restored to sight a lad who had been blind nearly from birth.   At Ferne's death he was elected first surgeon to St. Thomas's, and was appointed consulting surgeon to St. George's and the Westminster Hospitals.   He was eminent in every department of surgery, but it was as a lithotomist that his name first became known all over Europe. The operation he at first adopted was that called the high method, when the bladder is entered above the pubes, which he performed with considerable success, saving six out of every seven who were cut.   About this period, however, all Europe rang with the name of Raw, the famous Dutch lithotomist, who had adopted Frère Jacques's method, with improvements of his own, but kept his plan so profound a secret as to blind the eyes even of the famous Albinus, his assistant, as to the exact parts through which he cut. Cheselden, with Douglas, and other surgeons in London, who had met with less success by the high method, tried the mode described as Raw's by Albinus, in which the whole wound in the bladder was made beyond the prostate ; but they experienced such ill fortune that they felt assured the operation was not correctly described, and Cheselden, abandoning this, planned the lateral operation as it is at present performed.   He now met with such signal success, that Moraud, then one of the first surgeons in Paris, came over to this country purposely to learn the operation, and during his stay saw Cheselden cut twenty-seven patients without losing one. Cheselden's manners were exceedingly kind and gentle, and notwithstanding the extensive practice he had enjoyed, he always, before an operation, felt sick at the thoughts of the pain he was about to inflict; though during its performance his coolness and presence of mind never forsook him*. In alluding to this feeling, Moraud relates an anecdote of a French surgeon, who, on visiting the hospital, expressed great surprise at witnessing such an evidence of weakness, as he considered it, on the part of so famous a surgeon : after the operation was over, the visitor was invited by Cheselden to accompany him to the fencing school, whither he was going to see a sparring match; but here the tables were completely turned, for no sooner did the contest begin, than the stranger turned pale at the sight, and was obliged speedily to betake himself to the open air.

It was under this great man that Hunter received his first lessons in surgery,—a worthy master for so eminent a pupil ; and he continued to attend regularly at the Chelsea Hospital during the summer months of 1749 and 1750. Here he would have probably continued for some time longer, but in the following year Cheselden was obliged to resign his situation in consequence of an attack of paralysis, which entirely unfitted him for business. He repaired to Bath in the hope of amendment, but in 1752 he was seized with apoplexy, which put an end to his life, in the sixty-fourth year of his age. Besides his talents as a surgeon, Cheselden displayed considerable taste in the fine arts ; he was fond of poetry, and an intimate friend of Pope ; he had also made architecture his study, and it was from his plans that Putney Bridge, and the former Surgeons' Hall in the Old Bailey, were erected.

* Such feelings, in a less marked degree perhaps, are far more commonly experienced than is generally supposed, by the very best surgeons previously to undertaking operations of importance.

But to return to Hunter. We may consider him as now fully entered on his professional studies; and as he was not one who ever loitered over an undertaking, it is probable that his time was pretty fully occupied between the hospital and the dissecting-room. He was, however, fond of company, and as he had not, like Haller, forsworn the use of wine on commencing his medical studies, though he found it necessary to do so in after life, he mixed much in the society of young men of his own standing, and joined in that sort of dissipation which men at his age, and freed from restraint, are but too apt to indulge in. Here, as in graver matters, his ambition urged him to take the lead of his companions, amongst whom he went by the familiar title of 'Jack Hunter'. Nor was he always very nice in the choice of his associates, but sometimes sought entertainment in the coarse broad humour to be found amid the lower ranks of society. He was employed by his brother to cater for the dissecting-room, in the course of which employment he became a great favourite with that certainly not too respectable class of persons the resurrection men; and one of the amusements in which he took especial pleasure, was to mingle with the gods in the shilling gallery, for the purpose of assisting to damn the productions of unhappy authors, an office in which he is said to have displayed peculiar tact and vigour.

It must not, however, be supposed that it was to company like this, or to the society of wild young men, that Hunter was confined. His brother was a scholar, and possessed of gentlemanly manners, and though comparatively a stranger in London, he was already known as a man of much talent, and as likely to rise to eminence; he was also fond of society, and his house was consequently frequented by many of the first men, not only in his own but in other professions. It has therefore seldom fallen to the lot of young men to enjoy equal opportunities of cultivating their minds by association with men of talent ; and though there can be no question that by far the greater part of his future eminence was owing to the original powers of his mind, yet, in recording the history of his life, it will be proper to trace the means by which those powers were improved, and to show, as far as may be, the assistance he received in bringing them fully into action. It is the more necessary to do this, in order to correct an unfounded opinion which generally prevails, that Hunter should be classed with those untaught geniuses who have risen to the highest honours by their own unaided powers. This was evidently not the case, and the meagreness of his early history seems sufficiently to prove that it was at his brother's table, and in his brother's dissecting-room, that his ambition and his talents were first roused to activity : without such a stimulus his genius might have slumbered, or have taken a wrong direction. Nor does this detract from his real merit. There is perhaps nothing that more distinguishes the man of genius than the manner in which he turns to account the advantages which common minds would let slip without profit. Hunter was a man of extraordinary powers ; he was placed in circumstances the best fitted to excite these powers, and give them their full effect, and the result was such as could only have been produced by this fortunate combination of circumstances.

CHAPTER II.

1751 to 1763.

Hunter becomes a pupil of Pott.—Pott's character as a surgeon.—Hunter enters at St. Mary's Hall, Oxford;—enters as a pupil at St. George's Hospital;—discovers the mode of connexion between the placenta and uterus;—his conduct as a lecturer and demonstrator of anatomy.—Disputes of the Hunters with contemporaneous anatomists respecting the anatomy of the testes, the office of the lymphatics, and the hernia congenita.—Hunter traces the nerves of the nose;—his experiments on the subject of venous absorption;—commences the pursuit of comparative anatomy;—embarks for Belleisle;—is still ardent in the pursuit of science.—Jesse Foot and his Life of Hunter.

On the retirement of Cheselden from the Chelsea Hospital, Hunter entered as surgeon's pupil at St. Bartholomew's. To this hospital Pott had been elected surgeon about two years before, after having served as assistant from 1745. He was now in his thirty-eighth year, and was fast rising in reputation as a most able practical surgeon. As an author he was not yet known, for his first work of importance, the 'Treatise on Ruptures,' which was composed during his confinement with a compound fracture of the leg, did not appear until 1756. Nor had he at this time commenced the delivery of his surgical lectures. At the hospital, however, Hunter must have acquired many a useful lesson, from a comparison of the lenient practice of leaving much to the efforts of nature, which Pott's sound judgement had led him to adopt, with the rude and pernicious interference with these efforts, which Nourse and his other colleagues, according to the custom of their day, were in the habit of employing.

Surgery was at this time beginning fast to emerge from

the state of barbarism in which it had long existed. To this change the French Academy of Surgery greatly contributed, and they have left us, in their Memoirs, a fine example of men laying aside petty jealousies and uniting their powers for one common object,—the advancement of their common profession.

It was in the operative parts of surgery, as might be expected, that the chief improvements were first made, a result almost necessarily arising from the knowledge of anatomy becoming more diffused. Far less had been done towards simplifying the curative department. The actual cauteries and charcoal-pan were still considered an essential part of the dressing apparatus at the hospital, and a farrago of applications, going under the names of suppuratives, digestives, and sarcotics, were implicitly relied on for effecting those changes which Nature was all the while performing in spite of her injudicious allies.

Pott was the first surgeon in this country who successfully attacked these abuses, and, as usually falls to the lot of innovators, was laughed at by his colleagues for his attempts. Several of the improvements suggested by him were, no doubt, introduced after the time when Hunter was a student ; yet we may fairly suppose that the latter obtained many useful hints from those he witnessed, which, confirmed and improved on during his practice in the army, may have formed the basis of some of the philosophic views which we owe to his genius.

At this hospital Hunter attended regularly during the summer months of 1751, and occasionally in the winter, when any operation of importance was to be performed. During the next summer he was absent from town, on a visit to Scotland, whither he went, partly probably to enjoy some relaxation from his labours, but principally for the purpose of accompanying to London his sister, Mrs. Buchanan, whose husband had died not long before.

In 1753 Hunter entered as Gentleman Commoner at St. Mary's Hall, Oxford.   Neither of his biographers satisfactorily explains the motives which led him to take this step, but it seems probable that he was persuaded to it by his brother.   It was not yet decided what line of practice John should pursue, and if there were thoughts of his becoming a physician, as it seems there were, it was natural that William, who was a good classic, and valued literary attainments, should recommend his brother to devote some time to the cultivation of those branches of knowledge, which he had hitherto so entirely neglected.   He was also recommended, it would seem, to try his fortune as an accoucheur ; but neither this proposal nor the former was to his liking, and he eventually decided on confining himself to the practice of surgery.   In speaking of this period of his life some years afterwards to Sir Anthony Carlisle, then a student at the hospital, Hunter said : "They wanted to make an old woman of me ; or that I should stuff Latin and Greek at the University ; but," added he, significantly pressing his thumb-nail on the table, "these schemes I cracked like so many vermin as they came before me."   It was fortunate, probably, that he decided as he did, for though his future progress was slow, the roughness of his manners would have been a still greater impediment to him in either of the other branches of the profession.

Having determined, then, on adhering to the practice of surgery, Hunter naturally felt anxious to secure for himself a chance of election at some future day to one of the London hospitals.   His prospect of obtaining the situation of surgeon to the Chelsea was too uncertain and too remote to be calculated on ; and at St. Bartholomew's it would have been necessary for him to serve an apprenticeship of five years to one of the surgeons, which, at his age and with his occupations, was quite out of the question. Fortunately, no such obstacle offered at St. George's, where he accordingly entered as surgeon's pupil in 1754, and attended, as in the former instances, during the summer months, whilst the winter was devoted to his duties and studies in the dissecting-room. Two years after this he served the office of house-surgeon to the hospital, a most desirable post for a young man intending to enter on surgical practice, since, in addition to the immediate care of all the patients under the direction of the surgeons, in their absence, a great part of the treatment of fractures, and several of the minor operations of surgery, usually devolve upon this officer.

Hunter's extensive acquaintance with anatomy was now generally known and appreciated, and he was not unfrequently applied to by others to assist them in clearing up any difficulties they might encounter in their researches. It was on an occasion of this kind, and about this time, that the important discovery of the mode of connexion between the placenta and uterus was made. The honour of solving this anatomical problem was laid claim to by each of the Hunters, and the dispute to which it gave rise twenty-five years afterwards caused a breach between them that was never healed until William was on his death-bed; and scarcely, it would seem, in his mind, even then. The following is the account which John Hunter has given of the transaction in his work on the 'Animal Œconomy'.

In May 1754, Dr. Mackenzie, then an assistant with Dr. Smellie, had been particularly successful in injecting the arteries and veins of the uterus, in a woman who had died during pregnancy. The appearance being new, he applied to Hunter for his assistance in making the examination, who, after having dissected and made the whole into preparations, on his return home in the evening communicated what had been done to Dr. Hunter. The latter treated his brother's account at first with goodnatured raillery, but on seeing the parts was soon convinced of the truth of the statement. Some of the portions were given to the Doctor, who afterwards exhibited them at his lectures; but in what manner he mentioned the subject, or what credit he gave to John on these occasions, does not appear. In his work on the gravid uterus, published in 1774, he gives general acknowledgements to his brother for his assistance, but does not mention his name in connexion with this particular subject. As it will be necessary to recur briefly to this dispute at a later period, no more need be said at present, except to remark, that attempts have been recently made to show that this discovery, on which so high a value was set at the time, is in truth not a discovery, but an erroneous opinion.

The most distinguished anatomists and physiologists of the present day, on the Continent, take this view of the subject; still, the doctrine of the Hunters is supported by evidence too strong to be easily overset, and it is said that some recent minute dissections instituted by Mr. Owen, which have not yet been made public, still further confirm the truth of their opinion.

In the course of this year Hunter became a partner with his brother in the anatomical school, and a portion of the lectures was regularly allotted to him; besides which, he took his brother's station whenever he was unavoidably absent. The lecture-room was not, however, a place in which John Hunter was calculated to shine, as he had always great difficulty in delivering himself extempore, an acquirement almost indispensable in anatomical teaching. Hence, notwithstanding his extensive and accurate knowledge of anatomy, he never gained a popular manner, and could not but have appeared to great disadvantage when contrasted with the Doctor, who was so preeminently qualified as a teacher.

In the dissecting-room he felt himself more at home, and it was here that he spent all his leisure hours, in making preparations, and in pushing his inquiries in anatomy and physiology beyond the point which his predecessors had attained.

Since the time of Vesalius anatomy had been prosecuted with great zeal and success by eminent men, both in England and on the Continent, and the most important parts of the human body had been more or less accurately described. There still remained, however, many minor parts, the structure of which had not been fully made out, and the newly discovered system of the lymphatics was as yet but imperfectly known. The invention of various modes of injecting the vessels had of late greatly facilitated researches into the minute structure of parts. Many able anatomists in the various schools of Europe were ardently engaged in pursuing such researches, and by none were they carried on with more zeal than by the Hunters.

A natural consequence of this direction of many minds to one object was, that a new discovery was frequently made nearly at the same time by different inquirers, and it became difficult to apportion the degree of credit due to each. The eagerness of the claimants for honour often led to disputes, in which far more warmth was displayed than the point in question merited, so that on reading the annals of these paper wars, we cannot but feel surprise at the violence shown about matters of such little moment. Dr. Hunter himself was a very Achilles in this sort of warfare.

Impiger, iracundus, inexorabilis, acer.

Jealous of his supposed rights, and unwilling to admit

C

the possibility of a discovery occurring to two independent inquirers, he was far too apt to accuse his antagonists of plunder if they displayed as their own any of those anatomical trophies to which he could establish a prior claim.

In several of his encounters, the discoveries which gave rise to them were due in great part to John, who, being far more dexterous with the scalpel than the pen, left the defence of their common property to William, whose literary attainments better fitted him for the service, and who displayed considerable ability in its performance.

Two of these disputes were with the Munros : the one, as to the first successful injection of the tubuli testis with mercury; the other, as to the discovery of the true office of the lymphatics. In both cases Dr. Hunter fairly showed that he had taken the lead of the Munros. On the former question, indeed, he had been, to a certain extent, forestalled by Watson and by Haller ; but on the latter, though other physiologists may have somewhat earlier suggested that the lymphatics were probably absorbents, the merit of proving this by observation and experiment, and of pointing out the great importance of these vessels in the animal œconomy, is undoubtedly chiefly due to William and John Hunter.

The third encounter was with Pott, who was no favourite with the Scotch faction in London, of which William Hunter was a leading member. He accused Pott of stealing from himself and his brother the knowledge of the true nature of hernia congenita, without acknowledging it in the paper he published on the subject. Pott, however, denied the accusation, and we have no reason to doubt his veracity. Be this as it may, both had been anticipated by Haller, who had a year or two before explained the nature of the disease, and given it the name of congenital hernia.

There was a question, however, connected with this latter

subject which required to be cleared up, namely, as to the cause and mode of descent of the testis in the fœtus. The explanation of the process given by Haller and Pott was fanciful and unsatisfactory; and to John Hunter alone is due the merit of explaining the steps of this curious physiological problem in so full a manner as to leave nothing to be added by others on the subject. The details of this inquiry, which gained him great credit, were first published in Dr. Hunter's Commentaries, and are given more at length in John Hunter's valuable work on the Animal Œconomy.

In addition to the above researches, he about this time traced the ramifications of the first pair of nerves within the nose; and from his preparations the engravings were executed which he published in the Animal Œconomy, accompanied by some valuable physiological remarks on the nervous system generally.

In 1758, and the following year, he instituted a set of experiments, which are detailed in Dr. Hunter's Medical Commentaries, for the purpose of ascertaining whether veins possess the power of absorbing. These were ingeniously contrived, and, to the minds of all present, so satisfactorily decided the question in the negative, that they greatly contributed to confirm the opinion that absorption was carried on by the lymphatics and lacteals only, and apparently gave the death-blow to the ancient doctrine of absorption by veins. Here again, however, later physiologists, by new and more varied inquiries, have succeeded in throwing considerable doubts on the correctness of Hunter's inferences, and have brought forward evidence, which, if not decisive, yet affords strong ground for believing that the veins are to a certain extent absorbents. What are the relative parts taken by these two sets of vessels in carrying on this function, or whether the apparent absorption by veins is not a mere effect of simple imbibition, still remains to be discoverd.

It was at one time Hunter's intention to have made a series of preparations of the whole system of lymphatics, and to have published engravings of them. With this view he had completed a preparation of the lymphatics of the lower extremity, from which Rymsdyk had executed a drawing; but ill health, and a variety of occupations, prevented his carrying the plan into effect.

Hunter had now been ten years engaged in the study of human anatomy, and having found that there were many parts the structure and functions of which required to be elucidated by a reference to other sources, he began with the same diligence to pursue his researches in the wide field of comparative anatomy. His health, however, was beginning to suffer seriously from his incessant labours. In the spring of 1759 he was attacked with inflammation of the lungs, which left behind it symptoms that threatened to end in consumption. He was strongly advised, therefore, to leave London for a time, and seek a more southerly climate. With this view he applied for an appointment in the army, and was immediately made Staff-Surgeon by Adair, who was then Inspector-General of Hospitals.

Europe was at this time engaged in the seven years' war, one of the most sanguinary of those in which nations were formerly so often involved, by their mutual jealousies, or the ambition of their rulers. England was as usual amongst the foremost in the contest, and early in 1761, a powerful armament was sent from this country, under General Hodgson and Commodore Keppel, to lay siege to Belleisle, an island off the western coast of France. With this armament Hunter embarked; and as the siege, though short, was extremely sanguinary, he was at once furnished with ample opportunities for practice in the treatment of gun-shot wounds.

By the following year England had embroiled herself with Spain. British troops were sent out for the protection of our Portuguese allies, and with these Hunter proceeded to the Peninsula. Here he remained on active duty until the end of the year, when all parties being heartily tired of the contest, the preliminaries of peace were agreed on.

Notwithstanding his constant employment in the practical duties of his profession whilst with the army, Hunter found time to pursue those physiological researches in which he took supreme delight. He made several experiments on lizards and snakes, to ascertain whether digestion continues during their torpid state; and he was also engaged in some inquiries on the faculty of hearing in fishes. It was during these campaigns, too, that most of his observations on gun-shot wounds were made, and that many of the peculiar views which his work on inflammation unfolds, first suggested themselves to his mind, though they were not published until more than thirty years afterwards, as he constantly endeavoured during his whole life to confirm and amend them, and to build them up into a work on which his future fame should depend.

We have no authentic account of Hunter's private life during the time he was with the army. Jesse Foot accuses him of exciting jealousies and quarrels amongst his colleagues; but to Foot's statements no sort of credit is due. He wrote what he is pleased to call the Life of Hunter with the same view that he made all his other attacks on him, under the hope, namely, that he might succeed in dividing the town into two parties, and himself become the Magnus Apollo of one of them. His hope of rivaling Hunter was certainly sufficiently ridiculous, and it need hardly be added that he utterly failed in his aim. Whether he carried his abuse so far as to disgust those he wished to please, or that his talents were not equal to filling a high station, certain it is he never made much figure in his profession; and whilst Hunter's name and works have been year after year rising into higher and still higher esteem, those of his traducer, Foot, are already well nigh buried in merited oblivion*.

In the spring of 1763, peace having been proclaimed, Hunter accompanied the forces home, and on arriving in England immediately returned to the metropolis.

* When Hunter published his work on the Venereal Disease, Foot followed with a book of his own on the same subject, filled with abuse of the doctrine and practice of his predecessor. Hunter was too wise to give consequence to his petty foe by publicly replying to his attacks, but the following comments were written by him on a couple of scraps of paper, destined for pipe-lights, but rescued from the flames by Mr. Clift. "One may say of Jesse Foot as we say sometimes of young men, 'It was well their fathers were born before them.' It was well for Jesse Foot that I published my book before he wrote his." "Jesse Foot accuses me of not understanding the dead languages; but I could teach him that on the dead body which he never knew in any language dead or living." Foot's best work was the life of his relative Murphy, the translator of Tacitus; but by an unfortunate blunder in the motto prefixed, he has betrayed how little pretence he, at least, had for reproaching Hunter with his want of classical knowledge. This motto he solicited and obtained from Mr. Thomas Copeland of Golden Square, a gentleman as distinguished in his profession as he is for true taste in classic literature; but by an absurd mistake Foot perverted its meaning, and thereby entirely destroyed its beauty. The following is the motto as it stands in his work. "Non hoc præcipuum amicorum munus est, prosequi defunctum ignavo *quæstu*, sed quæ voluerit meminisse, quæ mandaverit exsequi." *Tacit. Ann.* lib. ii. By substituting *quæstu* for *questu*, as in the original, he has spoiled an elegant motto.

It is said that Foot received four hundred pounds from some of Hunter's enemies for writing his life; if so, he deserves only to be remembered in connexion with a homely remark of Hunter's, in answer to a gentleman who was condemning this sort of conduct, "O, sir! we all have vermin that live on us."

CHAPTER III.

1763 to 1771.

*Hunter settles in London.—Alienation between the brothers.—His strait-
ened circumstances;—his favourable position in other respects.—Patience and fortitude required of young surgeons.—Obstacles to Hunter's
success;—his contempt of humbug;—his thirst for fame and knowledge
greater than his love of wealth;—delivers lectures on anatomy;—his
persevering industry.—The state of surgery at this period.—The plan
of his vast future labours conceived and entered upon.—The Baconian
philosophy.—Earl's Court.—His encounter with a bull and two leopards;
—is made F.R.S.—His description of the Proteus;—ruptures his tendo
Achillis;—is elected surgeon to St. George's Hospital;—removes to
Jermyn-street.—Dr. Hunter's liberal offer to the Government rejected.
—Mr. Hunter's house-pupils.—The pupils of distinguished surgeons
themselves become distinguished.—Dr. Jenner;—his immortal discovery
of vaccination.—Mr. Hunter's treatise on the teeth;—his marriage.—
Mrs. Hunter.*

A TERMINATION having been put to the late war, at the
earnest desire of all parties, there was little probability that
Hunter would be again called into active service by a renewal of hostilities; and as his health was reestablished, he
determined on immediately settling himself in London.

The situation which he had occupied in Dr. Hunter's
school was now filled by Hewson, who had been taken
into partnership soon after Hunter quitted England; and
as this gentleman's talents, both as a lecturer and as a
practical anatomist, were of a high order, and enabled him
to fill the post with credit to himself and advantage to the
establishment, there was no prospect of a vacancy soon occurring in this quarter. It may indeed be doubted, even
if the situation had been open, whether Hunter would have
again entered into partnership with his brother; for it

would appear from Sir Everard Home's statement, that their
former connexion had not been one of entire harmony;
and that indeed the only tie which bound them together,
long after other considerations would have led to a separation, was John Hunter's extraordinary skill as an anatomist, and the valuable contributions which he was continually making to Dr. Hunter's museum.

For the future, then, Hunter was to depend on his own
unaided exertions; consequently, though his situation was
one of more independence than that he before occupied, it
must also have been one of more anxiety, as he had nothing
certain to depend on beyond his half-pay.

The circumstances under which he commenced his career in London must be considered, however, to have been
on the whole unusually advantageous. His age was sufficiently advanced to inspire his patients with confidence;
he had a brother established in extensive practice as a physician and accoucheur; and the abilities he had manifested
in his former situations had made him favourably known,
not only in the army, but to many of the most eminent
literary and scientific men of the day. With such advantages, it might have been expected that his unwearied industry and eminent natural endowments, improved as they
had been by an education under the first surgeons of the day,
and by the personal experience which three years of active
service had afforded him, would have certainly and speedily
introduced him into a large share of profitable practice.

Hunter was, however, destined to undergo a long trial
of those qualities of passive fortitude and active perseverance, of which few situations in life demand a larger share
than that of a young man commencing practice in the
higher branches of the profession of law or medicine in
London; for assuredly it needs no small degree of fortitude to bear up against the disappointment a young man so

placed must experience, in finding his merits overlooked, whilst the world is showering wealth on many around him whom he, at least, thinks far less deserving than himself. It requires, too, much steady perseverance constantly to keep in view the destined goal, resisting the allurements which have so often led men of superior talents to desert the arduous contest, and devote themselves to the pursuits of literature or of science; pursuits which, though delightful, can seldom be extensively followed without the neglect of objects more essential to those who seek for fortune, as well as fame, from the practice of a profession.

Various circumstances combined to render Hunter's success in practice far less rapid than might have been anticipated. Of these, one of the most obvious was that of the field being already occupied by several men of real merit in their profession, and who by their writings had contributed largely to the improvement of surgery. First of these, and *facilè princeps*, stood Pott, in the prime of life and in the zenith of his fame, who though he had never received, because he had never solicited, those titles and posts of honour which are usually bestowed on the leaders of our profession, yet had raised himself by his eminent abilities and industry, and by his gentlemanly manners, to the highest place in the esteem of his professional brethren and the public.

The second stations were ably filled by Bromfield and Sir Cæsar Hawkins, surgeons to St. George's Hospital; and Samuel Sharp and Warner, of Guy's. These divided amongst them the greater part of the civil practice, whilst Adair and Tomkins, from their long connexion with the army, enjoyed the chief share of what accrued from that quarter.

The narrowness of his income was no doubt also an obstacle to Hunter's success; for though his personal habits were very inexpensive, his scientific inquiries required more money than he could well afford. He was therefore obliged to be content with establishing himself in the plainest manner, and living a retired life ; and though this no doubt enabled him with more freedom to pursue those important objects in which he was about to engage, yet it would not be likely to conduce to his speedily increasing his professional connexions. It is in this respect that, *cæteris paribus*, a man commencing with a moderate share of fortune has a decided advantage over the fortuneless ; for though it has been truly said that " moneys are not the sinews of fortune, but the sinews and steel of men's minds, —wit, courage, audacity, resolution, temper, industry, and the like," yet even he who declared this, has allotted the second place to " wealth and means."

But besides these external difficulties which most men have to struggle with in a greater or less degree at the outset of life, there were in Hunter's case some great impediments arising out of his own character. He was deficient in those refined gentlemanly feelings, and those conciliating manners, which in all situations go far to win the good will of those whom we are in the habit of meeting in the daily intercourse of life, and are especially requisite in the medical profession. Conscious of great mental superiority, he was too apt to show this in a rude and overbearing manner, towards men who in station were his equals, and exhibited somewhat too large a share of that " pride of port" which the poet assigns to those

> Intent on high designs, a thoughtful band,
> By forms unfashion'd, fresh from Nature's hand.

Consequently, though the intrinsic excellences of his character insured him the friendship of a few, who knew and estimated his worth, this fault raised up against him many bitter enemies, and prevented him from ever becoming a general favourite with the profession. It might probably with justice be said, that of all who have attained to the highest rank as surgeons, no one ever rose so entirely by the pure force of superior talents as John Hunter, or was less indebted than he was for his success to the good will and assistance of his contemporaries.

Hunter had also a great contempt for those minor tactics, which constitute so large a part of what has been aptly called the art of rising in the world; and they who have carefully watched the progress of men to fortune, know full well how much of their success has often been due to the judicious management of these auxiliary means. It would be egregious folly to suppose that a man could ever attain to high repute as a surgeon in London, without possessing a large share of the essential requisites for the practice of his profession; but, on the other hand, it requires no great penetration to perceive, that the vast difference in the amount of her favours, vouchsafed by Fortune to her different votaries, must be accounted for in some other way than by the amount of professional talent possessed by each. "He that is only *real* had need have exceeding great parts of virtue," says Bacon, "as the stone had need be rich, that is set without foil;" and we need not a better illustration of the truth of this observation, than is afforded by Hunter's tardy progress in the path to fortune, compared with the rapid strides of others, who in professional attainments would be the first to acknowledge themselves but the humble disciples of this great master.

But after all, perhaps, the principal reason why Hunter was so long in obtaining a large share of practice was, that he looked not, as most men do, to the acquisition of fortune as the end for which he was labouring; but, on the contrary, considered wealth only as a means, by which he might advance the far more important objects he had in.

view. His powerful mind was unceasingly stimulated by an ardent desire to forward the acquisition of those branches of knowledge which to him appeared best fitted to promote the improvement of his profession ; to this object was devoted every hour that he could spare from his daily avocations, or snatch from the time allotted by others to sleep, and to promote this end he was always ready to sacrifice the claims of worldly prudence and self-interest. To witness an interesting or extraordinary case he would take any trouble, or go almost any distance, without a chance of pecuniary recompense ; but to the daily routine of practice he always returned unwillingly, and even when he had acquired a lucrative and extensive business, he valued it only as affording him the means of pursuing his favourite studies. This feeling he would often express to his friend Mr. Lynn, when called to see a patient, by saying, as he unwillingly laid by his dissecting instruments, " Well, Lynn, I must go and earn this d——d guinea, or I shall be sure to want it tomorrow*."

As a means of increasing his income, Hunter determined on delivering lectures on anatomy and operative surgery to a private class. These he continued for several years; but so far were his talents, and his enlightened views, from exciting the attention they merited, that his hearers never amounted to twenty. Amongst them, however, were numbered Cline, Lynn, Brande, Adams, Vaux, and Justamond. " Dr. Garthshore†, too," says our modern Democritus, the

* Hunter was much addicted to swearing, and constantly interlarded his conversation with expressions of this sort. In relating anecdotes respecting him, the author has generally omitted these expressions, since the objections to introducing them appeared to him greatly to outweigh any advantage that such verbal exactness could afford.

† Dr. Garthshore was quite a physician of the old school, always well dressed, and exceedingly polite, and a great favourite with the dowagers. He was intimate with John Hunter, who did not however treat him with much ceremony. One day the Doctor, on entering the dis-

late worthy and facetious William Wadd, "occasionally looked in, wound up his watch, and fell asleep."

Hunter's leisure hours were never allowed to remain unemployed. He returned to the study of comparative anatomy with increased delight; and to furnish subjects for his researches, he obtained the refusal of all animals which chanced to die in the Tower, or in those smaller zoological collections, which used at that time, more frequently than at present, to perambulate the country; and to insure the good will of the owners, he used to allow them a life interest in any rare animals he was able to purchase, on condition that their carcases were restored to him after their decease. All the money he could spare was devoted to procuring curiosities of this sort, and Sir Everard Home used to state, that as soon as he had accumulated fees to the amount of ten guineas, he always purchased some addition to his collection. Indeed, he was not unfrequently obliged to borrow of his friends, when his own funds were at a low ebb and the temptation was strong. "Pray, George," said he one day to Mr. G. Nicol* the bookseller, with whom he was

secting-room where Hunter was at work, began as usual with great *empressement*, "My d-e-a-r John Hunter"—"My dear Tom Fool," replied Hunter, looking up and imitating the tone and manner of the astonished Doctor.

* Mr. Nicol, bookseller to the king, and a highly accomplished scholar, was father to the present Mr. W. Nicol of Pall Mall, who probably owes his life to Hunter's interference. Mrs. Nicol, who was a sister of Cruikshank, had lost five children, and was in the family-way for the sixth, the present Mr. N. Hunter, in passing one day, dropped in, and asked Mr. Nicol whether he intended to kill this, as he had killed all the rest of his children. Mr. N., who was a North-countryman, had on false principles endeavoured to inure his children to cold and rough usage, thinking that if they could not survive this they would never live to be reared to manhood. Not understanding such a question, therefore, he demanded of Hunter what he meant. "Why," said Hunter, "do you know what is the temperature of a hen with her callow brood? because if you don't, I'll tell you." He then proceeded to explain the necessity of warmth to young animals, and convinced Mr. Nicol of the propriety of changing his plan; which he did, and with complete success.

very intimate, " have you got any money in your pocket? "
Mr. N. replied in the affirmative. "Have you got five
guineas? because if you have, and will lend it to me, you
shall go halves." "Halves in what?" inquired his friend.
"Why, halves in a magnificent tiger which is now dying in
Castle Street." Mr. Nicol lent the money, and Hunter got
the tiger.

It was probably about this period that Hunter laid the
plan of those vast researches into the animal œconomy, to
the execution of which the best hours of his future life
were to be devoted.

At the time he commenced his labours, surgery, though
holding a far more respectable station as a practical art
than it had done fifty years before, was yet destitute of
those sound general views of the nature and treatment of
disease which constitute the foundation of practice in the
present day, and the possession of which justly entitles it
to claim the rank of a science. The able men who, in this
country and on the Continent, immediately preceded Hunter, had succeeded, by the exercise of correct observation
and sound judgement, in removing a load of absurd prac-
tices with which the art had been clogged; but the improvements suggested by them depended for the most part
on isolated experience, and were deficient in a solid and
satisfactory foundation upon well known principles of the
animal œconomy. As yet little had been done towards
explaining the real nature of diseases, by showing in what
particulars they are allied to natural processes, and what
are the aberrations from those processes, which give them
their peculiar character. Nor were the actions by which

The justice of Mr. Hunter's remarks on this subject, which is one of
great importance, has been beautifully illustrated by Dr. Edwards's admirable experiments in his work " On the Influence of Physical Agents
on Life, &c."

Nature operates in the cure of diseases at all better understood, and the most vague notions prevailed respecting the important functions of nutrition and absorption, and the processes of adhesion, suppuration, granulation, &c.; the right understanding of which, forms as it were the very corner-stone of a good surgical education at the present day.

Hunter perceived the want of this knowledge, which in his opinion could alone furnish a sure foundation for the future improvement of surgery; and it was to contribute towards supplying the deficiency that his labours were hereafter to be unceasingly directed.

He clearly saw, that in order to obtain just conceptions of the nature of those aberrations from healthy actions which constitute disease, it was necessary first to understand well the healthy actions themselves; and these required to be studied, not in man alone, but throughout the whole animal series, and even to receive further elucidation by comparison with the functions of vegetable life. It was no less an undertaking, then, than the study of the phæno-mena of life, in health and disease, throughout the whole range of organized beings, in which Hunter proposed to engage; an undertaking which required a genius like his to plan, and from the difficulties of executing which, any mind less energetic, less industrious, and less devoted to science than his own would have shrunk.

In pursuing these researches, he strove not, like many of his more learned but less philosophic predecessors, to unravel the mysteries of nature by taking up some principle à priori, and seeking for facts to support his theory. On the contrary, he followed, in the strictest manner, the inductive method laid down by the great father of modern philosophy, as the only sure though arduous road to knowledge. He aimed not at discovering the essence of life, satisfied that this was beyond the province of philosophical

research ; but he sought to know how the various organs
are constructed, and how they act in accomplishing those
various processes by which the presence of this principle
is manifested.   Nor was he content to acquire his information at second hand.   Instead, therefore, of referring to
the discoveries detailed in books*, he appealed directly to
Nature herself, and rested nothing upon the facts related by
others, until, by the evidence of his own senses, he had
ascertained their truth.

As the labours of Hunter in this field of knowledge were
continued during his whole life, and as the various discoveries he made will require to be mentioned in noticing
his publications, and more fully in the chapter devoted to
a description of his museum, it will be unnecessary to
enter into a detail of them in this place.   As many of the
inquiries which he was desirous of instituting could not be
carried on conveniently, if at all, in the centre of a crowded
city, he purchased a piece of ground called Earl's Court,
at Brompton, about two miles from London, and built a
small house, where he used to spend much of his time, and
where he pursued most of those researches which form the
subjects of his papers in the Philosophical Transactions, or
are detailed in his work on the Animal Œconomy.   Here
it was his delight to spend an hour or two, amongst the
strange inmates congregated from all parts of the globe,
engaged in observing their habits and instincts, and amus-
ing himself in making them exert their various methods of
self-defence against his playful attacks.   As might be expected, he sometimes got himself into perilous situations
in his character of assailant.   On one such occasion he was

---

* It often, therefore, happened to him, as it has done to others, to find
that he had been anticipated in many discoveries : such confirmations,
however, of previously discovered truths are always valuable, particularly
when they depend on a distinct line of proofs.

thrown down by a little bull which the Queen had given him, and with which he had been wrestling; and had not one of his servants accidentally seen his danger, and driven off the victor, he would not have escaped without severe injury. In another of his adventures, still more serious consequences might have ensued. Two leopards, which he kept chained in an outhouse, broke from their confinement, and got into the yard with the dogs : a fierce encounter immediately commenced, the noise of which alarmed the neighbourhood, and quickly brought out Hunter to inquire into its cause. He found one of the leopards engaged with the dogs, whilst the other was making his escape over the wall, and instantly, though quite unarmed, he ran up and laid hold of both the animals, which fortunately submitted to be led back to their den and secured. When the danger was over, however, he became so agitated at the recollection of it, that he fainted.

In 1767 he was elected a Fellow of the Royal Society; and although persons, except on account of their rank, are not generally admitted members before they have furnished some paper of original research to be read before the Society, yet this custom seems not to have been rigorously enforced in Hunter's case, as the only communication he had made was an appendix to a paper by Ellis, on a new marine animal, the Proteus; nor did he contribute any entire paper to their Transactions until five years after: he was, however, a very regular attendant at the meetings of the Society, and, with Sir C. Blagden and others, used to meet and discuss papers, which had been presented, on topics of interest.

It is somewhat singular that John Hunter should have been elected before his brother William, who had been ten years longer in London, and certainly at this time occupied a higher station in public opinion than he did.

It was in this year that he ruptured his tendo Achillis

D

whilst dancing, after the muscles of the leg had been fatigued.   He did not confine himself to bed for this accident, but continued to walk about during the cure.   His
mode of treatment was to keep the heel raised, and to
compress the muscle gently with a roller, by which any
fresh separation of the ends of the tendon by spasmodic
and involuntary contractions of the muscles was prevented,
for he found that by no *voluntary* impulse could he excite
them to contract after the rupture of their tendon, " the
muscle refusing to act as if from a sense of imperfection,"
as he expressed it.   This accident led him to examine into
the process by which divided tendons are reunited.   He
divided the same tendon in several dogs, by introducing a
couching-needle under the skin at some distance from it,
and killed the dogs at different periods to see the progress
of the union, which was found to be similar to that of
fractured bones where the skin is not wounded.   It was ascertained at Mr. Hunter's death that the union of the ruptured tendon was by ossific deposition.

In 1768 a vacancy occurred at St. George's Hospital,
by the retirement of Gataker, the translator of Le Dran ;
and Hunter became a candidate for the situation.   He was
opposed by Mr. D. Bayford, but being supported by the
powerful interest which Dr. Hunter possessed, he was
elected surgeon on the 9th of December by a majority of 114
votes against 42.   Soon after this he was chosen a member
of the Corporation of Surgeons ; but he seems not to have
assimilated well with his brother corporators, for he gave
them but little of his society.   By his election to the hospital he was ensured the means of making his talents as a
surgeon more generally known, and was enabled to obtain
as private pupils, on advantageous terms, young gentlemen coming to town to complete their medical education*.

* Hunter received a fee of 500 guineas with each of his pupils, who
were bound to him for five years.

This was further facilitated by his removal to a more commodious house in Jermyn-street, which his brother had just vacated.

Dr. Hunter had, in the year 1765, in the most liberal way proposed to the then Ministry to build a public theatre of anatomy, at an expense to himself of 7000*l.*, and to endow a professorship of anatomy in perpetuity, on condition that they would grant a piece of ground in the Mews as a site for the building. But Lord Grenville and his colleagues, with the apathy which the English Government has too often shown to the interests of science, declined the offer. Lord Shelburne was desirous that the plan should be executed by subscription, and generously requested his name should be put down for one thousand guineas. Dr. Hunter's delicacy, however, led him to decline this proposal, and he determined to erect a building at his own expense. For this purpose, he purchased a spot of ground in Great Windmill-street, where he built a spacious house, with a theatre and museum, to which he removed in 1770, passing over the lease of his house in Jermyn-street to his brother John.

Amongst those gentlemen who successively became inmates of Hunter's house, as private pupils, were Dr. Jenner, Mr. Guy of Chichester, Mr. Kingston, Dr. Physick of Philadelphia, and Sir Everard Home. Mr. Lynn and Sir A. Carlisle, although not living in his house, were admitted there on the most intimate terms, assisted in his dissections, and contributed several valuable preparations to his museum. All of these gentlemen have risen to high reputation in their various stations, and it is not unworthy of remark, that of the eminent surgeons of which this country has had to boast, by far the greater number have pursued the most important part of their professional education under the roofs, and as the private pupils, of the most able of their predecessors in the art. This may no doubt, in some cases, be accounted for by supposing that the disciple had previously shown such talent as to lead his friends to seek the best situation for its improvement; but more has been probably due to the stimulus imparted to their energies by the examples before them, and still more to the advantages derived from daily witnessing the best modes of practice, and receiving information on those nicer distinctions in treatment which can never be fully conveyed in lectures, but the knowledge of which forms a distinguishing mark of the accomplished surgeon*.

It is to the credit of the gentlemen above named that they continued on friendly terms with Hunter until his death, for he not unfrequently conferred his friendship rather hastily on young men if he perceived any thing in their characters which pleased him, but as suddenly threw them off again on finding them to be of less sterling metal than he had anticipated†.

Dr. Jenner was amongst the earliest of Hunter's pupils,

* Thus we find that most of the surgeons who in the present day enjoy the largest share of the public confidence are, as it were, the direct mental descendants of the men who a century ago introduced the first important improvements into modern surgery. Cheselden, Nourse, and Douglas, were then the leaders of our profession, of whom Sharp, Pott, and the Hunters were the immediate pupils; they, again, became the instructors of Cline, Lynn, Home, Abernethy, Carlisle, Macartney, Sir James Earle, and Cooper; and from them the mantle has descended to a Brodie, a Lawrence, a Green, an Earle, and others, who now occupy with so much credit to themselves the places which their great predecessors adorned.

† Hunter set a high value on anatomical skill, and especially on dexterity in making preparations. Sir Anthony Carlisle stood high in his good graces on account of his ability in this art; but he used to abuse Sir Everard's clumsy fingers, swearing " that his fingers were all thumbs, and that he would never have sense enough to tie down a bottle." This was of course a mere sally of passion: his engaging him as his assistant, and leaving him the care of all his patients when unable to attend them himself, sufficiently proved the good opinion he entertained of the abilities of his brother-in-law, who was, there can be no doubt, a very skilful surgeon.

having become one in 1770, when he was in his twenty-first year, and Hunter in his forty-second. His mind was ever strongly impressed with respect and esteem for the character of his great master, whose vigorous and independent intellect excited the admiration, while his kind, free and manly nature insured the affection, of such a pupil. Their intercourse did not cease on Jenner's leaving London, but was kept up by letter until within a short period of Hunter's death. Many of the letters written by the latter have been published in Dr. Baron's Life of Jenner; and these, as well as some additional ones which Robert F. Jenner, Esq., of Berkeley, has kindly permitted to be introduced into this work, furnish interesting and truly characteristic memorials of the mind of him who penned them; for though generally but brief, and often faulty in orthography and in grammatical construction, they everywhere show the vigour and originality of his thoughts, and the untiring ardour with which he prosecuted his researches. Several of these letters will be inserted in the next chapter, but the following, though written two or three years later, may be introduced here, as evincing the interest Hunter felt in the welfare of a deserving pupil. Jenner, on the other hand, never mentioned Hunter but in terms of regard and affection; his usual appellation for him was "the dear man," an epithet which is used, in speaking of him, by others of his friends who still survive, and which shows how strong a hold he had acquired on the esteem of those who were on sufficiently intimate terms with him to know his real worth.

"DEAR JENNER,

"I received yours, and was extremely happy to hear of your success in business: I hope it will continue. I am obliged to you for thinking of me, especially in my natural history. I shall be glad of your observations on the cuckoo, and upon the breeding of toads: be as particular as you possibly can. If you can pick me up anythimg that is curious

and prepare it for me, either in the fish or flesh way, do it. Pictures*
have been very cheap, but the season is now over. There will be but
one sale, viz. Fordyce's ; but I believe all his pictures are exquisite,
and will go beyond you or me. Since you wrote to me I purchased
up a small landscape of Barrett's, of cattle and herd : I gave five pounds
seven shillings and sixpence: it is one of his eight-guinea pictures.
You shall have it or not, as you please. I have one of the same size,
that I bought of him some time ago.

"I saw the young lady, your patient: I do not know well what can
be done. If it is possible to pass a bougie from the nose up the duct
to the sac, it might be of service ; but nothing but a solid can be of any
use as a local application. Her general habit should be attended to,
such as sea-bathing, or cold bath, using a good deal of gentle exercise,
such as getting up early in the morning, riding, &c. She might take
gentle mercurials with the bark and cicuta. Let me hear from you
soon.

"Ever yours,

"JOHN HUNTER."

At the time this was written Jenner was practising as a
surgeon at Berkeley in Gloucestershire. Here he remained
for many years, and conducted those inquiries which led
to the introduction of vaccination. It seems that whilst
in London he frequently mentioned the opinion that prevailed in the dairy districts, that persons who had had
the cowpox were safe against the infection of smallpox.
Hunter considered the subject worthy of investigation,
mentioned the opinion occasionally in his lectures, and recommended Jenner to prosecute further inquiries into its
truth. There is no ground, however, to suppose that
Hunter assisted him in the investigation, as has sometimes
been insinuated. On the contrary, it is quite evident that
the merit of conducting every part of it belongs exclusively
to Jenner. As his letters to Hunter have been destroyed,
it is not possible to say what communications he made to

---

* Hunter was very fond of pictures, and valued himself on his con-
noisseurship in the art : his other pursuits, however, prevented his in-
dulging his taste by the purchase of many oil paintings, but of prints
he had a large and valuable collection.

him on the subject, for no allusion is made to the inquiry in Hunter's letters. It would seem that in 1788 Jenner was in London, and on that occasion showed a drawing of the vaccine pustule, as it appeared on the fingers of milkers, to several medical men, and amongst the rest, no doubt, to Hunter. Indeed there exists, amongst the Hunterian drawings, a rough sketch of the pustule, as seen under the above circumstances, on the envelope of a letter from Jenner, without date. It was not, however, until eight years after this, and three years after Hunter's death, that the question was subjected to the *experimentum crucis*, by actually inoculating a boy with lymph from the hand of a person affected with cowpox, and afterwards submitting him, without effect, to inoculation with variolous matter : and even then nearly two years elapsed before Jenner considered the inquiry sufficiently complete to be made public*.

* Various attempts were made to deprive Jenner of the credit of his discovery, but unjustly. That an opinion prevailed extensively in the dairy districts, that a person who had been infected with cowpox was no longer liable to smallpox, is certain; but no one who is acquainted with the utter groundlessness of many prevalent opinions on medical matters would put much faith in such an opinion until supported by direct experiments, instituted by a competent person. It would further appear, that a farmer Jesty had actually inoculated some of his family with matter taken from the teat of a cow; and claims to the discovery of vaccination were made on behalf of a Mr. Nash of Shrewsbury, on similar grounds. But was Dr. Jenner acquainted with either of these cases? And if not, how do they affect his merit any more than the existence of printing at an early date amongst the Chinese detracts from the merit of the discovery in Europe? With regard to Mr. Nash's case, Dr. Baron states that they were proved to have been cases of smallpox inoculation. But supposing them to have been cases of vaccination, does not his silence on the subject until the publication of Jenner's work argue either a want of faith in his own powers of investigation, or a want of courage to publish the facts? Does not the whole merit belong to Jenner of distinguishing the true from the spurious vaccine— of tracing the origin of the disease—of subjecting the opinion to the test of rigid experiment, and of conducting his inquiries to a triumphant conclusion, amidst difficulties and opposition of no ordinary kind?

In May 1771, Hunter published the first part of his ' Treatise on the Teeth *.' This contained the natural history of those organs in their healthy state, and was followed in 1778 by a second part, in which he treats of their diseases. It was the first work on the subject, which, in addition to an accurate anatomical description, furnished comprehensive views of the physiology and pathology of these organs. Like all Hunter's productions, it evinces marks of accurate observation and sound judgement; and though too brief in some of its descriptions, and not altogether free from errors and omissions, which subsequent inquirers have pointed out, it continues to hold its place as one of our standard surgical works. It needs, indeed, but to receive the additions and corrections of the able practitioner and accomplished naturalist who has undertaken to revise it for this edition of Hunter's works, to become one of the best treatises on the subject in this or any other language.

Hunter had for some years been engaged to Miss Home, daughter of Mr. Home, surgeon to Burgoyne's regiment of light horse, and sister of Sir Everard Home. As she was without fortune, and as his income, at the time they first became acquainted, was considerably under a thousand a year, and scarcely sufficed for his own expenses, their union was deferred until he was able to arrange his affairs sufficiently to allow of their marrying. This he had now succeeded in doing; and as his practice was yearly augmenting, they were married in July of the present year.

Mrs. Hunter was an agreeable, clever, and handsome woman, a little of a *bas bleu*, and rather fond of gay society, a taste which occasionally interfered with her hus-

---

* It is said that the proceeds of this publication, which came out only two months before his marriage, were appropriated to defraying the expenses attendant on that event.

band's more philosophic pursuits; for, though fond of mixing in society at his own house and at the houses of others, it was not exactly in such as is generally to be found at fashionable *soirées*. He sought company, not so much as a relaxation as because he preferred acquiring knowledge from conversation rather than from books ; and this being the case, he naturally preferred the company of able and scientific men, to that of the gay circle in which Mrs. Hunter's brilliancy was fitted to shine. So far was he indeed from finding relaxation for his mind in mixed society, that he really experienced fatigue from remaining long in company where the conversation wanted connexion ; and he therefore occasionally interposed his marital authority to check the inroads of these troops of idlers*. No serious disturbance to their concord, however, seems to have arisen from this very natural difference in the tastes of Mr. and Mrs. Hunter, and there is every reason to believe that this alliance was a source of great consolation and happiness to him during the remainder of his life. The fruits of their union were four children, two of whom died young ; the other two are still living,—John, his eldest son, and Agnes, who married Captain, afterwards Sir James Campbell.

---

* Hunter's mode of exerting this authority was occasionally somewhat too unceremonious. On returning late one evening, after a hard day's fag, he unexpectedly found his drawing-room filled with musical professors, connoisseurs, and other idlers, whom Mrs. Hunter had assembled. He was greatly irritated, and walking straight into the room, addressed the astonished guests pretty much in the following strain: "I knew nothing of this kick-up, and I ought to have been informed of it beforehand ; but as I am now returned home to study, I hope the present company will retire." This intimation was of course speedily followed by an *exeunt omnes*.

CHAPTER IV.

1772 to 1778.

Mr. Hunter's paper on the digestion of the stomach ;—his museum ;— his private practice ;—his illness, attended with a cessation of the heart's action ;—his correspondence with Dr. Jenner ;—his paper on the tor- pedo ;—his lectures on surgery ;—his character as a lecturer.—Hunter effects a revolution in surgery ;—his paper on the receptacles for air in birds, and on the stomach of the gillaroo trout.—The general character of his monographs.—Mr. Bell.—Mr. Hunter's warmth of temper ;— his method of employing his time ;—his punctuality.—Anecdote of Mr. Cline.—Dictates his various compositions ;—his domestic habits ;—con- templates the establishment of a school of natural history ;—his paper on the heat of animals and vegetables ;—is appointed surgeon extraordinary to the King ;—his paper on the recovery of drowned persons ;—Croonian lectures ;—correspondence ;—is attacked with an alarming illness, at- tended with peculiar symptoms ;—his visit to Bath ;—his character as an experimentalist ;—his second part on the teeth ;—his expenses and difficulties.

HUNTER had now been five years a Fellow of the Royal Society; but deterred, partly by the difficulty he experienced in literary composition, and partly by an unwillingness to make any of his observations public until he had thoroughly satisfied himself of their correctness, and investigated a subject in all its bearings, he had contributed no paper to the Philosophical Transactions since his election. About this time an opportunity offered for making known his opinions on a physiological phenomenon which had hitherto entirely escaped investigation, and on which, at the instance of Sir John Pringle, he was induced to communicate his thoughts in a memoir to the Royal Society. Pringle was at this period the President, and had distinguished himself in this honourable post by the learned and eloquent orations he had annually delivered, on presenting the Copley medal to those who had successively gained it by their important contributions to science. He and Hunter were on intimate terms, and occasionally met in consultation, and on the present occasion chanced to be engaged together in examining the body of a man who had died under Sir J. Pringle's care, of some disease in which the stomach was thought to have been not implicated. To Pringle's surprise, however, on opening this organ an extensive perforation was observed at its great end, an alteration of structure for which he could not account, until Hunter informed him that he had frequently met with such an appearance, both in men and animals, and attributed it to the action of the gastric juice on the coats of the stomach, after the death of this organ. This explanation forcibly struck Pringle, who was the more interested in the subject from having himself been engaged some years before in experiments on digestion. He accordingly urged Hunter to commit his thoughts to paper, and communicate them to the Royal Society, a request with which the latter, though somewhat unwillingly, complied. His memoir was accordingly presented, and read on the 18th of June, and was published in the Transactions for the year. This curious question in physiology did not at the time excite much attention. Spallanzani, who made several experiments, with a view to its further elucidation, concluded by rather throwing doubt on the possibility of this *post mortem* digestion, and the point was thus left *sub judice*. Of late years more attention has been paid to the inquiry, and though several continental pathologists, and amongst others Cruveilhier, have maintained that the appearance described by Hunter is always caused by morbid action going on during life, the experiments of Dr. Carswell, detailed in the Edinburgh Medical and Surgical Journal for October 1830, have fully proved the correctness of Hunter's explanation.   This gentleman killed several rabbits during digestion, and hung them up by the hind legs, when the depending part of the stomach was always found more or less digested.   The gastric juice of one rabbit was conveyed into the stomach of another previously killed, and digestion of a part of its stomach was the consequence.

· In the autumn of this year Hunter's brother-in-law, Mr., afterwards Sir Everard Home, became his pupil. He describes the museum as at this time beginning to assume an imposing degree of magnitude. All the best rooms in the house were already devoted to its reception; and though, from the increase of his professional engagements, Hunter had less time to devote to comparative anatomy, yet as he always spent three or four hours before breakfast, and as much time as he could spare during the remainder of the day, in the dissection of animals, he was constantly adding to its size and value.   His increasing reputation as a naturalist, also, facilitated to him the acquisition of objects on which to pursue his researches, as it induced scientific travellers to send him specimens of rare and curious animals, assured that they could not better forward the cause of science than by conferring them on one so ardently devoted to its promotion. " Hunter's private practice and professional character," adds Home, "were at this time advancing fast;" and yet his income, until 1774, never reached a thousand a year, a convincing proof how much his fame as a naturalist had outrun his fortune as a surgeon.

In the spring of the year following Hunter suffered under an alarming attack of spasm, apparently seated about the region of the pylorus, but attended with a cessation of the heart's action, which lasted three quarters of an hour, in defiance of various active remedies suggested by Dr. Hunter, Sir George Baker, Dr. Huck Saunders, and Dr. G. Fordyce;

who were hastily called in on the occasion. The complaint was probably of a gouty nature, for he had this year escaped a regular fit of gout, such as he had suffered from during the spring of the three preceding years ; but the immediately exciting cause was a violent mental affection, the nature of which Sir Everard Home does not mention. During this attack the sensation and voluntary actions continued unaffected, and Hunter continued to respire by a voluntary effort, with a view of keeping himself alive ; though, as he afterwards observed, the continuance of respiration was probably of no service, as the circulation had ceased*. This seems to have been the first warning he received of the existence of disease about the heart ; although it never again manifested itself by an exactly similar attack ; nor was it until several years after that this organ became permanently deranged in its actions.

It has been stated, in the preceding chapter, that soon after Jenner settled at Berkeley, Hunter entered into a correspondence with him, which was kept up nearly to the period of his own death. Hunter's letters alone have been preserved, and these consist, for the most part, of requests to his former pupil to procure for him various objects of natural history, which a residence in the country rendered easily attainable, or of directions respecting experiments to elucidate those inquiries into the vital actions, in which Hunter was constantly engaged, and in the prosecution of which Jenner was always ready to lend his valuable aid. The letters seldom bear any date, but when this can be

---

* This curious fact in physiology has never been satisfactorily explained. Bichat and his school insist on the necessity of arterial blood constantly circulating through the brain in order to the continuance of its functions, but here we find its functions going on though the circulation had ceased. In the collapse of cholera, the sensorial functions continue perfect for hours after all perceptible circulation has ceased, and when the blood is as dark as pitch.

ascertained, either from the postmark or from the nature of their contents, it will serve as the guide for their insertion in this and the succeeding chapters. The following one appears to have been written somewhere about this time.

" DEAR JENNER,

" I received yours, as also the cuckoo's stomach : I should like to have a few more, for they do not all show the same thing*. If possible, I wish you could remove the cuckoo's egg into another bird's nest, and tame the young one, to see what note it has. There is employment for you, young man! If you collect eggs, you should also collect the nests, and I do not care how many you send. I wanted a crow's nest, as also a magpie's, in the branches of the trees where they are built, but I am afraid it is now too late.

" This evening, looking into my book of patients to scratch out the name of one who had paid me, and whose name began with M, I saw a Mr. Matthews of Berkeley, recommended by you. He did not pay me. I forget whether he was recommended by you as a friend to serve him or me : if it was to serve him, I scratch him out of my book. Do you keep an account of the observations on the cuckoo, or must I refer to your letters? I want a nest with the eggs in it; also one with a young cuckoo; also an old cuckoo. I hear you saying, there is no end of your wants.

" Ever yours,
" JOHN HUNTER."

The phenomena of electricity had of late begun deeply to engage the attention of scientific men. Mr. Walsh was one who had devoted much attention to the subject, and who had been making experiments, to ascertain whether the shock communicated by the Torpedo is analogous to that of an electrical battery. Being anxious to learn the exact

* The internal coat of the cuckoo's stomach is found thickly set with the hairs of caterpillars on which it feeds. These hairs are laid circularly over each other in one direction, showing the circular motion of the two portions of the gizzard, on each other, in grinding the food. It is to this, probably, that Hunter alludes, as there is a preparation in the museum showing this fact. Jenner had now commenced his observations on the hatching and rearing of the cuckoo, which were communicated many years after to the Royal Society.

anatomical arrangement of the parts in which the peculiar power resides, he requested Hunter to examine them, a request with which the latter willingly complied, and in July communicated, in a paper to the Royal Society, an accurate description of the electric organs of the Ray, and pointed out the vast nerves with which they are supplied as the probable source of their peculiar power.

In the autumnal session of this year, Hunter for the first time delivered a course of lectures exclusively on surgery. These lectures were for the first two years given gratuitously to the pupils attending St. George's Hospital, but after that the usual fee for admittance was required.

It has been before observed that he appeared but to little advantage as a lecturer; his language, though forcible, was inelegant, and often coarse*; his delivery was heavy and unengaging, as he rarely raised his eyes from his book; and as, in addition to this, the doctrines he taught were new, and often obscure and theoretical, his hearers were never numerous. The many who found it troublesome to think, and desired only straightforward directions for every-day practice, sought other teachers; for notwithstanding the length of the course, which in late years extended to eighty-six lectures, he entered but little into the minuter details of practice, and gave little or no account of the operations of surgery, but confined himself almost exclusively to the theory and principles of the art.

It was an instance of Hunter's perseverance, that though his dislike to delivering himself in public was so great that he never commenced a course of lectures without having

---

* In speaking, for example, of a case of gun-shot wounds, he described the ball, as "having gone into the man's belly and hit his guts such a d—d thump, that they mortified." And in relating his own case, where secondary symptoms had ensued on inoculation with the matter of chancre, he repeated over so often, and in so peculiar a tone, "I knocked down the disease with mercury and I killed it," that the whole class at length burst into a loud fit of laughter.

recourse to laudanum to relieve his uneasy feelings, he notwithstanding continued the practice of lecturing for many years. He was induced to this by other motives besides the more obvious one of increasing his reputation: his opinions were for the most part peculiar to himself; he was desirous of subjecting them to the test of public opinion, and thought this the best mode of doing it, until they were sufficiently matured in his own mind to be committed to print; he felt also that the practice of lecturing was beneficial to himself, by discovering to him the amount of knowledge he possessed on any subject, and when this knowledge was deficient*. In this respect he was accustomed to compare the process of preparing a lecture to that of a tradesman taking stock.

Boldness and independence in the pursuit of truth, one of the striking characteristics of Hunter's mind, was well exhibited in these lectures. He attached no value to opinions, except they could be shown to be firmly based on fact: fallacious reasoning, though ingenious, he quickly saw through, and instantly demolished; and he was not more indulgent towards his own theories when he discovered them to be erroneous. To a pupil (Sir Astley Cooper) who asked with surprise, whether he had not the year before stated an opinion on some point, directly at variance with one he had just put forth; he replied, " Very likely I did; I hope I grow wiser every year:" and to the same purport he answered Professor Coleman (another of his pupils), who asked whether he had not written so and so; " Never ask me what I have said, or what I have written; but if you will ask me what my present opinions are, I will tell you." Occasionally, too, he would say to any of the pupils

* "Reading," says Lord Bacon, "makes a full man, conference a ready man, and writing an exact man." Public lecturing, and more particularly extempore lecturing, combines these advantages in a remarkable degree.

whom he saw taking notes, "You had better not write down that observation, for very likely I shall think differently next year:" and on one occasion, after lecturing for a considerable time, he stopped short, raised his spectacles, and said, "Gentlemen, I think you had better omit what I have been saying; the fact is, I had an idea when I wrote down this, but I have lost the train of thought connected with it, and I cannot now recall it*." Such a mode of lecturing was not likely to become popular; his class consequently never exceeded thirty, and not half that number derived much benefit by their attendance. Those, however, who would take the pains to understand what they heard, set a high value on these lectures, by which, perhaps even more than by his writings, Hunter originated that revolution in surgery, of the occurrence of which none can doubt, who compares the best surgical works written half a century since, with those of the present time.

We find, accordingly, that most of the eminent surgeons who immediately succeeded to the time of Hunter, were at one period or other attendants at his lectures; and that in effecting those improvements which they were the means of introducing into the practice of surgery, they pursued that path into which he had directed their steps at the very outset of their career. Besides those before mentioned, we must enumerate the names of Home, Carlisle, Abernethy, Astley Cooper, Wilson, Chevalier, Macartney, Coleman, and

---

* This was a difficulty he not unfrequently experienced. After thinking deeply, he would make short notes of his thoughts, on looking at which some time after, he would find them unintelligible until his mind was prepared to fall again into the same train of reasoning. It may fairly be questioned, when Mr. Hunter had got so deep, whether he had not got out of his depth. At least from the specimens we have of his hypothetical reasoning, we have no reason to regret that he did not oftener indulge in it. Dr. Beddoes observed: "John Hunter fancied that what he could not find words for was very profound: but he was mistaken; whenever he found himself at a loss for words, he was labouring with the delivery of nothing."—*Dr. Beddoes's Common Place Book.*

E

Physick; and others might no doubt be mentioned, who have, like them, done honour to the surgical profession in this century.

In 1774 two papers by Hunter were read before the Royal Society, and published in the Transactions. The first of these contains a general account of the receptacles for air which are found in the abdominal cavity, the cellular tissue, and bones of birds. In the second, a description is given of the stomach of the Gillaroo Trout, a peculiar species of trout found in some of the lakes in Ireland, the stomach of which is so thick and muscular, as to have led to the name of Gizzard Trout being applied to this animal.

There is another paper on the subject, in this volume of the Transactions, by Henry Watson, and it is not uninteresting to observe the different manner in which the two men have handled the same topic. Watson has contented himself with giving a plain anatomical description of the organ, from which he draws the conclusion that it is not properly a gizzard, but only a very muscular stomach. Hunter arrives at the same conclusion, but has given interest to a rather meagre subject, by introducing it with a general view of the various modes in which the preliminary process of digestion, that of comminuting the food, is effected in different animals. He points out the analogy between the gizzard of granivorous birds and the grinders of mammalia; shows how, by imperceptible gradations, we pass from the membranous stomach to the gizzard; and finally determines, that though the object to be effected in the stomach of the Gillaroo Trout is very much the same as in the gizzards of birds, yet that in structure it more resembles a true membranous stomach than a gizzard. The introduction of such general remarks was a common practice with Hunter in treating any anatomical question, so that the titles of his papers seldom afford us any adequate notion of their contents. He employs the subject treated of as a text, on which he freely expatiates, introducing valuable original researches of a physiological character as a prelude to some point in anatomy, which, separately considered, would possess little interest.

Hunter's increasing professional avocations began now to render it impossible for him to devote as much time as he desired to extending and perfecting his collection. The field of his labours, too, was considerably increased ; on the one hand, by the opportunities for the cultivation of morbid anatomy, which his connexion with a hospital, and his increasing private practice afforded him ; on the other, by the augmented stores of rare and curious animals, which the kindness of his friends, and the liberality of scientific men, continually accumulated on his hands. He therefore engaged Mr. Bell, a young artist of considerable merit, to reside in his house, and to devote himself, under his superintendence, to making anatomical preparations and drawings, and to the general care of the museum. Mr. Bell's engagement was for ten years, and he eventually remained fourteen, in the course of which time he became an accomplished anatomist, and added a large number of valuable preparations and several hundred admirable drawings to the collection. He was also frequently employed by Hunter as his amanuensis, and some of the catalogues now in existence are in his handwriting.

The fact that Mr. Bell remained so much longer with Hunter than he originally engaged to do, is an evidence that he was not dissatisfied with his situation. Probably, like most of those who were intimately acquainted with this great man, he gradually acquired a strong personal attachment to him, which led him to tolerate the violent sallies of passion to which the inmates of Hunter's house were not unfrequently subjected on very trivial grounds. Home states that "Hunter's temper was warm and impatient, readily provoked, and when irritated not easily soothed;" and this account is confirmed by most of those who were intimately acquainted with him. An intrusion on his studies, even by one with whom he was on friendly terms, would call forth expressions of strong disgust and impatience: an object of which he was in want being misplaced, would bring down all the vials of his wrath on the offender; and during these fits of passion he used to swear in the most outrageous manner, a vicious habit, which was not uncommon, even amongst men of education, fifty years ago, and to which Hunter was greatly addicted.

The accession of Mr. Bell to his staff did not lead Hunter at all to relax in his own exertions; on the contrary, every hour of the day, and of great part of the night, found him busily employed. He commenced his labours in the dissecting-room generally before six in the morning, and remained there until nine, when he breakfasted. After breakfast he saw patients at his own house until twelve*, when he made it a point to set forth on his rounds, even though persons might be in waiting for the purpose of seeing him; for, said he, "these people can take their chance another day, and I have no right to waste the valuable time of other practitioners by keeping them waiting for me." Hunter was a great œconomist of time, and was always very punctual in fulfilling his appointments, to ensure which he kept a regular entry of his engagements in a book at home, and carried an exact copy of this in his

---

* The following note shows that Mr. Hunter went out at an earlier hour at one period of his life:

" DEAR SIR,

" I can hardly be at home after 11 o'clock *any* day, but on Friday I will wait till half-after, and if that should not suit your convenience, and you do not come by that time, I will be at home by three to meet you.

" I am your most obedient servant,

" *Wednesday Evening*." " JOHN HUNTER."

waistcoat pocket, so that by a reference to the book he could always be found at any hour of the day, in the event of his being wanted. Any unnecessary discomposure of these engagements greatly annoyed him, and caused him to give vent to his feelings in no measured terms. The late Mr. Cline once excited his ire by an offence of this kind. He had engaged Hunter to meet him in consultation on a case in the afternoon, but in the course of his morning rounds saw another patient, respecting whom he wished to take Hunter's opinion, and accordingly, without giving him previous notice, appointed to call with him after the former engagement was ended. When the first visit was over, Cline mentioned the second appointment, on hearing of which Hunter got into a towering passion, and asserted that Cline had acted in the most unjustifiable manner in thus deranging the whole of his arrangements for the afternoon [*]. Cline, who was of a very placid temper, was amazed to see such a storm excited by so trifling a cause, and said what he could to appease it. In this he succeeded, and Hunter, soon recovering himself, turned to him, and in a very altered tone said, "Come along, then, let us go and see our patient." Hunter was equally strict in enforcing punctuality on his household : he dined at four, then the fashionable hour, and gave strict orders that dinner should be ready punctually whether he was at home or not. He was a very moderate eater, and set little value on the indulgence of the palate. During many of the latter years of his life he drank no wine, and therefore seldom remained

---

[*] This attention to punctuality was also displayed by Hunter's nephew, Dr. Baillie, in as remarkable a degree. When accidentally detained beyond his time, he made it a point to forfeit one appointment to save the rest. He used to say : "I consider it not only a professional, but a moral duty to meet punctually my professional brethren of all ranks. My equals have a right to such a mark of my respect, and I would shudder at the apprehension of lessening a junior practitioner in the eyes of his patient, by not keeping an appointment with him."

long at table after dinner, except when he had company; but then, though he abstained himself, he was not willing to allow his friends to follow his example*.

After dinner he was accustomed to sleep for about an hour, and his evenings were spent either in preparing or delivering lectures, in dictating to an amanuensis the records of particular cases, of which he kept a regular entry, or in a similar manner committing to paper the substance of any work on which he chanced to be engaged. When employed in the latter way, Mr. Bell and he used to retire to the study, the former carrying with him from the museum such preparations as related to the subject on which Hunter was engaged; these were placed on the table before him, and at the other end sat Mr. Bell, writing from Hunter's dictation. The manuscript was then looked over, and the grammatical blunders, for Bell was an uneducated man, corrected by Hunter†. At twelve the family went to bed, and the butler, before retiring to rest, used to bring in a fresh argand lamp, by the light of which Hunter continued his labours until one or two in the morning, or even later in winter. Thus he left only about four hours for

---

* "Come, fellow," said he, in his usual blunt way, to Mr., now Sir William Blizard, "why don't you drink your wine?" Mr. B. pleaded in excuse a whitlow, which caused him much pain. Hunter would not allow the validity of the plea, but continued to urge him and ridicule his excuse. "Come, come, John," said Mrs. Hunter, "you will please to remember that you were delirious for two days when you had a boil on your finger some time ago." This turned the laugh against Hunter, who now ceased from importuning his guest.

† Burke used to say that it was impossible for any man to arrive at great eminence by his own unassisted talents: the power to combine the assistance of inferior men, in subserviency to his own views, used always to constitute an essential part of his definition of a truly great man. This power Hunter possessed. All his pupils and intimate friends contributed more or less to the formation of his museum; fourteen years of Mr. Bell's life were devoted to this object; he called in the aid of the ladies of his family in the prosecution of his researches on the œconomy of bees, and he even carried this so far as to call on his coachman occasionally to act as amanuensis when Mr. Bell was otherwise engaged. There were no drones in his hive.

sleep, which, with the hour after dinner, was all the time that he devoted to the refreshment of his body. He had no home amusements, as cards, for the relaxation of his mind, and the only indulgence of this kind he enjoyed consisted in an evening's ramble amongst the various denizens of earth and air which he had congregated at Earl's Court, where he slept, and, with his family, spent the greater part of his time during the autumnal months.

In 1775 Hunter entertained thoughts of establishing a school of natural history, in which he purposed himself to take the chief part; but as it was necessary that he should obtain the assistance of some young man of talent in carrying on the undertaking, and as none was better qualified for the office than Jenner, he applied to him in the following letter to say if he felt disposed and at liberty to join him.

" DEAR JENNER,

" I have received many things from you, and will thank you in the lump; but while I thank you, I have a great scheme to communicate to you, and I want you to take part in it; but remember, it is as yet a most profound secret. My scheme is to teach natural history, in which will be included anatomy, both human and comparative. The labour of it is too much for one man, therefore I must have some one to assist; but who that person shall be is the difficulty. When running over a variety of people, you have come into my mind among the rest. Now if it is a scheme you would like, and a possibility of your leaving the country,—at the same time, able and willing to lay down one thousand guineas,—I will send you the whole proposals; but if you cannot leave the country on any' terms, then it is unnecessary to go any further; and all I have to beg is to keep it a secret. I would not have you mention it to Ludlow, ——, &c. I proposed it to L—— before he left London, but his father objected, I believe, to the money. I know the scheme will be to your taste. Before you ask any of your friends, consult with yourself, and ask, Can I go to London, and can I give one thousand guineas for any chance that may be worth it? Let me hear from you very soon.

" Yours,

" London, May 24th." " J. HUNTER."

Jenner declined the offer, for what reasons cannot now be known, as his letters have been destroyed; but it would appear, from Hunter's next letter, that the refusal was not unexpected, and we may judge, moreover, from his language, that he had already given up the project himself.

"DEAR JENNER, *August 2nd.*

"I received yours, in answer to mine, which I should have answered. I own I suspected it would not do; yet as I did intend such a scheme, I was inclinable to give you the offer.

"I thank you for your experiment on the hedgehog; but why do you ask me a question by the way of solving it? I think your solution is just; but why think? why not try the experiment? Repeat all the experiments upon a hedgehog as soon as you receive this, and they will give you the solution. Try the heat: cut off a leg at the same place; cut off the head, and expose the heart, and let me know the result of the whole.

"Ever yours,

"J. HUNTER."

It is probable that Hunter abandoned his intention on finding that it was not likely to be attended with success proportionate to the trouble and expense it would entail on him, since the number of persons who would have been willing to become pupils in a school of comparative anatomy was in those days extremely limited. This was probably the chief reason which weighed with him in determining to abandon his scheme; but we may gather, from the following anecdote, that he was also in part deterred by the difficulties of the undertaking itself. Hunter was one morning at breakfast, when a young man, who was on intimate terms with him as a friend and pupil, mentioned, as if casually, that he had some thoughts of giving a course of lectures on comparative anatomy. Hunter looked up, and drily replied, "Sir, that is a bold undertaking; I had thoughts once myself of doing the same thing, but the difficulties and necessary qualifications were so great that

I did not think myself competent to the task; but you, I dare say, may feel yourself quite equal to it."

In the early part of this year Sir C. Blagden presented to the Royal Society the details of some interesting experiments instituted by Dr. Fordyce, himself, and others, to ascertain how far the living body possesses the power of maintaining its standard heat when exposed to air at high temperatures. This drew from Hunter a valuable paper on the heat of animals and vegetables, containing an account of various experiments made some years before*, by which the counterpart of the above proposition was proved, namely, that living bodies possess a power of maintaining their heat against the influence of external cold, and this in a degree proportioned to their rank in the scale of organization.

In January 1776 Hunter received the appointment of surgeon-extraordinary to the King, the first and only one which brought him within the atmosphere of Royalty.

In the course of this year he contributed to the Philosophical Transactions a memoir on the means to be employed in the recovery of drowned persons. This paper was drawn up at the request of the Humane Society, then newly established. Its contents are so generally known, that it will be sufficient to remark, that the directions it furnishes are based on sound physiological principles, and still continue to guide the conduct of those who may be called to the assistance of a fellow-creature suffering under this form of asphyxia.

---

* Hunter's experiments were made with a view to discover if it were possible to restore to life animals which had been frozen. This was for some time a favourite inquiry, and he used to speculate on the possibility of freezing human beings, and thawing them to life two or three centuries after, a project which, if he could realise, he expected would make his fortune. Whilst his friends Lynn and Benjamin West, therefore, were warming themselves with a bout of skating on the Serpentine, Hunter staid at home freezing his fingers in pursuit of this his philosopher's stone.

He also commenced this year a series of six Croonian lectures, on muscular motion, which he had been appointed by the Royal Society to deliver.

In return for the assistance which Jenner afforded him in his pursuits, Hunter was enabled sometimes to give him the benefit of his professional advice, in such cases of difficulty as the former might encounter in his practice. The following letters are of this kind, and relate in part to the treatment of a case of *fungus cerebri* under Jenner's care.

"DEAR JENNER,

" I don't know any one I would as soon write to as you. I do not know any body I am so much obliged to. I thank you for a fish, but I should thank you more if you had let me know who it comes from.

" I beg for the future you will always write when you send me anything. Somebody sent me a cheese, with a fish upon it; perhaps it was you; you know I hate to be puzzled. Also let me know what things you have sent me lately. I have not received the cuckoo's nest yet. Now for your patient. I believe the best thing you can do is to do little. I would not touch the fungus with an escharotic, for fear the brain should be near: I would also use but very slight compression, as the fungus will be a bandage to the brain; and as to the fungus itself you have nothing to fear, for wherever the parts underneath are sound, the fungus will subside of itself. Keep your patient rather low, and quiet. Let me know how he goes on, and anything else you can.

" Ever yours,

" J. H."

"DEAR JENNER,   [*Post-mark Jan.* 10*th.*]

" You must think me very fond of fish when you send me cheese as much fishified as possible : however, it is an excellent cheese, and every country has laid claim to its birth. The fish is called ——*

" I have but one order to send you, which is, to send everything you can get, either animal, vegetable, or mineral, and the compound of the two, either animal or vegetable, mineralized.

" I would have you do nothing with the boy but dress him superficially : these funguses will die, and be damned to them, and drop off.

" Have you large trees, of different kinds, that you can make free with ? If you have, I will put you upon a set of experiments with regard to the heat of vegetables.

---

* There is an omission here, which Hunter probably intended to supply before closing his letter, but forgot to do so.

"Have you any eaves, where bats go to at night? If you have, I will put you upon a set of experiments concerning the heat of them at different seasons. I should have been extremely happy to have had the honour of a visit from Lord Berkeley.

"Ever yours,
"JOHN HUNTER.

"Anny sends her compliments, and thanks you for all favours. Write down the case."

"DEAR JENNER,   [*Post-mark Jan. 22nd.*]

"I did not understand that the funguses which you described were brain; and I should still very much doubt that they are brain, for their keeping into one substance would make me inclinable to believe that it is a new substance; but let it be what it will, I would advise you not to meddle with it: if it is brain, let it drop off; if it is fungus, let it either drop or waste off: therefore be quiet, and think yourself well off that the boy is not dead. You do not mention a word about bats. I have no particular experiments at present about fixed air; it is such a wide field that a man may make a thousand experiments before he determines anything. Have you got the bones yet of a large porpoise? I wish you had. Is ever the salmon spawn seen after she has parted with it? If it is, I wish you could get some: I want to examine the spawn of fish in the progress of the formation of the young one.

"I am, dear Jenner,
"Your most obedient Servant,
"JOHN HUNTER."

In the second of the preceding letters we have seen that Hunter expresses a wish that Jenner would undertake some experiments on animal and vegetable heat. This was a subject in which Hunter was much interested, and about which he continued for several years to institute experiments. The following letters, which appear to have been written early in this year, refer chiefly to this inquiry.

"DEAR JENNER,

"I received the box; also your letter. I am very much obliged to you for your kind attention to me, and how to reward you I do not know. Let that be as it will, I must still give you commissions. If you can get me easily salmon spawn, I should like to have it, and out of

different places, as it will be of different ages.   It should be put into
bottles immediately, with spirits.   The spirits should be proof, and
there should be rather more spirit than spawn.

"I will also take any specimens of fossils you may send me, or indeed
anything else.   Did I send you any of my publications in the Philosophical Transactions ?   If I have not, let me know.   I want to put you
upon some experiments this winter.   What do you think of examining
eels ?   Their sexes have not yet been found out, nor their mode of propagation ; it is a thing of consequence in natural history.   I began it,
but could not get eels immediately from the river, and to get them of
fishmongers, who buy them in custom, does not do.   My intention
was to examine several pretty large eels on the first and fifteenth of
every month.   If the eels are plenty with you, and if you like the proposal, let me know, and I will give you full instructions how to proceed.   Also, next spring, I would have you make the experiments on
the growth of vegetables ; and if you have no objection, I will set you
upon a set of experiments upon the heat of vegetables in the winter.
If, in any of these pursuits, you discover any principle worthy of the
public, I will give it to the Royal Society for you.   I must pick you
up a picture this winter.   I saw Mrs. Black* at Mr. Drummond's : I
suspect Mr. Black is dead, but I durst not inquire.   Cannot you get
me a large porpoise for love or money ?   What is the bird you sent me?
also the young animals, which I imagine to be guinea-pigs ?

"Ever yours,

"JOHN HUNTER."

"DEAR JENNER,

"I received your salmon, and very fresh, and just examined enough
to want another, but will wait till another season.   If I was to have
another, it should be one that had just spawned : I will take a cock
salmon when you please.   If you catch any bats, let me have some of
them ; and those you try yourself, open a hole in the belly, just size
enough to admit the ball ; put the ball down towards the pelvis, and
observe the heat there ; then up towards the diaphragm, and observe the
heat there ; observe the fluidity of the blood.   Do all this in a cold place.
Extraneous fossils are all vegetable and animal substances found in a
fossil state.   See if you can catch the number of pulsations and breathing in a bat without torture.   If the frost is hard, see what vegetables
freeze : bore holes in large trees, and see whether the sap runs out,

---

* Jenner's elder sister.

which will show it is not frozen. I am afraid you have not a proper thermometer: I will send you one.

> " Your very much obliged Servant,
> " J. HUNTER.

" I have not seen Dr. H., but I dare say he will be glad to have the cases."

The two foregoing letters appear to have been written in January or February. Hunter, in the multiplicity of his engagements, forgot to send the thermometer he had promised, and Jenner, after waiting for some time, began to fear lest he might in some way have offended his friend, and accordingly wrote to inquire the cause of his long silence. To this Hunter replied in the following letter, which bears the post-mark of April 12th.

" DEAR JENNER,

" I can never be offended with you. The reason for not sending the thermometer was I entirely forgot it, but it shall be sent next week. I shall be glad to present your paper if you mean to give it to the public. The large porpoise I would have coarsely stripped, and the bones put into a cask and sent; the young one, if not too large, put into spirits to be able to inject it. If the breasts of the old one were taken off and put into the cask among the spirits, I should like it. You will find the nipples on each side of the vulva, and the gland passes along under the skin of the belly, almost to the breast, so that it would be only preserving the belly part. Did I write to you some time ago about cuckoos? I have forgot : if I did not, I must give you a long order.

> " I am, dear Jenner,
> " Ever yours,
> " J. HUNTER."

" Friday night."

" I was at my club last night, and not coming home till twelve is the reason I did not write."

" DEAR JENNER,   [Post-mark April 16th.]

" I have received your fish, as also your letter ; for both I thank you. It came quite fresh, and it is under dissection and drawing. The bubbies of this are as flat as a pancake, but I have injected the ducts. Was the milk sweet ? Could you save some of it ? if but two drops, to see if it grows sour. Try it with the syrup of violets. Are the breasts demolished ? Are the kidneys demolished ? If not, could you send them ?

I will leave it to you what is to be done at present with the bones; either send them as they are, or steep them in water till the flesh rots off. If you could, send me the stomach and a piece of intestine, if the large one was different from the small; but if it had the same head, then you need not send them, as the present informs me of the class. I have got the thermometer, but let me know to whose care I am to send it. You did not in your last tell me if I wrote to you about the cuckoo.

" Ever yours,

" J. HUNTER."

Very soon after the date of the last letter, Hunter was attacked with an alarming fit of illness, brought on by anxiety of mind, at being called on to pay a large sum of money for a friend, for whom he had become security ; a call which his circumstances made exceedingly inconvenient. The most distressing feature of this complaint, which Sir Everard Home has described at considerable length, was a constant vertigo, which rendered him incapable of raising his head from his pillow for ten days : this sensation was accompanied by a morbid acuteness of the organs of sense, with a feeling of being suspended in the air, of his body being much diminished in size, and of every motion of the limbs or head, however slight, being both very extensive and accomplished with great rapidity. This complaint was unattended by fever. Various remedies were employed, but without any perceptible effect on the symptoms, which, at the end of ten days, began to disappear spontaneously. Sir Everard Home dates this illness in 1776 ; but in one part of his memoir he says it happened in the spring, and in another in the autumn. The following letter of Hunter's to Jenner, which, contrary to his usual practice, bears the date of the year, shows that it occurred in 1777.

" DEAR JENNER,

" I have before me two letters of yours, which I should have answered much sooner. Your friend Dr. Hicks I have not seen. I was not at home when he called, and I have not had time to wait on him, as he lived entirely out of my walk. I should have been glad to have seen him, but I suppose he stood upon ceremony. I received the fossils, and should be glad of any that you can get. If any bones of animals are found, be sure and get them for me. I should be glad to have some of the salmon-fry. I had the pleasure of seeing your brother, but only for a time. I received the bird: I am not acquainted with it: send me some more if you can get them readily. I sent with Mr. Jenner the thermometer: if you do not understand it, let me know.

"Not two hours after I saw your brother I was taken ill with a swimming in my head, and could not raise it off the pillow for ten days: it is not yet perfectly recovered. Have you begun the eels? No porpoises. No salmon spawn before it has hatched. You see I am very greedy. Be sure to keep an account of all outgoings.

"My compliments to Mrs. Black and your brother, and let me hear from you.

"Ever yours,

"*London, May* 11, 1777." "J. HUNTER."

In July he wrote again to Jenner, explaining the mode of using the thermometer, and treating of divers other matters, with his accustomed brevity.

"DEAR JENNER,

"Excuse me for not answering your letters as soon as you could wish. Send me all the fossils you find. What I meant by bones was all the bones that are found any depth below the surface of the earth: many are found in stones, &c. I suppose those skeletons are not complete, but send me some of them; and if any history can be given, send it also. The thermometer is a very useful one when understood. You will observe the scratch upon the glass stalk, perhaps about two inches from the globe, which is the freezing point: put 0, or nought, which is upon the ivory scale, two degrees below the scratch, then 0 becomes the thirtieth degree, and the scratch, being two degrees above it, stands at the freezing point; then, from that count upwards: or if the cold is below 30°, then put 1 or 2 at the scratch, and count down: every No. is ten degrees. What the devil becomes of your eels in the winter? but try them in summer, and see what you can make of them.

"I do not remember Dr. Fordyce's ever supposing a polypus vascular. I should rather believe that he supposed the contrary: you know it comes near my idea that the blood is the bond of union everywhere. But I should very much suspect that a polypus formed after death is not of that kind. I am pretty certain that I have injected them in arteries after amputation. I have a preparation which shows it, and which supports my theory.

" Yours,

" *London, July 6th*, 1777." " J. HUNTER."

Hunter was disposed to treat his late illness as one of trifling moment ; but his medical friends thought more seriously of it, and as he had never fully regained his health, urged his resigning business for a time and retiring to Bath. In compliance with this advice, he proceeded thither in the autumn, after having deputed Mr. Bell and Mr. Home, in his absence, to complete a catalogue of all the preparations in his museum with which they were acquainted, a task which had been hitherto entirely neglected. Before leaving London he announced to Jenner his intended visit to Bath in the following letter.

" DEAR JENNER, " *August 6th*, 1777."
" I just now found your last letter. I think I answered it, but am not sure ; if I did not, let me know. Is there any judging whose these human bones are? Let us have some of them, especially skulls, as complete as possible, with the lower jaw, &c. I am very well, but for all that I set out, in a few days, for Bath.

" Ever yours,
" J. HUNTER."

Soon after his arrival at Bath he was visited by Jenner, who was greatly shocked to perceive the alteration which had taken place in his appearance, and concluded, from the symptoms under which he laboured, that his disease was angina pectoris, an affection not then well understood, but which Jenner had been led to believe, by the dissection of former cases, depended on an organic change in the heart. He abstained from telling Hunter his opinion, as he feared the effect such an announcement might have on his mind, but communicated it to Dr. Heberden, one of Hunter's medical advisers, in a letter, which Dr. Baron has published in his Life of Jenner.

During the time Hunter remained in Bath he appears to have had frequent communication with his friend, and the following letter affords a good example of the familiarity which existed between them.

"DEAR JENNER,

" Till yesterday we did not know from whom the hare came ; but the cook found it out. We thank you : it was a very fine one. By your not taking any notice of my letter, I do suppose you did not receive it. Near three weeks ago I wrote to you to meet us at the Hotwells, Bristol. Some days after the date of my letter we went to the place appointed, by ten o'clock in the morning ; but no Jenner there. We breakfasted, we dined, we staid all night, and set out for Bath the next day. We would have came on to Berkeley, but we were afraid you might not be there. I am afraid it will not be in my power to come and see you, though I wish it much. I shall be obliged to take South-ampton in my way home. Are the hedgehogs so saucy as to refuse coming without coming for them ? See if you can coax them. We are alive here. The downs look like a beehive. Let me hear from you. Mrs. Hunter gives her compliments to you.

" Yours,

" *Bath*, 18*th*."   " J. HUNTER.

" My letter was sent to your friend in Bristol by the coach, but per-haps the coachman forgot to deliver it."

After remaining three months in Bath, he became very desirous to be at home again, and decided therefore on im-mediately returning to London, though his health was not fully re-established. Fortunately, he felt no inconvenience from this step, but continued to improve after his return, and shortly regained his usual state of health.

He now recommenced his ordinary pursuits with una-bated diligence, and appears about this time to have been chiefly engaged in confirming and extending his inqui-ries on vital heat. He was anxious to engage Jenner's assistance in conducting some of the experiments, for which his residence in the country afforded him the necessary facili-ties, and determined to write to him on the subject ; but

F

as he had received no reply to several of his late communications, his first letter was written to inquire the cause of Jenner's long silence.

" DEAR JENNER,

" I wrote to you twice from Bath since I saw you, and have had no answer to either; what the d—l is become of you? I have got your candlesticks: to where shall I send them? Let me know by return of post; and all the news you can.
" Yours,

" Nov. 6th, 1777."   " JOHN HUNTER."

Having ascertained, to his satisfaction, that Jenner had not become a subject of " Pluto's dreary reign," he forthwith transmitted him the necessary instructions for his guidance.

" DEAR JENNER,

" I have sent you the candlesticks as you desired. I hope you will like them. They cost five pounds and a shilling; so I owe you four shillings. I have received the hedgehogs. If you have time, see their natural winter haunts, and in the very cold weather run the thermometer into the anus, and observe the heat; then open the belly by a small hole, and pass the thermometer down towards the pelvis, and observe the heat; then towards the liver or *diaphragm*, and observe the heat: you may do all this in a very few minutes. Observe the fluidity of the blood, by comparing it with another that has been kept warm for a few days. I have heard of Mr. Cattgal's collection of fossils, and not till I came to London: I suppose he will not sell any. I shall think of your lymphatics; and if I can pick up a preparation or two, I will. I am sorry you did not get my first letter, as we intended going to Berkeley with you, but did not choose to come without an answer, as it was possible you might not be at home. I have seen your old master, who has given me the use of a very curious bone: I hope he will give it me altogether.
" Dear Jenner, yours,

" Nov. 23rd."   " JOHN HUNTER."

Unfortunately, his hedgehogs all died, either from exposure to cold or some other cause; he therefore referred the experiments, for the present, to Jenner, until he could learn what means were requisite to keep them alive.

" DEAR JENNER,

" I am always plaguing you with letters, but you are the only man I can apply to. I put three hedgehogs in the garden, and put meat in different places for them to eat as they went along; but they all died. Now I want to know what this is owing to; therefore I want you to find out their haunts, and observe, if you can, what they do; if they make a warm place for themselves; if they have any food by them, &c. I would have you kill one, and see its heat. First, make a small hole in the belly, and introduce the thermometer into it, first down to the pelvis, then up to the liver and diaphragm, and see the difference, for I believe they will answer the purpose as well as bats. See if there is any food in the stomach; what the intestines contain; examine if they are fat, and in the spring see if they are much leaner; see if the blood is as fluid as common, or if thicker. In short, make what observations you can. Let me hear from you when you have nothing else to do.

" Yours,

" *London, Dec.* 17."   " J. HUNTER."

His next letter, written in March 1778, is as follows :

" DEAR JENNER,

" Your letter of December has lain before me ever since I received it, to put me in mind that it was not answered. I am glad you liked the candlesticks: I thought them pretty. The fossils were none of the best; but I know you did not make them, therefore it is not your fault. The particular one you put the Q? on is only the cast of a bivalve. I wish I had seen E.'s collection. I am matching my fossils, as far as I can, with the recent. Have you made any experiments with the hedgehogs, and can you send me some this spring? for all those you sent me died, so that I am hedgehogless.

" Mr. Ludero sent me the bone; it is a very curious one : whether he will let me keep it or no I do not know. I received yours by Mr. Jones, with the bird. I thank you for thinking of me. Frogs live an amazing while after they are dead; as also all animals of that tribe. The directions I gave you about the blackbirds were, when you have a blackbird's nest, viz. with four young ones, take one and put it bodily into spirit by the head, extending the wings and legs. Observe when the feathers begin to sprout; then take another, and serve it in the same way; then a third, and a fourth, so as to get a series of the growth of the feather; but the last, or fourth, must not be so old as the feathers to cover other parts where feathers do not grow. This you will better understand when you come to make the trial. I have a picture of Bas-

F 2

san's that I lent a poor devil three guineas upon : he died and never redeemed the picture. I intend sending it to you : it is a good deal damaged, but some of the figures are very good. Get a frame for it, and hang it in a strong light. There are some experiments of mine publishing in the Philosophical Transactions, which I will send you with the picture ; accept them as a remembrance of the trouble I put you to. Let me hear from you when convenient. Mrs. Hunter desires her compliments to you.

" I am, dear Jenner,

" Your most obedient and most humble servant,

"*London, March* 29, 1778."   " JOHN HUNTER."

It is not very clear what are the experiments to which Hunter alludes in the foregoing letter as about to be published ; it seems most probable, however, that they were those contained in his second memoir on the heat of animals and vegetables, which he this year presented to the Royal Society. The only ground for doubting it is, that at the head of this paper, in the Transactions, it is stated to have been read in part on the 19th of June, and the remainder on the 13th of November, whereas the date of the foregoing letter is March.

This was one of the most valuable of the many excellent papers which Hunter furnished to the Royal Society, both on account of the importance of the subject treated of, and the valuable deductions he has drawn from his experiments. The inquiry was both new and complicated, and it is not therefore surprising, that whilst adding much to what was before known on the subject, he yet left some errors to be corrected, and many parts requiring to be extended and filled up by the labours of later physiologists. Hunter never contented himself with the character of a mere maker of experiments, but always aimed at drawing general conclusions ; and he perhaps occasionally fell into the error of generalizing from insufficient data. Hence we find that on the present subject his experiments are sometimes not sufficiently varied, and are defective, for want of those precautions against disturbing influences which characterize the inquiries of Edwards, Marshall Hall, and other physiologists, who have of late trodden in the same path.

Hunter does not seem to have considered his own inquiries on the subject as at an end, for he recurs, in many of his letters written after this time, to his experiments on hedgehogs, as the following letter, written about this time, evinces.

"DEAR JENNER,

"I received yours by Dr. Hicks, with the hedgehog alive. I put it into my garden: but I want more. I will send you the picture; but by what conveyance? or by what place? I have a picture by Barrett and Stubbs. The landscape by Barrett; a horse frightened at the first seeing of a lion, by Stubbs. I got it for five guineas: will you have it? I have a dearer one, and no use, for two of the same masters; but do not have it excepting you would like it, for I can get my money for it.

"I am glad you have got blackbirds' nests. Let me know the expense you are at, for I do not mean the picture to go for anything, only for your trouble.

"Ever yours,

"J. H.

"N.B. I should suppose the hedgehogs would come in a box full of holes all round, filled with hay, and some fresh meat put into it."

Jenner had, about this time, become involved in an *affaire du cœur*, which, unfortunately, ended in disappointment. Hunter had heard a rumour of his expected marriage, but not of the rejection of his addresses; and in his next letter expresses his hopes that his information may prove to be correct.

"DEAR JENNER,

"I don't know when I wrote to you last. I do not know if I thanked you for the cider. The hedgehogs came, with one dead, which was a female with young, and which I made a preparation of. I have since got the blackbirds, which I think will do vastly well. I have not yet sent the picture; it is packed up ready to go, and shall be sent immediately.

"I was told the other day that you was married, and to a young lady with considerable fortune. I hope it is true, for I do not know anybody more deserving of one. Let me know whether it is so or not. I hope you keep an account of all expenses. What is become of your paper on lead in cider? Let me have it, and I will send it to the Medical Society. How do the fossils go on?

Jenner was of a rather sensitive disposition, and as he had probably calculated pretty certainly on success in his suit, was much affected for some time by the disappointment. Hunter was, moreover, not exactly the person " to trust a love tale to," and Jenner accordingly delayed to reply to his inquiries until the receipt of the following letter, which requiring an immediate answer, he summoned courage to communicate the real state of affairs.

" DEAR JENNER,   ·   [*Post-mark Aug.* 30.]

" I hope this winter to be aole to get you some preparations of the eye and lymphatics; but Hewson's preparations are to be sold this month; now perhaps for four or five pounds some preparations may be picked up. If you have no objection to throw away so much money, let me know, and what subjects you would like best. I shall give you some commissions about heat, cold, &c.

" Yours,

" JOHN HUNTER."

On learning how Jenner's hopes had been frustrated, Hunter kindly expresses his regret, but, as might be expected, recommends to the lover a summary dismissal of the lady from his memory, and like a skilful physician, undertakes to find him other employment for his thoughts.

" DEAR JENNER,

" I own I was at a loss to account for your silence, and I was sorry at the cause. I can easily conceive how you must feel, for you have two passions to cope with, viz., that of being disappointed in love, and that of being defeated; but both will wear out, perhaps the first soonest. I own I was glad when I heard you was married to a woman of fortune; but ' let her go, never mind her.' I shall employ you with hedgehogs, for I do not know how far I may trust mine. I want you to get a hedgehog in the beginning of winter, and weigh him; put him in your garden, and let him have some leaves, hay, or straw, to cover himself with, which he will do; then weigh him in the spring, and see what he has lost. Secondly, I want you to kill one in the beginning of winter, to see how fat he is, and another in spring, to see what he has lost of his fat. Thirdly, when the weather is very cold, and about the month of January, I could wish you would make a hole in one of their bellies, and put the thermometer down into the pelvis, and see the height of the mercury; then turn it upwards, towards the diaphragm, and observe the heat there. So much at present for hedgehogs. I beg pardon,—examine the stomach and intestines. If Hewson's things go cheap, I will purchase some that I think proper for you; those you mention will, I am afraid, be everybody's money, and go dear.

"Ever yours,

"*London, Sept. 25th,* 1778." "J. HUNTER."

Hunter's next letter is dated in November, and relates chiefly to the physiological experiments which he had requested Jenner to make, and to another inquiry respecting the breeding of eels, to which he had directed Jenner's attention in a former letter.

"DEAR JENNER, *London, Nov.* 9, 1778.

"I received yours, with the eel. The spawn of the salmon was lost. I shall send you back the eel again, with the liver, stomach, and gut removed, and nothing left but a fringe which passes down the sides of the backbone, which I took, and still take to be the spawn; but I never saw any difference in it at any time of the year; and this one you have sent is similar to all I have yet seen. I think your stopping the eels a good plan, if you can; but I should suspect they would be more slippery than hedgehogs. I do not know if hedgehogs burrow. About a month hence examine another, and compare him with your notes and memory also. Examine his heat in the pelvis, diaphragm, &c.; a month after that another, &c. I like your experiment on the toad and snake; but bury them rather deeper, and let the ground be kept moist about them, especially in summer. I shall keep all your letters, but I expect in the end all your notes. I like your friend Ludlow much; he is a lively sensible fellow. I have got a few preparations for you; I am getting them put into a little order for you before I send them. Are there no bats in the old castle of Berkeley? I should like similar experiments to be made upon them to those of the hedgehog. Mrs. H. desires her compliments to you.

"Believe me to be, most sincerely yours,

"JOHN HUNTER."

Hunter this year completed his work on the Teeth, by

publishing the second part, containing an account of the diseases to which these organs are liable.

Mr. Home had now resided six years with Hunter, in which time he had completed his education; and as he had no emoluments to expect by remaining longer an inmate of his house, since, says he, " his expenses had always hitherto exceeded his income," he was glad to obtain the very eligible appointment of surgeon to the new naval hospital at Plymouth, where he was immediately called on to take charge of the men who had been wounded in the late action under Admiral Keppel.

It may seem surprising, that after having been so long in practice, and after acquiring so considerable a reputation as Hunter at this time enjoyed, his finances should still have been in an embarrassed state ; but it must be remembered that Hunter had for some years past maintained his two establishments in London and at Earl's Court ; to supply the wants of an increasing family, and, what was probably most expensive of all, to provide for the outlay required for the maintenance and extension of his museum. Mr. Hunter once declared to Mr. Lynn that the museum had cost him upwards of 70,000*l.* ; and when it is recollected that the whole of his professional income, which for the last ten years of his life was very considerable, was, with the exception of his domestic expenses, wholly devoted to this object, we cannot doubt that this estimate was near the truth : at least the sum of 15,000*l.*, voted for its purchase by Parliament, fell very far short of the actual outlay, to say nothing of the time and talent unceasingly devoted by himself and others to its completion. Rarely, however, have the labours of those great men who have advanced before the age they have adorned been duly appreciated, until another generation has arisen to weigh their merits in an impartial balance.

CHAPTER V.

1779 to 1788.

Mr. Hunter's paper on the hermaphrodite black cattle ;—his anxiety for rare specimens to enrich his museum ;—renewal of the disagreement between him and his brother.—Mr. Hunter's paper on smallpox during pregnancy ;—his paper on the hen pheasant.—Trial of Sir T. Boughton. —Croonian lectures.—His paper on the organ of hearing in fishes ;—removes to Leicester Square ;—assists in forming the Society for the Improvement of Medical and Chirurgical Knowledge.—Charlatanism.— Correspondence.—Mr. Hunter's notion of the immateriality of matter from the theory of colours ;—his paper on the inflammation of veins ;— his fame and practice at this time ;—his merits as an operating surgeon ;—his illness returns ;—his second visit to Bath ;—Mr. Home acts as his assistant.—Mr. Hunter's paper on the double-coned Terebella ; —his operation for popliteal aneurism ;—is appointed Deputy Surgeon-general to the Army ;—his treatise on the Venereal Disease ;—his work on the Animal Œconomy ;—prints his own works at his own house ;—his paper on the Wolf, Jackal, and Dog ;—his paper on Whales.—The giant O'Brien.—Obtains the Copley medal ;—opens his museum to the public. —Mr. Home and Mr. Keate appointed assistant surgeons at St. George's Hospital.—Sits for his portrait to Sir Joshua Reynolds.—Sharpe's engraving.—Death of Pott ;—comparison between him and Hunter.— Pott's character.

In 1779 Hunter's valuable memoir on the hermaphrodite black cattle, or free martin, was read before the Royal Society*. As usual, he has by no means confined himself to a bare anatomical description of the peculiar malformation

---

* Amongst those present at the reading of this paper was the illustrious anatomist Von Soemmerring, then a young man, as the following letter, written by him on his being elected a Fellow of the Royal Society, will show :

" *Franfurt am Mayn,*
" DEAR SIR, *20th August,* 1827.

" Feeling myself extremely honoured in being admitted as a foreign member by the very first literary Society in the world, I beg the more

of the genital organs in these animals, but has introduced the subject by a variety of observations on hermaphroditism in general, which render his paper a very important contribution to this branch of physiology.

It will be remembered that in his last letter to Jenner, Hunter had requested him to make some further experiments on the heat of the hedgehog during its torpid state. He had as yet received no communication on the subject, and accordingly wrote the following short note, as a spur to his friend's activity.

" DEAR JENNER,

" What are you doing ? How do the hedgehogs get on ? How cold are they in the winter ? &c. &c. Let me hear from you. I have not yet sent the preparations for you. I have added an eye to one of them of my own making.

" Yours,

" *London, Jan.* 16, 1779."   " J. HUNTER."

Jenner had not been idle, however, but was able to give so good an account of his proceedings that Hunter seems to have resolved not to allow so valuable a coadjutor to remain unemployed; accordingly, though he rarely put confidence in any experiments which were not conducted by himself, or under his own eye, he suggested to Jenner some further ones, respecting the state of the digestive powers during torpor.

---

from you the favour to return my best and sincerest thanks, as I always remembered with singular pleasure to have been present in the year 1788, at the reading of John Hunter's celebrated paper on the free martin, not imagining at that time once to become myself associated to that illustrious assembly, by whose exertions I profited infinitely in all my studies.

I am, dear Sir, with great respect,

Your obedient humble Servant,

SAMUEL THOMAS VON SOEMMERRING, F.R.S.,

Privy Counsellor to H. M. the King of Bavaria,

Knight of several I. and R. Orders.

To Dr. Young,
Foreign Secretary of the Royal Society."

"DEAR JENNER,

"I thank you for the trouble you have taken. I do not see another experiment to be made with the hedgehogs, but one: get a piece of meat into the stomach of one, during the very cold weather, and kill him twenty-four hours after, to see if it is digested, which I have done with lizards. This may be difficult; but suppose he was made lively in a warm room, and then fed, and put out into the cold immediately, with a little hay over him. If this does, two or three may be served in the same way, and kill them at different distances, respecting time. Observe their breathing when in the cold; if possible, the quickness of the pulse and fluidity of the blood. If you chance to get more than you use, I would take a few to put into my garden, to walk about in the evenings.

"Is there no chance to see you in London this winter? Do come and see us. I shall send you a paper of mine on the free martin, also one to Ludlow. I wrote to him in answer to his letter; I hope he received it. If a good deal of that air in the hog's guts* could be collected, see if a candle would burn in it as large as in common air. I had a letter from Mr. Cheston, of an ossified thoracic duct; I wish he would let me have it: you see how greedy I am. You will hear from me soon.

"Ever yours,
"JOHN HUNTER."

The above letter furnishes an example of the eagerness with which Hunter sought to draw all curiosities connected with his researches within the sphere of his museum. He was indeed a most resolute beggar for every specimen which particularly pleased him by its rarity, and which chanced to be in the possession of any of his friends. The late Dr. Clarke had a preparation of an extra-uterine pregnancy, in which the fœtus had been detained in the fallopian tube, and had there undergone partial development, when the mother died from internal hæmorrhage, consequent on the rupture of the tube. On this specimen he set a high value, and Hunter had often viewed it with longing eyes. "Come, Doctor," said he, "I positively must have that preparation." "No, John Hunter," was the reply, "you positively shall

* See an engraving in the 'Animal Œconomy.'

not." " You will not give it me, then ?" " No." " Will you sell it ?" " No." " Well then, take care I don't meet you with it in some dark lane at night, for if I do, I'll murder you to get it."

Winter returning, brought back Hunter's thoughts to his inquiries on vital heat, and we find him accordingly writing to remind Jenner to prepare for fresh operations against the hedgehogs.

"Dear Jenner,

" I have not troubled you with any letter this long time, nor have I heard from you. This moment, I do not know if I sent you the butter-flies ; if they are not sent, they shall this week. I want you to pursue the experiments on the heat of the hedgehog this winter ; and if you could send me a colony of them, I should be glad, as I have expended all I had, except two : one an eagle ate, and a ferret caught the other*. Mrs. Hunter and I were at Bath the other day, and came home by way of Gloucester ; we wished much we could have staid a day, to have waited on you. Let me hear from you soon.

"I am, dear Jenner,
"Yours,
"London, Nov. 8th, 1779." "John Hunter."

In 1780 that unfortunate disagreement took place be-tween the Hunters, of which mention has been made in a former part of this memoir. It commenced in John Hunter's presenting to the Royal Society a paper on the structure of the placenta, in which he claimed for himself the honour of discovering the true mode of union between this organ and the uterus, a discovery which Dr. Hunter had commu-nicated as his own, in his work on the Gravid Uterus. What could have induced Hunter to bring forward such a claim twenty-five years after the alleged discovery, and five years after the publication of Dr. Hunter's work, it is not

---

* Hunter's account of his hedgehogs reminds one of Magendie's re-mark on the dogs whose evil stars bring them acquainted with the in-terior of his physiological slaughter-house. " Vous savez, Messieurs," said the Professor to his class, " que les chiens ne s'amusent pas ici."

easy to say. The probable explanation seems to be, that something unpleasant had previously passed between the brothers, and that, under a consequent feeling of irritation, Hunter transmitted his paper to the Royal Society*. Whether his claims were well or ill founded ; whether any part of the discovery was his ; or what it was, it is impossible, from the evidence now before us, to decide. Dr. Hunter, in a letter to the Royal Society, denied having derived his information from his brother, and asserted that the discovery was the result of many years' patient investigation of the subject on his part†. To this a rejoinder was sent by

* Such an explanation has, in fact, been commonly given, but the causes assigned have been various. Some confidently allege that Hunter's resolute determination to marry Miss Home gave offence to his brother, who strongly remonstrated against his forming an alliance with a lady who had neither rank nor fortune, which, he asserted, would slacken his endeavours after fame, and mar his fortune. By others a dispute is said to have occurred between them respecting certain preparations, now in the Hunterian Museum at Glasgow, to which both brothers laid claim ; but through the inquiries of Professor Badham, who has kindly investigated the subject, it has been shown that no just grounds for this account exist, although such a tradition has certainly prevailed on the spot. It is needless at this time to scrutinize further into so unpleasant an affair, although it was one which probably affected Mr. Hunter's feelings more powerfully than any other event of his life.

† LETTER I.

"*Windmill Street*, Feb. 3, 1780.

"Dr. Hunter begs the favour that the Secretary to the Royal Society will read to the Society what follows.

"Mr. Hunter's account of the structure of the human placenta, explaining the connexion and circulation between the mother and the *fœtus in utero*, which was read at the last meeting of the Royal Society, informs us that it was a discovery which he made with Dr. Mackenzie, and that it was not claimed by me. The Society will be sensible that I am reduced to the necessity of taking notice of this mistake, when they are informed of the following facts :

"First. That the doctrine has been many years ago published in printed books as my discovery, and had been communicated as such by myself. See Baron Haller, for instance, in the second part of the eighth volume (p. 220) of his great Physiology, in quarto, printed thirteen or fourteen years ago.

"Secondly. Besides treating of it as my own discovery, in my lectures upon the subject, I have always done so for many years last past,

Hunter, reasserting the truth of the account he had given
of the transaction, but adding that as his brother seemed unwilling to allow him the whole merit, the former should
be welcome to share it, provided that a part at least of the
discovery was adjudged to himself; which, after all, would
have probably been the fairest mode of adjusting their
claims.

in the very first lecture of my course, which is the most public of all,
because the door is then open to every person whose curiosity prompts
him to be present.

"In the third place, occasionally both in what I have printed, and
in my lectures, I hope I have not overlooked opportunities of doing justice to Mr. Hunter's great merits, and of acknowledging that he had
been an excellent assistant to me, in this and in many other pursuits.
By doing so I always felt an inward gratification, shall I call it, or
pride? I had given him all the little anatomical knowledge which I
could communicate, and put him into the very best situation that I
could for becoming what this Society has for some time known him to
be. May it be presumed, then, that I stand possessed of the discovery
in question, till proofs shall be brought to dispossess me? I shall most
willingly submit to the pleasure of this Society. If they signify an unwillingness that this emulation (I will call it) should go on, I shall ac-
quiesce, and be silent. If curiosity, justice, or the laws and practice of
the Society should incline the Council to seek out and determine upon
the merits, I shall be equally ready to obey their commands. And if it
should appear reasonable to them, I would first beg to know the grounds
of Mr. Hunter's claim, as I am too well acquainted with his abilities
not to think that he must be able to support his claim by something
that I am ignorant of. And if I should receive that satisfaction, I shall
immediately show that I am more tenacious of truth than even of anatomical discoveries. But if that information should not alter my thoughts
upon the question, I shall show to the satisfaction of the Society, if I
can at all judge of my own employments and pursuits, that my pretensions arise out of a long series of observations and experiments, made
with a view to the discovery in question: that it was not a random conjecture, a lucky thought, or accidental occasion, but a persevering pursuit for twelve or thirteen years at least, the progress of which was
always publicly known here, and admits of the most circumstantial
proof.

"WILLIAM HUNTER."

LETTER II.

"To the President of the Royal Society.

"SIR,   Jermyn Street, Feb. 17, 1780.

"Though I know the constitution of the Society over which you pre-
side too well to suppose that they will give their judgement on any sub-

Here the discussion terminated. The Royal Society decided to take no further cognizance of the matter, and would not allow the offending paper to be published in the Transactions. Between the brothers, unhappily, the estrangement produced by the dispute continued undiminished until Dr. Hunter was on his death-bed, though, to John

---

ject, and respect it too much to think it a proper field for waging the war of controversy, I cannot avoid requesting you to lay before that learned body a short answer to the paper given in by my brother, Dr. Hunter, as silence on my part, after his charge, may be interpreted by my enemies into an acknowledgment that I have intentionally claimed to myself a discovery in reality his due. I am as tenacious as he is of anatomical discovery, and, I flatter myself, as tenacious, also, of truth. The discovery was made in the manner in which I stated it in my paper. Dr. Mackenzie had injected the subject, and being unable, as I conceived, to explain an appearance which he had found in dissecting it, sent for me. I came to him, and having examined it further, explained the appearance in question, then, for the first time, to my own satisfaction and that of Dr. Mackenzie; and in the evening of the same day, full of the discovery, I came to Dr. Hunter, and brought him with me to Dr. Mackenzie, to see and judge of the explanation I had given and Dr. Mackenzie had agreed to. This is my state of the fact upon which I ground my belief of myself being the author of this anatomical discovery; but as my brother thinks differently, after a period of twenty-five years, I am content to abolish all remembrance of the successions of time in the course of that day, and to suppose that Dr. Mackenzie, Dr. Hunter, and myself, inspected the parts together, and made the discovery: by which means the honour of it will be divided into three, one of which I may surely be allowed to take to myself, the other two may appertain to Dr. Mackenzie and Dr. Hunter, if they choose to claim and be content with them; though in this division we must make some reserve for the claim of several ingenious young men, at that time pupils, who were with us, and, of course, entitled to some proportional share in the discovery, though their present situations, settled at a distance from this town, have prevented them from getting early notice of the present claim, and, of course, of making application to the Society for their share. However, I may here declare, that if Dr. Hunter will produce to me any claim which I can allow of his having discovered this anatomical fact at any period of time prior to this conference at Dr. Mackenzie's, I shall first declare, in excuse for having troubled the Society, that I was not before acquainted with it, and immediately after declare that he is entitled to the sole honour of it, at least in preference to myself.

" I am, Sir,
" Your much obliged, and most obedient humble Servant,
" JOHN HUNTER."

Hunter at least, if not to both, it was often a cause of deep regret. During Dr. Hunter's last illness, which occurred three years after, his brother requested that he might be admitted to see him : this was acceded to, and he continued to visit him daily, and to afford him professional assistance until his death. Notwithstanding this apparent reconciliation, the feeling of soreness seems not to have been quite obliterated from the mind of Dr. Hunter, since it did not lead him to make any alteration in the previous disposal of his property, and he died without leaving any portion of it to his brother. Dr. Baillie, however, to whom Dr. Hunter left the family estate, with great generosity ceded it to Mr. Hunter, as soon as the will was proved.

Two other papers of Hunter's were read before the Royal Society, and published in their Transactions for this year. The first of these, which was presented in January, contained the account of a woman who had taken the smallpox during pregnancy, and passed safely through the disease, but some weeks after fell into premature labour, and was delivered of a dead child, bearing on its body an eruption precisely similar in its character to the smallpox in an advanced stage. To the details of the case are subjoined some valuable considerations, suggested by them to Hunter's mind.

The second paper contains observations on a phenomenon of not unfrequent occurrence amongst pheasants, and several other species of birds ; that, namely, of the hen bird's assuming a plumage like the cock's. This change is found to occur only when the hen has ceased from breeding, and, as Hunter supposed, only when the cessation was the result of old age ; but more recent researches have shown, that a disease of the ovary, unfitting this organ for producing eggs, may give rise to the change of plumage even in young hens.

The following letter to Jenner, dated 4th of March, appears to have been written this year, and, like most of the others, relates chiefly to various objects of natural history received or expected by him from Berkeley.

"DEAR JENNER,

"This very evening I was going to write to you, when behold a basket came with pea-fowls, lizards, and birds' legs. I know nothing of the natural history of the viviparous lizard, but shall ask Sir Joseph Banks, who, I dare say, knows; but I should like to have them when with young, therefore beg you will give a genteel reward to those who will bring you several; and let me know in what situations they are commonly found, that I may employ others to hunt for me. How did the puppy and you agree?

"Last night I looked over all your letters, to see the one giving me the account of the porpoise, but I could not find it; therefore I must beg your account of them, and the milk, &c., which I hope you will send soon. Lord Berkeley has not sent for his dog. Have you had any account of the bustard?

"Monday morning has produced nothing new; so good day to you."

"March 4th."   "J. HUNTER."

In March 1781 Hunter appeared as a witness at the Warwick assizes, in the famous trial of Capt. Donellan, for the supposed murder of his brother-in-law, Sir Theodosius Boughton. Great public interest was excited by this trial at the time, and the medical evidence adduced on the occasion has furnished subject for comment in almost every English work on legal medicine published since that time.

Sir T. Boughton, a young man, previously in good health, expired in convulsions about half an hour after taking a draught of rhubarb and jalap, sent him by his medical man, but with which it was supposed Capt. D. had subsequently mixed laurel water, as Sir T. Boughton's mother observed that the draught smelt of bitter almonds.

Suspicions of poison were excited, and about ten days after death the body was disinterred, and examined by several medical men, who, however, made but an imperfect inquiry, as they neglected to investigate either the brain or the intestines. At the inquest suspicion fell on Capt. Donellan, who was consequently arrested, and tried at the following assizes.

On the trial, four medical witnesses gave it as their opinion, from the symptoms, and the appearances on dissection, that Sir T. Boughton had been poisoned, and that laurel water had been the means employed.

Hunter, on the other hand, with that proper caution which resulted from his extensive knowledge, avoided drawing so hasty a conclusion. He asserted that the appearances described as having been seen on dissection, were such as might have arisen from putrefaction alone; and with regard to the symptoms, that they might have been caused by apoplexy or epilepsy as well as by poison, a point which an examination of the head would have gone far to decide. He allowed, on his cross-examination, that the occurrence of the symptoms immediately after taking the draught, was a circumstance in favour of its having caused them; and "*if*," said he, "*I knew the draught was poison, I should say that, most probably, the symptoms arose from that.*" But he very properly, and indeed with the direction of the Court, separated in his mind the circumstantial evidence adduced to show that the draught was poison, from the medical testimony he was called on to draw from the symptoms and dissection; and having done so, he said he felt it impossible to give any decided opinion as to the cause of death.

Mr. Justice Buller, who presided at the trial, seems to have lost his temper at not being able to draw a more decided opinion from Hunter as to the real cause of death, and on summing up, threw out some sarcastic remarks on the doubts he had suggested, and attached no weight whatever to them. The consequence was, Capt. Donellan was found guilty and executed. The circumstantial evidence against him, indeed, was rather strong, so that we ought not perhaps to consider this, as some have done, an instance of judicial murder: assuredly, however, there was not sufficient ground for conviction, and the conclusions of the medical men opposed to Hunter rested, for the most part, on completely unsatisfactory data, and should have had but little weight in the decision of the question.

In 1781 Hunter was elected a Fellow of the Royal Society of Belles Lettres at Gottenburg.

In 1782 he completed his series of six Croonian lectures on muscular motion*, of which he had annually delivered one since 1776, with the exception of 1777, when for some reason he did not give any lecture. In these discourses he unfolded many novel and ingenious views respecting the causes of motion in vegetables and animals, and on the various modes of progression employed by the latter, in swimming, flying, leaping, running, &c. At their conclusion the Royal Society expressed a desire of publishing them; but Hunter objected to it, as he did not consider his information sufficiently complete for this, and was accordingly allowed to withdraw them, with a view to pub-

---

* From the following letter of Hunter's to Sir J. Banks, it would seem that he experienced some difficulty in getting paid the money allotted for the support of the Croonian lectures. With whom the fault rested does not appear; but as Hunter was not fond of being troubled about money matters, to cut short the affair he applied to the President.

"Sir,   *Jermyn-street, July* 25, 1781.

"The last lecture on muscular motion which I had the honour to deliver was the fifth. Sir John Pringle made a point of my applying for the money allotted for such purposes, which I did; but there were reasons given for my not receiving it then. You have also desired me to apply, which I have done, both to Mr. Wegg and Mr. Robertson, but have been shifted from one to the other. I thought it my duty, both to you and the Society, to acquaint you of this.

"I have the honour to be, with great respect,
"Your most obedient and most humble Servant,
"JOHN HUNTER."

lication at some future period. He never found leisure,
however, to carry this intention into effect ; but some of his
observations were introduced into the work on Inflammation, and others Sir Everard Home embodied in his own
publications on comparative anatomy. The latter have met
with general approbation amongst continental physiologists,
but they have not always been traced up to their true author.

He also presented this year a paper on the organ of
hearing in fishes, in which he gives a general account of
the structure of the organ in this class of animals, and
shows that in the Ray tribe and some other fishes there
is an external opening. He was the first who pointed out
this fact, and, as appears by the following letter, was anxious to secure himself the credit of his discovery, which he
feared some other philosopher might run off with ; since,
from the date of the following letter, it would seem that his
paper had been given in the year before, but for want of
opportunity could not be read.

"Dear Sir Joseph,   1781.

"If it was possible and agreeable to read a little bit of my paper
upon the ears of fish, so as to be able to publish it, I should be glad, as
somebody now will rob me of the external opening in the Ray kind,
and in other fish*. I have left it open for future inquiry, because I have
a preparation of it, but cannot say what fish till I shall learn that by
future inquiries ; but all this I leave to you, as I know you have my
credit at heart.

"I am, dear Banks,
"Your much obliged,
"John Hunter."

In 1783 Hunter was elected a Member both of the Royal
Society of Medicine and the Royal Academy of Surgery in
Paris.

The lease of his house in Jermyn-street expiring this

* Dr. Hunter used to say that "philosophers lie like the devil." It
would seem that his brother thought they also thieved like the devil ;
and we must allow him to have had some experience.

year, he purchased the remainder of the lease of some more
extensive premises, now occupied by the National Reposi-
tory of Arts, on the east side of Leicester-square, consisting of a dwelling-house in the square, with a large portion
of ground extending to Castle-street, where there was a second smaller dwelling; between the two he determined on
building a museum. That this was a very imprudent transaction, in a pecuniary point of view, there can be no doubt.
His lease was only for twenty-four years, and the sum he
expended in the building was not less than three thousand
pounds. It seems, however, that his mind had been so
harassed with the difficulty of obtaining an eligible site,
that it was a relief to be able to conclude even such a bar-
gain as this. The new building was to consist of a room
above, for the reception of his collection, fifty-two feet long
by twenty-eight wide, lighted from the top, and furnished
with a gallery all round. Under this were two apartments, ,
one of which he designed to employ as a lecture-room; the
other, for which no particular use was at first allotted, afterwards became the place of meeting for the Lyceum Me-
dicum, a society which Hunter and Fordyce were the means
of establishing, and of which they were chosen two of the
patrons. All that Hunter could spare from his income was
for the next two or three years devoted to carrying the
above plan into effect, and he used often to complain to his
friends that he was now obliged to spend in bricks and
mortar what would have been otherwise expended in enlarging his collection. To the new building, the house in
Castle-street was subservient, and in the various apartments
of it the different departments of human and comparative ˙
anatomy were carried on. The house in Leicester-fields
was occupied by Hunter and his family.

Notwithstanding his architectural engagements, Hunter
found time to take an active part, with Dr. Fordyce and

others, in the formation of the "Society for the Improvement of Medical and Chirurgical Knowledge," which was established in 1783, and continued in existence about twenty years. This, like the present Medico-Chirurgical Society, had its appointed meetings for receiving and discussing treatises on medical subjects, and those which were judged worthy of it were reserved for publication. During the whole existence of the Society only three volumes of transactions were published; but these contain many valuable papers from the pens of Fordyce, Hunter, Baillie, Home, Blane, Wells, Abernethy, and others. Amongst the early contributors we also find the name of Jenner, whose attention had lately been turned to improving the mode of preparing the emetic tartar, and who communicated the results of his experiments in a paper to the Society. Several of Hunter's letters to Jenner, written about this time, relate to the subject, in which, as usual, he took a kind and active interest.

"DEAR JENNER,			[*Post-mark Nov. 14th.*]

"I received yours, with the experiments on heat and colours, but have not had time to pay sufficient attention to the colours. I also received your little publication with the Tart. Emet. I have a great deal to say about it. First, do you mean to take out a patent? Do you mean to advertise it? or do you mean to let it take its chance? I approve of it much, and will do all in my power to promote the sale; but I would advise you to give it a new name, expressive either of the composition, or of its virtues on the body, viz. sal antim., or sal sudorif., or sal antim. sudorif. I would also desire you to burn your book, for you will have all the world making it. Let me have your answer to all this.

"Ever yours,
"J. HUNTER."

The piece of advice given in the latter part of the foregoing letter affords an example of that want of high professional feeling occasionally displayed by Hunter. Perfect liberality in the communication of professional knowledge which may contribute to the general benefit should ever characterize the enlightened physician. It is this conduct which forms the honourable distinction between quackery and one of the noblest of human pursuits; and the practitioner who, in seeking after wealth, neglects to observe it, deserves to rank only with the venders of secret medicines and professors of secret modes of cure, who in all ages have found ready dupes amongst the ignorant and credulous, whether of high or low degree*. Jenner had too high. a respect for his professional character to follow the advice, and, accordingly, made his method generally known, by publishing it, as has been before observed, in the Transactions of the Society for the Improvement of Medical and Chirurgical Knowledge, a channel which, as will be seen in one of his future letters, Hunter himself recommended.

The following letter was probably written soon after this

---

* Notwithstanding some late notable instances of successful imposture, there seems fair ground for believing that quackery is on the decline in this country. We should hardly, in the present day, find a judge proclaiming from the bench his belief that a bone-setter was just as skilful and efficient in his business as any surgeon; nor can Sir Benjamin Brodie complain, as Mr. Pott did, that any Mrs. Mabb drives her carriage and four into London to take charge of the dislocated limbs of the nobility and gentry. It would appear, from the following anecdote, that in Hunter's time these worthies were even admitted into consultation by well educated professional men; and we know that certain departments of surgery, as the operations on the eye, &c., were still entrusted to men ignorant of the first principles of medicine. The Taylors of Whitworth were empirics who enjoyed much repute in treating diseases of the rectum. Thurlow, bishop of Durham, and brother of the Lord Chancellor, laboured under stricture of the rectum, for which the faculty promised little relief. The Chancellor invited Taylor to see his brother, and several medical men met him in consultation : Hunter came late, and Taylor was invited to proceed in the examination; but he bluntly refused, and said he would do nothing till Jack Hunter came, for he had no opinion of any but him. Hunter soon arrived : Taylor made his examination, and declared it a bad case; but passed a candle, besmeared with an ointment he had brought with him. Hunter took up the box, and asked what the ointment was made of. "That," said Taylor, turning to the Chancellor, "is not a fair question: no, no, Jack, I'll send you as much as you please, but I won't tell you what it's made of."

preceding, as it is filled with directions respecting experiments on colours, a subject on which, as we have there seen, Jenner had been making some experiments. The want of this gentleman's letters leaves us to guess at the object of the experiments proposed, but from their nature it may be inferred that they were to be conducted on an individual labouring under that incapacity for discriminating between certain colours which is not unfrequently found, in a greater or less degree, in different individuals. Hunter's object appears to be, to ascertain whether the incapacity arises from a general defect in the perceptive power, or whether certain primary colours fail to make their accustomed impression, and hence the compounds into which they enter appear different from what they really are.

"DEAR JENNER,

"I thank you for your last letter: I want you to pursue the inquiry considerably further; and to give you an idea of what I mean, I will first premise that there are in nature but three colours, viz. *red, blue,* and *yellow,* all the others being combinations of these three. First, present him with these three colours singly, and see what he calls them; then altogether (not mixed), and see how far they correspond with his first ideas of them: when that is ascertained, then begin to mix them; for instance, blue and yellow (which make a green), see what he calls that; then a yellow and red (which make a scarlet); next a blue and red (which make a purple). Now to explain the intention of these experiments. Suppose he has a perfect idea only of one colour; and although you mix that colour ever so much, yet he sees none of the other, but only that colour in the mixture. Suppose all the three colours, when seen singly, or unmixed, with him are blue; mix blue and red (making a purple), he will only see the blue, the red not being visible to him; and so on of the others, according as he sees them. Suppose that a simple colour makes no impression, but a compound one does, viz. green (which is composed of blue and yellow); then mix blue and red in all proportions, to see what the colour is. Then mix yellow and blue in all proportions, and see what colour these are: if he sees no green in any of them, then mix all the three colours in various proportions, and see what colours those make. When all the colours are mixed in various proportions, and the whole is a green, perhaps of different shades, according to the quantity of blue and yellow, then you may fairly conclude that it is the mixture of the blue and the yellow which produces it, the red never making any impression.

" If there is any other simple compound that he sees, as scarlet, which is the yellow and the Modena red; or a purple, which is blue and red; see if, when those two are predominant in the mixture, (although there are all three colours in the mixture,) that the compound becomes the visible colour.

" The drawing of the skull has been made ever since you desired it, but I had forgot it. I have a cast for you of the aneurismal varix, as described by Dr. Hunter. How shall I send both? Let me know.

" Ever your much obliged,·

" JOHN HUNTER."

The following letter, which was probably written about this time, relates to the metaphysical inquiry as to the nature of matter. It appears to have been hastily written, and certainly does not lead us to regret that Hunter did not more often quit natural philosophy for metaphysics. Both facts and reasoning are unsound.

" DEAR JENNER,

" I received yours, with the heron's legs. Could you not get a live heron or bittern,—or see how they make that noise,—and send them to me? I will pay expenses. By the by, you were to have sent me some hedgehogs. I am putting my things into some order, and shall find some Don Saltero's for you.

" My proof of the non-existence of matter is in colours, there being no such thing as a primary colour, every colour being a mixture of two, making a third. Thus, green is a mixture of blue and yellow; blue is a mixture of purple and green; yellow is a mixture of green and orange; and so on of the other colours. Therefore all colours are compounds. But what are they compounds of? Of nothing but themselves. And what are themselves? Nothing. If there were three colours that were permanent, (for with less than three we can hardly compound to any extent,) which could not be produced from any compounding of colours, then I would say, there is something immutable in matter, although metaphysicians might say this was only an immutable idea, or an idea of immutability; but that is only applying abstract reasoning to matter, or what we call matter; but when we·see that there is no such thing as permanency in one species of matter, viz. light, and that it can be proved from the matter itself, it then comes more home to our understandings than all the reasoning in the world.

" Yours always,

" J. H."

His next letter, written in December, relates almost entirely to Jenner's new medicine.

"DEAR JENNER,   [*Post-mark Dec.* 15*th.*]

" I have delayed writing longer than I intended, and longer than what I should have done, and even now I do not know well what to write. I love a new name so well that I could have wished it had been christened. Mr. Jones informed me that there was a man of some fortune making experiments with the same view; he may hit on some method better than the present, and which may or may not be as good as yours; or it may be thought to be as good. I asked Jones if he had any objection to have it advertised at his shop: he did not give me a direct answer, and he is now out of town. I should be glad to have a few of the printed accounts. I could send them to different people; to Black and Cullen, &c., amongst the rest. I like your experiment upon the dogs with it: if you make any more, let me have them. The experiment on the dog's thigh you did not finish. You told me he had extracted the plug, and that the ball of the thermometer went in with ease, but you did not say how high the mercury rose. Let me know what service I can be to you.

" J. HUNTER."

Hunter's next communication appears to have been made early in the year following. He again recurs to the tartar emetic; but other subjects are mentioned, especially the question as to the mode in which the young cuckoo is reared, a point which Jenner was at this time, at Hunter's request, endeavouring to clear up.

"DEAR JENNER,

" I am puffing off your tartar as the tartar of all tartars, and have given it to several physicians to make trial, but have had no account yet of the success. Had you not better let a bookseller have it to sell, as Glass of Oxford did his magnesia? Let it be called Jenner's Tartar Emetic, or anybody's else that you please. If that mode will do, I will speak to some, viz., Newberry, &c.

" You are very sly, although you think I cannot see it: you very modestly ask for a thermometer; I will send one, but take care those d—d clumsy fingers do not break it also. I should be glad to have a particular account of the cuckoo, and, as far as possible, under your own eye. To put all matters out of dispute, if the cuckoo's eggs were taken out of the hedge-sparrow's nest in which they were laid, and put into another's, by human hands, there could be no supposition that the parent cuckoo would feed or take care of them. I also want some young ones. I had a series from you, but a moth got in among them, and plucked them. Let me hear from you when you can.

"Yours,

"J. Hunter."

Jenner had been also engaged in making some observations on the migration of swallows, the result of which he communicated to Hunter, who, in his reply, suggests a difficulty with regard to one of the observations.

"Dear Jenner,

"To show you how much I am pleased to hear from you, I sit down to acknowledge the receipt of yours this evening. Somebody before told me of your experiment on swallows; but you should not have made the same experiment on both the old and the young of the same nest, for you do not know whether it was the old or the young that returned. I have been for some time going to write to you, to inform you there is a medical society set up here*, who intend to give papers in medicine and surgery, and also to receive. I think your paper on the Tart. Emetic would make a good paper, and probably the one on the ophthalmia, which you may probably take a little more pains about. If you should like to have them published, I can communicate them. If your account of the cuckoo is not so full as you see it may be, keep it to another year, for I am in no hurry.

"I am, dear Jenner,

"Ever yours,

"*Jan. 26th.*" "John Hunter."

In February Hunter's paper on Inflammation of the Veins was read before the Medical Society above mentioned, and is included in the first volume of their Transactions. Hunter was the first who understood and explained the nature of this affection, which he has described in several of its more usual forms. Little attention seems to have been

* Society for the Promotion of Medical and Chirurgical Knowledge.

excited by it at the time. Mr. Abernethy indeed, not long
after, contributed some additional information on the subject; but from that time until 1815, when Mr. Hodgson
recalled the attention of the profession to the question, no
pathologist had pursued the inquiry further. Since that
time much additional light has been thrown on the nature
of these affections by the labours of Carmichael, Travers,
Guthrie, Arnott, and Dr. Lee in this country, and
MM. Bouillaud, Velpeau, Breschet, and Ribes in France,
by whom it has been shown that many of the important and
dangerous symptoms following venesection, amputations,
parturition, &c., are due to inflammation of the internal
coats of the veins.

In May Hunter wrote again to Jenner, and requested
him to draw out his process for making tartar emetic, that
he might present it to the Society for the Promotion of
Medical and Chirurgical Knowledge.

"DEAR JENNER,

"You must excuse me if I am not very punctual in my answers: it
is my loss, not yours. In my last but one you mention my having anything of the porpoise I wanted. I should be glad of one of the nipples.
I hope you have got the thermometer. I want the cuckoo cleared up:
I am afraid it is now too late. I wish you would shoot an old one for
me, and send its gizzard in spirits.

"I wish you would draw out the process for making the tartar emetic.
The physicians that I have given it to speak well of it as a more certain
medicine than the other; however, I am afraid it will be too late for
this year's publication; but put it to paper. Your paper must be published before you can think of being a member, and then we will stir
for you.   Ever yours,

"*May 29th.*"   "JOHN HUNTER."

Jenner immediately complied with his directions, and his
paper was read at the first meeting of the Society, in June.

In the course of this year Mr. Home returned to London on leave of absence from Jamaica, where he had been
acting as Staff-Surgeon, and on his arrival was permitted to

exchange on half pay. " I found Mr. Hunter," says he, " advanced to a very considerable share of practice, and a still greater share of public confidence :" and he afterwards adds, " at this period Hunter may be considered as at the height of his chirurgical career ; his mind and body were both in their full vigour ; his hands were capable of performing whatever was suggested by his mind ; and his judgment was matured by former experience ;" in confirmation of which he goes on to mention some of the remarkable operations which Hunter successfully performed about this time.

With regard to this latter point, namely, Hunter's talents as an operator, a remarkable diversity of opinion exists amongst competent judges. By some, Sir Everard Home's account of his great skill is most fully confirmed, whilst by others his ability in this department of surgery is rated very low. In the opinion of Sir Astley Cooper, whose judgment on the subject must be considered as at least as likely to be correct as that of any man living, Hunter scarcely deserved to be considered a dexterous operator, certainly not an elegant one ; but his large experience, and his extraordinary skill as an anatomist, almost always enabled him successfully to complete any operation he undertook: though slow, he was sure. Hunter does not seem, indeed, to have been ever ambitious of particular renown in this field. He used frequently to say, " To perform an operation, is to mutilate a patient we cannot cure ; it should therefore be considered as an acknowledgment of the imperfection of our art."

The new building which Hunter had been erecting for his museum was completed in 1785; and Mr. Home, Mr. Bell, and Mr. Andre, whose services Hunter had engaged, were employed in superintending the removal of the preparations to their new site.

If Hunter's building-expenses had of late prevented his purchasing objects for his collection, he appears now to have again begun to add to its stores. We accordingly find him making his accustomed calls on Jenner for objects of natural history, and, amongst others, for a bustard, the largest and one of the rarest of English birds.

"DEAR JENNER,

"I am very much obliged to you for your attention to me. I will very readily give three guineas for the bustard, therefore give such orders as you think fit. I request the whole history of the cuckoos this summer from you. I have bought a house in Leicester-fields, and shall move this summer, when I shall be able to pick out some things for you. Give my compliments to Clench, and I hope to see him before he sets out for Newfoundland; if I do not, let him think of the white hares, to tame a buck and doe, and send them to me. Let me know in your next what you are doing. I hope to see you in London in about two years hence, when I shall be able to show you something.

"I am, dear Jenner,

"Ever yours,

"JOHN HUNTER.

"When the bustard arrives, I will write to you."

The bustard was accordingly procured and sent, and the receipt of it acknowledged in the following letter.

"DEAR JENNER,

"I have received the bustard safe, as also the bones. Your friend Mr. Hazeland has been very kind, for which I wrote to him and thanked him; but when you see him or write to him, express the same, as an indirect thank is better than a thousand direct ones. Are hedgehogs in great plenty? I should like to have a few. You must pursue the cuckoo this summer. I am employed building, moving, &c. I wish this summer was well over. When I am fitted up, I hope you will come and see me.

"Ever yours,

"April 22."   "J. HUNTER."

Soon after the date of the foregoing letter, Hunter began to suffer from a very painful and distressing affection of the heart and arteries; an affection, to the recurrence of which he was constantly liable during the remaining years of his life. He had been troubled, as usual, during the early part of the spring, with slight symptoms of gout; after a time these subsided, but were succeeded by irregular spasmodic affections of the face, arms, chest, and stomach, and finally, by a violent spasm of the heart, which, after half an hour of agonizing pain, ended in syncope. The faintness continued about ten minutes, at the expiration of which he started up, without any recollection of his previous illness. Similar attacks, though slighter in degree, returned very frequently for some time after, especially on occasion of any extra exertion or mental anxiety; and indeed the latter cause seems to have been mainly instrumental in exciting the first incursion of the disease, for when pressed by Dr. D. Pitcairn on this point, he admitted that his mind had been much harassed with a fear lest he should be attacked by hydrophobia, in consequence of a wound which he had received in the hand whilst examining the body of a person who had died of that disease. After a time the spasms became less frequent, though even now they were easily re-produced by a fit of anger, or by trifling anxiety of mind, as about the hiving of a swarm of bees, the fear lest an animal, which he wished to procure, might escape before a gun could be brought to shoot it, and similar causes. Various remedies were of course tried for the relief of his sufferings, but with scarcely any effect; and, amongst other means, he was advised to try the waters at Tunbridge. Thither he accordingly went in August; but after a fortnight's trial, finding himself rather worse, he resolved on repairing to Bath, where he had formerly derived much benefit. He arrived at Bath early in September, and in the following letter we find Mrs. Hunter communicating to Jenner the presence of his friend in his neighbourhood.

"DEAR SIR,   *Bath, Sept.* 13, 1785.

"I take it for granted you will not be sorry to hear Mr. Hunter is so near you, though you will lament that want of health is the occasion. He has been tormented with a flying gout since last March, and we are come here in hope of some favourable crisis before the winter. He has been inquiring for the post to Berkeley, and I find within this hour that it goes off this evening: as he is now asleep after dinner, I rather write myself than disturb his nap, to inform you of our being in your neighbourhood, and that Mr. Hunter will be glad to hear from you.

"I am, dear Sir,

"Your obedient Servant,

"*No.* 12, *South Parade.*"   "A. HUNTER."

Hunter remained in Bath about five or six weeks, and derived some little amelioration of his sufferings. At the end of that time he returned to London, and resumed his occupations.

During the whole of this illness, and of his absence from home, his brother-in-law, Mr. Home, was intrusted with the care of his practice. This gentleman therefore necessarily became an inmate of his house, and as Hunter's state of health, even after his sojourn at Bath, was too infirm to allow him to dispense with the presence of an able assistant during the performance of important operations, and to attend to night calls, Mr. Home continued to act in this capacity up to the time of Hunter's death.

Hunter's continued ill health had prevented his contributing as largely as usual to the Transactions of the Royal Society. The only communication which he made this year was an appendix to a paper of Mr. Home's on the Double-coned Terebella, an animal which he had brought with him from the West Indies. The infirmity of his body had not, however, abated his ardour for the improvement of his profession, and it was in December of the present year that he planned, and carried into execution, his famous operation for the cure of aneurism; that of tying the artery at a distance from the tumour, and between it and the heart, instead of laying open and emptying the sac, and then seeking for the orifices of the vessel, according to the old operation. He was led to propose this improved method in consequence of the frequent failure of the operation by the old mode, and thus introduced into surgery an improvement which has been more fruitful in important results than any since Paré's invention of the ligature for divided arteries.

Our Gallic brethren have striven hard to dispossess Hunter of the honour of this invention, and have adjudged the whole merit to their own countrymen. This of course. Three candidates, Guillemeau, Anel, and Desault, have accordingly been brought forward, to each of whom they have decreed a certain portion of the honour, and whose united services, as they assert, entirely forestalled those which it has been generally thought that Hunter rendered to surgery by his successful operations. The following are the grounds on which these pretensions rest. Guillemeau, a pupil of Paré, in a case of aneurism of the brachial artery, caused by a puncture in bleeding, tied the vessel immediately above the tumour, then opened and emptied the sac, and healed it from the bottom. Anel, about a century after, in a similar case, tied the artery as Guillemeau had done, but left the sac unopened. Desault, a few months before Hunter's operation, placed a ligature on the artery in the ham, above the tumour, in a case of popliteal aneurism : the sac inflamed, suppurated, and discharged its contents ; a fistulous sore remained, and the man died at the end of seven or eight months.

Now, of these three operations, that of Guillemeau appears to be absolutely devoid of any shadow of claim to be considered as even a first step towards Hunter's. It was simply the old operation reversed; instead of first opening the sac and then tying the artery, he tied the artery first, and opened the sac afterwards. Anel's operation undoubtedly

H

merits more consideration, and it must be admitted that he
first demonstrated the truth of one of the important principles on which Hunter's operation is founded, namely, that
*the impulse of the blood into the aneurism being restrained by
a ligature placed on the artery above the tumour, the further
progress of the disease will be checked,* without the necessity for a ligature being also placed on the artery below
the tumour.   Two other principles, however, remained to
be proved.   First, *That the powers of absorption would suffice for the removal of the coagula in the sac,* and the necessity for opening it be thus done away with.   Second, *That
the anastomosing vessels of the limb, in their natural state,
would be capable of immediately taking on such increased
action as would suffice for carrying on the circulation to the
parts below the point at which the main artery was tied.*

With respect to the first of these two principles, Anel's
operation proved nothing, for he succeeded, or thought he
succeeded, in first emptying the tumour of its contents by
pressure, before tying the artery.   Neither did Desault's
operation prove this point, for we have seen that the sac
burst, and discharged its contents.   It is true that the removal of the tumour, in the cases of natural cure of large
aneurisms, related by Valsalva, Guattani, and others, must
have depended on this power in the absorbents, but these
authors were not aware of this, and attributed their dispersion to the effect of pressure, resolvents, &c.   Nor was the
possibility of the coagula being so removed generally admitted by later authors, until after Hunter's operation. Although it would appear, therefore, that Desault intended to
trust to the action of the absorbents when he tied the artery in the ham, without opening the sac, yet it was Hunter's operation that really proved the sufficiency of this action.   With regard to the third principle, I think a candid
examination of the question will satisfy any one, that pre-

viously to Hunter's operation it was universally disbelieved that the anastomosing vessels, when not previously enlarged, would be equal to carrying on the circulation of a limb, after a ligature of the main artery. It was by acting in opposition to this general disbelief, and proving their sufficiency for this office, that his operation became the fruitful source of the numerous improvements in the treatment of lesions of the arteries which have since been introduced into surgery.

No doubt, both Anel's and Desault's operations required, for their success, that the circulation should be carried on by the anastomosing vessels, just as the old operation did; but that it was so carried on was accounted for by supposing that the anastomosing vessels in the neighbourhood of the tumour had undergone a gradual dilatation, in consequence of the pressure of this on the main artery. No one had hitherto generalized on the fact, and to place a ligature on the artery in the middle of the thigh, where no such dilatation of the anastomosing vessels had taken place, would have been, in the general opinion, to ensure mortification of the parts below. So deeply rooted was this opinion in men's minds, that some years after Hunter's first operation, we find Pott, in a case of popliteal aneurism, recurring to Desault's operation in the ham, rather than risk mortification by placing the ligature as Hunter had done; and his pupil, Sir James Earle, following his example as late as 1792: and even long after this, many of the French surgeons continued to employ various preliminary measures to cause a dilatation of the branches previously to operating, until repeated successes, without these precautions, had shown their uselessness. If, as it is pretended by French surgeons, Anel's operation was the prototype of Hunter's, how are we to account for the fact, that during the three quarters of a century which intervened between them the former was never once imitated, whilst the

latter was not only immediately imitated, but speedily led
to other most important improvements in the operations on
arteries?   The truth is, neither Anel, nor any other surgeon before Hunter, conceived that it was possible to make
those important modifications in the operation which the latter introduced, and which could alone render it generally
applicable ; modifications so important, as in fact to render
it a new operation based on new principles.   A convincing
proof of this is afforded in the very operation of Desault
which has been adduced to deprive Hunter of part of the
honour which is his due.   Had Desault believed in the fea-
sibility of tying the artery in the thigh, would he, in revi-
ving Anel's operation, have followed it so closely as to seek
the artery in the ham, where the operation is more difficult,
not only from the greater depth at which the vessel is placed,
but from the consolidation of parts by previous inflammation?   Assuredly not.   Another important advantage, too,
which Hunter's operation possesses over that of Desault, is
the greater chance it affords of finding the artery in a sound
state, a consideration so important as to have formed the principal inducement with Hunter to propose his operation.

The difference, then, between the operations of Hunter
and Desault, was not, as M. Velpeau pretends, merely that
of the ligature being placed two or three inches higher in
the one case than in the other ; they were essentially different in principle, and justice demands that we should vindi-
cate the claim of Hunter to the entire credit of inventing
an operation the importance of which was speedily estimated as it deserved, and which has led to those valuable
improvements in the treatment of the lesions of arteries of
which modern surgery is justly proud.

It will be seen in the account of the operation given by
Sir Everard Home, that Hunter committed some errors, in
the first two cases, in the mode of applying the ligatures,

which he afterwards corrected. He separated the artery from its connexions to a much greater extent than was safe, and this in order that he might apply four ligatures, which were intended to afford increased security; but so far from producing this effect, did in reality greatly augment the dangers of the operation. These points, however, belong rather to the history of surgery than to a memoir like the present, and as the observations on the subject have already extended to an almost undue length, I must hasten to resume the thread of this narrative.

In 1786, in consequence of the death of Mr. Middleton, Hunter was appointed Deputy-Surgeon-General to the army. In the early part of the same year he published his work on the Venereal Disease, which had been long expected by the public, and which met with a rapid sale. On this work Hunter had bestowed great pains, and before publication he submitted every part of it to a committee of his friends, consisting of Sir Gilbert Blane, Dr. Fordyce, Dr. David Pitcairn, and Dr. Marshall. It is said that the amendments introduced by these gentlemen were numerous; some have wished that they had been still more so, at least as regards the purely theoretical parts of the treatise. A great diversity of sentiment has prevailed as to the specific or non-specific nature of the disease. The former was decidedly the most prevalent theory at the time Hunter wrote, and he adopted it in all its latitude, and endeavoured to point out the peculiar laws by which it was regulated. Of late years the latter opinion has been gaining ground, and few would now be disposed to go the length which Hunter did when he proposed as a test whether certain diseases be or be not syphilitic, their requiring or not requiring mercury for their cure. Whatever may be thought, however, of Hunter's theory, it cannot be denied that his work contains many ingenious and striking views, and a variety of valuable observations on the various stages and forms of the disease:

hence, notwithstanding some improvements which have been since introduced into the treatment of these affections, Hunter's still remains by far the best general work, and requires only the corrections of the gentleman who has undertaken this part of the subject, whose experience of these affections has been of the most extended kind, to render it the universal book of reference on this complicated and Protean disease.

Towards the end of this year he published also his work on the Animal Œconomy*, consisting chiefly of a collection of his most important papers in the Philosophical Transactions, to some of which he has made considerable additions. Besides these, the work contains his paper on the descent of the testis in the fœtus, with large additions ; his account of the structure of the placenta, which the Royal Society had declined to publish ; and other shorter memoirs, of minor importance. This volume is undoubtedly one of Hunter's ablest productions, consisting as it does of accurate anatomical descriptions of various parts of the animal structure, together with original and ably conducted researches and sound and striking conclusions on some of the most important questions in general physiology. It has been before remarked, that we can seldom form an adequate notion of the contents of Hunter's various papers from the titles which he gave them. This remark is fully

* Hunter adopted the plan of printing the first edition of this work, as he did several of his previous works, under his own eye, and indeed in his own house. His reason for doing this was, that before the Irish Union it was no unfrequent proceeding with booksellers to send a copy of the manuscript, or else the proof sheets, of any valuable work to Dublin, where a cheap edition was hastily got up and imported to England so as to be ready for sale as soon as the original work, by which means the author was deprived of the profits which would have accrued to him from a second edition being called for. This proceeding, however, gave great offence to the booksellers ; and as some of them were old friends, with whom he did not wish to quarrel, he gave the publication of the second edition to Mr. Nicol, of Pall Mall, and Johnson, of St. Paul's Church-yard.

exemplified in those contained in the Animal Œconomy, a knowledge of which is necessary to such as desire to become well acquainted with the Hunterian museum, or with the style and strength of his reasoning on physiological subjects. We may also easily discern, in some of his remarks, the germs of important doctrines in physiology which have been since enlarged on and given to the world as new discoveries.

The correspondence between Hunter and his friend Jenner had gradually become more infrequent; not from any decrease of their mutual esteem, but from the increasing occupations of both. The following letters, however, appear to have been written during the latter part of this year, and refer to a subject which had been frequently mentioned before, namely, Jenner's researches respecting the cuckoo.

" DEAR JENNER,

" I·have been long expecting a long letter from you, informing me of your method of curing ophthalmias, history of cuckoos, &c. I received your dog-fish; are you sure that the spawn or egg came from her? there were none in her: if it did, then there is a species of dogfish oviparous. Let me hear from you soon.

Ever yours,

" Sept. 7th."

" J. HUNTER."

" DEAR JENNER,

" I have all your letters before me, but whether I have answered any of them or not I cannot recollect. First, I thank you for your account of the cuckoo, and what further observations you can make I shall be glad to have them, or even a repetition of the former will be very acceptable. I received the bird: it is well known; but I look upon myself as equally obliged to you. I also received your cocks, which were very good. I have bought the print of Wright, viz. the Smiths, which is his best. There is one more I would have you have, I mean Sir Joshua Reynolds's print of Count Ugolino; it is most admirable, and fit only for a man of taste. We had a sale of bad pictures lately, but there were some good heads: I gave a commission for them for you, thinking they would come cheap, but unluckily there were some that saw their merit as well as I, and they sold above my commission. Pictures seem to be rising again. I will not send you yours till I hear from you.

" I am told there is the skin of a toad in Berkeley Castle that is of prodigious size. Let me know the truth of it, its dimensions, what bones are still in it, and if it can be stolen by some invisible being. I buried two toads last August was a twelvemonth; I opened the grave last October, and they were well and lively.

" Have you any queer fish? Write to me soon, and let me have all the news, &c. &c.

" Anny sends, with little John, their compliments.

" From yours, &c.
" JOHN HUNTER."

Jenner having at length completed, as he supposed, his observations on the cuckoo, drew them up in the form of a paper, to be read before the Royal Society, and transmitted it for this purpose to Hunter, who, in the following letter, states the reasons why he had not already presented it.

" DEAR JENNER,   [*Post-mark April* 26.]

" I received your papers, and should have presented them to the Royal Society before now, but for almost the whole of this winter we have had nothing but disputes in the Society, and giving up of Secretaryships, &c., and are not yet settled; but when we are I will give in your paper, but shall take a copy of it, that in case they should not publish it in the Transactions, it may be probably published by the Medical Society, who will make it of more use than the Transactions. The person you mentioned, who was attempting to make the medicine, called on me and left his name. When you have anything new, let me hear from you.

" I pity poor Cheston, for the loss of his son.

" Ever yours,
" JOHN HUNTER."

Shortly after this Jenner's memoir was read, and would have been published in the Transactions for 1787, but since delivering it he had discovered the fact that the eggs and young of the hedge-sparrow are ejected from the nest by the young cuckoo, and not by the parent bird, as he had at first supposed ; he was therefore allowed to withdraw the paper, in order to correct this error, and its publication was put off till the year following.

Whilst Jenner was pursuing his observations on the cuckoo, Hunter, it would seem, was busied in trying to make pearls, by introducing extraneous substances into oysters, as nuclei, for them to form on. What success he met with does not appear, and indeed the following letter of his to his friend Sir J. Banks gives us all the information we possess respecting this inquiry.

"DEAR SIR JOSEPH, 1787.

"I have these two days been draining the pond, or rather fishing for pearls, the success of which you will see by the specimens. Those I had made the experiments on were dead, but there is one recent. I have a few alive that I mean to put under experiment; but I shall open the shell and put in the extraneous body. If any other method suggests itself to you, be so good as to inform me. I would not have you make Lady Banks a present of them; I hope to get better, at least as large as my thumb. I lately got a *tall man*, but at the time could make no particular observations. I hope next summer to be able to show you him.

"I am, dear Sir Joseph,

"Your much obliged,

"JOHN HUNTER."

Hunter presented two papers to the Royal Society in the course of this year. The first contains observations tending to show that the Wolf, Jackal, and Dog are of the same species. The second is a long and valuable treatise on the structure and œconomy of Whales, illustrated by a number of very excellent engravings. Hunter had pursued his researches on these animals with great diligence and success, considering his necessarily limited opportunities for making observations. In this paper he mentions a fact which shows how little he spared expense in the pursuit of his favourite studies. As he found it impossible to obtain proper subjects on which to pursue his inquiries to the extent he desired, he engaged a surgeon, at his own expense, to proceed to the North in a Greenland whaler, after having given him such anatomical instruction, and provided him with such other means as would, he supposed, enable him to obtain some valuable information respecting the Whale tribe. But his choice of a messenger proved an unfortunate one; for all that he got, in return for his trouble and expense, was a bit of whale's skin, with some barnacles stuck on it. This eagerness of his to obtain rare and valuable specimens for his museum, often led him to pay more than its worth for an object he desired to make his own, as the following account of the manner in which he acquired the skeleton of Byrne, which heads the osteological collection, will probably be thought to prove.

Byrne, or O'Brien, the famous Irish giant, died in 1783. He had been in a declining state of health for some time previously, and Hunter, anxious to procure his skeleton, set his man Howison to keep watch on his movements, that he might be sure of securing his body at his death. Byrne learned this, and as he had a horror of being dissected, determined to take such precautions as should ensure his not falling into the hands of the doctors: he accordingly left strict orders that his body should be watched day and night, until a leaden coffin could be made, in which it was to be inclosed, and carried out to sea and sunk. Byrne died soon after, and, in compliance with his directions, the undertaker engaged some men to watch the body alternately. Howison soon learned this, found out the house where these men went to drink when off duty, and gave information to Hunter, who forthwith proceeded thither with the view of bribing them, to allow the body to be carried off. He had an interview with one of the party at the ale-house, and began by offering him fifty pounds if he would allow the body to be kidnapped: the man agreed, provided his companions would consent, and went out to consult them. He returned shortly, saying that they must have a hundred pounds. Hunter consented to this, and thought the affair settled; but the men finding him so eager, soon came back with an increased demand, which was also agreed to ; when further difficulties were found, and larger and larger demands made, until, it is said, they raised the price to five hundred pounds! The money was borrowed from Pidcock to pay them ; and in the dead of night the body was removed in a hackney coach, and after having been carried through several streets, was transferred to Hunter's own carriage, and conveyed immediately to Earl's Court. Fearing lest a discovery should take place, Hunter did not choose to risk the delay which the ordinary mode of preparing a skeleton would require ; accordingly, the body was cut to pieces, and the flesh separated by boiling ; hence has arisen the brown colour of the bones, which in all other respects form a magnificent skeleton.

The Royal Society this year conferred on Hunter the Copley medal, as an honourable testimony to the importance of his discoveries in natural history. He also received, about the same time, another mark of the estimation in which his labours were held, by being elected a member of the American Philosophical Society.

The arrangement of Hunter's museum was now completed, and he had the gratification of opening it for the inspection of his friends and acquaintance during two months in each year ; in October to the medical profession, and in May to those noblemen and gentlemen who felt an interest in such subjects.

Hunter's private practice was now so extensive, whilst his bodily health had so much diminished, that he determined on applying to the Governors of St. George's Hospital to allow him an assistant. His colleague, Mr. Gunning, determined on making a similar application at the same time ; and we accordingly find amongst the minutes of the Committee for this year the following entry :

" Mr. Gunning and Mr. Hunter·present their compliments to the gentlemen of the weekly board, and beg the favour of them to summon a Special General Court for the purpose of electing two assistants, a favour which has been formerly shown to Mr. Middleton, Mr. Hawkins, and Mr. Bromfield, in consideration of their many years' services to the hospital.

"The persons whom they beg leave to recommend to this situation are Mr. Keate, Surgeon in ordinary to His Royal Highness the Prince of Wales, and Mr. Home, who has been bred up under Mr. Hunter.

"They flatter themselves the propriety of their recommendation will render this indulgence the less exceptionable."

The request was complied with, and these gentlemen elected, the Court suspending a by-law which forbade physicians or surgeons of the hospital to recommend assistants or deputies. Mr. Gunning and Mr. Hunter at the same time declared that it was far from their intention to give up the necessary attendance at the hospital.

Hunter's friends had long been desirous to engage him to sit to Sir J. Reynolds for his picture; but he had always hitherto declined to do so, not choosing that it should be done at the expense of others, and thinking the price too high for himself to pay. He was, however, at length induced to comply, chiefly to oblige Sharp, the eminent engraver, who had received much notice from Hunter, and was very anxious to be permitted to make an engraving from Sir Joshua's picture. Reynolds found Hunter a bad sitter, and had not been able to satisfy himself with the likeness, when one day, after the picture was far advanced, Hunter fell into a train of thought, in the attitude in which he is represented in the present portrait: Reynolds, without saying a word, turned the canvas upside down, made a fresh sketch, with the head between the legs of the former figure, and so proceeded to lay on over the former painting the colours of that which now graces the walls of the library at the College of Surgeons. From this portrait Sharp executed his engraving, which is admitted by the best judges to be one of the finest, if not the very finest specimen of the art ever executed. The doubt rests chiefly between this and another engraving by the same artist*, 'The consultation of the Doctors on the immaculateness of the Virgin,' after Guido, for both are thought to be superior to the best efforts even of Raffael-Morghen or Desnoyers.

Hunter's increased professional engagements prevented his continuing to be any longer so large a contributor as formerly to the Transactions of the Royal Society. During the next five years we find but one short paper of his, namely, a Supplement, in 1789, to his Observations on the

---

* Poor Sharp, though a man of extraordinary talent in his art, was singularly devoid of common sense. He was a devotee, and a firm believer in the pretensions of the prophet Brothers and the aged virgin Johanna Southcote; but at the same time a man of profligate habits. Hunter was a great admirer of his talents as an artist, and possessed a large portfolio of splendid engravings by Sharp and other eminent masters in the art. Sharp always considered his engraving of Hunter as one of his happiest efforts, and was found poring over it with admiration forty years after he had executed it. Hunter took fifty copies of the engraving, at two guineas each, and the plate proved a milch-cow to the artist. One of the means by which Sharp succeeded in attaining to such perfection in his works was the following: he always kept a number of engravings in hand at the same time, in various stages of their progress; it was his practice to commence working on those parts which required least delicacy in the execution, and when he had got his hand well in, or when he felt particularly in cue, immediately to transfer his operations to those plates which were in a state to require delicate manipulation. For the engraving of Hunter, which was prefixed to the first edition of his work on inflammation, edited by Home, and which is to be found amongst the plates accompanying this edition of his works, Sharp received fifty guineas, a large sum at that time. It is so exact a copy of the portion of the large engraving which it represents, that it was supposed by some to have been actually a portion cut out of the original plate; there is, however, every reason to believe that this latter is still in existence.

Wolf, Jackal, and Dog, given two years before. Nor do we find that he contributed anything this year to the Transactions of the Medical Society before mentioned; and for the future he generally entrusted to his brother-in-law the business of communicating an account of such improvements, or observations of a professional kind, as he thought deserved to be recorded.

We find also that his correspondence with Jenner for this year was confined to a single letter, and that principally in reply to a consultation respecting a case of disease of the urinary organs, which Jenner had under his care.

" DEAR JENNER, *May* 1788.

" I have been going to write to you some time past, but business and a very severe indisposition for three weeks past has prevented me; but when two guineas rouse me, I cannot resist. Have you tried a bougie, to find if there is any mechanical stoppage? As there is blood in the urine, is there no stone? Would it not be right to try both? But suppose no stoppage nor no stone, then I would push the cicuta: at the same time he should be very temperate in eating, drinking, and exercise; eat no salt nor made dishes; drink no fermented liquors; but plentifully of everything else, and be very quiet.

" Your paper has been read, passed the Council, and is in print, for I had a proof sheet this day, and I have ordered fifty copies, twenty-five for you and twenty-five for myself, to give to friends. I spoke to both Sir Joseph Banks and Dr. Blagden about your wish. Sir Joseph has not the least objection, and will give us all his assistance, but he thinks the paper had better be first printed and delivered, and let the people rest a little upon it, for he says there are many who can hardly believe it wholly. This will put off the certificate till the beginning of next winter, when we shall hang you up. I have received a box, with a wapping landlady and two lizards. Mrs. Hunter's and my compliments to Mrs. Jenner.

" I am, dear Sir,
" Your most obedient Servant,
" JOHN HUNTER."

In December of the present year an event occurred which left to Hunter the undisputed title of the first surgeon in

England; this was the death of the veteran Pott. It is true that for some years past Hunter had been in possession of a larger share of practice and of public confidence than any other member of the profession; but as Pott still lived, and, notwithstanding his advanced age, continued actively engaged in practice, the recollection of his former fame maintained to him a high degree of public esteem, and left it doubtful to which of these eminent men the priority of station should be adjudged. On the 22nd of December, however, this able surgeon and excellent man expired, at the age of seventy-five, after an illness of only a few days, having retained the full use of his faculties almost to his last moment. It will be recollected that Pott was amongst the earliest of Hunter's instructors in surgery, but in after-life they gradually assumed somewhat of a hostile attitude towards each other. A great dissimilarity existed in their characters and attainments; and as, from the position which each occupied, and from other circumstances, comparisons were often instituted between them, it may not be uninteresting to endeavour briefly to show in what this dissimilarity chiefly consisted.

Pott was a man of quick natural talents and of sound sense, which had been improved and strengthened by a good classical education, and by constant assiduous attention on his own part in after-life. As a surgeon he was thoroughly versed in the history of medicine in all ages, and knew well how to bring this knowledge to bear on the practice of his profession. His correct observation enabled him to discover many of the errors of his predecessors, and his ingenuity and judgment, to correct them; and thus, by the combined effects of his own and others' experience, he was the means of introducing many valuable improvements into the practical departments of surgery. He was not fond of employing physiological reasoning to guide his practice, but aimed rather at founding his treatment on immediate analogy and induction from established facts than on broader general principles ; the theoretical part of our profession, therefore, he did little to improve.   As an operator, Pott was eminently skilled ; as a lecturer, clear, energetic, and fluent ; as a writer, classically correct and elegant.   In society he was agreeable, witty, and abounding ·in anecdote, and at the same time kind and gentlemanly in his manners. Though hospitable in his mode of living, he was prudent in regard to pecuniary matters, and though he commenced his profession poor, brought up a large family liberally, and left them well provided for at his death.

The account already given of Hunter has sufficiently shown how destitute he was of many of those acquirements which added lustre to the character of Pott, and which mainly contributed to obtain for him the high esteem which he so long and deservedly enjoyed.   But in spite of these deficiencies, Hunter, by the force of his own genius, which was unquestionably of a much higher order than that of Pott, and by his unwearied industry, forced his way at length to the summit of his profession ; and, as Dr. Beddoes observed, " when one heard that Hunter was at length the first surgeon in London, one felt a satisfaction like that which attends the distribution of poetical justice at the close of a well told tale."

CHAPTER VI.

1789 to 1793.

WE have thus traced Hunter's career from the time when, as a raw and uneducated youth, he first made his appearance on the stage of his future labours and his future fame, upwards through

> " What rugged places lie between
> Adventurous virtue's early toils
> And her triumphal throne,"

to the period when, after forty years of almost unexampled industry, he had raised himself to the highest place, not only in the estimation of the public, but in the more valuable, because more discriminating, judgment of the most intelligent amongst the rising generation of professional men. By the latter he was looked up to as the author of a new æra in surgery; and his opinions were current, not only amongst those who had been his immediate pupils,

but amongst all the younger members of the profession who
aspired to keep themselves on a level with the advancing
state of medical knowledge.   Hunter's behaviour was well
adapted also to secure him the regard and the homage of
his junior brethren; for he was by no means backward in
encouraging the advances of young men of talent who desired to cultivate his acquaintance, but readily afforded any
slight attentions in his power to those coming to London
to finish their studies, and recommended such as had completed their education to situations in the army if he found
them industrious and intelligent.   It may be worth while
to mention a few instances of this sort, which, though trifling perhaps in themselves, will not be without value if
they tend to illustrate the character of this eminent man.

On his arrival in London, Mr. Thomas, in company
with Mr. Nicol, by whom he was to be introduced, called
on Hunter : they found him dressing. " Well, young gentleman," said Hunter, when the first ceremonies of introduction were over, " so you are come to town to be a surgeon; And how long do you intend to stay ? " " One year,"
was the reply.   " Then," said he, " I 'll tell you what, that
won't do ; I 've been here a great many years, and have
worked hard too*, and yet I don't know the principles of
the art."   After some further conversation, Mr. T. was directed to call again in an hour, which he did, and accompanied Hunter to the hospital, where he said to him, after

---

* It is a not uncommon practice with great men to conceal the
amount of labour bestowed by them on their works, in order to heighten
the opinion of their genius. Hunter seems to have been above this ar-
tifice ; he worked hard, and he cared not who knew it. His contemporaries might under-value his labours, because they could not understand
their object, but he never doubted their usefulness. " Ah, John Hunter,
what still hard at work ! " said Dr. Garthshore, on finding his friend in
the latter years of his life busy in his dissecting-room. " Yes, Doctor,"
said Hunter, " still hard at work ; and you 'll find it difficult to meet with
another John Hunter when I am gone."

the business was over, " Come to me to-morrow morning, young gentleman, and I will put you further in the way of things ; come early in the morning, as soon after four as you can." It was summer : Mr. Thomas kept the appointment, and found Hunter, at that early hour, busily engaged in dissecting beetles. Mr. Thomas afterwards became his dresser at the hospital, and was finally recommended by him as surgeon to Lord Macartney's embassy to China, on returning from which he found that Hunter had died during his absence from England.

Sir A. Carlisle, whilst a pupil at the Westminster Hospital, was anxious to become personally acquainted with Hunter. He introduced himself by calling and requesting his acceptance of a very delicate and well-executed preparation of the internal ear. Hunter was highly delighted with it, detained him to breakfast, and in the course of conversation encouraged him by saying, " Any man who will set about a business, and do it as you have done that ear, may do anything he pleases in London." On finding that Mr. C. had not yet attended his lectures, as a reason for which he assigned his not being sufficiently advanced in professional knowledge to profit by them, " That, Sir," said Hunter, "is very complimentary, but I will give you a perpetual ticket, and shall be glad to see you whenever you will call." This invitation was not neglected, and Mr. Carlisle's anatomical skill soon made him a favourite with Hunter, to whose collection he contributed several valuable preparations.

Nor did Hunter confine himself to such minor attentions as these, but occasionally assisted young men whom he saw struggling with pecuniary difficulties at the outset of their career, by sending them valuable patients ; or even extended his kind consideration still further, as the follow-

ing anecdote, which is not quite correctly related by Mr.
Abernethy in his Hunterian oration, will show.

Mr. Lynn, who was for many years on intimate terms
with Hunter, suffered a long illness in consequence of
having wounded his hand in opening the body of a man
who had died from a syphilitic affection. Hunter frequently
called to see him, and one day, after expressing regret at his
misfortune, and the obstruction it caused to his business,
offered to lend him two hundred pounds, adding, that
though he was the last man in the world to be able to do
such a thing, yet that he would stretch a point, in consequence of the esteem he had for Mr. Lynn. His friend had
been more prudent, however, than Hunter supposed, and
did not then require assistance, but said, that should he
have occasion for it he would not fail to apply to him.
" Nay," said Hunter, " what I offer I will do now, but what
I may be able to do a week hence it is impossible for me
to say." On his recovery, Mr. Lynn went to thank him for
his kindness. Hunter had forgotten the circumstance ;
" But," said he, " if I did say so, you may depend on it I
meant what I said."

But to resume the thread of my narrative. His old friend
Jenner had long ere this sufficiently recovered from the
effects of his first disappointment to plead his cause successfully with another lady, and he this year wrote to communicate to Hunter the news of the birth of his first child,
to which he requested him to stand godfather; and as Hunter had no more intention than other godfathers of bur-
thening himself with the performance of what he undertook,
he readily acceded to the request, as will be seen in his reply.

"DEAR JENNER,   [*Post-mark Jan.* 29.]   1789.
I wish you joy : it never rains but it pours. Rather than the brat
should not be a Christian I will stand godfather, for I should be unhappy

if the poor little thing should go the devil because I would not stand godfather. I hope Mrs. Jenner is well, and that you begin to look grave now you are a father.

"Yours sincerely,
"J. Hunter."

Two other letters of his, written in the early part of this year, to Jenner, show the diligence with which he promoted the interests of his friends ; they relate to the admission of the latter into the Royal Society, of which body he was made a Fellow, in consequence of his interesting communication respecting the cuckoo. The first is as follows.

"Dear Jenner,
"You are to be balloted for next Thursday. I think there can be no fear of success. You shall have a letter from me by the Friday's post.
"Yours sincerely,
"John Hunter.
"I have wrote to Dr. Glass."

The second communicates the intelligence of his election.

"Dear Jenner, London, Feb. 26th.
"You was this evening voted into the Royal Society. You will have a letter from the Secretary ; but as that may not be sent for some days, I thought it would not be disagreeable to have the earliest notice.
"I am, dear Jenner,
"Your most obedient,
"John Hunter."

His own contributions had, as we have before observed, become gradually more infrequent. The only paper he communicated this year was a supplement to his observations on the Wolf, Jackal, and Dog.

To the Transactions of the Society for the Improvement of Medical and Chirurgical Knowledge he furnished a paper on intussusception, where he ingeniously explains the mode in which the several forms of the disease are produced. In the same volume is contained the account of Hunter's operation for aneurism, as before given in the

Medical and Surgical Journal, and of a number of additional
cases operated upon by Hunter and others. This paper was
furnished by Mr. Home.

In the following year he furnished to the same Society
a paper on Paralysis of the Œsophagus, and pointed out
the mode of nourishing the patient, now commonly used in
this and some other diseases, by means of a tube passed
down the œsophagus. He also provided Mr. Home with
the materials for another paper, on the formation of Loose
Cartilages in joints, the presence of which he satisfactorily
explains by a reference to pathological preparations.

In 1790 Mr. White, Surgeon-General to the colony of
New South Wales, published a journal of his voyage to
that country, to which is added an appendix by Hunter
on the best mode of collecting and sending home animals,
and on the nomenclature and classes of animals, as also a
description of the kangaroo, and several other animals of
that country.

The following letter to Jenner relates principally to the
subject of the presence of hydatids in the body, a phenomenon to which this gentleman, and his biographer Dr. Baron after him, have attached much importance, as giving
rise, in their opinion, to the formation of many kinds of
morbid growth.

" DEAR JENNER,

" I have just received the favour of yours. I have, just now, forgot
the case of hydatids; but if there was anything that struck me, I dare
say it was laid by. They are frequently in the kidneys; but I should
doubt your oil of turpentine having any merit in bringing them away.
My reason for supposing them animals is because they move after they
have been extracted. I have taken them out of the head or brain of
a sheep, and they have contracted in different parts of them when put
into warm water. I should be glad to employ you if I knew in what,
but if anything comes across my imagination I will think of you. The
measly pork are hydatids.

" I am afraid of your friend Mrs. L. There is a hard tumour that almost fills the pelvis, most probably the uterus. How does Mrs. Jenner do ? Do you bring her to London ? What family have you got ? My compliments to Mrs. Jenner ; and believe me to be, dear sir,

"Your most obedient and most humble Servant,

"*Dec. 8th*, 1790." "JOHN HUNTER."

Hunter's health had continued very precarious ever since his severe attack of illness in 1785 : in December 1789 he suffered under a sudden and entire loss of memory, which lasted half an hour, and then as entirely left him. The spasms about the præcordia were frequently re-produced by very slight causes, as trifling bodily exertion or mental irritation. The latter cause was the most frequent, to which the uncontrolled hastiness of his temper rendered him particularly obnoxious ; and so sensible was he of the risks to which it exposed him, that he was accustomed to say that " his life was in the hands of any rascal who chose to annoy and teaze him ;" a painful thought, that one possessing a mind of such intellectual vigour should, from neglecting earlier to check this infirmity of temper, at length have allowed it " so to over-master reason" as to reduce him to hold his life on such a tenure.

Notwithstanding, however, his ill state of health, Hunter continued to *enjoy* life ; his constant employment prevented *ennui*, and his natural vigour and courage enabled him to bear up against attacks which would have dispirited weaker minds. He does not seem, like his contemporary Dr. Johnson, to have been oppressed with a fear of death ; but neither had he, any more than the great moralist, any longing to " shuffle off this mortal coil ;" and when a gentleman at his table spoke of Dr. Hunter's expressing, in his last moments, a feeling of satisfaction in dying, Hunter replied, " Ay, 't is poor work when it comes to that." Indeed, he had sufficient reason for being anxious that his life should be prolonged. As yet he had made no provision for his family; and his museum, on which he had expended so much, and to the sale of which he chiefly looked as the source of such a provision, was as yet greatly deficient in proper catalogues, a want which could not but greatly detract from its value, and to supply which formed one of the chief objects of his attention during the remaining years of his life.

Although Hunter considered his pursuits too important to allow of his devoting much of his time to general society, yet he was hospitably disposed, and, as soon as his income allowed of it, lived in rather a handsome style, kept a carriage and footman for Mrs. Hunter, entertained his friends at dinner, and opened his house to his medical acquaintances every Sunday evening. His house at Earl's Court had been gradually improved and enlarged since his marriage, and some of the rooms had been tastily fitted up under Mrs. Hunter's direction ; the drawing-room, in particular, was ornamented with moveable panels, elegantly painted in water-colours, and representing the story of Cupid and Psyche. Here he used to spend a good part of his time during the autumnal months, returning to London in the morning after breakfast, and retiring to dine and sleep with his family at Earl's Court. The grounds were, as usual, stocked with various denizens of earth and air, collected from all quarters of the world, and the garden was well furnished with wall fruit; but this was considered the sole property of his bees, several hives of which were contained in the conservatory, where he used to pursue his observations whilst at home, and leave some of his family to mount guard during his absence. His fondness for bees was very great, from whence he derived a common but expressive metaphor, which he was in the habit of employing, that " his head was like a bee-hive."

When residing in London his establishment was very

numerous; and as he had generally workmen engaged about
the premises, not less than thirty persons usually sat down
to dinner in his house.

In conversation he seldom displayed wit; but his remarks
were often wonderfully pointed and forcible, and showed
him to be an original thinker. In politics he was as stre-
nuous a Tory as Dr. Johnson or the renowned Christopher
North could have desired, and was not more lenient than
they towards those who differed from him in opinion. He
used to say, that " he wished all the rascals who were dissatisfied with their country would be good enough to leave
it." He had a great dislike, as may be easily imagined, to
taking part in any public procession or displays of any kind,
and fairly wished Sir J. Reynolds and his friends at the
d—l when called on to take part in the funeral of this eminent artist and delightful author*.

In 1792 Hunter contributed his last paper to the Philosophical Transactions. This contained the results of his
observations on the hive bee, continued, with various inter-

---

* Hunter, with Sir G. Baker and Mr. Home, attended Sir J. Reynolds in his last illness, the nature of which was very obscure, and is
said not to have been understood until a fortnight before his death, when
it was ascertained to depend on enlargement of the liver. The following is a copy of the *post mortem* examination, the original of which is
in the possession of my friend Mr. Palmer, the great-nephew of Sir
Joshua, and editor of the present edition of Hunter's works.

" In examining the body of the late Sir Joshua Reynolds, we found
no marks of disease in the cavity of the breast, except only a slight adhesion of the lungs to the surrounding membrane on the left side.

" In the cavity of the belly the only diseased part was the liver, which
was of a magnitude very uncommon, and at least double of what is natural: it weighed eleven pounds, and was of a consistence which is
usually called scirrhous. It had lost its natural colour, and become of
a pale yellow.

" We found the optic nerve of the right side shrunk, and softer than
natural. There was more water in the ventricles of the brain than what
is generally found at so advanced an age.

" G. BAKER,
" JOHN HUNTER,
" 24*th Feb.* 1792." " E. HOME."

ruptions, during a period of twenty years. The variety of
his employments rendered it impossible that he should devote such continuous attention as some others, and especially Huber, have since done to the habits of these very
interesting animals ; nevertheless, his keen observation did
not fail to detect several errors which preceding naturalists
had fallen into, especially with regard to the formation of
the wax, which he proved to be secreted, not collected, by
the animal; and on the whole his paper added largely to
the general stock of knowledge respecting the œconomy of
the bee.

He had not confined his attention to the hive bee only,
but intended, as will be seen by the following letter to Sir
J. Banks, which accompanied his paper, to treat also of the
hornet, the wasp, and several of the solitary bees ; and we
cannot but greatly regret that his intentions were left un-
fulfilled.

" SIR,   *February* 21, 1792.

" Allow me to present to you a paper on the natural history of the
common bee. It contains the result of experiments and observations
occasionally made in the course of the last twenty years. They have
been frequently interrupted by my other pursuits, which prevented me
from following this subject regularly through any one season, and consequently obliged me to renew it in others. Unforeseen accidents have
considerably retarded my progress : a very sultry day melting the comb,
the bees removing some eggs or maggots, or a hive dying under experiment, have destroyed the chain of my observations for a whole season.

" It was my intention to have added some remarks on the management of bees in this country, but I am induced, from the length of this
paper, to reserve them for another opportunity. If you and your learned
Council think them worthy the attention of the Royal Society, I shall
hope to have them honoured with a place in your valuable Transactions.

" As I have gone a considerable length into the natural history of
this tribe of insects, I hope next winter to give you the account of the
wasp, and probably the hornet. I shall afterwards be able to give the
wild or humble bee, and many of those called solitary bees, in which I

have made considerable progress; and in time I hope to complete the history of the British bees.

"I am, Sir, your much obliged and most humble Servant,

"*Leicester Square.* "JOHN HUNTER."

"To Sir J. Banks, Bart., P.R.S."

He this year resigned to Mr. Home the office of delivering his surgical lectures, and for this purpose passed over to him all his manuscripts, the greater part of which have unfortunately been either lost or destroyed. On the fly-leaf of each of these lectures were inscribed references to the different preparations which he employed for the illustration of his opinions, which, did they exist, would manifestly afford great aid in determining the specific object of many of these preparations. The loss of these lectures has been lately remedied in part by the publication of the late Mr. Parkinson's notes of them by his son, under the title of "Reminiscences of John Hunter;" and Mr. Palmer will be able, in the present edition, still further to repair the loss, by collating a number of copies, of different dates and by different hands, with each other. To this foundation furnished by Hunter, Mr. Home added a number of new lectures on particular diseases, and on the operations of surgery, which he continued to deliver for a few years, but was never a very popular or diligent lecturer.

Mr. Hunter's chief reason for declining his lectureship at this time was, that he might have more leisure to devote to the completion of his work on Inflammation, which, in justice to himself, he felt it was now time he should make public. As it happened, he did not live to see the entire work through the press, a portion of it still remaining at the time that he died, the office of correcting which devolved on Mr. Home and Dr. Baillie. It was published in 1793, together with a life of the author by Mr. Home.

This work is the one on which, above all his other writings, Hunter's fame has hitherto rested; perhaps too exclusively so, since it has arisen from the circumstance that, with the exception of the treatise on syphilis, his other works have been less generally read than they deserve, in consequence of their having been published either in an expensive form or in detached treatises, scattered through the volumes of the Philosophical Transactions, or of the Medical and Chirurgical Society. There are not, however, any of his writings which do not well deserve the attentive perusal of professional men, not only for the information they furnish, but as models of bold and sagacious reasoning; and hence the present edition, which places within the reach of every professional man the whole of his works, heightened, too, in value by the commentaries of the able men to whose revision they have been severally entrusted, cannot fail to be viewed as a tribute justly due to the merits of Hunter, and as a highly important accession to our medical literature.

The treatise on Inflammation and Gunshot Wounds must be considered as comprising the results of forty years' assiduous attention to the subject, since, from his Introduction, we learn, that the doctrines it unfolds first suggested themselves to his mind at the time he was a student in the London hospitals, and were based on observations collected during that period. These doctrines he continued during his whole professional career to submit to the test of his own increasing experience and the experience of others, to whom he taught them in his lectures, ever carefully and candidly correcting them where more accurate observations proved them to be faulty, and extending them where fresh information showed them to be deficient; and having thus brought them to as high a degree of perfection as his abilities and opportunities would permit, he at length submitted them to the test of public opinion in the condensed and systematic form in which we now possess them.

Notwithstanding the time and attention he had devoted to the completion of a work on which his future fame was mainly to depend, he was himself fully sensible of its still possessing many defects, and rather desired it to be considered " as a new figure composed from rough materials, in which process little or no assistance could be had from any quarter," than as a perfect work which no further experience could have amended. It must indeed be acknowledged that it does, in many parts, exhibit imperfections of style and diction, as well as repetitions, which not unfrequently obscure the author's meaning; and illogical errors, such as that of confounding proximate and final causes, or employing such imaginary causes as the " stimulus of necessity," " the stimulus of death," " the force of a negative impression," &c., to account for certain effects ; phrases which cheat the ear with a seeming explanation, but leave the mind no whit the wiser as to the real causes of the phenomena to be accounted for. These defects, though they do unquestionably detract somewhat from its value, are, however, trifling in comparison with the great and varied excellence of this work, which, for the originality and variety of its experiments, the accuracy of its observations, and the importance of its deductions, can with difficulty be paralleled in the whole range of medical literature.

About this period the London Veterinary College was first projected, and being liberally supported by several influential noblemen, was speedily established. Hunter felt much interest in its formation, and, with several other gentlemen, took shares in it to the amount of two hundred pounds, and, furthermore, granted to the pupils attending there a free admission to his lectures.

In addition to the honorary distinctions which he before enjoyed, Hunter had this year conferred on him the title of Member of the Irish College of Surgeons, and of the Chi-

rurgo-Physical Society of Edinburgh; but neither these
nor any others did he ever append to his name, preferring
the simple appellation of John Hunter, which he was fully
conscious was better able to confer honour on most Societies than their initials to add importance to it.

We have now arrived at that period when it becomes necessary to notice the unhappy disagreements which had for
some time past existed between Hunter and his colleagues
at the Hospital, and which now broke out into more decided
measures of hostility. It would have been more agreeable,
had it been proper, to have passed over these without notice,
since they reflect little credit on either of the contending
parties; but they are so intimately connected with the fatal
event which terminated Hunter's life and labours, that it
seemed absolutely necessary, in the present narrative, to
notice them somewhat more fully than his former biographers have done.

Mention has already been made of the blunt and overbearing manner which Hunter not unfrequently displayed
towards men of his own standing in the profession. Devoted as he was to physiological pursuits, and firmly persuaded that without an improved knowledge of physiology
it would be impossible to attain to correct general principles
in surgery, which he looked on as still in its infancy, he
viewed with contempt those who were content to guide
their practice by past experience alone, or by the erroneous
theories of their ancestors. On the other hand, the majority of Hunter's contemporaries considered his pursuits to
have little connexion with practice, charged him with attending to physiology more than surgery, and looked on
him as little better than an innovator and an enthusiast.
There could be little harmony between such discordant
elements, and as it was with his colleagues at the hospital
that Hunter most frequently came into collision, it was

between him and them that mutual want of respect most easily and surely ripened into animosity.

At the commencement of 1792 Hunter's colleagues at the hospital were, Gunning, who was his senior, a man of good talents and high spirit, and leader of the opposition against him; Walker; and Charles Hawkins, the son of Sir Cæsar, and a remarkably dexterous operator. Early in the year Hawkins resigned his situation, and a contest for the vacancy ensued between Keate and Home. The latter was of course supported by Mr. Hunter, whilst all the remaining medical officers, with the exception of Dr. Baillie, lent their interest to his opponent. The contest was perhaps the warmest in the annals of hospital electioneering, and several of the Royal Dukes attended in person to vote for Mr. Keate, who was chosen by a majority of 134 against 102.

A contest like this, however it might have ended, could scarcely fail to heighten existing animosities; and soon after, Hunter, actuated far more by a spirit of hostility to his opponents than by any desire of pecuniary benefit to himself, announced to them his intention to discontinue the practice of dividing equally amongst the surgeons the admission fees of all the pupils attending the hospital, and for the future to retain for himself the money of those who should enter under his name as pupils; a preference which is determined by various circumstances, and which has never been regarded in any other light than as a compliment. As a reason for this step, he alleges his wish to stimulate the other surgeons to pay some attention to the education of the pupils, which, as he asserts, they were far from doing, but on the contrary had brought disgrace on the hospital by their neglect.

This measure his colleagues resolved to resist, and determined to submit the matter to the decision of the Governors, a step which seems, from the following letter, to have met with Hunter's full concurrence.

"GENTLEMEN,

"As the time approaches when you propose referring to the Governors of St. George's Hospital my determination respecting the money arising from the surgeons' pupils, I beg leave to acquaint you that I entirely agree with you in the mode that you have proposed, a mode I did not myself adopt, as it took from you the power of acceding to my proposal, and made me appear to the Governors as an accuser. But when you bring it before them I shall meet it fairly and very willingly.

"I am, Gentlemen,

"Your most obedient Servant,

"*Leicester Square, Feb.* 8, 1793."   "JOHN HUNTER."

"Messrs. Gunning, Walker, and Keate."

A Special Court was accordingly summoned to meet in March following. Before the day of meeting, Hunter forwarded to each subscriber, for his information, a pretty long printed letter, explanatory of his reasons for the alteration which he had determined to make. In this communication, which is certainly not remarkable either for its liberality or modesty, he gives an account of the various efforts he had made, since his connexion with the hospital, to induce his colleagues to improve the system of instruction ; efforts which, he says, all proved ineffectual : one man " did not choose to hazard his reputation by giving lectures," and another " did not see where the art could be improved." Disgusted at his want of success, and resolving not to encourage the indolence of others, he had consequently slackened in his attention to the pupils, and an immediate and constant falling off in their numbers had been the result. He shows how large a majority of the whole number of students had always entered as his pupils, argues on the propriety of each surgeon profiting according to his labours, and therefore justifies his present intention, which cannot justly be ascribed to any avaricious feeling, seeing that the whole number of those entering at the hospital is now so small. Finally, he deprecates the considering this as a party question, affirms that he is actuated by the most disinterested feelings, and expresses his readiness to submit to the decision of the Court.

To this letter the hostile triumvirate replied, by denying the correctness of Hunter's account. The increase of pupils after his accession to the hospital, they attribute to the breaking out of a war, and not to his presence; the subsequent decrease they state was caused by the establishment of medical schools at the other hospitals, and not by Mr. Hunter's neglect. They admit that the number of pupils entering with him has been larger than with either of themselves; but this has been owing to his connexion with the anatomical school in Windmill-street, and his power of conferring posts in the army, and not to his superior attention to the pupils. To the charge of neglecting their duty, brought against them, they reply by stating that they have continued the usual plan of instruction long followed in the hospital. That if the students have neglected their duties there to follow physiological researches, it was not their fault. A proposal they state had been formerly made, that each of the surgeons should give six lectures at the hospital, for which extra instruction the admission fee was to be raised from twenty to five-and-twenty guineas, but for the following rather curious reasons the plan was not put into execution. 1st, Because they thought the old plan of instruction best for surgeons. 2ndly, Because copies of the lectures might be taken by the pupils, and might get abroad! 3rdly, Because, though the pupils might be pleased for a course or two, the lectures would lose their effect ultimately, and might, from the numbers being lessened, in consequence of the rise of price, in the end prove disadvantageous. They then go on to show, that a manifest disad-

K

vantage to the pupils would arise from the proposed measure;
for whereas they had hitherto enjoyed the benefit of instruction from all the surgeons, they would for the future be
limited to the instruction afforded by the surgeon alone under
whom they entered, should Mr. Hunter's intention be carried into effect.

The decision of the Governors was given against Mr.
Hunter; for though his opponents neither fully disproved
his statement, that he had been the means of increasing
the number of pupils at the hospital, nor could deny that
he had done more towards their instruction than any of
themselves, yet the disadvantage of the plan he proposed
was so obvious, as pointed out by his opponents, that nothing but confusion and discord could have been expected
from its adoption. A Committee was subsequently appointed to draw up a code of rules for regulating the admission and instruction of pupils; and a set of proposals
was submitted to them by Mr. Hunter's colleagues, which
was agreed to without his having been even consulted on
the occasion! Many of the regulations adopted continue
in force to the present day; others, and especially those
relating to the better instruction of the pupils, soon fell into
disuse; and some seem to have been especially directed
against Mr. Hunter. Amongst these latter was one which
determined that for the future no person should be admitted as a student of the hospital without bringing certificates
that he had been educated to the profession; a regulation
which was probably designed to exclude Mr. Hunter's
countrymen, who sometimes came up to town recommended
to him, and entered as his pupils at the hospital, without
having had any previous medical instruction. Nor was this
clause long in taking effect; for in the autumn two young
men, who had come up to town ignorant of this new regulation, applied to Hunter to be admitted under him at

the hospital. He informed them of the law which had been passed, but undertook to press for their admission at the next Board-day, and directed them to furnish him with a statement of their case in writing. On the 16th of October the Board was to meet, and Hunter prepared to fulfil his promise, though he was so well aware of the risk he incurred, in undertaking a task which he felt would agitate him, that in mentioning the circumstance to a friend who called on him in the morning, he expressed his apprehension lest some unpleasant dispute might occur, and his conviction that if it did it would certainly prove fatal to him. At his accustomed hour he left his house to commence his morning rounds, and by accident forgot to take with him his list of appointments; he had left the house but a few moments when it was discovered, and Mr. Clift, who was then residing in his house, hastened with it to York-street, St. James's, the first place on the list, where he found the carriage waiting. Hunter soon made his appearance, took the list, and in an animated tone called to the coachman to drive to St. George's. Arrived at the hospital, he found the Board already assembled, and entering the room, presented the memorial of the young men, and proceeded to urge the propriety of their being admitted. In the course of his remarks he made some observation which one of his colleagues thought it necessary instantly and flatly to contradict. Hunter immediately ceased speaking, retired from the table, and struggling to suppress the tumult of his passion, hurried into the adjoining room, which he had scarcely reached when, with a deep groan, he fell lifeless into the arms of Dr. Robertson, one of the physicians of the hospital, who chanced to be present. Dr. Baillie had immediately followed him from the Board-room, and Mr. Home, who was in the house, was also summoned to his assistance. Various attempts were made for upwards of an hour to restore animation, under the hope that the attack might prove to be a fainting fit, such as he had before experienced, but in vain ; life had fled ; and all their efforts proving useless, his body was placed in a sedan chair and conveyed to Leicester-square, followed by his now vacant carriage.

This most distressing event of course put an end to the business of the meeting ; the Board broke up, and the only notice to be found on the books of that day's proceedings is the following minute :

" Resolved,—That Mr. Hunter's letter to this Board relating to two of the surgeons' pupils, which was received this day, be preserved for future consideration."

The body was examined after death*, when the viscera of the belly and head were found loaded with blood, but otherwise nearly in a natural state, with the exception of the carotid arteries and their branches within the skull, which were in parts thickened and ossified.   In the chest, the left lung had become attached to the costal pleura by old and firm adhesions ; but the heart was found to be the chief seat of disease.   The pericardium was unusually thickened, but did not contain much fluid.   The heart itself was small, appearing too little for the cavity in which it was contained, its diminished size being the result of wasting, and not of strong contraction of its fibres.   Two opake white spots were seen on the left auricle and ventricle. The muscular structure of the organ was pale, and loose in its texture.   The coronary arteries had their branches

---

* It has been supposed by some that Hunter had the same antipathy to the scalpel of the anatomist as was felt by his brother; but this was by no means the case ; on the contrary, he always spoke of it as a matter of course, and used, in the strongest language, to express his condemnation of those who should neglect to examine his body and preserve his heart.   It is to be regretted that no relic of this sort has been preserved.

which ramify through the heart converted into long tubes, with difficulty divisible by the knife. The mitral valves were much ossified. The aorta was somewhat dilated, its valves thickened and wanting pliancy, and the inner surface of the artery was studded with opake and elevated white spots.

Hunter's body was interred in a private manner, in the church of St. Martin-in-the-Fields, accompanied only by a few of his medical friends.

Some time after his death Mrs. Hunter felt anxious to erect a monument to his memory in Westminster Abbey; but the fees demanded for permission to occupy a niche within that venerable fane were too great for her reduced fortunes, and she therefore abandoned her intention. It may be thought that the author of the Hunterian museum needs no other memorial of his worth than the proud one he has himself erected; nor does he, to perpetuate his fame: still, it would be a fitting act of respect to his memory, from those who enjoy the benefits of this rich legacy of his genius, to enrol his name amongst those of the other gifted men whose worth stands recorded in Westminster Abbey.

Thus, in his sixty-fifth year, died John Hunter, celebrated alike as a surgeon and as a naturalist; in neither of which capacities has he had many equals,—in his combined character, none.

In person he was about the middle stature, of a vigorous and robust frame, and free from corpulency; his shoulders were high, and his neck short. His features were rather large, and strongly marked; his eyebrow projecting, his eyes of a light colour, his cheeks high, and his mouth somewhat under-hung. In dress he was plain and gentleman-like; and his hair, which in youth was of a reddish yellow, and in his latter years white, he wore curled behind.

On considering what was the distinguishing character of

Hunter's mind, we perceive that it was rather that of general strength and vigour than of a marked predominance of any one faculty, especially adapting it for excellence in some particular kind of pursuit. Johnson says "a true genius is a mind of large general powers, accidentally determined to some particular direction;" a definition which, though certainly not universally true, seems thoroughly descriptive of Hunter's mind. To talents for observation naturally acute, and heightened to an extraordinary degree by constant practice, Hunter added strong reasoning powers, a sound judgment, and an imagination which, though not brilliant, was sufficiently active to aid him in his researches, whilst it rarely drew him far aside from the sure paths of induction into the regions of hypothesis. Hence, though it might be difficult to name any employments better fitted to call the faculties of his mind into full action than those in which he was engaged, yet it cannot be doubted that there were many in which those faculties, aided by his extraordinary powers of application, would have as certainly raised him to a pre-eminence above other competitors as they did in medical science and natural philosophy.

With regard to Hunter's moral character, though it was adorned with many noble features,—as undeviating honesty, an eminent love of truth and candour, and a humane and generous spirit*,—and though as a friend he was warm and disinterested, and as a husband and a parent kind and affectionate, yet his character was defective for want of that control over his passions and his temper, the possession of

* In regard to fees Hunter was extremely liberal. He used generally to reply, when asked to say what was due to him, "Why, that you must determine yourself; you are the best judge of your own circumstances, and it is far from my wish to deprive you of the comforts of life." He never allowed himself to accept any remuneration from non-beneficed clergymen, professional authors, or artists of any sort, and sometimes returned large fees when he found that the parties were in embarrassed circumstances.

which is absolutely necessary to the attainment of moral excellence and true happiness.

It is related of Mr. Pitt, that when asked in his last illness by the Bishop of Lincoln if he had any objection to receive the sacrament, he replied, "None whatever. I will take it readily, if you wish ; but, my dear Lord," he added, "the whole of my life has been devoted to Politics ; and as I have had no time to attend to religion, I must now trust to the mercies of God." As regards his attention to the all-important subject of Religion, it is to be feared that a similar answer must have been given to a like question by Hunter, whose mind had been directed with no less intensity and devotedness to his peculiar pursuits than had that of the great statesman before mentioned.

In forming an estimate of Hunter's professional character, and of the influence which his labours have had on the improvement of surgery, we are not, as with ordinary minds, simply to enumerate the various practical amendments of which he was the immediate author. His claims are of a far higher nature ; and in as much as he was the first who taught us to bring the lights of physiology to bear upon the practice of our art, and by his writings, his teaching, and his example stimulated the minds of numerous able followers to pursue the track he had pointed out, he justly merits to be considered as the author of a new æra in the history of our profession.

In the character of a naturalist it is impossible for us to form a full estimate of Hunter's labours, either from his published works, or from his incomparable Museum as it at present stands. In the course of the numberless dissections which he prosecuted during thirty years of unwearied diligence, he necessarily made a great variety of isolated observations, which, though not immediately applicable to the objects he had in view, would doubtless have constituted important contributions to the general stock of knowledge in comparative anatomy. Such observations he always recorded carefully in appropriate volumes ; but by Sir Everard Home's extraordinary destruction of his manuscripts science has been deprived of these fruits of his industry, of which scarcely the smallest portion now remains in existence. But even in cases where the records of his researches have been preserved, either in the form of preparations or by means of drawings forming part of his museum, the want of proper descriptive catalogues has often caused them to be overlooked, whilst more modern naturalists have been reaping the honour of discoveries which were due in the first place to Hunter.

Nevertheless, though we cannot estimate the full extent of his labours, enough remains to entitle him to a place in the highest rank as a natural philosopher*. His various papers in the Philosophical Transactions and elsewhere give sufficient evidence of the original and masterly manner in which he handled every subject of inquiry ; and the arrangement of some departments of his museum shows, that whilst his great contemporary Linnæus was extending and perfecting his beautiful but artificial arrangement of living objects, Hunter had made considerable advances towards

* The following extract from the obituary of Hunter, in the Gentleman's Magazine, is much more flattering to the author, and affords a curious specimen of the *stuff* which these memorials often consist of :—". . . . As a man of letters, independently of his profound scientific studies, he had traced the practice of surgery to the earliest ages. He was well acquainted with every practitioner mentioned by Pliny, with all the Greek and Roman authors who had written on the subject, as well as with every modern one who had contributed to the perfection of the art. . . . . As a man well versed in ancient history, the Egyptian chronology was familiar to him, as far as related to the antiquity of anatomy : as a scholar, distinguishably classic, he knew that Homer was an anatomist, at least had ideas of anatomy, as well as an epic poet," &c.—One would imagine that the biographer had purposely selected the weak points of Hunter's character, in order to parody them.

that natural classification of the animal world which Cuvier has so admirably effected in modern times.

By his will, of which Dr. Baillie and Mr. Home were the executors, Hunter bequeathed the estate of Kilbride to his son. Earl's Court he directed to be sold; and the proceeds, after payment of his debts, to be divided equally between his widow and two children. His Museum he ordered to be offered, in the first instance, to the British Government, (therein following the example of his elder brother,) and on such terms as might be considered reasonable ; and in case of their refusing it, he directed it to be sold either to some foreign state, or in one lot, in such manner as his executors might think proper.

On examining, however, into the state of his affairs, it was found that his property, exclusive of the Museum, would scarcely suffice to pay his debts ; and it was accordingly to the produce of the sale of this that his family had to look for their future support. The disposal of it to the British Government was on all accounts most eligible; but it was no easy task to bring this about. The attention of Parliament and the nation was wholly directed to the events of the French Revolution, and there was a great unwillingness to expend money on any objects not essential to the conduct of the war. When Mr. Pitt was applied to on the subject, his reply was, " What! buy preparations! Why I have not money enough to purchase gunpowder." And it was not until three years after that Parliament could be induced even to institute an inquiry into the value of the Museum, with a view to deciding how far it might be desirable to make it national property. In the mean time Hunter's family were in very straitened circumstances. Through the kind interposition of Lord Auckland, Mr. Pitt was prevailed on to bestow a portion of His Majesty's bounty on Mrs. Hunter during the first two years of her widowhood; but the Act of parliament forbade its being given a third year. The greater part of Hunter's household goods were therefore sold to meet the current expenses of his family and pay for the conservation of the Museum*; and it is to be regretted that amongst these were included his library†, and a valuable collection of crystallizations, both of regular and irregular forms, which he was accustomed to use in his lectures to exemplify the difference between the laws which regulate the growth of organic and the increase of inorganic bodies. Whilst, however, we must regret that these objects were irretrievably dispersed, we must entirely exempt his executors from the blame which has been sometimes attached to them for allowing this to take place. Neither of them were in circumstances to defray from their own resources the expenses necessary for the maintenance of his widow and children ; and as there seemed little prospect of soon disposing of his collection, they were obliged

* Amongst these were a variety of valuable objects of *virtù* which Hunter had collected from various quarters ; ancient coats of mail, weapons of various dates and nations ; and a very beautiful turning-lathe, which had belonged to the Duke of Cumberland. With such articles as these Mr. Christie, the fashionable auctioneer of the day, who presided at the sale, found himself quite at home ; but when he came to dispose of a curious mask, which Hunter had constructed to protect his face whilst making his observations on bees, the renowned auctioneer was completely non-plused. At length, after turning it round and round, and surveying it on all sides, he said, " This, ladies and gentlemen, is a covering for the face, used by the *South Sea islanders* when travelling, to protect them against the *snow storms.*"! It would appear from a sale catalogue (in the possession of Mr. Upcott), dated July 31, 1794, to which the prices are affixed, that the produce of this sale could not have been considerable.

† It has been already observed that Hunter found he could employ his time more profitably in studying nature than in reading books, whence it arose that his library was small, and consisted principally of presentation copies. Its dispersion would not of itself have been a subject of regret, if it were not that Mr. Hunter was in the habit of annotating largely in the margins of those books which he read. He has made references to Borelli, Hamberger, Goddard, Glisson, Swammerdam, &c., in his Croonian Lectures, which he would probably not have done if he had not carefully consulted these authors.

to have recourse to the sale of objects which, under other circumstances, they would have gladly held sacred*.

In 1796, all the personal efforts of Hunter's executors having failed to induce the House of Commons to think of purchasing the Museum, Lord Auckland kindly undertook to interest himself in the affair, and accordingly applied, in the following letter to Sir J. Banks, to know how far he would be disposed to lend his assistance in calling public attention to the subject :

*" Eden Farm, near Bromley, Kent,
Jan. 25, 1796.*

" My dear Sir,

" I wish, in the fewest words possible, to engage your attention to a subject interesting both to friendship and philosophy. I know that the pleadings of two such advocates will be most congenial to your feelings.

---

* These difficulties were entirely removed, after some years, through Dr. Garthshore's kind interference. He engaged Mrs. Hunter, whose exemplary conduct during her widowhood had gained her the esteem of all parties, to reside in the house of two young ladies of large fortune, who were wards of his, where she continued until her death in the receipt of a very handsome salary. During this time she published a volume of poems, which possess considerable merit as light compositions. In 1804 she composed the following Epitaph, with the design of having it inscribed on a marble tablet to be placed over the remains of her late husband in St. Martin's church ; a design, however, which it was intimated to her by Dr. Hamilton, the rector, was contrary to the rules of the church :

" Here rests in awful silence, cold and still,
 One whom no common sparks of genius fired ;
Whose reach of thought Nature alone could fill,
 Whose deep research the love of Truth inspired.

" Hunter! if years of toil and watchful care,
 If the vast labours of a powerful mind
To soothe the ills humanity must share,
 Deserve the grateful plaudits of mankind,—

" Then be each human weakness buried here
 Envy would raise to dim a name so bright :
Those specks which in the orb of day appear
 Take nothing from his warm and welcome light.
                                    " Anne Hunter."

" Our late friend John Hunter left *nothing* for the support of his widow and children, after the payment of his debts, but his collection of comparative preparations. From respect for his memory, and from regard for Mrs. Hunter, whose conduct in such a position has been highly becoming, I have concurred with the Chief Baron during two years in obtaining for her, through Mr. Pitt, the aid of His Majesty's bounty ; and I have been of some use to her in other respects. But the Act of Parliament does not allow the King's bounty to be given a third year. In the mean time the Trustees of the Collection (Mr. Home and Dr. Baillie) have not been able to induce the House of Commons to purchase it, or even to consider the subject. In truth, the agitations of their minds amidst the great scenes which are going forward, as well as a general impression that all avoidable expenses not essential to the purposes of the war should be postponed, have combined to make it difficult to recommend the purchase to the public. The delay is most distressing to the family, who have no other resource : the mere expense of keeping the collection is an overwhelming weight to those who have nothing.

" I do not pretend to be able to form any adequate idea of the value and importance of the collection to science ; it is quite out of my line of observation. But I have always understood that you scientific leaders concur in thinking it highly curious, and well calculated to do service in the school both of medicine and of natural philosophy in general.

" I trust that as the worthy President of the Royal Society, as an old and respected friend of a distinguished person whose family is left destitute, and, in short, as a man of science and of benevolence, you will turn this subject in your thoughts. If the purchase could be properly and effectually recommended, with the King's approbation, to the House of Commons and to the Minister at the head of the Treasury, it would be the best result.

" If you would like to have a consultation at your house of any number of Mrs. Hunter's friends, and of persons of other descriptions, I shall be glad as an individual to attend your commands in Soho-square. I propose to return to town about the middle of next week.

" I wish you would re-settle the seasons, which seem to be under a revolutionary government. I do not remember an instance of so long a prevalence of southern gales in the depth of winter.

" Believe me, my dear Sir,

" Most sincerely yours,

" AUCKLAND."

In his reply to this application Sir J. Banks, as will be

seen, expresses his readiness to take part in endeavouring to bring about the desired purchase of the Museum ; but at the same time seems to intimate that the College of Surgeons had been backward in interesting themselves on the subject, although they were the parties to whom it would prove most serviceable.

" MY DEAR LORD,

" Had I thought my friend John Hunter's collection an object of importance to the general study of natural history, or indeed to any branch of science except to that of medicine, I hope that two years would not have elapsed without my having taken an active part in recommending to the public the measure of purchasing it. I was consulted in the first instance by the gentlemen concerned, who, if I rightly understood them, agreed with me in thinking that the history of diseases was the only interesting and valuable part, and the natural history was not of consequence sufficient to be brought forward as an object of public purchase.

" Concluding that the history of diseases arranged itself naturally under the protection of the College of Surgeons, and knowing that the corporate mansion of that learned body was roomy enough to receive the collection ; being well aware that matters of abstract medicine did not come within the province of the Royal Society, knowing that the apartments of that body are scarce able to contain the property they already possess, and thinking the museum, to which, from the nature of its institution, students could not have a convenient access, an improper deposit, I declined, with the full approbation, as I thought, of the parties concerned, taking any lead in the matter.

" Regard for my deceased friend, however, has always made me desirous of doing all I could do, without interfering too much in a business evidently out of my province ; I offered, therefore, at that time all the secondary assistance in my power. I shall be happy, therefore, whenever your Lordship or the Chief Baron, who have hitherto taken the lead in this business, do me the honour to think I can be of use, to obey either of your summons, and meet you when and wherever either of you shall choose to appoint." . . . . . .

Soon after this the question was at length properly brought before the House, when a Committee was appointed to take the petition of Dr. Baillie and Mr. Home into consideration, and to inquire into the value and probable expense of keeping up the Museum. Several of the most eminent physicians and surgeons, as well as other scientific men, were examined, who strongly recommended the purchase of the collection, which they estimated at a much higher value than 15,000*l.*, the sum named for it. The Committee having satisfied themselves on this point, and made a report to the House, the above sum was voted by Parliament on the 13th June 1799. Instead, however, of being immediately transferred to the Corporation of Surgeons, it is reported that an offer of the collection was first made to the College of Physicians*, who, foreseeing the expense of maintaining so large a number of preparations, demurred to accept it, unless accompanied with such additional grants of money and lands as should be adequate to its support. The disinclination which was thus manifested by the College of Physicians to become the guardians of this noble collection, and to incur those public and private liabilities which were necessarily incident to the charge, might equally have been justified on the part of the Surgeons. The funds of the Corporation of Surgeons at this period were in an extremely low state ; nor were the fame and public reputation of this body in a much more flourishing condition. It is therefore greatly to the credit of the Council of this Body that they came to the *unanimous* vote, on Dec. 23, 1799, to accept the Museum on the terms proposed by the Government, especially when we reflect that the costs for maintaining and augmenting the Collection, up to August 1833, amounted to not less than 36,000*l.* It would manifestly, however, have been in the highest degree improvident in the Surgeons to have acceded to the offer

---

* It would appear also, from a letter addressed by Dr. Baillie and Mr. Home (Nov. 1799) to the Lords of the Treasury, that thoughts were afterwards entertained of making it a part of the British Museum.

of Government, with the conditions annexed, if they had not foreseen some method of replenishing their finances. This method consisted in obtaining a new charter from the Crown, which should entitle them a ROYAL COLLEGE, with permission to examine for diplomas; and in this hope they were not disappointed. In the course of the ensuing year a charter was obtained; and although the applicants for diplomas during the first two years did not amount to more than 300, yet this number had increased to 770 in the two years ending August 1833; and the average receipts to the College derived from this source alone, during this latter period, did not amount to less than 11,116*l.* per annum. This increase of public reputation, and consequent wealth, must no doubt mainly be attributed to the celebrity which necessarily accrued to the College from possessing a new charter, and from being appointed the public guardians of the Hunterian Collection. It would be unjust, however, not to say that these circumstances alone would have been insufficient to attain the objects in view, if they had not been strongly supported by the zeal and talents of several members of the Council, who more particularly interested themselves in the management of the affairs of the College at that period.

This valuable collection was not entrusted to the Corporation of Surgeons unfettered by conditions; and that these conditions might be duly performed, a Board of Trustees was appointed, whose duty it was to supervise the general management of the collection.

The principal of these conditions were,—

" 1. It was incumbent on the College to preserve the collection in the best possible state at their own expense.

" 2. That the collection should be open to the inspection of the Fellows of the College of Physicians and the Members of the Company of Surgeons, and persons properly introduced by them, four hours in the forenoon two days every week.

"3. That a catalogue should be made of the preparations, and a person appointed whose business it should be to explain it to such persons as visited the collection.

"4. That a course of twenty-four lectures on comparative anatomy, &c., should be delivered annually at the College."

The admirable manner in which the first and last of these conditions have been complied with will not be questioned by any one who has visited the Museum or attended the lectures. As for the second and third, as it is impossible to offer praise, so it may be more prudent to refrain from animadversion. The parties who were most to blame in this business have long since gone to another tribunal, and any comment upon this subject would be useless.

CHAPTER VII.

The Hunterian Museum.

THE museum of Hunter having been entrusted by Government to the care of the College of Surgeons, the Council, in July 1800, appointed from their body a Board of Curators, consisting of seven members, to whom was given the charge of superintending the preparation of catalogues of the objects in the collection, and of drawing up regulations for its management.

During the first six years the collection remained in the gallery in Castle-street, which had been built by Hunter for its reception; but in 1806, the lease of the premises having expired, it was resolved by the Board of Curators to deposit it temporarily in a house in Lincoln's-inn-fields, adjoining the College of Surgeons, the Council having at the same time come to a resolution to erect an appropriate building for its reception, and to apply to Parliament for assistance in accomplishing the work. Plans were accordingly drawn up, and the expenses of the undertaking were estimated at 15,000*l.* This sum was liberally granted by Parliament, and the building was commenced in the course of the following summer. The work does not, however, appear to have proceeded very rapidly; the real cost of the structure, it was found, would be treble that of the estimated expense; and a second application to the legislature was resolved on. This elicited a second grant of 12,500*l.*, and the remaining deficiency (equal in amount to the sums voted by Parliament,) was made up out of the funds of the College. At length, in the year 1813, the edifice being com-

L

pleted, and the necessary arrangements made, the museum was opened to the inspection of visitors*.

In the year 1806, in compliance with the conditions of agreement under which the Hunterian museum was entrusted to the College of Surgeons by Parliament, the Council took the necessary steps for instituting two annual courses of lectures, the one on surgery, the other on anatomy. These were delivered for the first time in the spring of the following year, and have been continued annually ever since. The number of lectures in each course amounted to fifteen ; and as the chief object aimed at in their institution was the elucidation of various parts of the museum, it has been customary to select from thence most of the preparations introduced by the Professors in illustration of their doctrines.

In 1813 Dr. Baillie and Sir Everard Home, the trustees of Mr. Hunter, provided for the delivery of an annual oration on his birthday. By this an opportunity has been yearly afforded of paying a tribute of respect to the memory of those practitioners of surgery who have contributed during their lives to the advancement of our profession†.

---

* During the time that the museum continued in Castle-street, it was open, under certain limitations, to the inspection of the public, and during the short peace was visited by many eminent scientific foreigners; amongst whom were MM. Du Fresne, Parmentier, Abbé Gregoire, Jean Baptiste Huzard, Dr. Gärtner, Dr. Stöll, Professor Aldini, and Dr. Frank. The first of these gentlemen was highly delighted, and expressed his satisfaction in a paper in the first volume of the *Annales du Muséum.* In 1813 Cuvier visited England, and for the first time saw the Hunterian museum, to which he paid the greatest attention, and had thirty or forty drawings made of different preparations by a gentleman who accompanied him.

† It may be worthy of consideration whether it would not be better that these orations should occur less frequently. It is a hopeless task to seek for something new every year on so limited a subject. Mr. Lawrence's late able oration might seem to contradict this remark ; but it will be observed that he wisely quitted the accustomed track, and sought for interesting matter in other countries and in the collateral field of natural history.

To these lectures all the Members of the College have of course a right of entry; and the senior pupils attending the London hospitals are by courtesy allowed to be present.

From the time when the museum first became the property of the College up to the present day, valuable additions have been continually made to its contents. These have accrued chiefly from two sources: on the one hand, from the purchase of appropriate objects contained in other collections, as the British Museum, the Leverian Museum, and the collection of the late Mr. Brookes; on the other, and this has proved by far the most copious source, from the liberal donations of public bodies and private individuals, amongst which those presented by some of the leading members of the Council hold a conspicuous place. Many valuable preparations have also been added by the diligence of the Conservator and of the Assistant-Conservator. The additions from these and other sources amount at present to nearly one third of the whole collection.

It is intended in the present chapter to give some account of the contents of this noble monument of the genius of Hunter; a work which stands unrivalled in its kind*, and the contemplation of which must ever call forth the highest respect for the indefatigable industry and extraordinary talents of its founder.

---

* This opinion is not only that of Englishmen, who have had an opportunity of comparing the admirable manner in which the preparations are displayed in the Hunterian museum with that of some of the most famous on the Continent, and, amongst others, of the Jardin des Plantes, but of foreigners also. Soon after the conclusion of the late war, the Emperor of Russia sent a body of scientific men to make the tour of Europe in pursuit of science. Those who came to England had previously visited the collections on the Continent. Their patience was inexhaustible; and of the many individuals who have visited the Hunterian museum, none ever examined it with so much care, or brought a larger share of previous information to the work, than they did. When they had concluded their inquiries, they unhesitatingly declared that this collection far excelled any other in Europe.

The original design of Hunter, in the formation of his museum, was to furnish an ample illustration of the phenomena of life exhibited throughout the vast chain of organized beings, by a display of the various structures in which the functions of life are carried on.   His collection, therefore, at its commencement, was strictly physiological in its character ; and though in the course of time various other departments were added to the original one, they were all in a manner subservient to this primary design.

Amongst these accessory departments we may mention, first, the collections of dried preparations in comparative anatomy, and the collection of comparative osteology, as being both nearly allied to the subject of general physiology. Next to these may be placed the collection of monsters and malformations, which is not less so.   To the subject which the latter is designed to illustrate much attention has of late years been deservedly directed, since the study of abnormal productions not only leads to a knowledge of the fact that nature is subjected to certain laws, even in her most striking deviations from the usual order of things, but also helps to throw much light on the laws of normal or natural formation.

In addition to the above, the museum contains a large collection of specimens in natural history, of which the greater number are preserved in spirits, and others are stuffed ; whilst those animals, or parts of animals, which require no such preparation, as shells, zoophytes, and insects, form a separate department.   Nor did Hunter confine his attention to the animal forms now in existence, but, not long before his death, collected a large number of valuable fossils, illustrating the structure and form of animals of a former age.   Another highly valuable portion of the museum illustrates the actions of living parts when in a state of disease.   This portion contains two large collections of pathological preparations, the one containing specimens of diseased parts preserved in spirits, the other specimens in a dry state ; and a collection of the inorganic products of diseased action, as calculi, concretions, &c. A numerous assortment of valuable drawings, oil paintings, and casts completes the whole; of these the former are the most valuable, since, from the excellent style in which most of them are executed, an accurate notion is afforded of the recent appearance of parts, when this has been destroyed in the original subjects, either by time or by the action of the spirits in which they are preserved.

In describing more in detail the various parts of the museum, each department will be successively treated of in the order in which they have been mentioned above. Before proceeding, however, to this description, it will be requisite to say a few words respecting the work on which Hunter was engaged at the time of his death, and which he designed as an exposition of the contents of his museum ; and also to make some remarks on the formation of the Catalogues which are now in the course of publication by the Council of the College of Surgeons, and from which the summary I am about to give will be principally derived.

It would seem that for many years Hunter was accustomed to trust chiefly to his own memory for a history of the specimens contained in his museum ; but when his health and faculties began to fail, under repeated attacks of disease, he became exceedingly anxious to complete the arrangement of its various parts, and to commit to writing an exposition of the whole. The reflection that he should probably die before this labour was completed, and leave his collection, the sole provision he had made for his family, in a condition which would greatly detract from its value, was a source of painful anxiety during the last years of his life.

It would appear to have been Hunter's intention, had he lived, not simply to form a catalogue of the numerous preparations contained in his museum, but to record, in one comprehensive work, the results of his labours and observations in each department, together with such general reflections as he had been able to deduce from them. In this work would have been included the anatomy of the whole animal kingdom, as far as he had investigated it, and there is sufficient evidence that few forms of animated nature had escaped his notice. He would have stated at large his views on the nature of animal life, on the particular uses of the several organs, and on their relations to one another. The laws of abnormal formations, as far as he was acquainted with them, would also have been unfolded ; and from these various data would have been deduced a classification of animals according to their natural affinities. The fossil remains of past ages had also occupied much of his attention, and his opinions respecting them would have filled an important place in his purposed work. It was his intention also to have entered into a full account of the several sections of his museum which are more directly connected with the practice of surgery, those, namely, which contain the pathological preparations ; and it must ever be regretted that we have been deprived of his exposition of these departments, in which would have been combined enlarged and scientific views of the nature of disease, with the sound practical information which his great experience and acute observation would no doubt have furnished.

Such was the work in which Hunter designed to embody the knowledge acquired during five-and-forty years spent in the diligent investigation of nature ; and let it not be thought that the above sketch figures forth an undertaking which it would have been beyond the power of any single man to complete ; an immense body of materials had already been prepared for different parts of it, and the regularity and rapidity with which he pursued his labours would almost certainly have insured its completion within a few years. Had he completed it, " this work," to use the language of one who has had ample means of knowing what were the intentions of Hunter, and of estimating the extent of his labours*, " would have reflected equal honour on its author and on the country and age in which he flourished."

Hunter died, however, before this his last undertaking could be completed, but not before enough had been accomplished to furnish us with means from which to form some judgment of what the whole would have been.

Of his labours in the field of comparative anatomy, which for variety and extent have probably never been excelled, he kept accurate and full minutes. These alone extended to ten folio volumes of MSS.†; and besides these there were catalogues of certain portions of the physiological department, with interesting general observations of his own prefixed to each series. To the account of the pathological preparations of the bones, Hunter had also devoted especial attention, as he purposed (according to the late Mr. Cline,) to publish a work on the diseases of these parts, and had collected an immense number of drawings in pursuance of this intention.

The whole of the above valuable documents passed into the hands of the College along with the preparations to which they referred; and it was the intention of the Council,

---

* Mr. Owen.

† Nine of these were on animal, and one on vegetable anatomy. They were written by Mr. Hunter's assistants, at his dictation, and contained the result of his observations upon whatever was new and interesting in the course of his individual dissections. It may be looked upon as a proof of the value which Hunter set on these, that he had them introduced into his portrait by Sir Joshua Reynolds. His cases of surgery and dissections, of which the College possesses four or five manuscript volumes, presented by Sir Everard Home, were recorded with equal accuracy.

with the aid which they afforded, to have prepared a descriptive catalogue of the whole museum. Before this work was far advanced, however, the ten volumes of minutes of dissections, along with many other valuable papers, were taken from the museum by Sir Everard Home*, without any previous permission from the Trustees, but with the alleged intention of employing them in preparing a catalogue, which he undertook to do gratuitously. Time, however, passed on, and no catalogue was forthcoming; repeated applications were made by the Council to have the MSS. restored, but were as often evaded, and at length, to the astonishment of all, it was ascertained that Sir Everard Home had actually committed them to the flames!

The announcement of such a proceeding of course drew upon him the bitter reproaches of the Trustees and of the the Council, against which he defended himself by maintaining his legal right to the papers, which he asserted formed no part of the museum, as no mention was made of them in Hunter's will; and he added further, that in burning the papers he had acted in accordance with the directions of his late brother-in-law. The first of these statements it was of course not worth while legally to contest, seeing that the objects in dispute were now no longer in existence. To give credence to the latter was somewhat difficult for those who knew how high a value Hunter had set on these papers. To such it seemed incredible that he should have ever seriously meditated the sacrifice of these memorials of the labours of his life; and it was justly urged, that if he had ever, in a moment of irritation, given expression to such a wish, Sir Everard Home should have felt that he would not only be justified in neglecting to fulfill it, but was bound to do so, for the honour of his patron and preceptor, and

* This was in 1812, when the collection was placed in the new building.

for the interests of science. Was it not also somewhat strange, it was asked, if such a direction was given, that Sir Everard Home should have neglected to execute it during the time the papers remained in his hands previously to the purchase of the collection by Parliament, and should have delayed its accomplishment until every one else supposed that these documents had, to all intents and purposes, become the property of the College? Rumour, as usual, assigned reasons for this act beyond the one alleged, and it was broadly asserted, that if the MSS. could be recovered, they would be found to have furnished the substance of many of Sir Everard Home's numerous papers in the Philosophical Transactions *.

Whatever may have been the cause of this extraordinary proceeding, the effects are irreparable. The difficulties experienced in the formation of a catalogue were so much increased by the loss of these papers, that those whose duty it was to superintend the work seem thenceforward to have despaired of ever carrying it into effect. At least such is the conclusion we must come to, when we recollect that nearly thirty years were allowed to elapse from the time the museum became the property of the College before the Council took effectual steps to supply such a catalogue. Whether this state of hopeless inactivity was excusable may well be doubted, when we see how satisfactorily the work will, in all likelihood, be completed, now that it has been resolutely undertaken. For though there can be no doubt that the establishment of the Zoological Society, and the liberal manner in which they have granted the bodies of the animals dying in their collection for the use of the College, have greatly facilitated the execution of some parts of the catalogue, it will yet scarcely be credited

---

* Sir Everard Home contributed more papers to the Royal Society than any other single Member of that distinguished Body since is foundation.

that the Council, had they been in earnest, could not have
found individuals long ago willing to undertake the task,
and able to have executed it, if not as well as it will now
be executed, yet in a manner which would have greatly increased the value of the collection to the profession at large.
As it is, they will hardly free themselves from the imputa-
tion of want of zeal in discharge of their trust, and of
having shown a culpable indifference to the honour of their
great master and to the cause of science in this country.

Happily, the Council were at length induced to take active measures for supplying the deficiency so long and
justly complained of, and two gentlemen were appointed to
assist the conservator, Mr. Clift, in preparing complete catalogues of the museum.   These were the late Mr. Home
Clift, the son of the conservator, and Mr. Richard Owen*,
who is well known as one of the first comparative anatomists
in this country.   Certain departments were allotted to each
of these gentlemen, of which they were directed to draw
out catalogues as speedily as might be consistent with correctness.   The first of these was published in 1830, since
which time five more numbers of the general catalogue,
and two numbers of a descriptive catalogue, on a more extended scale, have appeared.   It is understood that we are
indebted to the respected conservator, Mr. Clift, for the
first and second parts of the general catalogue, containing
an account of the pathological preparations in spirit and in
a dry state.   To Mr. Home Clift, his son, whose untimely
death was lamented by all who knew him, we owe the third,
fifth, and sixth parts, containing catalogues of the human
and comparative osteology, of monsters and malformations,
and of the vascular and miscellaneous preparations in a
dried state.   To Mr. Owen was allotted the task of preparing the fourth part of the general catalogue, which furnishes
an account of the preparations of natural history in spirit,

* Mr. Owen was appointed in 1827.

and the still more important and difficult duty of forming a descriptive catalogue of the first two divisions of the physiological gallery. The whole work, as far as it has yet appeared, reflects credit on the Council, under whose auspices it has been published, and by whom the above appointments were made, and on the gentlemen to whom the business of preparing the catalogues was intrusted, for the talent displayed in the performance of the several parts. It is, however, to be regretted that a fuller account of the pathological preparations was not given, since the want of a history of the cases often deprives them of more than half their value. It is understood, however, that the Council have it in contemplation to publish descriptive catalogues of the whole museum, which will probably extend to twenty volumes, and no doubt the present deficiency will then be amply supplied*. With regard to that portion of the descriptive catalogue which is already before the world, too much praise cannot be given to Mr. Owen for the very able manner in which he has performed the difficult task of preparing it. When it is recollected that a great many of the preparations in this department had not even a tittle attached to them, and afforded no clue beyond their situation in the collection, and their general appearance, for ascertaining what they really were or whence derived, and consequently that a search was to be instituted for their likeness in the great book of nature, it will be readily granted that no little talent and diligence were required in overcoming this first difficulty. But, in addition to this, the object which Hunter had chiefly in view, in the forma-

---

* The conservator has long been engaged in the preparation of such a catalogue, which at the present time extends to five times the length of that published by the Council. The urgency of the demand for a catalogue on the part of the public and the Board of Trustees, was the only reason why the Council confined themselves to the fulfilment of their *literal* engagements.

tion of several of the series, was to be sought amongst his various publications, or, where these did not furnish the requisite information, to be deduced from the writings of others, or from the observations of Mr. Owen himself; and from each of these sources have been drawn the valuable observations prefixed to several of the subdivisions. That Mr. Owen has been successful in overcoming these difficulties, the catalogue itself affords sufficient evidence, and the students of natural science will owe him a debt of gratitude should he succeed in that portion of his work which is yet unfinished as ably as he has done in the part which has already been published.

Having thus given a general account of the museum up to the formation of the catalogues, I shall now endeavour to furnish as accurate an account of its contents as the means in my power and the nature of the present work will admit.

The first, and fundamental department of the museum, that, namely, which is contained in the gallery of the present building, is, as has been said, devoted to the illustration of the science of life itself.

" It consists of dissections of plants and animals, in which the structures subservient to the different functions are skilfully and intelligibly displayed.

" These structures are taken from every class of organized matter, and are arranged in series, according to the function, in the order of their complexity, beginning with the simplest form, and exhibiting the successive gradations of organization to the most complex.

" The series are disposed in two divisions : first, those illustrative of the functions which minister to the necessities of the individual ; and secondly, those which provide for the continuance of the species.

" The first division commences with a few examples of the component structures of organic bodies, and then extends into a series embracing the active and passive apparatus for progressive motion. It is succeeded by analogous series, illustrative of the functions of digestion, nutrition, circulation, respiration, and excretion,—or the functions immediately connected with the internal œconomy of an organic being. Then follow the organs which bring the animal into relation with the external world, viz. the nervous system and organs of sense, which are the peculiar characteristics of the animal kingdom. After these come the parts which complete the system of an animal body, such as the connecting and adipose tissues, and the various modifications of external covering; and lastly, those instruments which, not being immediately related to any of the vital and animal functions, constitute peculiarities in the œconomy of particular species.

" The second division commences with a series of the generative organs of plants and animals in the passive and unimpregnated state : first, of such as complete the function of generation by the simplest kind of hermaphroditism ; second, of those in which a necessity for reciprocal impregnation co-exists with the possession of both the sexual systems in the same body ; and lastly, of the male and female organs, as they are exhibited separately in distinct individuals.

" The next subdivision contains the female organs in a state of fructification or impregnation ; it exhibits the generated organism in its different stages towards mature development, together with the various temporary structures destined for its support during fœtal existence ; and lastly, the organs in the parent which supply the young with food, or afford it shelter during the helpless period of its existence*."

* Introduction to the Descriptive and Illustrated Catalogue of the Physiological Series : 1833. By Mr. Owen.

Such is a brief summary of the contents of this part of the museum, which consists of 3745 anatomical specimens, of great delicacy and beauty, and for the most part in an admirable state of preservation.

FIRST DIVISION OF THE GALLERY,

ILLUSTRATIVE OF THE FUNCTIONS WHICH MINISTER TO THE NECESSITIES OF THE INDIVIDUAL.

That portion of the descriptive catalogue which has been published furnishes an account of 841 of these preparations, which form the two first subdivisions of the first division, and are designed to illustrate the functions of locomotion and digestion.

THE FIRST SUBDIVISION
ILLUSTRATES THE SUBJECT OF LOCOMOTION.

To the elucidation of this subject thirteen series are devoted, of which the first exhibits the component parts of vegetables and animals, as bark, wood, blood, tendon, elastic ligament, cartilage, bone, &c. &c.

To these succeed examples of different kinds of sap and blood, the former arranged according to their degree of vitality, as shown by their tendency to coagulate: from these we ascend to the colourless blood of crustaceous animals, the cold blood of reptiles and fishes, and lastly, the warm blood of the mammalia.

With the third series, we enter on those parts of vegetables and animals which possess evident motion. Motion in vegetables Hunter considered to depend on a property analogous to irritability in animals: it may be caused either by the irritability being excited, as in the mimosa and other sensitive plants; or by the cessation of irritation allowing an antagonist force to take effect, as in the sleep of plants.

The fourth series contains preparations of the muscular fibre, which, says Hunter, "is one of the simplest forms of an active solid." The various modes in which these fibres are arranged in various muscles are shown ; and to these succeed several preparations illustrative of the application of muscles, and the manner in which certain parts of the body, as we ascend in the scale of animals, come to be specially devoted to the production of motion, either actively, as in the case of muscles, or passively, as in that of the skin of worms and of the larvæ of insects ; of the hard covering of crustaceous animals ; of this combined with an internal skeleton in the testudines ; or of the latter alone in fishes, birds, and mammalia.

The application of elastic powers in the animal frame is next illustrated. These act either in opposition to muscular force, as in the hinge of bivalves, or in aid of it, as in the ligamentum nuchæ of various mammalia.

The five succeeding series illustrate the particular properties of the organs of passive motion. These organs, as is here shown, may be formed either of membrane, horn, cartilage, calcareous earth, or of various combinations of these. The growth and composition of shells are next illustrated, for though shells for the most part serve as organs of defence, "they are in many cases used as levers for the muscles to act on." Most of the preparations illustrating this subject have been added of late years, and the varieties they exhibit in chemical composition, &c., are explained in the Catalogue, by extracts from Mr. Hatchett's papers on the composition of bone and shells. The structure and growth of bone is next unfolded. The differences which bones exhibit in consistence and composition in different classes of animals, the mode in which ossification commences, and the superior vascularity of growing bone, are amply developed. Next follow twenty-four preparations,

exhibiting the growth, perfection, and casting of the horns
of deer. And lastly, the increase of size in bones is shown
to take place, not by the insertion of new particles amongst
the old, as Duhamel supposed, but by the addition of new
parts to the extremities and circumference of bones, whilst
the form of the bone is preserved by the removal of superabundant parts by the absorbents. The former fact is shown
by preparations of the leg-bones of fowls, into which
shot had been inserted at given distances from each other
whilst the bones were growing, which distances were found
not to have varied when the bones had much increased in
length. A fuller illustration of both facts is afforded by
feeding young animals on madder, which tinges all fresh
deposits of bone, and thus points out exactly where and to
what extent these have been laid down. There are several
preparations which originally *exhibited* these points very
clearly, but as the spirit has destroyed the colour, the assistance of Mr. Bell's drawings is required for their explanation, and engravings of these have been accordingly given
in the Catalogue. After the growth of bone, are displayed
the various positions of the skeleton in various animals;
and the last of the five series illustrates the composition of
the skeleton. This may be formed of one piece, as in the
cuttle-fish; of several unattached pieces, as in the pennatula
and other zoophytes; or the several pieces may be connected by elastic joints, as in the spine of cartilaginous
fishes; by ligamentous fibres attached to the whole articulating surface, as in the lower jaw of the whale; by capsular ligaments; by capsular and inter-articular ligaments,
as in the hip joint; or with interarticular cartilages, as in
the joint of the lower jaw; or by the three combined, as in
the human knee-joint.

The various mechanical contrivances by which the power
of muscles is augmented, so as to combine neatness, which,

as Hunter observes, "is often a principal object in the formation of a limb," with the requisite degree of power, form the twelfth series.

The thirteenth and last series of this subdivision shows the form and arrangement of parts in the various organs adapted for progressive motion; for swimming; for flying; for creeping, as serpents, in which animals the progressive motion is effected by means of the ribs, which have strong muscles attached, and are moved much in the same way as the centipede moves its legs; for burrowing; for climbing; for leaping; for walking or running; and lastly, for tearing the prey of the animal.

THE SECOND SUBDIVISION
ILLUSTRATES THE FUNCTION OF DIGESTION.

Teeth.—Of the organs which minister to this function the teeth are first treated of. The series in which the nature and offices of these organs are shown consists of 170 preparations, derived from all parts of the animal kingdom, the account of which in the Catalogue is preceded by some general observations by Mr. Hunter on their nature; on their analogy to the beaks of birds; and on the varieties they exhibit in number, form, structure, and situation, according to the food of the animal; as also on the mode of their formation and growth; on the manner in which the place of those which are lost is supplied; and on their relation to the stomach. These several points are illustrated in a number of subseries, of which the three first exhibit the structure and growth of parts analogous to teeth in various tribes of animals, as the calcareous teeth of some mollusca, the bills of birds, and the whalebone in whales. The fourth subseries exhibits the mode of growth of various teeth. 1st, Of such as are limited in their growth, and which, when lost, require to have their places supplied by

M

new teeth; and this is effected in a variety of ways.   2nd,
Of such, as are continuous in their growth, as the incisors
of rodentia and the tusks of boars.   The amount of animal
matter contained in various descriptions of teeth is shown
in a set of preparations, in which the calcareous part has
been removed by the use of dilute acids.   The manner in
which the teeth are shed, and their places supplied by
new ones, in different orders of animals, is next shown.
In some the teeth are shed but once, and those of the new
set are formed on distinct pulps, as in most mammalia; in
others, as in the shark, teeth are successively formed at
the back part of the mouth, and brought forward by the
absorption of the fore part of the jaw.   In the crocodile
there is a constant succession of new teeth, which are
formed on the same conical projecting pulp which the former occupied: in many kinds of fish the new ones are
formed in rows of distinct pulps, and these may be situated
either within or without the rows in use, but in either case
are brought into action by the absorption of the opposite
side of the jaw.

The last subseries displays the varieties in the situation
of the teeth, which may be placed either on the jaws, the
tongue, the palate, or in the stomach.

We next come to the principal organ of digestion.

Stomach.—This organ Hunter considers to be the essential part of every animal.   In its simplest form it is a
mere bag, secreting a liquid capable of dissolving and animalizing its contents, and possessing the power of absorbing the nutritious parts of the food, and rejecting that which
is indigestible.   In many cases such a bag constitutes the
whole animal, as in the hydatid; but in most animals other
parts are superadded to assist in the process of digestion.
These parts vary exceedingly in different tribes, and " would
serve as a ground for the classification of them."   A co-

pious illustration of the above facts is furnished by a number of preparations selected from the various orders of animals, commencing with the most simple, in which the stomach has but one orifice for the reception and rejection of foreign matter; and ascending through the radiated animals, where two orifices are found, and the digestive cavity is divided into stomach and intestines; to the insect tribe, where, in addition, a crop is sometimes found, for retaining the food previously to its undergoing digestion; or, in the case of the bee, to its being deposited in the hive. To these succeed the stomachs of mollusca, ascending from the ascidians, or soft-shelled mollusks* as Hunter aptly called them, through the acephalous tribe to the gasteropoda and cephalopoda of Cuvier.

The stomach of fishes is next displayed, which is for the most part a simple capacious bag, between which and the large and muscular œsophagus there is often scarcely any distinguishable separation. In some fishes, as in the Gillaroo trout and mullet, the stomach is a strong muscular organ, fitted in the former for breaking the shells of testaceous animals, on which it feeds; and in the latter, to grind down with sand the vegetable substances of which its nutriment consists.

In reptiles we find great diversities in the form of the stomach. In the ophidians, both this and the œsophagus are capable of great distension, for the reception of bulky animals, on which they prey. In the chelonians it is broad and flat, like the body; whilst in the crocodile it is divided

---

* Hunter had paid great attention to the anatomy of these animals, as also to that of the cirripeds, on both of which Cuvier has also published memoirs. The beautiful engravings attached to this portion of the Catalogue show how accurately and fully Hunter had unfolded the structure of the various organs, and how correctly, for the most part, he had made out their several offices.

M 2

into two cavities, a cardiac and a pyloric, much as we find
it in some of the carnivorous birds.

Birds are furnished with a proventriculus, or glandular
cavity, which receives the food before it passes into the
stomach, or gizzard; and in the crane tribe we find a pyloric cavity between the gizzard and duodenum, as in the
crocodile. The gizzard varies much in the strength of its
muscular coat: this in carnivorous birds is much weaker
than in granivorous; but if a bird of the former kind be
fed on grain, the gizzard will become gradually more developed, as is shown by the preparation of a gull's stomach
which had been so fed.

To the stomachs of birds succeed those of mammalia.
In many of these the stomach consists of a simple cavity,
which in the ornithorhynchus takes the general form of a
gizzard, the cardiac and pyloric orifices being close to each
other, as in birds.

In the porcupine, the stomach is partially divided into
three cavities; in the peccary the division becomes more
complete, the œsophagus opening into the middle one,
whilst the cavity of the fundus takes a bifurcated form.
In ruminating animals, however, a still greater degree of
complexity exists: in these we find four cavities, the first
two of which receive the food prior to rumination; but
after rumination the food is prevented by a peculiar sensibility of the sphincter, which closes their orifices, from re-
entering them, and is passed on by a sort of canal to the
psalterium, or third cavity, and from thence to the abo-
masus, or fourth cavity.

In the llama and camel the muscular fibres of the first
two cavities are disposed reticularly, and the mucous membrane forms sacculi between the meshes: into the sacculi
of the second cavity water is received, and is preserved there

for a long time in a pure state. In the whale tribe we find the stomach assuming a loculated form, and consisting of from four to seven cells, disposed in a row one after the other.

In this series are also deposited several preparations illustrative of the digestion of the coats of the stomach after death; a fact which Hunter first pointed out and explained.

Intestines.—The Third Series displays the structure of the intestines in various tribes of animals, arranged in the same order as is adopted for the stomachs.

Glands.—The Fourth Series exhibits the varieties which exist in the form and composition of the glands which aid in the process of digestion.

First, of the salivary glands: these in many mollusks are found in the form of tubes, blind at one end, and opening by the other into the buccal cavity, or œsophagus, and gradually as we rise in the scale assume the form of conglomerate glands.

Next, of the pancreas; which in like manner is first seen under the form of cæcal tubes, opening into the upper part of the intestine.

The same may be said of the liver at its first appearance as a separate organ. It soon, however, as in the mollusks, assumes the form of a conglomerate gland, and is in these of a large size. In the lower animals the bile is secreted from arterial blood.

After the liver, the gall bladder and ducts are exhibited. In many of the lower animals, and in some of the higher, there is no gall bladder. In the squalus maximus, for example, twelve ducts convey the bile from the huge liver to a receptacle six feet distant, and lying in contact with the duodenum, into which it opens. This, however, is not supposed to be analogous to the gall bladder, as a similar receptacle is found in the elephant, which possesses a gall bladder.

Next follow preparations of the spleen, and other appendages of the alimentary canal, and these complete the division devoted to the function of digestion.

Absorption.—The function of absorption is the one which is next illustrated. In vegetables this function is shown to be performed by simple tubes commencing in the roots, of an equal diameter throughout, and without branches.

The first traces of the absorbent system in the animal tribes are found in certain of the medusæ, as the rhysostome, on which vessels are found opening on the fringe, like appendages of the stem. These take up nourishment from the water, and coalescing into larger trunks, empty their contents into the digestive cavity.

In the aphrodita the absorbents consist of small capillary vessels, arising from the cæcal appendages of the intestine, where they take up the chyle, and convey it to various parts of the body, without the intervention of a heart.

The next step is to the lacteals of the higher animals, which terminate in the venous system. But the absorbents are employed not only in taking up nutriment for the supply of the body, but in conveying away the effete particles ; and these are termed excretory absorbents. Amongst the preparations illustrative of this function is one on which Mr. Hunter set a high value, as affording demonstrative evidence that the absorbents perform the above office. This is a preparation from the head of a spermaceti whale, where the lymphatics are seen filled with this animal oil, which they were in the act of taking up.

Circulation.—The organs of the circulation are next exhibited, in an ascending order. First, in those animals in which there appears to be no heart, as the leech, where we find two sinuous ventral vessels and a small dorsal vessel, each giving off lateral branches. In the amphinome, which has external branchiæ on each ring, small vessels convey the aërated blood from them to the dorsal artery: this gives off other branches, and, amongst others, one which courses along the upper side of the intestine, whilst the corresponding vein to which its branches pass runs along the under side, and with the other veins enters the ventral vessel, from whence lateral branches are sent off to the branchiæ.

The situation of the heart in different animals is next shown. This, as Hunter observed, depends on the situation of the organs of respiration, which it always follows.

In insects the heart is a long tube, placed in the back, and extending from head to tail.

In the lobster and other crustaceæ it consists of a single cavity, also seated in the back, and of about the same extent as the roots of the branchiæ. In bivalve mollusks it is seated in the centre of the back. In the gasteropods, in various parts of the body, following the branchiæ. In fishes, just at the lower angle of the gills, &c.

Its composition becomes more complicated as we ascend in the scale of organisation, beginning with the dorsal vessel of insects, which receives the blood through valvular openings in the sides of the vessel, from the irregular venous sinuses which permeate the adipose tissue, and distributes it to the body through lateral branches, as shown in the injected preparation of a large caterpillar. In the ascidians, or soft-shelled mollusks, there is a single long ventricle, which receives the blood at one extremity and distributes it from the other end to the branchial sac and body. In bivalves we find a single ventricle, sending the blood to the branchiæ, from which it passes to the body, and is received back into two auricles, which supply the ventricle. In the snail we have one ventricle and one auricle. In the cuttle-fish we find both a systemic and a branchial ventricle, and the latter indeed is divided into two portions, one seated at the base of each of the branchiæ. Two auricles receive the blood from the branchiæ, and empty themselves into the systemic ventricle.

In fishes we find a branchial ventricle and a single auricle. In some of the cartilaginous fishes the heart is largely supplied with valves; in the lophius europæus, for instance, the veins opening into the auricle are seen to be guarded by valves: the auriculo-ventricular opening has semilunar valves, and the opening from the ventricle into the bulb at the root of the main artery is surrounded with valves. In the sturgeon there are no less than three rows of valves in the bulb.

In reptiles we find two auricles, one receiving blood from the lungs, the other from the body, and a single ventricle supplying both. The ventricle, which in frogs and other batrachians is a simple cavity with one aorta, in the ophidians, chelonians, and saurians becomes more and more divided into different cells by imperfect septa, the general effect of which is to prevent the aërated blood from mixing equally with the whole mass of circulating fluid, and to direct it rather towards certain parts, as the head and upper extremities.

In birds we attain the most perfect form of heart, consisting of two ventricles and two auricles, as exhibited in the hearts of the ostrich, emu, &c.

The same form of heart prevails in mammalia; and under this head we find preparations of the huge heart of the elephant with its three venæ cavæ, and of the far more enormous heart of the whale.

To the foregoing preparations succeed others, in which the structure of the blood-vessels is exhibited; the nature and form of their valves; the several coats of which they consist; and the varieties in these displayed in different animals. The outer of these coats may be deficient when the vessel passes through cartilage, as is shown in the cervical vertebræ of the squalus maximus.

Respiration.—The organs in which the aëration of the blood is effected are exhibited in the succeeding series. This process may be effected,

First,—By its exposure to the air contained in water.

The simplest form of the organ is where a certain portion of the general mass is especially devoted to this object, as the thin edge of the disk in some kinds of medusæ. In some of the annulose animals, as the amphinome, the organ consists of a bunch of rays seated on either side of each ring. In others, as the amphitrite, the branchiæ are collected on the rings of the neck. In the lobster and other crustaceæ, the branchiæ are attached to the legs, and are covered by a lateral extension of the dorsal shell. In bivalves they form foliated appendages on either side of the body, between it and the mantle. In the gasteropod and other mollusks the branchiæ assume very various and often elegant forms, and are variously placed on the body.

In the myxena, lamprey, and other cartilaginous fishes, the gills consist of a row of sacculi, varying in number, and placed on either side of the neck, each sac having an external orifice and an opening into the œsophagus, and its internal membrane being variously laminated, to afford larger surface for the aëration of the blood. In the bony fishes the gills are supported on bony arches, and covered by an operculum; these arches differ in form, and in some instances assume a very elegant appearance, as shown in preparations of the branchiostegal bones from the devil fish of the Antilles and others.

Secondly,—For the exposure of the blood to the air in water, and to the atmosphere.

The fœtus of the squalus alopeceus is shown to be furnished with external branchiæ when first born, as well as with gills; the former drop off after a time. In the siren and proteus there are external branchiæ and lungs, and both are persistent.

Thirdly,—For the exposure of the blood to the atmosphere.

Amongst the reptile tribes, we find that snakes are furnished with a single lung, consisting of a long bag, the upper part of which has vesicular parietes, whilst the lower serves as a reservoir of air, to be employed during the time in which the animal is swallowing its prey and its trachea is obstructed. In frogs the lungs appear like a conglomeration of transparent sacculi. In the turtle these sacculi are much smaller, and more numerous, so as to give the lungs more the appearance of those of the mammalia, which are last shown. The series is completed by twenty preparations of the tracheæ and organs of voice in birds and mammalia.

Kidneys.—The organs for the depuration of the blood, or the kidneys, are next exhibited, and some of their most remarkable differences in situation, number, form, and structure in the vertebrated animals are shown.

Brain.—To this succeeds a series, containing about ninety preparations, in which the development of the brain and spinal marrow, from the knotted cord of insects and crustacea, with a small ganglion above the œsophagus; representing the brain upwards through fishes, reptiles, and birds, to the perfect brain and spinal cord of the mammalia. This series is perhaps one of the least complete, and this has arisen from the small degree of importance which these organs obtained in Hunter's physiology compared with that attached to them in the present day.

ORGANS OF THE SENSES.

To the series illustrative of the central portions of the nervous system succeeds one consisting of not less than four hundred preparations of the several organs of the senses.

Of Feeling and Touch,—Exhibiting the cutis increasing in vascularity in proportion as its sensibility increases ; the varieties in compactness, density, &c., which the cutis exhibits in different animals ; the slowness with which it decays under certain circumstances, as illustrated by a preparation of the right hand of a body, said to be that of John of Gaunt, in which the cutis is perfect ; lastly, its retention of marks made in it, as in the tattooed skins of South-Sea Islanders or British sailors.

Of Taste,—Exhibiting the tongues of animals, arranged according to their secondary uses ; to which succeed fifteen preparations of some of the principal varieties of the mouths and fauces of different animals.

Of Smell.—In fishes the organ of smell assumes the form of laminæ, arranged in various order around the nasal cavity. In reptiles the cavity is divided by folds of the olfactory membrane, as in the higher animals ; but these do not contain bony plates between their layers : the organ is exhibited in the turtle and other animals of this class. In birds the extension of the nasal cavity becomes greater, especially in birds of prey, and canals leading from it communicate with the air-cells of the head, as shown in the

swan and eagle.   In mammalia it becomes still more complicated.

Of Hearing.—In this collection are contained several
good preparations of the ear in fishes, to which Hunter had
paid much attention, showing the semicircular canals, the
sac in which they terminate, and its ossicles, varying in
number from one to three.   In most fishes the ear has no
external communication; but in the ray, the squalus, and
other cartilaginous fishes a canal leads from the sac to the
surface of the head, where its orifice is closed by a membrane.   In reptiles, birds, and mammalia the organ becomes
gradually more complicated by the development of the con-
cha and addition of the tympanum and external ear.

Of Sight.—The structure of the eye and its appendages
is developed in a hundred and fifty preparations.   The peculiarity in the eye of the cuttle, which Cuvier has since
pointed out, namely, that the choroid coat is placed in front
of the retina, had attracted Hunter's notice, and is shown in
several preparations.   The structure of the eye in fishes,
fitting them for seeing in a medium of high refractive power,
is shown; as also the peculiar fulcrum on which the eye re-
volves in cartilaginous fishes.   The plicated arrangement
of the retina in birds, enabling them to see at vast distances;
the tapetum lucidum, the membrana nictitans, and the various forms of the pupil in several mammalia, adapted to
their habits of life; and lastly, the structure of the eye in
man, are all exhibited in this series.

Cellular Tissue.—To the organs of the senses succeeds
a series in which the various forms which the cellular tissue assumes are well shown, as also the varieties of oil and
fatty matter contained within its cells in different animals.

External Coverings.—The external covering alone remains to complete the list of parts fitted for providing for

the necessities of the individual, and the various forms which this assumes constitute the subject of the next series. We commence as usual with the vegetable tribes, of which the texture and appearance of the cuticle is first shown, and next of the animal tribes. The colour of the skin in the latter is seen to depend on the rete mucosum, and this in the dark varieties of mankind assumes more of a membranous character than in the lighter varieties. The arrangement of the external covering, in the form of hair, bristles, feathers, &c., is exhibited, and the mode in which the latter are formed is developed in several excellent preparations. Several other specimens exhibit the cuticular lining of the œsophagus and stomach in various animals. In others the external cuticle is shown to become thicker where parts are exposed much to the action of external bodies, or to assume the form of scales, nails, hoofs, and spines, or of beaks, horns, or spurs, according as defensive or offensive weapons may be required.

Individual Peculiarities.—This division of the Museum is completed by a series of about one hundred and eighty preparations of some of the most distinguishing peculiarities of individual species or of classes of animals in the vegetable and animal kingdoms. Amongst the former may be noticed the elegant natural ewer of the pitcher plant, and the apparatus at the joints of the leaflets, subpetioles, and petioles of the sensitive mimosa, causing these parts to collapse on the slightest touch. As examples of the peculiarities amongst animals are exhibited the casting off and regeneration of the external covering and cuticular lining of the stomach in crustaceous animals ; and of the cuticular covering in serpents. The regeneration of entire members in crustacea, newts, &c. The green bones of the gar pike, or belone vulgaris of Cuvier. The dark periosteum of the African fowl. Peculiarities in the intestines, arterial system

and urinary bladder in various animals.   Local deposits of
fat for specific purposes.   The tentacula of the cuttle tribe,
with the suckers which enable them to secure their prey.
The termination of the elephant's proboscis.   The substi-
tution of whalebone for teeth in the whale.   The orna-
mental appendages of the male in some species of birds.
The peculiar glands of animals, whether for internal uses or
opening externally, as the oil-bags of birds, the odoriferous
glands of the peccary, &c.   The air-bladder of fishes.   Feet
in mammalia adapted for swimming.   Fins in fishes for
flying.   Coralline formations.   The stings of insects, and
poison-teeth of serpents.   The electric organs of the torpedo and electric eel, &c.

THE SECOND DIVISION OF THE GALLERY,

ILLUSTRATIVE OF THE FUNCTION OF RE-PRODUCTION,

Contains about fifteen hundred preparations, admirable
alike for their delicacy and beauty as works of art, and for
the accurate and extensive information they afford on this
interesting department of physiology.

They are arranged, according to the Synopsis of the
Museum, in ten series.

The first series, which contains preparations of the
sexual organs in hermaphrodite plants and animals, commences with an elegant selection of subjects, exhibiting
some of the most striking varieties in the form and arrangement of these parts in hermaphrodite flowers.   To these
succeed preparations of the organs in self-impregnating
animals, as the asteriæ, the cirripeds ; and lastly, of hermaphrodite animals, which perform a double coitus, as the
snail, slug, and other gasteropod mollusks.

The second series of this division exhibits the form and
structure of the male organs, commencing with the sta-

mina of plants ; then ascending to the animal kingdom, and
exhibiting, first, the testes and penis in insects, as the bee,
the scorpion, &c. ; then in fishes, amongst which we find
two distinct forms : in osseous fishes the testis, or milt, is
a cellular sac, varying greatly in size at different seasons,
which opens by a common orifice with the kidney, immediately behind the anus. In the ray and squalus it is a
granular mass, having more of the form of the testis in the
higher animals, and opens into the cloaca. Several preparations exhibit the testicle in the toad, increasing in size
in the season of coupling, and attended with an increase in
the size of the tubercle of the thumb, which is employed in
retaining the female. The testis and penis of snakes and
lizards are next shown, the latter of which organs is seen
to be double. In the crocodile and turtle it is single, and
assumes the general form which it exhibits in mammalia ;
but the urethra, instead of forming a canal, consists of a.
groove only, in the dorsum penis. In birds the size of the
testis varies very much at different seasons ; this fact is
shown in the sparrow. The urethra is a groove, as it is
in reptiles, but the form of the penis varies much. In the
ostrich it is straight and large ; in the goose, duck, &c., it
assumes a spiral form when thrust out from the sheath.
The structure of these organs in mammalia is shown in several injected preparations, and in others where the semi-
nal tubes have been unravelled to show their great length ; .
and the series is completed by several specimens, which
exhibit the form and structure of the accessory glands, as
the vesiculæ seminales, prostate, and Cowper's glands, in
different animals.

The third series consists of preparations of the female
organs in plants and animals. A few specimens of the
pistils of plants head the series ; and these are followed by
the ovaries and ducts in molluscous animals ; in insects ;

in fishes, whether bony or cartilaginous; in reptiles; in birds, where only one ovary is developed; and in the ornithorhynchus. Next follow the ovaries and uterus in mammals, amongst which the latter organ is simple, or divided into two cavities, or furnished with horns. In the marsupial animals the horns are seen opening into a central or third cavity, which does not communicate directly with the vagina, but intermediately, by means of two lateral curved canals. The last eighteen preparations of this series exhibit the form of the clitoris in mammalia, and the occasional appearance of a hymen in them.

The coitus in some of the lower animals is exhibited in the ten succeeding preparations.

The development of the ovum forms the subject of the three following series. First, in plants which have no evident seeds; next, in gemmiparous animals, as the hydatid; next, in cryptogamous and phanerogamous plants; and lastly, in hermaphrodite animals, whether self-impregnating, as the asteria, the barnacle; or mutually impregnating, as snails, slugs, and other gasteropods.

The sixth series of this division contains about four hundred and fifty preparations, illustrating the various conditions in which the eggs of oviparous animals are placed for the purpose of being hatched, and of the changes which take place in the young animal during the fœtal state. The ova of some animals, as certain of the univalve mollusks, are deposited previously inclosed in a membranous nest. In others the eggs are retained in clusters, as is the case with the sepia, the ova of which resemble a bunch of grapes; or with the roes of osseous fishes. In the insect tribes the young undergo certain metamorphoses before they attain the perfect state: these changes are exemplified in about ninety preparations of the larva and chrysalis state of different insects, and in about the same number, forming a regular series of the changes in the silk-moth. The caterpillar state of several other insects is shown, and these are followed by preparations of the nidus which many insects prepare to receive the egg and contain it during its transformation. The ova of some animals are carried in the arms of the mother until hatched ; in the crustacea they are fixed to the scales beneath the tail. In osseous fishes they are clustered in masses ; in the ray the eggs are deposited singly, each, as it passes through a glandular enlargement of the oviduct, having a horny shell secreted on its surface ; this is shown in several very elegant preparations : in the shark the ova are hatched before they leave the oviducts. In Batrachian reptiles the young are furnished with gills, which are cast off when they leave the tadpole state. Of snakes and lizards, some are seen to have the eggs hatched in the body, and others externally. The turtle and crocodile deposit their eggs on the ground, where they are hatched by the warmth of the sun. In birds they are hatched under the mother. The formation of the egg in birds is next shown ; and the series is completed by about forty preparations, exhibiting the progress of incubation in the egg. These, which were originally beautiful preparations, have, from their delicacy, been somewhat injured by time ; but happily the deficiency is more than compensated by a series of exquisite drawings, made under Mr. Hunter's eye by Mr. Bell. These will be published along with the descriptive catalogue of this part of the museum ; and if the engravings should be executed, as there is every reason to hope they will be, in a manner worthy of the originals, they cannot fail to excite a very high opinion of Mr. Bell's talents as an artist, as well as serve to show with what masterly skill Hunter prosecuted his researches in this branch of physiology.

N

The Seventh Series illustrates the development of the ovum and its contents in Mammalia.   The changes which the ovary undergoes subsequently to impregnation are first shown, in various animals.   Then the changes going on in the uterus ; first, in such uteri as have horns, where the several ova are seen to occupy separate compartments ; next, in uteri without horns, under which head are arranged a number of preparations of the uterus in woman, at different stages of pregnancy ; and these are followed by others, showing the changes which the uterus undergoes subsequently to parturition.   The series is completed by a number of preparations designed to elucidate the structure of the placenta, and its connexion with the uterus, a point which has given rise to so much discussion of late.

The Eighth Series shows the principal peculiarities of structure in the young animal during the fœtal state, such as the yolk-bag, and its connexion with the fœtus ; the fœtal circulation in birds ; the horny knob on the beak used in breaking the shell ; the reception of the yolk into the stomach ; the umbilical cord in Mammalia ; the open foramen ovale ; the ventricles of the heart of equal thickness ; the situation and descent of the testes ; the membrana pupillaris, and the large thymus gland.

The Ninth Series illustrates the growth of the young, whether in plants or animals.

The Tenth and last series shows some of the various modes in which food and protection are furnished for the young animal ; as, for instance, the glandular structure in the crop of pigeons, which secretes a kind of milk ; the lactiferous glands of Mammalia ; the young lodged in temporary cells on the back of the mother, as in the pipa frog; or carried in a pouch, as in the marsupial animals ; or preserved in nests, as in birds, insects, &c.

Having entered into so full an account of the Physiological Gallery, the remaining departments of the Museum must be treated of but briefly.

DRY PREPARATIONS.

That which comes next to be noticed is the collection of objects in Comparative Anatomy preserved in a dry state. This department contains 745 specimens, of which 617 belonged to the original Museum as left by Hunter. These are arranged in eleven series, which successively exhibit preparations of the heart and blood-vessels ; of the absorbents ; of the respiratory organs ; of the digestive organs ; of the male urino-genital organs ; of the same organs, with the lactiferous apparatus, in the female ; of the nervous system ; of the organs of vision ; and of the cutis. The tenth series contain smodels, casts, &c. ; and the eleventh, several mummies. Various interesting and curious preparations are comprised under these several heads : the first affords a pretty full illustration of the various modes in which the aorta and its first branches arise in different animals ; the sixth consists of the admirable preparations of the nerves which accompanied Mr. Swan's prize essay on this subject ; in the tenth series are three wax models by the celebrated Clementi Susini ; and amongst the mummies the most remarkable is that of Martin Van Buchell's wife, which was prepared by Cruikshank according to Dr. Hunter's directions, and given many years afterwards to the College by her son.

The Catalogue of this department forms the fourth part of the General Catalogue in the course of publication.

OSTEOLOGY.

The department of Human and Comparative Osteology is that which I shall next briefly notice. To the specimens here contained, very large and valuable additions have been made since Mr. Hunter's death. The original collection consisted of 963 preparations, to which 973 have since been added. The sources whence these have been derived are very various; the most abundant has been that of donations, but many of the rarest and most valuable skeletons were purchased by the College at the sale of Mr. Brookes's Museum. Only a fifth part of the valuable specimens contained in this department has yet been displayed, from a want of room in the present building; and upwards of 400 boxes, containing either the whole or a portion of the skeleton of various animals prepared by Mr. Hunter, remain shut up from public view. Of these, a manuscript catalogue is in the course of publication. The arrangement adopted for this department is that of Cuvier in his *Règne Animal*. At the head of the collection stands the skeleton of Charles Byrne, who measured eight feet four inches in height at his death; and as a contrast to his gigantic remains, we find here the skeleton of Mdlle. Crachami, an Italian dwarf, who, at the age of nine, when she died, measured only twenty inches in height. The order Bimana is further illustrated by a large collection of skulls, exhibiting the characters of the five great varieties of the human race, the Caucasian, Mongolian, American, Æthiopian, and Malay. The preparations from which the engravings in Hunter's work on the teeth were made are also deposited in this collection. Under the order Quadrumana we find the skeleton of the adult pongo, the chimpanze, and ourang-outang, and a few specimens from the family of lemurs.

The large order Carnivora also contains many valuable skeletons, principally from animals of the true carnivorous tribes, as the Plantigrada, Digitigrada, and Amphibia. The Cheiropterous and Insectivorous genera are but scantily illustrated.

The order Rodentia contains about a dozen skeletons, with several skulls of some of the rarer species.

In the order Edentatá we find a few valuable skeletons, amongst others one of the Rufous Ornithorhynchus. There are also several specimens of the Marsupiata.

The order Pachydermata exhibits various specimens of the tusks, teeth, and skulls of elephants, as also the skeleton of Chuni, the large male elephant, whose violence necessitated his destruction some years since at Exeter 'Change; a skeleton of the hippopotamus, of the single-horned rhinoceros, and of the two-horned rhinoceros; as also the tapir, and of several of the smaller Pachydermata.

The order Ruminantia is rich in skulls and horns of the antelope tribes, and of other genera, but contains few skeletons.

There is no adult skeleton of any of the larger species of the Cetaceous tribes except one of a young whalebone-whale, and about half a dozen skeletons of the smaller animals of this race.

The class Aves, though illustrated by several valuable skeletons and a large collection of skulls, affords ample room for the donations of liberally disposed individuals.

The same remark holds good of the class Reptilia.

The class Pisces is very meagrely supplied with skeletons, which no doubt chiefly arises from the difficulty experienced in preparing and preserving in place the bones of these animals.

The Catalogue of this department forms the third part of the General Catalogue.

MONSTERS.

The department which next claims our attention is that containing preparations of monsters and malformations. These are disposed in two divisions, according as the preparations are preserved in spirit or in a dry state, and each division comprises four series, as arranged by Hunter.

The first series contains examples of the preternatural situation of parts. The second, of the addition of parts. The third, of the deficiency of parts. The fourth, of herm-aphroditism. Several curious and valuable preparations are contained in this collection; many have been added since Hunter's death. Amongst the latter are to be numbered two in the first series, which exhibit curious instances of one fœtus becoming inclosed in the belly of another. The first is that which occurred to Mr. Highmore, of Sherborne; in which the fœtus was encysted in the belly of a young man of seventeen. In the second, which occurred to Mr. G. Young, the containing child was six months old when it died. The histories of both have been published.

Under the second head we find various examples of double parts in animals; amongst others, of a double uterus and vagina in a woman, and one of the uteri containing a fœtus of seven months.

The case of deficiency of parts is exemplified by preparations of the heads of pigs and lambs, in the former of which animals malformations appear to be very common. In several of these the whole of the face which lies anterior to the ears is wanting; in others there is but one eye, in the centre of the forehead, with a proboscis from the forehead. Pigs so constructed go under the name of elephant pigs.

The fourth series contains preparations from the herm-aphrodite cow, or free-martin, on the generative organs of which Hunter wrote a paper in the Philosophical Transactions; as also of the organs of generation in hermaphrodite sheep and dogs. The organs of the hen pheasant, which has taken on the plumage of the cock, are also here exhibited.

Amongst the series of dry preparations the most curious is that of a double skull, which belonged to a child of six years of age. The skulls are united by their vertices ; the upper one was supplied by blood-vessels passing through the united portions ; and from the account given by eyewitnesses, the upper head seems during life to have experienced sensations, and to have exhibited mental operations, distinct from those of the lower head.

These preparations are described in the fifth part of the General Catalogue.

NATURAL HISTORY.

1. *In spirit.*—The next department of the Museum contains 2098 specimens of natural history preserved in spirit, of which 1743 belonged to the Hunterian collection. As yet only a catalogue of the invertebrate animals has been published, which amount to 614 in number. "This division," says Mr. Owen, who prepared the catalogue, "originated in the preservation of natural objects transmitted to Mr. Hunter for dissection, which accumulating as the reputation of the illustrious founder increased and extended, and as the requisite leisure for their examination became abridged, at length enabled him to exhibit in a series the most remarkable differences in the outward forms of the animal kingdom. They were arranged by him in the ascending order ; this order has therefore been adhered to, and best accords with the position of the several classes of animals whose structures are shown in the Physiological Gallery. With a few exceptions, the classes and orders of Cuvier and Lamarck have been adopted. The invertebrate animals are arranged in two series, one ascending through the inarticulate, the other through the articulate classes."

The Tunicata are arranged according to Mr. MacLeay's method. The Entozoa, after Rudolphi. The Cirripeds, after Dr. Leach. His genera have also been adopted for the Crustacea; but the families and the orders are arranged according to Latreille's method in Cuvier's. *Règne Animal.* After the latter also the Insecta are arranged.

2. *Stuffed.*—In addition to the specimens of natural history preserved in the foregoing department, the Museum contains a small collection of stuffed animals *, and about 1000 dry specimens of insects, shells, zoophytes, &c., of which no catalogue has yet been published.

3. *Fossils.*—The collection of fossils contains 1415 specimens, of which two hundred have been added since the death of Hunter. There exists a manuscript catalogue of this department, with introductory remarks by Hunter, but this has not yet been published.

PATHOLOGY.

Having thus taken a rapid sketch of the natural history departments of the Museum, a brief notice must now be given of the department of pathological anatomy. The preparations here contained are arranged under three heads. The first contains specimens of diseased parts preserved in spirit. The second, pathological preparations in a dry state. The third, the inorganic products of disease, as calculi, concretions, &c.

1. *In spirit.*—Under the first head are arranged 1392 specimens, of which 1084 constituted the collection as left by Hunter. They are disposed in three divisions, of which the first illustrates the actions of restoration and of disease in the various structures of the body. Examples of union by the first intention are first exhibited; to these succeed specimens of adhesive inflammation; of suppuration, under

---

* An application is at present before the Privy Council for leave to dispose of the larger stuffed animals, which take up disproportionately the room of the Museum, while they only indirectly subserve the primary object of its formation.

various circumstances ; of ulceration, in its different forms ; of granulation, as seen on different tissues ; of cicatrization ; of the union of fractured bones. These are followed by a series illustrative of the effects of inflammation in bone, of diseases in joints, and of dislocation of bones. Diseases arising from pressure are next exemplified ; then the collection of fluids in cavities ; diseases of the circulating system ; tumours not encysted ; and finally, encysted tumours.

In the second division the effects of specific or peculiar diseases are shown, as of scrofula, cancer, fungated ulcer, smallpox, gout, syphilis, gonorrhœa, hydrophobia.

The third division contains specimens of disease, arranged according to their locality, beginning with diseases of the œsophagus, and proceeding to those of the stomach, intestines, and anus ; of the liver and gall-bladder ; of the spleen, kidney, and urinary bladder ; of the uterus and its appendages, in the impregnated and unimpregnated state ; of the brain and its membranes ; of the spinal cord and nerves ; of the eye ; of the gums and teeth ; and lastly, of the air-passages and lungs.

2. *Dry.*—Under the second head we find a large collection of dry preparations, illustrative of the actions of disease and restoration in bones, on which subject Hunter was preparing a work for publication at the time of his death. He bestowed great pains on the arrangement of these specimens, and left behind him very complete explanatory documents relating to them ; but these, it is supposed, were committed to the flames by Sir Everard Home, along with the manuscripts which have been mentioned before. Besides the above specimens, we find under this head specimens of diseases occurring in teeth ; of diseases in the blood-vessels, lungs, intestines, and urinary organs ; besides a variety of casts, and other miscellaneous objects.

3. *Calculi.*—The collection of calculi and concretions con-

tains 1781 specimens, of which more than two thirds have
been added since the death of Hunter.   A manuscript catalogue of the whole has been completed, but the chemical
composition of several of the specimens remains yet to be
ascertained.

I have endeavoured in the above outline to furnish a
general conception of the character and contents of the
Museum of Hunter.   That it conveys but a faint idea of
the real merits of this noble monument of his genius I am
well aware.   The brevity with which I have been compelled
to speak of the several parts has necessarily prevented my
entering into those details which would have given interest
to the account, and under any circumstances a written description could furnish but an inadequate notion of the
merits of this work.   He that would fully appreciate these
must not only see the collection, but must examine each part
with minute attention ; for in this way alone can a correct
idea be acquired of the skill displayed in the execution of
the several parts, and of the comprehensive genius and indefatigable industry, the combination of which alone could
have enabled him to plan and to execute so great an undertaking.

Without doubt it is by this work, above all others, that
Hunter has immortalized his name.   In his writings we
occasionally find an obscurity in the expression of his
thoughts, a want of logical accuracy in his reasonings, and
an incorrectness in his language, resulting from a deficient
education.   In this work no such failings are apparent ;
Nature is here made to be her own expositor, and the treasures she has poured forth come fresh to the mind from the
fountains of knowledge, unimpaired by passing through the
imperfect medium of language, and unimpeachably proclaiming the genius of him by whose labours they were brought to
light.   That Hunter should have still left this work incom-

plete, after so many years devoted to its construction, will not surprise those who reflect that the stores of Nature are in truth inexhaustible. He has raised a noble edifice, the magnitude and beauty of which all must admire who consider that it was the work of one mind; but there is still ample room for the labours of others in adding to or completing its various parts; and those to whose care this invaluable collection has been committed could not have better forwarded the interests of science than by devoting, as they have done, some of the ample funds at their disposal to judiciously increasing its treasures, and to making those treasures more extensively useful by publications, such as those by which they are now illustrating them.

It has long been a subject of just regret that the building in which the Museum is at present contained does not afford room for the display of more than one half of the whole collection. The Council have therefore determined on increasing the accommodation, by the incorporation of the two adjoining houses, so as to form one uniform building, in which particular attention has been paid to ensure the complete illumination of every part, a point in regard to which the present premises are remarkably defective*.

This building is now rapidly advancing, and will probably be completed in about a twelvemonth, by which time also the remaining parts of the General Catalogue will be far advanced. In addition to this the College has provided, at an expense of upwards of 10,000l., a magnificent library,

* It is perhaps to be regretted that the Council of the College should have come to the resolution of building upon their present site, where they are confessedly so much cramped for room. The accumulated and yearly funds of the College, amounting in 1832 to upwards of 66,000l. in hand and 11,000l. per annum, might justly have warranted a more enlarged plan, commensurate with the trust reposed in their hands, and with the expectation of further increase, which they have a right to entertain. The building, however, which is now in progress will form a noble object in the metropolis, and be a great improvement upon the former one.

to which valuable additions are now being made; so that when these and the before-mentioned arrangements are completed, the surgical profession in England will have reason to boast of possessing one of the noblest scientific establishments which the world can exhibit.

APPENDIX.

Chronological List of Mr. Hunter's Writings.

1762.	1. On the Descent of the Testis.	Medical Commentaries, by Dr. Wm. Hunter, Part I. p. 75; and Animal Œconomy.
——	2. On Absorption by Veins.	Med. Comm. p. 42.
1766.	3. An account of an amphibious Bipes, by J. Ellis, with supplement by J. Hunter.	Phil. Trans.
1771.	4. Treatise on the Natural History of the Human Teeth, Part I.	
1772.	5. On the Digestion of the Stomach after death.	Phil. Trans., and Animal Œconomy.
1773.	6. Anatomical Observations on the Torpedo.	Phil. Trans.
1774.	7. An account of certain receptacles for air in Birds, which communicate with the lungs and Eustachian tubes, &c.	Phil. Trans., and Animal Œconomy.
——	8. Observations on the Gillaroo Trout, commonly called in Ireland the Gizzard Trout.	Phil. Trans., and Animal Œconomy.
1775.	9. An account of the Gymnotus electricus.	Phil. Trans.
——	10. Experiments on Animals and Vegetables, with respect to the power of producing heat.	Phil. Trans., and Animal Œconomy.
1776.	11. Proposals for the recovery of people apparently drowned.	Phil. Trans., and Animal Œconomy.
1776 to 1792.	12. Croonian Lectures on Muscular Motion (never printed).	
1777.	13. On the Heat of Animals, &c.	Phil. Trans., and Animal Œconomy.
1778.	14. Treatise on the Natural History of the Human Teeth, Part II.	

1779. 15. An account of the Free Martin. Phil. Trans., and Animal Œconomy.

1780. 16. Account of a Woman who had the smallpox during pregnancy, and who seemed to have communicated the same disease to the fœtus. Phil. Trans.

—— 17. An account of an extraordinary Pheasant. Phil. Trans., and Animal Œconomy.

1782. 18. Account of the Organ of Hearing in Fishes. Phil. Trans., and Animal Œconomy.

1784. 19. Observations on the inflammation of the internal coats of Veins. Transactions of a Society for the Improvement of Medical and Chirurgical Knowledge, vol. i.

1785. 20. Description of a new Marine Animal, in a letter from Mr. Everard Home to J. Hunter, F.R.S., with a postscript by Mr. Hunter, containing anatomical remarks upon the same. Phil. Trans.

1786. 21. Treatise on the Venereal Disease.

—— 22. Observations on certain parts of the Animal Œconomy, being a republication of certain papers above mentioned, in the Phil. Trans., to which were added the nine following:

23. A description of the situation of the Testis in the Fœtus, with its descent into the scrotum.

24. Observations on the glands situated between the rectum and the bladder, called vesiculæ seminales.

25. On the Structure of the Placenta.

26. Some observations on Digestion (almost an entirely new paper).

27. On a secretion in the crop of breeding Pigeons for the nourishment of their young.

28. On the colour of the Pigmentum nigrum in different animals.

29. The use of the oblique Muscles.

30. A description of the Nerves which supply the Organ of Smelling.

31. A description of some branches of the fifth pair of Nerves.

1787. 32. Observations tending to show that

1794.	50. Observations on the Fossil Bones presented to the Royal Society by the Margrave of Anspach, by the late Mr. J. Hunter.	Phil. Trans.
1794.	51. Treatise on the Blood, Inflammation, and Gun-shot Wounds.	
——	52. The case of a young Woman who poisoned herself in the first month of pregnancy, by Thomas Ogle; to which is added an account of the appearances after death, by the late J. Hunter.	Transactions of a Society, &c., vol. ii.
——	53. Mr. Hunter's opinion concerning the Anatomy of the Camel's Stomach.	Natural History of Aleppo, by Alexander Russell, Esq., 2nd Edit. vol. ii. p. 419.
——	54. Notes on the Anatomy of the Jerboa, by Mr. Hunter.	Ibid., vol. ii. p. 419.
1798.	55. Experiments and observations on the growth of Bones, from the papers of the late Mr. Hunter, by Everard Home, F.R.S.	Transactions of a Society, &c., vol. ii.

Some account of the Editions of Mr. Hunter's Works.

TREATISE ON THE NATURAL HISTORY OF THE HUMAN TEETH.

1st Edit. $\begin{cases} \text{Part I. 4to. 1771.} \\ \text{Part II. 4to. 1778.} \end{cases}$

On the occasion of the publication of Part II. a new title-page was added to Part I., and the two (being bound together) were sold as the *second* Edition.

2nd Edit. 1778.—The circumstances of this Edition are explained above.

3rd Edit. 4to. 1803.

A few unimportant alterations in the disposition of the prefatory parts of the work are made in this edition. No pains seem, however, to have been taken to rectify any of the errors of the former editions.

The drawings from which the engravings were made having been marked by Mr. Hunter with the initial capital letters A, B, C, &c., instead of by the Roman numerals I. II. III., &c., the engraver mistook the I for the J, &c., and thus innumerable errors in the references arose, which rendered the explanations to several of the plates absolutely unintelligible in all the former editions.

TREATISE ON THE VENEREAL DISEASE.

1st Edit. 1786. 4to.
2nd Edit. 1788. 4to.
The alterations in the Second Edition were mostly verbal. Both the First and Second Editions were printed and published at Mr. Hunter's own residence.
3rd Edit. 1794. 4to. with Notes by Sir Everard Home.
This was printed by some mistake from the First, instead of from the Second Edition, and is therefore chargeable with all those errors which Mr. Hunter was at so much pains to correct. The Editor has not only added notes at the foot of the page, but has incorporated his own remarks in the body of the text, without the insertion of any marks by which they may be distinguished. He has also omitted whole paragraphs, or parts of paragraphs, in several parts of the work, without any apparent authority for so doing. The work is illustrated by the original plates.
4th Edit. 1810. 1 vol. 8vo. with Notes by Dr. Joseph Adams.
This is a pretty correct reprint from the Second Edition. Dr. Adams, however, was too enthusiastic an admirer of Hunter to admit of his seeing any defects in the works of his favourite author; and consequently his notes rarely apply themselves to the real difficulties or defects of the work, but rather manifest a determination to uphold the opinions of his *friend* at all events. The plates which illustrate this edition are reduced from the 4to plates, and cannot be commended.
5th Edit. $\left\{ \begin{array}{l} 1809. \\ 1810. \end{array} \right\}$ 4to. with Notes by Sir Everard Home, Bart.
Being the *Second* Edition by this Editor, in which, however, few deviations from the First are observable. A supposititious title-page, purporting to be the *Third* Edition, seems to have been added in 1810, in order to increase the sale.

OBSERVATIONS ON CERTAIN PARTS OF THE ANIMAL ŒCONOMY.

1st Edit. 1786. 4to.
2nd Edit. 1792. 4to.
Both these Editions were printed and sold at Mr. Hunter's own residence. The Second Edition contains two additional papers, as well as some additional plates illustrative of the papers contained in the First Edition. The alterations are exceedingly numerous in every part of the work, and, upon the whole, considerable additions are made.

TREATISE ON THE BLOOD, INFLAMMATION, AND GUNSHOT WOUNDS.

1st Edit. 1794. 4to.
Was about one third through the press when Mr. Hunter died. It possesses no index. Its punctuation is extremely erroneous, the language often obscure, and the printing very inaccurate. These defects must be ascribed to the circumstance of

O

Mr. Hunter's death, and the neglect which the work afterwards suffered. A Life, by Sir Everard Home, is prefixed.

2nd Edit. 1812. 2 vols. 8vo.
3rd Edit. 1818. 2 vols. 8vo.
4th Edit. 1828. 1 vol. 8vo.

These are merely reprints of the errors as well as of the other matters contained in the first 4to Edition. The plates are reduced from the 4to plates, and cannot be praised as specimens of the art of engraving. None of these Editions contain any Index, or Life of the author.

Mr. Hunter's Evidence on the Trial of JOHN DONELLAN, *Esq., for the wilful Murder, by poison, of Sir* THEODOSIUS EDWARD ALLESLEY BOUGHTON, *Bart., at the Assizes at Warwick, on Friday, March 20,* 1781*.

(Taken in Short Hand by J. Gurney, Esq.)

Mr. JOHN HUNTER *sworn : Examined by* Mr. NEWNHAM.

Q. Have you heard the evidence that has been given by these gentlemen ?—*A.* I have been present the whole time.

Q. Did you hear Lady Boughton's evidence ?—*A.* I heard the whole.

Q. Did you attend to the symptoms Her Ladyship described, as appearing upon Sir Theodosius Boughton, after the medicine was given him ?—*A.* I did.

Q. Can any certain inference, upon physical or chirurgical principles, be drawn from those symptoms, or from the appearances externally or internally of the body, to enable you, in your judgment, to decide that the death was occasioned by poison ?—*A.* I was in London then ; a gentleman who is in Court waited upon me with a copy of the examination of Mr. Powell and Lady Boughton, and an account of the dissection, and the physical gentlemen's opinion upon that dissection.

Q. I don't wish you to go into that ; I put my question in a general way.—*A.* The whole appearances upon the dissection explain nothing but putrefaction.

Q. You have been long in the habit of dissecting human subjects. I presume you have dissected more than any man in Europe ?—*A.* I have dissected some thousands during these thirty-three years.

Q. Are those appearances you have heard described such, in your judgment, as are the result of putrefaction in dead subjects ?—*A.* Entirely.

Q. Are the symptoms that appeared after the medicine was given such as necessarily conclude that the person had taken poison ?—*A.* Certainly not.

Q. If an apoplexy had come on, would not the symptoms have been nearly or somewhat similar ?—*A.* Very much the same.

---

* See Life, p. 81.

Q. Have you ever known or heard of a young subject dying of an apoplectic or epileptic fit?—*A.* Certainly; but with regard to the apoplexy, not so frequent: young subjects will perhaps die more frequently of epilepsies than old ones; children are dying every day from teething, which is a species of epilepsy arising from an irritation.

Q. Did you ever, in your practice, know an instance of laurel-water being given to a human subject?—*A.* No, never.

Q. Is any certain analogy to be drawn from the effects of any given species of poison upon an animal of the brute creation, to that it may have upon a human subject?—*A.* As far as my experience goes, which is not a very confined one, because I have poisoned some thousands of animals, they are very nearly the same; opium, for instance, will poison a dog similar to a man; arsenic will have very near the same effect upon a dog as it would have, I take for granted, upon a man. I know something of the effects of them, and I believe their operations will be nearly similar.

Q. Are there not many things which will kill animals almost instantaneously, that will have no detrimental or noxious effect upon a human subject; spirits, for instance, occur to me?—*A.* I apprehend a great deal depends upon the mode of experiment; no man is fit to make one but those who have made many, and paid considerable attention to all the circumstances that relate to experiments. It is a common experiment, which I believe seldom fails, and it is in the mouth of everybody, that a little brandy will kill a cat: I have made the experiment, and have killed several cats, but it is a false experiment; in all those cases where it kills the cat, it kills the cat by getting into her lungs, not into her stomach; because if you convey the same quantity of brandy, or three times as much, into the stomach, in such a way as the lungs shall not be affected, the cat will not die. Now in those experiments that are made by forcing an animal to drink, there are two operations going on; one is, a refusing the liquor by the animal, its kicking and working with its throat to refuse it; the other is, the forcing the liquor upon the animal: and there are very few operations of that kind but some of the liquor gets into the lungs; I have known it from experience.

Q. If you had been called upon to dissect a body suspected to have died of poison, should you or not have thought it necessary to have pursued your search through the guts?—*A.* Certainly.

Q. Do you not apprehend that you would have been more likely to receive information from thence than any other part of the frame?—*A.* That is the track of the poison, and I should certainly have followed that track through.

Q. You have heard of the froth issuing from Sir Theodosius's mouth a minute or two before he died; is that peculiar to a man dying of poison, or is it not very common in many other complaints?—*A.* I fancy it is a general effect of people dying in what you may call health, in an apoplexy or epilepsy, in all sudden deaths, where the person was a moment before that in perfect health.

Q. Have you ever had an opportunity of seeing such appearances upon such subjects?—*A.* Hundreds of times.

Q. Should you consider yourself bound, by such an appearance, to impute the death of the subject to poison?—*A*. No, certainly not; I should rather suspect an apoplexy: and I wish in this case the head had been opened, to remove all doubts.

Q. If the head had been opened, do you apprehend all doubts would have been removed?—*A*. It would have been still further removed, because, although the body was putrid, so that one could not tell whether it was a recent inflammation, yet an apoplexy arises from an extravasation of blood in the brain, which would have laid in a coagulum. I apprehend, although the body was putrid, that would have been much more visible than the effect any poison could have had upon the stomach or intestines.

Q. Then, in your judgment, upon the appearances the gentlemen have described, no inference can be drawn from thence that Sir Theodosius Boughton died of poison?—*A*. Certainly not; it does not give the least suspicion.

Mr. JOHN HUNTER, *cross-examined by* Mr. HOWORTH.

Q. Having heard the account today that Sir Theodosius Boughton, apparently in perfect health, had swallowed a draught which had produced the symptoms described, I ask you whether any reasonable man can entertain a doubt that that draught, whatever it was, produced those appearances?—*A*. I don't know well what answer to make to that question.

Q. Having heard the account given of the health of this young gentleman on that morning, previous to taking the draught, and the symptoms that were produced immediately upon taking the draught, I ask your opinion, as a man of judgment, whether you don't think that draught was the occasion of his death?—*A*. With regard to his being in health, that explains nothing; we frequently, and indeed generally, see the healthiest people die suddenly, therefore I shall lay little stress upon that: as to the circumstances of the draught, I own they are suspicious; every man is just as good a judge as I am.

Court.—You are to give your opinion upon the symptoms only, not upon any other evidence given.

Mr. Howorth.—Upon the symptoms immediately produced, after the swallowing of that draught, I ask whether, in your judgment and opinion, that draught did not occasion his death?—*A*. I can only say, that it is a circumstance in favour of such an opinion.

Court.—That the draught was the occasion of his death?—*A*. No: because the symptoms afterwards are those of a man dying, who was in perfect health; a man dying of epilepsy or apoplexy, the symptoms would give one those general ideas.

Court.—It is the general idea you are asked about now, from the symptoms which appeared upon Sir Thedosius Boughton immediately after he took the draught, followed by his death so very soon after; whether, upon that part of the case, you are of opinion that the draught was the occasion of his death?—*A*. If I knew the draught was poison I should say, most probably, that the symptoms arose from that; but, when I don't know that the draught was poison, when I consider that a number of other things might occasion his death, I cannot answer positively to it.

Court.—You recollect the circumstance that was mentioned of a violent heaving in the stomach?—*A.* All that is the effect of the voluntary action being lost, and nothing going on but the involuntary.

Mr. Howorth.—Then you decline giving any opinion upon the subject?—*A.* I don't form any opinion to myself; I cannot form an opinion, because I can conceive if he had taken a draught of poison, it arose from that: I can conceive it might arise from other causes.

Q. If you are not at all acquainted with the effects and operations of distilled laurel-water, whether the having swallowed a draught of that would not have produced the symptoms described?—*A.* I should suppose it would: I can only say this of the experiments I have made of laurel-water upon animals, it has not been near so quick. I have injected laurel-water directly into the blood of dogs, and they have not died; I have thrown laurel-water, with a precaution, into the stomach, and it never produced so quick an effect with me, as described by those gentlemen.

Q. But you admit that laurel-water would have produced symptoms such as have been described?—*A.* I can conceive it might.

Mr. Newnham.—Would not an apoplexy or an epilepsy, if it had seized Sir Theodosius Boughton at this time, though he had taken no physic at all, have produced similar symptoms too?—*A.* Certainly.

Q. Where a father has died of an apoplexy, is not that understood, in some measure, to be constitutional?—*A.* There is no disease whatever that becomes constitutional but what can be given to a child. There is no disease which is acquired that can be given to a child; but whatever is constitutional in the father, the father has a power of giving that to the children; by which means it becomes what is called hereditary. There is no such thing as an hereditary disease, but there is an hereditary disposition for a disease.

Mr. Howorth.—Do you call apoplexy constitutional?—*A.* We see most diseases are constitutional: the smallpox is constitutional, though it requires an immediate cause to produce the effects. The venereal disease is hereditary. I conceive apoplexy as much constitutional as any disease whatever.

Q. Is apoplexy likely to attack a thin young man who had been in a course of taking cooling medicines before?—*A.* Not so likely, surely, as another man; but I have, in my account of dissections, two young women dying of apoplexies.

Q. But in such an habit of body, particularly attended with the circumstance of having taking cooling medicines, it was very unlikely to happen?—I do not know the nature of medicine so well as to know that it would hinder an apoplexy taking effect.

Court.—Give me your opinion in the best manner you can, one way or the other, whether, upon the whole of the symptoms described, the death proceeded from that medicine or any other cause?—*A.* I do not mean to equivocate; but, when I tell the sentiments of my own mind, what I feel at the time, I can give nothing decisive.

Extract from Mr. JUSTICE BULLER's *Charge.*

"For the prisoner you have had one gentleman called, who is likewise of the faculty, and a very able man. I can hardly say what his opinion is, for he does not seem to have formed any opinion at all of the matter. He, at first, said he could not form an opinion whether the death was, or was not, occasioned by the poison, because he could conceive that it might be ascribed to other causes. I wished very much to have got a direct answer from Mr. Hunter if I could, what, upon the whole, was now the result of his attention and application to the subject, and what was his present opinion; but he says he can say nothing decisive. So that, upon this point, if you are to determine upon the evidence of the gentlemen who are skilled in the faculty only, you have the *very positive* opinion of four or five gentlemen of the faculty that the deceased did die of poison. On the other side, you have what I really cannot myself call more than the *doubt* of another; for it is agreed by Mr. Hunter, that the laurel-water would produce the symptoms which are described. He says, an epilepsy or apoplexy would produce the same symptoms; but, as to an apoplexy, it is not likely to attack so young and so thin a man as Sir Theodosius was; and, as to an epilepsy, the other witnesses tell you, they don't think the symptoms which have been spoken of do show that Sir Theodosius had any epilepsy at the time."

LECTURES

ON THE

PRINCIPLES OF SURGERY,

BY

JOHN HUNTER, F.R.S.

WITH NOTES

BY

JAMES F. PALMER,

SENIOR SURGEON TO THE ST. GEORGE'S AND ST. JAMES'S DISPENSARY, FELLOW
OF THE ROYAL MEDICAL AND CHIRURGICAL SOCIETY OF LONDON, ETC.

PREFACE.

THE following Lectures are printed from a very full and accurate copy, taken in short-hand by Mr. ~~Nathaniel~~ *Henry* Rumsey of Chesham, to whom I am indebted for the permission to make them public. They were delivered in the years 1786 and 1787, after which period I have not found any copy, excepting a very short and imperfect one in the Museum of the Royal College of Surgeons, dated 1791, by Mr. James Pearce. There are also in the College Museum five other copies, which are respectively attributed to Mr. Twigge, Mr. Hopkinson, Mr. Parkinson, and Mr. R. Keate; the fifth being only a partial transcript of a copy by Dr. Joseph Adams, Mr. Hunter's biographer. Of all these Mr. Parkinson's is by far the most full and accurate, although in these respects it falls very far short of the accuracy and fullness of Mr. Rumsey's copy, from which the ensuing lectures are printed. Indeed, from the fullness of the latter, one might almost suppose that the writer had had access to the Hunterian manuscript; for, besides being generally more full, it never omits examples and illustrations in proof of opinions, which the former ones frequently do. The style also is characteristically Hunterian.

I am also indebted to Sir Benjamin Brodie, to Professor Macartney, and to Mr. Frederick Tyrrell, for the use of copies in their possession, the first of which is ascribed to Mr. Howison, the second was taken by the Professor himself, and the third by Mr. Robert Lees. The last of these (bearing date 1785 and 1786) is the most valuable, being not only the most full, but abounding with interlineations, which there is every reason to believe were added during an attendance upon a second course of the same Lectures. These last-mentioned copies, as well as Mr. Parkinson's, have been had recourse to whenever occasion required, but in general, and with very few exceptions, the printing has been conducted from Mr. Rumsey's. Occasionally it has been found necessary to retrench redundancies and repetitions, and to substitute one word for another having a synonymous signification.

The value of these Lectures, I suppose, will not be questioned, nor the interest which attaches to them denied. Besides the luminous general views on Physiology and Pathology which they contain, they also abound in useful facts and the most valuable practical suggestions. In some respects they may be regarded as amplifications of his published opinions, but in other respects they enter upon entirely new subjects of the greatest interest to the Surgeon.

The notes which accompany these Lectures are not numerous; for as many of the subjects treated of will again come under consideration in the course of the Treatises, it seemed more convenient to refer any observations that might be required, to those parts of the work, in which the Author has expressed his opinions in his own undoubted language. In the few observations which the Editor has deemed it necessary to make, he has sometimes had recourse to authorities, which he has not always thought it necessary to mention particularly. He trusts, however, that this general acknowledgement will obviate the suspicion of his wishing to appropriate unjustly the labours of other men.

JAMES F. PALMER.

38, Golden Square, April 1835.

CONTENTS.

LECTURES

PRINCIPLES OF SURGERY.

CHAPTER I.

INTRODUCTION.

Introductory remarks.—These lectures to contain the results of Mr. Hunter's own observation ;—intended to explain the general principles of the art;—these the necessary guides to practice.—Mr. Hunter's opinion of operations ;—motives for lecturing.—To commence with some account of physiology.—Preliminary observations on matter ;—its general properties ;—our perception of matter ;—attraction ;—repulsion ;—properties added to constitute organized matter.—Of animal and vegetable matter ; —its origin in, and return to, common matter ;—but distinguished from it by peculiar properties ;—growth ;—propagation of the species ;—existence under two states, the living and the dead ;—three modes in which it may be considered : 1st, Living ; 2nd, Chemically when dead; 3rd, In a state of decay, and return to common matter.—Errors of former physiologists, in explaining vital actions by mechanical or chemical operations ; —this error to be corrected.—Consideration of animal matter in particular ;—and especially of the human body ;—but information to be drawn from other animals and vegetables ;—also from diseases and malformations.

MR. HUNTER used generally to commence by stating that it was his intention, in these lectures, to give only the results of his own observations and experience, because the opinions of others might be found in their works. I do not mean, said he, that all I say in this course will be entirely new, and that none of the opinions and observations which I shall deliver are to be found in any publications, for there are many facts too obvious to have been overlooked in the most ignorant days of physic. I intend in this course to include some of the most interesting parts of surgery, principally those subjects on which I have had opportunities of making many new, and I hope useful observations, so as to put our art, in many respects, in a new point of view. Many of my ideas, and the arrangement of my subject, are new, and consequently my terms become in part new, for two ideas cannot be expressed in the same terms. I am led to suppose my ideas are just, because they have in some measure stood the test of time; and what is the most incontestible proof of their correctness is, that they have been adopted by others; and I hope my *terms* will be found expressive of the things meant, and that they are so appears evident, from their having been employed in several late publications on surgery.

I do not intend to give my lectures as a regular course, but rather to explain what appear to me to be the principles of the art, so as thereby to fit my pupils to act as occasion may require, from comparing and reasoning on known principles. I shall suppose you already acquainted with the structure of the parts of the human frame, and must observe, that a knowledge of the healthy and diseased actions, or, in other words the principles of our art, are not less necessary to be understood than the principles of other sciences; unless, indeed, the surgeon should wish to resemble the Chinese philosopher, whose knowledge consisted only in facts. In that case the science must remain unimproved until fresh facts arise. In Europe philosophers reason from principles, and thus account for facts before they arise. Too much attention cannot be paid to facts; yet too many facts crowd the memory without advantage, any further than that they lead us to establish principles. By an acquaintance with principles we learn the *causes* of diseases. Without this knowledge a man cannot be a surgeon. Surgeons have been too much satisfied with considering the effects only; but in studying diseases we ought not only to understand the effect, as inflammation, suppuration, &c., but also the cause of that effect; for without this knowledge our practice must be very confined, and often applied too late, as in many cases it will be necessary to prevent the effect. In the bite of a mad dog, for instance, the disease will be prevented by removing the part; in the venereal disease, in the case of chancre, we must not only know how to cure the chancre, but also to prevent its effects on the constitution, which is done by giving mercury internally. On the other hand, it would be often proper to increase the effect, which can only be done when we know the cause*. In many cases, where the

* [By the "law of nature" is meant the invariableness or uniform constancy of certain results following certain given conditions, the agents (which for the most part are

effect could not be prevented, or afterwards either removed, diminished, or increased with advantage, it will be proper to change it to some other more in our power to remove, as, for instance, by converting the venereal into common inflammation. If the disease is already formed, we ought to know the modes of action in the *body* and in *parts*, in their endeavour to relieve themselves; the powers they have of restoring themselves, and the means of assisting those powers. Or, if these prove insufficient, we judge, by all the attending circumstances, how far excision may be necessary, and what condition of the constitu-

unknown and invisible,) being denominated the *cause*, the resulting phenomena the *effect*, and the conditions under which that effect is produced, the *law*. Thus, all bodies fall to the earth, and all bodies also suffer an expansion of their particles by the application of heat. Here the principles of gravitation and heat are the causes, the descent and expansion of the bodies the effects, and the rates according to which these effects take place, the laws of gravitation and heat. Causation is attributed merely in consequence of the invariableness of the phenomena, and not in consequence of any knowledge which we possess of the intimate relation of causes and effects.

It is not in general difficult to deduce the laws of physical agents, in consequence of the power which we possess of simplifying and varying the conditions of our experiments, so as in the first instance to separate all extraneous influences or disturbing causes, and in the second place to verify the results thus obtained by every possible combination of opposing circumstances. Such certainty, however, is rarely attainable in regard to organized bodies, in consequence of the reaction of the parts of which they consist upon one another, and the consequent impossibility of observing the effects of organic agencies in their simple state. The conditions under which any given class of phenomena are observed are continually varying, and a variety of extraneous causes are mixed up in almost every case, so that, from the most careful experiments, it is still extremely possible to mistake the conclusion, and to deduce laws which are expressive only of a part of the facts. These circumstances afford no just ground for undervaluing physiological principles, although they are calculated to inspire a wary caution in arguing with too much positiveness from principles of this kind. We would say, "Est quodam prodire tenus si non datur ultra."

It is scarcely necessary to observe that causes differ greatly among themselves. It would be absurd to confound the principle of heat, the expansion of steam, and the machinery by which the power thus generated acts, as causes of the same kind. The remote and the proximate cause in such a case have no immediate relation, but are connected together by a number of intermediate circumstances which, like the steps of an argument, unite the conclusion to the premises. It is very necessary to bear this in mind in physiological reasoning, in consequence of our almost total ignorance of these intermediate links in the chain of causation. In the instances above adduced by the author, we have no knowledge of the *mode* in which the poison of a rabid animal, or the poison of syphilis, produce their effects on the animal body; nor how mercury and other medicines should tend to eradicate the latter from the constitution. We are unable in these cases to advance a step further than to perceive the necessity of absorption of the poison, after which all is conjecture. A full perception of the whole sequence of effects would doubtless at once discover the precise nature of the remedy, as well as the proper cases in which it should be administered.

These few observations have been made in consequence of the indefinite and not very philosophical manner in which Mr. Hunter sometimes employs the word *cause*. The final and efficient causes are frequently confounded.]

tion is most favourable for an operation. To determine on this last point is exceedingly difficult, and in some instances exceeds our present knowledge. I lately saw a patient die in a few hours, of no other operation than the excision of a small tumour from the arm; another, by the removal of one from the abdomen; a third, by castration; and within these two days I assisted at an operation for fistula in perinæo, sixteen hours after which the patient died. Now all these patients seemed previously in good health, and perhaps the cause of death, and the particular circumstances of the constitution which render operations thus hazardous, will never be understood.

This last part of surgery, namely, operations, is a reflection on the healing art; it is a tacit acknowledgement of the insufficiency of surgery. It is like an armed savage who attempts to get that by force which a civilized man would get by stratagem. No surgeon should approach the victim of his operation without a sacred dread and reluctance, and should be superior to that popular *éclat* generally attending painful operations, often only because they are so, or because they are expensive to the patient.

Mr. Hunter next mentioned his motives for lecturing; showing that he did not do this with a view to pecuniary gain, since the time thus expended might be employed more profitably in extending his connexions and enlarging his practice. I have seen, said he, as much practice, and made a larger collection of diseased preparations than perhaps any man in Europe, all of which I find to correspond with the opinions I have formed of the nature of the respective diseases. In the years 1761 and 1762, having been already engaged ten years in the profession, I attended the army, without which I should have been unable to give my opinion concerning gunshot wounds, which rarely occur in civil practice. In the year 1768 I was called upon to be a teacher of anatomy, but I congratulate myself that I did not become so, as it could not have failed of engaging my attention too much to admit that general attention I have been able to pay to surgery; and the necessity I should have been under to read might have occupied me too much, and prevented my forming habits or established modes of thinking. In the years 1772, 1773, and 1774, I had frequent opportunities of giving my opinion in private, and had generally the satisfaction to be heard with candour. Since I have lectured, I have scarcely found a pamphlet without some of my opinions, and often my very language, as adhesive and suppurative inflammation, &c. But what more than all induced me to lecture, was the great advantage every one finds by putting his thoughts into writing. A man can never tell how much he knows till he arranges his knowledge, and then he can tell how defective it is; hence it is that almost all the authors of any consideration in physic have been public teachers.

In the present lectures it is my intention to begin with the physiology of the animal œconomy in its natural or healthy state; and then to come to pathology, or the physiology of disease, which may be called the *perversion of the natural actions of the animal œconomy*. Amongst the latter I shall treat first of *accidents* the most simple or natural, or *diseases spontaneously arising*; next, of the *means of restoration*, on which I shall be particularly full,—of these the first is *adhesive inflammation*, commonly called healing by the first intention; then of inflammations tending to *suppuration, granulation*, and *cicatrization*: after these I shall consider the *specific diseases*, as *locked jaw, scrofula*, &c.: the *poisons* next, as the *venereal disease, cancer*, &c.

Of Matter; and first of the Distinction between Animate and Inanimate Matter.

I must now beg the close attention of the gentlemen present, as I shall be a little abstruse in the present lecture, which I intend as an introduction to all animal matter.

Before we endeavour to give an idea of an animal, it is necessary to understand the properties of that matter of which an animal is composed; but the better to understand animal matter, it is necessary to understand the properties of common matter; else we shall be often applying our ideas of common matter, which are familiar to us, to animal matter, an error hitherto too common, but which we should carefully avoid.

By our senses alone is matter demonstrable. If a man did not see, he would have no conception that there was such a thing as light; if he was deaf, he could have no idea of sound; if he had no touch, no taste, no smell, in short if he had no sensation at all, (which is easily conceivable,) he would not know that there is such a thing existing as matter. On the other hand, it is from matter alone that we come to a knowledge of our senses; so that the only proof of the existence of either is by their reciprocal effects.

An animal, then, must be composed in such a manner as to be susceptible of impression, which impression consists of an alteration in the part impressed; and matter must make the impression on us before we can become sensible of its existence. Matter is in itself, however, only an abstract idea, and it is not the matter itself but some of its properties which make the impression, as sourness, heat, &c. When we see

a man, it is not the man himself or the matter of the man that makes
the impression, but the light which he reflects, and which our eye has
the power of collecting to one point, so as to give a determinate shape
on the organ of sight.   Now the act of seeing is that impression made
on our eye which gives us an idea of a body exterior to us, exactly similar to touch; it is an impression made of a given figure.   Every man
might be able to see simply with every part of the body as well as with
the eye; for if you were to place before my skin a refracting glass, so
that the image should be thrown on my body of the same shape as that
which is exterior, if my feeling was so very delicate as to distinguish
this shape, it would give me the same idea as seeing.   A drum has no
sound in itself, but it has the power of putting the matter of the air into
action, which produces the idea of sound by its impression on the organ
of hearing.   The sense of touch would appear most to contradict the
above statement; but touch only arises from the resistance of matter,
which resistance alters the form of the part touching, and the alteration
causes feeling.   If it was the matter itself which caused the sensation,
we ought to have as many kinds of matter as we have of sensation;
but our sensations correspond with the different properties of matter,
not with the different kinds.

But to return to my subject: by matter we mean all that composes
this globe of the earth on which we live, and which is probably formed
of only a few substances differing in specific properties from each other,
but which when compounded produce a very great variety, and of course
these cause a great variety of sensations in us.   Matter, thus compounded, appears to us in one of the three following states, a state of
solidity, fluidity, or vapour.

The first, or solidity, appears to be the natural state of matter; the
other two seem to involve a kind of *force*, especially vapour.

The first of the various properties of matter is attraction : of this
there are many kinds, of which I shall first mention elective attraction,
which is a disposition in all matter to unite with some particular kinds
of matter rather than with others, forming with them a compound, which
at the same time that it is a compound, seems homogeneous.   Elective
attraction can only take place when bodies are in a fluid state or in
vapour; it would appear to be a kind of choice, and it is one of the
most refined properties of common matter, producing new compounds
by a species of generation, but annihilating the old by the same action.
This property is given to matter for the purpose of forming various regular solids and fluids of which the world is composed, and it is this
that gives us such variety.

Secondly.   By a particular attraction, or by an increase of the same attraction, these parts are brought into closer approximation : this we call the attraction of cohesion, by means of which attraction bodies are kept in one mass. When bodies are so subdivided as to be reduced to their constituent particles, still each particle has its centre of gravity on which it may be said to move, from whence arises fluidity. So that a fluid would appear to be a body reduced to its original parts ; the attraction of cohesion is destroyed, but each particle has its centre of attraction or of gravitation. As the centre of the globe attracts every particle of matter that is in it, so every mass of matter, simply as matter, has an attraction in its centre, by which it can bring bodies to it or keep them in contact with it. If we were to let drop some quicksilver, and it met with no resistance, it would assume a globular form : this is not from the attraction of cohesion, but from the attraction of gravitation. It must be observed, however, that where the attraction of cohesion is but slight, as in fluids, this will not take place, unless there is some affinity, as between acids and water, spirits of wine and water, &c. Water and oil will not unite by this species of attraction when in a fluid state.

There are other general properties which arise out of the attraction of cohesion, such as figure, magnitude, &c. These properties are those which make bodies fit subjects for mechanics, but they are not the only ones necessary. A clock may be made correctly, but yet it will not go until we bring in some active power, such as gravitation, the raising of water into steam, &c. Thus we find something like the life of mechanics, which is not matter, but a property belonging to it ; what is simply mechanical, that is made of inert matter, must have, as it were, a soul to put and continue it in motion.

When all these properties have their full effect they produce various other effects, and become the regulators of the whole mass, confining its motion, space, &c.

These are some of the properties of common matter. How far repulsion is a universal principle I am not able to determine ; I should much suspect that it is not so general as the others. That there is such a principle in nature is evident, because neither fluidity nor vapour could take place without it ; perhaps heat is the great repulsive property, at least it counteracts attraction and produces repulsion amongst the particles of matter when diffused through it.

Thus the matter of the globe is in general so regulated, by properties stamped on it at first, that in its common actions it cannot err. But we find that matter has been carried much further in some other properties than in those just mentioned ; it has undergone changes not in the least connected with or arising out of them, and its properties are of course entirely different; seeming, as it were, a monstrosity in the combination of matter. Its mode of continuance, by preparing within itself matter similar to itself, is entirely different.

These changes produce the animal and vegetable or organic portion of the world.

Of the Matter of Animals and Vegetables.

Animal and vegetable matter has certainly arisen out of the matter of the globe, for we find it returning to it again. Both are subject to the laws mentioned above as regulating common matter, but they are so different, from their peculiar modification, as to appear at first like originally distinct species of matter; but they will be found, on investigation, to be only a new modification of matter.

This change in the original principles of matter seems to be equally distinct both in animal and vegetable matter, and the first principle of action of those two substances seems to be in great measure the same; however, there are marks by which they can be distinguished. The connexion of these two modifications of matter with common matter has never yet been traced, nor has the gradual transition from one to the other been imagined; and if those substances had not reverted into common matter by their decomposition, it never could have been suspected that they were originally composed of the same materials. For these reasons they have been ranked by themselves.

Animal and vegetable substances differ from common matter in having a power superadded, totally different from any other known property of matter, out of which arise various new properties.

Animals and vegetables have a power of action within themselves, are capable of increasing their own magnitude, and possess the power, as it were, of working themselves into form and a higher state of existence. This power of action and capability of increase require a supply of materials, as well for the increase as for the waste arising from action. This supply appears not to be wholly the same in both, though perhaps it may be. The idea of a supply always supposes a resource distinct from the thing supplied, and no waste parts can ever perfectly revert into the thing itself without first going through all the changes which first brought it into a fit state.

This supply is furnished by the materials of the globe. Vegetables alone appear to have a power of immediately converting common matter into their own kind. Animals probably have not that power, therefore are removed further from common matter; so that a vegetable seems an intermediate step between common matter and animal matter. But observation will show that vegetables can readily convert both animal and vegetable matter into their own substance, as in the case of dung, which increases the natural growth of plants*.

Both have a power of propagating their kinds by a production out of themselves, by which means the stock is replenished.

Both are capable of being in two states : one of these is the living state, which we have been considering, the other is the dead state.

Hence both animals and vegetables are capable of being considered in three ways. 1st, In their power of continuance and production, when possessed of their natural powers of action or life. 2nd, In their nature chemically as matter, which can only be considered when they are dead. 3rd, In their decay, or spontaneous reduction to common matter, when life is gone†. In all these operations they are totally different from common matter. The first distinction, or life, in which consists the power of self-preservation, is the antidote to the two last, since before either of these can take place the whole part must be deprived of the living principle. When in the first state, their actions are either natural, the whole being in harmony, and every part acting in concert with the rest, which is called health; or they are unnatural, which constitutes disease, the tendency of which is to destroy the whole.

When chemically considered, both animal and vegetable matter are found to be acted on by different substances, or are capable of solution

---

* [It is highly probable that the different proximate elements of vegetable and animal substances hold different ranks in the scale of organized substances, in the same manner that one animal ranks higher in the scale of organised beings than another. Thus, starch, sugar, and woody fibre among vegetable substances, and gelatin, albumen, and fibrin among animal substances, are *raised*, as it were, from one to the other by successive processes in the animal or vegetable œconomy; so that fibrin may be regarded as the substance most highly animalised, or as possessing the distinctive properties of an animal substance in the highest possible degree. In this view, vegetable life, which subsists almost exclusively on carbonic acid gas, and graminivorous animals, which are able to extract nutriment from vegetable substances, may be regarded as subservient processes, intended to prepare the common elements of matter as nutriment for the more perfect animals.—which, however, afterwards undergoes a series of further processes in the bodies of these animals, in order to fit it for all the purposes of the œconomy. Sennebier and Saussure have satisfactorily shown that decayed organic remains do not nourish plants by being absorbed in their unmodified state, but by affording a more abundant supply of carbonic acid gas, which, in combination with water, forms the principal aliment of vegetables. There is no process in vegetables corresponding to digestion in animals, and hence the food of plants is spontaneously evolved by the natural processes of fermentation and putrefaction.]

† [There are many other distinctions between organized and inorganized bodies, which, however, it is unnecessary to consider in this place.]

in other bodies, as concentrated acids, alkalies, &c., in which respect they are pretty similar to one another. Both are capable of being acted on by fire; but in this process we find each yielding some substances peculiar to itself;—animal matter when distilled yields water, volatile alkali, empyreumatic oil, and calcareous earth;—besides these there is a small proportion of iron, which does not appear, however, to be a constituent part of the whole animal body, being chiefly procurable from the blood; a small proportion of other substances may also be found in the blood*.

In their decay, both animals and vegetables go through a series of regular spontaneous changes, the succeeding one arising entirely out of the first, and the next out of this, until the whole return to common matter from whence they arose, for to the earth they must return from whence they came.   In this natural process we find animals and vegetables yield many substances not to be found in them before these changes, also not to be found in common matter.   This process I call fermentation, and it is peculiar, I believe, to vegetable and animal matter.

The processes carried on by chemistry and fermentation, which can only take place when the parts are dead, have been introduced by physiologists into the living animal œconomy; and, not satisfied with this, they have brought in mechanics to account for many of the operations of vegetables and animals. But, for the purpose of distinguishing more accurately between mechanical, chemical, and vital operations, and the circumstances under which the two first are applied to the living body, let us consider them a little further.

The actions and productions of actions, both in vegetable and animal bodies, have been hitherto considered so much under the prepossessions of chemical and mechanical philosophy, that physiologists have entirely lost sight of life; and perhaps they have been led to this mode of reasoning because these properties are much more familiar, more adapted to our understandings, and more demonstrable than the living properties of organized beings. But unless we consider life as the immediate cause of all actions occurring either in animals or vegetables, we can

---

* [Vegetable substances are nearly all composed of oxygen, hydrogen, and carbon,—carbon, for the most part, being the preponderating ingredient. In some few examples nitrogen is likewise present. The proximate principles of vegetables, or those substances which exist ready formed in plants, are exceedingly numerous, as gum, starch, sugar, &c., amounting in the whole to not less than forty-five or fifty substances, characterized by different properties. Animal substances, on the contrary, at least all the principal animal substances, contain nitrogen as well as oxygen, hydrogen, and carbon, and the proximate elements are not so numerous as those of vegetables. The animal fats, which are considered by many as a natural store of nutriment, contain no nitrogen, and therefore approximate to vegetable products.]

have no just conception of either vegetable or animal matter. No wonder, then, that the theories of the older physiologists are ill built and ill supported, their principles being false. Many of the effects both in animals and vegetables might at first sight appear to be chemical, or the consequence of fermentation. The production of many juices of plants, such as gums, acids, sugar, &c., would seem to be of this kind ; but all arise from natural actions of the vegetable, and do not belong to chemistry. No chemist on earth can make out of the earth a piece of sugar, but a vegetable can do it. Digestion, the formation of the blood, and all the secretions of an animal, might at first appear to be of this sort ; but that they really are not chemical products I am clearly convinced. If an ingenious man undertook to account for every change in matter by fermentation, there is no change in nature that might not be brought within his definition. The living principle itself would be shown to arise from fermentation ; brain, muscles, bones would grow from fermentation, since they are all formed from the blood, and yet the blood is not found in them.—Of all things on the face of the earth definitions are the most cursed ; for if you make a definition you may bring together under it a thousand things that have not the least connexion with it*.

---

* [By the fermentation here spoken of is not meant that process of spontaneous decomposition, occurring under the conditions of heat and moisture, to which the appellation is restricted by modern chemists, but a vague chemical disturbance, in the course of which a new and undefined arrangement of the elements was imagined to take place.

Mr. Hunter, in his zeal for the vital principle, has probably gone too far in excluding the agency of chemical causes. There is not the least reason for supposing that the vital principle is able to confer new properties on matter, or to transmute one matter into another, so as indiscriminately to employ other substances than those which it does for the repair of the body and its various secretions ; on the contrary, there seems every reason for believing that the elementary particles exert the same affinities under the influence of vitality that they do in the laboratory of the chemist, and that if it were possible to present these to each other out of the body under precisely the same circumstances that they are presented in the body, and in the requisite states and proportions, the same combinations would take place, and the same results would be produced. The vital principle may not perhaps improperly be compared to the principles of heat and electricity, which exert an influence over the affinities of matter without essentially altering its nature ; but the great distinction between organic and ordinary chemistry is not less in the nature of the agent than in the minute and appropriate apparatus by which that agent operates. All the processes of organic life, referrible to this head, are executed, as it were *atomically*, by an arrangement of parts infinitely small ; by which the affinities of the acting bodies are brought together in modes which cannot artificially be imitated by the chemist. The following observations by the reviewer of MM. Tiedemann and Gmelin's Treatise on Digestion apply to the present question :—
" Je suis loin de nier qu'il y ait dans les actes du corps vivans quelque chose de special, quelque chose qui reconnaît d'autres lois que celles qui régissent les corps bruts ; mais

What I call fermentation, only takes place in animal and vegetable matter when dead. It is that change which takes place in the substances themselves out of their own spontaneity, without any external assistance. Chemistry is a kind of force on things to decompose them. In the process of fermentation, vegetable matter goes through intermediate stages, in which it is neither vegetable nor common matter; the same with animal matter during putrefaction. But in all the productions of a living animal or vegetable, the substances produced are animal or vegetable matter. The only substance produced in an animal which cannot be called animal matter is the earthy matter of bones, and of some diseased parts* : it appears also that, in some of the secretions of animals, the products produced have none of the original properties of animal matter, as the sugar of milk, the bitter principle in the bile, these not having been found in any of the natural solids or fluids by any process whatever. But this does not come up to my notion of fermentation, for no process of fermentation of animal or vegetable matter ever produced either one or the other; and even in vegetables, where sugar seems to constitute part of the plant, it is formed by the action of the vegetable. If ever any matter is formed in any of the juices secreted in any part of a vegetable or animal body similar to what arises from fermentation, we may depend on it it arose from that process, but we may also depend on it that there is a defect of the living principle in those cases.

The conversion of water into vegetables, which is vegetation, or of vegetable and animal matter into animals, which is animalization, is not a change taking place according to the nature of the substance, but is effected by the actions of the vegetable or animal. The different juices formed from the blood, called secretions, differ not from the nature of the blood as animal matter, all giving nearly the same substances when analysed, or subjected to fermentation. Nor can the substances formed in a vegetable be formed, by any process that we know of, from water†. We might suppose that fermentation would produce an animal from a

---

ces dernières interviennent, sans aucun doute, plus qu'on ne le pense généralement dans les functions de nutrition ; et c'est mieux servir la science de la vie de reconnaître cet intervention, et de l'etudier jusqu'à son extrême limite que de voir partout de la vitalité sans attacher à ce mot un véritable sens."]

* [It is a question with some geologists whether lime is not essentially an animal product.]

† [The refinements even of modern chemistry have not yet enabled us to form any animal or vegetable principle *ab origine* from any combination of the ultimate elements. The substance called oxalamide, obtained by Professor Faraday from the oxalate of ammonia, approaches in character to an animal product, although it is not actually so. A few other examples of the same sort might be mentioned.]

vegetable, because in this change "a decomposition of matter and a new combination" is effected; but fermentation never could bring back dead animal or vegetable matter to living, so that it does not correspond to the above definition which has been given of it. This single circumstance throws more light on the power of the stomach than we are yet aware of, for dead matter subjected to it is not obliged to undergo any change as matter, but goes through that process which produces life*.

In treating of an animal body I shall always consider its operations, or the causes of all its effects, as arising from the principle of life, and lay it down as a rule that no chemical or mechanical property can become the first cause of any of the effects in the machine. But as all animals have form and motion, which motion is directed by that form, these motions become mechanical, so that every motion may be truly called mechanical. Mechanics are therefore introduced into the machine for many purposes. The living principle, however, in itself is not in the least mechanical, neither does it arise from, nor is it in the least connected with, any mechanical principle.

Having thus given a general idea of these singular combinations of matter, I shall now confine myself to animal matter. But before I treat of the diseases of the animal body, which is the intention of these lectures, it will be necessary to give such general ideas of the subject, and to lay down such axioms and propositions, as will enable you to follow me through all the necessary descriptions of preternatural actions of the machine. This matter we must consider in two points of view: 1st, in its production; 2ndly, in its continuance. This leads me into a new field, and exhibits properties very different from all the other properties of matter. It will be necessary, I say, to have clear and distinct ideas of the difference between animate and inanimate matter, in order to know when and where the animal principle acts, and when other prin-

---

* [There are grounds, I think, for believing that the first rudiments of life, or the revivification of dead animal matter, actually commences in the stomach. Digestion, however, is a complicated chemical process, and not of that simple kind that might be inferred from Mr. Hunter's language. (See Tiedemann and Gmelin, and Prout.) The transformation or passage of common matter under the empire of physical laws to living matter which exists in defiance of those laws, is a mystery which will perhaps never be completely understood. So far as observation has gone, the steps of this transformation are gradual and complicated; the products of each successive process always advancing from a lower to a higher degree of animalization. If therefore we regard life as a superadded principle, we cannot but observe that it is communicated to common matter only in proportion as this matter is animalized. In short, certain conditions of the recipients of life seem necessary before it can be communicated, and the higher the manifestations of life the higher are these conditions. The manifestation of intellect in proportion to the development of the brain presents an example very analogous.]

ciples are made use of in an animal body in accomplishing all the different purposes of life. The human body is what I mean chiefly to treat of; but I shall often find it necessary to illustrate some of the propositions which I shall lay down from animals of an inferior order, in whom the principles may be more distinct and less blended with others, or where the parts are differently constructed, in order to show from many varieties of structure, and from many different considerations, what are the uses of the same parts in man; or at least to show that they are not for the uses which have been commonly assigned to them; and as man is the most complicated part of the whole animal creation, it will be proper in the first place to point out general principles common to all this species of matter, that I may be better understood when I come to the more complicated machine, namely, the human. Besides having recourse to many of the inferior orders of animals for the elucidation of some of the phenomena of the more complicated orders, we are also obliged to Disease for many of our hints on the animal œconomy, or for explaining the actions of parts, for the wrong action of a part often points out what the natural action was, and itself gives an idea of life. Disease often corrects our imagination and opinions, and shows us that such and such parts cannot have the uses commonly attributed to them, and therefore brings us a step towards the knowledge of the true use. Monstrosities contribute to rectify our opinions in the same if not in a more intelligible manner. A monster is either from a deficiency of parts which can be produced from art (and often is from necessity, as in operations), or else from a modification caused by a wrong arrangement or construction of parts, which will produce an unnatural action, by which means the natural action may be known.

CHAPTER II.

ON THE VITAL PRINCIPLE.

Difficulty of conceiving of this principle ;—complex in its effects, but simple in its essence ;—not the result of any perceptible arrangement of matter ; —may result from a peculiar arrangement of the ultimate particles, giving rise to a principle of preservation ;—this the simplest idea of life ;—illustrated by magnetism in iron.—Erroneous comparison of life to mechanical powers.—Action not an essential property of life.—Life without action ;—vitality of an egg ;—experiments ;—but action promotes the continuance of life.—Seeming exceptions to the preservative power of life ;—peculiar form of putrefaction in certain bodies ;—death of a part of the body previously to general death.

ANIMAL matter is endowed with a principle called, in common language, life. This principle is, perhaps, conceived of with more difficulty than any other in nature, which arises from its being more complex in its effects than any other ; and it is therefore no wonder that it is the least understood. But although life may appear very compounded in its effects in a complicated animal like man, it is as simple in him as in the most simple animal, and is reducible to one simple property in every animal *.

I have observed that animal matter may be in two states ; in one it is endowed with the living principle, in the other it is deprived of it. From this it appears that the principle called life cannot arise from the peculiar modification of matter, because the same modification exists where this principle is no more. The matter abstracted from life appears at all times to be the same, as far as our senses and experiments carry us. If life arose out of this peculiar modification, it would not be destroyed until the modification was destroyed, either by spontaneous changes, as fermentation, or by some chemical processes ; and were it destroyed by the last, it might sometimes be restored again by another process. Life, then, appears to be something superadded to this peculiar modification of matter ; or this modification of matter is so arranged that the

---

* [It is considered by many, and perhaps truly, that we are not yet prepared for a generalisation of so high a kind, or at least that it would be more convenient for the analysis of vital phenomena to consider life as made up of several principles differing in their nature.]

principle of life arises out of the arrangement, and this peculiar disposition of parts may be destroyed, and still the modification, from which
it is called animal matter, remain the same. If the latter be the true
explanation, this arrangement of parts, on which life should depend,
would not be that position of parts necessary to the formation of a whole
part or organ, for that is probably a mechanical, or at least organical,
arrangement, but just a peculiar arrangement of the most simple particles, giving rise to a principle of preservation ; so that matter so arranged could not undergo any destructive change till this arrangement
were destroyed, which is death. This simple principle of life can with
difficulty be conceived ; but to show that matter may take on new
properties without being altered in itself as to the species of matter,
it may be not improper to illustrate this idea by such acquirements
in other matter. Perhaps magnetism affords us the best illustration
we can give of this. Iron appears at all times the same, whether endued with this property or not : magnetism does not seem to depend on
the formation of any of its parts. A bar of iron without magnetism
may be considered like animal matter without life ; set it upright and it
acquires a new property, of attraction and repulsion, at its different ends.
Now is this any substance added ; or is it a certain change which takes
place in the arrangement of the particles of iron giving it this property?
If we take a piece of glass, it is transparent ; we break it into a thousand
pieces and it becomes white. Whiteness is not a new matter added to it,
but a property arising from its being composed of a number of small
pieces.

It was not sufficient that animal matter should be endowed with this
first principle, the principle of preservation, it was necessary that it
should have action or motion within itself. This does not necessarily
arise out of the arrangement for preservation ; on the other hand, the
arrangement for preservation, which is life, becomes the *principle* of
action, not the *power* of action, for the power of action is one step
further. The *power of action* must arise from a particular position of
those living parts, for before *action* can take place the matter must be
arranged with this view. This is generally effected by the union of
two or more living parts, so united as to allow of motion on each other,
which motion the principle of action is capable of effecting when so
disposed. A number of these simple acting parts, united, make a muscular fibre ; when a number of these are put together they form a muscle, which, joined with other kinds of animal matter, as tendon, ligament, composes what may be called an organ. Thus, too, by the arrangement of the living particles, the other organs of the body are
formed, their various dispositions and actions depending on the nature

of the arrangement, for action is not confined to muscle, the nerves also have action arising from the arrangement of their living particles*.

The principle of life has been compared to the spring of a watch, or the moving powers of other machinery; but its mode of existence is entirely different. In a machine the power is only the cause of the first action or movement, and thereby becomes the remote cause of the second, third, &c.; but this is not the case with an animal; animal matter has a principle of action in every part, independent of the others, and whenever the action of one part (which is always the effect of the living principle,) becomes the cause of an action in another, it is by stimulating the living principle of that other part, the action in the second part being as much the effect of the living principle of that part as the action of the first was of the living principle in it. The living principle, then, is the immediate cause of action in every part; it is therefore essential to every part, and is as much the property of it as gravity is of every particle of matter composing the whole. Every individual particle of the animal matter, then, is possessed of life, and the least imaginable part which we can separate is as much alive as the whole.

The first; and most simple idea of life, I have observed, is its being the principle of self-preservation, preventing matter from falling into dissolution,—for dissolution immediately takes place when matter is deprived of it; and the second is its being the principle of action. These are two very different properties, though arising from the same principle, the first being capable of existing independently of the second; for it may be observed, that it is not necessary for the preservation of animal matter that there should be action in all parts, for many parts of an animal appear to have little action, yet they are as much endued with life as the more active parts; such, for instance, as tendons, elastic ligaments, &c.

A fresh egg is a body which, it must be allowed, has no vital action; yet an egg is as much alive as an animal, which I shall endeavour to

* [This opinion concerning the unity of the principle of life has already been shortly adverted to. It may perhaps be illustrated by referring to the powers of common matter, which are not one, but many. There seems good reason for considering the different kinds of attraction as modifications of a higher principle, and the best reason for believing that magnetism, common electricity, and galvanism proceed from the same source, or at least are essentially identical; the same is highly probable in regard to the powers of life: in analysing physical phenomena, however, it is found far more convenient to consider the powers above mentioned separately, and it cannot be doubted that physiologists would derive equal advantage from pursuing a similar method. According to the author's representation, the modifications of life result simply from differences in the organized apparatus, through which it manifests its effects, nearly in the same way as mechanical force may be made to produce the most different effects, according to the kind of machinery which is employed.]

illustrate by observation and experiment. I was led to this opinion in the year 1757, when I was making drawings of the growth of the chick in the process of incubation. I then observed, that whenever an egg was hatched, the yolk, which is not diminished in the term of incubation, remains sweet to the last, and that part of the albumen which was not employed in the growth of the chick was perfectly sweet some days before the hatching, though both had been kept at a temperature of 103° in a hen's nest for three weeks. But if the egg did not hatch, I observed that it became putrid nearly in the same time that other dead animal matter does.

To determine how far eggs would stand other tests of the presence of the living principle, I made the following experiments : I put an egg into a freezing mixture about zero, and froze it, and then allowed it to thaw. From this process I conceived that the preserving power of the egg must be lost, which proved the case. I then put the egg into a freezing mixture at 15°, and with it a new-laid one, to make the comparison on that which I should call alive, and the difference in the time of freezing was seven minutes and a half, the second one taking so much longer to freeze. 2nd. I put a new-laid egg into a cold between 17° and 15°; it took about half an hour to freeze : when thawed I put it into an atmosphere only at 25°; it froze in half the time, which it should not have done, nor even in half an hour, if it had not been killed by the first experiment, for the atmosphere now was not so cold as in the first experiment by nine degrees. These experiments show that the egg, when living, has a power of resisting cold, which, when killed by freezing, it has not.

To determine the comparative heat of a living and dead egg, and to determine whether a living egg be subject to the same laws with the more imperfect animals, I made the following experiment.

I took a fresh egg, and one which had been frozen, and put them into a cold mixture at 15°. The thawed one soon came down to 32°, began to swell and congeal : the fresh one sunk to 29½°, as happens to living animals, and in twenty-five minutes after the dead one froze. Another reason for supposing it dead was, that before freezing took place it rose to 32°, as other fluids do which are brought below their freezing point.

From these observations and experiments, it must appear that a fresh egg has a power of resisting heat, cold, and putrefaction; and similar results are come to by similar experiments on some of the more imperfect animals, which we shall have occasion to notice hereafter.

It would appear, then, that life is not *action*, but it is continued or supported by it when it takes place. Action creates a necessity of support, and furnishes it. It is not necessary that *action* should continue in all parts ; in some it is only necessary that the principle and power of action should be continued, but in others it is necessary that *action* should take place even for the preservation of the principle of action. Action is necessary for the various purposes for which the animal is intended, and if one species of action takes place, it brings the whole into action, as all the parts and actions of an animal body are dependent upon one another.   If the heart acts, the lungs must fulfill their part ; the stomach must digest; the other parts subservient to this organ must be put in motion, and the secretory organs, nerves, and voluntary muscles. The whole is thus set in motion to produce some ultimate effect, which appears to be the propagation of the species, for preservation (of the individual) cannot be called the ultimate effect.

I have asserted that life simply is the principle of preservation in the animal preserving it from putrefaction ; but there is a curious circumstance attending life which would appear to be contradictory to itself. Life is the preserver of the body from putrefaction, and when life is gone putrefaction would appear soon to begin. But this is not uniform ; it is sooner in some cases than in others ; therefore there must be some other cause than the simple deprivation of life to account for this difference of time.   In the most striking instances of rapid putrefaction after death, it does not appear to arise from the process of putrefaction having gone to some length before total death took place, for in those who die of putrid fever the smell becomes less offensive before death, and when life is gone they do not go into putrefaction as soon as might have been expected, and not nearly so fast as many who had not the least tendency this way before death.   The tendency to putrefaction in those whilst living would appear to be part of the disease, but does not become putrefaction, and on dying they appear to lose that tendency, and to become like other bodies.   However, it is disputed whether, in putrid fever, there is really any putrid matter formed*.

But there is a process or an action in life which predisposes the body for many diseases, and which becomes the remote cause of them ; and there is an action in life which disposes the body for a species of putrefaction (or decomposition) when dead, and very probably death is the effect of this action in these cases.   In these cases the body immediately after death becomes emphysematous ; this emphysema, though it does not occur during life, would yet appear to be an effect of life, for it depends on disease as the body is dying.   It is not genuine putrefaction ; for, when the process is ended, the body keeps nearly as long as if no such process had taken place.   It occurs immediately after death, or perhaps in the act of dying. The process itself seems to con-

---

* [The offensive exhalations here alluded to may probably, in great part, be referred to the excretions, which show a great tendency to run into rapid decomposition.]

tinue when the body is warm; after a time it stops, and the body remains stationary, until it sets out, as it were, for a second time to become putrid. What diseases this is to be classed with I do not know. To ascertain the causes of it with precision, it would be necessary to know the persons when alive, the disease of which they died, and the time when the putrefaction occurred after death. I have myself seen several very remarkable instances of its occurrence. The first was that of a young lady about four months gone with child, who in March or April, about two or three in the afternoon, was suddenly taken ill with a fit, of which she shortly died. She was opened the next morning at seven o'clock, when the body was found swelled with air extravasated in the cellular membrane; the mesentery, intestines, liver, and heart were loaded with air, the blood worked out of the larger vessels mixed with air, and the body had become very offensive.

Another case of the kind occurred at St. George's Hospital, in a man who had an encysted tumour in the upper belly of the right rectus muscle, which contained a fluid: it was opened on Friday, and on the Monday following, in the evening, he became ill, and died at one o'clock. He was opened seventeen hours after death, and was found emphysematous, just as in the former case.

This appears to be similar to what is commonly termed sphacelus, being a species of mortification occurring before death, or in the act of dying.

That the mode of dying assists the process of putrefaction is evident in common mortification, which will be noticed when on that subject, and I may illustrate it further by relating what took place in a case of operation for aneurism.

A man at St. George's Hospital had the operation for popliteal aneurism performed. The artery was tied just where it passes through the tendon of the triceps muscle. The case went on well till the sixth day, when ulceration took place in some part of the artery which was not united: considerable bleeding took place, and recurred several times afterwards, by which so much blood was lost as to become in the end the cause of death. Immediately after the first bleeding, I observed the foot and leg of the diseased side to become cold as high as the middle of the calf, while it was warm about the knee, ham, and upper part of the leg. The lower part of this leg ever after remained cold, and did not in the least change in appearance, from which I conjectured that it was *dead*, not *mortified* (for there is a material difference). I suspected it was *dead* as in common death. He became weaker and weaker every day, and died about four days after. Before he died, the upper parts of the leg, which had gone on with life a little longer, were mortified, that is, they showed evident signs of such a change taking place; a vesication formed, discharging a bloody serum, and they became darker, as if blood was diffused in the cellular membrane, and œdematous, or, rather, emphysematous. A very short time after death these parts became putrid, while the lower part of the leg and foot remained unaltered as in common death. Here was a part which just died for want of circulation, therefore no action took place in that part; but above, where there was action, a very different change took place, producing a tendency to putrefaction after total death had taken place. The part which died naturally without any action did not become putrid, while the part in which that peculiar action took place became putrid directly, though it died later. I took off the two *feet*, to see which of them would become putrid first; for some time it was difficult to perceive any difference, but about sixteen days after, the foot on the sound side began to turn green, and went on to putrefy much faster than the other.

The whole of this part of the case is extremely curious. First, that part of the leg which retained life longest became putrid immediately after death, because during life it took on actions which were productive of putrefaction. The foot of the diseased side, which died early, was not allowed time to take on any actions while living, excepting perhaps that resulting from the stimulus of death, and did not become putrid so soon as the foot on the sound side, which may be said to have died a natural death, and which died later. This I think may be accounted for by supposing that the latter, from surviving some time longer, took on some of those actions which gave the tendency to putrefaction. It may be necessary to explain what I mean by the stimulus of death. Death itself produces an action in all the muscular parts when there is nothing to prevent it. If a man's head be cut off, he becomes stiff; he is not stiff while there is real life : for there is a difference between visible life and real life. A part may be living though not in action; but whenever death takes place it excites an action in every part that is muscular : they contract, and this is the action of death. To cease breathing is not the action of death, though certainly it is the first step towards it, and gives rise to the other. The action of real death is that which takes place in the stiffening of the body, and till then it is not dead (except when killed in a peculiar manner—killed universally before the stimulus of death can be given,—and then it remains lax).

I suppose, then, that this foot, which died first from the loss of blood, became stiff; that is, took on action resulting from the stimulus of death, all the muscular parts contracting ;—that in the other foot the stimulus of death was in some measure lost, from the longer continuance of the diseased state, and the consequent action was less strong. What would be the consequence of this? I take a man in perfect health, and cut off both his legs; to one I give a stroke of electricity sufficient to kill the part before it contracts, and no contraction takes place; the other I leave to itself and let the stimulus of death produce contraction: this latter shall not become putrid so rapidly as the former.

CHAPTER III.

THE BLOOD.

Reasons for its fluidity ;—erroneous views respecting its nature.—Anima-lization and vivification two distinct steps in the conversion of foreign matter into part of a living body.—Blood not merely fluid animal mat-ter ;—has also become vivified ;—arguments for this opinion.—Coagula-tion of blood ;—its importance in determining the nature of blood ;—varieties in the process.— Case proving the life of the blood.—Death of the blood preventing coagulation.

WHAT I have had hitherto principally in view has been the solid animal matter, its formation, and its arrangement by which it is endued with life, composing, as it were, the whole visible body. The fluid part of the compound now remains to be taken notice of.

Blood is the material out of which the whole body is formed and out of which it is supported*. It is fluid that it may be capable of moving to the very minutest part of the solid with ease, and may with less dif-ficulty be divided for the increase and repairs of the different parts of the machine ; easy of division and separation, to form various secretions, and also to bring back what was superabundant, and to carry off the parts which were useless.

This part of the body has been considered as a passive, inanimate, moving fluid, found everywhere in the body, deriving motion from the heart for the various purposes of the whole, then returning to the heart to be sent out again. Those who have formed this idea of the blood have no adequate notion of the manner in which it is capable of per-forming those great uses above mentioned. Some, in considering this fluid, have been in a great measure satisfied with examining the spon-taneous changes which it undergoes out of the circulation. This might have led them to draw some natural conclusions, since all natural phe-nomena are facts, and teach enough of a thing to enable us to draw sound conclusions. Others have attended to the chemical analysis, which teaches nothing with respect to its use in the living body ; for blood gives no analysis excepting that of common animal matter†.

---

* [The expression of Bourdon is peculiarly elegant: "*Le sang est de la chair coulante.*"]

† [This observation is no longer true. Some important additions to physiology have of late years been obtained from chemical investigation of the blood with the present improved means of analysis; and with further improvements we may expect still more light to be thrown on the subject. The subject will be more fully considered when the ' Treatise on the Blood,' &c., comes before us.]

Some inquirers have laid great stress on its appearance when viewed with a microscope, as if forms of parts would explain first principles : this they cannot do unless in operations that are mechanical. This inquiry could be carried no further than to investigate such parts of the blood as have form and opacity, if there are such, and that which appears to have both is called red blood : in a great number of animals, therefore, the knowledge of the operations of the blood in the animal body rests nearly in the same state that it did some centuries ago. The two last points of investigation, namely, the chemical analysis of the blood and the form of the blood globules, though very proper to be made by physiologists, have hitherto explained nothing in the animal œconomy.

Before I explain my opinion of the blood, it may be not improper first to state some facts from which I draw my conclusions.

I have endeavoured to show that animal matter differs from common matter in many circumstances; that this animal matter has a principle peculiar to itself, which I call *life*, and this life is the second step or process of animal matter. Animalization is the first; vivification the second. To prove this, I observed that an animal is increased and supported by many substances which previously had not the properties of animal matter, and of course not the principle called animal life ; I observed, too, that it was also supported by substances which were of animal origin, but which had not then the living principle : in other words, an animal can be supported on dead vegetable and animal matter. In the next place it was remarked that these substances, before they can increase or support the animal, must all be converted into animal matter ; and lastly, that the substances must be so prepared, or animalized, as to become part of the body, and of course to be endued with the living principle.

It is now necessary to trace these changes in the food till it becomes part of our solids, and observe as we go along when it is most probable that life begins.

Blood is not simply fluid animal matter, it is animal matter particularly arranged, for it differs in every respect from fluid animal matter produced by art. The first change that takes place with vegetable matter before it is rendered blood is its conversion into animal matter. This change I call animalization. With animal matter it might be supposed that no change was necessary to produce animalization ; but we find the change, whatever it may be, the same in both ; and the process in both is probably similar, for the produce from the digestion of animal matter is as different from common animal matter as anything can be : were it not so, animal substances rendered fluid by chemical operations, as jellies, &c., would answer the same purpose as blood. But the necessity for a total and similar change in both is evident, for out of this change life is to arise, digestion being the first step towards vivification. It may be supposed that the first step in the digestion of vegetables is that of animalizing them, and that they go through the next of chylification with animal matter; but this we cannot allow, for it would be supposing two different actions going on in the stomach at the same time, which I should very much doubt.

The second process, vivification, must take place somewhere before the blood becomes an active part of the machine. We shall first premise that animalization may take place without vivification—(how far this is the case is not easily determined,)—however, we may say with certainty that vivification cannot be prior to animalization. Let us first trace animalization.

Animalization begins in the stomach, and in common language is called digestion, the immediate produce of which is called chyle. In the change of food into chyle we do not see why it may not have received the living principle, for the change is such as renders it capable of becoming alive. But it may be supposed that this process is reserved for the lungs, where the chyle is so much exposed to the air : the air may be imagined to act on it like heat on an egg, or moisture and warmth on seeds, giving a power of growth to their particles. In these cases, however, it is not the principle of life which they give; they only give life its action.

Again, blood may be supposed not to become alive till it be made into a solid, when it becomes part of our body, and loses the property of blood, and there its life is indisputable; but I am apt to believe that the living principle takes place sooner, which I imagine will appear in investigating the properties of the blood, with the many phenomena that attend it in the living body.

I have already observed that the organization of animal matter is not necessary for life*, only for its actions ; therefore fluidity is no objection to the blood being alive. My reasons for supposing the blood to be alive in a fluid state are the following : 1st, It may be observed that it appears to carry life to every part of the body, for whenever the whole or a part is deprived of fresh blood it very soon dies. This blood, however, must be such as has undergone some change in the lungs ; for if the

---

* [This has ever been a *quæstio vexata* with physiologists, and will probably long continue so. The instance of the egg which has been already adduced, and of the blood, which now comes under consideration, were supposed by Mr. Hunter to demonstrate the existence of vitality *independently* of organization. Although, however, the fact of the vitality of the blood and of the egg should be admitted, it yet remains to be proved that the globules of which they both appear to consist do not present incipient traces of organization: but the question is not one which can be entered into here.]

blood did not undergo this change it would probably soon die, therefore would not be capable of keeping up the living principle in other parts. This effect arising from the want of fresh blood is so evident that it needs no illustration ; I may therefore conclude that it is the only cause and support of life, the nerves having no other part in it but to produce some of the actions,—not life itself, for without this support the nerves themselves die. 2ndly, We may observe that whilst circulating, or in useful motion, it is always found in a fluid state. Hence I think I may be allowed to say, as it is never found in a solid form in the cavity of the blood-vessels, that it has not the least tendency to become solid; that such a state is contrary to its nature. This must arise from some principle which is probably both in the blood and the vessel. The want of disposition to coagulate whilst moving in the living vessel does not arise from the motion, for in many places where the motion is extremely slow the blood remains fluid. We have instances of this in the veins of the leg, where the crural artery has been tied, in which case the blood only moves through a few small collateral branches below, and back again by the larger veins. Now, a small quantity of blood being sent into these larger vessels, the motion in them must be next to stagnation ; yet, while there is any degree of motion, the irritation of imperfection is not given ; there is consciousness of its being an useful part ; by which is meant that the harmony between the solids and fluids is kept up. It is curious often to see the small quantity of motion which shall keep up this mutual harmony. In cases where people have been days, or even weeks, in trances, where there is not the least perceptible motion in the blood, it has retained its fluidity, because both solids and fluids retained their life, though not their actions. The want of disposition to coagulate in such situations does not arise from any property in the blood simply as animal matter, for simply as animal matter (whose alterations arise out of its composition, as fermentation,) it would not vary in its effects from circumstances that do not in the least alter the nature of the compound.

Dead animal matter acts on the living body as any other foreign or extraneous matter ; therefore, the blood being in perfect harmony with the living principles of the solids when both are in perfect health, is a presumption that the blood is alive. However, this argument is not conclusive, for we find in the blood heterogeneous parts which do not destroy this harmony ; most probably those heterogeneous bodies are introduced simply as stimulants to the living principle, as extraneous objects are to the sensitive.

This harmony of the blood with the solids is more observable in some parts than others. The parts with which it is in the greatest harmony are the vessels; this is evident from its retaining its fluidity longer in contact with them without motion than in any other part of the body, though equally inclosed in living parts.

All the diseases which act on the solids act on the blood, causing it to effect those changes which arise spontaneously from rest out of the body; so that blood is as capable of diseased *actions* as the solids are. If the blood did not change in the diseased states of the solids, it would lose the natural harmony I have been speaking of. This change is according to the state of the solids, which shows the intimate connexion between the two; it is not a primary diseased alteration of the fluids, but a consent with the diseased disposition of the solids*.

On the other hand, the solids are affected by diseases of the blood: I even suspect death in the blood can take place independently of the solids; but the death of the solids will soon follow.

The blood when at rest has a disposition to separate into several parts, viz. coagulable lymph, red particles, and serum; the red part being retained in the coagulable matter, and the serum squeezed out in the act of coagulation. This disposition in one of the parts to coagulate when at rest, from whence the above changes are produced, is more or less strong, according to circumstances.

This property of the blood deserves particular attention, as it throws more light on its nature than any point of view in which it can be considered, it being spontaneous and natural. It is by this change that the solids are formed, and it seems to me so important that I think it almost the only thing necessary to be considered more fully; indeed the power of coagulation in the blood throws so much light on the nature of a disease, so far as the blood is concerned, that it is almost the only part we have recourse to in the examination of the blood after bleeding,

---

* [How far the blood can originate an *action* within itself, for the purpose, as it were, of bringing itself into harmony with the changed condition of the solids, is a question which I think will generally be answered in the negative. That the blood *does* harmonize with the solids is an incontestible fact; but then the cause of this harmony is in the solids themselves, either directly by an impression communicated to the blood by the vessels, or indirectly from some defect in the processes of nutrition and sanguification; some retention or vitiation of the secretions; some introduction of deleterious matter, or some fault in some one or more of the vital actions. According to Mr. Hunter's own definition (p. 231), action requires organization, and yet the great difficulty which he is even now combating is, how the blood, an *unorganized* fluid, should possess life. In short, there is the strictest kind of reciprocity between the solids and fluids; not, however, arising as parallel effects, but as cause and effect; the solids, being altered, necessarily modify the blood, and the blood, being modified, as certainly reacts upon the solids. In this point of view, to employ the words of Andral, "On ne trouve plus de sens aux disputes des solidistes et des humoristes: l'économie ne paraît plus qu'un *grand tout*, indivisible, dans l'état de santé comme dans l'état de maladie."]

when we look to see whether or not the blood is buffy, that is, whether there has been a disposition for the red globules to sink faster in such blood; or rather, perhaps, that from such blood being longer in coagulating, the red globules have time to sink to the bottom, and leave the coagulable lymph atop free from red globules, and this causes the buff of the blood*. It is by this coagulation also that we perceive whether the blood is cupped or not, that is, whether the coagulum draws together and its edges rise; and then we say that the blood is not only inflammatory, but highly so, showing great strength in the constitution: if, on the other hand, it lies flat in the cup, and makes an even uniform surface, we know it is rather loose in its texture (although it may be still buffy), which shows that the powers of the constitution are weak.

The red globules abstracted, or the red blood abstracted from the other parts, need hardly be considered, as they hardly explain anything.

The serum also explains but very little; there may be more or less of it than common, but in itself it explains very little.

The power of coagulating in the blood is greater when out of the circulation and exposed to common air, even more than when extravasated in some cavities of the body, the necessity or use of which is evident, for by this it becomes more effectual in stopping extravasation. A striking instance of this kind happened in the crural artery of a boar. I cut it through and allowed it to bleed; but before the animal became weak, or at least had the appearance of weakness, the bleeding became less and less, till at last it stopped. On examining the artery, it was found to have a quantity of coagulated blood opposing and surrounding its cut end like a mop, through which the blood could not pass.

This power of coagulation, especially when exposed, enables the blood to unite external wounds more readily, and of course preserves the living principle better, and keeps the internal parts from exposure in many wounds which otherwise would become external: by this means they are united by the first intention.

---

* [The buffy coat is undoubtedly mainly due to the cause which Mr. Hunter has assigned. Dr. Davy, however, has remarked, and I think the observation will be borne out by the experience of every one, that this phenomenon is sometimes exhibited, even in a marked degree, although the coagulation shall have taken place more rapidly than usual; nay, a blueish and transparent lymph may often be observed to have separated from the other parts within thirty seconds after the blood is drawn, and consequently much sooner than under ordinary circumstances. There seems, therefore, reason for believing that the buffy coat is referrible in some measure to a greater relative difference in the specific gravities of the coagulable lymph and red globules than natural, as well as to the slowness of the coagulation. Mr. Hunter partly also accounted for the appearance of buffy blood, by supposing that "the blood has an increased disposition to separate into its component parts;" a supposition which I cannot but think is borne out by many facts.]

In all inflammatory dispositions in the solids, whether universal or local, the blood has an increased disposition to separate into its component parts, the red globules become less uniformly diffused, and their attraction to one another becomes stronger, so that the blood when out of the vessels soon becomes cloudy or muddy, and dusky in its colour, and when spread over any surface it appears mottled, the red blood attracting itself and forming spots of red. This is so evident in many cases that it is hardly necessary to wait till the whole coagulates to form a judgment of it. I think I can say when the blood is coming from the vessel, by its appearance in the stream, whether it will be sizy or not. When the blood has not an inflammatory disposition the stream has a degree of uniformity and transparency in its appearance : but it is only an eye accustomed to it that can make this distinction.

If the inflammatory disposition of the solids arises from fever, this disposition in the blood is universal. If there is universal inflammatory disposition, from some local irritation, the blood is still universally affected. But if the inflammation is local, and the constitution is not affected, the disposition in the blood is not universal : how far there is local inflammatory disposition of the blood I do not know, but there is reason, however, to suspect it, from the ready union of parts under inflammation. If the blood does become inflamed in passing through an inflamed part, we must suppose that it immediately loses that disposition when it meets with parts in perfect health*.

These properties, namely, increased disposition to separate, and a disposition to become a firmer solid, always show increased disposition for action in the living principle, and also, most probably, increased power. It is one of the signs of strength of the living powers, although the materials for action are weak.

The use of this change in the blood is evident, since it is made fitter for uniting parts by this means ; and it is from this disposition that the blood retains its living principle sufficiently long till union takes place.

---

* [That the blood undergoes peculiar changes, losing its globular character, its transparency, and the vividness of its colour, as well as its motion, in the vessels of inflamed parts, is evident, from the observations of Levret, Kaltenbrunner, Dollinger, and others, who have microscopically investigated this subject. These changes are most likely due to the influence of the vessels upon their contents; but to suppose that the blood itself can be the subject of inflammation, is to suppose it endowed not only with life and organisation, but with life and organisation of a high degree, for from the best observations which have been made it does not seem probable that those animals which are lowest in the zoological scale are capable of inflammatory action. Certainly we can form no definite idea of inflammation, except as connected with vascular and organised parts, although, from what is said further on, Hunter did not carry his ideas of the blood to that extent.]

Unless the stimulus of necessity for coagulation is given by the solids, the extravasated blood will not coagulate, it will only act as an extraneous body, which often happens where union is unnecessary, improper, or hurtful, as in cases of contusions, where the blood remains fluid in the cellular membrane.

This disposition to coagulate when out of the vessels, or when retained in them without motion till the consciousness of the use of motion, and of course of fluidity, is lost, is one of the effects of the life of the blood.

I have used the word *consciousness* because we have no language existing answerable to all my views of the animal œconomy, and to coin words would not answer the purpose, because then I must have a dictionary of my own. I have not a word for expressing the cause of those actions which take place in the body, as if it was conscious that such and such things were going to take place. There are actions in the body which come the nearest to consciousness of the mind of anything that I can conceive, and therefore I make use of this word; but it is commonly applied by philosophers only to the mind.

Coagulation is a species of attraction arising out of this irritation*. It may be considered as a species of generation, for it is the first action or establishment of a power of action within itself, so as to form itself into muscular fibres, the only powers in an animal: these, again, with other parts, form organs to act on the materials from which they arose, for their own support.

I will relate a case in proof of most of the arguments which I have employed respecting the life of the blood. It is one of many.

A man came to St. George's Hospital who had a hydrocele, for which he was tapped with a lancet. The water was clear serum: when this was evacuated, the testicle to the feel was found to be larger than natural. About a month after, the tunica vaginalis became as full as before: the radical cure was now determined on, the tunica vaginalis was slit up its whole length, and the fluid, which was now bloody, was evacuated. The testicle, on being exposed, was found larger than natural, and was extracted. On the body of the testicle,

---

* [Hunter uses the term *irritation* in place of the *exciting cause*. His meaning, therefore, seems to be that the *consciousness of necessity* is the *exciting cause* of coagulation, or that coagulation arises from the *irritation* of this *consciousness*. This is an instance of false logic, or of reasoning from final causes, which he not unfrequently displayed: he has described the objects to be attained by coagulation, and he here states that the necessity of effecting these objects is the cause of the coagulation, which is much the same as to say it is so, because it is so. It is evident that this does not in the least help us to discover the proximate causes of coagulation.]

and nearly in the direction of its long axis, and opposite to the orifice in the sac made by the lancet when the water was first evacuated, lay a coagulum of blood, dark in colour, almost like a leech when that animal is shortened, about two inches long, and of the thickness of a common-sized little finger. In the angles between the epididymis and body of the testicle lay another coagulum, adhering in some places to the epididymis, in other parts loose to the body : it was attached only at one end. The adhesions of the large coagulum to the body of the testicle were firm, although it would admit of separation. This was made at one end, when fibres were plainly seen running from the testicle to the coagulum. The adhesion of the small coagulum was in many parts still firmer. All over the tunica vaginalis there were a great many vessels full of blood, and in many parts coagula of blood like extravasation. In this state I had a drawing made of it, and a small part magnified, to show the vessels and the dots of extravasation as they then appeared. By being put into water all these vessels and dots disappeared, and the parts became white. I then injected the testicle by the spermatic artery, which succeeded extremely well. On examining the part, I observed the following appearances. The surface of the testicle and tunica vaginalis had resumed the former appearance, only with this difference, that the injection was of a lighter red than the blood to the naked eye, and much more so to a small magnifier. The vessels on the surface were very distinct, and the dots, where the extravasation of injection was as if there had been extravasation of blood. The coagulum on the tunica vaginalis now appeared vascular ; the surface of the adhesion, for about one twentieth of an inch, was injected and extremely full of distinct vessels. The smaller coagulum was injected in many places through and through its whole substance, in the other only for a little way.

If it should be asked, How came those coagula there? The answer is, the blood from the wound made by the lancet in the tunica vaginalis passed into the cavity, and then coagulated on the testicle directly opposite to the wound, and a small quantity of the blood which got down to the chink between the testis and epididymis coagulated there also. That this is the most probable way of accounting for it is, I think, strengthened by another case, where the tunica vaginalis was found adhering to the testicle, when performing the radical cure, at the very part where he had before been tapped. In half a year probably this coagulum would have become wholly vascular, and probably in a little longer time the whole would have been taken away ; because, being vascular, it would have had absorbents, which would have taken it all, as a useless part, into the constitution.

The tunica vaginalis filling again so rapidly in this case was perhaps the reason why it did not adhere to the coagulum on the other side, so as to produce a union between the two parts.

Quære, For what purpose did this coagulum become vascular ?* for no visible purpose could be answered by it, as absorption, we may suppose, might have taken place as easily in a coagulum as in the cellular membrane. But perhaps absorption not going on here was the cause of the collection of water; and adhesive inflammation evidently took place here that it might be able to absorb itself.

Thus, then, the materials of which the blood is composed are joined with the living principle; in consequence of which the blood, if properly disposed, is capable, when extravasated, of forming itself spontaneously into parts fit for motion, and for performing all the offices of any part of the living whole, successively receiving the stimulus of nature from the surrounding parts to form itself into a similar part, as bone, cartilage, &c.

In many diseases not inflammatory, namely, those called putrid, where the solids have a tendency to fall into those changes natural to animal matter deprived of its preserving principle, the blood has no disposition to coagulate, nor the solids any power of raising inflammation, both having taken on the same disposition. In such a disease both the principle and power are diminished, so that life is hardly able to preserve the matter from falling into its natural changes, though it has still a disposition to keep the vital parts or body moving.

Many kinds of death as well as putrid diseases produce this effect on the blood; an instance of which was met with in a gentleman, who being in perfect health, died instantaneously from passion, this having been so violent as to produce death in every part at once, and his blood did not coagulate.

A healthy woman was taken in labour of her fourth child. As the child was coming into the world the woman died almost instantly. On

---

* [The opinion that coagulated blood can become vascular, and so afford the common basis of union by the first intention, was firmly entertained by Mr. Hunter; but the proofs which are here adduced in favour of such an opinion are by no means so conclusive as they should be to establish so important a doctrine. For, not to mention the length of time which elapsed, in the present cases, between the injuries received and the appearances observed, the situation and definite form of the coagula would rather favour the idea that they proceeded from effused lymph, which became more or less intermixed with effused blood. Such an intermixture is generally observed in cases of wounds and operations, but I am not aware of any unequivocal example of pure coagula which have been observed to become vascular, although it is scarcely possible that this should have escaped observation if it were at all frequent. See Plates XVIII. and XIX. for the appearances alluded to in the text.]

opening the body next day, there appeared no cause for death whatever, every part being natural and sound; but the blood was in a fluid state, nor did it coagulate on being exposed.

A soldier, a healthy young man, confined for desertion, received a blow on the pit of his stomach from one of his comrades, from which he dropped down, and died almost instantly. On opening the body, no preternatural appearance was observed, but the blood was in a perfectly fluid state, and did not coagulate when taken out of the vessels and exposed a considerable time.

In animals struck dead by lightning the blood does not coagulate nor the muscles contract, both being killed at once.

There are other instances. Two deer were hunted to death, in which case they acted until the very power of action ceased, and of course death ensued. On opening them the blood was fluid, only a little thickened, and the muscles were not rigid, as we find them, where they are capable of acting, from the stimulus of death. In both cases the life of the solids and of the blood was destroyed at the same time and at once*.

The observation that animals hunted to death are tenderer than those killed by other means is not uncommon.

There is a natural action of the living body which destroys the life of the blood in the act of extravasation; this is the discharge of the menses in women. If that discharge is natural and healthy, the blood does not coagulate; but, on the other hand, if the extravasation is not a healthy one, the blood coagulates as it is extravasated, and comes away in clots. This perhaps is best demonstrated in cases where the hymen is unperforated and the menses are accumulated. This observation leads us to understand something of the nature of the menses; for, depend on it, where a woman has her menses come away in clots, it is not a natural but a diseased discharge.

To prove that the blood and the solids correspond very much in their actions of death, we shall only generally observe, that when an animal dies in the common way, it is by the vital actions being first destroyed; but life still exists, for the muscles contract and the blood coagulates.

---

* [The diversity of circumstances under which the blood remains fluid after death at present renders any generalization upon the subject impossible. This is so much the case that many able physiologists of the present day are disposed to ascribe the incoagulability of the blood to a cause the very reverse of that assigned by Hunter, viz. to a greater residual vitality in the blood and vessels than in ordinary death, by virtue of which the fluidity of the blood is preserved until the disposition to coagulation is lost. But this explanation, like the former, explains only half of the cases. See Notes to the Treatise on the Blood and Inflammation.]

But if we destroy life instantaneously, or along with the vital actions, then the muscles will not act, and the blood will remain fluid*.

These changes in the blood, which appear spontaneous, are not really so; they arise from irritation in the blood itself as much as any actions in the solids. This irritation excites the natural action of the blood, which produces these effects and all the properties we see the blood possesses in either a healthy or diseased state.

We cannot suppose the blood has a power of communicating sensations, as it cannot have nerves; its living powers are therefore those of simple life, and it is similar in that respect to the solids of many animals.

As sensation is a principle superadded, and intended to convey fixed intelligence, it is unnecessary for a moving part to have it; but when it becomes a fixed and solid part it opens a communication with the mind.

Thus far I have endeavoured to show that the blood is as much endued with life as the solids are; and the only difference between the two is that the solids have construction, called organization, producing considerable visible effects, while the blood, not having this construction, does not produce these visible effects. The truth of this theory will appear more evident in treating of the diseases of the animal body†.

---

* [In Bichat's language, the animal life dies first, and after that the organic life. The muscles stiffen by organic contractility.]

† [The reader will form a better idea of the greater copiousness of the present copy of Lectures as compared with Mr. Parkinson's "*Reminiscences*," when he is informed that the whole of the preceding pages are comprised in less than seven pages of the latter. The consideration of the blood is less fully entered into here than in the Treatise on the Blood and Inflammation; but the reader will not fail to observe that Mr. Hunter often speaks with less reserve on many points in the former than in the latter; although in judging of his opinions, those contained in his Treatise on the Blood should undoubtedly be preferred, as being the result of his last and most deliberative judgment.]

CHAPTER IV.

ORGANIZATION AND ACTION.

General views of organization and action.—Arrangement of matter into certain forms to answer the end required;—these structures combine to form organs;—organs arranged according to certain laws constitute animals.—Organization and life distinct from each other.—Action exists in every part of an animal;—depends on contractility.—Of two kinds;—common—and peculiar.—These are mutually dependent;—of the first kind, all involuntary;—of the second, nearly all so;—cessation of the latter in disease;—Mr. Hunter's own case.—Of the second, digestion, circulation, and respiration are most closely connected with the first;—others, as motion of the limbs, more distantly.—Motion may be caused by elastic forces reacting, as in ligaments.—Conclusion.

FROM what I have said above, it must appear that original or common matter has been first so decomposed, and then again so combined, as to become animal matter. This animal matter next became so arranged as to become alive. Now I shall observe that these combinations and arrangements are differently modified, so as to produce the various kinds of animal substances; some of which have their parts so disposed as to have motion among themselves, as muscles; others to have sensation, as brain and nerves; and in others the living parts are so disposed as to acquire other properties, as elasticity, rigidity, &c.

Solidity, in a certain degree, is necessary for self-motion; for parts cannot produce motion in one another without some resistance or fixed point of motion. We therefore find the acting parts of an animal composed of solids, or the parts which compose them could not coalesce together by the attraction of cohesion; and it is necessary that it should be so, as without this no determined action could be produced.

Now we have gone so far with the materials of an animal, let us next examine how these materials are disposed so as to form an animal. These materials may now be considered in a mechanical point of view, like the component parts of a machine, each of which has its destined use and own peculiarity of form. These are united with each other to form parts, the whole forming organs of various kinds to produce the mechanical effects required. These organs, again, united according to certain established rules, form animals. This compounding of animal matter is what should be understood by organization.

Now if this idea of organization is just, organization and life are two different things; for, according to this definition, a dead body is as much organized as a living one, for in the dead body the same mechanism exists as in the living one.

Organization, then, comes nearest our ideas of the mechanical formation of parts, and the ultimate effect must be mechanical; for it is impossible to produce motion in matter without having a mechanical effect.

Having considered simple life, and the general idea of what is called organization, we shall next consider *the Actions of an Animal*.

We have said that animal matter is so constructed as to be endued with a power of self-motion, as in a muscle; and as we can hardly conceive any part of an animal entirely passive or free from motion, since all parts grow and are nourished, we must suppose this muscular structure very universal in an animal body, though this power has been considered principally in regard to muscles, properly so called, whose actions are plainly visible to the eye*.

The different necessary circumstances attending the composition of a muscular fibre, with the mode of action of a muscle, we shall not touch upon, the field being too large for my present purpose. I shall only observe that they are the animal powers by the immediate actions of which every, the smallest, part of an animal is moved†.

Every machine has its power; a clock has either a spring or weight, and so on. In mechanics the parts are dependent on one another, so that some *one* power is necessary to put the whole in motion; in mechanics too there is commonly but one ultimate effect produced, whereas in an animal body there are a thousand. The powers therefore of an animal body are differently placed and circumstanced from what they are in an inanimate machine: it is not one power that is setting the whole to work, because if that were the case an animal's actions would always be the same, but he is at rest in one part, moving in another, and so on; and as this is the case, he must have power in every part,

---

* [The author has elsewhere (See Introd. to Inflam.) defined life to be that power which renders the body "susceptible of impressions which excite action;" a definition which, however brief, exhibits in miniature the leading features of Bichat's celebrated hypothesis, according to which all the actions and phenomena of life are ultimately referred to two primary principles—namely, sensibility and contractility.]

† [The reader is referred to Mr. Hunter's Croonian Lectures on Muscular Motion, in the *fourth* Volume, where will be found a more full account of this subject.]

so that his powers are diffused through the whole animal, which is almost composed of powers.

· The actions of an animal, considered as a whole, should be divided into two kinds. 1st, Those actions common to every part alike, such as those which are employed in the internal operations of the machine, as growth, alteration, building up, taking down, &c., every individual part (the smallest conceivable*) acting for itself only, which actions may be called immediate. These are probably performed by the ends of vessels, whether the terminations of arteries or the beginning of absorbents; likewise the actions of the brain are of this kind. 2nd, Those actions which are of whole parts, and which vary according to their composition or construction, being employed chiefly respecting other matter, not for the immediate use of themselves, as in those above mentioned, but still absolutely necessary for the first.. These actions are of whole parts, as the stomach, heart, organs of respiration, organs of sensation, mind and will. That these actions differ from the first is evident, because the organs in which they are found have also the first, and are indebted to the first for their existence, in the same way that the first are indebted to the second for their continuance : the stomach, lungs, heart, and other organs of life, may be said to be continually supplying materials with which the first are employed in building and repairing the system. The second kind may be called labourers, being subservient to the first, which, as being engaged in laying down and taking up parts, may be called the bricklayers. It is the first which compose the movements of the true animal, being those which are immediately employed about itself. It is the operations of these which properly constitute the animal œconomy respecting itself, and it will be principally these which I shall consider.

The whole of the first kind of actions are involuntary, the will having no power over them, the mind being not even conscious of them, although it has involuntarily considerable influence over them under circumstances of diseased and irregular action. Most of the actions of the second kind are subservient to the first, and are absolutely necessary to the continuation of their existence. These have therefore a

---

* [It seems now to be generally admitted by microscopical observers that even the globules of the blood possess an inherent power of motion, in their quality of organized parts. Wolff, Dollinger, Treviranus, Kaltenbrunner, &c. have noticed a variety of movements of this kind, which are principally of a rotary or volvular kind.—See Revue Méd. vol. ix. 1828, and Journ. des Mag. des Sciences Méd. vol. viii. 1828, and also the Treatise on the Blood and Inflammation, where this subject is further considered. Tiedemann calls the blood-globules "the elementary organic forms;" and several of the French physiologists have thought that they might not improperly be classed with the infusorial animalculæ.

R 2

certain degree of regularity, and according to the relationship or immediate necessity of the second to the first are these second permanent
and constant; indeed we seldom find in them any intermission, perhaps never in health; however, in disease they are sometimes stopped.
There have been instances where the motion of the heart has ceased,
and also the involuntary action of breathing :—this once happened to
myself.

I had the gout in my feet three springs successively, and missed it
the fourth.   In the fifth spring, one day at ten o'clock in the forenoon,
I was attacked suddenly with a pain nearly about the pylorus : it was
a pain peculiar to those parts, and became so violent that I tried every
position to relieve myself, but could get no ease.   I then took a tea-
spoonful of tincture of rhubarb, with thirty drops of laudanum, but
still found no relief.   As I was walking about the room, I cast my eyes
on a looking-glass, and observed my countenance pale, my lips white,
and I had the appearance of a dead man looking at himself.   This
alarmed me.   I could feel no pulse in either arm.   The pain still continuing, I began to think it very serious.   I found myself at times not
breathing; and being afraid of death soon taking place if I did not
breathe, I produced a voluntary action of breathing, working my lungs
by the power of my will.   I continued in this state three quarters of
an hour, when the pain lessened, the pulse was felt, and involuntary
breathing began to take place.   During this state I took madeira,
brandy, ginger, and other warm things; but I believe nothing did any
good, as the return of health was very gradual.   About two o'clock I
was able to go about my business.

Here, then, was a suspension of the most material involuntary actions,
so much so that the involuntary action of breathing stopped, while sensation and all the voluntary actions were as strong as before.

Quære, What would have been the consequence if I had not breathed?
At the time, it struck me that I should have died; but that most probably would not have been the consequence, because, most probably,
breathing is only necessary for the blood when it is circulating; but as
there was no circulation going on, so no good could have arisen from
breathing*.

---

* [It is probable that the circulation, although enfeebled, still continued to be carried on in this case as in Lipothymia, occurring from severe and sudden injuries to
vital parts.   It would be contrary to every fact with which we are acquainted to suppose that the animal and organic functions could be executed or maintained in an
active state without a due supply of fresh blood.   The respiration is almost if not altogether suspended during the state of hybernation; but then the animal functions, and
as far as we know the organic functions also, are suspended.   The same thing likewise
occurs in those states which have been denominated trances and in cases of Asphyxia.]

The stomach appears to have been the seat of this affection. Affections of the stomach appear to have more influence on every part of the body than any other one part has on another; and this sympathy is reciprocal, for every part has a power of affecting the stomach, which shall be more fully treated of hereafter.

Of the second kind of actions, those which may be considered as having the nearest relationship to the first, are digestion, circulation, and respiration; these are all secondary actions of the machine. Those which are not so closely connected with the first, but respect more the actions of other parts of the same body, or what may be called remote parts of the animal œconomy, are the actions of muscles in moving the limbs, sensations, and voluntary actions employed on external objects, as progressive motion, modes of catching food, &c. We may just observe, that in a muscle itself which has the power of moving other parts, we find the two kinds of actions; first, growth and support as in every other part; and secondly, the action peculiar to the muscle itself. The first kind of actions arise immediately from the living principle, and have always been ranked as involuntary actions; the second are either involuntary, as the actions of whole organs,—the stomach, the heart, &c.,—or are voluntary and dependent on the will, as common muscles &c.: but these last I shall leave till I have spoken of the brain and nerves.

Besides this action in parts, which I have said is confined to muscles, there is another mode of action introduced, that of parts having the living principle which yet have not a power of self-action like muscles; these are the elastic ligaments.

The elasticity of these parts does not depend on life, for it exists equally in dead as in live parts. Ligaments are employed to assist muscles in keeping certain parts in their places, the position of which is long continued. They may be considered as producing a secondary action in the machine. These are more common in some parts in some animals than in others; such as the neck of quadrupeds, especially those with long necks, as the camel; and on the abdomen of some animals, as the elephant: this power is also introduced in the vascular system.

There are other parts introduced into the machine which possess no action that can affect any other part, but have a kind of passive use in the machine. These vary in their consistence according to the uses made of them, some being extremely firm, as bones, tendons, &c., which sustain the actions of different parts of the animal, and without which it could not subsist; others are less firm, and are employed in uniting the various parts as cellular membrane.

From all that has been advanced, we see that by the juxtaposition or union of living parts organs are formed, which gives us the first mode of action, and the form of bodies gives the secondary mode. By the union of these various parts compound motion is produced. In this manner the whole of the most complicated animal machine is produced. The power of self-action which animal and vegetable matter possesses, distinguishes it from matter endued with any other properties than life, and also distinguishes living from dead matter*.

---

* [Muscular contractility, which bears not the slightest analogy to any other power of matter, was yet frequently confounded at the time of Hunter with the principle of elasticity. Hunter was the first to show that this was never the source of actual power, like muscles, but depended on a reaction in bodies in a contrary direction to the original impressing force, and always in proportion to it.

It is still, however, very difficult to refer to their true causes many of the phenomena presented by skin, membranes, fibrous coats, &c., which obviously contract and relax in various degrees under different conditions of the system. Most frequently these phenomena are to be accounted for upon the principle of *tonicity*, a power analogous to muscular contraction. Some, however, have been disposed to assign elasticity as the sole cause. (See Bostock's Phy., Vol. I. ch. iii., and Majendie's Lect. 8—10. *apud* Lancet, Vol. I. 1834-5.)]

CHAPTER V.

FUNCTIONS OF NUTRITION AND ABSORPTION.

The Stomach;—peculiar and essential to animals;—intimately connected with other vital organs;—less with parts not vital;—sympathy with internal parts greater;—compared with the sympathy of the brain with external parts;—greater with ligaments and tendons than with muscles. Sympathy of the stomach with the mind.
Vascular System;—its actions necessary to be understood.—Arteries;—secretion.—Veins;—formerly supposed absorbents.—Absorbents.—Relative offices of the three systems of vessels.—Various kinds of absorption;—modelling absorption, as during the growth of bones;—absorption of entire parts.—Supposed solvent.—Mouths of absorbents.—Alterations of matter absorbed.—Table of absorption.

Of the Stomach.—Every animal body, however compounded, must have the means of support, especially as it is by gradual increase to complete its own magnitude. To this end the living parts fitted for preparing nourishment are thrown into the form of a bag, which is adapted for retaining the food; and this bag is endued with the power of secreting a matter which has the property of converting many vegetable, and all animal, substances into a substance of one kind. This part is called the stomach, and in the less perfect animals it not only makes a considerable part of the whole animal in respect to size, but also in respect to its use in the machine, being the most considerable part of the whole. It may be considered as the first part of an animal, ever becoming more and more simple as the animal becomes more simple; and also as the animal becomes more simple, becoming proportionately the larger part of the animal.

The stomach is the distinguishing part between an animal and a vegetable; for we do not know any vegetable that has a stomach nor any animal without one. It is the converter of the food by hidden powers into part of ourselves, and is what may be called the true animal, no animal being without it; and in many, perhaps in most, it is what constitutes the principal part of an animal. A polypus is little more than stomach. An animal can exist without any senses, brain, or nervous system, without limbs, heart, or circulation, in short, without anything but a stomach. But for the continuance of the species you must have parts of generation; and a polypus is a stomach and parts of generation in one*; and the complicating an animal is no more than adding other parts for various purposes†. To one animal which has a brain and nervous system, you have ten thousand without them.

The power and operation of digestion is perhaps as curious a part of the animal œconomy as any whatever; at present, however, it is not for me to explain these operations, but it is necessary for me to take some notice of the connexion between this viscus and the animal œconomy in general; in doing which we shall find it to be as much the seat of universal stimulus and irritability as the brain is of sensibility. This connexion, as in the case of sensibility, is much greater in some parts than in others: the connexion that all the vital parts have with the stomach is much greater than between the others, which may be called voluntary, which is only saying in other words that the connexions among the vital parts is more immediate than between the vital parts and those which are not vital.

In diseases the brain seems to be intimately connected with the stomach, and *vice versâ*. It was as necessary for the stomach to be connected with the whole body as for the brain, although not in so marked a manner; but that it is as immediately connected with the body as the brain we may certainly say. The affections of the stomach with the body are not so strong as those of the brain, the mind being made sensible of the least injury done to a part, while the stomach is not at all affected under many partial injuries of the body.

The stomach is more affected from the internal œconomy of the animal than from external influence, which is the reverse of the brain; for external influence in general can only be local, and local injury does not affect the stomach unless it be previously disturbed, or unless the injury is in certain parts, as the brain, the testes, and many of the vital

---

* ["Nothing more is necessary to complete an animal than the power of continuing the species, which power is superadded to this bag in many."—Hunterian (MS.) Cat., Phys. Series, vol. i. p. 113.]

† [Nothing can be more simple than the apparatus for digestion in the lowest animals; but in the higher animals "the parts preparatory and subservient to digestion become more complicated, and indeed so much so, that there is hardly any system in an animal more complicated in itself; and when we consider the varieties of these complications which take place in the various animals, they appear to be almost without end.

"The parts subservient to digestion in the complicated animals bear a great relation to the other properties of the animal," so that "animals in general might be tolerably well classed by these organs."—*Ibid.*]

organs, which, as I observed, have a more intimate connexion with the stomach.

The strongest natural affections of the stomach, as respects the body are those connected with nutrition. These are of the greatest consequence in the machine, and may be said to be of two kinds, namely, want, and the contrary. Want has often been known to produce madness : the contrary may be divided into two kinds,—repletion, and the want of health rendering nourishment unnecessary; and under such circumstances of the machine it is refused to be taken in. Perhaps repletion may be only a negative affection of the stomach with the body; the other is a positive one, and is often carried so far as to produce a sensation in the stomach, namely, sickness.

The stomach is affected by injuries in parts of the body which have no connexion with nutrition, and more especially with parts which have the least action in the machine. Although it may be difficult to understand why it should happen, yet we find that the stomach is more readily affected by injuries done to tendinous parts, and those which have little sensibility, than by injuries of muscular parts, especially of muscles under the controul of the will. This is very remarkable in strains of tendons and ligaments.

The stomach is no less connected with the brain in the internal operations of that viscus concerning external objects or mental operations than in cases of real injury done to that part. A man cannot hear a horrible story or behold distressing circumstances but he will often experience sickness, vomiting, or purging, especially the latter.

The Vascular System.—In many animals, especially the more perfect, the nourishment, or whatever is taken into the system, is taken up and carried from the stomach to the heart, and from thence is thrown out to all parts of the system, through tubes; and from the system it is again returned to the heart by other tubes or vessels. It is absolutely necessary for the surgeon to have a tolerably clear idea of the operations of these vessels. The teaching of the structure and offices of these different vessels more properly belongs to the anatomist than to the surgeon; but as there is one use of the absorbent vessels not generally known, and which is of great importance in many local diseases, and has also an immediate connexion with the original formation of the body, it will be necessary that I should explain this : at present, however, I shall do so but slightly, and trace the action more at large in speaking of local diseases. For the better understanding the whole action of the absorbents, it will not be improper to give a short sketch of the vascular system.

An animal body has in general been considered under the idea of an hydraulic machine, because it appears to be almost wholly composed of tubes in which fluids move. I shall not at present enter into all the different opinions concerning the uses of these tubes, especially of that system called arteries; how they are variously affected, and how they produce their various actions, according to the different stimuli either of health or disease; but shall only give some general ideas of the most important uses of the three different sets of vessels, namely, arteries, veins, and absorbents.

Arteries.—These carry the blood from the general reservoir, the heart, to all the different parts; the veins bring it back again. The arteries constantly dispose of a part of the fluid which they contain in the different operations of the body, according to the different functions of the parts: adding to the whole where growth is necessary; making up losses where the whole is either improper or destroyed; and throwing out of the direct line of motion parts of that fluid, which, according to the different affections and actions of these arteries, become considerably altered in the process: this is called secretion.

Juices so secreted are intended for various purposes in the machine: some for stimulants, as the bile; some for mechanical purposes, as the tears, synovia, saliva, &c.; some for a store of nourishment, as the fat, &c.; while others are thrown out of the body as useless, because they have already performed all their purposes, as the urine, &c.

Veins.—The other set of vessels, the veins, are considered as less active, being principally employed in bringing back the red part of the blood, after it has lost its most salutary parts, or done those offices, whatever they are, for which it was sent out. This, of carrying back red blood, was not considered as the only office of the veins; many of their beginnings were supposed to arise, not from the terminations of arteries, but from most if not all the surfaces of the body, internal and external; making so many inlets into the general system, and bringing matter into the common mass of fluid for the support of the whole, and also to bring back many of the parts secreted by the arteries from the blood for the different purposes of the machine, such as synovia and lubricating fluids of all kinds; which fluids, having answered their different purposes, and having become unfit for every other use in the machine, were obliged to be brought back again into the circulation, to be thrown out of the circulation by the arteries.

Absorbents.—Such were considered to be the uses of the veins before the discovery of the lacteals; but by the discovery of these they were deprived of part of their supposed offices, namely, that of absorbing the chyle; still they were thought to absorb matter from the cavity of the intestines for the secretion of bile. The other part of the absorbent system, called the lymphatics, though long known, was not in the least suspected of performing the operation of absorption, but was still supposed to be the terminations of the extreme ends of the arteries, not large enough to carry red blood but only serum or lymph, though from their similarity to the lacteals, which were known to be absorbents, it became at last evident to common sense that they must absorb.

Before this idea was started, the general opinion of the vascular system ran thus. The arteries were supposed to carry blood for nourishment, secretion, &c. throughout the machine; the veins to return the red blood, as also to absorb from every surface of the body; the lymphatics to return the lymph or blood which came along the arteries; and the lacteals to absorb part of the chyle from the intestines.

But some experiments which I made to ascertain whether the veins of the mesentery absorbed, proved that they had not the power of absorption*. I do not suppose the veins, even in an erection of the penis, to have the power of absorption; but I consider the corpora cavernosa as veins through which the blood is constantly flowing from the arteries, and that other veins carry off the blood from the corpora cavernosa; that in erection there is a spasm on the extremities of these veins, which prevents the blood from flowing into them, in consequence of which an accumulation and distension takes place, which causes an erection, and this ceases with the spasm on the veins. By tying the veins of a dog's penis, I found I could cause an erection at pleasure, while the arteries continued free†. Now, therefore, the offices of the three systems of vessels were as follow. The arteries remain as before; the veins reconvey the blood to the heart, for a continuance of the actions of the arteries as before, but have lost their supposed power of absorbing; the absorbents alone are employed to take up whatever is to be carried into the circulating system. Now let us consider what are the substances always allowed to be absorbed. 1st, Extraneous matter, in

---

* [See the details of these experiments in Vol. IV.]

† [In 1830 Mr. Houston announced the discovery of a muscle in the human subject which arises from the ramus of the pubes, and, crossing the dorsum of the pœnis to unite with its fellow in the mesial line, effectually compresses the dorsal vein whenever this muscle is brought into action. (Dub. Hosp. Rep. Vol. V. p. 459.) A similar muscle, but more perfectly developed, was much earlier discovered by Cuvier in several of the mammalia, to which that eminent anatomist assigned the true use (Anat. Comp. Vol. V. p. 102); in addition to which we may mention that the tongue of the chameleon possesses a highly erectile tissue, and is provided with a similar pair of muscles adapted to fulfil the same object.

Tiedemann, Cuvier, Moreschi, &c. have confirmed the accuracy of Hunter's opinion respecting the structure of these tissues, namely, that they consist of veins enlarged at their origins, and not of a system of cells as has generally been supposed.]

which is included nourishment. 2nd, Secreted, superfluous, and extravasated matter, whether natural or diseased. 3rd, The fat. 4th, That portion of parts which, being absorbed, causes the waste of parts, as muscles becoming smaller, bones lighter, &c. Although these two last effects were perhaps not expressly said to be carried on by absorption, either by the veins or the other system of vessels, yet we must suppose it was understood.

So far the absorbents have been considered as an active part in the animal œconomy; but, from a further knowledge of these vessels, we shall find that they are of much more consequence in the body than has been imagined, and that they are often taking down what arteries had formerly built up, thus becoming modellers of the body; and that they are also removing many diseased parts, which were beyond the power of cure.

As these vessels are productive of a vast variety of effects in the animal œconomy, which are very dissimilar in their intention and effects, they may be viewed in a variety of lights, and admit of a variety of divisions. We shall first consider them under two views. 1st, As absorbing matter which is not part of the machine. 2nd, As absorbing the machine itself.

The first is a well-known office of the absorbents, and is of two kinds: a, the absorption of exterior matter, in which may be ranked everything that is applied to the skin, as also the chyle; b, the absorption of interior matter, such as many of the secreted fluids, the fat, the earth of bones, &c. It may be necessary to observe that I do not consider the fat and earth of bones as part of the animal, as they have no action within themselves, and have not the principle of life*.

These actions of absorption are principally employed with a view to the nourishment of the animal, as also to answer many other purposes, as in the absorption of foreign matter, which is extremely extensive and is very important; for, besides its salutary effects, it is often the cause of a thousand diseases, especially from poisons; all which is not to our present purpose.

The second office of the absorbents which we are to consider is that of removing parts of the body itself, which may be of two kinds. The

---

* [In regard to the earth of bones, we may observe that its particles are arranged in a determinate and specific manner—constituting an organized body in the most extensive acceptation of that word as distinguished from inorganic matter generally, and from the amorphous ossific depositions which sometimes occur in membranes, muscles, glands, tumours, &c., in which no definite structure is observable. The peculiar stratification and fibrous texture of bone may easily be observed by calcination. This being the case, are we warranted in saying that the earth of bones, forming an organized part of the body, is not alive?]

first of these is where only a gradual wasting is produced, either of the whole machine, as in atrophy, or of a part, as in the muscles of a leg or arm, from an injury done to a nerve, tendinous part, or joint: this I call interstitial absorption, because it is the removing a part of the body out of that part which remains, leaving the part still a whole or complete part; a muscle, for instance, that is wasted remains still a perfect muscle. The second is where the absorbents are removing whole parts of the body, and this may be divided into natural and diseased. In the natural, these vessels are to be considered as the modellers of the original construction of the body; and if we were to consider them fully in this view, we should find that no alteration can take place in the original formation of many parts, either in natural growths or in parts arising from disease, without the absorbents being in action to take a considerable part in it. This kind of absorption I shall call modelling absorption. If I was to consider this function in these lights, it would lead me to a vast variety of facts, as extensive as those connected with any principle in the animal œconomy, for bones cannot be formed without it, nor probably many other parts.

A part which was of use in one stage of life, and becomes entirely useless in another, is removed. This is evident in many animals: the thymus gland is removed, the ductus arteriosus and membrana pupillaris are removed. This process is perhaps more remarkable in the changes of insects than in any other animals. The changes in an insect are very curious. The insect is first a maggot or caterpillar, then goes into the chrysalis state, and comes out a butterfly. Whilst in the chrysalis state it is totally changed, the old parts are almost wholly taken up, and new parts formed; and it is this modelling process that occasions these changes*.

Bones do not grow by having new particles put into the interstices of previously formed parts, so as to remove these to a greater distance from each other, by which means they should grow larger,—as, for instance, if I put a sponge into water, the water getting into all the interstices makes it larger,—but they grow by the addition of new bone on the external surface†.

---

* [It must be remembered, however, that in insects, where these changes, as Hunter observes, are the most striking, no proper absorbent vessels exist, and indeed the vascular system generally is very imperfect. The changes that take place in the insect transformation have been since ascertained to be rather a development of parts previously existing in a rudimentary state than a total change of parts. In the caterpillar are to be found the rudiments of the future butterfly.]

† [See Vol. IV. for a paper detailing the whole of Mr. Hunter's experiments on this subject.]

I took a pig of a very large breed when young, bored two holes in the tibia, and put a shot into each, measuring on a card the distance of each from the other. I allowed this pig to grow up to its full size, then killed it and took out the bone, and I found the two holes at exactly the same distance from one another as at first. Now if the bone had grown in all its parts these two shot would have been removed to a distance from each other proportionate to the growth of the bone.

This fact is also ascertained by feeding animals on madder at different intervals, by which means we shall get strata of red and white bone.

Since we know that bones do not grow by fresh matter being put into all parts, so as to push the old matter to a greater distance, but by new matter laid upon the external surface, let us see whether it is possible for bone to grow and retain its form without being taken down. Let figure 3, Pl. XX., represent the head of the thigh-bone of a fœtus. Now if the increase was accomplished by superimposed layers, one over the other, as in figure 4, the head of the bone would necessarily become of an enormous size, and in time would come down so as to occupy the middle of the bone, while the cavity in the centre would not be enlarged. Absorption, therefore, must necessarily go on to keep the bone of its proper shape. Hence I call this the modelling process, for without this combined action of absorption and deposition the animal could not grow as it now does.

The absorbents possess the power of removing complete parts of the body, in consequence of disease, an operation which is somewhat similar to the first of this division, or the modelling process, but very different in the intention, and therefore in the ultimate effect. This process of removing whole parts in consequence of disease, in some cases produces effects unlike what it produces in others, one of which is a sore or ulcer; in other cases no sore or ulcer is produced, although the whole part is removed. The first I call ulcerative absorption; but for the other I have not been able to find a term.

This process of the removal of a whole solid part of the body, or that power which the animal œconomy possesses of taking part of itself into the circulation by the absorbent vessels when necessary, is a fact that has not been in the least attended to, nor even been supposed possible; and as I now mean to give a general idea of it, I may just be allowed once more to observe, that the oil or fat of the animal, and the earth of bones, have always been considered as subject to absorption, and some other parts of the body most liable to waste have been supposed to suffer by absorption; but that any solid part should be totally absorbed is a new doctrine. This use of the absorbents I have been able to demonstrate. The first hint I received of it was in the waste of the sockets of the teeth, and also of the fangs of the shedding teeth, which was in the years 1754 and 1755 (see Treatise on the Teeth, first and second parts). This opinion was strengthened by what I observed in the process going on in the exfoliation of bones.

It may be difficult to conceive how part of the body should remove itself, but it is just as difficult to conceive how the body can form itself. They are both equally facts. The knowledge of their mode of action would perhaps answer but little purpose.

This, at least, I may assert, that when any solid part of the body undergoes diminution, brought on in consequence of disease, it is the absorbent system that has done it; they are the thieves.

The remote cause of absorption of whole and living parts implies the existence of two conditions, the first of which is a consciousness, in the part to be absorbed, of the unfitness or impossibility of remaining under such circumstances, whatever they be, and therefore they become ready for removal, and submit to it with ease. The second is a consciousness of the absorbents of such a state of the parts. Both these concurring, they have nothing to do but to fall to the work*.

Now the part that is to be absorbed is alive, it must feel its own inefficacy and admit of absorption. The vessels must have the stimulus of imperfection of this part, as if they were sensible that this part were unfit; therefore take it up. There must be a sensation in both parts.

When the part to be absorbed is a dead part, as nourishment and extraneous matter of all kinds, then the whole disposition is in the absorbents†.

This is the only mode in which this power is capable of producing such effects, and, like all other operations of the machine, arises from either stimulus or irritation, all the other modes of destruction being either mechanical or chemical.

[It is by the progressive absorption that matter, or pus, and extraneous bodies of all kinds are brought to the surface of the body. It is by this process that bone exfoliates and sloughs are separated. It is the absorbents which remove whole bones while the arteries are forming new ones. It is this operation that removes the alveolar processes

---

* [The reader, I imagine, will scarcely refrain from smiling at the *naïveté* with which our author here ascribes consciousness and intelligence to an animal body, to an extent little inferior to Boerhaave, Van Helmont, or even Stahl. It were devoutly to be wished that the *body politic* possessed a similar consciousness of what ought to be done, and an equal will and power to carry its resolutions into effect.]

† [It is difficult to conceive how the absorbents can act on detached solid substances, incapable of solution, as bone, for example; yet portions of dead bone are often observed to be entirely absorbed in cases of necrosis; and in some experiments made by Mr. Thomas Blizard, in which disks of bone were bound on over ulcers; the surfaces of these disks were found to be eaten out, or destroyed, just as in common caries.]

when the teeth drop out of themselves, or are taken out by art; as also the fangs of the shedding teeth, which allow them to drop out; and it is by this means also that ulcers are formed.

It becomes in many cases a substitute for mortification, in which cases it seems to depend upon a degree of strength and vigour superior to that where mortification happens; and in many cases it finishes what mortification had begun, by separating the dead part. From all this, we must see that the causes of the absorption of whole parts are many.

Pressure appears to be one of the greatest causes of absorption, and it is commonly a cause of the progression. It produces its effects not in all cases in proportion to the pressure, but according to the pressure and other circumstances combined; for we find very different effects from the same quantity of pressure: thus, under one circumstance, pressure shall give signs of strength, and produce an increase, or thickening; but under another circumstance the same quantity of pressure shall produce waste, or an absorption of the parts. This difference in effect, from the same quantity of pressure, depends upon the pressure being from without or within, for the first effect of the irritation of pressure from without is the disposition to thicken, which I have asserted is rather an operation of strength; but if it exceeds the irritation of thickening, then the power appears to give way to it, and the absorption of the parts pressed gives way to it.

Pressure produced by an extraneous body surrounded on all sides, such as pus in an abscess, acts equally on every side of the surrounding parts, and therefore, every part being pressed alike, ought, from this cause singly considered, to produce absorption of those surrounding parts equally on all sides, supposing the parts themselves similar in structure, or, which is the same, equally susceptible of being absorbed : but we find that one side only of the surrounding living parts is susceptible of this irritation; therefore one side only is absorbed, and this goes on in regular progression. The side of the cavity which is susceptible of this irritation is always that which is next to the external surface of the body; therefore we have always extraneous substances of every kind determined to the skin, and to that side of the body on which the extraneous substance lies, or to which it is nearest, and that without having any effect upon, or producing the least destruction of, any of the surrounding parts. From this cause we find abscesses whose seat is in or near the centre of a part readily determined to the surface or side in preference to another; and whenever the lead is once taken, absorption goes on there only. But as some parts of the body are more susceptible of this irritation than others, we find that such parts are often absorbed, although they are not in the shortest road to the skin; and of such structure is the cellular membrane. We find exfoliations of bones, as well as all other extraneous bodies, approaching the skin in like manner, and from the same cause. But the progressive absorption is always more or less attended with the interstitial, and assisted by it.

The vessels in general would appear to have more powers of perfecting themselves when injured than any other part of the body, for their use is almost immediate and constant, and it is they which perform the operation of restoration on the other parts; therefore they themselves must first be perfect. They would seem to have more of the polypus in them than any other part of the body. This is perhaps more in the absorbents than in the arteries and veins, for we can conceive a part injured by accident, and, as it were, standing still for a little while; but we see ulceration going on very rapidly, which proves an immediate formation of vessels for absorption *.]

---

* The preceding paragraphs are transcribed from the Hunterian Catalogue (Phys. Series, vol. ii. p. 5), and are also partly repeated in the work on Inflammation. They are in Mr. Hunter's own words, and serve to complete this subject.

A long and interesting note is added to this part of the Catalogue by the author,

The knowledge of the use of the absorbent vessels is of late date, and the knowledge of their different modes of action still later. Physiologists have endeavoured to account for their modes of action on the principle of capillary tubes at their beginning, and this is the most common notion, because it is a familiar one. But this is too confined an idea for an animal machine; nor can it account for every kind of absorption. But as solids are often absorbed, as indurated tumours, coagulated blood, earth of bones, &c., they were driven to the necessity of supposing a solvent. This may or may not be so; it is one of those hypotheses that can neither be proved nor disproved, and must for ever rest as an opinion. My idea is, however, that nature leaves as little as possible to chance alone, and that the whole operation of absorption is performed by one action in the mouths of the absorbents.

But even under the idea of capillary tubes, physiologists were obliged still to have recourse to the actions of these vessels, to carry on the matter absorbed; therefore they might as well have extended the action to the mouths of the vessels.

As we know nothing of the mouths of these vessels, it is impossible we can for many opinion that can be relied on; but as they are capable of absorbing substances in a state of solidity and fluidity, it is reasonable to suppose that they have different modes of action; for although any construction of parts that is capable of absorbing a solid may also be such as is capable of absorbing a fluid, yet I can suppose a construction capable of absorbing a fluid that is not fitted for the absorption of a solid, though this is not likely.

To see the possible correctness of this notion more forcibly, let us only recollect the variety in the mouths of different animals, and I will venture to say that the mouths of all the different animals have not a greater variety of substances to work upon than the absorbents have; and it may be observed, that with all the variety in the mouths of different animals, this variety is only for the purpose of adapting them to the forms of solids, which admit of great variety, every one being capable of absorbing fluids, which admit of no variety.

I have often said, on this point, that if we could see the mouths of these vessels, we might perhaps class the modes of absorption as animals have been classed, by their teeth, &c.

Matter taken into the constitution by the absorbents is capable of

---

asserting the claims of his brother, Dr. William Hunter, to the discovery of the lymphatics, in opposition to the pretensions of M. Noquez. The whole note is very characteristic, and affords an excellent specimen of critical and sound judgment, of a certain combativeness of disposition, and of that homely but vigorous mode of expression for which Hunter was distinguished.

being altered in its nature from what it was out of the constitution. Although this may have been conjectured or imagined, it never has been absolutely known, and even now the only proof we have of it is the change produced in venereal matter. If the matter of chancre or gonorrhœa be absorbed, it produces disease: this disease is not similar to the original; it is not pocky matter which is produced from the ulcers, but this matter has been changed from its original nature in the circulation; although the change was of such a kind as still to retain its power of stimulating and producing disease: but as it was changed, the disease produced was not similar to that from whence it came.

That there is a change in venereal matter is very evident, for if venereal matter out of the constitution be applied to a living part, it always produces an effect according to the nature of the part, which part may be one of two kinds, either, 1st, a secreting surface, producing then gonorrhœa; or, 2nd, a non-secreting surface, producing then a chancre.

That this process of altering substances in the constitution is not a universal principle and common effect of all kinds of matter which enter the circulation, is evident; for we do not as yet know, for certain, of any other matter being altered.

TABLE OF ABSORPTION.

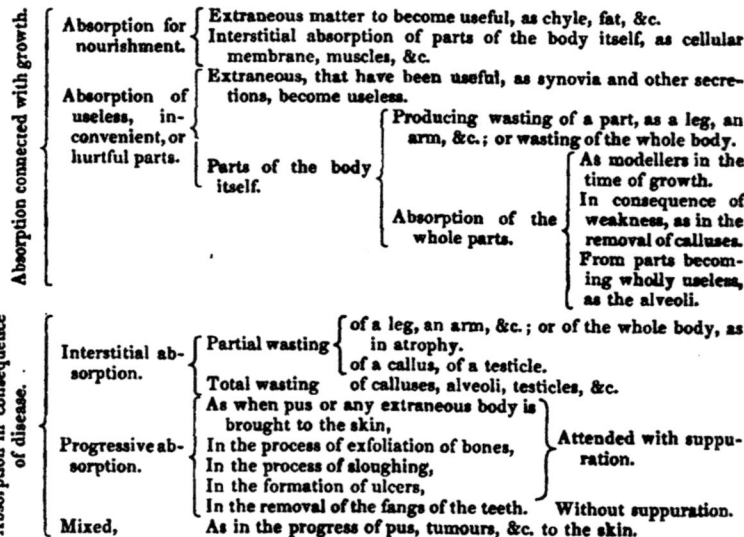

CHAPTER VI.

OF THE BRAIN AND NERVES.

Passive and active states of the brain ;—too much influence attributed to the brain in the bodily actions ;—actions of the brain ;—five modes of impression on the nerves, or senses.—Voluntary action becoming involuntary, as in chorea.—Of sensation.—Connexion of the actions of the brain and nerves with life.—Of sleep ;—its importance in the animal œconomy.

WE have hitherto traced animal matter from its change from common matter to animal matter, the particles of which have possessed such an arrangement as to produce life; still it has other modes of arrangement, out of which arise other modes of action, and which only take place in some animals. These are the brain and nerves, which produce sensation, out of which arises mind and reason; for without sensation the mind could not be formed, nor could we reason; it being always about some object that the mind is affected, or that we reason.

In sensation the brain is passive, only receiving the impression from the nerves, according to their actions, called so many sensations. In mind it is active. Mind arises from a peculiar quality in the sensation, being expressive of some quality in the body which is the object of sensation, and which gives an action to the brain answering to those qualities, as agreeable and disagreeable, with all their different species, as love, joy, hatred, anger, &c.; which actions of the brain, or states of the mind, become the causes of particular modes of action in the body affecting both involuntary and voluntary actions. The heart beats quick or slow according to those states; sickness may be produced; purging, contraction of the bladder shall take place; the voluntary muscles hardly obeying the will, but performing involuntary actions, according to the state of the mind.

Reason, by influencing the will, becomes the cause of the voluntary actions; and by this connexion all these principles can affect one another.

Now the brain appears to be capable of two modes of action, and out of these arises every property of the brain. We may call the actions of the brain, mind; objects shall affect our senses so as to form a peculiar state of mind: this I call mental impression. Again, the mind can reason and exercise volition respecting objects. The former is involuntary, and belongs also to brutes; the latter is voluntary. For instance, I am

s 2

challenged to fight a duel, volition, and reason determine me to go to it; but when at the place, my joints tremble, my stomach turns sick : this is the effect of mental impression, or feelings of the mind. The two operations are very different ; and in general the feelings of the mind, if strong, will prevent all reasoning.

Much more has been given to the brain and nerves than they deserve*. They have been thought to be the cause of every property in an animal body; that independent of them the whole body was a dead machine, and that it was only put in action by them.

But although their actions are absolutely necessary in the machine, they are not so universally so as has been imagined. They are not the cause of growth, nor do they even preserve a part from death, although the whole as a whole cannot live without them.

The nerves have but one mode of action, namely, that of conveying impressions ; but this in two different directions : one from their extremities in the body towards the brain, conveying impressions made on them to the brain, in order to excite actions suitable to these impressions ; the other, from the brain to the extremities, conveying the mandates of the will, &c.

That mode of action which is from the body towards the brain is of two kinds. One is the internal feel of the body, of perfection, imper-

---

* [It may here be remarked, that the author, on the whole, lays less stress on the nervous system in his physiology than it probably deserves, at the same that he gives disproportionate importance to the stomach. Modern experiments have shown that the functions of digestion, nutrition, secretion, circulation, respiration, &c. in the higher animals are intimately dependent on the integrity of the brain and nervous system ; and though in some of the lower animals no traces of this system are discoverable, yet may we safely infer, from the irritability which these animals manifest, that something corresponding to a nervous system actually exists, constituting the *materia vitæ diffusa* of the author. Something analogous to this has been suspected in regard to the stomach itself, in certain species of zoophytes, in which either there are no visible stomachs or else the parts which are generally considered as separate and independent animals are regarded by others as merely a multiplication of stomachs belonging to the same individual. Some experiments also have lately been performed in America which show that undressed animal food undergoes a species of imperfect digestion when inclosed in fresh wounds : from which it seems probable, that notwithstanding the centralization of the vital organs in the higher orders of animals, the separate parts still exhibit traces of those vital endowments which in the lowest order of animals are diffused through the whole body, very much in the same manner as in vegetables. The proper objects of comparison however, in the present case, are the stomach with the great sympathetic nerve or nerves of the viscera rather than with the cerebral masses. The superaddition of the latter has reference principally to the organs of external relation, very few of which exist in zoophytes and the simpler forms of beings. Physiologically, it is as difficult to conceive of sensibility and contractility without a nervous system, or something analogous to this system, as it is to conceive of nutrition without digestive and circulatory organs.]

fection, power, want, &c. The other is of those feelings of the body which are to call forth the powers of the will to perform what are called voluntary actions, for the subsistence of the body, or to effect the actions which it cannot perform.

The actions of the brain towards the body are also of two kinds: one in consequence of the feelings or state of the mind at the time, whether the actions of fear, courage, anger, love, &c.; the other, in consequence of the command of the will, called voluntary actions.

Those of the body to the brain are the first in order; for it is the receiving the impressions that gives rise to the others. Of the latter, the first are the feelings of the mind, and the second the will and its consequences, namely, voluntary actions, or all those actions, directed principally to external objects, for which muscles are provided.

As the nerves are perfectly passive till impressed by external objects, no one could have any sensation except while an impression is made on some of the senses. Therefore a man should not feel that he exists but in thought; nor could he do that if he had never received impressions to think about, for thinking is no more than the memory of impressions put into order by the mind; nor should he have those actions which naturally arise from the brain till the brain makes the impression on the nerves.

The impression is made on the body, but the sensation is in the brain, for the effect (of a person's feeling in a part to which a nerve is distributed) on cutting or otherwise injuring a nerve, proves that sensation is in the brain, and not in the body; for if it was in the body, the sensation would be referred to the part injured; but sensation being in the brain, and brought from the brain by the action of the nerves, or sensation being formerly in the brain, the action of the nerves we find is referred to the beginnings of that action by the combination of the other senses; otherwise it would be only in possession of the sensation without any reference. The reference produces a feeling in the mind receiving sensation, by joining it with the seat of impression.

There are five modes of impression of nerves, or perhaps rather five modes of construction of parts, which are adapted to so many kinds of impression. These are called the five senses; but there are a great many kinds of sensation conveyed to the brain or sensorium.

The five senses are no more than parts constructed so as to be capable of receiving impressions, or so many properties of matter. Perhaps all are capable of receiving the impression of touch, or pressure, if it could be applied to all, so that every nerve may be said to feel*.

---

* [It would seem that Mr. Hunter thought that all the nerves of the senses were capable of conveying the sensation of touch or pressure, in addition to the sensation

But, besides pressure, there are other properties of matter. Many bodies have qualities besides being tangible ; some only when in solution making an impression on the tongue and causing taste ; the same bodies when thrown into vapour give smell : air, besides being tangible, has a peculiar motion, arising from its repulsive quality, called vibration, which strikes the ear and produces hearing. There arises another property in another species of matter, called light, which we know less of than any other, which has a power of pervading some bodies, called transparent, and gives us the sensation of sight ; and from peculiarity in the formation of those transparent parts light becomes more determined in its direction.

The sensation of the glans penis, tickling, and itching would seem to belong to feeling. The first, however, is certainly a different mode of action of the nerve from common feeling, and both itching and tickling require a particular mode of impression to produce them.

An animal can bear with ease a certain quantity of common sensation, which quantity being particularly applied will give pleasure ; but if common sensation be increased beyond certain bounds, it gives great pain ; so that pain is no more than an increased sensation, such as the sense of violence committed to a part *.

All the five senses are subject to the same mode of sensation when applied in the same way, namely, by touch, and if the impression is too strong, give the sensation of pain. For instance, if the retina be hurt, it gives pain, but not light ; if the ear be hurt, it gives pain, but not sound ; if the nose be hurt, it gives pain, but not smell †. But there

_____

which they are specially fitted to convey. This opinion is not warranted by more recent discoveries. An impression on the retina, of whatever kind, excites the sensation of light. Majendie found that on touching the retina with a couching-needle no pain was excited, but the sensation of light: a blow on the eye has the same effect. If pressure be made with the finger on the sclerotic, a dark spot will be seen immediately at the point of pressure, where the function of the nerve is probably impeded, with a halo of light surrounding it. Of the auditory nerve we know little; and on the tongue and nose the gustatory and olfactory nerves are so intermixed with the fibres of the fifth or nerve of feeling, that it is not easy to distinguish between their actions in such an experiment; but galvanism, which excites a pricking sensation in the skin, causes a peculiar flavour when applied to the tongue; and the smell of the electric fluid is well known.]

* [If this were the case, we should expect to find pain differing only in degree, but not in kind. Some structures, as bone, ligament, and the fibrous structures generally, exhibit no *common* sensation, although they are acutely alive to pain under circumstances of injury and disease.]

† [To each of these organs are distributed branches of the fifth nerve, or the nerve of sensation ; it is by means of these that common sensation is furnished to the organs of sense, and through them that lesions excite the feeling of pain. See the preceding note.]

are exceptions to the two first, for a blow on the eye often produces light, and on the ear sound. And besides, those senses are subject to diseases, where the sensation often arises without impression from without.

The common actions of the body, that commonly arise from the will, often become involuntary, as in palsies, St. Vitus's dance, &c.; but I suspect that these actions still arise from the brain or mind, though not the will, because they do not take place in sleep; nor do we find the same diseases in any animal but the human.

Our senses being such, have their peculiar degree of sensation and their peculiar mode of receiving impressions, and when this is carried to too great a length, they become extremely uneasy: but it is an uneasiness different from pain; it is the peculiar sense carried beyond what the mind can bear.

Sensation is in proportion to the impression made on a part, joined with the susceptibility with which the nerve is ready to act. But for distinct sensation two things are necessary, namely, time and space. It is necessary that the impression should be some time in performing, because an impression may be too quick to excite sensation, or quicker than any action in the nerves, such as a ball passing through a man's body without his feeling it; but he is capable of feeling it afterwards, which arises from an action of the injured part, not from the violence itself. Neither must the time be too long, for an impression or an injury may be so slow as not to affect the nerves at all, so as to throw them into any action. A person, for instance, shall become dropsical, and the belly shall fill with water so gradually as to give no pain from the stretching of the muscles, peritoneum, &c.; but if you were to attempt to stretch the belly of another person in a given time to such a degree, it would produce pain in proportion to the violence.

The space must also be determined, for a given quantity of impression may be concentrated so as to be within bounds of sensation; for it would appear that a single nerve or a very few nerves are not capable of conveying sensation, however affected; for instance, a given quantity of light may be concentrated into such a small point as not to be seen.

Every sensation, every mode of sensation, and every sense appear to depend on the quantity of nerves acted upon, and in a given time; therefore we have a great quantity of nerves going to parts that are allotted for strong sensation, that no impression may be made without affecting a great many nerves at the same time.

The uneasiness arising from too strong impressions we can easily assign a reason for, as it becomes a means of avoiding that violence; but itching and tickling appear not to be so very necessary: however they must be of service iń the animal œconomy. I can conceive itching becomes a cause of our keeping ourselves clean, free from vermin, &c., and becomes a substitute for pain : it naturally leads us to the cure, which gives pleasure ; and the performance of it is almost similar to the indulgence of our natural appetites.

This principle of sensation is our director with respect to all other external actions, but has no absolute power over the internal œconomy of the machine. But this first principle we shall find can influence the others very materially, and thus a compound principle will be produced.

The brain and nerves also give the body a consciousness of its own muscular powers. This is more remarkable in other animals than in man : thus, a horse will at once know what he can leap, and will leap no more, nor attempt it ; and indeed a man can for the most part tell. A nobleman (the Duke of Queensbury) who had broken his tendo Achillis was fearful of walking about his room ; but I advised him to do it as well as he could, assuring him that his gastrocnemius muscle, knowing its own business better than its master, would refuse to act if he walked, and that the action would be performed by other muscles. This he found to be true. But in the night time, I told him, I could not be answerable for what his muscles would do, therefore I thought proper to put the leg into a fit posture and secure it by a bandage.

As the brain and nerves are composed of animal matter, and as that animal matter has life, or the first principle of action, in common with all the other matter composing the whole body, there arises necessarily an intimate connexion between those principles, and, though totally different in their peculiar actions, yet they become blended with each other, so that one seldom acts perfectly unless the other is in perfect order, each of them calling on the other to do its part ; and when both these principles are in vigour and in perfect harmony the whole machine is in health.

Life is coeval with the existence of the animal or vegetable matter itself ; but sensation is a later principle, does not take place until birth, when a new œconomy is set up, in which sensation is called in by the living principle for the support of the whole, beginning first in the stomach by sympathy, and then going on in a series of actions. These compound actions, therefore, cannot take place until sensation takes place ; and it is reasonable to suppose that a child in the womb has no sensation, for it is just as well formed in all its parts without brain as with it, and the nerves are indebted to the brain for their formation *.

---

* [This statement is incorrect. The nerves may exist without the brain or spinal marrow, which are accessory not the fundamental parts. The same law obtains in regard to the heart and blood-vessels: and indeed it may be observed generally in regard to the progressive development of the higher animals, that at first they follow the

But the moment a new mode of action takes place, actions arising from sensation must be performed for the support of this; and an animal must die if these sensations are not produced, which cannot be produced if there is no brain*.

Actions arising from the union of the two principles, life and sensation, are extremely evident; being all those actions which constitute a state of mind, or those feelings of the mind from which instinct arises.

Sleep.—A singular result of our being possessed of the sensitive principle is sleep. Perfect sleep is an annihilation of the power of present sensation, of the power of thinking, and all traces of the past, or what we call memory. We find that there is, of course, a cessation of all voluntary actions; the will itself is in every respect at perfect rest, and we are at this time, in respect to ourselves, in a state of non-existence. But sleep has its degrees; perhaps in all cases there is a considerable loss of these principles, especially sensation; but the effects of sensation are not always lost, namely, those operations of the mind which produce actions which are very nearly voluntary. During sleep, therefore, the mind may be thinking, which forms what we call dreams; but as our present sensations do not become directors of those actions which the mind is employed about, no such action takes place as the mind forms to itself. It is even possible to dream when awake; it is only necessary for the thinking power to take possession of the mind, and proceed with an action with which the present sensation has nothing to do, so that a person neither sees objects, hears sounds, nor feels anything that touches him; and when the mind ceases to act and sensation returns, we call it a dream. Now whenever the body loses

type of inferior animals, but afterwards advance to those which are still higher and higher in the zoological scale. Hunter in the main was well acquainted with this law of development as regards the higher animals, as will appear from the following passage, in which we may remark that he has anticipated many of the leading discoveries on this subject by modern anatomists. The passage occurs in the introduction to the description of the drawings relating to incubation. " If we were capable" (he says) " of following the progress of increase of the number of the parts of the most perfect animal, as they first formed in succession, from the very first, to its state of full perfection, we should probably be able to compare it to some one of the incomplete animals themselves, of every order of animals in the creation, being at no stage different from some of those inferior orders; or, in other words, if we were to take a series of animals, from the more imperfect to the perfect, we should probably find an imperfect animal, corresponding with some stage of the most perfect." (Hunt. Cat., Phys. Series, vol. ii. p. iv.) Many other passages might be adduced which evince that Mr. Hunter's extensive acquaintance with comparative anatomy had enabled him to deduce the true principles which regulate the formation of the body and the coexistence of the different systems of parts in the same individual organism.]

* [Mr. Hunter must have been aware of many examples of fœtuses without brains which have lived for some time after birth. He must here mean the medulla oblongata, without which respiration cannot take place.]

the consciousness of its own existence, it may be called a waking dream, and this is often the case when people are in deep thought. Sleep appears to be to the sensitive what I have already described to take place in the living principle when I mentioned my own case; but that arose from disease, while sleep is necessary.

When both these principles undergo a cessation of their actions it is called a swoon. Here there is a cessation of all actions which naturally arise in the body, but still a capability of having them reproduced. Now in a fainting fit there seems rather a cessation of the actions of sensation, the animal becoming totally insensible to itself; but in a swoon we have this carried further: the cessation takes place not only in the sensitive but in the living principle itself, for we shall have people fall into a trance or swoon, and they shall remain in it without any kind of motion,—respiration, circulation, digestion, and every operation of the body at total rest; and if the disease, or the cause of cessation of that action, should continue a long time, they may lose the power of reproducing this sensation again. Fainting, from bleeding, fear, &c., is a swoon in a certain degree, for these principles are diminished, especially the sensitive. Sleep is not only a cessation of voluntary action, but produces cessation of involuntary action of voluntary parts, arising from their diseases, as in St. Vitus's dance, &c.

Sleep is of such material consequence to the sensitive principle of the constitution,—namely, sensation, mind, and will,—that it may be said to constitute one third of its duration. As it is only an annihilation of sensation and all its consequences, one might suppose that it was of little consequence to the machine; but it is as essential to it as food.

Sleep, or rather a cessation of sensation, thus taking place, while the action of life is going on, shows that there must be a peculiar structure, and a principle arising out of that structure superadded, making a compound which is endued with life; for life for a time can go on without sensation, but cannot always go on without it.

Sensation, then, is a fatigue to life; and in proportion to the exertion of sensation, in a given time, the sooner is life wasted. For this reason, when we are in health, sensation stops at proper times; life then appears at ease. This slighter effect of health is often increased preternaturally, as in cases called lethargy*.

---

* [Dr. Marshall Hall found that the muscular irritability of hybernating animals was greatly increased during their state of torpor. In the same way, sleep, "nature's second best course," seems to be intended to recruit the exhausted irritability of the system after the labours of the day; and accordingly during the condition of sleep the organs both of animal and vegetative life are in a state of repose, the one completely, the other only partially so. Various causes have been assigned for this state, none of which is completely satisfactory.]

CHAPTER VII.

OF SUSCEPTIBILITY OF IMPRESSIONS; OF STIMULI; OF DISPOSITIONS OF THE BODY; OF HABIT AND CUSTOM.

Difference between impressions on animate and inanimate matter ;—of internal susceptibilities.—Of stimuli ;—carried too far they become irritants ;—animals susceptible of stimuli at one time and not at another. —Of dispositions of the body ;—less well understood than those of the mind ;—in health arising from impression ;—in disease without it.—Of dispositions in the mind ;—their ultimate effects are on the body.—Of dispositions of the body compared with the preceding ;—both compared with the actions of machines.—Want of balance betwixt the parts of animals ;—parts weakest when at a distance from the sources of power ; —why.—Of the memory of impressions ;—to be found in the body as well as the mind ;—example.—Of the effects of repetition of natural actions. — Definition of habit and custom. — Of custom ; — lessened effects from repetition of impression ;—increased effects.

EVERY species of matter, whether inanimate or animate, is capable of impressions, and the effects of the impression are according to the nature of the impression and the part impressed. All matter is not capable of acting or reacting according to the impression, which passiveness belongs to inanimate matter, though not to all. A piece of dough receives impressions, but seems chiefly passive, not having the power of reacting, and making but little resistance. Elastic bodies receive impressions, which they restore in a contrary direction, producing ultimately various effects, which I have said are the soul or life of mechanism.

In animal bodies the effects of impressions are more various and complicated than in inanimate matter, because the most simple animal is more various and complicated in its susceptibilities of impression, and of course more complicated in its dispositions for action.

In inanimate matter there are no actions within itself excepting the disposition to reinstate itself, as in elasticity ; therefore impressions are not rising up within itself, in consequence of its own actions, as in animals, so as to produce consequent dispositions and actions, unless we could conceive that chemical and fermentative operations were of this kind. But animal matter having internal actions, these actions are producing impressions which are forming dispositions to action in the parts impressed; and, secondly, it is capable of being acted upon or impressed by common inanimate matter, in both which cases the impressions will be according to the nature of the impressions and part impressed conjoined.

When a man is so affected as to feel within himself that he cannot live, which is very common, it arises from the mind being made acquainted with the state of the body; the living powers are become weak, inactive, &c., and the nerves are communicating the intelligence. Accordingly, their actions are expressive of the extinction of life going on, and the action of the brain is expressive of such actions of the nerves; and as death is a something we know takes place, and this sensation of ours is not such as we feel in health, we conclude, from an habitual species of reasoning, that we cannot live, and we are often not deceived. This effect is often so quick that it may exceed the sensation of it, or at least may hardly afford us time to communicate these sensations to others.

The internal susceptibilities, with the consequent impressions and dispositions, are, first, of want, and, second, of repletion; and all the other internal operations of the machine arise naturally from these two, especially repletion, as digestion, circulation, respiration, secretion, the intercourse of the sexes, &c. But the first movement of these actions appears to require the impression of external matter, the powers of digestion being excited by food being thrown into the stomach, in consequence of which circulation, respiration, secretion, &c. all follow, arising out of the internal operations of the machine; all which have nothing to do with the sensitive principle, but are wholly dependent on the living principle. The desire of food, or susceptibility of the stomach to digest it, arises not from external objects, but from its own organization.

The second kind, susceptibility of external impressions, affects principally the sensitive principle, but may also affect the living principle, as in medicines. These are called stimuli; and when both principles are affected they may be said to have the management of the machine*.

Impression, or stimulus, produces a disposition to act, or rather action may or may not take place. But all impressions, either on the living or sensitive principle, are not stimuli; some go beyond stimulus, and become irritants†; and other impressions are from their nature not sti-

---

* [It is impossible to avoid remarking here the similarity of this view of Hunter's to Bichat's division into organic and animal actions.]

† [It may safely be said that almost all stimuli, when applied in excess, operate as irritants, and, if carried to their utmost point, as direct sedatives. Thus, electricity, which in a moderate degree irritates the system or rouses it to an unusual degree of

mulants, but produce a disagreeable impression either to the mind or body, and are also irritants.

Stimuli.—An animal, I have observed, is susceptible of impressions; which impressions, I shall now observe, are to become causes either of immediate or remote disposition to action, either in the part impressed, or some other by sympathy. These impressions, which excite or increase the disposition, are called stimuli; therefore we may say that a part is stimulated, or such an application, substance, or object is a stimulus; and a part either readily increased in action by impression, or brought into action, we say is very susceptible of stimuli. I could wish we had some one word expressive of this condition of the part stimulated, as stimulable, and also of the stimulus, as stimulative, to answer to irritable, sensitive, &c.

An impression which becomes a stimulus by sympathy may have been carried so far as to have been an irritator of the part to which it was applied, as a mote in the eye irritates the tunica conjunctiva, which irritation acts only as a stimulus to the lachrymal gland, for this gland can only act by sympathy. The power of a stimulus must be according to the nature of the stimulus and of the part jointly, for as almost every part of a body has a peculiarity in its mode of action, every part must have its peculiar stimulus.

An animal is so constructed as to have its parts susceptible of stimuli at one time and not at another. An animal has a power of improving its parts so as to make them susceptible of such stimuli as are adapted to the disposition of the parts: for instance, an animal improves all those parts peculiar to the sexes. When those parts are perfect, which is called the age of puberty, they stimulate the mind and various other parts connected with that, giving rise to the passion of love or the appetite of lust.

On the other hand, want becomes the cause of impression: a part becomes susceptible of such want, so that the ultimate effect or stimulus

---

action, in a concentrated form immediately extinguishes life. Cold and heat have the same effects, and so have most other stimulants. The same remark applies to those stimuli which in a healthy state proceed from the mind and produce agreeable impressions; as, for instance, joy, which may be exalted to ecstacy, and so occasion sudden death.

It is probable that the same principle obtains in regard to the internal œconomy, and that those powerful sympathies which are the result of disease are many of them merely to be regarded as exaltations of natural impressions primarily subsisting between the different parts, which may be carried to any conceivable extent, so as to produce increased action, pain, or an entire destruction of the function. A different class of affections will, on the other hand, arise from a deficiency in these impressions.]

is completely produced, and an appetite arising from such stimulus takes place. Thus, the stomach when empty is susceptible of the stimulus of hunger. This kind of stimulus may be carried so far as to excite a diseased action, and must then be considered as an irritant.

Of Dispositions of the Body.—It may be difficult to define a disposition of the body, but that the body has dispositions is undeniable; and without knowing this, and therefore coming at or endeavouring to come at the knowledge of these dispositions of the body, a man must be a very confined surgeon in his practice. But the term disposition is more commonly applied to the mind than the body. In the mind it is more easily comprehended, because the mind has the power of investigating its own feelings or dispositions, also the power of communicating them, by means of the body, to the minds of others, so as to be understood or felt by those minds.

Every man has felt perhaps every disposition that can arise in the human mind, and is therefore perfectly sensible of those dispositions when they occur in others. But in the present inquiry the mind has no intelligence of the feelings or dispositions of the body, and is obliged to compare the effects of the one with those of the other, and where they are similar to suppose that the causes are also similar.

A disposition either in the mind or body, when in health, always arises from some impression; but as both mind and body are capable of seemingly spontaneous actions, these may arise from diseased dispositions in both, producing madness in one case and strong disease in the other.

As disposition may arise in consequence of some impression, it is capable of being destroyed by a counter-impression, which in disease is the method of cure that will be called specific. Many dispositions wear themselves out, or are such as the body or part cannot go on with.

A disposition is different from a visible action, yet it is possible it may be itself an action. If we compare the actions of the body with those of the mind (which is comparing from analogy, and perhaps the only mode we have), we shall gain a pretty good notion of them.

A disposition of the mind, then, certainly arises either from some action of the brain, or a certain position of the parts of the brain takes place, giving them an inclination to produce action. But this action, or the position which produces the inclination to action, we know nothing of; it is only a sensation of the mind, or rather a consciousness of the mind of such inclination, which sensation, or consciousness, is different from the sensation of the brain, arising from other actions of this viscus : and also knowing that such action of the brain as produces such sensation in the mind, is endeavouring to set other parts of the body into action which may be called voluntary, or rather actions in voluntary parts ; and that when such actions of the brain have taken place, such dispositions of the brain are lost; I say, knowing so much, we may, from analogy, form some idea of bodily dispositions. But the dispositions of the body appear to differ in this respect from those of the brain, that in the brain there is only the disposition, the ultimate or consequent action taking place in the body. But this is, perhaps, because we are not much acquainted with the immediate effects of the disposition in the brain, being led away by the visible actions which take place in the body.

To explain this, let us suppose that I have an impression made on my body in such a manner that my sensitive principle is sensible of it ; if, for instance, a man gives me a knock on the head that makes me angry, I form a disposition from that for resenting it : that disposition in my mind produces an action in my brain which forms a peculiar state of the mind, which is anger. If it was an action of some other kind, it might be affection or gratitude. The brain can do nothing by way of retaliation, whether it be gratitude or revenge which directs, but to set parts of the body to work. Having received a blow on my head, the disposition in my brain to produce the action of revenge sets my hands to work to give my enemy another blow, and then the disposition is at an end. So that whenever the action has taken place, the disposition is gone*. The ultimate effect is made sensible to us, and we are apt to imagine that it is the immediate act of the disposition of the brain; but it is only that the immediate action which took place in the brain made other parts of the body act secondarily, so that three actions are. necessary to the ultimate effect; but they are not all three actions of the brain. There is, 1st, the action which produces the disposition ; 2nd, the action of the nerves in consequence of the disposition ; 3rd,

---

* [The disposition does not cease because the action has taken place, but because a new feeling, that of gratified revenge, has arisen in the mind, and taken the place of the previous disposition. Had the blow of retaliation missed its aim, the disposition would have continued, notwithstanding the action had taken place, until a second and more effectual one had been given. This mode of reasoning from metaphysics and false analogy is extremely unsatisfactory, although it must be admitted, that many striking analogies exist between the powers and actions of the mind and those of the body, which Hunter seems to have studied with attention, and of which he has adduced some apt examples.]

the action of the voluntary muscles in consequence of the action in the nerves: but only the two first actions belong to the brain*.

Let us see how far this disposition and consequent action of the brain correspond with the dispositions of the body and the actions arising in consequence of these dispositions.

If on any part of an animal an impression is made, a disposition is formed suitable to that impression, which is the first; and an action in the same part suitable to that disposition may take place, which is the second, and is the ultimate; but if a sympathetic action takes place, it becomes somewhat similar to the ultimate effect on the body, arising from a disposition in the brain.

We may, with great propriety, compare the disposition and action of either the brain or the body with the disposition or action of an elastic body. An elastic body, when acted on, (which is similar to an impression made on the body,) acquires a disposition or inclination, which, if allowed, will produce action in all parts of the elastic body, which destroys the disposition. The disposition to action, and the action, are two very different things in themselves, even in the elastic body: when the elastic body has performed its action, it remains at rest until acted upon again; but it always requires action to destroy disposition.

We must make a material distinction between a disposition and an action in diseases, for what will cure an action will have no effect on a disposition.

Every machine is composed of very different parts, yet all tend to some ultimate effect. Every machine, whether natural, as an animal body, or constructed by art, however simple it may be, yet is always composed of more parts than one: and it must be observed, that no two parts have the same action, although all are tending, even in the most complicated, to produce some one ultimate effect.

For instance, some machines of art are intended for the division of time, as a clock, which may be so simple as to perform that effect by one wheel, the effect being expressed by an index. Some, again, are much more complicated, all the parts, however, being employed to the same ultimate effect, namely, the movement of this index, which expresses the ultimate effect; and the different parts composing the clock may be called organs.

So it is with natural machines; some animals are so simple as to have apparently but one operation, and that is support, and these may

---

* [Or rather to the sensitive principle, which he supposed to be seated in the whole of the nervous system.]

be called one organ. Others are complicated, being composed of different parts, whose actions and effects appear complete in themselves, as the action of a kidney, a liver, &c. : yet all combine to produce an ultimate effect in the machine, namely, the preservation and continuance of the species.

To produce the ultimate effect in any machine, there must be a succession of actions, one naturally arising out of another, each part taking on the action peculiar to itself; the preceding action being always the stimulus to the next succeeding one; and thus the parts go on acting in regular succession until the ultimate effect is produced, and then the whole is at rest until stimulated into action again. In some parts this is almost immediately, as in the heart, organs of respiration, &c.; thus, when the heart has thrown out its blood, it has done its business; when we inspire and expire, the organs of respiration have done their business, but there is a necessity for a recurrence of the operation again, and so immediately that it seems almost constant. But in others there is a greater distance of time before the action is renewed, as in hunger, evacuation of the fæces, urine, &c.

An animal body so constructed gives us an idea of perfection, for as each part has its particular appointment, one should naturally expect equality or powers suitable to these appointments would be found through the whole. But this certainly is not the case, at least in the more complicated animals, whatever it may be in the more imperfect or simple. We find this in the more perfect, where life depends for support on the action of some one part, as the heart; also where many actions of the animal depend on the powers of another part, as the voluntary actions on the brain; and not only the simple voluntary actions of the body depend on this viscus, but their real strength depends on it, for whenever the power of the brain is taken off, they waste; and this wasting does not arise from the brain supplying these parts with nourishment, and that being now cut off they lose their future support, but it arises from want of necessity to keep these parts in a state fit for action* when action cannot take place, because the will cannot now stimu-

---

* [If the exercise of every part is its natural stimulus to perfection, as it certainly is, by exciting the natural actions of which every part is capable, then the want of exercise is the cause of this wasting. The same effect would equally be produced, although the parts should be supposed perfectly capable of executing their proper functions if called upon to do so. The stomach that has long fasted, or the eye which has long been deprived of light, lose the power of performing their ordinary functions just in the same manner that a joint which has long been confined in one position loses its suppleness and strength, and the muscles waste. This tendency on the part of our author to suppose a sort of intelligential understanding subsisting among the different parts of the body has been already adverted to.]

late them to action; and the same thing takes place in a proportionate degree when a joint is simply rendered, either wholly or in part, unfit for motion, where no injury has been done to the nerves. Hence it must appear, that as the power of support is in one part of the machine, and the power of many actions in another part of the machine, it is possible that all parts of the body may not be equally served by the first, namely, the heart; nor equally influenced by the second, namely, the brain; and we do find that the more distant parts from these sources of power are the weakest. This, perhaps, is better illustrated in disease than by any actions of health. We may just observe, that all the vital parts are near the one, and all the acute sensations near the other. In disease we see a mortification arising in the extremities more than in the other parts, and more especially if the person is tall, so that the heart is not capable of propelling the support of life to those distant parts in such a state of the constitution.

How far the blood may lose its power of nourishment before it reaches the extremities, I will not say. If our acute sensations are near to the brain, it is reasonable to suppose that proximity of parts adds to the power of the nerves in communicating sensation; if so, it is reasonable to suppose that proximity of parts will also add to that power which the brain has over the actions of voluntary parts by means of the nerves.

On Habit and Custom.—Memory, or recollection of past impressions, has, I believe, principally been applied to, or supposed to be an attribute of, the mind only; but we know that every part endued with life is susceptible of impressions, and also that they are capable of running into the same action without the immediate impressions being repeated. Habits arise from this principle of repetition of, or becoming accustomed to, any impression, and the same thing exactly takes place in the mind. The memory of the body is of much shorter duration than that of the mind. The mind not only goes more readily into action the second time of an impression, though a considerable distance of time has taken place since it went into the same action before, but seems to take up the action with more ease, from merely collateral causes, from a recollection of the similarity, or often without any possible recollection whatever, as if the actions, in consequence of the former impression, were taking place in the brain again. This does not appear to be so much the case with the memory of the body, for this only arises from immediate impression, but goes into action a second time more readily than at first. Possibly, however, the action arising from the first impression may be repeated from some collateral or similar impression to the first; if so, it comes very near to that of the mind, though not so strong.

A gentleman rubbed in mercurial ointment for the reduction of two buboes; he had only used it a few times when it affected his constitution so much that he was obliged to leave it off: he became feverish, the fever being of the hectic kind, with a small quick pulse, debility, loss of appetite, no sleep, and night sweats. He took the bark, with James's powder. As the effects of the mercury went off, and his buboes were advancing, it was necessary to have recourse to mercury again: he now rubbed in a considerable quantity without its having the least effect on his constitution or mouth; but the buboes spreading, made me order it to be left off again, and they were opened. He had recourse to the ointment the third time without its producing any disagreeable effect. The buboes took on a healing disposition, but then became stationary. I ordered him to leave off the ointment, to go to the sea, and bathe, and then they began again to heal. In about three weeks it was thought necessary to rub in again: when he began, it almost immediately affected his mouth very violently; he left it off till his mouth was a little better, when he began for the fifth time, and it had not so much effect, and he was able to pursue the mercury. Now in this case he had lost the mercurial habit during the time he was at the sea, the parts had forgotten the mercury altogether, and the mercury coming on such a state of constitution, produced the same effect as it would have done if he had not taken mercury. So that the body had, as it were, lost the remembrance of the effect of the mercury on it in so short a time; but the mind would not have lost it.

Custom is with me the negative of habit: by custom comes an insensibility to impression, the impression diminishing although the cause is the same, and the parts becoming more and more at rest; whereas from habit there comes an increased facility to go into action, as also an acquired perfection in the action itself, the impression continuing the same though the cause is diminishing.

These may be reckoned as secondary principles in an animal, and produce two very opposite effects, both according to their modes of impression.

Habit is the continuance of actions we have been accustomed to produce, without any immediate assistance, or even continuance, of the first cause, as a body set in motion continues to move after the cause of motion has ceased to act.

Custom arises from external impressions, either in the mind or body, and is of two kinds, one when, the cause continuing, the impressions, and consequently the actions, are diminished, the parts becoming habituated to the impression. We shall see the effect of this in our applications. If we apply a medicine to a sore, which shall affect it in one way or another, (it is immaterial which for the principle, but we will

suppose it heals,) from becoming accustomed to that application, it shall
lose the impression, and shall at last do nothing; therefore you will be
obliged to make the application more stimulating, more active, or change
it for something else.　It is exactly so with the mind; if a man goes
into a strange place he is affected by the new objects about it; the next
time he goes he is less struck; the third time less, till at last, when he
goes into the place he can hardly perceive anything strange in it.
These very different effects arise from a difference in the degree of impression resulting from the state of the mind or body at the time.　In
the first instance, if the impression or cause be very slight, so as hardly
either to alarm the part or the constitution, they will get familiar with
it, and will become insensible to it; a ring on the finger, the use of
snuff, our very clothes, and physic itself are striking and daily instances
of this.　The habit of insensibility will soon be formed if the sensations
of the mind and body be not very acute.　If the first impression be
violent, and such as produces considerable effect, it is not necessary that
the same degree of violence should be inflicted to produce a similar effect a second time.　One can easily imagine that these impressions may
be continued until the parts continue to act without the impression,
which would then become habit.　If a dose of an emetic be given, which
affects the stomach much, the same quantity is not necessary a second
time to produce the same effect; the second must be given, however,
before the stomach has lost the impression of the first perfectly*.

The same effect is produced on the mind as on the body, for whatever
has made but a slight impression, soon wears out, and we think no
more upon it.　On the other hand, if an animal has met with anything
that has affected its mind much, as fear, &c., it is not necessary for the
object to appear in the same manner to produce a similar effect.

Those effects will be more or less, according to the state of the body
or mind at the time of the first affection; the more irritable or the more
ready it is to fall into the first action at the time, the more readily will
it take it up the second time, although it may not be particularly irritable or susceptible of this particular action.

---

* [This arises partly from habit and partly from the fact that the emetic has produced an irritable state of the stomach, which renders it more susceptible of the action
of any irritant.　It would appear that mere impressions, or the passive part of habits
(called by Mr. Hunter custom), always diminish in intensity by repetition, but that the
actions or thoughts that are put in train by those impressions recur more easily the
oftener the impressions are repeated.　The reader who is desirous of pursuing this subject is referred to Bishop Butler's admirable treatise on the Analogy of Natural and
Revealed Religion, Part I. Chap. V., a book which, like Hunter's treatise on Inflammation, was the product of upwards of twenty years' labour, and is stamped in every
page with characters of the most profound genius.]

Habit.—A habit of acting arises from a repetition of acting, which repetition of acting is custom, and which becomes the cause of the continuance of the same action. So that custom is always prior to habit, or, as it were, forms habit, which may be ranked as one of the secondary principles in the machine.

The first action being produced by a disposition in, or force upon, the part, this being repeated or continued a sufficient length of time, the action at length goes on, when that original disposition or force is gone, until some other power counteracts it, or it wears itself out. The more we have been in the habit of thinking on any object, the more readily does the train of thinking relating to that object recur. This principle in the animal is similar to the vis inertiæ in matter, for by it a motion begun is continued, and their remaining at rest is from the same cause. This principle becomes the cause of the actions of the mind; it does not allow men to think differently from what they have been accustomed to think. Men in general go through life with the same modes of thinking, and thus it becomes a cause either of the retardation or improvement of the understanding. It retards improvement, because it gets the better of even present sensations, and does not allow men to wander into novelty. It promotes improvement, because it makes men perfect in what they have been long employed about.

CHAPTER VIII.

OF THE HEAT OF ANIMALS.

The principle of heat a great principle of action in nature ;—nature of, unknown ;—opposed to cold ;—unequal distribution of on the earth ;—measures of sensible heat ;—absolute heat of bodies, unknown ;—of the sensation of heat ;—destructive when in a high degree, as is cold.—Natural heat of animals capable of diminution without loss of life ;—certain functions first cease ;—propagation of the species first ;—digestion in some animals, as reptiles.—All animals endowed with heat, but in different degrees ;—erroneous notions of its causes ;—cases in which the function was remarkably deranged ;—experiments, showing the power of animals to generate heat in proportion to the necessity ;—order of cessation of functions from cold ;—diminution of heat during sleep.—Experiments on hedgehogs.—Heat of lower animals varying with temperature of the air.—Standard heat of higher animals not exact.—Experiments to ascertain whether cold acts as a stimulus to the production of heat.—Resistance to external heat ;—experiments ;—those by Fordyce.—Observations on animals having a standard heat ;—differences in the capability of different animals to produce heat.—On differences of climate resulting from temperature ;—other causes also act.

THE principle of heat is one of the first principles of action in nature; it is that which unlocks matter, and allows it to act according to its natural properties, or according to its combinations. It may be even said to compel matter to action. But that idea arose, I imagine, more from the effects which extreme heat has both on our sensations, and its immediate effects on our bodies seeming to produce a species of violence, for we do not annex this idea to moderate heat, although moderate and immoderate heat act on the same principle of putting matter in such a position that certain actions in the matter must take place, all which arises from the nature of the part heated. How far it is an active principle is not easily ascertained, though we must allow it has every appearance of being one.

The term heat meant originally simple sensation, arising from a property of matter capable of producing that sensation, which is only an effect of that property. But philosophers having inquired into the causes and effects of this matter, have, from a poverty of language, applied the word which was at first only expressive of a quality to the thing itself, so that by heat now is also meant the matter of heat abstracted from the sensation which it occasions*. This is so much the case, that Dr. Black† makes use of the term latent heat to signify that heat which a body contains without imparting it to the senses, as we might call the water which goes into the formation of salt latent water; in other words, that water which the salt contains without losing its solidity.

It has been much disputed whether heat is matter, or only a property of matter. If it is simply matter, then wherever there is heat there must be that matter present. If heat is a property of matter, there must be both matter and property present. If heat is only an action in a particular matter, then there is that matter with its action, as also the body which throws this matter into the action‡.

Heat and cold are opposite principles, and cannot inhabit the same place§. They occupy different parts of the globe, and in some places alternately; these, therefore, are subject to the variations of temperature, which cause varieties of climate. These will be further spoken of hereafter.

Heat, although not equally distributed all over the globe, yet exists in such a degree as to pervade all matter, and is therefore to be found in some proportion everywhere. Heat destroys attractions of all kinds, by which means it becomes the principle of fluidity, and consequently

---

* [The sense of this inconvenience has given rise to the general use of the term caloric for the agent which produces the sensation of heat.]

† [In connexion with the name of Dr. Black, we may mention that it was not until this able philosopher had completed his train of researches on the subject of heat that the true theory of respiration began to be understood, or the connexion which subsisted between this function and the production of animal heat. Previous to this time the lungs were considered merely as the agent for cooling the blood.]

‡ [Whether heat consists of a highly attenuated subtle matter which pervades all things, or of a vibration among the atoms of matter, has not yet been decided. Its leading feature is evinced in the repulsion which it produces among the particles of matter, in which respect it is the proper antagonising force to attraction. Whatever it is we do not know anything of the principle itself, or of the manner in which it produces its effects.

The subject of animal heat occupied a great deal of Mr. Hunter's attention, in consequence of which he made it the subject of two express papers in the Philosophical Transactions, besides recurring to it again very fully in the Treatises on Inflammation and the Animal Œconomy. The reader is referred to these works in the third and fourth volumes for fuller information.]

§ [Cold was formerly thought by philosophers to be a positive principle, like heat, instead of a mere negation or absence of heat, as it is at present almost, if not quite, universally considered. It is in the former view that Mr. Hunter speaks of it.]

the reverse of the cohesive attraction, or principle of solidity. By means of this effect, motion is allowed to take place among the particles of matter. We have no other idea respecting the variations of heat, except as regards quantity. The quantity of heat has always been estimated by some visible effects, at first probably by our sensations alone, but afterwards by its effects on the expansion of bodies, especially of metals*, all of which is called sensible heat. But it has been discovered lately that many bodies retain more heat than can be made sensible by any of the commonly constructed instruments; therefore a body may have the matter of heat in it without its producing any sensible effects. Hence heat has now been divided by some into sensible and absolute heat. It may be possible that many bodies may have their whole heat made sensible; if so, then their sensible and absolute heat are the same. But it is most probable that the absolute heat of a body can never be known, for the measure of the quantities of heat from every experiment is always by sensible heat, which can never be a proof of the absolute heat in a body.

The real increase of heat must alter the position of parts so as to produce the sensation called heat; and as this heat is diminished, the texture or position of the parts is altered the contrary way, which, when carried to a certain degree, becomes the cause of the sensation of cold. Now these sensations could not take place without a real increase or decrease of heat in the parts. When heat is applied to the skin, it becomes hot in some degree, according to the application. This may be carried so far as actually to burn the living parts. On the contrary, in a cold atmosphere a man's hand shall become so cold as to lose the sensation of cold altogether, and change for that of pain†.

---

* [It has lately been discovered that minute variations of temperature, utterly inappreciable by the ordinary instruments founded on the principle of expansion, may be rendered evident and estimated by means of electro-magnetical currents, which are found to traverse certain arrangements of the metals when unequally heated. The degree in which the needle deflects from its mean position indicates the quantity of caloric which has entered the heated body, and may be measured by an index of degrees.]

† [It is improbable that the sense of heat and cold depends simply on an "alteration in the [texture or] position of the parts," for if this were the case the same temperature, by inducing the same condition of parts, should always produce the same sensation, although it is well known that this is far from being the case. What to one hand, just removed from a vessel of hot water, feels very cold, shall feel very hot to the other hand just removed from a vessel of cold water; or a part shall feel hot or cold when the reverse of these states is actually present. The sense of change, or the intensity of the impression, is estimated in relation to the previous state rather than to its absolute quantity, or else depends on some peculiar and morbid condition of the sentient organ. Thus, the eye which has long been secluded from light is oppressively affected by the

Real heat and cold may be carried so far as to alter the texture of parts on which the actions of life depend. Nature has allowed the heat of most animals to come much lower than the heat necessary for performing all their natural functions. This is most so in the more imperfect animals, although it exists in a considerable degree in those possessed of a better regulated standard of heat, as the most perfect.

This answers the wisest purposes, for by allowing the heat to come to that degree in which many actions are suspended, or annihilated, the state of the animal is adapted to the state of the atmosphere, which is such as would render the effects of those actions unnecessary or of no effect.

The first action that is suspended is the propagation of the species; for if birds were to hatch, or animals to bring forth their young, in winter, there would soon be an end to propagation in the temperate and frigid zone, as animals in general only breed once a year.

Cold also annihilates the powers of digestion in all those animals whose food is rendered impossible to be procured in the winter, and which have not power of emigration, such as frogs, lizards, snakes, bats, hedgehogs, &c.

The power of generating heat was the first considered; the possibility of generating cold being hardly suspected, because most people who made observations on this subject lived in an atmosphere colder than their own body. They observed, that in almost all animals there was a standard of heat, which in common language has been called blood heat. However, they extended their observations a little further, and called a certain number of animals the cold-blooded animals, but made no experiments either to ascertain the effects or the principle on which they depended.

If we examine any class of animals, we shall find them, more or less, endowed with this principle, though varying from one another very materially in this respect. The heat of the human body being always considerable, even in the coldest climate, it has necessarily attracted a good deal of the attention of philosophers and physiologists, and various have been the opinions which they have formed respecting its cause.

Friction being a cause of the production of heat in many bodies, was supposed to be the cause of heat in animals, especially, too, as they

---

common light of day; and the same thing may be asserted of stimulants and their effects universally.

It is a singular fact that excessive cold should produce effects very similar to those produced by excessive heat. Frozen mercury, for instance, occasions a sensation of burning, and destroys the life of the part which touches it if the contact is prolonged only a few seconds.]

thought it could be easily explained on this principle, for they observed there was sufficient motion in the body for such an effect, which motion was principally that of the blood. They calculated the size of the internal surfaces of the arteries, which increases as they divide. They calculated the size and number of the red globules; all of which furnished an amazing extent of surface for friction; and when they calculated the velocity of the blood moving on this extent of surface, as also of the globules on one another, they thought they saw a sufficient cause for the heat of the body, especially as they saw that when this motion was increased, as in fevers, the heat was to appearance greater. But we may say at the same time, that they did not see the objections to this theory, which are many.

Dr. Stevenson* observed, that there was another cause for the production of heat besides friction, viz. fermentation, and on this principle he accounted for animal heat. But the fermentation of animal substances does not produce heat.

The superstructure built on the foundation that the friction, from the motion of the blood, is the cause of animal heat, falls immediately to the ground on the observation that fluids have no power of generating heat; nor have two solids, if kept asunder by the intervention of a fluid of any kind. If this had not been a fact, still friction probably would not have accounted for all the variety in the production of animal heat. Nor could the principle of fermentation account for all the phenomena which attend the heat of animals; therefore some other principle must be referred to as the cause.

It being discovered that the absolute heat of bodies differs very much in different substances, and perhaps in the same substances differently combined, it was thought that this would account for the production and continuation of animal heat. It is supposed that the air which we inspire has much more absolute heat than the same air has when we expire it, and that the superabundant heat of the inspired air is given to the animal. But this chemical method of accounting for heat will not account for all the varieties in the heat of animals at different times, especially in disease, when the breathing does not equally vary or correspond with the heat of the animal.

A remarkable case fell under my observation of a gentleman who was taken with an apoplectic fit. He lay insensible in bed, covered

---

* [Edin. Med. Essays, vol. v. Part II. p. 806, et seq. These can only be regarded as specimens of the opinions and modes of reasoning adopted by the mechanical and chemical physiologists of the last and the preceding centuries, to the subversion of which the efforts of Hunter, united with those of Haller, Stahl, and Cullen, mainly contributed.]

with the blankets. I found his whole body would become extremely cold in every part, and continue so some time, and in a short time would become extremely hot. While this was going on, several hours alternately, there was no sensible alteration either in the pulse or the breathing.

A man fell from his horse, and pitched on his head, and produced all the symptoms of a violent injury. There was concussion and perhaps extravasation of blood, but no fracture could be seen. The pulse was at first 120°, but came to 100, and sometimes to 90, and was strong, full, and rather hard. He was very hot in the skin, but breathed remarkably slow, only half the common frequency.

His breathing, pulse, and heat therefore did not correspond with this theory of heat.

February, 1781.—A boy about three years old appeared not quite so well as common, being attacked with a kind of shortness of breathing in the night. It had become exceedingly oppressive about five o'clock on Sunday morning, so difficult that he appeared dying for want of breath. In this state he lay till ten o'clock when I saw him. He was breathing so slowly that I thought every breath would be his last, about two and a half inspirations, or even less, in a minute. (The common rate of breathing in such a boy is about thirty inspirations in a minute, and about twenty in a man.) When he drew his breath it was with a jerk; but his expiration was extremely slow, generally continuing through five seconds. I often could not distinguish the pulse, at other times it was very manifest, although very faint and slow, not more than sixty. On tying up the arm the vein did not rise in the least, so that the blood did not go its round. His eyes were turned under the upper eyelid; while his body had a purple cast, especially the lips, which is easily accounted for,—it was owing to the blood not getting the scarlet red in its passage through the lungs, and whatever it might get there was lost in its slow motion through the arteries of the body. He had a fine warmth on the skin all over the body, although in a room without a fire, not covered with more clothes than common in the month of February, with snow falling at noon.

Here it cannot be said that the heat of the body, which was neither great nor deficient, could arise from the constant supply furnished by respiration.

It appears from the account given in the Philosophical Transactions of the experiments made in the heated room, under the direction of Dr. George Fordyce, that Dr. Cullen long ago suggested many arguments to show that life itself had a power of generating heat, independently of any common mechanical or chemical means; though we may observe, that the experiments here related only tend to show the power of producing cold, which they effectually do.

I own I had formed an opinion on this subject. I rather supposed that animal heat was owing to some decomposition going on in the body, and in pretty regular progression, though not the process of fermentation.

In consequence of an experiment made on two carp, to explain another principle in the animal œconomy, (where every common action was meant to be wholly suppressed, or so far suppressed as to render them incapable of producing heat,) I found an effect produced while the animals were under the experiment which I did not suspect. I began, in consequence, to suspect some other cause of heat than the common or natural actions of an animal; for during the experiment I observed a remarkable reproduction of heat taking place in these two animals. Until this time I had not an idea that there was a possibility of calling the principle forth, or that cold could excite it.

Experiment. In the year 1766 two carp were put into a glass vessel with common river water, and the vessel was put into a freezing-mixture. The water surrounding the fish froze very rapidly on the inside of the glass all round. When the freezing-process approached the fish it became as it were stationary; and the remaining water not freezing fast enough, in order to make it freeze sooner I put in as much cold snow as made the whole thick. The snow round the carp melted. I put in more snow, which melted also. This was repeated several times, till I grew tired, and I left them covered up to freeze by the joint operation of the mixture and the atmosphere. After having exhausted the whole power of life in the production of heat, they froze; but that life was gone could not be known till we thawed the animals, which was done very gradually. But with their flexibility they did not recover action, so that they were really dead. Till this time I had imagined that it might be possible to prolong life to any period by freezing a person in the frigid zone, as I thought all action and waste would cease until the body was thawed. I thought that if a man would give up the last ten years of his life to this kind of alternate oblivion and action, it might be prolonged to a thousand years; and by getting himself thawed every hundred years, he might learn what had happened during his frozen condition. Like other schemers, I thought I should make my fortune by it; but this experiment undeceived me*.

---

* [Blumenbach observes that the pupæ of many insects are in winter so thoroughly frozen as to ring like glass or icicles when allowed to drop on the ground, and yet without any injury to the torpid animal within. " The eggs of silkworms and butterflies hatch after exposure to a cold of 24° below zero. On the other hand, insects may

This experiment laid the basis of many of my future conjectures on animal heat.

I think we may observe in the common occurrences of life that for the actions of an animal a certain quantity of heat is necessary; and this quantity I find to be in some degree according to those actions, the greatest degree of heat being always wanted for the least essential action in every order of animals. However, every order of animals in general requires a heat peculiar to itself, though not always so, some admitting of a much greater variety than others even of the same order, as in the insect tribe.

The actions of an animal may be placed in the following order with respect to its heat, which is the inverse order to that of their immediate use in the machine. Propagation first; digestion; sensation, in which may be included wakefulness; secretion; circulation; each requiring its degree of heat for complete action. Propagation requires the greatest, digestion may be carried on with a degree less, secretion in two degrees less than propagation, and so on.

In the insect tribe there is a difference between a bee and a wasp and many flies. A bee at all times requires a heat above 90 (?) degrees* to support life with ease, while a wasp can allow its heat to vary with the atmosphere without losing life.

When the external heat is so much diminished that it does not assist the natural powers of an animal, and it is obliged to vary its proper standard and become colder, then many of the actions are either lessened or totally suspended, not being necessary: generation is suspended, and insensibility takes place, commonly called sleep; but it is not sleep. Sleep is an effect which takes place in all degrees of heat and cold, though when a man is asleep he is colder than when he is awake, and I find in general the difference is about 1½ degree, sometimes less†. This difference in the degree of heat between sleeping

---

be frozen repeatedly, and recovered as soon as thawed." (Elliotson's Physiology, p. 247.) This faculty of enduring cold is infinitely less surprising than that referred to by the last-mentioned author, which allows beetles and other insects to survive being boiled. See note.]

* [Hunter found the thermometer rise to 93° or 98° in a hive of bees in spring; to 104° in summer; to 82° when the air was at 40°, and to 73° in winter. (See his Paper on Bees in Vol. IV.)]

† [There is the same close relation between the ordinary sleep of animals in general and the ordinary sleep of hybernating animals, as there is between this last and absolute torpor. In the 1st, the respiration is diminished and the temperature lessened 1¾°; in the 2nd, the respiration is still further diminished, and the temperature reduced to within a few degrees of the external medium; and in the 3rd, the respiration is altogether suspended, and the temperature reduced to the surrounding medium. Cold is evidently a

and waking is not the cause of sleep but the effect; for many diseases produce a much greater degree of cold in an animal, without any tendency to sleep. Besides, many of the operations of perfect health are going on in the time of natural sleep, at least in the perfect animals, as digestion, secretion, &c., while none of these operations are going on in the tribes called sleepers during their torpid state*. In these animals, where a great many actions are suspended, it appears an effect arising from a certain degree of cold acting as a sedative.

Now this degree of cold in some cases seems to act as a stimulant: the animal powers are roused to action for self-preservation. It is probable that most animals are under this influence of cold, and that every order has its degree of cold in which many of their actions can be suspended.

In some countries, where there is summer and winter, there are some animals whose actions are suspended during the winter. This suspension of several of their actions seems natural to them, being part of the œconomy of such animals. In other animals, where a suspension of several of their actions takes place from cold, it seems a force on those actions, as it rather seems to lead to the destruction of the animal than the preservation of life. We cannot give a stronger instance of the forcible power of the suspension of actions in animals from cold than what happened to Dr. Solander and others in their voyage round the world.

Returning from a hill in Terra del Fuego, they were suddenly surprised with a degree of cold beyond what they ever felt before. Dr. Solander advised that they should immediately make their way to the ship as fast as possible, and he himself would bring up the rear. However unnecessary it might appear, Dr. S., who had crossed the mountains in Switzerland, well knew the danger of being left, and told them that they would soon be attacked with an almost irresistible propensity to sleep; that whoever gave way to the feeling would sleep, and whoever slept would die. But after this very serious caution, the doctor was the first who felt the sensation he described, and could scarcely be

---

predisposing cause to all these states. Cuvier, however, has remarked that in some warm latitudes, as, for example, in the Isle of France, there are certain animals which fall into a state of torpor only during the hot months.]

* [There is a good deal of difference in this respect in different animals. The hedgehog and dormouse awake every three or four days when the weather is mild, and during the interval of activity pass the urine and fæces freely, which could not be the case if they did not digest and secrete during their state of torpor. This has never been observed of the bat, because the bat is an insectivorous animal, and would awake in vain if there were no insects. The circulation, however, is continued even in the bat at the rate of twenty-eight strokes in the minute during the state of torpor. (See Phil. Trans., 1832.)]

persuaded by the united efforts of Mr. Banks and the others to proceed. Mr. Banks's black servant, Richmond, was the next whose desire of sleep was very great, so much so that, notwithstanding the consequences, he begged that he might be left to die. The Doctor only begged to sleep a little, and promised that he would then proceed. Mr. Banks, finding the case grow more serious every moment, sent forward four of the company to the first place where they could light a fire, the rest staying and endeavouring to bring up the few who had lain down. The Doctor was awaked, but their efforts were less successful on poor Richmond. In the midst of their endeavours to rouse him, they felt the same symptoms stealing on themselves very fast; it was in vain to attempt carrying, every one being scarcely able to carry himself. Having proceeded about a quarter of a mile, they met two of their party with the welcome news of a fire being kindled at the distance of half a mile. These two were dispatched in search of Richmond. Having warmed themselves, and becoming apprehensive for the fate of the two, a party set off in search of them. They had missed their way, and become victims to the malady from which they had endeavoured to restore the black. Richmond was found just crawling, and brought back, but no means had the least effect on the other two*.

Winter.—I took two hedgehogs, not full grown, from their huts: the weather for some days preceding had been severe and frosty; the heat of the atmosphere was 44°. In one the thermometer was introduced at the pelvis, and the mercury stood at 45°; and at the diaphragm at 48°. In the other I found the heat in the pelvis 46°, and at the diaphragm 50°.

The degree of heat of these animals being so low, it was compared with the heat of a puppy. The heat of the atmosphere during this experiment being 50°, a thermometer was introduced into the belly and pelvis of the puppy; the mercury stood at 102°, and also at the diaphragm.

Summer.—Atmosphere at 78°. A thermometer was introduced into

---

* [Many thousands of Napoleon's army are reported to have perished nightly from the same cause during the retreat from Moscow.

Sir B. Brodie classes the effects of cold in the following order:

" 1st, It lessens the irritability and impairs the functions of the whole nervous system.

" 2nd, It impairs the contractile power of the muscles.

" 3rd, It causes contraction of the capillaries, and thus lessens the superficial circulation and stops the cutaneous secretion.

" 4th, It probably destroys the principle of vitality equally in every part, and does not exclusively disturb the functions of any particular organ."

(MS. Notes of Lectures by Sir B. Brodie *apud* Paris.)]

the belly of a freshly-caught hedgehog. In the pelvis the mercury rose to 95°, at the diaphragm to 97°.

From the foregoing experiments we find that the temperature is allowed to fall lower than the standard, which is productive of no evil excepting suspending such functions as require the standard degree of heat for their actions.

Animal matter endowed with the living principle, whether endowed with action or not, or whether of the first or second order of animals, as far as I am acquainted, admits of the temperature going somewhat lower than would serve for the congelation of the same matter in a dead state.

The more imperfect animals vary their heat according to the atmosphere in some degree.

I made the following experiments on fowls, which I considered to be one degree above the amphibia, and one degree below what are commonly called quadrupeds.

I introduced the ball of the thermometer successively into the rectum of several hens, and found the mercury at 103°, 103½°, or 104°. Cocks furnished the same results. In hens during incubation the heat was the same. Living eggs under the same hens raised the thermometer to 99°; an addled egg only to 97°. So that the living egg had some power of generating heat. In the more perfect animal, as the fowl, the heat is not allowed to come so low as in the more imperfect.

The power of generating heat keeps the higher animals as near one standard as possible; but it was not necessary that this standard should be very exact, therefore we find that they are in some degree influenced by external heat and cold, somewhat similar to inanimate matter and the more imperfect animals*.

As parts recede from the common mass, as extremities, fingers, toes, the combs of cocks, &c., they are more subject to be affected by cold, and will raise or sink the thermometer in some measure according to the external degree of heat or cold applied; though not in a proportional degree to this application, as would be the case in inanimate matter.

I put the ball of the thermometer under my tongue, and kept it there

---

* [In the more perfect animals the temperature of the vital parts is more easily elevated above the natural standard than depressed below it. Thus, it was found in Capt. Parry's second voyage, that out of sixteen foxes, which were killed while the thermometer was from 3° to 32° below zero, the temperature of eleven varied from 100° to 106¾°: and so in other cases it has been observed that the temperature of the blood at the heart bears no relation to the external cold; a fact which cannot equally be affirmed in regard to heat.

for some minutes, when it rose to 97°, but would not go higher. I then took several pieces of ice and put them in the same situation, allowing them to melt. This I continued ten minutes, and found on introducing the thermometer that it fell to 77°, and gradually rose again to 97°.

I thought the urethra would do still better, and I introduced the ball of a thermometer into a man's urethra. At one inch from the extremity the mercury rose to 92°, at two inches to 93°, at four to 94°; at the bulb of the urethra it rose to 97°. Thus we see that projecting parts are subject to have their heat lowered by surrounding cold.

To render this experiment more conclusive, I endeavoured to render this part colder by applying a colder medium to the penis than the common situation. This part was immersed in water at 65° for a minute. The thermometer, introduced an inch and a half, rose to 79°.

To find if there was any difference in the quickness of heating and cooling between living and dead parts, as also what difference, I made the following experiments.

I procured a dead and a living penis: the heat of the living penis, an inch and a half in, was 92°. I heated the dead one to the same degree, then immersed both in water at 50°. The dead one cooled fastest, but only two or three degrees; the living one coming down to 58°, while the dead one came down to 55°. I repeated the same experiment several times with the same result.

The standard heat of the human body is about 99°, and I believe that degree is pretty regular; however, this regularity in some degree arises from there being in every body a considerable mass of matter which causes less consumption of heat. This standard is necessary for the more material actions of life.

The heat of the more imperfect animals is not the same in every part of the body, even when there appears an equal mass of matter. To ascertain this, I took a healthy dormouse, the atmosphere being at 64°. I put the thermometer into the belly, nearly in the middle between the thorax and the pelvis; it rose to 74°: at the diaphragm it rose to 80°, against the liver to 81¼°.

As there is some difference between the heat of an animal at the source of the circulation and that of the mouth, pelvis, and rectum, we must make an allowance in judging of the heat of the heart by that of these parts.

I next wanted to ascertain if cold applied to an animal would act as a stimulus, and therefore greater heat be produced than the common standard.

I took a healthy mouse,—atmosphere 64°,—introduced the ball of

the thermometer between the thorax and pelvis. The mercury rose to
74½°, at the liver to 81½°. I put the mouse into an atmosphere at 30°,
and when the ball was again introduced into the belly the mercury rose
to 92°, at the liver 93°, the animal being still very lively. Here was
an increase of 17½° in the belly, and 11½° at the liver, and this produced
by the application of cold to the skin.

Of the Resistance to foreign Heat above the standard.—We have found
that animals evidently possess a power within themselves of producing
heat when in a cold atmosphere, so as to keep their bodies in a temperature suitable to the œconomy of the animal. But as animals are often
placed in an atmosphere much hotter than their standard heat, I wanted
next to see how far they have a cooling power, or, if they have not, to
what degree the heat of an animal might be increased, and what might
be the consequence of that increase, supposing it possible; for *à priori*
we should suppose that the standard heat, or that heat at which all the
animal functions are best carried on, would be the medium heat of the
animal. But I find from experiment that the standard is generally
within a degree or two of the ultimate heat that the animal can bear.
As allowing the heat to rise above the standard could answer no wise
purpose, Nature has put a check to it by making the stimulus of heat the
cause of its own annihilation, just as the stimulus of cold produces, on
the other hand, an increase of heat*.

This would appear to take place in two different ways: one is by
evaporation, which arises from the action of the living powers; and the
other by an immediate power of destroying heat. So that animals have
two means of destroying heat, while it would appear that they have only
one for the production of it.

I put a viper into an atmosphere at 108°, and allowed it to stay in
seven minutes, when the heat in the stomach and anus was 92½°, beyond
which it could not rise in the above heat.

The same experiment was made on frogs with nearly the same
success†.

I now tried to what degree of heat I could bring a more perfect
animal; and as I found the penis the best part for trying the experiment with cold, I imagined it would be the best for the trial of heat.
The experiments were made in the same manner with the former, only

---

* [The *cause* of animal heat is considered in the Treatise on Inflammation, Part II.,
chap. iii., sect. 3; and the mode by which the temperature is regulated, at sect. 4. The
reader is referred to this part of the Work, as well as to the author's paper on this subject in Vol. IV.]

† [According to De la Roche, the temperature of frogs does not rise above 80° to 82°
in a medium of 110° or 115°. (Journ. de Phys., tom. lxiii.)]

the water was now hotter than the heat of the man. These were only simple experiments, but I chose to make a comparative one with a dead penis.

A living and dead penis were immersed in water gradually made warmer and warmer, from 100° to 118°, and continued in this heat for some minutes. The dead penis raised the thermometer to 114°, while the living could not raise it higher than 102½°. It was observed by the person on whom the experiment was made, that about a minute after the part was put in water the water did not feel hot, but on the water being agitated it felt so hot that he could hardly bear it. On applying the thermometer to the sides of the living glans, while in the water, the mercury fell from 118° to about 104°, while it did not fall above a degree when put close to the dead penis, so that the living glans produced a cold space of water about it*. This experiment may furnish a useful hint about bathing in water, whether colder or warmer than the heat of the body; for if it is intended to be either colder or hotter, as it will soon be of the same temperature with that of the body, the patient, if in a large bath, should move from place to place, and in a warm bath there should be a constant succession of water of the intended heat†.

The experiments made by Dr. G. Fordyce in heated rooms prove, in the clearest manner, that the body has a power of destroying heat.

The action of evaporation produces cold, and in proportion to the quickness of the evaporation is the cold produced; and from experiment we find that the evaporation of spirits of wine produces cold faster than that of water, and of æther faster than spirits of wine. On this principle we suppose that evaporation is one means of producing cold in the living body‡.

It appears from Dr. Fordyce's experiments that the living powers were very much assisted in generating cold by evaporation, but that evaporation was not the sole agent in keeping the body cool. There is

---

* [These experiments on *parts* of the body are evidently inconclusive, in as much as any elevation of temperature is necessarily prevented by a continual influx of fresh blood, which carries off the heat.]

† [Upon the same principle the Sirocco and scorching winds of the African deserts are so destructive of animal life. In the expedition to discover the N.W. Passage, the sailors found a temperature at zero attended with a breeze far more difficult to resist than a temperature at 50° below zero attended with a calm atmosphere.]

‡ [The influence of evaporation in producing this effect has been fully investigated by De la Roche, who arrived to the general conclusion that evaporation from the lungs and skin is the *main* cause by which the temperature is regulated in all cases, and the *sole* cause by which this effect is produced when the body is exposed to a temperature above its own natural standard. (See Journ. de Phys., tom. lxiii. lxxi. and lxxvii. See also Treatise on Inflammation, loc. cit.)]

therefore a further provision of Nature for enabling animals to support great heat. In order to keep up a just balance of temperature, it is probable that the living powers exert greater effort as evaporation is deficient, and less effort as evaporation increases. In emergencies, evaporation is not sufficient: when a greater power of producing cold than ordinary is required, the powers of the animal are called forth.

As animals can only destroy a certain quantity of heat in a given time, so the time they can continue the full exertion of this destroying power seems also limited. It is probable that both the power of destroying heat, and the time in which that power can be exerted, may be increased by frequent exercise.

When Dr. Fordyce was in the heated room, his hand became so hot as to make his body feel cool to it*. It is probable that that part, from its habit of changing its degree of heat, is more ready to take on different degrees of heat applied. It is found from experiment, in the application of cold, that all the extremities are more subject to the laws of inanimate matter than the body; and the nearer the source of circulation, the greater the deviation is from these laws. Possibly the same may be observed with regard to heat.

In animals which have a standard heat it would appear to be more natural to form than to destroy heat, (although the power of destroying it appears to be much greater than that of producing it,) for we may observe that they live with much more ease to themselves when in an atmosphere considerably lower than their standard, in which they must constantly be generating heat, than in an atmosphere even of their own temperature, in which it cannot be necessary for them to form heat; so that either this action simply of generating heat, or being in such a degree of cold as makes this action necessary, proves salutary to the constitution†. Perhaps the medium between their extreme heat, which is 98°, and the lowest degree they can come to, is the proper and most wholesome temperature of the atmosphere, and this is about 63°.

Some of these animals which are endowed with this property of a standard heat have this power of generating heat much stronger than others, and are always best in those situations where this power can be exercised: we should naturally suppose that this power always requires a necessity for that exertion equal to its power, so that the power and the necessity should always be proportioned. This cannot be the case

---

* [This effect probably arose from the superior denseness of the cuticular covering of the hand preventing perspiration.]

† [It is certainly a remarkable proof of Hunter's penetrating sagacity that he should have been able to arrive at so general a truth without being acquainted with the true cause of animal heat, or the intimate connexion which subsists between this function and that of respiration. (See Treatise on Inflammation, loc. cit.)]

with those imperfect animals which have little or no power of forming heat, but are obliged to the atmosphere for heat.

When we consider the white bear, the fox, and wolf, in the more northerly climates, inhabiting countries where the temperature is below zero, yet having a power of preserving their noses, feet, tails, &c., while man, with all his care and art, loses his extremities in the same degree of cold, we must acknowledge that those animals have by much the greater power of generating heat of the two. When we compare the above animals with the lion, tiger, monkey, &c., we find the proportion in the power of generating heat between these two classes of animals still greater; for if the human species finds it impossible to generate heat like the white bear, &c., the lion and tiger must find it impossible to generate heat equal to man : for though they may not lose parts of their bodies when in cold that is tolerable to the human species, they lose their lives in the end*.

It may be desirable to inquire into the proper temperature for each of those classes above mentioned, that is, the temperature in which they carry on their ultimate actions†. This must be ascertained with great difficulty ; perhaps the temperature suitable to the white bear, &c. is about 50° ; for the human species about 60°; for the lion, tiger, &c. about 70° ; and there may be some which require a still higher temperature, though probably none will require a lower than 50°‡.

---

* [Habit in this instance has great influence, so that the calorific function actually increases or strengthens in winter and diminishes in summer, (Edwards, De l'Influence, &c., pp. 162 seq., 242 seq.) an effect which we cannot but observe in those who have resided in the East and West Indies returning to an European climate.]

† [By ultimate actions Hunter probably means generation, as he has stated the continuance of the species to be the ultimate end for which the vital powers are given to animals.]

‡ [" Vegetables and animals are prepared for almost all climates, and for temperatures higher than the heat of any country. Dr. Reeve found larvæ in a spring at 208°; Lord Bute, confervæ and beetles in the boiling springs of Albano, that died when plunged into cold water. A species of chara will flower and produce seed in the hot springs of Iceland, which boil an egg in four minutes. One plant, *uredo nivalis*, which is a mere microscopic globule, is said to grow and flower under the snow.

" Some cold-blooded animals bear heat very badly. Dr. Edwards says that frogs die in a few seconds in water at 107°. [but Dr. Marshall Hall states that a frog plunged into water at 120°, " first struggles violently, then experiences convulsive movements, and then promptly dies, whilst the limbs become exceedingly and permanently rigid. After apparent death, all sensibility and motion having ceased, the heart is found to beat for a considerable time, presenting the singular phenomenon of an animal dead to animal life and maintaining a sort of vegetative existence only." (Hall on Circ., p. 174.)—*Editor.*]

Yet a species of tænia has been found alive in a *boiled* carp ; but then the carp which it inhabits will live in water as hot as human blood.

" The germs of many insects, &c. are unaffected by a great range of temperature. I

On the Effects of Climate.—By climate we mean that state of the atmosphere which is peculiar to any particular part. Climates vary as much as anything in nature. Their difference may be said to arise chiefly from the influence of the sun, from their moisture or dryness, which will depend partly on the shape of our globe and its oblique direction with regard to the sun, and also from the nature of the surface, whether hilly, or flat, or woody. The different seasons are dependent on the form of the earth and its motion round the sun. Between the tropics the variations of seasons are less; still there are kinds of seasons, and the climates are very various. The greatest variety of climate is near the tropics. The world there, being chiefly if not altogether heated by the sun, works very hard to gain as much of its influence as possible; it exposes itself to it as much as possible in every direction. The air of the equator is very different from that of the poles; few can live in the climate of the poles, either animals or vegetables, and even of those which can live many become torpid during the winter. It is wonderful, considering the necessity of heat to animalization and vegetation, and how partial Nature has been in the distribution of it, how both these processes go on so well as they do*. Nature, however, has been obliged to adapt animals to their different climates as well as vegetables, except the bramble, which lives between the tropics and at the poles.

Some animals become torpid during the cold, others even of the same order do not; this seems to be because the food of the first is not to be found during that season: so Nature formed them either animals of passage, as some birds; others she constituted so as to become torpid. Animals of passage, however, seem to have their peculiar climate; fish, which wander more than most animals, have their climate, and the general cause of their moving south is for the purpose of propagation. So herrings come from the North Pole to the coasts of Europe and America, for no other purpose than to lay their spawn. Quadrupeds seem the best formed for variations of climate, though their heat is more stationary. There are exceptions, as the dormouse, bat, &c.; but men, dogs, deer, horses, &c. live tolerably well, though not without disease,

---

know a gentleman who boiled some honeycomb two years old, and after extracting all the sweet matter, threw the remains into a stable, which was soon filled with bees. Body lice have appeared on clothes which had been immersed in boiling water. Spallanzani found long ebullition in the open air favourable to the appearance of the animalcules of vegetable infusions; and the application of great heat in close vessels, although it prevented the appearance of a larger kind of animalcule, did not that of a smaller." —*Elliotson's Phys.*, p. 246. See note, p. 284.]

* [Cold, however, interrupts the growth and nutrition of organized bodies, as may be seen in the short stature and small size of the Greenlanders, Laplanders, Esquimaux, &c., as well as in all the plants and animals of cold and mountainous regions.]

between the tropics and also far north. Nature has furnished some animals with mechanical means for adapting them to climate, as hair, feathers, &c. The use of hair is clearly to preserve warmth: the porcupine of Italy has no hair, but only quills; and the southern bears have only bristles, without hair. There are some animals furnished with proper non-conductors of heat, as seals, sea-cows, &c., whose hair can be of little use to them while living in the sea, and is therefore only useful to them perhaps while on land. Those animals, as whales, which, from living constantly in water, could derive no advantage from hair, have an immense quantity of fat, which is a worse conductor of heat than water by nine to one*.

External heat and cold produce diseases peculiar to themselves. Men are the only animals which go to climates not congenial to themselves, and consequently they are alone subject to the consequences of an unfit climate. Too much heat produces diseases of the liver, though, as Dr. Blane observes, this must depend on some other cause than mere heat, as these complaints are not so frequent in the West Indies as in the East†. Diseases of the bowels and tetanus are also often produced by heat; it also tends to produce fevers. The diseases produced by cold are chiefly those of debility, as chilblains, scurvies: also diseases of the lungs, which are more dangerous than those of the liver. Cold also increases some diseases, as the lues venerea; and changes from heat to cold produce some diseases, as scrofula.

As heat is able to volatilize almost all bodies, the impurities of the atmosphere must very much depend on it; but, as Dr. Blane remarks, the same heat which volatilizes bodies will very often decompose them. The plague has not been known between the tropics, nor the jail fever, and very warm climates abound much less with diseases of a putrid kind than temperate climates. How does the atmosphere affect the body? Is it by the lungs or by the skin? This question it is perhaps impossible to solve. The purest air seems, *cæteris paribus*, to be the

---

* [The white hair, white skins, and white flowers which characterize the productions of the frigid zone are designed for the same purpose, in as much as heat radiates from white bodies more slowly than from those which are coloured. In the same manner, all the finer furs and downs come from the high latitudes, whereas cats, rabbits, and other animals change their fur into hair when they are transplanted to a meridional climate.]

† [If, as Tiedemann and Gmelin conjecture, the functions of the liver and lungs are, in one sense, correlative, viz. that they both tend to free the blood of its carbon, then it is not difficult to understand the greater tendency to diseases of the liver in these climates. The blood equally requires purification, and yet this cannot be effected by the lungs without the production of more animal heat than is required; in consequence of which the liver is called upon to fulfill this extra duty, and from over-exertion falls into disease. In the West Indies the sea-breezes materially tend to prevent those consequences which take place in the inland continents of the East.]

coldest; and the worst, the warmest, especially when moist, where the situation is low, and where animal substances suspended in it are allowed to putrefy. In a very hot air substances may be volatilized so rapidly that decomposition cannot take place; this air will prove destructive by different modes: 1st, By preventing respiration; for if many substances are volatilized, the air containing them will not reach the lungs, except in too small quantities for the support of animal life*. 2ndly, By specific poison, producing a variety of diseases, often sedative, as debility and agues, in marshy grounds; in other places, fluxes and different kinds of poisons. 3rdly, The effects of an impure atmosphere are found in jail distempers and hospital diseases; very few of the former places are ever free from foul air, and most hospitals are more or less affected with it. There are different modes in which these poisons may affect. A stranger in a marshy country is much sooner affected than a native or an inhabitant. A person who has not long been used to a jail will earlier, and with more certainty, be affected with jail distemper. An instance of this occurred at Salt Hill in 1760. The effects were at first attributed to the wine; but they were evidently caused by a few paupers, who were examined by some gentlemen, although the paupers did not appear to be affected. In 1775 some prisoners were examined at the Old Bailey who infected the whole Court, and many died; the judge on the bench, the jury and evidences, &c. Many poisons are of this kind: a person may carry the infection about with him without being affected himself†. The air is capable of carrying most poisons, and communicating their irritations. The venereal poison cannot be thus raised in a state of vapour, or if it can, it loses its effects in the change.

Perhaps next to never coming within the influence of such effluvia at all, it is safest to live surrounded by them in large cities, where, either from the habit of being exposed to their action, or from one effluvium destroying another, the effects are prevented from taking place to the extent that might be expected. However, if the atmosphere, being impure, produced an effect only on those coming into it, all the old residents would be equally healthy as the strangers who come to reside for a time only; yet this is not the case, for they are by no means all robust; therefore what may be styled its unfitness produces a debility, and the persons are neither so strong nor so healthy as those resident in a

* [It is extremely improbable that a case of this kind ever occurred, considered merely in respect of climate.]

† [The catalogue of infectious diseases is much curtailed in modern times, actually as well as speculatively; at least, the non-contagionists are now the prevailing sect. The infectious miasm probably consists of some compound in which hydrogen is an ingredient. This appears from the facility with which the odour and noxious qualities of putrid exhalations are destroyed by the vapour of chlorine.]

healthy atmosphere, though they feel not the sudden effects with which strangers are attacked*.

We have a kind of atmosphere which spreads over various countries or climates in particular seasons only, as lately over England. These have had different names at different times; we call it the influenza: it affects at first dogs, then horses. In 1775 the dogs were all ill; and afterwards the horses, before men, felt the influence of it.

The atmosphere is the menstruum for various substances, some of which are held in a state of solution, and others in a state of mixture only. Water is held in solution in the atmosphere, and when much of this is suspended, it renders it heavier, as the barometer shows; and when a decomposition of the solution takes place, the water is precipitated as rain or snow, and the air is made lighter, as the barometer also shows. This decomposition may take place, although neither snow nor rain is produced, and this in consequence of a fresh combination taking place before the ultimate end is produced. When the above decompositions take place, the birds and beasts seek their shelter; and an effect is produced on wounds, particularly when in a healing state, and in diseases and ailing parts of the human body, so that persons become, as it were, a weather-glass. We have lately been informed by a German that the variations of the magnetic needle have appeared so much to take place with change of weather, that as much might be learned from it respecting the prognostics of the weather as from the barometer itself. Winds may be easily supposed to bring with them the effluvia of disease. Extraordinary effects are produced by the Harmattan wind, a wind which blows off the interior part of Africa to the coast of Guinea. It generally comes three or four times a year, at certain seasons; it is always attended with a fog, which has no taste, nor could anything be discovered in it by means of glasses thinly covered with molasses. The fog is thickest on the beach, and gets tolerably thin about four miles inland. It lasts often for a fortnight, and produces a pain and dryness in the mouth and nostrils, not as if from mere dryness, but from some acridity: if it continues three or four days, the scarf skin falls off, and the tongue applied to that part of the skin denuded of cuticle is sensible of an acrid taste. Though very prejudicial to vegetable life, it is salutary to animals, curing fluxes and other epidemic disorders, and often restoring weakened constitutions. Fevers which had been imprudently

---

* [The late population returns have exhibited in a striking light the serious effects of crowded houses and a crowded population, in doubling, and in some instances in trebling, the rate of mortality, a fact which is still more strongly exemplified in some of the capital cities of Europe. See Count Chabrol's statistical account of the department of the Seine.]

reduced by bleeding, got well in spite of the doctor. The smallpox always yields to it, while it prevented the inoculation from taking effect in some African slaves. Such as were inoculated before the Harmattan set in had the smallpox, and all did well; but such as were not then seized with the symptoms, and these were sixty in number, never felt any other affection but a slight fever and nausea during the continuance of the wind; after which it showed itself in twenty of them: the others were reinoculated, and all did well.

CHAPTER IX.

GENERAL PRINCIPLES OF DISEASE.

Disease the consequence of unnatural impression ;—may arise from faulty primary arrangement.—Diseased actions often established on the same principles as healthy actions ;—some diseases end with the cause ;— others continued from habit.—Diseases common to all parts, or peculiar to some ;—obscurity of the physiology of disease.—Of susceptibility to impression and consequent action ;—difference of susceptibility in different individuals.—Distinction between susceptibility and disposition ;— predisposing causes only susceptibilities.—Susceptibilities of constitution and of parts for different actions.—Universal susceptibility producing local diseases.—Susceptibilities almost specific.—Temperament.—Of diseased dispositions.—Dispositions unnatural, but not diseased ;—dispositions for restoration ;—of necessity ;—and of disease.—Diseased dispositions have an allotted time for action.—Action.—Disease a disposition for wrong action ;—action the effect of disposition ;—symptoms the result of action.—Action, healthy or diseased ;—diseased action of two kinds.—First symptoms of disease.— Diseased actions arising without proper stimulus.—Too great action ;—too little action.—Diseased actions simple.—Of wrong actions.—Habit of diseased actions.—Of sedatives and stimulants.—Irritability.

Now that I have treated of some of the properties of the animal in health, I shall go on to treat of its imperfections, or diseases. To understand these it was necessary, in the first place, to describe its perfect or healthy state. To describe the parts in a healthy state belongs to the anatomist; their actions in this state to the physiologist; but the diseased state of these actions, and the restoration of parts to health, to the physician and surgeon.

It is hardly to be supposed that disease is ever natural to an animal; it can only be the consequence of some unnatural impression which interferes with the natural action of the body, which impression may take place at the very first formation, or original arrangement of the animal, so as to stamp a permanent unnatural action; or it may take place in the first life, namely, in utero; but much more frequently after birth, when it is exposed to a thousand variations, all which are impressions, and are contrary to the natural actions of the animal, or are, as it were, a forcing it to take on actions which are either to remove those impressions or to destroy itself.

It is most probable that diseased actions are established on nearly the same principles that the actions of health are. They are at least similar in a great many of their principles : they destroy the dispositions of parts ; they produce growth ; they produce the power of removing natural parts ; they are ruled by habit ; they are affected by every external influence.

An animal is so constructed as only to continue some diseases so long as the immediate cause lasts, as in scrofula, when it arises from climate ; or which is so constructed as to continue other diseases from habit, as a gleet, so as to go on with a disease, although the first cause is gone; and this may be only for a time, as in gonorrhœa ; or it may be for ever, as in lues, cancer, &c.

Diseases are either common to all parts alike, or are peculiar. They are common to all parts alike, as inflammations of all kinds ; as, also, tumefaction, scirrhus, dropsies, &c. The peculiar are those in which there is a fault in the peculiar actions of a part, as involuntary action of voluntary muscles, too much or too little secretion from any of the glands, in short, wrong actions of any part in its peculiar mode of action.

After the disposition, the action which should destroy the disposition takes place ; the action having taken place, the disposition ceases and the natural action of the parts returns. But this is not always the case. The disposition may be affected in one of the following ways : 1st, The action may destroy the disposition, for instance, in gonorrhœa (and perhaps in many other complaints) ; in this case the action destroys the disposition, or the inflammation destroys the disposition of the virus. 2ndly, The disposition is destroyed for a time, and returns at intervals, or after certain spaces, as in all periodical diseases, or others where the disease ceases for a time, and the disposition continues. 3rdly, Where the action takes place, yet does not destroy the disposition, as the venereal disease, which goes on till it is cured or kills, and the action of it never destroys the disposition*.

Many diseases often require their full action before they produce their effects, as the gout and many agues. Vomiting is the action fol-

---

* [It is scarcely necessary to observe that this dogma respecting the venereal disease is no longer entertained ; and indeed it may be questioned whether there is any disease, unattended with actual change of structure, which is not susceptible of a natural cure. This at least seems to be the broad and leading distinction between curable and incurable diseases, although in practice it is often extremely difficult to say what does and what does not constitute change of structure, the simple consequences of inflammation being always excepted.]

lowing the disposition to sickness, and is often its cure, for without it the nausea and disposition will continue. Sometimes chronic diseases will be cured by acute ones, in which case, the full action being given, the disposition is removed.

General Observations on Susceptibility and Disposition, constituting Constitutions, and on Actions forming Symptoms.—The physiology of disease is more extensive, more obscure, depends less on general laws of nature (being often a prevention or perversion of those laws), and is therefore more irregular than any part of science, and is of course less understood.

The most simple idea I can form of an animal being capable of disease is, that every animal is endued with a power of action and a susceptibility of impression, which impression forms a disposition*, which disposition may produce action, which action becomes the immediate sign of the disease; all of which will be according to the nature of the impression and of the part impressed.

That every action, whether natural, preternatural, or diseased, arises from this susceptibility of impression, I think we must allow, which susceptibility may exist without even disposition or action, if no impression or stimulus is made; for the disposition is only formed in consequence of some impression, and the action is only the consequence of the disposition being so strong as to incline a part for action rather than for resolution. Therefore action is the ultimate consequence of impression being made on a part endued with a susceptibility of impression and the power of action, which impression gives them the disposition to act. For from what was said above, parts having susceptibility do not necessarily have the disposition; the disposition arises from some impression, which will, in its turn, produce the action, and this action, or disposition to action, must be sufficient to overcome the natural and habitual actions of the part or whole, just as force overcomes the vis inertiæ of matter. But susceptibilities are in some so strong as almost to approach a propensity to act, which is probably as strong as the disposition, or often probably stronger†.

* Susceptibility has been too often called disposition. A man is said to be well disposed, or parts are said to be well disposed when they are only susceptible. Disposition is a degree further than susceptibility.

---

† [The reader will probably agree with the Editor that the distinction which is here drawn is not tenable. The author, for instance, says, (p. 310) that action is not disease, but the effect of disease; but what proof is there that the disposition (which according to the author seems identical with the disease,) exists at all, except from the action which it produces and the visible effects of that action? And, particularly, what proof is there that this *latent disposition* differs from susceptibility? A part may be more or less prone to or susceptible of inflammation, but can a part have the disposition to

The actions of the body, and the cause of these actions, with their effects, are exactly similar to those of the mind, and as we are sensible of the actions of the mind themselves, abstracted from their causes or effects, we reason about them as much as we can reason about their causes and effects. This is not the case with the actions of the body, for in them we are only acquainted with the causes and effects, not the action itself; therefore our minds are only reasoning about them from analogy.

The susceptibility for action of the mind is not known to the mind itself, but by the consequence of such susceptibility. Some minds are much more susceptible of certain actions than others; thus, some men are more susceptible of anger, others of love. But this does not imply that one mind is always in anger, another in love, &c.

With this susceptibility of mind, a stimulus must be applied to produce the disposition to action. A stimulus of one kind will produce anger, of another kind, love. The action of the mind employs other parts to complete the whole, as when the actions of the mind are employing other parts to produce the ultimate effects. But these are not necessary to the action of anger, for anger could exist without the action of employing other parts, and indeed continue longer; for this tends to destroy the action of anger, because the effect being produced the cause ceases.

Every animal has a variety of susceptibilities which admit of a variety of impressions, each impression producing a disposition peculiar to itself. Also every animal has some of those susceptibilities stronger than it has others, out of all which a vast variety of diseases is produced. Each tendency to a peculiar mode of action gives the character of the animal respecting disease. The sting of a bee, for instance, affecting some people much more than others, demonstrates that there is a susceptibility in some for such actions more than in others. In many the susceptibility will be so strong as only to require a stop to be put to the natural actions, when the disposition and the disease too will take possession of the part or of the whole. An instance of this we have in

---

inflammation (in Mr. Hunter's sense,) without showing the action of inflammation? If it can, then where is the proof of its existence, except from the proneness or readiness of the part to act in that particular manner? which is the idea conveyed by the term susceptibility. I offer this criticism with diffidence; at the same time I cannot but regard the whole argument, so far as it is founded on this distinction, as based on a metaphysical subtlety which ought not to be admitted in philosophical discourse.

As there can be little doubt that Mr. Hunter formed these opinions from observing that the disposition (so called) to the venereal disease often remained after the visible symptoms had been apparently cured, the reader will naturally turn to this part of his works for further information.]

scrofula, for it often happens that common accidents, as strains, bruises, fevers of all kinds, produce the disease even in situations the most calculated to prevent it, as in the West Indies. Even poisonous dispositions are produced in this way, a blow on the breast or testicle shall produce a poisonous mode of action, e. g. cancer.

From this account no animal is formed with a disposition for the action of disease. The natural actions are for the good of the animal; but they can be perverted, they can be made to destroy the whole. These circumstances are similar to those of the mind; some minds are more susceptible of some impressions than they are of others, which produces a disposition to act, which action will be according to the impression. The susceptibility of the constitution may be increased, so as almost to be similar to a new formation, but is never originally formed, by art*. Where the susceptibility is weak, it may be increased and kept so much on the brink of forming the disposition, that it shall only require the least increase, or some other immediate cause, to produce the effect or form the disposition, as a man not naturally fearful may be worked upon so that the least thing may alarm him. Susceptibilities may be so increased as almost to deserve the name of acquired; constitutions long habituated to particular climates will form a scrofulous habit, or an aguish habit, and a certain way of life will produce a rheumatic or gouty habit. On the other hand, persons naturally susceptible may be made by degrees considerably less so, by being gradually accustomed to the immediate cause, beginning within the degree of impression necessary to excite disposition to action.

There is no such thing, strictly speaking, as a predisposing cause. What is commonly understood by a predisposing cause is an increased susceptibility to form disposition to action. When I say I am predisposed for such and such actions, it is only that I am very susceptible of such and such impressions, which impressions must form the disposition; or if it is intended to dispose a person for such and such actions, it is only to render him more and more susceptible of such and such impres-

---

* [If by *art* Hunter means the influence of external agents, this statement does not appear to be correct. When, for example, hospital gangrene is prevalent in a ward, probably three fourths of the inmates would be attacked by this disease, after any operation performed on them. The susceptibility of the disease has surely here been generated, yet they would probably have escaped, if the operation had not come to convert this acquired susceptibility into action. The operation under different circumstances would not have been followed by similar consequences; the body, that is, is not *naturally* susceptible of this disease, in the same way that it is susceptible of inflammation or smallpox, without previous preparation; a new state of the constitution must first be induced,—a point which is clearly admitted by the author in his Treatise on Inflammation.]

sions. The susceptibility must always precede the disposition. A disposition is a determined thing,—a thing formed,—a kind of resolution.

Of Susceptibilities of Parts and Constitutions for different Actions.— Every constitution is more susceptible of some constitutional actions, both natural and diseased, than it is of other actions, whether natural or diseased; and every constitution is more susceptible of some local actions, natural and diseased, than it is of others.

Every constitution is compounded of parts whose natural actions are very different from one another. Thus, the natural actions of the liver are very different from those of the lungs. Therefore we also find the diseased actions of one are often different from those of the other; although every part of the body may be subject to some one or more common diseased actions, as e. g., the liver and lungs, which may be subject to common inflammation, or they may both have the same specific disease, as scrofula.

Every constitution being composed of different parts, whose natural and diseased actions are different from one another, as above mentioned, these actions being according to the nature of each part, and each part in some constitutions being more susceptible of natural actions peculiar to itself than the same part in other constitutions, so also in some constitutions each part is more susceptible of its diseased actions than the same part is in other constitutions. Thus, as the liver in some constitutions is more susceptible of secreting bile, which is its natural action, than it is in others, so also it is more susceptible of its peculiar diseases in some constitutions than it is in others. Constitutions may be said to be more or less susceptible of this or that universal action, among the first of which may be marked the irritable and the indolent.

Secondly, some constitutions are more susceptible of some diseases than others are of other diseases.

Thirdly, some constitutions are more susceptible of some diseases than others are. And those constitutions not susceptible of this or that disease may be at the same time more susceptible of some other diseases than the first-mentioned constitutions are. For example, some constitutions are more susceptible of inflammatory fevers than of any other fevers; others are more susceptible of putrid fevers; while either one or the other of these constitutions might have some other disease, either violently or mildly, as smallpox, measles, &c.

Constitutions may be more susceptible of some one specific disease than the same constitution of other specific diseases, e. g., some constitutions are more susceptible of smallpox than of measles, or *vice versâ*.

Some constitutions may be more susceptible of some specific diseases than other constitutions are, e. g., some constitutions are more susceptible of the smallpox than others are, and yet have the disease mildly.

All of which characterize the constitution at large.

Of universal Susceptibility to produce local Diseases.—Bodies may be said to be both constitutionally and locally susceptible of diseased action. The erysipelatous fever, which is constitutional, being attended by the erysipelatous inflammation, which is local, is a strong instance of this.

Constitutions are more or less susceptible, both universally and locally, of the same disease, as the smallpox fever, when violent, has more violent and extensive local effects; when mild, more mild local effects.

Constitutions may be said to be more or less universally susceptible of this or that local action, when one part takes on action without any visible immediate cause, or when any injury (whether constitutional, as fever, or local, as accident,) makes parts so injured run into a much worse diseased state than the same injury would have done in others; many parts even taking on specific diseases, whenever the immediate cause is produced, as scrofula, venereal gonorrhœa, &c.

Constitutional susceptibilities for diseased actions may be divided into three kinds, and there are also others which are mixed*.

1st, *An original constitutional*; that is, where there is a universal susceptibility for diseased action of one kind or another, in which, however, the whole must be in action, as inflammation, fever, smallpox, &c.; also sympathetic fevers of all kinds. Persons may be very susceptible of the whole of these, or only of one or more.

2nd, *Original local*; that is, where the whole is so constructed as to be universally susceptible of going into diseased action in any one part;

---

* [There is probably not a more abstruse subject in physiology than that of susceptibilities, which most frequently depend on causes with which we are entirely unacquainted. Mr. Hunter has classified susceptibilities according to their effects and remote causes, without attempting to explain the physiological conditions on which they depend. But we ought not, I conceive, to repose here, as if further progress were impracticable, but to ascertain, if possible, the actual conditions of the organisation on which they depend, or the particular manner in which the functions reciprocally react on one another so as to produce them. The pathologist should seek to trace the remote cause to its utmost effects, so as to arrive as near as possible to the immediate efficient cause of the susceptibility in question.

An example of this kind has been already adduced in regard to the susceptibility of the liver to diseases in hot climates, (see note, p. 295,) arising from a reciprocity of function between it and the lungs, of which many similar instances might be given in respect of the other organs. The heart and the brain are said to be more susceptible of disease now than they were formerly, although this may solely depend on the complicated interests and passions of modern life, which necessarily induce particular physical conditions of these organs which directly tend, on known principles, to the production of disease. The constitutional susceptibilities are, in general, far more obscure, and scarcely at all admit of this mode of explanation.]

but the actions will be always local and independent of every other part, as scrofula, gonorrhœa, or chancre. Hence the venereal disease is worse in one than in another, and yet is local ; the same with scrofula.

3rd, A susceptibility to fall into universal indisposition, as if there was something teazing the whole ; which then can call on a part, and that relieves the whole, as in gout, rheumatism, and perhaps all those diseases where the local action is critical. Most of these can be relieved by a universal facility to action, or retarded by the contrary, which will affect either the local action or the constitutional one.

Strong susceptibilities of a constitution to take on diseased disposition and action, whether of the whole as such, or a local effect of a constitutional disease, (which last I call an act of the constitution,) only require the impression of the immediate cause for the disposition and action peculiar to these susceptibilities to take place. These immediate causes may not be the same in two constitutions, although both have a strong susceptibility for the same action ; for what will produce the action in one constitution may not produce it in another. One constitution will require one immediate cause and another another, though both constitutions may have a susceptibility for the disease. Two men equally susceptible may be exposed to the cause of an ague : one may have the disease, the other not. It is exactly similar with the mind : two men may be naturally or constitutionally equally susceptible of anger, but each must have his immediate cause ; what will bring bring forth action in one will have but little effect on the other, and e contrario. It is the same thing with every effect of the mind.

Most susceptibilities are so much of a specific nature in themselves that each susceptibility shall be brought into action, in nineteen people out of twenty, in one way, and probably in the twentieth it has been prevented by what produced it in the others. This accounts for the same diseased action in people arising from so many different causes, and also accounts why such disease, though having a specific mode of action, may be varied in the same person in different ways, still more in different people, and even often require different modes of cure.

This theory may be illustrated by every disease that takes on full specific action ; whether a full constitutional action, as an ague, or a local one, as the gout. As an ague is a well-known and well-marked disease, this theory will of course be illustrated by this disease.

Every constitution has more or less susceptibility to fall into an aguish habit ; but there must be in all an immediate cause to produce the disease. The immediate cause may be such as will make nineteen people out of twenty fall into aguish action ; but many constitutions, though they have a susceptibility of falling into an aguish habit, yet when the immediate cause takes place, may have no disposition to take on the full action of that disease ; by which means the constitution is teazed by what is called a badly-formed ague. If the immediate cause be some local disease in the body, as diseased liver, spleen, &c., then the cure must be effected by the cure of the liver, &c.

This reasoning may be taken in another point of view. Suppose twenty people having different susceptibilities;—introduce something that shall endanger the constitutions of the whole number, and each shall take on the disease that he was at that time most susceptible of, whether ague, gout, or any other.

But often that which would become the immediate cause in those already susceptible of action, or already predisposed to it, by repetition or continuance becomes the predisposing cause in others not susceptible. If two men, one so susceptible as only to want the immediate derangement, the other not at all susceptible of an ague, be sent into the fens of Lincolnshire, the first shall have an ague immediately, because he only required the immediate cause of it ; the other, if he does not get the better of the climate by habit, shall become aguish in time, because the country will become both a predisposing and an immediate or exciting cause.

We may substitute for the disease of ague some other disease, and the whole of the above reasoning will be perfectly applicable. But where it is the nature of the disease to take on local action, as in gout, there must not only be a universal disposition for such disease, which is the original, but there must also be a local preference, or rather a local susceptibility superior to the rest; and when the immediate cause takes place, so as to form the disposition, that part takes on the whole action, which relieves the constitution of such disposition, except it should produce another constitutional effect by a vital part taking it up, by which means it would affect the whole constitution similarly to any of the affections of this vital part, where a diseased disposition is formed, but does not take on the regular type of the disease, or does not take on the full and complete action ; as in the aguish disposition not having gone through the regular stages of the ague, or gout not having formed a regular fit.

In those diseases that become local, as gout, some attention is to be paid to the seat of action ; for if a vital part takes it up, it must be much worse than when there is only a constitutional affection.

The qualities of periodicity and regularity in constitutional diseases, or the power of a constitutional affection to become local, are, I believe, but little understood.

Susceptibilities for dispositions and actions appear to me to be the same with what are usually understood by temperament. Temperament is the state of the body fitting it for the disposition or action it is then in, whether it is only a state of susceptibility, of disposition, or action. The action is always the best test of that state ; but, although the action is the best test, yet there are some circumstances attending animals that either dispose them for, or are concomitant upon, such and such susceptibilities ; and from these circumstances we can say beforehand, although only in a general way, what are the most predominant susceptibilities for certain actions in this or that animal. We see that even colour in animals depends on a difference in their temperaments, or is concomitant with temperament ; for animals with fair skin and hair are more susceptible of cold than the dark, as also of pain. This is well known in the army, where we find that the power of bearing violence committed on the body is in proportion to the darkness of the individual. Fair people are more irritable in their minds, more susceptible of anger, and probably of all other passions. Fair people are also more susceptible of certain diseases than the dark, as of scrofula. This may arise from their not being able to bear the vicissitudes of climate ; for it is in changeable climates, especially where there is cold, moisture, &c., that scrofula is most predominant. The irritable inflammation also is more common in the fair than the swarthy. As the fair are less able to resist cold than the dark*, it might be supposed that the dark are less able to resist heat, therefore more ready than the fair to run into diseases which warmth has a tendency to bring on. But from the estimate made by Dr. Young in the Island of St. Vincent's, it would appear that there is some reason to suppose the contrary ; from which it would appear that the dark-coloured are rather fitter for all kinds of climates.

Of diseased Disposition.—Dispositions are natural or unnatural, including diseased. The natural belong to the healthy animal, therefore are not to our present purpose.

Dispositions may be unnatural (and of course the actions arising from them unnatural,) and yet not diseased.

Unnatural dispositions and actions we shall divide into three kinds, or they may arise from three causes, which are remote.

1st. The disposition of restoration, in consequence of some injury done, which is also a consequence of every disease which is curable.

2nd. The disposition arising from necessity, as the thickening of parts from pressure, ulceration of every kind. This includes a great variety.

---

* [This must be understood with some limitation. The inhabitants of high northern atitudes, who are often very fair, are far less susceptible of scrofula than the darker-complexioned races of more southern countries ; as, on the other hand, the African and the half-caste are more liable to this disease when transplanted to a northern latitude than the natives. It is not merely cold, but cold and moisture, associated with a variable climate, which predispose so strongly to this disease.]

3rd. Diseased dispositions of all kinds, which also includes a vast variety.

From this division we see that there are two preternatural dispositions that are not diseased, so much so that the first may be reckoned a disposition of health; therefore there is but one preternatural disposition to action which can be called diseased, namely, the disposition to destruction, and which is to be cured by substituting the first disposition.

Diseased dispositions may arise from some fault in the animal powers themselves, or some extraneous matter in the constitution or circulation, as in the case of many poisons, or from many substances acting on the stomach called poisons, or from some substances being applied externally to the body which disagree with animal life in general, as too much cold, too much heat, &c.

Every diseased disposition most probably has its allotted time for action after the impression, or after the formation of the disposition. This is remarkably the case in specific diseases; but yet this will differ according to the susceptibility. The same with poisons: the smallpox is about six, seven, or eight days at a medium; the measles the same. The venereal disease has a medium, although it varies. But some specific diseases shall remain a considerable time before the action takes place; and this will be much longer in some than in others, according to the nature of the diseased disposition and parts. In cancer it is often very tedious. I have seen instances where it was years after all continuance of the cause was removed before the glands in the armpit had taken on diseased action after contamination.

A girl at St. George's Hospital, fourteen years of age, born in the West Indies, left that part of the world when ten years of age. About a twelvemonth ago she had an eruption on the skin in several parts of the body, especially on the face, arms, and hands. The eruption arose like warts, or like large moles, about the size of half a crown piece, above the surface of the skin, irregular in their base, some standing single, others running into one another, of a browner colour than the common skin, which was clear and of a firmer texture.

Now this was a West Indian disease; therefore I say that the girl was contaminated in the West Indies. The impression was made there which was the first cause, and the disposition was formed; but the disposition did not come into action for three years after. The removal to a cold climate, though it could not remove the disposition or prevent its effects, yet protracted them.

It may be further remarked, in specific diseases and in poisons, that if the specific disease or poison is such as is capable of contaminating different parts, whose powers or readiness to act is different, the same disease will show itself at different intervals in these places in the same person, though perhaps every part is contaminated at the same time. Thus we have the venereal disease appearing in different parts at different intervals in the same person, arising from the natural susceptibility for action in some parts being greater than in others. The skin and tonsils being most susceptible of contamination, as also of action, are therefore affected soonest; the bones and tendons less so, and are therefore later in taking on the action. The disposition simply does not seem to affect either the constitution or the part, (see note, p. 301) for either shall go on well with all their natural functions, and powers of restoration when injured or affected with diseases of every other kind, although at the same time in the disposition of some other disease.

Dispositions of one kind may be restored after being destroyed for a time by a more powerful impression, or such as the constitution is more susceptible of, which shall supersede the first disposition, and go on with its actions; and when its action is completed, the first disposition shall again take place, as will be illustrated when we come to talk of actions simply.

Action.—I have explained that a disease is a disposition for a wrong action, and that the action is the immediate effect of the disposition, and that either the actions, or the effects of those actions, produce the symptoms which are generally called the disease, such as sensations, which are commonly pain of all kinds, sickness, alteration visible or invisible in the structure of the part or parts that act, and sympathy.

The animal, or part disposed to act, generally takes on action, which is of three kinds: natural, restorative when injured, and the diseased; each arising from the corresponding class of dispositions, and therefore divisible into the same.

The actions of health arise from a disposition to act properly, that is, according to the combined laws of the machine, which may be either universal or only partial; for a man may be wholly in health, or only so in part. The actions of restoration are for the falling back into the above natural actions, and which will be according to the nature of the injury done and the parts combined. The diseased actions are many, but may be ranked under the following heads:

1st. Improper actions of natural parts, as spasms of muscles; irregularity in the times of action of a compound part. The nerves have the credit for being the remote cause of all these.

2nd. Unnatural or improper actions of the vessels; and these may be either attended with an increased or diminished action.

The ultimate and visible effect of disease is action; but this is not the disease, for the action is only an effect, a sign, or symptom of disease. But the disposition being only discovered by its effects, we are apt to go no further in our inquiry, the cause being to many only an object of curiosity. However, the effect must be attended to, for it is this which leads us to the cause. These actions may arise from poisons, or substances improperly applied to the surface; from cold; from substances taken into the stomach: these usually give a sensation to the animal, so that it can judge that the parts are diseased. But sometimes the action is too slow to give an alarm to the part; or the disease is felt through the irritation; or by a part remote from the diseased part sympathizing, as worms in the intestines, producing convulsions, an itching at the nose, &c. When the hip or loins are affected, the sympathizing part, before the disease is felt in the original seat, is the knee. Passing a bougie has caused sickness before it was felt in the urethra, as has a clyster before the rectum was sensible of any inconvenience.

Often the internal feeling of health is the forerunner of disease. People just before a disease shall be in better spirits, and feel strong, so as to take notice of it themselves.

A gentleman had better health before a spitting of blood came on.

A boy had more spirits than usual the night before he was attacked with the cold fit of fever.

Perhaps the cause of disease gives the first feeling of health or vigour: the animal powers are called up on the first alarm of disease; and when they sink, which is the second stage, they produce cold, or shivering, which is generally supposed to be the first symptom. In children I have often observed that the smell is affected before diseases. The first impression here is made on the olfactory nerves.

Some diseases come on extremely rapidly, producing at first very violent symptoms, called acute; others come on slowly, and do not produce any sensible first symptom.

I have already observed, that all the actions in a healthy state are only produced by their proper stimulus; but sometimes we have actions without proper stimulus, which are diseased actions. In all organs I have observed there is a regular succession of action, as in the secretion of different substances, according to the wants of the parts which become the stimuli; but they may perform this office without the stimulus. The vessels are very active parts, and have often wrong actions, producing diseases in a great variety of parts, and are peculiarly active in the operations of disease.

Too great action will produce disease, according to circumstances. As the powers are equal, or greater, the action is universal or local: if universal, as in inflammatory fever, it will either produce resolution or death; if local, as in inflammation, either resolution or suppuration;

or if the action is greater than the power, irritability: or it may keep up a constant inflammation; or if very violent, produce mortification. Too great action will often in the end produce too little action; but not often *vice versâ*. General action or fever may produce local, as inflammation; or local inflammation will produce general, as fever. They often attend one another from accident, and then they generally increase one another.

Too little action arises from a disposition to act within the necessary bounds of health, which produces real weakness and a bad state of health, with debility, without any visible state of disease, as we often see in fine ladies. If the part debilitated be not necessary to life, it only produces its effects on that organ. Too little action may subject the person to many more diseases than what the active are subject to. Even the habit of indolence in the mind, joined with inactivity of the voluntary actions (which is generally produced from an indolent state of the mind), produces the same effects, especially as we see in women. So that weakness is attendant on many diseases, and although somewhat necessary to many, yet it is not actually the disease itself. For instance, weakness attends the scurvy, and is necessary before the full effects of the specific disposition, namely, the action, can take place. The same in locked jaw, scrofula, &c. Weakness becomes one of the causes of irritability, as will be explained. Weakness, too, produces an increase of the disease. It may be local or universal, for many parts of an animal body may be weak, while others are strong; and if the weak parts are not essential to life, then the effect is only debility in performing the function, and the vital parts may not suffer. If the nerves are weak, the voluntary parts suffer; if the stomach, then the whole will suffer, or there may be a weakness which includes the whole without destroying it. It sometimes seems that the suspension of action for a time, increases the power afterwards; and lessening the power of action, increases the real strength at other times.

All diseased Actions are simple.—A disposition of one kind may and shall exist in a part or whole, while an action of another kind is going on; and when the action ceases, the disposition, or dormant action, if we may be allowed to call it so, shall then come into action.

There are certain natural actions arising in an animal body in consequence of every irritation, whether appearing as a spontaneous injury or from accident. These common actions I shall illustrate by inflammation.

Inflammation, then, is one of these simple actions; but we find inflammation may be joined with a specific quality which shall not alter its apparent mode of action, yet shall cause its ultimate effect to vary; thus, though the mode of action *is* altered, the action itself is not altered.

It appears to me that every disposition must be simple, and therefore be only capable of producing a simple action. Parts so disposed may be irritated by something that alters the disposition. If the old disposition be destroyed, a new one must be produced; but if the disposition be only altered in part, there may be the two dispositions in the same part, the old in part and the new in part. But it is possible that a new disposition may be formed out of the two, different from either of the two which formed it; still it must be considered as a simple disposition.

This is plain in the cure of the venereal disease; a third disposition (namely, the healthy,) arises out of the two, that of the disease and that of the remedy. This is likewise shown in the action of Dover's powder, for neither vomiting nor sleep is produced, but a third action, namely, sweating.

But a constitution or part may have equally a susceptibility to a variety of diseases, as venereal, scrofula, &c., some of which may have a common cause, others a specific, as lues; yet the constitution can have at the same time only one specific action. As there are susceptibilities for dispositions, so there must be also dispositions for actions; yet two of these cannot exist at the same time in the same part or constitution.

Two children were inoculated for the smallpox. Their arms inflamed; but about the third or fourth day from the inoculation symptoms of fever arose, and the measles appeared, and went through their progress as usual. During this time the inflammation in the arm was arrested; but when the measles were completely gone, the smallpox took place, and went through its progress.

Here a disposition for the measles had taken hold of the body, but although it had done that previously to the smallpox, yet it was not in such a way as stopped the progress of the smallpox. The smallpox matter was capable of contaminating, and produced inflammation, which went to a certain length, but the moment the measles changed their disposition into action, as the two actions could not go on together, the action of the smallpox was suspended till the measles had gone through its action, and the moment the constitution got free of this, the smallpox began to act again.

A lady of rank was inoculated by Mr. Sutton. A few days after a fever came on, of the languid or putrid kind, but without any eruption, except a few petechiæ on the breast: she went through the process of a low fever, and afterwards the smallpox commenced; yet when the pustules maturated they spread wide and were very large; also a different set of eruptions succeeded, so that thirty days passed before the skin was clear of the eruptions.

These cases show that but one mode of action can take place at the same time ; yet I could conceive that two actions might produce a third one, which might have been a new poison, as the last case in some measure seems to show.

Of wrong Actions.—I have already mentioned, under the animal œconomy, the two different kinds of action in an animal : 1st, The natural powers of growth, modelling, &c. ; 2nd, The powers peculiar to each part, voluntary or involuntary. Now, the first may act improperly ; it may push forth unnatural and unnecessary growth in some parts, and too little in other parts. They may also act in such a manner as to obstruct the necessary actions of the machine, as by unnecessary masses called tumours, increase of the bones, &c. The second may also act wrong, that is, may act without the necessity for action, as in spasms, locked jaw, over-secretions, palpitation of the heart, &c. This is in every respect similar to the former, only the improper action is on a different part. If, then, improper actions fall on a part of importance to the machine, they produce disease ; or they may act too little, and thus produce diseases of a different kind.

Diseased actions, like the actions of health, become accustomed to impressions, and we see many of them subject to the same laws. This is of two kinds : first, where the diseased part becomes less and less affected by stimulus, from a continuance of the application ; second, where the whole body, or a part, becomes more easily affected by the stimulus, from a repetition of the application.

People constantly exposed to the cause of certain diseases become less affected, or less liable to be affected. Perhaps the best way to prevent being affected by some infectious diseases would be to live constantly where the infection was. People coming out of the country into the town are more liable to be affected by certain infections, as the small-pox, than those who live constantly in large towns. The constitution having once felt the stimulus of the smallpox, is not afterwards affected by it ; yet I can readily conceive that if a man were to live two hundred years he might arrive at that period when he would again be susceptible of the impression.

Of Sedatives and Stimulants.—Perhaps there is no idea of any principle, simply as an idea, more correct than that conveyed by the word sedative, stimulus, irritation ; yet I think it is probable that there is no idea so little understood in practice ; and it may be a very difficult task, and next to an impossibility, to say what real state the body or part is in, or can be brought into, to be affected in either one or the other way. This arises from our imperfect knowledge of the true state of the body or parts, or of their œconomy ; for what might act as a sedative at one time, might be a stimulant at another, or even an irritant ; or what might be a sedative to one part, might be either a stimulant or irritant to another, which we shall see to be really the case, for whatever will excite action, even the common action of parts, will be a stimulus, and whatever will excite actions beyond the real strength of the body will be an irritant; and this cause of excitement beyond the common action may be no more than what at another time would act as a sedative.

For example, without heat, probably no action could take place either in common vegetable or animal matter. Heat admits of becoming an exciter to action; but as heat, in so far as it can, only excites natural actions, and, in due proportion to the strength of the parts, it may be called sedative; for we may suppose that by sedative is not meant an unnatural reduction of action, (for which, indeed, we have no expression,) but the production of a natural action from too great an action. It may increase or diminish action, according to circumstances. But to ascertain the precise degree of heat suitable to every state of body or part, so as neither to increase nor diminish action, is probably impossible.

When animals are extremely weak, their actions should be suitable to their strength. Or if an animal is only moderately weak in the whole, considered as a whole, yet there will be parts that will be very weak; and if those parts are under disease, care should be taken that those parts are not thrown into action above their strength.

The temperature of the body, or parts respecting heat and cold, should be in proportion to this weakness, which will regulate the action, and to apply warmth at such time would be applying a stimulus; and if the body was still more reduced, warmth might become an irritant; or if the body was not able to act up to this stimulus, it would be an irritant.

To lower actions suitably to the state of the constitution, whatever this may be, is the use of a sedative; but in some constitutions it may be requisite to bring it even lower. So it is often necessary to produce fainting; but this cannot be called a sedative; it is probably only weakening.

Irritability.—There is no word perhaps more improperly applied than irritability; it is often used for stimulus, and stimulus often used in place of it. Indeed we must allow that there is a resemblance between them in several of their properties, both exciting actions of the living parts; but they differ very much in the consequent action, as, indeed, irritability appears to be nearly allied to susceptibility.

I have already explained, when on the animal œconomy, (p. 269,) that stimulus excites or increases natural actions; but an irritation either excites an unnatural quantity of a natural action, or an entire new one; and susceptibility is the readiness with which they can be excited.

Some constitutions are so easily excited, or, in other words, so susceptible of diseased impression, as to take up actions so readily as to make them appear natural, which in others are only brought on by disease. That a natural action may be increased beyond its natural bounds we see every day. Salivation is an instance of this. That irritation produces new action is perhaps more evident than the former. Accidents of all kinds are of this kind. Blisters act on this principle. In short, every new action which takes place may be said to arise from an irritation produced in the part, or something similar. Irritations are often producing salutary effects, and therefore may be said to terminate in a stimulus, which is owing to a kind of irritation, such as those which are in consequence of many accidents, which new action produces a restoration of the part injured, as in wounds, compound fractures, &c.

There are new modes of action taking place every day that would appear to arise spontaneously (therefore from no possible irritating cause, which, on the contrary, most probably arises from this new mode of action). The immediate cause may be so slight as hardly to approach to an irritation. Such constitutions are called irritable, which is only saying that one part may be irritated by what would have no effect on another. Those unnatural spontaneous actions often arise from a want of power to act properly, with a strong disposition to action, which is the reason why weakness, or want of power, becomes the cause of irritation, which produces new action, which new action will be according to this want of power and the nature of the part combined.

Necessity often becomes the cause of irritation, as when a small opening is made into a large cavity, and not allowed to heal by the first intention, the whole becomes under the necessity of taking on a new action to restore the whole; therefore irritation often produces salutary effects.

Many of the preternatural actions are so slow in their motions that we can hardly make them accord with our ideas, which ascribe them to irritation, especially in those that seem to arise spontaneously, as the formation of many wens, encysted tumours, &c.

Irritation may be divided into common, specific, and poisonous: 1st, Common, is that which will affect all animals; 2nd, That which will affect only the same species; 3rd, Is also very much confined to species; one only, as far as I know, being excepted,—the bite of a mad dog. So that the disease of one animal, although communicable to another of the same species, is not so to one of another species. Smallpox, chickenpox, venereal disease, measles, hooping-cough, jail-distemper, itch, scrofula, are peculiar to the human. The disease of black cattle is confined to them; the rot to sheep; glanders to horses; mange to dogs*.

---

* [There are some of the above diseases which are now known to be communicable to other animals.]

CHAPTER X.

OF SYMPATHY.

Disposition to action arising from sympathy;—without direct impression.—
Sympathy of two kinds;—connexion of principles of action in the living
body;—sympathies of sensation doubtful.—Sympathy between differ-
ent bodies.—Sympathy natural or diseased;—not always reciprocal
between parts;—generally single;—common or uncommon;—similar or
dissimilar;—partial or universal.—Varieties of partial sympathy;—
varieties of universal sympathy;—fever, inflammatory, hectic.—Certain
parts sympathize more strongly than others.—Of similar and dissimilar
sympathies;—of simple sympathies;—difference of sympathies from
modes of impression.—Sympathy of body with affections of the mind;—
of the mind with the living principle;—use of sympathies.—Of delu-
sion;—explanation of it;—delusion in dreams.

I HAVE endeavoured to show that there are two principles in the higher
animals, namely, life and the action of the nerves, which last is called
sensation and volition; or rather, perhaps, there is but one principle,
life, which becomes the basis of the other and of every action of the
body. I also endeavoured to point out that sensation arose from
feelings in the mind, which produce action in the body. I attempted to
show that the more simple actions arose independently of sensation or
of the actions of the nerves; that the nerves, from their specific actions,
only become the cause of many actions, but are not the principle of those
actions; that from their termination in the brain they produce sensations
there from which is formed mind, and that they also give rise to the
will, and form the basis of reasoning. I showed that the mind becomes
the cause of many involuntary actions in the body, as reason becomes
the cause of the voluntary; and that thus the actions of life, of the
nerves, of the mind, and of the will arise from impressions being made
on each so as to affect their principles.

In speaking of the general principles of disease, I divided the living
power into susceptibility of impression, impression, dispositions arising
in consequence of such, and action consequent on disposition; all which
I observed were immediate or primary. But there is a secondary sus-

ceptibility, disposition, and action arising from, or in consequence of, all, by necessity, called sympathy; actions, as it were, playing amongst themselves, each becoming a stimulant to the other, or each being affected by the other.

By this principle of action, called sympathy, an action arises without an immediate impression in a secondary way, either acting in conjunction with the part immediately impressed, or taking the whole action on itself. This action without immediate impression is one of the most complicated principles in the animal body, especially the more complicated animals, because it is the compounding of actions.

Sympathy may be divided into two species: 1st, A local with a local disease; 2nd, A universal with a local. The first may be called local sympathy; the second universal. But all sympathies must arise from a local cause. Sympathy is not confined to the same actions of the same person, but is transferable from one person to another*.

In the investigation of this subject, we shall find all the principles of action in an animal, even in the most complicated, have a connexion with one another; for instance, the living principle, the action of the nerves, and the mind: and that the same principle in one part shall be affected by the same principle in another; and this is the simplest kind of sympathy I can conceive. Thus, the living principle of one part sympathizes with the actions of life in another part, as must be the case in all animals which have no nerves†. The nerves of one part sympathize with the actions of the nerves in another, which may produce sensation.

---

* [For some curious examples of this sort, see Dugald Stewart's " Elements of the Philosophy of the Human Mind," p. 153, et seq., and Edin. Med and Surg. Journ., vol. iii. p. 434, et seq., respecting the mode in which some convulsive diseases were propagated in Scotland. A strong collateral argument may be derived from this species of sympathy in favour of that opinion which makes the intervention of the sensorium commune a necessary condition to the existence of sympathy. See Whytt's Works, p. 140, and Dr. Alison in Edin. Med.-Chir. Trans., vol: i. p. 165. That the nerves, however, are capable of a reflex action through the medium of the spinal marrow as well as through the brain, is rendered certain by the experiments of Dr. Marshall Hall and by many morbid phenomena. See Med. Gaz., vol. ii., 1832-3, p. 769.]

† [What the real conditions of the organization are on which sympathies depend are unknown, although there seems every reason to ascribe this agency *solely* to the nervous system. To ascribe it to the living principle is merely eluding the question by a sort of abstraction. The difficulty still returns—what is the intermedium through which distinct and dissimilar parts are thus associated? Some intermedium there must be; and as to the difficulty respecting those beings which have no nerves (p. 260, note), the same is equally felt in regard to the higher animals, in which the most powerful sympathies exist, although no anatomical connexion is to be traced between the parts, nor any relation of function or structure observable. Indeed, those structures, such as fasciæ, membranes, &c., which apparently have no nerves, are those very parts which give rise to the strongest and most marked sympathies.]

The mind sympathizes with the mind, which of course can only take place in animals that have mind, and perhaps not in all of them; and it is more than probable that such minds as are capable of sympathy are capable of other complications of affections. Probably what might be called the disposition to action of one principle in one part may produce action of another principle in another part. Thus sensation in another part may be produced, while simple life only is affected in the part immediately impressed. This would appear to be owing to the nature of the sympathizing part. Thus, if an injection is thrown into the urethra in a man, it shall not give pain in the urethra, not even the common sensation of the part, yet the stomach shall be affected and sickness produced, which last is a sensation. I have known a stimulus in the rectum, which did not produce pain in the part, produce sickness and pain in the small intestines, and even stop digestion. Such pain certainly arises from action in the part. On the contrary, simple pain in the finger shall produce a greater action of the living principle in another part, as making the heart beat oftener.

The principle of sympathy itself I shall call a genus, of which the above make three species, namely, sympathy of the actions of life, of the nerves, and of the mind. Each of these have their varieties in action, each being susceptible of varieties of impressions, affections, and actions, and all being capable of sympathizing with one another.

It may admit of dispute, and probably will be difficult to settle, whether there is sympathy between sensation and sensation simply; for sensation must arise from some impression made on a part, or some action of nerves similar to those arising from impression. Therefore every sympathy which only produces sensation must still arise from impression on, or action of, the nerves; and the same with the sensation in the sympathizing part. Sensation is only the natural consequence of such action, for sensation is only the intelligence of action, either from impression or arising from the spontaneous action of the nerve itself.

I suspect that all those which would appear to be sympathies of sensation only, without action, are a delusion of the mind, a wrong reference of the mind to some other than the part affected, which I shall explain when upon the subject of delusion.

From what has been said above, it must appear that sympathy is a principle in animal bodies so intimately connected with every possible impression, affection, and action, that we cannot have a proper conception of the animal œconomy respecting diseases without taking this principle into consideration. It is one of the secondary principles when applied to the body itself, being the effect of some impression, affection,

or action in some other part of the same body.   Sympathy arises from
every part of the body being ready to fall into affections and actions in
consequence of an impression, affection, or action having taken place in
some other part.   Sympathy is one part taking part in the impressions,
affections, and actions of another part.

Sympathy is not confined to actions of the same persons amongst
themselves, but is transferable from one person to another, in whom it
cannot be called a secondary action, as it arises from an impression
being made on some of the senses.

Yawning is a species of sympathy; and all actions peculiar to country,
places, family, &c., are so many sympathies.   Dancing may be included
among the sympathies, for it is not simply an imitative action arising
from the will, but it is an irresistible impulse arising from a state of
mind produced by musical sounds.   If there were no sounds, or, in other
words, not a sense of hearing, there would be no dancing; for seeing
would not produce it, probably rather retard it.   There is, first, sensation; then a state of mind formed in consequence of that sensation;
and then the action of the limbs excited by that sensation.

The idea of sympathy may be stated differently: instead of saying a
part sympathizes with another, we may say one part under stimulus or
irritation is capable of stimulating another part of the same body into
sensation, action, &c., which I think is the most natural idea or position.

Sympathy may be divided into two kinds, the natural and the diseased.   The diseased is when sound parts sympathize with the diseased,
and probably the diseased with the diseased, which is what I mean to
explain.

The sympathy of one diseased part with the diseases of another part
will include the idea of revulsion, as revulsion consists in the production of a disease in one part to cure a disease in another part; which
shows that this one part, while under disease, can be affected by a diseased action being produced in another part, or the cessation of one
action in consequence of another having taken place in another part.

Natural sympathy takes place more readily, and its actions are more
strongly marked, in proportion as the powers of the machine are capable
of repairing an injury received.   On the other hand, it takes place more
slowly, and is less evident, as the powers of life are more languid.

In many diseased states the condition of the whole body is often such
that it more readily falls into sympathy at one time than at others.
Thus we find people at particular periods much affected by slight causes,
while at other times considerable mischief received will hardly affect
them.

Some people are naturally more readily affected than others, as will be evident in disease.

Sympathy sometimes proves fatal, as in children from teething. But this depends in great measure on the parts sympathizing, or the number of parts that sympathize.

Sympathies are often not reciprocal: the liver never sympathizes with the shoulder, nor the urethra with the testis; nor when the glans penis is affected does any irritation pass to the bladder: but often they are, as, for example, between the head and the stomach.

Sympathies are generally simple; we hardly ever find two parts sympathizing with the same cause: however, the spasmodic convulsion of both hands, or hands and feet, &c., as sometimes takes place, may be called a double sympathy.

Sympathy is common and uncommon. The first is where it takes place more readily between some parts than it does between others, as between the stomach and head, the stomach and the skin, the testes and the urethra. Sympathy may be called uncommon when parts sympathize with diseased parts that were never known to sympathize in health.

A gentleman had a sore on the inside of his thigh, which itched so intolerably that he could not avoid scratching it, and when he did, it always produced tightness in his chest and shortness of breathing, which he never had but at these times.

Lord Cavendish's father always felt pain in the left arm from a stone in the bladder. This pain was the only indication of a want to make water.

Sympathies are either similar to the cause or dissimilar. The similar can be but of two kinds: where the modes of affection or action of the sympathizer are either wholly similar to the modes of affection or action of the parts diseased, or the sympathizer has one of its modes of affection or action similar, and which is the one that sympathizes. Dissimilar sympathy may be of so many kinds that it is probably hardly possible to be completely master of the whole of the particular varieties.

Sympathy may be said to be either partial or universal. Sympathy is partial, from local diseases, when the causes of action in one part become the cause of action in a distant part, as when anything tickles the nose the muscles of respiration act; or it may be partial from a universal disease. But local sympathy with the constitution has its order of parts, as the stomach sympathizes with the whole body in an incipient fever.

Sympathy is either natural or diseased. Natural sympathy always tends to produce some salutary purpose, as the breasts of women increasing with the size of the uterus during gestation.

As no part of the body is entirely independent of the rest, in all particular injuries the whole must sympathize more or less; but as every individual part has a more intimate connexion with some particular part than with others, these parts sympathize more readily.

Local or partial sympathies we call continuous, contiguous, or remote. Continuous is only an extension of the same action, as in most inflammations spreading from the centre; otherwise, in an injury, the part which received the first impression would alone become inflamed. Contiguous is where one part sympathizes with another where the parts are only in contact with each other, without any continuity of parts, as the contents of the abdomen with the abdominal muscles*. Remote is where one part sympathizes with another part, though at some distance from it.

Universal sympathy is when the whole becomes affected in consequence of a local disease, and is of two kinds. One is where every part of the body sympathizes with any one part stimulated, as the sympathetic fever in consequence of local inflammation, as also eating substances that disagree with the stomach, convulsions from worms, teething, &c.; or, secondly, where particular parts, being stimulated, more readily produce universal sympathy than any other.

Constitutional sympathy may arise in many cases from local sympathy, and not from the effect of the first injured part. This is very remarkable when the sympathizing part is a vital part, though the first injured part be not vital. If the stomach sympathizes strongly with any part of the body, this sympathy of the stomach produces a morbid state of the constitution.

In universal sympathy there appear three stages, but all equally belonging to this principle: 1st, inflammatory fever; 2nd, hectic fever; 3rd, dissolution. These take their rise from the different stages of the local disease. There may be marked a fourth, which may be called nervous, spasmodic, or hysteric; but this is not particular to any one of the states of the local disease from which the others arise, but from peculiarity of constitution, and sometimes it exists when the others do not.

Local or partial sympathy is found more in old than in young; whereas universal sympathy is more in young than in old. Sympathy is less determined in young persons, every part being then ready to sympathize with other parts under disease. This is remarkable in the

---

* [Of this kind also are the actions of membranous muscular cavities, as the heart, stomach, or intestines, when their lining membranes are stimulated, and of the muscle of the skin in animals when the skin is irritated.]

teething of children, for in them universal sympathy seems the first mode of sympathy arising from local irritation.

When a local disease takes place in a part when the patient is very young, it is capable of giving a general disposition to sympathize, by which means symptoms become more uncertain than in those of more advanced age, often putting on the appearances of a great variety of diseases.

As the child advances, the power of sympathy becomes partial, there not being now in the constitution that universal consent of parts, but some part, which has greater sympathy than the rest, falls into the whole irritation; therefore the whole disposition to sympathy is directed to some particular part. The different organs acquire more and more of their own independent actions as the child grows older.

We find in children the symptoms from sympathy often more violent than those of the parts affected. In adults when cutting teeth there is only an affection of the part, or only a continued sympathy, that is, a swelling of the cheek, &c. In adults the pain is often very great, but in children the pain is little, and the action of the part moderate, but the action in the sympathizing parts is very great, namely, in the voluntary muscles.

Sympathetic Inflammatory Fever.—In consequence of considerable local injuries, as a compound fracture, or operation of consequence having been performed, that accident or operation shall be followed by inflammation, suppuration, &c. In consequence of this local injury fever shall arise in the system, which is universal sympathy, commonly called symptomatic fever.

Convulsions often arise from considerable local injuries called irritation. Permanent contractions are also often the consequence of local injuries or irritation, as tetanus.

If another mode of action takes place in the part sympathized with, namely, the cure of the injury, then the inflammatory sympathetic fever will subside.

Sympathetic Hectic Fever.—If parts have not a power to effect a cure, the constitution sympathizes in another way: it is teazed, as if conscious that the disease is incurable; and this teazing constitutes the greatest part of what has been called hectic fever. But if this incurable part is removed, the hectic fever will cease.

I have seen a wound in the knee keep a man awake several nights with pain and constant purging, and the patient becoming hectic; and by amputating the part he slept well the same night without opium, the purging immediately ceased, and costiveness ensued. A man had a wound in the elbow-joint, and was affected exactly in the same way, the pulse quick and hard : within ten minutes after the removal of the arm the pulse became slower and softer.

This universal sympathy, of whatever species, is greater when certain parts are diseased. The sympathetic fever will more readily take place from an injury done to the involuntary parts, as the stomach, intestines, testicles, &c., than if the same mischief had been done to the voluntary parts, as the muscles of the arm, for instance.

When vital parts are diseased, there is more sympathy among vital parts than among others.

Universal sympathy is greater if the injury received is further from the source of life, namely, the heart, than near it, provided it be a part of the same nature in both cases.

Sympathy is similar to sensation, action, motion, &c. : it can, and often does, cease instantaneously. Every sympathy ceases after the cause is gone, although its effects may remain, as tumefaction*.

Some parts of the Body sympathize more than others.—The stomach appears to have this connexion with the body more than any other part. It would appear that the stomach was the seat of universal sympathy, sympathizing with every part of the body, and most parts of the body sympathizing with the stomach.

Every part of the body seems to have some susceptibility of sympathy; but although there is universal sympathy between the stomach and whole body, yet the stomach sympathizes more readily with a complaint in the head than with one in the toe; more with the testicle than with many other parts. Also some parts of the body sympathize more readily with the stomach than many other parts, as the head, skin, &c. The skin sympathizing with the stomach is often very evident, from the effect some food has on the stomach, producing disease of the skin. A glass of cider in some shall produce a flushing in the face immediately; and spirits, in the end, we know, produce inflammation and suppuration over the whole face, called pimples, especially on the nose. But whether the stomach loses part of this property I am not certain. It appears that other parts lose that susceptibility to sympathize with the stomach, as the skin, for that part does not seem to be so readily affected in the old as in the young.

The stomach sympathizes with the skin in many of its affections. Cold or wet feet will immediately affect the stomach. But the most striking instance is seen in the leech when its stomach is full of blood,

---

* [It often happens, however, that parts acquire a *habit* from long-continued sympathy, which does not cease upon the cessation of the cause.]

by throwing salt on it, when, from sympathy of the stomach with the skin, it immediately rejects all the blood.

The intestines, especially the upper parts, have also sympathies over the whole body. Cases of worms show this perhaps more than anything.

Observations on Sympathies of the different Principles with one another, producing similar and dissimilar Sympathies.—Continued sympathy is more commonly similar than the remote, as it is an extension of the same action, and commonly in a similar part which can act alike, as indeed most parts do in most of their common actions, although the peculiar actions of the part may be dissimilar*. Thus, chancre on the scrotum, if it was to spread to the testicle, would produce the same mode of action in the testicle as in the scrotum, though it might at the same time produce effects peculiar to the testicle, as stoppage of the secretion, &c.

But the remote, local, or partial, is both similar and dissimilar, varying according to two circumstances: 1st, According to the nature of the part diseased and the nature of the sympathizer. 2nd, According to the species of properties in each part; as one property in the part diseased producing sympathy in another property in the sympathizer; disease in one part producing increased natural discharge in another part, which makes sympathy very complicated.

Let us take sensation as an illustration: although we have no sympathetic sensation, it being wholly delusive, yet sensation is an absolute guide. We know that the sensations in the brain are not similar to any other sensations in the body, at least not similar to many of them; also the sensations of the stomach are unlike to many of the brain, if not to the whole of them; also that many of the sensations of the stomach are not similar to the sensations of other parts; also that all sensations of the stomach are not the same; also that an action of one part shall produce sympathy of another, whose mode of action is not similar: we must see therefore at once why the two modes of action become not

---

* [To this head may be referred, 1st, Those sympathies by virtue of which parts become successively diseased *in pairs*, as two eyes, two similar parts of the skin, or two testicles. 2nd, Those which give rise to disease in consequence of similarity of *function*, as ulceration of the cartilages, inflammation of the synovial membranes of joints, &c. 3rd, Those which affect particular organs from *forming parts of the same general system*, as disease of the bladder affecting the kidney, of the uterus affecting the breast, or the spinal marrow the brain, &c. And 4thly, Those which arise from *similarity of structure*, as inflammation of fibrous and mucous membranes, &c.

We may observe, once for all, that any-philosophical classification of sympathies is impracticable. Mr. Hunter has probably made his division of sympathies too complex; but he has amply redeemed this fault, if it be one, by the able manner in which he has treated the subject.]

similar, and why the sympathy is not similar to the cause, producing by this means another cause of complication, and consequently a variety in the first principles of sensation and action respecting sympathy. Again, difference of properties may produce dissimilar sympathies between two different principles, as the principle of life and that of action. For as sensation in one part may produce sympathy in a part whose actions are dissimilar from that other part, the sympathy produced will be dissimilar, and this resulting from the difference in the properties of the principle of action.

Also when we consider that many parts have more modes of action than one, as the stomach, which has a variety of actions, and of course is capable of producing a variety of sympathies in other parts, or can sympathize in a variety of ways with other parts, so that any one of these peculiar actions in one shall produce an action or sympathy in that suitable to the first action of the disease, which of course will be similar to the action of the diseased parts; while another action in the same part, and from the same principle, shall produce another mode of sympathy in the sympathizer; when we consider all these, they will at first sight appear inexplicable : as an illustration, we may observe what a variety of sympathies are produced from one mode of irritation, as teething, or worms in the intestines.

This connexion of every part of the body with the others, by sympathy, becomes one of the extensive principles of action in the animal œconomy, indeed is the basis of most of the compound impressions, affections, and actions.

Similar Sympathy.—Sympathy must be similar to the affection of the part first affected when between parts whose affections are wholly similar; similar in action when between parts whose actions are wholly similar.

Sympathy may be similar in disease when between parts endued with a variety of affections and actions, provided they are endued with the same affection or action, as irritation in one part producing irritation in another, which thus produces inflammation, as an injection into the urethra producing swelling and pain of the testicle.

Continued sympathy, I believe, in all cases is similar to the disease, at least the action is so, even though it may spread to a dissimilar part. If inflammation attacks the diaphragm, and extends to the liver from continuity, that inflammation of the liver will be similar to that of the diaphragm. The same also if disease extends from the testicle to the scrotum, &c.

Dissimilar Sympathy.—Sympathy is dissimilar when the affections or actions of the part impressed are not similar to the actions or affections of the part which sympathises; thus, sickness at the stomach cannot produce sickness anywhere else; or, secondly, where parts diseased are susceptible of a variety of affections or actions of which the sympathizer is not; or, thirdly, even in parts where both the part diseased and the sympathizer are susceptible of the same varieties of stimuli and modes of action, which varieties in themselves are similar to one another, yet the sympathizer shall not be the corresponding affection or action to that which is excited in the part diseased; for example, a medicine taken into the stomach shall produce flushing of the face or inflammation, though the stomach is liable to the same disease as that of the face, namely, inflammation. So that in this case the difference does not arise from the mode of action being different from that of the stomach, only that the face does not run on to the same degree of action as the stomach. In inflammation of the liver the pain in the shoulder is different from inflammation, though the shoulder and liver are equally susceptible of inflammation. So that many parts have a variety of actions in themselves which are similar to some actions in other parts; therefore sympathy shall or shall not be similar to the action of the diseased part, being according to the stimulus applied to such part, or mode of action of the diseased part joined with the mode of affection. Therefore simple stimulus, action, or affection shall not only be the cause either of similar or dissimilar action, but both, according to the variety of affections and different parts that sympathize. A stimulus in the testicle shall produce sickness in the stomach, which shall produce vomiting, which is an action; so that a double and different compound sympathy takes places from the same stimulus.

Of the simplest Sympathies.—In vegetables we evidently see actions taking place in consequence of actions having taken place in another part; but how far vegetables have a variety of properties and actions is not perfectly known: however, we can hardly doubt that they have a great many, for they produce a vast variety of effects, all these actions and effects arising from the principle of life. So that sympathies of vegetables may be complicated, and even dissimilar, but still more simple than the most simple animal. The succession of motions in a sensitive plant are no more than a succession of sympathies, or a succession of stimuli in consequence of those preceding. Here, then, we have an exact similarity in the actions of the sympathizers with the part first acted on.

The most simple sympathy is perhaps to be found in vegetables, these being much more simple than the most simple animal. Vegetables have the same properties as animals without brain or stomach. Take away, therefore, the sympathies of the stomach with the body, and of the body with the stomach, and those between the brain and the body, reducing the sympathies of the animal to the simple properties of life, and an animal will be exactly similar to a vegetable; and this I know from experiments made on trees.

The motion of the sensitive plant I have said is produced by a succession of simple sympathies: something like this may be found in the more imperfect animals; but no animal can be so simple in all its sympathies, though it may in some. I shall at present suppose that every part of an animal is liable to be affected by the stimulus of agreeable or disagreeable sensations, and the more simple the animal the more likely it is to be under the same simple sympathy. A polypus is the most simple complete animal, and therefore must be most similar in its sympathies; but I can conceive a child in the womb to be still more so, being capable of one stimulus only, namely, want in the system; and perhaps it has no sympathy even with this, as it has no demand on any part of its body for the supply. This simplicity of stimulus is found not only in the simple animals, but in some degree also in the more complicated. The similar sympathies may be compared to the unison in sounds.

A polypus, though so simple an animal, is susceptible of four different stimuli, disagreeable and agreeable, propagation of the species, and want of repletion. In the last the stomach becomes the original sympathizer, and produces action in the other parts, so that here is a sympathy as in plants, but not so simple, for the stomach first sympathizes with the whole body when it wants repletion, and afterwards by a reflex sympathy the body is called into action and its little arms are erected.

Difference of Sympathies in the Sympathizer arising from difference in the mode of Impression.—Difference of affection and action of the sympathizer from that of the part affected does not always arise from difference in the nature of the two parts, but often from difference in the nature of the stimulant, or mode of impression; for a stimulant of one kind shall produce a mode of impression of its own kind in the part, from which shall arise a peculiar sympathy, while a stimulus of another kind will produce an impression of another kind, which of course will produce a sympathy of another kind in the part that sympathizes. Thus, when the stomach is stimulated in a particular way, the head shall ache, which is often the case when something is taken which disagrees with the stomach; and if stimulated in another way, the headache shall be removed, namely, by exciting vomiting*. There will be, therefore,

---

* [This illustration is incorrect; the headache is removed, not because another mode of stimulation, that of the emetic, takes place, but because the original one is removed; thus spontaneous headaches terminate in sickness, and get well.]

a variety in the actions of the sympathizer, arising from varieties in the specific modes of action, created by different stimulants, which may also produce similar sympathy in dissimilar parts, for parts very dissimilar in their natural actions shall be put into similar actions by sympathy. When the stomach is stimulated in one way, an action shall be brought on in the muscles of respiration and of the belly for the expulsion of the irritating matter; or if stimulated in another way, sweating shall be brought on in the skin; or if stimulated in another way, universal debility takes place; a blow on the stomach may even kill.

Hence it appears, that a stimulus of one kind produces sympathy in one part of the body, while a stimulus of another kind applied to the same part produces sympathy in another part, each mode of action in a particular part having other parts distinct from each other which sympathize with it.

I should suspect that specific inflammations are not able to give to the sympathizer their specific virtues, though they may be liable to give them others. In *continuous* sympathies the affection is similar, but not in the remote. A swelled testicle in venereal gonorrhœa does not partake of the specific nature of the original disease. In a cancerous breast, the glands in the axilla will often inflame and subside again, which they would not do if they were affected with cancer.

Sympathies of the Body arising from Affections of the Mind.—The living principle of the body sympathizes with the mind. Strong affections of the mind will produce involuntary motions, even of those parts commonly at the command of the will. This must be by means of the nerves, for the body has no connexion with the brain but by the nerves. Fear will produce action of the involuntary parts, as purging, discharge of urine, &c.

I suspect that particular parts may sympathize more readily with the mind than others; therefore in such cases sympathies may be called local or remote, but they are, I believe, in most cases universal.

Sympathies of the Mind with the Living Principle.—The third principle, mind, is capable of sympathizing with the first, or actions depending on the living principle, for I should think that a state of the body often forms a state of mind; however, it is not so readily affected by what does not produce sensation as by that which does. A man in pain not only feels pain as a sensation, but becomes depressed; or if the actions of life can produce sensation in any part, then the mind becomes affected, as when the whole body is in want of food the stomach sympathizes strongly with the whole, and the sympathy of the stomach causes a sympathizing mind. This is not sympathy immediately with the first principle, but sympathy with the sympathizer, or second, which, however, arose from the first. There are, however, instances where the mind sympathizes with the first, or life, for there are many instances where the mind is depressed without a sensible cause, called hypochondriasis, and also where the mind is light or easy without any sensible cause. I suspect that both these states arise from the living principle being either diseased or at rest.

Sympathy of the mind with the voluntary parts is curious. If the voluntary parts are rendered useless, the will has no longer any power over them; it produces a state of mind which prevents the will putting the parts into action. Thus, when the tendo Achillis is divided, the person cannot put the muscles attached to that tendon into action by the will; but as soon as union takes place and grows strong, the mind allows the will to take possession of its action over the muscles.

Use of Sympathies *.—Sympathies are designed for very important ends. They produce a communication between the three principles of the animal œconomy. The use of sympathy is often very evident. If there is an uncommon irritation in the lungs or throat, the muscles of respiration act with uncommon force, and the offending substance is thrown up. The irritation is frequently in the lungs, then it is transferred to the larynx, the muscles of respiration sympathize with the latter, and cough is excited either to get rid of the disease or of its consequence, which is increased and morbid secretion. In pregnancy

---

* [To enumerate all the uses of sympathies in an animal body would evidently be impossible in the present state of science. Nothing is more certainly ascertained, however, than that every part of the frame is connected in some mysterious manner with the whole, and the whole with every part, in consequence of which a sort of community of feeling is established between all the parts and functions of the machine. This is most remarkably exemplified in those organs which are associated in some common function, as, for example, in the organs of generation, digestion, respiration, &c., which reciprocally act and react upon one another on all occasions, in health and in disease.

Ascending to still higher generalities, as, e. g., to the great centres of organic life, the stomach, the brain, and the heart, the same relationship and dependence is observed to exist, still more strongly developed; while these again may be regarded as so many primary *foci*, to which all the impressions of the body tend, and from which, by a sort of reflex operation, they radiate to the most remote parts of the system. A balance of power and action is thus established which it is easy to see must be of the most essential importance to the general œconomy of the animal, whereby the weakness of individual parts is reinforced by the reaction of the whole, or, on the other hand, the over-action of one organ divided and broken by participation with another. Upon this principle it is, also, that one disease becomes the cure of another, and that revulsives and counter-irritants operate. This *consent* of parts, or interchange of sympathy, in virtue of which the parts of a complex animal body vibrate, as it were, in unison, preeminently distinguishes an organized being from any work of human art, especially when we add

the breasts become swollen, preparatory to their secreting milk in parturition. In labour the uterus is stimulated by the child, now become fit for expulsion, and the muscles of the abdomen sympathize with the uterus.

Sympathy in diseases, by becoming the symptom of disease, often leads us to the cause, especially when the cause is in a deep-seated part, as the pain in the knee when the hip-joint is affected.

We find that the sympathizer in some cases relieves the part irritated or under diseased action, as the testicle relieves the urethra; but there appears to be nothing gained by this, as the sympathy is the worse disease of the two.

By the sympathizer often relieving the part diseased, and sometimes even curing it, it becomes similar to a constitutional affection becoming a local one, as in the gout; and, as in the swelled testicle from gonorrhœa it often changes sides almost instantaneously, it is in this exactly similar to gout.

Some sympathies are opposite in their action to the original action: pain in the liver is depressing, that in the shoulder rousing. Nature is incapable of sustaining the former, and sets up the rousing pain in the shoulder to continue life.

Delusion.—A simple sensation in the mind of a local disease in the body which does not correspond with the seat of the disease itself has,

---

to this the further fact that it carries within itself its own resources of repair whenever it is injured. The full perception which Hunter had of this extraordinary co-operation of parts led him to employ a language borrowed from the operations of the mind, as if *consciousness* resided in an animal body, and was capable of directing its operations as it were by *anticipation.* (See pp. 232, 255, 260, 264, et passim.)

The prevailing opinion is, that this connexion of function is established by means of the great sympathetic nerve, which is supposed to accompany the arteries in their most remote ramifications. Whether this is so or not is not susceptible of proof; we may at least venture to say that our knowledge of this set of nerves has hardly kept pace with other branches of physiology, and that in fact our actual knowledge of the subject is exceedingly imperfect. In the greater number of cases the intervention of the brain or spinal marrow seems to be an essential condition to the propagation of sympathy; and probably in those cases where this is not necessary, the same condition is fulfilled by the ganglionic masses of the sympathetic nerve. Nothing certain, however, can be affirmed on this subject.

Some physiologists have excluded from their definition of sympathy all those phenomena which depend on obvious anatomical connexion, functional relation, or continuity of structure, restricting the term to those cases only in which no functional or mechanical connexion is to be traced. I apprehend, however, that this distinction is not tenable, and that these two sets of phenomena will be found to depend on the same principle, and insensibly to merge in one another.]

I believe, been always referred to the principle of sympathy. Thus, sensation of pain in the shoulder from disease in the liver has been always supposed to arise from the shoulder sympathizing with the liver. The sensation of the glans penis from a disease or irritation in the bladder has been referred to the same cause. But I believe it is a delusion in the mind; for the nerves of the part are not the seat of the disease, and irritation could not communicate to the mind the sensation of pain in the part affected excepting they (the nerves) take on the same action, which they must do when they produce the sensation of pain of that part. But if the nerves of the part which is the seat of sensation in such cases do not act at all, it cannot be called sympathy.

That there is such a delusive principle in the animal œconomy we see every day, and that it not only exists between mind and body, so as to lead us astray from the real subject, but between the mind and other bodies with which it has no immediate connexion, not even by the common senses. But we must allow that certain sensations can form a peculiar state of mind, called a sympathizing mind, for we are capable of transferring the sensation of another person to ourselves, which is like a dream. A delusion in the mind is an object appearing to be where it is not.

To account for this delusion in sensation in ourselves may be difficult, but we may conceive it to be in this way. We may suppose that when the seat of sensation in the brain only takes on part of the action of sensation in the brain, it may be in this way:

Suppose E, (Pl. XVII. f. 3.) the brain; A B, two portions of the brain; G H, two nerves; F, communication between these two nerves; C D, two different parts of the body.

The nerve G is inserted into part of the brain A; the nerve H into the other part B. F is a communicating nerve between G and H. A and B are the two parts of the brain to which sensation from C and D is conducted. C is the disease or part impressed. But from the connexion between C and D, by means of the nerves G F H, B will become the seat of action of the nerve G as well as of the nerve H, and the sensation be in part referred to D as well as to C. For if the nerve H is stimulated, in consequence of these connexions, to take up part of the action of the nerve G, and B is sensible of it as well as A is of the sensation of C, then the sensitive principle of the nerves A B is made sensible of both the disease of the part of impression as also of the sympathizer D, which become the two impressions in the sensorium. If anything stimulates G, part of the action is communicated to H; this goes on with the action to B, so that both A and B become sensible of the disease C. If there is disease in C, the mind is made sensible of it, because G always communicates the sense of C to A; but if a small portion of it is brought over to H, and this nerve carries on the action to B, B becomes sensible of it also, and B refers it not to C, but to D, because it is to that point that it has been accustomed to refer all its sensations.

I do not know whether this explanation may be the true one or no, but it is one mode of explaining how we may feel both the disease and the part of sympathy. But how is it in those cases where the sympathizer takes on the whole action, affection, or sensation ? In this case we must suppose that not only a part but the whole of the sensation passes by the communicating nerve F to B, and thus the disease appears to be in D only. But it is possible that nervous sympathy is not effected by the nerves communicating with one another in the body, but from their connexions in the brain; as from the point B sympathizing with the point A, taking on the whole of its action, and referring its sensation to D*.

Delirium.—It will be very difficult to prove whether delirium is a disease of the brain or nerves; it appears equally easy to prove that it is from one as from the other.

A delirium is a dream arising from disease, whether the dream is in the brain itself or in the body; only it is worthy of consideration, as dreams arise from sleep, and as a delirium is a diseased dream arising from what may be called diseased sleep, whether it may not be first necessary to give a short definition of sleep.

Perfect sleep is a cessation of susceptibility of sensation, and of course of all its actions; the consequence of which is a cessation of consciousness in the animal of its own existence; and also, of course, of the consciousness of the relation it bears to itself and every other

---

* [Thus, if a *branch* of a nerve be irritated (being in connexion with the spinal marrow), it is capable, by a reflective operation, of exciting all those muscles supplied by the *trunk*, although if the spinal marrow be destroyed this effect does not take place.

Sympathies of simple sensation are probably as *real* as sympathies attended with visible action, and to be referred to the same general law. This appears from the same cause producing one or both effects, according as the cause is less or more intense. Thus toothache and tic douloureux will occasion pain *or* inflammation of the face; diseased hip will produce pain of the knee, *and,* as I have frequently seen, inflammation of that part; gonorrhœa will occasion pain *or* inflammation of the testicle; disease of the bladder pain *or* morbid change of structure in the kidneys. Many other examples might be adduced to show that the same cause is capable of producing simple pain or pain accompanied with visible effects: which is evidently inconsistent with the opinion which ascribes simple sympathetic pain to a misdirection of the mind.]

thing. But whether this cessation of the susceptibility of impression arises from the brain not then having power to receive impressions of the actions of nerves, or whether the nerves are not then capable of acting or conveying their action to the brain in the state of sleep, is not so easily determined.

Dreams are actions of the mind in sleep; therefore may be independent of any immediate information or impression, but are always independent of the relative connexion between body and mind, or consciousness of the existence of that relationship between the two. For the connexion between the two enables the mind to distinguish perfectly what is sensation and what is only thought, without which all would be a dream. In a delirium, as in sleep, we find the susceptibility of external impression lessened. Whilst sensation is continued sleep is kept off; delirium may be also lessened by arousing the mind from that particular state by external impressions; so far delirium appears similar to dreams, but it widely differs in other respects. In natural sleep the more the brain puts on that peculiar state the less we have of dreaming; but the more the other state is put on the greater the delirium. Dreams often do *arise* from sensations of the body being conveyed to the brain, it being in an imperfect sleep; but the consciousness of the connexion between our own body and our own mind being cut off by the state of sleep, the sensation may or may not be referred to our own body: it may be referred to some other body*. In some cases it is not referred to the part of the body where the impression is made; and the same thing happens in delirium, where the connexion

---

* [One of the most remarkable properties of dreams is, that we have no idea of time or place, or sometimes of our personal identity; in consequence of which we commit the most ludicrous anachronisms, imagine ourselves dead and alive, or in two places, at the same time, or else that our spirits have transmigrated into some other bodies. In consequence of the absence of external perception in sleep, the ideas and associations of the mind acquire an overpowering vividness which leads us to mistake them for realities; while the absence of reason and volition permits the imagination to revel in its own creations under the simple guidance of association. There are, however, many phenomena respecting dreams, delirium, and that variety of the former called somnambulism, which do not admit of any plausible explanation: the will, the senses, and voluntary motion are still exercised, under certain modifications; whilst it must be in the experience of every one that the reasoning faculty is still also capable of exerting itself, so as in some rare cases to engage in, and even to accomplish, the analysis of complicated problems which it could not have achieved during its waking state.

There is one point in which pure delirium and sleep differ from insanity. Persons may be roused by a strong impression from the former to a right perception of their situation, whereas in the insane person truth and error are inextricably blended together, so that when seen side by side they are not distinguishable by the patient.]

is cut off: these not distinguishing between real sensation and thought, what the mind thinks about appears to be real.

But even where the mind is in full possession of the consciousness of its connexion and relationship with the body, we have in some cases this delusion, as the appearance of the turning round of the objects about us whilst they are really fixed, and that in consequence of our having turned about quickly; giddiness from going to a height, or from riding backwards in a coach. Delusion is also an effect of intoxication and disease. Whilst awake and in health, impressions produce sensations, which are conveyed to the brain, and from these the mind reasons: but suppose the mind to have lost, or as it were forgot, its former connexion with our body, then the above false reference takes place.

A gentleman came into this country in 17—; his memory was imperfect, and a particular kind of delirium began whenever he was going to sleep, but afterwards continued whilst wide awake; and for a week before his death he was not quiet from this delirium a moment, but whilst his impressions were forced on him by external objects. His delirium was of this kind: he was constantly talking of former circumstances of his life, but referring them to the present moment and to some other person. There was a revival of past ideas in his mind, but from a want of connexion between his mind and his body, he was not enabled, by his present impressions, to infer how little relationship they bore to the present time, or to those persons to whom he referred them: at the same time, it really appeared more a want of connexion between the mind and the body than the mind itself being hurt, for he determined rightly what should be done in those circumstances which he supposed present, and would express his sentiments in really elegant language. That it depended more on want of connexion than on disease of the body, appeared, from his being sensible of impressions, and referring them to the part where they took place, but supposing that to be in any other body than his own. Thus, he would tell his nurse or the bystanders that they were hungry or thirsty; but upon offering food or drink, it appeared plainly by his eagerness that the idea had arisen from a sensation of hunger in his own stomach. He would show great signs of distress or anxiety, which he would say was because his nurse wanted to go to the close stool, but was restrained by his presence; and this from his sensations also. He had a violent cough, in which he would sympathize with some bystander, proceeding in his story after the cough, no otherwise disturbed than by sympathizing with the person whom he thought so unfortunate as to have it. The objects about him were more to him than his own sensations.

A gentleman who was fond of his bottle referred all his own weaknesses and feelings, as he became intoxicated, to those around him; and upon his going home would insist upon undressing all his family and putting them to bed, declaring that they were too drunk to do it themselves; and this happened not only once, but whenever he was intoxicated. I myself once experienced what I have since thought must have proceeded from this want of connexion between the mind and the body. I was reading a remarkable case, and reasoning with myself upon it, when I found the letters and words made an impression on the retina, but that I was incapable of affixing a meaning to them: this I thought might proceed from want of sleep; but that was not the case: I tried repeatedly, but without effect, and at last I went to bed, from which I did not move for three weeks, a violent affection of the head following this extraordinary circumstance. It may not be amiss to say, that the case I was reading was that of the late Mr. Foote, who was not able to command his attention to more than one action or circumstance at a time: thus, if he took his snuff-box out of his pocket and held it in his hand, it was all very well, until he attempted another action, such as taking a pinch of snuff out of it, and then the box fell immediately out of his hand; in fact, he was going back into a state of second childhood, for a child is not capable of commanding his attention to more than one circumstance or action at a time: give him a stick to hold, and call his attention to another object, and the stick will be dropped; for it is by habit we become capable of attending to several actions at a time. If a person is blindfolded and put into a coach, he will think he is riding forwards though really moving backwards. An impression from any part, either healthy or diseased, may be conveyed, yet there may be no consciousness of the mind from which part of the body it was conveyed, the mind having full possession of the impression, and a perfect idea of it, but having nothing to direct it right in its reference of it. It must refer it somewhere, and is more likely to refer it to another than to itself. Thus, A (Pl. XVII. fig. 3.) does not refer the sensation to C as a cause, nor will B sympathize with A so as to refer it to D.

A gentleman, a medical man, dreamed he had given a patient too strong an injection for gonorrhœa, and that it had produced a total stoppage of urine: he awoke, and found an erection of the penis, and that he could not void a drop of urine. Here was an impression without the consciousness, and he referred the impression to another person.

A gentleman, upwards of ninety years old, suddenly lost his senses, and in consequence of this there was a reference of all the ails which he might be supposed to feel to his wife, who had been dead some time, but who he now thought to be alive, and ordering the utmost silence to be preserved, lest by noise her illness should be increased. The new-born child has probably sensation without this consciousness. The contrary takes place when a person refers the sensations of others to himself, or when the idea of sensation is supposed to be sensation itself, as happens in those who are affected by animal magnetism. I was asked to go to be magnetized, but at first refused, because the spasm on my vital parts was very likely to be brought on by a state of mind anxious about any event. Thus, at my country box I have bees, which I am very fond of, and I once was anxious about their swarming lest it should not happen before I set off for town; this brought it on. The cats teaze me very much by destroying my tame pheasants, partridges, &c., and rooting up my plants. I saw a large cat sitting at the root of a tree, and was going into the house for a gun, when I became anxious lest she should get away before my return; this likewise brought on the spasm; other states, where my mind is much more affected, will not bring it on. Now I feared lest my anxiety for the event should bring on the spasm, and that should be imputed to animal magnetism. But considering that if any person was affected by it it must be by the imagination being worked up by attention to the part expected to be affected, and thinking I could counteract this, I went; and accordingly, when I went, I was convinced by the apparatus that everything was calculated to affect the imagination. When the magnetizer began his operations, and informed me that I should feel it first at the roots of my nails of that hand nearest the apparatus, I fixed my attention on my great toe, where I was wishing to have a fit of the gout; and I am confident that I can fix my attention to any part until I have a sensation in that part. Whenever I found myself attending to his tricks, I fell to work with my great toe, working it about, &c., by which means I prevented it having any effect on me.

CHAPTER XI.

OF LOCAL AND CONSTITUTIONAL DISEASES.

Difficulty of distinguishing between strictly local diseases and local diseases arising from constitutional affection.—Diseases constitutional;—local; —mixed.—The first universal, as fever ;—or constitutionally local, as gout.—Local diseases.—Mixed diseases.—Diseases common or specific. —The latter do not always depend on a specific cause.—Of diseases peculiar to ages.—Effects of climate on diseases ;—of seasons ;—of temperature;—of the moon.—Of humours, erroneous notions of them ;— effects of substances contained in the blood ;—experiments of injecting medicines into the blood ;—no specific diseases produced.—Of diseases supposed to arise from humours.—Of hereditary diseases ;—hereditary nature of natural and of acquired properties ;—hereditary dispositions; —latent hereditary principles ;—similarity of children to their parents; —dispositions hereditary, but not diseases ;—more permanent than accidental dispositions ;—scrofula ;—gout ;—supposed hereditary.—Symptoms of disease local or universal ;—variation of local symptoms ;— universal symptoms affecting the circulation ;—secretions ;—nerves.— Combinations of symptoms.—Irregular symptoms.—Delusive symptoms.

IT may be difficult in all cases of local diseases to distinguish between one truly local and one arising from the constitution; that is, one arising entirely in the part diseased, and one arising entirely from the constitution. For as one can and often does affect the other, which may be called mixed, it becomes the more uncertain where the disease originated*.

Diseases may be called constitutional, local, and mixed. Diseases may be originally constitutional and originally local; that is, diseases

---

* [Mr. Abernethy, in speaking of the evil effects arising from the separation of medicine from surgery, makes the following observation: " The effects of local disorders upon the constitution have in consequence been too little attended to; and, indeed, I know of no book to which I can refer a surgical student for a satisfactory account of those febrile and nervous affections which local disease produces, except that of Mr. Hunter." See his Essay " *On the Constitutional Origin and Treatment of Local Diseases.*"]

may take place in the same person from constitutional or local causes, and be totally independent of each other; but they may affect one another.

The first, or constitutional, is either a universal action of some kind, as fever, or where there is a universal susceptibility for an action, but the action is local. Therefore they are divisible into two kinds, 1st, universally constitutional, and 2nd, constitutionally local.

Universally constitutional is when there is universal action of some kind, as fever, where every part of the body is under some diseased action, which will be according to the nature of the influence which produced the fever, as inflammatory fever, putrid fever, &c.

Those arising from external influence will in some degree reduce all constitutions to some one mode of action; and whatever difference there is between one and the other must only arise from a peculiarity in constitution.

If an inflammation is produced in any part by violence, it will always be as the constitution is. If a man has a fever, a cut will partake of the disease, and the inflammation will be erysipelatous*, or so on, according to the fever. But if the fever is of some specific kind, super-added to the nature of the constitution, as smallpox fever, a cut will not partake of the specific quality of that fever, but will be exclusive of the specific quality. Nor will a cut on any part of a pocky patient be venereal.

Constitutional diseases are of various classes, which are known by their effects. A constitutional disease is a universal diseased action, as fever, every part taking on more or less of the diseased disposition. Such diseases, I apprehend, have no disposition for local action, though it is commonly supposed they have, as where fever produces abscess. This I hardly believe, though an abscess may form in the time of that fever, and is caused by it, or is an effect of that fever; but it is not an act of the constitution, according to our third division, therefore does not relieve the constitution of that fever. What I call an act of the constitution relieves the constitution, as gout falling on a part; but in abscess from fever it is only that this part has been so disturbed in the time of the fever that it has gone into inflammation and suppuration.

The second of the universal is the constitutionally local, that is, when there is universal susceptibility of body to produce peculiar local

---

* [There are many exceptions to this observation, as, for instance, in several cutaneous diseases, gout, rheumatism, &c. These diseases may exist in an active state in some parts of the body at the same time that common inflammation is produced in other parts by accidental injury. On the other hand, the erysipelatous inflammation seems to give way to common phlegmon when incisions are made into erysipelatous parts.]

z 2

complaints, but not the action, till disturbed ; requiring an immediate cause, which may at the time be either universally disturbing, as fever, or in the part only, as an accident. Thus the whole constitution may be affected with a gouty disposition, but the disease becomes local and is cured. We see constitutional or universal diseased affection excite local, as fever exciting scrofula, not as a termination of that fever, but because the part affected was partaker of the universal affection, and being disturbed by that universal affection or action, it took on the mode of action it was most susceptible of. It would do the same thing on being locally disturbed ; therefore, as to its diseased action, it is the same whether it is disturbed as part of a whole, or only by itself. The scrofula goes no further than a susceptibility for diseased action, until it is brought into action by the local injury or constitutional fever.

Perhaps there is no term so vague or undetermined in the mind as the term constitutional. Universal action of every kind may be called constitutional, even when arising from some local cause, which I have called one of the mixed ; or one capable of producing local effects, which we have also called one of the mixed. But a true constitutional disease is one arising, as it were, spontaneously in the constitution, partaking of the nature of the constitution itself.

Local disease I would consider in two lights : 1st, When it is a natural local action, being a kind of violence on a part, there being no constitutional local affection. In this case the disease takes on no specific quality of the constitution, either from the constitution having none, or the disease not being affected by it, being such as either arises from itself in a part from a local cause, and may take place in any constitution, or may be produced by accident or violence where the constitution was never affected. 2nd, Which will more properly come under the head of mixed, where the local affection either affects or is affected by the constitution.

The mixed may be said to partake of the first and second, and is often the consequence of either, namely, original constitutional producing local, or original local producing constitutional ; therefore they are often of two kinds, and such as may be called secondary actions either of the constitution or part, as universal sympathy with local disease, yet not what generally comes under the idea of common sympathy, as sympathy of part with part. Of the mixed, the first kind is where original constitutional produces local ; the second where it influences local already produced. Therefore this kind is divisible into two species.

It may be difficult to say certainly when a constitutional disease really produces a local ; but it may be set down generally that there will be a distance as to the time of appearance of the two diseases.

The first of these two species is of various kinds, perhaps belongs more to specific diseases than to common, and is where the constitution from its nature produces a local one, and is necessarily relieved by it, by what I have called an act of the constitution. Of this kind are small-pox, measles, fevers producing critical abscesses, erysipelatous fevers, gout, &c., and on this is founded the doctrine of revulsion.

Local diseases produced by an act of the constitution may be illustrated, I think, by the growth of plants. A plant or tree appears to have a disposition and power of producing either only a top shoot, or a number of shoots, called branches, which are according to the nature of the plant. If the top is cut off, then a new branch sprouts, and it serves as a top; so that the disposition is taken up by some other part most susceptible of action. The same thing happens in those plants which grow by branches. So that the removal of a part in action gives the disposition of action to parts not before disposed to act, but next in order of susceptibility.

The second of the mixed is where the original local produces constitutional, and which may alter the constitutional disease already existing, or cure it. This may be of three kinds.

1st, The immediate; 2nd, Less determined as to time; 3rd, The remote. Of the first there appear to be two; of the second but one, though it may appear in different forms; of the third probably only one.

Of the immediate we shall reckon that which is called symptomatic fever. Delirium I shall reckon the second, though it is not always the second as to time. The third, or remote, is hectic, to which may be added symptoms of dissolution, which last stage may be the consequence of either of them, or of any other disease.

The first of these is generally called symptomatic fever, but I choose rather to call it sympathetic inflammatory fever. It is sympathy of the constitution with the first stages of local disease, which is the action of alarm on the constitution, rousing up its powers to produce action.

The second, or delirium, appears to arise from an affection of the brain or sensorium, producing sympathy of action of the brain with the nerves of the part; not sensation, as headache, but an action producing ideas without uniting sensation, which is therefore delusive.

The remote, namely, the hectic, is a sympathy of the constitution with local disease, but sympathy of another kind; it is sympathy with the operation of an incurable disease, where the constitution is conscious of inability of the part to perform a cure, by which means the constitution is at last, as it were, worn out, producing dissolution if not removed.

Dissolution is the last stage and consequence of all, whether local or constitutional.

Diseases are common or specific.—All diseases are either common or specific, but it is more than probable that most diseases have some specific qualities. A common disease is such as will attack every constitution, and perhaps every animal, and rather appears to be an increased action, as common inflammation, common inflammatory fever, &c.

Many diseases may be reckoned specific, in their mode of action, though not in their cause. An ague is a specific action, but its causes are various. Gout is a specific action, but its causes various. Cancer is a specific action, though its immediate causes are various; but it is capable itself of becoming a true specific cause, by forming a poison. The cause of scrofula varies, though its action is specific. The remote cause of all is a greater susceptibility of such actions.

A specific is a peculiar mode of action, differing from every other mode of action. A true specific disease is one that probably cannot arise but from one cause, and which probably belongs only to morbid poisons; for although gout, scrofula, ague, &c. may be ranked among the specific, yet they can and do arise from a thousand causes.

There seems a specific susceptibility for those diseases in those that have them. But in poisons there must be a specific cause, which may be attended at the same time with specific susceptibility of such, as some have a greater tendency to smallpox than others.

Specific diseases are such as we cannot increase, for they always act with the full force of the readiness in which the constitution is at the time. If the constitution can be made more susceptible of action, the action will be increased.

Every specific disease has two modes of action—namely, the common and the specific,—joined to it. There are specific inflammations, specific suppurations; or, in other words, there are inflammations and suppurations with specific properties, or which have specific properties superadded; thus, in smallpox there is common inflammation, with the specific qualities superadded. Specific diseases may be either universal or local; universal, as fevers of particular kinds; local, as scrofula; others are mixed, as agues, rheumatism; and these admit of cure from a variety of medicines.

A circumstance worthy of notice takes place with respect to local specific diseases: parts appear susceptible of them as to take on their action so readily, that were it not for another very curious circumstance we might soon expect them to spread over the whole body; but the favourable circumstance I refer to is where the disease is spreading very fast, affecting parts which the disease has not yet touched, whilst in the centre this diseased action no longer takes place. Those parts which have already suffered this action appear to have lost their susceptibility of it, whilst the surrounding parts are contaminated by sympathy with those parts already affected: this property belongs to many, as erysipelas, herpes, &c. I have seen the same thing take place in ulcerated bubo, spreading over the whole belly and thigh, but healing in the centre. Another circumstance is to be added to what I have mentioned as hindering the disease from extending over the whole body, which is, that the constitution itself alters or loses that peculiar susceptibility before such an event takes place.

Different parts differ very much in their power of resisting diseases, as well as in the power of curing themselves, or getting rid of the diseased action and putting on a curative one: this seems to be according to the strength of the circulation in the part; where this is less the power is less; thus, there is greater power of resistance in a muscle than in a tendon. But in specific diseases I should suppose there is little difference in this respect, in consequence of a difference in structure, although we know that specific diseases affect some parts more than others, as the smallpox affects the skin; the measles, the skin and surface of the lungs; hooping-cough and hydrophobia, the throat; &c.

Diseases peculiar to Ages.—Particular ages have their particular diseases. These diseases peculiar to age are perhaps more of the specific than of the common kind; and age is little more than a natural or remote cause, there being some immediate cause acting so as to produce the disease, as in scrofula. But this is not the case with all of them, e. g. cancer, for this appears often to arise without any peculiar immediate cause. How far particular ages are more or less susceptible of particular poisons we do not know.

· The age of man may be divided into three parts: 1st, The age of growth; 2nd, The stationary age; 3rd, The age of decline. The first and last are absolute, but the second is not so easily ascertained, it not being very easy to say where the first ends and the last begins. The young subject and old are more susceptible of many diseases than the full-grown, or stationary, but they are not subject to the same diseases. The young are more susceptible of sympathy, both universal and local; more susceptible of scrofula than the middle-aged, but particularly more than the old; and this scrofula may produce consumption, which we know is peculiar to youth. Children are more disposed to have affections of the bowels, and worms, perhaps, from a peculiarity in their way of life. They are also more subject to water in the head than those who are older. The young have few affections of the mind, excepting those arising from natural passions, or immediate sensations of the body.

The middle age would appear to have but few diseases peculiar to it, excepting nervous affections and hypochondriasis, &c. The middle age, gets into an imaginary region, a region of romance, which produces diseases of the mind, and also affects the body. However, it is, as it were, accidentally affected with the diseases both of youth and age, with which it is gradually intermixed. The foundations for the diseases of old age are often laid by intemperance during the middle age.

In the old we have perhaps as great a variety of diseases as in the young. In the old the power and necessary action are not well proportioned, even in health, much less, therefore, in disease. This produces a degree of irritability often increasing inflammation, and terminating frequently in mortification. In the old we have the gout, which, seldom takes places in the young. Cancer is peculiar to the latter part of the middle age, and still more to the old. Gall-stones are to be found chiefly in the middle-aged and old. Ossifications of arteries are rarely found in young persons. The bladder becomes less disposed to stretch, and more irritable; hence old people make water oftener than young. The prostate gland is more subject to indurations. The mind gradually becomes more attached to [Quære, *detached* from?] this world and the things that are in it the nearer it approaches to a separation from it.

Effects of Climate on Disease.—Climate in general only becomes the immediate cause of disease; however, it is sometimes sufficient to produce the whole disease. Climates are of three kinds: hot, cold, and temperate. Hot climates carry on the natural operations both of animals and vegetables with much more rapidity than either of the others.

It is almost impossible to rear young animals in cold weather; therefore most animals bring forth their young in spring and summer. Animals of the same species do not grow to the same size in cold climates as in warm. It is almost impossible to fatten an animal while it is kept in the cold.

Warmth produces action beyond its power of generating strength.

Parts more readily yield to any power in summer than in winter. Mr. Jones, the inventor of the machine for correcting distorted spines, observes that they produce more effect in summer than in winter.

Hot climates produce diseases in the liver, but these diseases are more frequent in the West Indian islands than on the continent of South America or India*. They also produce violent vomitings and other disorders in the stomach; also violent affections of the bowels:

---

* [The very reverse of this observation is, I believe, the fact; see p. 295.]

and fevers and diseased actions, like the natural, are much more rapid than in temperate climates, it being no unusual circumstance for diseases to run through all their stages in a few hours, ending in death, which is speedily followed by putrefaction. Heat produces indolence in the voluntary actions, which is injurious to health, but generally increases the involuntary action or actions of life, which is always hurtful. Cold climates retard many actions, both of vegetables and animals; but cold, when only in a certain degree, and continued for a certain length of time, excites action; but that is the action of strength, the action of resistance or defence, not the action of luxury or ease. Cold climates produce their diseases, though it would appear that they have not equal effects with warm, nor are capable of producing such variety. Whatever diseases are produced by cold are not so rapid as those produced by heat; and after death putrefaction does not take place so rapidly. We may observe a curious gradation in this process: in cold climates, after visible death, absolute life will remain for some time; the muscles will retain their power of contraction, and the blood be kept from coagulating. But in hot climates death is as rapid as disease; for it is action that consumes life. In cold the action is less; in heat it is so great that the body can hardly support it, and death comes on. Cold climates lead to voluntary actions, which generate heat, and this is much more healthful than heat derived from external sources.

In temperate climates there is perhaps a greater variety of diseases than in either the hot or the cold; for the temperate is a very irregular medium, sometimes very hot, sometimes very cold, and often in the middle state; and these changes are not at regular periods. This irregularity produces some irregularity in the wetness or dryness, so that in such climates we have a great mixture. These changes in temperate climates give rise to scrofula, colds, &c., which are the forerunners of a thousand diseases. Agues are also much more frequent in temperate climates.

Seasons.—Seasons which arise from the variations of heat in a climate, produce diseases which will be in some degree similar to those both of hot and cold, and also temperate climates; for seasons are, as it were, a change from one climate to another. Seasons have, besides, diseases peculiar to themselves; they produce an increase of old diseases, arising simply from the change, and call forth those diseases which only want an immediate cause to produce them. The spring and autumn are two of the most unhealthy seasons in the year; the spring the most so, although from reasoning alone, without observation, it is supposed to be the most healthy, and therefore people do in the spring whatever will allow of a choice of time, as inoculating, &c. This idea probably took its rise from observing vegetation, that at this time the plants appear to come into life and action. But, even in vegetables, this season is the most unhealthy : blights much more frequently take place in spring than in summer. Of every disease that can be called constitutional, that is, where there is a strong susceptibility for such disease, we find spring becomes the immediate cause, exciting it to action ; thus, scrofula shows itself, or increases in spring ; the same with rheumatism and scurvy : hence spring is said to set the humours afloat by those who are favourers of the humoral pathology.

I should doubt much whether there is any diurnal influence on our body, further than that which the habitual modes of acting produces ; consequently, I doubt if daylight or darkness produces any effect. It is, however, certain that the increase of action which commonly takes place in the day, increases diseased action, producing exacerbations in continuous diseases. It is probable, therefore, that it may bring on the paroxysms of those diseases which are periodical, and may bring on the first fit of a disease for the same reason.

Effects of the Moon.—The moon has certainly considerable effects on the human body. We find it often become the immediate cause of diseased actions, especially those of the mind. Mad people are certainly more affected at particular periods of the moon than at other times. The full of the moon has the greatest effect ; it not only affects those who have a natural predisposition, but also some who have had injuries done to the brain by external violence.

A lamplighter, by a fall, injured his head ; upon examination I found a fracture, which appeared to run through the foramen magnum of his occiput ; he recovered, but he was seized every spring with a phrenzy at stated intervals, and this was found to be at the full of the moon.

A gentleman had an ankylosed knee and ankle-joint from scrofula, and he is always deaf at the full of the moon, except in autumn, when his sores discharge plentifully.

This effect of the moon is increased at certain seasons ; in spring it is greatest often. Intermitting and remitting fevers often arise, recur, or become exasperated about the time of the full or new moon, more especially in climates fitted for giving rise to such diseases*.

Of Humours.—The term humour has been applied to the animal body, especially the human, both literally and metaphorically. When literally, it is used in two senses, either as expressive of an extraneous

---

* [Dr. F. Balfour has fully confirmed this observation as to the effects of sol-lunar influence on the billous remittent fevers of hot climates.]

substance existing in the blood, or as meaning the blood itself. When used metaphorically it is applied only to the mind, and is therefore more applicable to the human than any other animal.

Nothing can be more vague, nothing more unphilosophical, nothing more misleading in science, than to employ the same term to express two or more different meanings. In whatever sense the term is used, however, whether as applied to the mind or the body, it always is meant to express the cause of an unnatural or uncommon action or effect.

At present we shall only consider humours in their literal sense, in order to ascertain how far the notion is just or imaginary. I have just said that the word is used in two senses, either as something in the blood, but foreign to it, or else as implying a vitiation, of the whole mass of the blood itself. Among physical people we find such expressions in common use as " the humours are afloat in the blood"; " sharp humours in the blood"; " the whole humours being in a bad state"; " the whole blood must be altered or corrected"; and a variety of such expressions without meaning. They even go so far as to have hereditary humours, as gout, scrofula, &c., and make us the parents of our own humours, saying that we breed bad humours. Accidents, or even the application of poultices, have been supposed to bring bad humours to a part, because the part in which the accident happened, or to which the poultice was applied, would not readily heal. Humours are even supposed to gravitate to the legs slowly; and, in short, the whole theory of disease has been built upon the supposition of humours in the blood, or of the blood itself being changed. I cannot conceive what is meant, unless it be that a strong susceptibility to a specific disease exists; as smallpox may bring on scrofula, or a strain the gout: if in these cases by humour is meant a susceptibility of either of the diseases, I can conceive that any kind of accident may bring it on. The smallpox introduced may excite action, and so bring on the scrofula.

I shall now consider the notion of humours afloat in the blood. If I have a just idea of the meaning of this expression, it signifies something extraneous or foreign, something that does not belong to the blood itself. That foreign matter is received into the blood-vessels is certain, and that so received it produces disease is also certain; but simply foreign matter being introduced into the blood, either produces no effect or no permanent and specific disease: the constitution, or some part, can be disturbed only as the constitution or part would be disturbed from any accident. Medicines, applied either externally or internally, is a proof of this, for all enter the circulation more or less, therefore are in the state of something extraneous, or of humours in the blood. Indeed, chemical analysis of the blood shows the existence of foreign matter, for it discovers substances that form no part of the animal, as sea-salt, iron, earths, &c.; yet these substances produce no ill effects by their presence.

The following experiments show the effects of foreign substances in the blood.

Experiment 1. I injected into the crural vein of a dog, towards the heart, a weak solution of sea-salt, which produced no effect. I then made as strong a one as possible and threw that in also, but no effect was produced. The quantity of salt thrown in might be about two teaspoonfuls.

Experiment 2. I threw a strong solution of Glauber's salts into the the vein of a dog,—about two drachms of salt. It produced no effect. The dog ate and drank and had his stools as before.

Experiment 3. Two ounces of a saturated solution of salt of tartar thrown into the vein of a dog had no effect.

Experiments 4, 5. Two drachms of sal polychrest in solution produced no effect.

Experiment 6. An ounce of water, in which a scruple of borax was dissolved, was thrown into the veins without effect.

Experiment 7. An ounce of vinegar and water, in equal proportions, was thrown into the veins of a bitch half gone with pup. This brought on an immediate disposition for miscarriage, which took place in about six or eight hours.

Experiment 8. Water, rendered about as acid as the vinegar and water, with vitriolic acid, was thrown into the veins, and produced little or no effect,

Experiments 9 and 10. The same experiment was made with nitric and muriatic acids with the same result.

From the above experiments it is evident that substances of considerable power may exist in the blood and produce little or no effects of any kind. We shall find, from other experiments, that there are many substances which have considerable effects when thrown into the blood; still, none of them produce any particular disease, though by repeating them, and increasing the quantities, a man may destroy his health, or even his life, by destroying the natural actions of the body.

But all this is not producing any specific disease; it is reducible to the effects of local applications, which is similar to an accident, producing no specific or permanent disease but what an accident would do, nor lasting any longer than the application lasted.

Experiment 11. I threw about two teaspoonfuls of a strong solution of opium, two parts water with one of opium, into the crural vein of a dog. The dog seemed to be very sensible of it at first, for he was extremely uneasy, and soon became convulsed, but did not lose sensation, for when touched he started and seemed frightened, and drew back his face when a hand was presented to it; so that irritability was rather increased. I then threw in as much more, which made him still more quiet, and in great measure produced loss of the use of his limbs, so that he could not stand; his breathing became slow and laborious, but his pulse very quick; when he attempted to get up he reeled, and came down as if asleep or drunk.

Experiment 12. I threw into the veins of a dog two teaspoonfuls of common gin. He showed no sense of uneasiness, but became soon vastly quiet, and not in the least irritable, showing no signs of fear when touched. He seemed wholly relaxed; his breathing was easy, and his pulse slow. He continued above an hour in this way and then began to recover.

Experiment 13. I threw about two teaspoonfuls of laurel water into the veins of a dog. The pulsation in the vessels became tremulous; he seemed very ill, and could hardly raise his head, but he recovered.

From these last experiments it appears obvious that many substances, having peculiar modes of stimulus, will, when taken into the blood, produce their effects there; but this effect will last no longer than the presence of the stimulus; and we shall find in general that their effects in this way are similar to what they are when taken into the stomach. We find also, by the above experiments, that many substances thrown into the constitution by the veins produce the same local specific effects on the intestines with those produced by the substance when taken in by the mouth.

Experiment 14. I threw into the veins of a dog an ounce of infusion of ipecacuan, made with five grains of the powder to two ounces of water. The dog immediately became very sick, and was retching before I could untie the mouth, and as soon as it was untied he threw up all that was in his stomach. He continued sick for some time, and gradually recovered. I can hardly suppose that the injection had gone beyond the heart, or even to it, when it began to act.

Experiment 15. An ounce of infusion of jalap, made with twenty grains of jalap to two ounces of water, and steeped for twelve hours; was thrown into the veins of a dog. In less than a minute he vomited a little and then seemed well. Thinking that no more effect would be produced, I threw in the remaining ounce. This did not produce any vomiting, nor did he at first seem much affected; but at last he grew weak on his legs, lay down at times, and then rose again. About two hours after the infusion was thrown in he had a stool, and after this another, which was loose. He remained sensible the whole time and then got well.

Experiment 16. In a similar experiment the dog vomited, had some loose stools, and in a few hours got well.

Although many substances do produce similar effects on the stomach and intestines when thrown into the blood as when taken by the mouth, as appears from the above experiment, yet this is not the case with all. In the second experiment, for instance, we find that Glauber's salt had no such effect when thrown into the blood as when taken into the stomach. In like manner,

Experiment 17. An infusion of rhubarb, thrown into the veins of a dog, produced no effect but that of increasing the urine, which it did plentifully.

Many substances thrown into the blood produce much more violent effects in this way than when taken into the stomach, and even cause immediate death.

Experiment 18. I threw into the veins of a dog a little æther, and he died immediately. On opening the body the thorax had a strong smell of æther. However, this effect may depend on the strength of the medicine, as we shall see by the following experiments that the reason why death did not take place in experiments 6, 7, 8, 9, was the weakness of the solution.

Experiment 19. I threw some common vinegar into the veins of a dog, towards the heart. He died before I supposed it could have got to the heart. Now vinegar, when diluted, as we found before, had no such sudden effect. In the same manner, nitrous and vitriolic acid, diluted to about the strength of vinegar, produced almost immediate death.

Air killed immediately. We should therefore be very careful in making experiments, when we inject substances into the veins, that air does not enter with the substances, and cause the death which we impute to the latter*. The Abbé Fontana committed many errors in this way : in short, before any man pretends to determine what will kill, he ought to have killed at least a thousand animals. A poor devil† was lately hanged at Warwick upon no other testimony than that of physical men whose first experiments were made on this occasion.

Experiment 20. I threw into the veins of a bitch half gone with pup

---

* [Air in small quantities, introduced at once, or even in large quantities gradually admitted, is not generally fatal. See Treatise on the Blood, &c.]

† [Captain Donellan. For an account of this transaction, and of Hunter's evidence on the trial, see Life, and the Appendix to the Life, pp. 81. 194.]

a quantity of serum, taken from the blister of a person who was ill of a putrid fever, and soon after died. It made her instantaneously sick, and she vomited. She soon miscarried, but in two or three days recovered perfectly.

From all these experiments we may, I think, at least draw, as a probable conclusion, that extraneous matters taken into the constitution do not produce any specific or permanent disease, that they operate as direct stimuli, producing immediate effects, and that when these are violent they arise from too great a quantity of the stimulating or irritating substance being thrown in.

Poisons come nearest to the idea of humours, but still are not what is meant by humours, nor have ever had this term applied to them. Natural poisons will act somewhat as the substances used in the foregoing experiments did, that is, either stimulate the whole, or part, to increased natural action; or irritate the whole, or part, into some unnatural action, but which will last no longer than the poison is present. The sting of a bee affecting some more than others demonstrates that there is a greater susceptibility in some for such actions than in others, and that it cannot be imputed to humours in the blood, unless we could suppose a humour similar to the poison of a bee, which then might act without that cause.

I suppose that bugs bite everybody, but some they do not affect and others they do.

This is not so readily demonstrable in the poisons that enter the constitution, though even they cannot be said to be assisted by any humours in the blood. Other poisons, which we call morbid, produce a specific disease similar to the original; but all this does not come up to the idea of humours. A humour is something which is supposed to go on teazing the constitution if not extracted, and is even supposed to be capable of leaving one part and going to another.

What comes nearest this idea of a humour, but only so in its effects, is a surfeit; yet though its effects may resemble those which are entertained of humours, we know from the mode of their origin that they are not caused by a humour. It is a mode of action taking place in the skin from a stimulus or irritation being applied to the stomach. Drinking cold water when a person is hot will produce it. In a similar case, I have seen inflammation come on in the heart and lungs; but they being less able to bear the action than the skin, it proved fatal.

The method of cure of those diseases supposed to arise from humours gives us no idea of the disease having arisen from extraneous matter in the blood-vessels. Can we form any idea how bark should extract humours, when it rather stops all evacuations? And yet it cures many

diseases.   Would bathing in the sea cure those eruptions of the skin
which are supposed to arise from humours if they were really caused by
them ?   Can we suppose that electricity extracts any humours, when it
cures an ague ?

· It is not easy to account for the blood having been supposed to be
the cause of disease, excepting from it appearing in a bad state after
bleeding, and this is always a *secondary* symptom.   Sometimes, when
this diseased state has not been very great, medicines have been given
to sweeten the blood*.

---

* [In connexion with this subject, it may not be uninteresting to mention the following facts, which prove that the blood is capable of being greatly vitiated, either by
the actions of the body or by foreign substances being introduced into it.

An animal body may be divided into those parts which form and those which con-
sume the blood.   The former consist of those organs which minister to digestion, sanguification, &c.; the latter, of those structures which perform the offices of nutrition.
Increased action also (although perhaps always attended with increased nutrition,) rapidly induces an alteration in the qualities of the blood, and renders a more frequent
renewal of it necessary.   Whatever, therefore, influences the regularity of those processes upon which the formation and consumption of the blood depend, so as to destroy
their just balance, must necessarily influence the constitution of this fluid.   The following observations, drawn from disease, serve to confirm this view of the subject.

In the first place, then, the varieties in the aspect and sensible qualities of the blood
prove that the condition of this fluid varies remarkably under different circumstances,
being either buffy, firm, soft, diffluent, tarlike, or wholly incoagulable.   It is of various
colours and odours ; it requires different times for its coagulation; it putrefies sooner or
later in one case than it does in another ; and the relative proportion of its constituents
is very different in different cases.

There are, however, other changes to which this fluid is subject which are not equally
obvious to the senses, but which are rendered evident by their effects on the body or
by chemical investigation.   Thus, urea has been detected in the blood in cholera, in
certain cases of dropsy in which the urine is albuminous, in considerable abundance in
cases of suppression of urine, and in dogs in which the ureters have been tied or the
kidneys extirpated ; sugar in cases of diabetes ; and cerebriform, and melanoid matters
in persons suffering from these diseases.   The injection of putrid or ill-conditioned pus
into the blood is found to give rise to a train of symptoms resembling those which are
produced by inflammation of the veins, so as to render it highly probable that pus is
taken into the blood in the latter cases ; but as this is an important point, I shall offer the
following considerations in proof of the fact.

1st, Pus is frequently formed in the cavities of inflamed veins and lymphatics at the
same time that these vessels are perfectly open towards the heart.   2nd, Pus is frequently found in the lacteals in ulceration of the intestines.   3rd, Large abscesses are
sometimes observed to disappear suddenly, which could not happen except the pus
were taken up by the absorbents and carried into the circulation.   4th, In inflamed
veins, smallpox, and *secondary* inflammations, there is reason for believing that pus is
taken up and deposited in distant organs, as if by metastasis.   5th, Immediate relief
of the constitutional symptoms ensues when ill-conditioned abscesses are laid open.
6th, M. Gendrin has observed a mucous sediment (*couche muqueuse*) in two cases at the
bottom of the vessel containing serum, in the first of which the patient was affected with
empyema, and in the second with a large abscess of the thigh.   7th, MM. Duploy,

On Hereditary Diseases.—Hereditary, in the animal œconomy, is applied to properties or peculiarities communicated from the parent to the child.

This principle, according to the common notions, may be divided

---

Andral and Rostau have noticed other cases in which the blood, throughout the whole venous system, appeared to have undergone spontaneous purulent decomposition, to which head may also be referred those cases of polypoid concretions in the vessels in which a purulent fluid is found in the centre, generally occurring at the same time with suppurative inflammation in some other part of the system. 8th, The physiological fact, that the actions of absorption and deposition antagonise each other, and are continually taking place in all the shut sacs of the body, which is proved by the rapid disappearance of injected matters.

M. Lecanu has detected the colouring-matter of the bile in the blood in cases of jaundice, which is well known to tinge the structures and secretions of the body of a yellow colour, and to give rise to drowsiness and other symptoms. M. Andral has referred to cases in which the principles of the bile were found to be accumulated in the form of depositions in several organs of the body. Many cases are related of vicarious discharges, especially of the urine, and menstrual discharge, when the organs which afford these secretions have been obstructed. In cases of obstructed lactation, M. Dance observed symptoms referrible to the absorption of the milk, of which sort is a case described by Professor Graaf, in which a substance exactly resembling caseum was found in the fluid of an ascites, brought on by suppressed lactation, although in a subsequent tapping six weeks afterwards no caseum was discoverable. Milky serum, depending on the presence of oleaginous matters, apparently diffused through it in the form of an emulsion, is not uncommon, while Blumenbach considers it as not improbable that the ferocity of animals during the rut, as well as man's superior courage, greatly depend upon the reabsorption of secreted semen into the circulation.

Besides these instances, there are others of a still more obscure nature, which have chiefly been insisted on by the humourists. Gout and rheumatism, for example, used generally to be referred to a vitiated condition of the blood; an opinion which is certainly favoured by the constitutional and, above all, the metastatic nature of these diseases. In the former there is a disposition to secrete uric acid in superabundance, both in the urine and in the neighbourhood of the joints; a highly azotised principle, corresponding to the highly azotised nutriment which is known to predispose to the arthritic diathesis. In the latter the cutaneous discharges are known to manifest a peculiar acidity. The formation of calculi, the tendency to ossific depositions, and the disease called scurvy appear to depend upon the superabundance of particular salts in the blood. Duhamel has related cases of the most violent effects, followed by gangrene and death, depending upon inoculation with the *blood* of overdriven animals or of persons labouring under putrid forms of fever. M. Gendrin inoculated a cat, and on another occasion a dog, with the *blood* of a patient labouring under a putrid fever with eruption of gangrenous pustules, both of these animals soon after dying with analogous symptoms. Dupuy and Lauret have recorded many similar instances in regard to the horse. The following case was related to me by Professor Coleman, and is an interesting proof of the manner in which disease may be communicated through the medium of the blood. One of his pupils having accidentally inoculated himself whilst dissecting a glandered horse, was taken ill, with a set of anomalous symptoms, for which he was bled. The blood which was drawn was injected into the veins of a healthy ass, and produced the

into two kinds: the transmission of natural properties, and the transmission of diseased, or what I shall call acquired or accidental, properties. The last is not hereditary in all its causes, for it always requires an immediate cause before the action will take place; therefore its cause is not similar to the first. To produce an exact hereditary effect, there must be an hereditary cause or causes; and as in all animals of

---

same disease in it as in the horse, notwithstanding that every precaution was used to obviate the possibility of any source of error. Mr. Hunter has related a case in which a child was born with the variolous eruption, and I have myself known a case in which a woman had seven children in succession (six of whom died) affected with venereal blotches on the nates a few weeks after birth, although she herself had been married upwards of ten years, and during that period had never been affected with any syphilitic symptom, although she admitted that she had had the disease previously. These and similar facts incontestibly prove that the blood is capable of being vitiated by the actions of the œconomy, in consequence of which it is rendered capable of propagating disease to others as well as of perpetuating it in regard to its own self. The following are some further instances calculated to show the influence of the nervous system in producing these effects.

Dupuytren found that the change from venous to arterial blood was not effected in the lungs when the eighth pair of nerves was divided; Dupuy, that the fibrin was relatively diminished by the same operation, at the same time that the blood was so much altered in quality as to give rise to dangerous symptoms when injected into the veins of other animals; Mayer, that the fibrin and hæmatosin had a disposition to separate under the same circumstances, and the blood in the whole pulmonary system to coagulate. The coagulation of the blood in mortified limbs, the stagnation of the circulation in inflamed capillaries, the incoagulability of the blood in cases of sudden death, and the spontaneous concretions which sometimes take place in the living veins, are also to be regarded as proofs of the influence of the nervous system.

But the blood may be vitiated by extraneous matters. The existence of many of these substances in the blood is *inferred* from their effects, but we have distinct chemical demonstration of the presence of others. Among the former we may reckon madder, which tinges the bones of a pink colour; the alkalies and acids, which correct the opposite states of the urine; ergot, which produces gangrene; salt provisions, or the long-continued use of the alkaline carbonates, which produce the sea scurvy; mercury, which excites ptyalism; arsenic, which inflames the stomach; turpentine and asparagus which communicate their odour, and rhubarb and many other substances their colour, to the urine. Alkoholic liquors pass off by the pulmonary exhalation; garlic and many other substances become sensible by the same means. Carbazotic acid and nitrate of silver dye the tissues, the former of a yellow, the latter of a purple colour. Dr. Graves has noticed a case in which sixty leeches, successively applied to a female who had lately taken hydrocyanic acid, all immediately perished; and Dr. Christison has related a similar case, occurring six hours after a dose of oxalic acid. Vernière poisoned an animal with nux vomica, and afterwards a second animal with the blood of the first. These examples afford the highest presumption that medicines actually enter the circulation before they produce their effects on the constitution; a conclusion which is further confirmed by observing that they equally produce their specific effects, whether administered by the mouth, applied to the skin, inhaled by the lungs, or injected into the veins. The following are demonstrative proofs of the correctness of this conclusion:

distinct sexes, in their propagation, there are two causes acting to produce a third, the first and second causes ought to be exactly similar in
all their dispositions and powers of action, or else the hereditary effect
must be a mixture of both, either in equal proportions, or one side may
preponderate more than the other. And this we find to be the case.
A true and perfect hereditary cause is such as will produce its effects

Iodine has been detected in the blood, saliva, sweat, urine, and milk; mercury, in the
blood, crassamentum, saliva, and urine; lead, in the liver, spinal chord, and muscles;
copper, in the liver and perspiration; camphor, sugar of lead,'sal ammoniac, verdigris,
and hydrocyanic acid, in the blood; sulphur, in the skin, &c. The authorities for these
and many similar facts may be seen in Dr. Christison's admirable work " On Poisons."

That medicines should enter the circulation, and thereby produce their effects upon
the constitution, is what we should expect; the extraordinary effects, however, of certain poisonous substances excite our astonishment. Sir William Herschel has shown
in regard to common matter that a power 50,000 times the power of gravity is generated by alloying mercury with $\frac{1}{10000000}$th part of sodium. The same or greater
effects follow the introduction into the blood of certain infinitesimal atoms of organic
matters. Thus, the Woorara and Ticunas poisons; the poisons received in dissection of
recently dead bodies; of hydrophobia, syphilis, and smallpox; of vipers and other
venomous animals; and that proceeding from exhalations from the surface of the earth
or from objects of disease, produce effects which, in reference to their causes, seem in-
finite. As we are not able to point out the distinguishing characters of these substances
when they are presented to us in a concentrated state, it cannot be demanded that we
should adduce direct proofs of their existence in the blood. Reason and analogy irre-
sistibly conduct to this conclusion, as well as the fact that the blood, in most of these
cases, is altered in its sensible qualities, is not disposed to coagulate after death, and
speedily putrefies after extravasation. The following are additional impediments to the
discovery of extraneous matters in the blood.

1st, The rapidity with which they pass off by the secretions; 2nd, Their diffusion
through 15 or 20 lbs. of blood; 3rd, Their disposition to locate themselves in particular
organs; and, 4th, Their actual chemical union with the elements of the blood. Mr.
Hunter indeed doubted of the possibility of this latter circumstance taking place; but,
not to mention the presumption which arises from other circumstances, the following
experiment by Dr. Christison puts the matter beyond doubt. He injected eight grains
and a half of oxalic acid into the veins of a dog, which was sufficient to kill the animal
in 30 seconds; but although the blood was immediately tested after death, no traces of
the oxalic acid could be discovered.

Whatever may be thought of these facts as proofs of the humoral doctrines, they
plainly establish the fact that the blood is capable of considerable vitiations. In general, I believe, these vitiations ought to be regarded as effects, and not as causes, of
disease. I conceive, however, in many cases the real cause of disease primarily exists
in the blood, and is in that sense truly constitutional; and although we should regard
these vitiations of the blood in other cases as merely *secondary* effects, yet we must
admit that they will react on the original disease, and in this point of view be well
deserving of the consideration of the practitioner. It is not unreasonable to expect that
modern chemistry will throw considerable light on this subject, and discover some
general principle by which the scattered facts which now exist relating to the blood
will be connected and explained. In the present actual state of science these facts are
practically useless.]

under all circumstances of life, not requiring the influence of any external circumstances whatever. It is hereditary for every animal to produce its own species, which may be reckoned the first hereditary principle. It is hereditary for every animal to produce the proper sexes, whether hermaphrodite or of distinct sexes. Of these distinct hereditary species we have varieties; and if the varieties, whether original or accidental, are such as can be communicated to the young, they are then hereditary qualities. Of this kind we may reckon shape, both of the whole body or of parts, the varieties of which come nearest to the original hereditary principle of shape. Size is a similar principle, as we see it is common for tall or short persons to have children of their own stature. Colour is another of these varieties, for we find this may become part of the principle of propagation, though not so permanent as some others. This property belongs to the epidermis, with all its appendages, as hair, nails, &c., which is subject to greater varieties perhaps than any other part: and those hereditary susceptibilities for certain dispositions and actions of the mind are perhaps as much hereditary as any other property in an animal.

These are what we may call permanent hereditary principles, becoming part of the constitution, and as subject to be produced in the offspring as any effect in nature. They are such as will take place under every external influence, as season, climate, &c. It is from these varieties being hereditary that we have a continuance of them from parent to child. When both parents are constitutionally alike, they will produce children like one another, and also like themselves, though this is not absolutely certain, for a less marked hereditary principle may arise so as to produce children very unlike the parents. But if the disposition to produce similarity in the children to the parents be different in the two parents, it is impossible to say what the produce may be like.

Hereditary varieties will often last for some generations, and then become extinct, seeming, as it were, worn out. A large nose shall be continued in a family for several generations, and then cease. A peculiar gait, the turning in of one or both feet, shall in the same way continue hereditary for some generations; and it is very possible that if such children were to intermarry with one another, the hereditary disposition would never be lost.

There are latent hereditary dispositions, which pass over one or two generations, and start up again in the second or third.

Children are generally more like one another than like either parent, because they have the united principles of the parents, which are dissimilar, but united will produce the same results.

Parents may not be at all times disposed to form children alike. This difference seems to be owing in some degree to the time between the births of the children; for we may observe that twins are more like each other than like those born a year or two apart, and these latter more alike than those born at the distance of several years.

If the varieties, as white, black, &c., are not original, they must be monstrosities; and then we may say that the disposition to produce monsters continues and becomes hereditary. The white negress, who may be called a monster of the black variety, being supposed to be born of black parents, and being herself white, with woolly hair, is a remarkable instance of the different dispositions of parents at different times. This woman married to a white man, and had three children, one quite black and the others tawny.

A gentleman had two children, both born with a disposition to exostosis; the son showed it earliest, and had exostosis on each thighbone, and indeed an increase of every bone in his body. The girl was little better off. Neither of the parents had any disease of the kind, but gave the disposition to their children by joint operations.

Of the acquired Hereditary Principle.—In these cases the principle is such as to require accident, or some external cause, to produce the disposition in such as have the susceptibility. In this case the susceptibility only is hereditary; but the disposition and action require the application of external influence before they will appear, and are therefore accidental. The action in this case is generally some disease.

As the susceptibility is in some degree hereditary, the immediate cause has been in some degree overlooked, and the disease has been called an hereditary disease; but it is impossible for a disease to be hereditary when one of its causes cannot be hereditary. It may be hereditary for a man to be irritable, one man may be more readily put in a passion than another, but no man goes spontaneously into a passion, there must be some violence committed on the mind; and so various are our minds, that some shall be put into a violent passion at a circumstance which would only slightly, or perhaps not at all, excite another.

The natural susceptibility for diseased action is so strong in some as to require only a slight secondary cause to put it into action; in others so weak, that it requires great violence as an immediate cause to bring on the effects.

All hereditary dispositions must be more prominent than those that are acquired or accidental; therefore people who have an hereditary susceptibility for any diseased mode of action will in general have it constantly, at least it will not vary so much as some others. It will not be of that kind which has a great tendency to disease at one time and not at another: such fluctuating dispositions cannot be hereditary.

Scrofula is one of those diseases which is supposed to be hereditary; but it is only the readiness to fall into this peculiar action, when properly irritated, that is hereditary; and when such a cause does not exist we find no scrofula.

Gout is another disease which is supposed to be hereditary, and there is often great reason in appearance for supposing that it is so. This is a diseased action which perhaps every one is susceptible of; but some fall into it much more readily than others, and this readiness may be hereditary. But this readiness never takes on action of itself; it must have the immediate cause to excite it, which is a stimulus of a particular kind. We find gout attacking people whose parents for many generations have not had it, and often never. We see it starting up in countries where luxury is introduced, where it was never known before. However, there are many instances where it would appear to be hereditary, as in the case of young men of fifteen, the sons of gouty men. But I suspect that this does not arise simply from the father's having had the gout, but from the circumstance that most people who have had the gout severely have deserved it, and that children have inherited the disposition for the way of living as well as the susceptibility for the disease, and will therefore be more liable to fall into the disease than children at large.

On this principle of the hereditary nature of diseases, if it be just, every disease under the sun will be hereditary; but many diseases having a stronger visible cause has made the hereditary susceptibility in them to be overlooked. Thus, the smallpox is as much hereditary as scrofula or gout, but from its arising in all cases from poison communicated, and evidently not in a spontaneous manner, is the reason why the hereditary susceptibility has been overlooked. But on our principle the smallpox is as hereditary as any other, only requiring the immediate cause to act to produce it as in any other disease. We may make the same observation with regard to the venereal disease, for we see some persons much more susceptible of this disease than others are, and suffering more severely from it when they get it.

I do not know that we have an instance of observation which proves that the circumstance of a person's having had the disease renders him more liable to communicate that susceptibility to his offspring than if he had only the susceptibility for the disease, without the action having taken place. If it was a fact that the parents having simply had the disease, in some degree entitled their offspring to it, the human species would soon become extinct in those places where such diseases arose ; and if the parents having had the disease increased the susceptibility in the offspring, both smallpox and lues would have become incurable by this time. So that the immediate cause, whatever this may have been, does not in consequence of its having had its full effect either give or even add to the disposition for such action.

The only difficulty I find, in stating this as a universal doctrine, is in the case of madness. This is allowed to be hereditary, and is I believe as much so as many, yet I cannot find the immediate cause in many cases. It would appear that the disposition to produce action is so strong as to go into action without the application of an exciting cause. It would be worth while to see whether people in a state of nature ever go mad : if they do not, then the state of mind in the civilized state is the immediate cause.

A gentleman informed me that he had paid particular attention to the diseases of Indians, and that he never heard of an Indian going mad.

On the Effects of Mind on Diseases.—When on the animal œconomy, I observed that the mind was formed by the senses, as also the will; that the will produced the voluntary actions, but that the mind produced actions both of the voluntary and involuntary parts, which actions are often very irregular and undetermined. On the state of the mind, therefore, the latter will depend, or at least they will change with it, and even the former may be affected by it; indeed there is not a natural action in the body, whether involuntary or voluntary, that may not he influenced by the peculiar state of the mind at the time, and every particular mode of the mind has some parts that are more readily influenced by it than others. The skin is affected by the feeling of shame; the secretion or even the non-secretion of the testicles takes place under certain states of the mind. Palpitations of the heart and quick respirations are brought on by some states; purging and increased secretions of the urine by others.

In voluntary parts we can also perceive the influence of the mind. It often produces actions independently of the will, especially when these actions are begun by the will, and when the mind is affected by a recollection of them; or even contrary to the will. Thus, fear produces a vibratory contraction of all the voluntary muscles, while the will is doing all it can to stop it. Since the mind has such power over the natural actions of the body, we might suppose it would have considerable effect in disease; and this we actually find it has, especially in those who have a strong susceptibility for such actions as the mind can most easily affect. We should naturally expect that it would be diseases principally connected with the nerves that the mind would most affect, though we do find that there are other diseases, with which they appear to have little connexion, that are much affected by the state of the mind; and I believe that it is principally those diseases in which the alteration is in the action of parts, not in their structure.

Minds which are particularly irritable are most subject to such diseases, having the acting parts more under the control of the mind, and less under that of the will; also the involuntary powers are more under the influence of the state of mind, as the heart, &c. These diseases are called nervous, and more peculiarly belong to women, who being less acquainted with the real properties of natural things, are more apt to imagine preternatural ones; and their reasoning powers not being so strong, they indulge the actions of the mind more, and allow it to take possession of the body: for the mind can often prevent diseases of such a nature as are contrary to health, and depend on voluntary actions, of which take the following instance. A woman, aged forty-six, of a good-natured disposition, had been troubled for some years with a drawing of the neck to one side, by the contraction of one of the mastoid muscles: this it was always in her power to prevent, by contracting the opposite muscle, when she sufficiently recollected herself. The right muscle, the one affected, did not contract of itself, unless by some accident she of her own accord contracted it a little, after which it continued contracting till it produced its full effect. When her mind was agreeably engaged she seldom felt it, or when conversing with an intimate friend or reading; but fear and every other unpleasant state always produced it. If she expected to see any stranger before whom she was particularly anxious to hide her defect, she had it always more violently than usual. This circumstance of the mind's continuing action when it has once taken it up, is remarkable in hiccup, which is often produced by laughing; thus hiccuping, which is an involuntary action, is produced by laughing, which is a voluntary one. But as the state of the mind is thus capable of producing a disease, another state of it may effect a cure: so the hiccup may be cured by producing fear. There are other diseases which a state of the mind may cure, though they have not been brought on by it, as agues have been cured by charms which have been used with a thorough conviction of their being a sovereign remedy. I am apt to suppose that a spider's web, when taken for an ague, cures in the same way, at least in one case; for on giving it without the patient's knowledge, it had not the slightest effect; but by persuading the patient that it was a spider, the effect was produced, at least the disease did not return. Even tumours have yielded to the stroke of a dead man's hand.

It often happens that there is a suspension of some actions in an animal body, and those actions return again. Thus, we have epilepsy, which is a suspension of the sensitive principle's actions: sometimes we have suspension of the heart's actions. It is perhaps impossible to know the cause of these suspensions, and equally so the cause of their return. I am apt to suspect that suspension of natural action becomes the stimulus to the powers to put themselves in action again; or, in other words, the suspension becomes by its continuance a force imposed on parts to act, and they act to relieve themselves. Thus, by stopping respiration we have such a stimulus raised in consequence that we can no longer live without the action, and the action takes place.

I suspect that opium often produces a struggle between the necessity of action and the consciousness of the preternatural suspension, which rather rouses. Death, which is the ultimate suspension of all actions, seems to explain that, as a person seldom dies without a struggle or convulsion. Convulsion appears to me to be an action arising from a consciousness of debility; as if there was an endeavour to act to preserve life, but not being able to preserve it, they give up the contest.

Of Symptoms.—A symptom is a sensible effect of a diseased action. The first mode of sensation is when the disease is shown directly, without the medium of any other reference, and is known only to the patient; of this kind is pain. The second is where it is given by a reference to some other sense, as that of touch, smell, &c., and is common to the patient and others; of this kind is the swelling of tumours, the redness of inflammation, &c. The third arises from a deficiency of sensation, and can be known only to the patient himself. It is by description and the second set of symptoms that the practitioner receives his information. Local disease may produce only the first mode of intelligence, as pain; or it may proceed to the second, as inflammation; or the second may be produced without the first, as indolent tumour, not known till felt by the hand.

Pain is a simple sensation which is common to many diseases, and is divided into several kinds, as sharp, sore, numbing, heavy, &c. The sharp pain is that produced by cutting with a knife; the sore, from inflammation and ulcers; the heavy, that which takes place in rheumatism; the numbing, from pressure on a nerve. The sharp and sore depend on what I shall call vibration of pain, particularly the latter. The heavy seems to be a continued pain, or where the repetitions are so quick as to appear continued; but probably all of them are owing to a succession of actions of the nerves. We refer all the sensations we can to those senses which give us the greatest intelligence. We call them sharp pains from their giving the sensations of anything that bites, or stings, as bees, or acids on the tongue; heavy, from their giving us the sensation of bearing a weight on the part. A gentleman who had a hemiplegia said his sensation was similar to an acid on the part, that is, to that feeling on the tongue.

We have often a bad taste in the mouth, or a bad smell; this is not always a sign that the saliva or mucus is altered in its qualities, as it is in salivation from mercury, which appears to be from the taste and smell of the mercury, but it is sometimes produced by a morbid action of the nerves, We have these symptoms, together with ringing in the ears, commonly in the beginning of diseases, and probably they arise from the actions of the disease in the nerves of the part.

Neither susceptibility nor disposition for diseased action can produce a symptom; it must be preceded by action; though I believe that there will sometimes be an unnatural feel in a part before action has taken place, as before a fit of the gout attacking the foot an indescribable sensation is sometimes felt, and when the action takes place the constitution is relieved.

Symptoms are either local or universal. Local, as chancre, cancer, &c.; universal, when they accompany universal diseases, as fever. Local symptoms may produce universal ones, which is a means either of increasing the local symptoms or of curing the disease. Local symptoms will vary according to the nature of the disease; its violence or its situation, as inflammation, will produce different sensations in different parts. Universal diseases will produce some of the following symptoms: affection of the pulse, which arises from the heart's sympathizing and partaking of the disease; the alterations are very various, as full, strong, weak, small, &c. The secretions are altered, as in fever; the tongue becomes covered with its own secretion, at first white, afterwards brown, or sometimes black, which last colour arises from blood being mixed with the secretion. The tongue also contracts in size, and we have often thirst without its being dry, and sometimes, as in low fevers, very dry without thirst, which last is owing to a diminution of sensation in the nerves, and is an unfavourable symptom. The urine is high-coloured, without sediment, owing to its being retained long in the bladder, from debility of that organ or from blood being mixed with it. The respiration fails, from debility in the lungs. The heat of the skin is altered from too great or too little action of the vessels. The colour of the skin in some diseases changes, as from white to yellow, in a very short space of time, not from jaundice, the white of the eye not being changed; nor could jaundice be so quick in coming and disappearing; it is probably a change in the rete mucosum of the skin, such as takes place in the chameleon and some other lizards: veins of the skin are enlarged by any tumour seated beneath them; as in hydrocephalus, tumours of the breast or of the uterus during gestation, the veins of the head, chest, or belly will be found enlarged.

The feeling of the part is the first mode of intelligence. Suppose a stone in the kidney; it may produce three symptoms : 1st, Pain in the part ; 2nd, Vomiting, which is symptomatic ; 3rd, Bloody urine. Now these symptoms may occur in other diseases, independently of stone; if they are combined, they afford a pretty certain diagnosis of the presence of stone, but any one or two of them leaves it doubtful. These symptoms attend the passing of a stone through the ureter, as well as when in the kidney; and when a stone gets from the ureter into the bladder the symptoms abate, and a different pain is felt, and this change occurring confirms us in the opinion we had before formed of the existence of a stone.

Anomalous Symptoms.—These are not immediately expressive of the disease, but make the diagnosis doubtful. They are very numerous, taking in all the symptoms which occur from dentition, worms, &c. Many of them are from sympathy, which we mentioned before.

Delusive Symptoms respecting Sensation.—This delusion of the senses makes disease seem where it really is not, from the different seat of the symptoms and of the diseased part. Thus, diseases of the liver are referred to the shoulder, of the testicles to the back, of the hip to the knee, and even in some cases, as was before observed, they are referred to some other person. When the trunk of the nerve is injured, the pain is referred to the termination of it, as, after amputation of the leg, pain is felt in the toes. When pressure is made on a large nerve, the most acute sensation will be at some distance below the part pressed on.

A gentleman complained of a pain in the hip, running down the outside of the leg and foot. Supposing it rheumatism I gave him James's powder, Dover's powder, and volatile tincture of guaiacum, but with no good effect. A liniment of opium to the leg and foot gave some relief. He at last perceived a tumour by the os ischii, just at the posterior edge of the gluteus maximus. This tumour increased, and the person died. The tumour was found to fill a part of the pelvis, and had made its external appearance at the foramen magnum ischii, being filled with coagulated blood; but the pain in the limb seemed to have been produced by its pressing on a great branch of the nerve, but chiefly perhaps from the great ischiatic nerve being stretched very tight over the upper surface of the tumour. Here that happened which may often be observed ; that is, the impression made on the trunk of the nerve gave a sensation as if it had been on the extremities of the nerve. The first action of a nerve is at its extremity, and the last in the brain; and this last in the brain refers the sensation receiving the first impression; and if, after the brain has become accustomed to refer any sensation to the extremities of the nerves, any impression be made on the trunk, the brain receives the impression in the same point where it was accustomed to receive the impressions made on the extremity of that nerve, and therefore the mind refers the sensation to the same spot, that is, the extremity of the nerve. This happens when the part to which the sensation is referred does not exist, as a person, having had an amputated limb, will for a long time refer his sensations to the fingers or toes.

In diseases the general character of the patient should be known, which is essentially necessary before we can judge of every symptom; for besides what we can know by the symptoms of a disease, yet peculiarity of temperament, &c. will occasion great differences in the character of the disease. For our being informed by the first mode of intelligence, the patient's sensations, the patient must be in his right senses, otherwise he may be deluded, and delude us. But even where the patient is perfectly sensible, many symptoms may appear to the physician which the patient is not sensible of, as wild looks, quick pulse, &c. The brain may not be conscious of them, and a false conception of their feelings is then present; and this may be called half-delirium. A complete delirium is an action of the mind directed by no sensation whatever. But we do not know how to distinguish between these two deliriums, the former being an action of the mind from sensation, but which sensation is incapable of directing its influence to the senses, and refers it to other parts or other objects. These should be well understood in practice, as in half-delirium the patient will have the sensation, but will direct it to some one else, or to the wrong part, which if we know we may be able to afford them the relief they want. The history of everything relative to a disease should be known, as symptoms alone are often not enough to direct us; we should, therefore, get the history of it and of prior diseases, of peculiarity of constitution, manner of living, &c.

CHAPTER XII.

GENERAL PRINCIPLES OF INFLAMMATION.

Frequency of inflammation;—nature of;—enlargement of vessels;—several species;—simple or compound;—three results from inflammation in a healthy constitution:—adhesion,—suppuration,—ulceration.—Adhesion;—nature of the uniting medium;—partakes of the quality of the diseased solids;—its uses.—Suppuration;—differs in degree according to the exciting cause.—Ulceration;—its uses.—Exciting causes of inflammation;—accidental or specific.—Remote causes of inflammation. —Comparative susceptibility of parts to inflammation.—Effects of inflammation on the constitution.—Of the pulse;—varies with the states of the constitution;—varieties of pulse;—causes of the varieties.— Effects on the constitution according to the state of the inflammation; —rigors.—State of the blood in inflammation;—colour, heat, coldness, pain of inflamed parts.—Declension of inflammation.—Ecchymosis;— varieties of;—termination of.

THE operation in the body called inflammation is one of the most common and most extensive in its effects, and requires our greatest attention. It is the cause of many effects, both salutary and diseased, producing abscesses, fistulas, diseased bones, &c., and in many diseases is the first step towards a cure; so that it becomes a first principle in surgery.

Inflammation would appear to be produced by an *increased action* of the vessels, but it is most probably in the smallest vessels, for it may be confined almost to a point where none but the smallest vessels exist. What the particular action is, or in what it differs from the common action of vessels, is not easily ascertained, we being more able to judge of the effects than of the immediate cause.

Inflammation may be considered as a genus, of which there are many species. It may be divided into healthy and unhealthy. The healthy is that which will always take place in a healthy constitution or part, and is rather to be considered as a restorative process than a disease. Unhealthy inflammation is that which takes place in an unhealthy constitution or part, and will vary according to the kind of unhealthiness of that constitution or part.

Inflammation is either simple or compound; simple, when there is only one mode of action in the part inflamed, as in its first stage; compound, when there are two or more modes of action. The compound produces three great effects, namely, adhesion, suppuration, and ulceration, which I shall call adhesive, suppurative, and ulcerative inflammation. The last is only an effect of inflammation, for the process takes place in a different set of vessels.

I shall place the adhesive first in order, though it is not always so, for with respect to priority of these effects of inflammation, it depends principally on the nature of the parts, with the degree of violence of the inflammation. To explain this more fully, I shall consider inflammation as it affects, 1st, The cellular membrane in general, and the circumscribed cavities ; 2nd, All the outlets of the body, i. e., the excretory outlets and ducts of glands, as the mouth, nose, tunica conjunctiva, &c., which have been called mucous membranes, and which I shall treat of in their proper order.

When inflammation takes place in the first order of parts, it is commonly the adhesive ; but it will be according to circumstances whether the suppurative or ulcerative follows first, and probably according to the degree of inflammation. But it sometimes happens that the suppurative takes place almost immediately, probably from two causes, either from the inflammation exciting the suppurative almost immediately after the adhesive, or from the inflammation having little or nothing of the adhesive in it. I suspect that the erysipelatous has little of the adhesive in its nature, no adhesion taking place before suppuration, whilst in phlegmonous inflammation of the cellular membrane it does ; so that the erysipelatous might be called œdematous inflammation. When inflammation occurs with violence on the surface of the skin, the ulcerative process takes precedence of the suppurative, although in the cellular membrane the reverse of this is the case. In the second order of parts the suppurative takes place first, and the adhesive does not take place, unless the inflammation is carried to a great height.

· When the inflammation is in the first order of parts, the suppuration and ulceration are so many actions superadded to the first, or adhesive, and arising out of the effects produced by that which now become new causes, especially of the ulcerative, which is an action of the absorbents. All these actions arise from the first irritation or cause.

The adhesive or suppurative, either in the first or second order of parts with their varieties, may have a fourth character superadded, such, for example, as the scrofulous or venereal disposition, or other specific disease.

These three modes of action, when carried on perfectly, are the effects of a good constitution, and constitute what I would be understood to mean by common inflammation.

The union of cavities in an animal body is formed by a uniting medium, which appears to be the coagulable lymph, which, by the inflammatory disposition of the vessels, is separated from other parts of the blood and thrown out on these surfaces. That this is the case appears from the following observations. In all large cavities where we can make our observations with certainty, we find when they have been inflamed that a substance similar to the coagulable lymph when separated from the serum and red particles, is diffused all over the sides or through the cavity. When we cut into an inflamed part after death, we find it firm and solid, like the section of a lemon, or some œdematous tumour, where we know extravasation has taken place; and this appearance arises from the cells of the cellular membrane being loaded with extravasated coagulable lymph.

This mode of separation of coagulable lymph is not peculiar to this species of inflammation; it is separated on many other occasions to form tumours*, where inflammation does not seem to be the leading cause.

It is probable that the coagulable lymph undergoes some change in its passage through the inflamed vessels which obliges it to coagulate sooner than it otherwise would, for in those cases of inflamed arms, after bleeding, we find that the cavities of the veins are in many places furred over, and in others united by coagulable lymph, which must have been thrown out by the vasa vasorum, and coagulated immediately. Hence it is reasonable to suppose that in this separation the lymph must have undergone some change, arising from the vessels, and that it is not simply such coagulable lymph as is circulating in the blood, else it would be carried off by the circulating blood passing through the

---

* [As we are not acquainted with the mode in which the process of nutrition is accomplished in its natural state, it is not to be expected that we should be able to account for those aberrations from the healthy state which constitute tumours. If the formation of tumours depended upon the organisation of effused blood or lymph, we should expect to see them much more frequently than we do, since few persons escape effusions at one time or other; and we should likewise expect to see them differ in their incipient and in their advanced stages. Observation, however, discloses nothing of this kind; on the contrary, the peculiar structure of tumours is as well characterized at first as when they become more fully developed: the blood or lymph which is effused in inflammation or by accident is generally absorbed, and in the great majority of tumours we are unable to refer to any previous injury or inflammation to account for their origin. See Home (*Trans. of a Soc. for the Imp. of Med. and Chir. Knowledge*, vol. i.,) and Abernethy (*Works*, vol. ii.), who have advocated the opinion in the text, and Lawrence (*Med.-Chir. Trans.*, vol. xvii.), who justly, in my opinion, objects to the statements of these gentlemen.]

vein. This change I suppose to arise from sympathy with the inflamed vein. The lymph seems, however, to retain the living principle, and probably in a greater degree than under common circumstances, and is, therefore, better fitted to become a living solid. It does not seem, however, absolutely necessary that coagulable lymph should first undergo this change in the extravasating vessels, for, as I have before said, blood extravasated from ruptured vessels is perhaps equally efficacious in this respect*.

It does not seem necessary for both surfaces that are to be united to be in a state of inflammation, but only for one, to throw out the coagulable lymph ; nor indeed does inflammation of either seem necessary, for union by extravasated blood may take place without inflammation.

Extravasated coagulable lymph, which produces either adhesion or tumours, always partakes of the nature of the diseased solids that produced it; if the case is venereal, the new substance is of the same nature ; if cancerous, cancerous ; for the absorption of this effusion from a cancerous breast will produce cancerous axillary glands.

The intention of the adhesive inflammation is in some degree to set bounds to or prevent the necessity of its own larger extent. In large cavities the inflamed parts adhere, and thereby exclude or prevent the other parts from the necessity of falling into the same irritation. But the chief intention is to confine the suppuration to those parts where it takes place, for where the adhesions are perfectly formed the operations of inflammation appear to be completed, so that the suppurative process does not spread : it also serves to confine the matter to the cavities where it is formed.

Inflammation often goes no further than adhesion, and then subsides and goes off, which is termed resolution. This cannot take place in all inflammations, but only in those where the parts can be brought into contact, for if the part in which it takes place is an open cavity, suppuration will take place.

When the adhesive inflammation is not capable of resolution, suppuration takes place. The immediate effect of this process is the production of matter from the inflamed surface, which appears under such circumstances to be a leading step to the formation of a new substance, called granulations, which granulations are the second method of restoring the first order of parts to health. But on all internal canals suppuration does not necessarily lead to granulation.

In order for spontaneous inflammations to produce suppuration, they must be much more violent than those inflammations (suppuration being

---

* [See note, p. 238, and Treatise on Inflammation, Part II. Chap. J.]

equally necessary,) arising in consequence of an operation or accident; and those inflammations from either operations or accidents, if they have not produced death in the part operated on, are more violent and of greater extent than those in which death of a part has been produced. Thus, the inflammation of a boil or bubo is more violent, and commonly more extensive, than that in consequence of a cut, or even amputation of the leg; and the inflammation arising from these latter will be more violent than that from a gunshot wound or the application of caustic. It may not be easy to account for all these differences: however, it is possible that in spontaneous inflammations the inflammation is more necessary for the ultimate effect than the suppuration; as in gout, the inflammation is the mode of carrying off the action of the disease. It is curious to remark, that in gout nature seems to produce all the purposes and effects intended by inflammation, but unaccompanied by either adhesion, suppuration, or ulceration; and although the inflammation runs much higher here than in many other cases, and although it is attended with all the common appearances, yet no adhesions are formed here; for the lymph is taken up, and chalk [urate of soda] is deposited in its place. In spontaneous inflammation, parts are either naturally more susceptible of the inflammation, or become so by disease. When inflammation is produced by the stimulus of the death of a part, or of effused blood, the inflammation is commonly slow; but that from a bruise is often quick and violent, but then the injury has not produced death. If caustics do not act with vigour, they will irritate and inflame much sooner than if they had immediately killed the part; but irritating applications must be continued some time to produce inflammation. After operations where inflammation must take place for the union of the wounds, suppuration is more necessary than inflammation, and we find it is soon produced.

The ulcerative inflammation is that which takes place in consequence of suppuration, therefore is not so much the original inflammation as the consequence. It is that inflammation which disposes parts to absorb themselves, and which brings matter or any extraneous substance to the surface to be discharged, the absorbents removing all the parts lying between the matter and the surface. This process has been erroneously ascribed to the melting down or dissolution of living solids with the pus.

From the foregoing general account of inflammation, it may be said to arise in all cases from injury done to the solids, where either the natural conformation of parts on which natural actions depend is so destroyed that they are not able to support themselves in that state, or from the natural actions or functions of a part being materially ob-

structed, the texture not being primarily affected. The first state
arises from causes that are visible or external, such as the application
of any irritating matter, as a blister, heat, or even cold, which acts as
a sedative when applied only in a certain quantity; but when in too
great a quantity, the parts, finding that they are losing their action, are
roused to action beyond that which is natural, in order to destroy the
irritating cause. Inflammation may also be produced by causes not
known or suspected, or from a constitutional disposition being determined to some part, producing local effects. I need hardly mention that
fever is thus often a cause of local inflammation.

Inflammations from the constitution are of two kinds : one may be
called accidental, as those arising in common fever; the other are determinate, depending on the species of fever which may be called specific, as small-pox, &c.

These inflammations are thought to be critical, but I very much
doubt the truth of this opinion. The smallpox and chickenpox are
the only diseases that can be brought in proof of it, with perhaps the
inflammation of measles; but even these pustules or abscesses are, perhaps, not necessary, as critical abscesses, to carry off the fever, for specific fevers cannot exist beyond a certain time, though no eruption appears; which time depends on the nature of the poison, and the constitution. And in these fevers we have large abscesses as often formed
as after any other; and certainly I cannot suppose those abscesses to
be critical, for they possess nothing of the specific nature of the preceding disease, and must therefore be common; or, where the constitution possesses a susceptibility for scrofula, they may be scrofulous,
but not critical; and as the preceding disease has already been followed by pustules or abscesses, which, if any deserve to be termed so,
certainly ought to be termed critical, we shall find that these inflammations and abscesses depend on the state of the constitution and part
at that time, and are an effect of simple fever abstracted from every
specific peculiarity. Fever is at all times a disturbed action, which may
have a specific action joined with it or not. The inflammatory fever is
perhaps, the most simple fever; and the putrid fever is, perhaps, only
the same fever occurring in a constitution predisposed to its peculiar
actions. This opinion may be illustrated by what occurs in the smallpox : two different people having this fever from the same infection,
the effect in one will be benign smallpox, with only simple inflammatory fever; in the other it will be erysipelatous or confluent smallpox,
with a tendency to putridity or gangrene. This difference cannot depend on the specific poison, as this can have but one mode of irritating.
Now, since every fever is capable of producing inflammation and ab-

scess, and as I have shown that in specific diseases they have no right to be termed critical, they certainly cannot be supposed critical in common fever.

Inflammation may arise from one of four causes, which may be called remote : 1st, From accidental force applied to a part ; 2nd, From some irritation, which does not destroy the texture of a part, but simply the natural actions, as friction, blisters, heat, cold, and often fevers of various kinds ; 3rd, From some particular disposition in the part itself, as boils arising spontaneously ; 4th, From the general state of the constitution affecting some particular part, as gout falling on the toe, or the irritation of fever on the lungs, liver, or any other part, producing adhesions or abscesses ; but such, I suspect, are of the scrofulous kind, and not in the least critical, and therefore belonging to the second cause. To these, I think, we may add specific causes, as scrofulous, venereal, &c., as a 5th ; and the stimulus of defect or imperfection of parts, especially cavities, as a 6th.

Obstruction of the blood's motion in the small vessels has been long supposed to be a great cause of inflammation, but is, I believe, now pretty generally rejected. This was certainly too confined an idea : it reduced all inflammations to one species. The only distinctions of inflammations must then have arisen from the nature of the constitution ; but this doctrine never could account for the peculiar action of any specific disease or poison. It was also too mechanical. If they had said that any obstruction to the natural actions of the parts which could stop the blood's motion in the part became the cause of inflammation, they would not have been so much out as to a possible cause of inflammation. In such a case the stagnated blood would cause irritation of the vessels, and suppuration would be produced to get rid of it. The immediate operation of these inflammations cannot be called disease, though their remote causes may, as smallpox, &c. ; for they may arise from the part being only disturbed, and hardly exceeding the idea we have annexed to that of being disturbed. It is the cause producing inflammation, then, which is the disease, and not the inflammation*, for

---

* [That is, inflammation with a specific character is the only inflammation which can be denominated disease. The meaning of the author I conceive to be simply that pure inflammation is a restorative action, in contradistinction to the actions of disease which tend to destroy (pp. 215, 308) ; and to this general statement there can be no objection, although it must be borne in mind that the rule of judging from final causes cannot be applied absolutely without excluding from the list of diseases a great many affections to which it would be absurd to deny this title, such as sickness, purging, increased secretions, ulceration, mortification, &c., the tendency of which on many occasions evidently is salutary, or to get rid of some noxious matters : still there is sufficient ground I think for the general observation.]

all inflammations that can be called diseases have specific causes; and, indeed, even these can be hardly called diseases, for in smallpox, where the inflammation goes on well, it is merely the action of health; if diseased, it would be erysipelatous, &c. Sometimes, by amputating a leg, more than simple disturbed action is produced, for it is a great loss to the constitution; but yet when the constitution is in a healthy state, we generally find a healthy inflammation and digestion of the wound take place: it will not go into an inflammation which is unhealthy. Specific inflammation as well as simple inflammation partake of the nature of the constitution. Some constitutions are more disposed to certain specific actions than others, and will fall into that specific kind of inflammation, as the erysipelatous, the scrofulous, &c.; and every aggravation is an aggravation of the specific nature of the inflammation; thus it happens in scrofula, cancer, &c. But some specific irritations bring all constitutions to their own nature, as the plague, jail-fever, &c. Here it is not a specific joined with a simple inflammation, but a thorough change of constitution, and the patients generally die, all suffering alike. The inflammation arising from these causes may be either the adhesive or the suppurative. From all which we may conclude that irritations either produce inflammation according to the disposition of the constitution or of their own nature, of which last is the plague.

The specific diseases will change, according as the constitution changes; for instance, after receiving the smallpox, if the constitution, then healthy, should by any means become disposed to show putrid symptoms, the smallpox will have the same appearance; but if the constitution is altered from this tendency, the eruption will also alter. Now the knowledge of this fact is very useful in the treatment of specific diseases: for example, if with a venereal chancre the constitution be erysipelatous, we may have an erysipelatous inflammation in addition to the chancre, which will spread over the whole penis. Now, in this case, we must make use of mercury against the one, and of bark against the other of these specific diseases, until we bring it to the simple ulcerative inflammation. Again, in the smallpox, when simple, the pustules retain their specific distances, but if an erysipelatous inflammation be joined to it, it becomes of the confluent kind. In the irritable constitution we find from continuous sympathy the inflammation will extend itself very far; but in general we find that considerable inflammations confine themselves very much.

Some parts are more susceptible of one kind of inflammation than of others; some admitting only of one kind, some two, and some all three, which difference appears to be according to the situation in the body of the inflamed parts, and also according to the nature of the parts inflamed. The deeper-seated parts, especially the vital, admit very readily of the adhesive inflammation, as is proved by dissections, for we hardly ever open a human subject that has not had considerable adhesions in the circumscribed cavities; but they do not so readily pass into the suppurative, which is fortunate, otherwise internal inflammation would oftener kill. But if the inflammation comes on at once with great violence, it would appear to pass almost at once over the adhesive, and to take up the suppurative action, and in this case we may sometimes have the erysipelatous added.

The external parts of the body are more susceptible of the suppurative inflammation than the internal, but they always begin with the adhesive. This greater susceptibity of the superficial parts to suppuration is shown in the passage of pins, bullets, and other extraneous bodies to the surface: if deep-seated, they will remain a long time inactive, inclosed in a cyst, and produce no inconvenience until they work their way to the skin, when suppuration will be produced. It is very remarkable of the cattle which feed in the bleaching-fields, and are always found after death to have a number of pins in them. (The stomach of a bull was shown, in which several pins were sticking, and which were not known to have caused any inconvenience.) Perhaps this does not altogether depend on the situation of the part, but also on the degree of irritating power possessed by the extraneous substance: thus, metals and glass seem to produce such a disposition in the part, that it becomes satisfied with the adhesive inflammation. A gentleman had a piece of glass in his hand for many weeks, which produced no pain, except on pressure. This insensibility of deep-seated parts to extraneous substances, depends on a sac being formed around these substances, possessing a peculiar degree of insensibility. Nature acts here with her usual care, preferring the least evil by securing the extraneous substance in a part possessing peculiar insensibility, rather than calling up the vital powers to produce suppuration, which must be considerable to reach the surface, and might expose parts which would be attended with considerable danger; but when they become external, then she chooses the other, to get rid of them as soon as possible.

In my division of parts, as regards inflammation, into two orders, I have made a distinction between the cellular membrane and circumscribed cavities on the one hand, and the ducts, canals, and outlets which are lined with what has been called a mucous membrane on the other. In the first order of parts, inflammation proceeds in this order; adhesive, suppurative, ulcerative: but in the second order of parts, the order of inflammation seems to be inverted as regards the two first; as may be seen in internal canals. In these, if the inflammation is but slight, the suppurative takes place almost immediately, not being retarded by the adhesive going before; as we see in gonorrhœa, catarrh, &c. It has been said that these discharges are not purulent, but in my opinion they certainly are; the purulent matter being only a change in the natural secretion, and its thickness or thinness depending on the degree of the inflammation. If the erysipelatous inflammation should come on in these parts, then the movement takes place from the suppurative to the ulcerative. In the mucous membrane ulceration will take place, probably from the violence of the inflammation having produced coagulable lymph, which acts as a stimulus, and the parts having been weakened, are unable to support themselves: this is sometimes the case in the mouth, from salivation; in the tongue, &c. in scurvy; in the intestines in dysentery, &c. Mr. Hunter endeavoured to produce adhesive inflammation in the vagina of an ass. He first, by moderate stimulus, could only produce suppuration, but by a very active stimulus, as a solution of corrosive sublimate, he produced the adhesive, causing coagulable lymph to be effused, which afterwards became membranous and inseparable, as was seen in the preparation of the parts which he exhibited. (See Pl. XXIII.)

Strength and weakness of the constitution, or of the part affected, will produce very different effects in inflammation. Strength produces good effects, and renders the disease more manageable, for it lessens irritability. Inflammation is most manageable in parts in the following order: muscles, cellular membrane, and skin, and the more so the nearer the source of circulation. In other parts, as bones, cartilages, ligaments, &c., which have but little power in themselves, it is less manageable, though the constitution be good, for the constitution feels conscious of the weakness of these parts, by which affection of the constitution they become further weakened. In vital parts, inflammation also is very unmanageable, though these have power in themselves; but in consequence of their being affected, the universal health is destroyed, and hence the disease is less manageable. If the stomach is inflamed, no operation of the body can go on well, the powers of restoration becoming weaker than ever; hence the greatest danger is to be apprehended.

Strength of the constitution and parts affected, when under inflammation, produces the following effects: viz., a more ready and quick termination, whatever it be. Thus, a wound in a healthy constitution unites more readily by the first intention; adhesive inflammation more readily terminates by resolution. If inflammation have got beyond the first stage, it passes sooner on to the suppurative inflammation; nature going through her operations with greater facility and dispatch in such a state of constitution.

Weakness of the Constitution and Parts.—When a wound is made in a person of a weak habit, the union is more difficult, and the inflammation is more likely to continue; and this not from there being a greater disposition to inflammation, but from want of a power and disposition to heal, nature needing greater and longer exertions to produce the intended effect.

In this state of the constitution and parts we often find that parts seem hardly capable of taking on either adhesive or suppurative inflammation; and in some of these habits inflammation will hardly even follow a solution of continuity. As in dropsy, I have observed that the puncture made by tapping or scarifications will hardly heal; a degree of inflammation does take place, but not sufficient to procure a healing of the wounds or suppuration, but mortification soon comes on. If in such a constitution a wound is made, the blood not coagulating sufficiently to heal it by the first intention, dies, and becomes an extraneous substance, causing irritation; suppurative inflammation succeeds, and often mortification, which mostly proves fatal.

Effects of Inflammation on the Constitution.—The sympathy of the constitution upon an act of violence to a part, is probably the most simple act of a constitution. But this will vary in different constitutions, because all constitutions do not sympathize equally. It will vary according to the stage of the inflammation, and according to the disposition of the parts inflamed.

We find the effects of inflammation on the constitution as various as any other circumstances, which appear to arise from the following causes: first, from the nature of the constitution; secondly, from the nature of the inflammation, whether common or specific; if common, according to the stage of the inflammation, whether adhesive, suppurative, or ulcerative; if specific, according to the kind, although I believe specific irritations do not produce much variety in the constitution, except the plague, which entirely changes it, and such as by their long continuance weaken the constitution, as lues, when of long standing; but this will be similar to any lasting disease, for at first it certainly does not affect the constitution so as to alter the disposition of a wound made on any part : thirdly, from the nature of the part inflamed, whether vital or otherwise : and, fourthly, from the different situation of similar parts, as of the muscles or cellular membrane in the legs or arms, &c.

In inflammation we have seldom more than the continuous or the universal sympathy, but sometimes the remote. The continuous causes the inflammation to spread. The general is when the constitution becomes affected. The remote is seen in pain of the shoulder, from inflammation of the liver.

As the effects which inflammation has on the constitution are by sympathy, they will be in proportion to the readiness it has to go into that action; and this is much greater in some constitutions than in others: moreover, every constitution sympathizes more readily with some parts than others. The kind of constitution least affected is generally the most healthy where sympathy hardly takes place, the surrounding parts even seeming hardly to feel what is going on in those nearest them.

The nature of the inflammation produces, I believe, but little variation in these effects; for of whatever kind, the sympathy will be in proportion to the violence of the inflammation, and its rapidity. Hence as the inflammation which produces healthy suppuration is more rapid, it generally produces more violent effects on the constitution than any other.

The effects which inflammation has on the vascular system, and which are chiefly discoverable by the pulse, are very remarkable. In considering the peculiarities of the pulse, it is always necessary to remark that there are two powers acting to produce it, viz., the heart and the arteries. That one part of the pulse belongs to the heart, another to the arteries, and a third is a compound of both. The stroke, which is the pulse, (as regards the number of strokes in a given time, the regularity or irregularity as to time, and the quickness of these strokes,) belongs to the heart. The vibratory pulse and slowness of the systole, with the fulness and smallness of the pulse, belong to the arteries.

As the pulse arises from the actions of the solids on the machine, it is of course according to the nature of the machine at the time; therefore is capable of being in one of two states, natural or diseased.

In most diseases of the constitution, whether original or arising in consequence of diseases of parts in which the constitution becomes affected by sympathy, the pulse is altered from the natural to the diseased state which is according to those affections.

The varieties of which the pulse admits are numerous. It may be increased or diminished in the number of strokes; regular or irregular as to time; quick in its stroke, or diastole, and slow in its systole; or it may be hard in its diastole. In all cases probably, when the constitution is in a state of irritation, the pulse will be quick and frequent in its number of strokes in a given time, and the artery being hard, from the constant contraction of its muscular coats, will give a feeling of hardness to the touch; besides which the diastole of the artery is not uniformly and regularly the same, but there are a vast number of stops or intermissions, which are so quick as to give the feeling of vibration, or what we call thrill. In such a disposition the pulse may be either full or small. These two opposite effects do not seem to arise from the difference in the quantity of blood, as might at first be supposed; but arise, I rather suspect, from the difference in the degree of strength and quantity of irritability that the patient possesses at the time, which, when joined, give an antidiastolic disposition to the arteries, so that when the arteries have a full power of contraction and are in a state of irritation at the same time this effect will always take place.

It is certain that arteries in such a state of constitution do not dilate so fully and freely as at other times; and as this varies quickly as the state of the constitution varies quickly, it is more reasonable to suppose that the effect is immediately from the arteries than from an increase or decrease in the quantity of blood. If this is really the case, we should naturally suppose that the motion of the blood in the arteries would be increased in proportion to their diminished size, unless we should also suppose that the systole of the heart should be diminished in the same proportion, which I think is probably the case, as we find the blood forsakes the surface of the body in such a state of constitution, which must therefore be collected in the larger veins about the heart. But if the heart were to throw out its whole contents at each systole, the velocity of the blood in the arteries would be immense, and must be then forced into the small vessels on the surface of the body, which it certainly is not. A quick hard vibratory pulse is generally attendant on inflammation. The fullness or emptiness of the pulse depend greatly on the parts that are affected, which either increase or decrease the irritability.

Different Parts produce different states of the Pulse.—In inflammation of common parts, as the skin, cellular membrane, muscles, &c., the pulse will be full and strong, and the symptoms acute, especially if near the heart. Ligaments, cartilages, tendons, and bony parts produce symptoms which are less acute; the pulse is not so full, but quicker, there being in these cases a greater degree of irritability. In the vital parts of the second order, as the brain, the pulse is soft and slow; but in the stomach and parts with which it sympathizes greatly, as the testicles, upper part of the intestines, &c., the pulse is small, quick, and contracted.

Of the Sensations arising from Inflammation in different parts.—When the injury is in the head, the pain is often dull and attended with sickness; when in the heart and lungs, the pain is more violent. When in the stomach or upper part of the intestines, it is a heavy depressing pain, and attended with more or less of sickness. When in the colon it is more acute, but attended with less sickness. When the liver, ligaments, or bony parts are affected, the pain is much the same as when the stomach is affected, that is, heavy and depressing: the pain is acute and rousing when the skin, cellular membrane, or muscles are inflamed.

Inflammations in vital parts do not all produce the same effects on the constitution, which would seem to arise from their greater or less sympathy with the stomach; but it is certain that a given quantity of inflammation in a vital part or its sympathizer will produce much more considerable effects than a greater quantity in another part, and the blood will be more sizy. When the heart is inflamed, its actions are irregular; if the lungs only are inflamed, the heart still seems to sympathize, and is irregular in its actions, as well as weak. If the stomach is inflamed, the patient feels a depression and a defective action in the heart as well as in every part; simple animal life, or the living principle, seems then to be depressed, as the sensitive from inflammation in the brain, and the pulse is low and weak. In inflammation of the uterus the pain is very acute, and the pulse quick and low, the stomach sick, &c. When inflammation occurs in these parts the symptoms come on very quickly; and if it proves fatal, it runs through its stages very fast, debility beginning very early. All this may depend on the stomach being, as it were, the central seat of sympathy, whence the actions of life are interfered with. However, universal sympathy soon takes place here, and the sympathy being similar to the first action, a fever of a depressing kind is produced, and death soon succeeds.

Inflammations of parts not vital, of such violence as to affect the actions of life by general sympathy, render the pulse full and strong. The constitution in this case is strong and not irritable; for when weak and irritable, the pulse is quick, hard, and small in the beginning, as it is in inflammations of vital parts, and the blood though sizy is loose in its texture.

Difference from different Nerves.—One cause of the difference in the inflammation of vital parts seems to be the different systems of nerves by which they are supplied. In all those parts supplied by the par vagum, inflammation affects the patient with lowness from the first, these nerves supplying the parts of involuntary motion, and therefore possessing the living principle in the highest degree; whence an inflammation of these parts becomes peculiarly depressing.

Situation of the Blood in the commencement of Diseases.—In some diseases the blood at first forsakes the skin, extremities, and lips, and the parts shrink and diminish in bulk; this is particularly evident in the eye, and arises from want of power in the constitution, all the powers being called to the citadel, or source of power, and the outworks left. This happens in fainting, agues, hectic, &c., and does not seem to arise from debility at first, but from a novelty of action, and a consequent inability to perform it. In putrid fevers the external parts first lose their living power, from having a less resisting power.

Of the Effects on the Constitution from different stages of Inflammation.—The constitutional effects arising from inflammation, independent of the difference of parts, situation, nerves, &c., are more or less according to the stage of the disease. When inflammation is in the adhesive stage, it has but little effect on the whole system, and that effect is generally an increase of animal actions. This stage is the one which should be considered as truly inflammatory, as in it the constitution appears to be more regular, more determined, and more at ease, for it is more steady, more capable of continuing the time of action than in any other, hardly any varieties taking place in the time of this stage of the disease. When the suppurative stage comes on, the effects on the constitution are much more considerable and more various. Cold fits or rigors are generally felt on the commencement of suppuration; but they are not lasting, and are often succeeded by hot fits, both being more or less according to the greatness of the present inflammation and the suppuration that is likely to follow, as indeed with the nature of the parts, and their situation, whether vital or not, &c.

Cold fits show plainly the commencement of some new action, as the beginning of fever, the absorption of poison, or even from simple irritation, as pricking the finger with a clean needle. They may also be produced by disagreeable sensations and disagreeable states of the mind. These rigors are probably dependent on the stomach, which being the seat of simple animal life and the seat of sympathy, takes part in every constitutional alteration, and we observe how much this viscus is affected by loss of blood, disagreeable sights, &c. What nature intends to effect by this sympathy with the rest of the body it is hard to say, but it is worthy inquiry whether she may not intend to relieve herself by rousing the actions of life by means of vomiting. Rigors seem to be the effect of any new action in the constitution, and not at the commencement of a disease only, for even at the close, changing from a diseased action to a healthy one will cause rigors to take place. In a strong constitution, where rigors occur in consequence of a well-formed fever, the consequent actions of a hot fit and sweating go on regularly; but in a weak constitution there is much loss of power by each rigor, and they will not be followed by a hot fit, but only perhaps by a little sweating.

A boy was attacked with rigor, followed by sweating, and he afterwards continued getting sensibly worse and worse : pulse quick and full, blood sizy, tongue white.　He was worse every other day.　After being ill a fortnight, he was again attacked with rigor, hot fit, and sweating, which, contrary to my expectation, who supposed these would be repeated, carried off the disease with that single fit.　I think I have seen other cases where Nature has attempted something like this, but has failed.

. In many cases the rigor is the first apparent symptom, and is followed by a hot fit, and then sweating, and when these whole actions of the disease have taken place the patient becomes well ; but this is not the case where, from weakness, &c., the whole regular actions do not take place, but, as at the commencement of the boy's case above related, the hot fit does not succeed the rigor, and he continued ill afterwards until Nature again took on the rigor, and he was able to go through the stages regularly, and one fit carried off the disease.　The boy above mentioned was also a striking instance of the crisis of a disease being like its commencement.

Rigors from a local affection are seldom followed by a hot and sweating stage, and the bark in such cases can be of little service.

The ulcerative stage seldom affects the whole system ; but that rigors take place on the commencement of ulceration is, I think, certain, although it cannot be well perceived in all cases, for ulceration will follow so close on suppuration in most cases that it will be difficult to distinguish which was the cause of the rigors.　But when suppuration has taken place, and the abscess been opened, (so that the act of suppuration is finished,) yet not so opened as to afford a ready outlet to the matter, the pressure of the matter against the most depending part of the abscess will cause ulceration, and thereby rigors will take place ; but these rigors will not take place for some time after the first opening, for the first opening will for a time remove the disposition for ulceration all over the surface of the abscess ; but when it finds this opening not sufficient to take off the pressure, it then sets to work to make another, and the rigors return.　Many have supposed from these rigors that new matter was forming.

Exacerbations are other symptoms, which have a great affinity to the foregoing, and are common to most constitutional diseases, and to some local ones.　They are repetitions of the first attack, but seldom so strong as the first.　These have been supposed to be owing to the disease acting on the constitution at stated times ; but we must search for some principle in the animal œconomy to account for this, for we cannot suppose an increase and decrease in the cause of disease to account for it.　Agues exist in the constitution as much between the fits as in them. If the constitution is strong, the exacerbations are regular; if weak, irregular. These may be partly owing to the fact that an animal cannot exist for long together in the same state; life cannot always be affected in the same way.

Of the state of the Blood in Inflammation.—It is reasonable to suppose that the blood is affected in the same manner with the constitution, and that disease has nearly the same effect on it that it has on the body, because the same living principle runs through the whole. We find this to be really the case; for till the disease has affected the constitution the blood continues the same as before; but as the constitution becomes affected the blood also becomes affected, and undergoes changes which are probably owing to contiguous sympathy between the vessels and the blood. So that we shall find that the changes in the blood are often as expressive of disease as in any other part of the body. When the action of the solids is of the inflammatory kind, or, what is perhaps the same thing, when there is too great action of the solids, the blood under such a disease more readily admits of a separation of its component parts (see p. 235, *note*); the red particles subside more to the bottom of the coagulum, and the coagulation of the lymph, though more slow, is firmer; the upper part of the coagulum being of an opake white, in which state the blood is said to be sizy. It is not easy to say whether this change in the blood is not the first produced, and that the constitutional is not an effect of the change. I have before said that I can conceive the death of the blood to take place independently of the solids, and it appears to me that the diseased state of the blood is capable of coming on as suddenly as the corresponding state of the solids.

A man received a stab in the abdomen. I saw him a little time after the accident, when there was no degree of fever or constitutional affection, but he complained of considerable pain; I therefore took away some blood from him, which was entirely in the natural state: in about a quarter of an hour constitutional disturbance came on, and the blood appeared very sizy.

Whether the disposition for inflammation and the change produced in the blood arise from a real increase of animal life, or whether it is only an increase of the disposition to act with the power that the machine is already in possession of, is not easily determined; but it appears certain that it is either the one or the other. However, some circumstances incline me to suspect that it is the last, because we often have inflammation when the powers are but weak, where there appears to be only an exertion of very weak powers, arising from some irritation produced. This appears to be equally the case in local inflammation and

inflammatory fever, or the symptomatic fever.   On the other hand, there
are some reasons for thinking it may be a real increase of animal life,
for women who are breeding, and who are in perfect health, have yet
sizy blood; and this is the case with all animals in a similar situation.
Now it would appear necessary for an animal, when put into a situation
where greater powers are wanted, that these powers should be increased.
In breeding females there is a process going on which, though natural,
is uncommon, and which requires a greater quantity of power than usual;
therefore we have greater powers produced.

If these observations are just, the blood should not be inflammatory
blood, but blood whose powers of life are increased.

On the other hand, where there is great debility in the solids, where
the powers of preservation are less, and therefore action weak, where
the body must therefore have a tendency to dissolution, we find the
very reverse of the former appearance in the blood; there is no distinct
separation, but the whole mass continues mixed.   This effect takes
place in those who die instantaneously, and I suspect that the blood
dies first, and instantaneously.

When the pulse is quick and hard, and has a kind of vibratory thrill,
we generally have sizy blood.   This may arise from fever, or such inflammation, &c. as affects the constitution or the vital parts, these being
diseased, so as to keep up a constitutional irritation, which will always
be an attending symptom.

But when we have neither a quick nor hard pulse, but rather small,
no visible fever nor inflammation, but perhaps some strange and undetermined symptom, such as pain, which is moveable, sometimes in one
place and sometimes in another, yet seeming to impede no natural
function, we shall nevertheless, on bleeding, find the blood sizy, as happened in a gentleman who had severe pain shifting about, with a small
slow pulse: he was blooded, and the blood found sizy.   After the
bleeding the blood became fuller and harder, and did so after every
bleeding, which, on account of this circumstance and the continuance
of the pains, was repeated several times.   Something like this is observable when an oppressed pulse becomes liberated by bleeding; but
what was remarkable here was its increasing in hardness.   We may
even have the blood contract so strongly in these cases as to cup.   So
that the pulse and the appearance of the blood do not always agree
with one another.

The manner in which inflammation begins is generally from a point.   It
afterwards spreads from this in proportion to the violence and the disposition of the surrounding parts.   This is the case in accidents; the
accident is limited, but the inflammation arising from it is not: it is

most violent in the first point and gets weaker and weaker as it spreads from this until it is lost insensibly in the surrounding parts. This extension is owing to sympathy; and hence, according to the susceptibility of sympathy will be the spreading; and from the difference of disposition to sympathy will result great differences as to the diffusion of inflammation: the more healthy the less the sympathy.

Swelling of the parts in inflammation, like the inflammation itself, is greatest in the middle, and gradually lessens from that till it is lost in the surrounding parts. It is owing to the extravasation of coagulable lymph and some serum, the serum being squeezed out as the coagulable lymph thickens, and is deposited around the inflamed part, causing œdema, which is less in proportion as the parts are healthy.

Of the colour of inflamed parts.—The colour of an inflamed part is visibly changed from the natural hue, whatever it was, to red. This red is of various hues, according to the nature of the inflammation; if healthy, of a pure scarlet red; if less healthy, the colour is rather more of a purple, and so on till it shall be of a blueish purple.

This increase of red would appear to arise from two causes; first, dilatation of the vessels, by which a greater quantity of blood is sent into those vessels which naturally admit only serum or lymph (an example of which we have in the conjunctiva of the eye when inflamed); and secondly, the formation of new vessels in the extravasated uniting coagulable lymph. From which circumstances there is a greater quantity of blood in the part than in a natural state, according to that law of the animal œconomy, that where a part has more to do than to support itself, red blood is thrown into it in larger quantities.

The true inflammatory colour is scarlet, that colour which the blood has in the arteries; hence we should suppose that the arteries were chiefly dilated, or if the veins are equally distended, that the blood undergoes no change in such an inflammation in the passage from the arteries into the veins, which last I think most probably the case.

Heat of the inflamed part.—The inflamed part is hotter than common; but this is most obvious in the skin, from its being a part most disposed to carry these sensations to the brain. Heat, I imagine, is a sign of strength and power in the constitution, though it may often arise from increased action in weak constitutions or weakened parts. It is an immediate action, while cold is the reverse, and often arises from a diminished action of strong parts. 'It has not been considered whether an animal has this power equally in every part of his body, though from what is generally advanced on this subject, it is probable that it exists in every part. Nevertheless, I am inclined to suspect that there is a principal source of heat, though I do not think with many that this

source is in the blood, but rather that this is affected by the source of
the blood being near to the source of heat.

That this principle resides in the stomach is probable ; at least of this
I am certain, that affections of the stomach will produce either heat or
cold.   Eructations often give a sensation of heat, but whether this is
increased heat, or only a sensation, it is difficult to say.   Certain substances taken into the stomach produce a glow.   Certain affections of
the mind also produce a glow.   This would appear to contradict my
opinion, but I suspect that the stomach sympathizes with the mind.   ·

We find that inflamed parts become hotter ; but let us see how far
the increase goes.   From all the observations I have made, I do not find
that a local inflammation can produce local heat above that which is
natural to the animal ; and when in parts whose natural heat is inferior
to that which is at the source of the circulation, it does not rise so high.
A man had the tunica vaginalis laid open for the cure of hydrocele : I
introduced a thermometer into the wound, and placed it in contact with
the testicle, and it stood at 92° ; by night it had risen to 98¾°, a rise of
6¾° ; but this is not greater than the heat of the blood at the source of
the circulation.   A wound was made in the belly of a dog, and the bulb
of the thermometer immediately applied to the diaphragm, which gave
101°, and did not increase above that.   Another dog's rectum gave 102°,
and when inflamed very much, which it was by injecting a solution of
corrosive sublimate, the heat was not increased a degree.   The rectum
of an ass, 98°, was injected with a strong infusion of mustard and ginger
several times repeated, but without increasing the heat at all, nor did a
strong solution of corrosive sublimate have this effect ; at last a much
stronger one was injected, which brought on a very violent inflammation,
but the heat was only increased to 100°.   A similar experiment was made
with nearly the same result on the vagina of the same ass.   Also a wound
was made deep in the gluteus muscle of the same ass, and in no stage
of this wound did it raise the thermometer above 100°.   A wound was
made in the belly of the same ass, and an injection of a strong solution
of common salt thrown into the belly, which produced violent inflammation, and even symptomatic fever ; yet the heat of the part was very
little altered.   From all which observations and experiments I do not
find that a local inflammation can increase local heat above the natural
heat of the animal ; and when in parts where the natural heat is inferior
to that at the source of the circulation, it does not rise even so high.
Yet, that in some instances the heat of parts may be increased beyond
its natural degree in those parts which have the greatest natural heat,
is certain, from the following experiment : the bulb of the thermometer
being held in the stream flowing from the abdomen of a man tapped for

dropsy, raised the mercury to 104°. In most of the above experiments there seemed a difference of 1° between the heat at night and in the morning, and this difference seems to exist in the natural state of the body.

I suspect that the blood has an ultimate standard of heat in itself when in health, and that nothing can increase that heat but some universal or constitutional affection, and that the whole power of local inflammation is only to increase it a little in the part, but cannot bring it above the standard heat of the constitution, nor even to it in parts far from the source.

Of Cold.—The production of cold certainly is an operation which the more perfect animals have a power of performing. (See p. 291, *note.*)

I suspect that coldness in disease arises from weakness of the whole constitution, joined with a peculiar mode of action at the time. That universal or constitutional cold arises from the stomach is evident, for whenever we are made sick universal coldness takes place. This is best proved by producing sickness in animals that we can kill while under the influence of the affection of the stomach. I threw three grains of emetic tartar into the stomach of a bitch, and repeated the experiment with a grain more: she vomited and strained very hard, and brought off a good deal of froth, that is, mucus, from the stomach, mixed with air in coming up. I opened her body, and, contrary to what we generally observe, I found the intestines, liver, and heart not warm. I have known people who had affection of the stomach say that they had plainly a feeling of coldness in their belly. I knew a gentleman who said, whenever he threw wind off his stomach it felt cold even to his hand.

Affections of the mind also produce general coldness, but such effects arise from the sympathy of the stomach with the mind, producing there such a sensation as we mean by the expression "turning the stomach with sickness": the sensation proceeds to the shoulders, which, with the rest of the body, are put into motion by what we term shuddering.

Of Pain in Inflamed Parts.—The immediate cause of sensation is an alteration in the natural position of the solids, arising either from violent action or mechanical or chemical effects*, joined with its being produced in a given time; for this alteration may be produced so slowly as

---

* [It must be confessed that we are very much in the dark respecting the proximate cause of pain; for being ignorant of the ultimate distribution of the nerves, as well as of their mode of action, we cannot say in what manner they may be affected; indeed, we cannot positively say that pain depends on the nerves at all, for those parts which are most painful when inflamed have the fewest nerves, and these do not enlarge in consequence of inflammation in the same manner that the vessels do.

Pressure is a well-known cause of pain, and therefore has been assigned as the cause of pain in inflammation, for not only are the minute vessels distended from within and

not to keep pace with sensation, as in many indolent tumours; or, on the other hand, this alteration in the natural position of the parts may be so quick as to exceed sensation. (See p. 262.)

Pain is not the same in all the stages of inflammation. In the adhesive stage it is generally but inconsiderable, especially if it is to go no further, and is perhaps more a heavy than an acute pain. But when the inflammation is passing from the adhesive to the suppurative, the parts are undergoing greater change, and the pain gets more and more acute until it becomes very considerable and becomes pulsatory, being increased during the dilatation of the arteries. The nerves, too, acquire a degree of irritability which renders them much more susceptible of impression than in a natural state. When suppuration has taken place, the pain in some degree subsides; however, as ulceration begins, it in some degree keeps up the pain, and this more or less according to the quickness of the ulceration. The pain attending ulceration gives more the feeling of soreness.

Of the Subsidence of Inflammation.—Whatever disposition it is which produces inflammation, and whatever the actions are which are produced by this disposition, yet when the disposition arises either from the constitution or part, it can be removed, and of course the actions raised in consequence of it cease.

---

pressed upon without, but the natural sensibility of the parts is exalted by the increased vascularity. This is further confirmed by the exquisite pain occasioned by inflammation when it occurs in any unyielding texture, as the teeth, the bones, the periosteum, the serous and fibrous membranes, &c., as well as by the relief which is afforded by such means as tend to diminish the tension of the inflamed parts, as bleeding, scarifications, fomentations, &c. It may, however, be urged on the other side, that the pain is not proportioned to the quantity of nerves, as in fibrous membranes, bone, teeth, &c.; nor to the quantity of effusion and consequent swelling, as in serous membranes; nor to the quantity of inflammation present, as in gout, rheumatism, &c.: that the difference in the quality of the pain is inconsistent with any mechanical explanation, which would occasion differences in degree but not in kind; that it is irreconcileable with the sudden transition of pain from one part to another, as in metastasis; that chemical substances cannot be supposed to act in this way; and finally, that pain often occurs without its being possible to assign any probable source of pressure as a cause, as in colic, tic douloureux, toothache, and many other forms of nervous disorders.

It seems, therefore, most probable that pain depends on some peculiar action of the nerves with which we are unacquainted, but to which pressure stands in the relation of an exciting cause.

Pain is the most general symptom of inflammation. What other purpose does it answer besides that of inducing the patient to repose the inflamed part? Does it answer any *direct* purpose in the œconomy? Intense pain occasions increased vascularity of the affected part, and if continued, excites inflammation. This is seen in toothache and tic douloureux, which inflame the face, and in disease of the hip, which occasions inflammation of the knee; on the other hand, whatever diminishes the pain diminishes the inflammation also.]

If the disposition for inflammation has taken place, and the vessels, which are the active parts, should have dilated thoroughly, they will allow the blood to enter them, so that the part shall look red; but no hardness or fullness shall be observed, and the whole will subside before adhesions have taken place : or if inflammation is gone so far as to pro-. duce swelling, which is the adhesive state of the disease, yet by certain methods it can be assuaged, and suppuration be prevented from taking place, and then the parts will fall back into their natural state, which is called resolution. And as the first symptom of inflammation is pain, the first symptom of resolution is the cessation of pain.

Why an inflammation of any kind should cease after it is once begun is very difficult to explain, or even to form an idea of, unless it is on the principle of what I call custom that the parts adapt themselves in time to their present situation; and therefore, in order to keep up inflammation, it is necessary that the cause should increase in proportion as the parts become reconciled to their present circumstances. But this will not account for their returning to their original state when this increased irritation ceases. We may suppose that the removal of the original cause is sufficient to stop the progress of inflammation; and when stopped, the parts cannot easily remain in the inflamed state, but by their own efforts begin to restore themselves to health, like a spring which is bent by a weight, but the moment the weight is removed the spring returns to its former state.

Restoration of injured parts.—All alterations in the animal frame arise from a disposition to act, and these preternatural actions, in consequence of injuries, may be caused,—1st, by a disposition to restoration, in consequence of injuries, which is the most simple; 2nd, by a disposition of necessity, as thickening of parts, ulceration, &c., which is rather more compounded; 3rd, by disease, which is the most complicated. (p. 308.) There are a great many cases requiring the assistance of a surgeon but which cannot be strictly called disease, but are injuries done to the body. In disease there is a disposition to wrong action, which goes on until the disposition is worn out, or is put a stop to by remedies; but the actions in consequence of accident are widely different, for here, by reason of the stimulus of imperfection in the injured part, a disposition to restoration is excited, and action, different from the former, comes on. In disease the restoration to health is produced by a prevention of the continuance of diseased action ; in injuries, or alteration of structure by violence, something is required different from the ordinary and natural actions, which will differ in some respects according to the nature of the violence and of the part ; and this alteration is of the most simple nature, being the action in consequence of a disposition

2 c 2

to restoration, and consequently, if it requires any assistance from art, it is of the most simple kind. The affections from accidents may be divided into two kinds, those which take place in sound parts, and those in parts before diseased. The first I shall only treat of now. Accidents, then, may be divided into two kinds; first, those which do not communicate externally, as bruises, sprains, ruptured tendons, simple fractures, &c.; secondly, those which have also an external communication, as compound fractures, wounds, &c.: yet these may be, and often are, brought under the first head. Bruises, which have destroyed the life of a part, might be considered as forming a third head. The first class, when in a simple state, requires a most simple treatment; but they may be so complicated as to require our utmost exertion. The most simple of these is the bruise, when the continuity of parts is not broken through; here the parts have nothing to do but recover themselves. The rupture of a small vessel is next, the blood being effused into the cellular membrane; but the vessel must not be in a part of any consequence to life, or the extravasation may kill, as in the arteries of the brain. The cure in this case will be next in simplicity, the vessel being closed by the contraction of its muscular coats, and the union effected by means of coagulable lymph, and the extravasated blood being taken up by the absorbents. The differences in these cases will arise from the magnitude of the injury and the nature of the injured parts. Some accidents of the first class, as fractures, will require the aid of a surgeon to restore the parts to their natural situation, and then nature falls to work and completes the business. Sometimes the quantity of blood extravasated is so large as to prevent nature from going through these processes directly, and forms a tumour called an ecchymosis. Ecchymosis may be said to be of two kinds; one is where the blood coagulates; the other is where it does not. That which coagulates commonly subsides gradually, from the blood being absorbed, and gives but little trouble, which is likewise the case sometimes with those in which the blood does not coagulate, though not generally. I have seen where a small wound has led to the cavity containing the coagulum, which not being meddled with, the sides of the cavity have gradually contracted, and have as gradually squeezed out the coagulum.

A woman fell with the labium pudendi on the edge of a pail. I found a very considerable tumour, which I thought was of blood; there was evidently a fluctuation. I bled her, and ordered a poultice, but did not open it, as I thought the presence of the extravasated blood might serve to stop the orifice of the vessel. In a little time the tumour burst, with a small opening, and on examining with a probe I found the coagulum filling a space the size of a goose's egg. The cavity grew less and less, but always kept exactly filled with coagulated blood; and thus it continued diminishing until the orifice healed. Thus the blood being allowed to remain in the cavity, and not acting there as an extraneous body, nor even allowing the stimulus of an imperfect cavity or inflamed surface to take place, the cavity continued to contract all round the blood until the whole had disappeared. Now what would have been the consequence if I had followed the old method of laying open the tumour, scooping out the blood and dressing the internal surface with turpentine? I should have had a sore of the whole extent of the tumour, and given considerably more trouble both to the patient and to myself.

The second species of ecchymosis, or that where the blood does not coagulate, does not always terminate so well as the former. It has often the appearance of an encysted tumour, but from being the immediate consequence of some accident to the part its nature is understood. The cause of this blood not coagulating must arise, I conceive, from some peculiar mode of action of the vessels arising from the injury, for I apprehend that in such cases the blood dies as it is extravasated, or in the act of extravasation, like the menses. This species of ecchymosis happens very commonly to children in birth under the scalp. In such cases nothing should be done but to wait with patience, and the whole will be absorbed. In many cases the accident has been so violent as to deaden the cellular membrane under the skin, or as to produce inflammation in the surrounding parts; these sometimes resolve, but they are seldom allowed to do so, for surgeons are led to open them early, from seeing the inflammation and feeling fluctuation, two strong enticements to use the lancet when all circumstances are not well attended to. But in such cases I should wait until I saw the signs of suppuration, viz., thinning of the skin over the matter and pointing of the contents, which are the only true marks of the formation of matter and of its approaching the skin.

Sometimes ecchymoses are removed by pressure, which without this would remain. Parts cannot bear pressure, so that the extravasated blood being pressed against the sides of the cavity, the absorbent vessels are under the necessity of absorbing it.

When ecchymoses are not absorbed, but suppurate, abscesses are formed, which must be treated as abscesses in common, only waiting with a little more patience than when wholly the consequence of inflammation. In many of those cases of accident not only the skin shall be deadened, in consequence of which it will slough and leave a sore, but often the skin shall preserve its living powers, and only the cellular membrane underneath shall be deadened and slough, and produce an abscess, which was not at first expected. In cases where the skin in one part is killed by a blow, and the cellular membrane in another part, while the skin over it remains sound, the deadened skin will come off, granulate, and heal kindly; but then inflammation shall take place, perhaps, an inch or two from it, where the cellular membrane was deadened, and an abscess shall be produced.

If these injuries are not very great, little effect will be produced on the sensitive principle, no sympathy or irritation taking place; but sometimes the accident will, by its irritation, produce another action of the parts, causing inflammation, the end of which is either adhesion of the divided parts or suppuration for getting rid of the substances become extraneous. The most simple accident may be attended with such circumstances as will prevent the more simple process of nature from taking place; such, for instance, as the magnitude of the vessel ruptured, or a fractured rib wounding the lungs, &c.

The second division I made was where wounds communicate externally. These are subject to greater variety than the former, yet often admit of the same mode of cure. A wound may be either simple or compound. The simple, which is what I mean to speak of now, is a solution of continuity in a part, which must be made with a cutting instrument. In such cases a number of vessels are always divided, blood is effused, and the cells of the cellular membrane exposed, as well as other internal parts. The former class required only rest, but in these there is a necessity for replacing the divided parts. The present class admit of both a natural and an artificial cure. By the natural is meant union by the first intention; when this cannot be obtained, a new bond of union takes place—adhesive inflammation*; and if this is lost, a third mode—granulation. In that by art we have to imitate the natural, we are to bring the divided surfaces into contact; the living extravasated blood, being then retained and coagulating, unites them; the mouths of the vessels shut, and the remaining blood is absorbed: the red globules are indeed absorbed, and only the coagulable lymph remaining becomes the bond of union†. This is an imitation of nature; but surfaces cannot always be brought to unite in this manner, and the blood in some parts loses its living principle, and then it becomes a source of irritation, ex-

---

* [Union by the first intention and adhesive inflammation are in the present day generally considered to be synonymous.]

† [It has been before observed that the blood does not become vascular, but only the coagulable lymph which is subsequently effused. The blood at first serves the useful purpose of uniting the divided parts; but beyond this it unquestionably is an impediment to union by the first intention. Wherever, therefore, union by the first intention is desired, the incised surfaces should first be cleansed of adhering blood previously to their being put into apposition. This rule of practice is universal.]

citing inflammation, which is the case sometimes in simple fractures, and which I shall call, for distinction's sake, simple compound fractures.

The best time of replacing the divided parts is perhaps during the time that the extravasation continues, but it may also be done when the discharge of coagulable lymph in the adhesive or first stage of inflammation takes place. Sometimes the inflammation runs so high as to get into the suppurative stage; the extravasated fluids may lose their living principle, and become a stimulus exciting inflammation.

By adhesive inflammation different parts of the body may be united to another by coming into contact; but the most extraordinary union is that of removing parts from one body and uniting them to another. Here is the testicle of a cock, separated from that animal, and put through a wound, made for that purpose, into the belly of a hen; which mode of turning hens into cocks is much such an improvement for its utility as that of Dean Swift when he proposed to obtain a breed of sheep without wool. The hen was afterwards killed, and the testicle was found adhering to the intestines, as may be seen in this preparation, where the parts are preserved. Here is another preparation, in which the spur of a cock has been inserted into the comb of another; and here a human tooth, inserted into the same part, and united by means of vessels, which you see injected, from one to the other. These living bodies thus applied to each other produce adhesive, not suppurative inflammation. In the same manner, the eggs of one animal laid in the flesh of another do not excite suppurative inflammation. This would not be the case if the inserted body did not contain the principle of life, for the part would run into suppurative inflammation, as would be the case with a pea so introduced. While the guinea-worm is endowed with the living principle it gives but little trouble; yet if killed, it gives the stimulus of an extraneous body, which produces suppuration through its whole length.

In this preparation you see a maggot deposited, just below the skin, on the back of a reindeer: here the first stage of inflammation took place only; coagulable lymph was poured out, which has formed a chamber in which the insect resided. A similar power is observable in vegetables. Here is an oak leaf, which I picked up in my garden; you observe on it seven or eight protuberances, exactly circular and uniform. These have been formed by the insertion of the eggs of an insect into the leaf; and I cannot but think the process would have been different if any substance not possessed of the vital principle had been inserted. It is on this principle of union by the first intention that the union of parts by suture has been recommended, which has been found the best practice where it can be done. The dry suture in superficial wounds answers very well, the quilled is sometimes useful, and the interrupted is very often useful. The two last are properly called sutures. In many cases it is improper to keep the surfaces together, as when the wound has been attended with considerable contusion, which generally occasions sloughing of the parts. When much blood is extravasated, suppuration becomes necessary, in consequence of the blood acting like any other extraneous body; but when laceration only is present, union by the first intention may take place, especially when on the head and over other superficial bones, as Mr. Cline has observed. The machine is not at all disturbed by this most simple operation : there being perhaps even no local action except the contraction of the vessels, the union being performed by the blood only.

CHAPTER XIII.

OF ADHESIVE INFLAMMATION.

Natural tendency of inflammation.—Definition of inflammation.—Seat of inflammation.—Adhesive inflammation ;—why limited, and how ;—its tendency ;—arising more easily in some parts than others ;—lymph affected by the state of the parts secreting it ;—appearances of inflammation ;—redness ;—swelling ;—pain.—Adhesive inflammation ;—its use, in large cavities ;—in the cellular membrane ;—in the lungs ;—compared with erysipelatous inflammation ;—sometimes imperfect ;—consequences of this imperfection ;—constitutional effects of this inflammation.—Of resolution ;—cases in which it is supposed to be improper ;—modes of by constitutional means ;—by weakening ;—by temporary weakness ;—by lessening irritability.— Venesection ;—medicines ;— local applications.— Treatment of adhesive when about to end in suppurative inflammation.

ALTHOUGH inflammation is an action produced for the restoration of the most simple injury in sound parts that exceeds union by the first intention, we must still look upon it as one of the most simple operations of nature. It is to be considered only as a disturbed state of parts, which require a new but salutary mode of action to restore parts to that state in which the natural mode of action will be necessary. But this same operation can and does vary, and is often carried much further than union, according to circumstances ; and is often attended with disease, and that of various kinds, by which means it becomes more and more complicated. It becomes therefore necessary to begin by describing it in its most simple form, and with its most general effect, and to particularize further as we go on.

I shall call everything inflammation that produces the following local effects, viz., pain, swelling, and redness, all depending on one cause, and occurring at the same time. Out of inflammation arise many other local effects, which may be called secondary ; such as adhesions, suppuration, ulceration, and even death or mortification in the part, and universal affection, such as sympathetic fever, and universal death.

The act of inflammation is, as I have said, most probably in the smaller vessels. What the action is, or in what it differs from the common action of these vessels, is not easily ascertained; for we are better able to judge of the immediate effects than of the immediate cause.

Hitherto I have only shown that this inflammation takes its rise, and is capable of uniting parts, when preternaturally divided; but we shall find that it is capable of arising from very different causes, and that it is capable of producing adhesions in whole parts, or in natural separations, such as common cellular membrane, large circumscribed cavities, joints, &c., and these effects will be found to answer very important purposes.

As the adhesive inflammation precedes the suppurative in every par-excepting the outlets, and the suppurative the ulcerative, the propriety of following this order of nature in treating of them will appear evident.

ADHESIVE INFLAMMATION.—If the actions of adhesive inflammation were allowed to extend themselves, it would prove more hurtful than any good that could arise from it; hence there are natural obstructions to its extending, which we shall first consider.

Natural Causes of the limiting of Adhesive Inflammation.—I have already observed that exposure of internal surfaces becomes the immediate cause of inflammation; that when it extends further than the exposed surface it is by continuous sympathy; and that when a whole cavity is wholly exposed, the whole would take on inflammation. We may now observe, that whenever a cavity is opened, the simple contact of its sides, or even the simple contact of these with any other living part, will set bounds to the immediate cause, which is the exposure.

To explain this further, we may observe that there is no such thing in an animal as an empty space in any of the circumscribed cavities of the animal body, exclusive of the outlets or reservoirs, which are imperfect, not being circumscribed. Every other part of an animal is either connected by the cohesion of one part with another, or by simple contact. This holds good too in the cellular membrane as well as the circumscribed cavities; for if a wound is made into either, we find that the surfaces of both, beyond the cut edges, are entire, and generally in contact with one another.

To explain this position, let me instance a case. If we make a wound into the cavity of the belly, in a sound state of those parts we shall find every viscus is in contact with some other viscus, and that the whole inside of the peritoneum is in contact with the viscera, so that no space is unfilled. If this wound is not allowed to heal by the first intention, still we find that no inflammation will take place, or extend further than the attachment of those parts to the cut edges, excepting what is owing to continuous sympathy. If this were not the case, every part of the cavity must inflame, because every part would be equally exposed; and if the contact were removed at the time of receiving the wound, or at any time afterwards, the whole cavity must inflame, every part being in the same predicament as regards exposure.

The same thing would happen in the cellular membrane, if those cells were not in a natural state in contact, and inflammation would as readily extend over the surfaces of each cell as air does when blown into part.

Inflammation, then, takes place at the edges of the exposed parts in order to preserve this contact, as well as to serve as a basis for future operations: and in cases of spontaneous inflammation of circumscribed cavities, we find that where this contact is completest the inflammation and its consequences are the least; as in the belly, in cases of peritoneal inflammation, the inflammation is greatest in the angles between the viscera, where the parts are not so well in contact.

The effect of simple contact, in excluding the irritation from extending, was well illustrated in a woman who had the Cæsarian operation performed. After the child was extracted, the wound could not be brought together well, therefore so far gave rise to peritoneal inflammation; but the belly closing and falling in on its contents, the whole came in contact as before. The woman lived twenty-six hours, which gave time for the inflammation to take place. After death, it was found that the intestines were united to the peritoneum all round the wound, for above half an inch in breadth, and the surface of the intestines, which lay unattached at the bottom of the wound, was inflamed, while every other viscus, as also the peritoneum beyond the adhesions, were free from inflammation.

The adhesive inflammation seems to be nearly of the same nature, whether it arises from the constitution, from a particular disposition of the part, or from some violence inflicted on the part; the final intention being nearly the same in all these cases, for in all it is an effect that has a tendency to repair an injury, as is evidently shown in many cases of violence, though it may not in all. Its utility is most obvious in those cases which arise from the constitution, or from disease in a part. When the adhesive inflammation arises from the constitution, it may be from some disease of that constitution; and, if so, it may be supposed to be of service to it, especially if it should be supposed to be the termination of an universal irritation in a local one, and by that means relieving the constitution of the former, as in gout. But where it is only a simple adhesive inflammation, I am rather apt to think that it is more a part of the disease than an act of the constitution, or termination of the disease. When it proceeds from a disposition in a part, it must be considered to arise from a disease of that part.

Although in all cases and in all parts the adhesive inflammation is not absolutely necessary and preparatory for the suppurative inflammation, yet if it is in the cellular membrane or a circumscribed cavity, then its effects will prove salutary. It may indeed be considered absolutely necessary to prevent greater mischiefs, for very bad consequences would arise without it. The object of it in these parts is to unite the parts together for their future benefit by means of the coagulable lymph and serum thrown out, by which the extension of the suppuration will be limited.

It would appear from observation that some surfaces of the body have a much stronger disposition to throw out coagulable lymph than others; or we may view this effect in another light, that some surfaces of the body do not so readily unite by exudation of the coagulable lymph as others do, and therefore on such surfaces there is commonly a much larger quantity thrown out than probably would have been if union would have readily taken place. Thus we see in inflammations of the heart that the coagulable lymph is thrown out on the external surface in vast quantities, while at the same time the heart shall not adhere to the pericardium. This extravasated matter is always of the same nature with that of the parts which produced it, which is a curious fact. If the disposition of the part is cancerous, the extravasated coagulable lymph is a poison, for on being absorbed it contaminates the absorbent glands, producing cancer; and probably the same takes place in every poison that is capable of irritating to inflammation and extravasation.

Appearances of Adhesive Inflammation.—The part inflamed becomes redder than common, and redder and redder as it advances; the red being of a scarlet hue when the inflammation is healthy. The part becomes apparently more vascular than in a natural state, and most probably is really so, both from new vessels being set up in the old parts, and from the adventitious uniting substance becoming vascular. These new vessels become of use both in the state of adhesion and of suppuration; in the first to give powers of action to this new substance which assist in preventing suppuration, in the second to form a basis for the future granulations. In consequence of this extravasation the parts swell, which is generally in proportion to the inflammation, the swelling being probably most where the inflammation is greatest, that is, at the point of irritation, and it is gradually lost in the surrounding parts. The whole swelling appears like a part of the body a little changed, without containing any extraneous matter, and indeed is simply formed by extravasation of fluids, without their having undergone any material visible change.

Such inflammations as approach to the skin often produce vesications, which are filled with serum and often coagulable lymph, both which are sometimes tinged with red blood. This arises from the violence of the inflammation producing an apparent degree of weakness, approaching to a death, in the connexions between the cuticle and cutis, the life being in this part very weak, for in the beginning of mortification and of the putrefaction of dead bodies it is produced. This connexion of the cuticle is more or less destroyed in every inflammation of the skin. We seldom see an inflammation attack the skin but the cuticle comes off sooner or later. We generally observe it peeling off in flakes after the inflammation has subsided.

The pain attending inflammation would not appear to be in all cases very acute, for many have very visible inflammations which do not give very much pain. However, this will vary according to the violence of the inflammation, or rather according to the quickness of its progress and its approach to suppuration ; for when there is a quick dilatation of the vessels, and rapid extravasation of the juices, the sensations arising from such will be increased ; but in cases where its progress is slow, as from indolent tumours, the mind is hardly sensible of its progress. That it must sometimes be very trifling is shown by the fact that on opening dead bodies we often find strong adhesions where the friends of these persons had never heard during life of a single complaint. We also see cases in which this inflammation arises from violence, where it gives very little pain. A man shall be shot through the abdomen, and, if none of the contained parts are materially hurt, the adhesive inflammation shall take place in all the internal parts contiguous to the wound, yet no degree of pain is felt from this process. In many bruises and in simple fractures the pain from the inflammation is very trifling, although there may be much laceration of the parts*.

---

* [Redness, heat, pain, and swelling may each of them exist independently of inflammation; and when they arise from inflammation, they may exist in every possible relative proportion among themselves. In judging, therefore, of the presence or degree of inflammation, it is necessary to look at the whole symptoms collectively. The *redness* and *heat* are generally in proportion to the original vascularity of the part conjoined with the momentum of the circulation; the *pain* is greater in proportion to the denseness and inextensibility of the inflamed part, added to the acuteness of the attack and the quantity of nervous supply ; the *swelling* is generally greatest where the reverse of these circumstances exists. Structure, however, is not the only circumstance which modifies these symptoms; they depend greatly on the specific nature of the inflammation: the sting of a wasp produces infinitely more pain and swelling than an attack of erysipelas.]

Of the Uses of Adhesive Inflammation.—This inflammation may be said to arise in all cases from a state of the parts which they cannot remain in; therefore an irritation of imperfection takes place. It may be looked on as the effect of wise counsels proceeding from a consciousness of imperfection: nature is taking all the defensive precautions possible, for in all cases we shall evidently see it answer wise purposes, such as checking the suppurative inflammation, by making parts adhere which must otherwise fall into that state; and where this effect does not fully take place, it acts as a check to the extent of it, as we see in circumscribed cavities. In the tunica vaginalis, after the operation for hydrocele, the parts often collapse and unite to other parts of the same sac by adhesive inflammation, which prevents the suppuration extending over the sac, so that partial collections of water again take place *. In still larger cavities, as the abdomen, where partial inflammations often take place, as after child-bearing or wounds of this cavity, we find this adhesion takes place, which either prevents suppuration altogether or unites the parts around it, and as the abscess enlarges the adhesive inflammation spreads, and thus excludes the general cavity. The same thing happens in inflammation of the pleura or surface of the lung. The cellular membrane everywhere in the body is united exactly in the same manner; the sides of the cells, as it were, sweat out the uniting matter, which, coming into contact with the opposite surfaces, joins them into one mass.

The lungs are subject to two modes of action in inflammation; being so circumstanced as to partake of the character of both orders of parts, the circumscribed cavity, and the secreting surface or outlet. The cellular membrane of the lungs readily admits of adhesive inflammation, like the cellular tissue elsewhere; but the inner surface of the air-cells, like the urethra, passes directly into the suppurative inflammation, and the matter which is thus formed is obliged to be coughed up. It is, perhaps, impossible to produce inflammation of the one without the other, which is, perhaps, the reason why inflammation of these parts is treated with such bad success.

We cannot give a better illustration of the use of the adhesions arising in consequence of this inflammation than to contrast it with the erysipelatous. How far this disease is to be ranked amongst inflammations I will not at present say; but it has some of the character., as swelling, redness, pain, &c. The swelling arises, not from extravasation of coagulable lymph, but from serum: and it has other pe-

---

* [The old operation is here referred to, in which the tunica vaginalis was exposed by incision, and suffered to suppurate.]

culiarities, as being generally superficial, andspreading along the surface with an abrupt edge, which is, perhaps, owing to its specific character being always confined to the part affected. It has nothing of the adhesive character attending it which was not necessary; because this inflammation, being confined to the skin, seldom produces suppuration. But it sometimes happens, when erysipelatous inflammation attacks deeper-seated parts, that it suppurates; and when it does so, it appears often to be a forerunner of mortification.

A man was attacked with an inflammation on each side of the anus. It had such an appearance as might have been expected from the suppurative and erysipelatous inflammations joined: it had an œdematous appearance. He was bled, and the blood appeared very sizy: he took physic, and was fomented. The next day the inflammation had reached the scrotum, where a fluctuation, with a gurgling of air, was felt. I now made an opening near the rectum, and in the scrotum, and let out a quantity of dirty-coloured matter. It continued to spread over the loins, scrotum, bottom of the abdomen, &c., where I made openings, and out of which the cellular membrane hung like wet tow. In this case, the suppuration was diffused for want of the adhesive process preceding or accompanying it, by which means it would have been limited.

Adhesive Inflammation sometimes imperfect.—Sometimes it happens that the adhesive inflammation is so imperfect that it cannot set bounds to itself, and still less to the suppurative. This may be owing to two causes; first, the violence of the inflammation and quickness with which suppuration ensues, that is, before the parts have sufficiently united; secondly, the inflammation may be, as I suspect it is, of the erysipelatous kind, especially when there is a tendency from the beginning to mortification. This mixture of the suppurative with the adhesive, or hurrying on of the suppurative, I have often seen in the abdomen of women who have been attacked with peritoneal inflammation after childbirth; and when these circumstances become the cause of death, we find matter mixed with coagulable lymph, as if formed together.

The adhesive inflammation also takes place in cases where it is impossible it should produce the same good effects; as in wounds which are not allowed to heal by the first intention, as a stump after amputation, and many other parts. But it is one of those fixed and invariable principles of the animal machine, that, on all such irritations, the uniting process should be produced, although, like many other principles in the same machine, it cannot always produce the same salutary effects. So that although the wound is not allowed to, or cannot, heal by the adhesive inflammation, yet the parts go through the common actions consequent upon being wounded; first, they throw out blood, as if to unite the parts by the first intention; and then, the vessels contracting themselves, coagulable lymph, with serum, is thrown out, which has the effect, even in such wounds, of preventing a great extension of the inflammation, while the contraction of the vessels prevents the inflammation from running along their inner surfaces*.

Effects of Adhesive Inflammation on the Constitution.—These effects are very slight, even when the inflammation arises from violence; but the effects of those inflammations which are indolent in their progress are still more trifling in the constitution. This arises from the slowness of the alteration produced in the part, as it were, insensibly stealing on the constitution.

We know that one effect of adhesive inflammation is the uniting of parts not intended by Nature to be united, and which must thus be made less moveable on one another; in fact, they must at first have little or no motion on one another, as occurs in the cellular membrane and circumscribed cavities: but it happens that motion is again obtained after a time by the elongation of the connecting part, which is effected by the repeated endeavours for motion. These uniting media are seen to become vascular. They are perhaps often the cause of many indescribable sensations, which cannot be called pain. In the heart they are the cause of palpitation, &c.

On the Resolution of Inflammation.—Since an animal body can be made to act improperly by impression, we can see no reason why, when acting improperly according to such impressions, it should not be made to act properly by the same mode, namely, by impression.

The cure of inflammation is resolution, and an attempt towards it, when in the adhesive state (for this is intended to prevent suppuration taking place), must be in general made only under the following circumstances, namely, when inflammation arises constitutionally, or from disease of the part. In cases of accident where there is no exposure, as also where there is, but that exposure is removed in time by bringing the parts into contact, and where the life of the parts has not been destroyed, in all such cases we find that resolution will readily take place.

It is commonly supposed that there are a great many local inflam-

---

* [One of the most remarkable good effects of the adhesive inflammation consists in the gluing of parts together previously to the discharge of hurtful matters from the body, as gall-stones, fæces, urine, &c., which are frequently discharged in this way; the ulcerative and adhesive processes proceeding *pari passu* to effect the discharge, at the same time that the latter always keeps a little ahead of the former. If it were not for this beautiful provision of Nature, the great cavities of the body would frequently be exposed to fatal inflammations from such causes.]

mations which should not be resolved. An inflammation arising from a preceding indisposition in the constitution, commonly called critical, has always been classed amongst those which are not to be resolved; it has been insisted on that the inflammation should rather be encouraged, and suppuration produced. But in such treatment it is always under the idea that the inflammation is in such parts as will readily admit of cure when suppuration takes place; for if the disease is otherwise situated, the cure of the constitution by suppuration will be a mode of cure which will reflect back another disease on the constitution, under which it will sink; therefore resolution in such situations should, if possible, be brought about. Many deep-seated inflammations, if allowed to suppurate, will, of themselves, most certainly kill: gout also, in the head or stomach, should always be resolved, and left to settle in some other part less connected with life. If inflammation is really a concentration of the constitutional complaint, and if, by not allowing it to rest there, the same disposition would really be diffused over the whole animal again, and would be liable to affect some other more important part, it would certainly be better to encourage it when in a proper part. Still it does not appear necessary that it should suppurate, for suppuration is only a consequence of inflammation; not an immediate effect of the original constitutional disease, but a secondary one. As suppuration, therefore, is only a thing superadded, and as we shall generally find that inflammation subsides as suppuration comes on, I see no reason why inflammation should not in the present case as well subside by resolution as by suppuration. It may, however, be supposed, that as this suppuration is not a natural or immediate effect of the disease, yet as it is a continued local action, that it is capable of diverting the disease to the part. I hardly know an instance where inflammation from violence may not with propriety be resolved, and prevented from going into suppuration, except where it relieves the constitution from any prior disease. Thus, Mr. Foote was cured of a violent pain in his head by amputation of his leg; but he afterwards died with a different complaint in his head. Might not the first diseased action in the head be altered in this case, and an action of a different kind induced, which proceeded to the degree of effecting his death?

Of the Resolution of Inflammation by Constitutional means.—If the inflammation is of the true adhesive kind, the only thing to be done is to lessen everything that has a tendency to keep it up, because we know of no method that will entirely quiet or remove the inflammatory disposition, or mode of action*; there is no specific against inflammation

---

* [Mercury and colchicum are perhaps exceptions to this observation; at least they certainly subdue inflammatory action with extraordinary rapidity in many cases.]

that we are acquainted with. Whatever will lessen the power or disposition will lessen the effect.

There appear to be three methods which tend to remove inflammation: first, by weakening; secondly, by producing temporary weakness; thirdly, by lessening or soothing the irritability.

That which absolutely weakens is bleeding, purging, quietude, and low diet. The temporary weakness is produced by sickness at the stomach, faintness, &c. The soothing effect may be produced by sedatives, antispasmodics, &c., such as many sudorifics, anodynes, &c. The first will have the greatest, most immediate, and most lasting effects; the second and third act as auxiliaries; the second probably will come nearest to lessening the cause, while the other will assist so far as irritation is a cause; they should go hand in hand, for wherever we lessen the power we should at the same time lessen the disposition for action. But neither bleeding, sickness, nor purging can possibly lessen the original inflammatory disposition*: by lessening the power of action of any disposition you only lessen or protract the effects, which, however, will be of singular service, as less mischief will be done, and will often give the disposition time to wear itself out.

Bleeding, then, at first may be necessary; but this must be done with some restriction. If inflammation arises from real powers, then bleeding freely is absolutely necessary; but if from too great action of weak parts, bleeding should be no more than what will just lessen the violence of the blood's motion, or remove the feeling in the part inflamed of too much to do. The quantity, therefore, must be according to the symptoms and other circumstances, that is, according to the visible indications. The indication for bleeding is, first, according to the violence of the inflammation, joined with the strength of the constitution; secondly, according to the disposition to form blood; thirdly, whether the disease is in a vital part; fourthly, its situation, whether near the heart or not; fifthly, according to the duration and the extent to which it has affected the constitution†.

---

* [In this instance the author has allowed reasoning and hypothesis to usurp the place of observation and fact. It is certainly not uncommon to witness the almost complete destruction of an inflammatory attack by a single copious venesection.]

† [The propriety of bloodletting is indicated by many other circumstances besides those pointed out in the text. I shall only mention three of these at present: the *first* arises from the structure of the part affected. Thus, serous and fibrous membranes require and bear venesection to an extent which would be perfectly unwarrantable in regard to mucous membranes. The *second* arises from the probable demands which will be made on the constitution during the future progress of the case. It would be extremely imprudent, for example, to bleed a patient with a severe compound fracture to the same extent which would be perfectly justifiable in inflammation of the eye. The *third* is derived from the act of venesection itself, as whether the blood flows freely and the state of syncope is easily induced; for it has been justly remarked that those

With respect to the first kind, in which the constitution is strong and the inflammation is violent, bleeding largely is proper, and in many cases bleeding near the part will answer better than from the general habit; less may be taken away in this way with an equal effect on the part inflamed, and of course with less effect on the constitution, as bleeding from the temporal artery, or the jugular vein, for complaints of the brain, or cupping or applying leeches near the part, as, for example, to the temples in inflammation of the eyes.

The same mode of practice is to be followed with regard to the second, third, fourth, and fifth. It seldom happens that one bleeding will be sufficient in a considerable inflammation. The first blood taken affords a symptom of the disease; if it is buffy, thick, and considerably cupped, future bleedings may be used with less caution. On the other hand, there may be indications for bleeding sparingly; first, from there being too much action with weakened power; secondly, from a disposition to form little blood; thirdly, from the part being far from the source of the circulation.

A gentleman had a violent inflammation of the eye; the blood was sizy, but though sizy the coat was exceedingly tender, and so slight as not to bear its own weight when raised up. He was blooded plentifully several times, without any good. Here was not, then, much power, the blood putting on the sizy appearance in consequence of there being increased action in the vessels of this part of the body.

A lady with inflammation of the tonsils was blooded; the blood was sizy, but loose; and after three bleedings the blood became so loose that the bark was given, which did service. The disorder returned again, and the same mode was used; the blood was sizy only in the first bleeding: the bark was obliged to be again given.

In such cases bleeding is very seldom necessary. Where it is necessary, it should be as near the part as possible, in order that it may have the greatest effect on the part with the least damage to the constitution. If local bleeding be used, leeches will answer best, because but little inflammation follows their bite*; however, this can only be put in practice in inflammations which are pretty much external. In many cases

---

inflammations which most require venesection *support* the constitution under considerable losses of blood, and enable it to bear them much more easily than it could have done in a state of health. In most cases of acute inflammation it is advisable to take such quantities of blood at first as shall make a decided impression on the constitution; one effectual bleeding being of infinitely more service in checking the disease than a number of successive bleedings to a smaller amount, at the same time that the powers of the general system are much less reduced.]

* [Cupping will generally be found more effectual where it is practicable, on account of the blood being more rapidly removed.]

we cannot take it immediately from the part, and must be content to go as near as we can, as in bleeding from the temporal artery or jugular vein, in affections of the head. Sometimes of course even this will be impossible, as in inflammations of the liver and stomach.

Too much action with small powers may often, if not always, be classed with the irritable, and bleeding here should be performed with very great caution. When inflammation is far from the source of the circulation the same precaution is hardly necessary, as in general it can be taken away from the part.

We cannot depend on sizy blood alone as a proof of the propriety of repeating the bleeding; we must take into consideration also the strength of action.

The pulse is a great indication for bleeding in inflammation, but is not always to be relied on. In inflammations that are visible, the knowledge of the kind of inflammation is in some degree ascertained, in which cases it has been supposed that we go on surer grounds in our indications for bleeding. But all inflammations are not visible; therefore we require some other criterion. If we could ascertain the pulse peculiar to certain appearances in visible inflammations, and were sure that universally the same pulse attended such appearances, we should then suppose we had the true indicative criterion to go by, and be able to apply it to invisible inflammations, and judge of these by the pulse. But when we consider that the same kind of inflammations in every part of the body will not produce the same kind of pulse, but very different pulses, not according to the inflammation, but according to the nature of the parts inflamed, and many of these parts are invisible, we see that we at once lose the criterion of the pulse as a guide. There may be every symptom of inflammation and the pulse be soft, and not quicker than usual, and yet the blood when taken away will be sizy and cupped.

A lady had this kind of pulse (soft and not quick), and at the same time had a violent cough, with tightness of the chest and stitches in the side; bleeding was ordered, when the blood was found sizy, &c.; nor did the illness subside till the sixth bleeding.

A hard quick pulse is generally an indication for bleeding, being frequently accompanied with sizy blood; but even these signs are not always to be depended on as furnishing a criterion. The kind of blood is of consequence to be known, for although it should be sizy, if it is not firm in its texture, but lies squat in the dish, bleeding must be performed very sparingly.

As the pulse simply, independently of all other considerations, is not an absolute criterion to go by, and as a sizy and strong coagulum is only an afterproof, let us see if there are any collateral circumstances that can throw some light on this subject, so as to enable us to judge, *à priori*, whether it is right to bleed where the pulse does not of itself indicate it.

When speaking of inflammation of various parts, I took notice of the pulse peculiar to each part, which I may now be allowed to repeat. First, I observed in inflammation of parts not vital, or such as the stomach did not sympathize with, that if there was great power and not much irritability, the pulse was full, frequent, and hard. Secondly, on the contrary, in inflammations of the same parts, if the constitution was weak, irritable, &c., that then the pulse was small, frequent, and hard, although, perhaps, not so much so as when, thirdly, the inflammation is in a vital part, as the stomach or intestines, or some part with which the stomach readily sympathizes ; then the pulse is quick, small, and hard.

Now in the first of these dispositions bleeding is absolutely necessary ; but in the second, where the pulse is small and frequent, bleeding should be performed with great caution : though the person may be of strong constitution, yet in inflammations of these parts the constitution appears to be more irritable, and to have a greater sense of weakness. We should bleed to two or three ounces by way of trial, which could do no harm.

The urine will throw some light on the disease ; if high-coloured, and not much in quantity, it may be presumed, with the other symptoms, that bleeding will be of singular service ; but if pale and copious, though the other indications may be strong for bleeding, it may be necessary to do it with caution.

Bleeding, however, is a remedy of so much importance that it should be employed in all cases with great caution ; yet not more than appears really necessary.

I cannot perceive why bleeding should have such an effect on inflammation as it often has. We cannot account for it simply on the mechanical principle of lessening the quantity of blood, because this can never remove the *cause* of inflammation.

Medicines.—Medicines which have the power of producing sickness lessen the powers of life universally, because every part of the body sympathizes with the stomach ; and when they are intended to produce this effect they should not be given in doses sufficient to produce anything more than sickness, for the act of vomiting is rather a counteraction to that effect, and I believe has rather the effect of rousing, as few are so weak as not to be able to bear sickness. Purges have been much recommended, under the idea that there were humours to be carried off ; such practice answers best in the cases in which bleeding is useful. In irritable habits, where inflammation becomes more diffused, greater caution is necessary, as nothing tends to weaken the habit more. A single purge has been known to produce death in dropsy. In such cases bark may be required to bring the constitution into a proper state, either for resolution or suppuration, by increasing the powers and diminishing the action; and thebaica may be a good assistant as a soother or sedative with the bark.

Modes of Resolution by external applications.—Whether we have any external applications which have really a tendency to resolve an inflammatory disposition, is not well ascertained. We are in possession of many that can weaken, so as to lessen the powers, (most of which appear to be of the soothing kind,) and thus lessen the action, though the cause may still exist; by which means the effects are lessened, and the inflammation is either cured or protracted, until the disposition wears itself out. Perhaps cold is one of the greatest weakeners, but it should not be used too freely, as it may produce a worse disease, which is indolence. Lead is supposed to have considerable effects in this way; but I believe much more is ascribed to it than it deserves. Its properties appear to be to lessen the powers, and therefore it should not be used except when the powers are too strong. Applications to weaken should not be applied to irritable parts; on the contrary, the parts should be strengthened, which can only be done through the constitution.

Whatever power external applications possess, they must act in one of four ways: first, which is the immediate or truly local; second, by repulsion; third, by revulsion and derivation; fourth, by sympathy, which is probably the same principle in the animal œconomy as revulsion and derivation.

The first, or local effect, may be of two kinds: 1st, simply such as is an antidote to the action of the part, as cold, sedatives; 2nd, such as destroys the first irritation, by exciting a second. This is most applicable to specific diseases, as the action of mercury in a venereal sore: but all specific diseases will not allow of it; a gonorrhœa in a scrofulous habit is an instance of this. In some cutaneous affections this mode of cure is very useful. Sedatives are less useful as local applications than counter-irritants, but both of them may have another effect, viz. repulsion or derivation, which must be from a constitutional affection, such as I have called an act of the constitution, as in gout. If the constitution is determined to have a local complaint, by which she throws off a constitutional disposition, then these revulsions do not rid the constitution of the disposition. It is difficult to say what will merely repel and what will cure. Repulsion, however, is a cure of the part, whatever effect it may have on the constitution. Surgeons were formerly greatly afraid respecting repulsion. They were even afraid of curing a gonorrhœa, lest they should drive it back into the constitution and produce a pox; but they did not consider that it does not arise from the constitution, and has nothing to do with it.

Revulsion and derivation appear to me to depend on the same principle in the constitution as sympathy, and, like the latter, have the greatest effect in habits which are irritable or nervous, and in diseases which are nervous, as cramp; not in such as change the structure of parts. I knew a nervous girl cured of pain in one arm by rubbing the other. These terms were used under the idea of removing humours by inviting them from other parts, as making an issue to remove eruptions. They probably act by causing an irritation in one part to cease when an irritation in another is excited; and this latter may be made greater than the original one, though in a part less dangerous, and where it can be more easily cured, as burning the ear cures the tooth-ache; vomiting, the swelled testicle; blisters, pleurisy, &c. In some of these, as the vomiting to cure the testicle, no new disease is excited, but only the action of the part. The cures performed by these modes are in many cases preferable to those by means of local applications, and they will succeed where the others fail; thus, vomiting will cure hernia humoralis, when other applications have had no effect. The cure by revulsion, or sympathy, is in some respects the reverse of that by derivation, yet it is probably from the same consent of parts, but from a different action. In these a remedy is applied to a sound part to cure a diseased, which is either contiguous, continuous, or remote, and the action is either similar or dissimilar. The cure of continuous parts by similar sympathy is by the application of such remedies as we suppose would cure if applied to the part. That of remote parts by dissimilar modes of action, is by stimulating a part in such a way as that the sympathy shall act in the same way, and yet the action in the diseased part be not at all similar to that in the sound part: suppose, for instance, a part in any mode of action, a medicine applied to it would increase that action, but by applying it to another part it will remove the first. The contiguous is different from the two former, and can only be applied to surfaces, as a blister to the scalp to remove headache. These may be either stimulating, or soothing, or specific.

Treatment of Adhesive Inflammation when Suppuration must take place.
—The treatment must, in some measure, be the same as in the foregoing in accidents where the powers are very great, and the inflammation violent, namely, bleeding, purging, sickness, &c.; but when the constitution is irritable, bark, &c., as before directed. In cases where there is considerable sympathy, sudorifics, as Dover's powder, seem de-

sirable, as they tend to keep up the harmony between the skin and the stomach. Opium in peculiar constitutions increases irritability; but in others, where there is not this peculiarity, it is highly useful in soothing and diminishing irritability.

Different applications have been made to the inflamed parts, as fomentation, washes, poultices, &c. The mode of applying heat and moisture by fomentation appears more efficacious than in the form of a fluid; it certainly gives ease at the time of the application, but the symptoms generally recur between the times of using it, and with nearly the same violence. How far the application of a medicine for fifteen minutes out of the twenty-four hours does good, I hardly know.

Washes are fluid applications, and are more commonly used to inflamed internal surfaces than to the common integuments. I am afraid we are not much acquainted with their true specific virtues, the use of them being very vague. For inflammation of the eyes we use astringents, as alum, vitriol, &c. For inflammations of the throat we gargle with port wine, vinegar, &c.; yet how absurd it would be, in the opinion of any surgeon, to use the latter applications to the eyes; and yet if the two inflammations are the same I do not see why we should not use the same remedies to both parts. These, like the former, have only temporary effects.

Poultices are constant applications, and may be either simple or medicated; their effect is greatest locally, but it extends likewise to surrounding parts, by sympathy. They may be medicated with lead, opium, &c. Simple poultices are the best application where we have no particular object in view.

CHAPTER XIV.

OF SUPPURATIVE AND ULCERATIVE INFLAMMATION; GRA-NULATION, SKINNING, HECTIC FEVER, AND DISSOLUTION.

Suppurative inflammation ;—difficulty of tracing the chain of causes leading to it ;—not arising from the access of air ;—nor from external violence ; —occurs most readily in canals.—Peculiar pain attending it ;—rigor ;— diminution of the inflammation.—Cure of suppurated parts ;—abstraction of matter by absorption, or by external opening ;—granulation ;— cicatrization.—Of pus ;—its formation ;—gradual changes from lymph to pus ;—breach of substance not necessary to its existence ;—erroneous notions of its formation and uses.— Of absorption of the whole or parts of the body, in consequence of disease.—Interstitial and progressive absorption.—Interstitial of two kinds;—1st, wasting ;—2nd, complete removal.—Importance of the latter ;—and of progressive absorption.—The two sometimes mixed.—New parts most subject to be removed.—Causes which render parts liable to absorption.—Relaxing process of the skin over an abscess.—Absorption with or without suppuration ;—Ulceration ;—progressive and interstitial absorption combined ;—almost always accompanied by inflammation ;—seldom affects the constitution.—Whitlow.—Granulation ;—not always attended with suppuration ;—does not appear till abscess has been opened ;—arises on one surface ;—nature and structure of granulations ;—colour an index of the state of the parts and constitution ;—contraction of granulations ;—followed by cicatrization ; —an assistance to this process.—Of skinning.—New skin generally arising from old skin ;—œconomy of nature in forming new skin.— Hectic ;—when arising ; causes numerous ;—symptoms ;—erroneous notion of cause.—Treatment ;—incurable ;—when from local disease in removeable parts, they are to be removed.—Dissolution, definition of the term ;—when occurring ;—symptoms ;—incurable.

WHEN an inflammation exceeds the adhesive state, and has got beyond the power of resolution, and when the adhesive has set bounds to the suppurative inflammation, the suppurative begins ; or in internal surfaces, where the adhesive cannot take place, the suppurative begins. The irritation which is the immediate cause of suppuration is the same, from whatever cause it may have been produced : it is a similar process, going through the same stages, whether it takes its rise from external violence, or from the constitution, or from disposition for disease in a part, if all other circumstances are equal. It is very difficult to give a true and clear idea of the whole chain of causes which lead to suppuration. Irritation simply is not always sufficient; it often only brings on the adhesive inflammation. Violence done to a part is one of the great causes of suppuration, but this alone is not sufficient: it must be with a prevention of union by the first intention, or by adhesive inflammation; it must be attended with death in the part, as in bruises. The application of air to internal surfaces has generally been assigned as a cause of inflammation, when it happened in consequence of destruction of a part; but air has certainly no such effect, for a stimulus would arise from a wound were it even contained in a vacuum; nor does it get to the parts forming circumscribed abscesses, which yet suppurate, in consequence of inflammation, as readily as exposed surfaces. In many cases of emphysema, where the air is diffused over the whole body, we have no such effect, excepting there is produced an exposure of some internal surface for the air to make its escape by, and then the wound inflames. In birds we find the cells in their bones communicating with the lungs, so that they have at all times more or less air in them, although they never inflame; but if these are exposed by a wound, the stimulus of imperfection is given, and inflammation begins, and suppuration may succeed. The same observation is applicable to a wound made in the abdomen of a fowl, for there the wound inflames and unites the intestines, to make the cavity perfect again; but if the union is not allowed to take place, more or less of the abdomen will inflame and suppurate. How should we account also for suppuration taking place in the nose during catarrh, since it is not more exposed to air then than at other times? Air, therefore, is not the cause of suppuration.

We are at a loss to say, with regard to spontaneous inflammation, whether it is a disease in which the constitution will be injured, or whether it is a salutary process in which Nature is endeavouring to relieve herself; and it is evident that the same action may arise from different causes.

Suppuration does not depend on the violence of the inflammation; for that circumstance, simply considered, rather tends to produce mortification; and we see that in gout, which does not suppurate, there often is more violent inflammation than in many other cases that do; and in true scrofula we have suppuration without any visible inflammation: so that this does not seem essential to suppuration. Although we find that inflammation and suppuration from injury are very violent, yet that which occurs spontaneously generally exceeds it in violence. In inflam-

mations of the breasts in women and of the testicles in men, the quicker
the inflammation proceeds the better; for where it is slow it gives the
idea of specific inflammation, as this generally proceeds slower than
simple inflammation.

Suppuration takes place more readily from the surface of canals than
in either the cellular or investing membranes; the same degree of inflammation which will produce suppurative in the first-mentioned parts
will only produce adhesive in the latter. If a bougie be introduced into
the urethra, it may produce suppuration; but if introduced into the tunica vaginalis or abdomen, it will only give a disposition for adhesions.

Symptoms of suppurative Inflammation.—The sensations arising from
a disease generally convey some idea of its nature. Some diseases give
what is called a heavy, a dull, or a gnawing pain, &c.; but the suppurative inflammation gives as much as possible the idea of simple pain,
without having relation to any other mode of sensation: this pain is
increased at the time of the dilatation of the arteries with the sensation
called throbbing.   The part now becomes more swelled by the greater
dilatation of the vessels and a greater quantity of extravasated fluid
being poured out, and the scarlet colour increases from the admission
of red globules into vessels not naturally conveying them and the formation of new vessels, and an œdematous appearance, like that in erysipelas, takes place.   One, two, or three parts of the inflammation lose
the power of resolution, and take on exactly the same disposition with
that of exposed surfaces, or a surface in contact with an extraneous
body. If it is in the cellular membrane that this disposition takes place,
or in the investing membrane of circumscribed cavities, the vessels
now begin to alter their disposition and mode of action, and continue
changing till they bring themselves to that state which fits them to form
matter. But as this change does not take place all at once, some parts
may for some time continue to discharge coagulable lymph, as in the
adhesive state, whilst those parts which have taken on the suppurative
action pour out matter; and hence, if the tumour be now opened, it
will be found to contain both matter and coagulable lymph: in which
state it has always been imagined that the matter had not arrived at a
state of ripeness by those who supposed its purulence to depend on its
confinement and stay.   It would appear, from matter forming from the
investing membranes of internal cavities and from mucous surfaces, that
matter may be formed without any breach of surface.

There is a certain period in inflammation when suppuration begins,
and which is discovered by new symptoms, as shivering, &c.; and though
the change is pretty quick, time must be allowed for the vessels to be
fitted for the suppurative state. The effect of inflammation seems to be

the producing the suppurative disposition, or that state of parts which disposes them to secrete pus : in doing this, inflammation seems to be carried to such a length as to destroy that state of parts on which itself depends ; the consequence of which is that they lose the inflammatory and come into that disposition which fits them for throwing out matter. That the suppurative is very different from the adhesive inflammation is plain from this, that if a wound in a suppurative state, yielding good matter, has by irritation of any kind the adhesive inflammation produced in it to any degree, the discharge lessens, and the wound puts on appearances very different from what it had before. It seems a fixed and useful law in the animal œconomy, that when inflammation has gone to the length of destroying the natural functions of parts, so as to prevent their returning by a retrograde motion to that state from which they set out, suppuration should come on to give them a disposition for a second mode of cure.

Treatment of Suppuration.—Suppuration may sometimes be removed by producing action in other parts ; thus, I have seen a bubo cured by a vomit, and similar effects are producible on scrofulous tumours. When suppuration cannot be stopped or resolved, in most cases it is to be hurried on towards the skin, which generally is the first step taken by surgeons.   How far suppuration can be increased by medicines or applications I do not know, but attempts are generally made ; hence we have I think, in the pharmacopœia, (though I do not read many books,) suppurating cataplasms, maturating, &c., but I doubt if they have considerable effect in this way, for the same applications applied to a sore would hardly increase the discharge of that sore.   However, in cases where the parts are indolent, and hardly admit of suppuration, by stimulating the skin more salutary inflammation may be produced, and of course quicker suppuration ; but with true suppuration, preceded by inflammation, it is I believe hardly necessary to do anything with respect to the suppuration itself.   Nevertheless it has perhaps been found by experience that these applications tend to bring matter faster to the skin, even in the rapid suppurations ; only, however, in those cases where the inner surface of the abscess is within the influence of the skin.   This effect, too, may arise from another mode of action being produced than that of quicker suppuration, which is the hastening of an ulceration. Poultices of bread and milk are commonly used to inflamed parts when suppuration is known to have taken place : this application can have no effect, except that of lessening the inflammation, or rather making the skin easy*.

* [The immediate effects of poultices and fomentations to inflamed parts are, 1st, to soothe the pain and irritation ; 2nd, to augment the local perspiration ; and, 3rd, to

Of Suppuration without Inflammation.—I have hinted that thickening of parts took place sometimes without inflammation, and also that the suppurative inflammation might take place without being preceded by the adhesive. Many indolent tumours, slow swellings of the joints, swellings in the lymphatic glands, tubercles in the lungs, and swellings in many parts of the body, are of the first kind, namely, thickening without visible inflammation; and the contents of some kind of encysted tumours, the matter of many scrofulous suppurations, as in the lymphatic glands, and in the joints of the foot and hand, for instance, and in the hip-joint, called hip cases, of the loins, called lumbar abscess, the suppuration of tubercles in the lungs and in many other parts of the body, all exhibit the formation of matter without any previous visible inflammation. They come on insensibly, the first symptom being a swelling in consequence of the thickening, (which is not the case in inflammation, for there sensation is the first symptom,) and this swelling is increased by the formation of matter*.

The nature of the matter is another distinguishing mark between suppuration in consequence of inflammation and that without it, the latter being generally composed of a curdly substance mixed with matter. The curdly matter is, we may suppose, the coagulable lymph deprived of serum, the thinner part is true pus, having the globules and specific properties of pus, and is often as thick as the common pus formed in consequence of inflammation.

All parts which form pus of any kind, whether in consequence of inflammation or otherwise, must go through similar processes to produce the ultimate effect or cure. The first step, in either case, is the evacuation of this matter, for till that is effected nature cannot take means towards a cure; the second step is granulation; the third, cicatrization.

There are three modes of doing the first; one is the absorption of matter, which is very common in the scrofulous kind, but not in those

---

diminish the tension. The addition of sedatives and narcotics certainly increases their soothing effects, and their continued application certainly promotes the suppurative process.]

* [Those singular deposits of purulent matter which occur in the joints, the serous cavities, the viscera, and the cellular membrane, during the progress of phlebitis and secondary inflammations, are examples of the same kind. I have, on several occasions, found all the principal joints of the body filled with an apparently healthy pus, although during life there were no symptoms of inflammation, nor after death any indications of increased vascularity.

The question, therefore arises, Does suppuration ever occur independently of inflammation? I think it does. The formation of cartilage antecedently to that of bone is a parallel case, and yet instances every now and then occur in which ossific depositions are formed independently of this condition.]

suppurations which are the consequences of inflammation, and which produces no alteration of the part except the gradually creeping into a sound state; the other modes of discharging this matter are, either opening the abscess, to allow it to pass out, or allowing ulceration to take place on the inside to produce its escape; which process, in the present case, having peculiarities different from those arising from inflammation, it is necessary to explain still further.

Ulceration in consequence of suppuration arising from inflammation, is very rapid, especially if the suppuration is very rapid; but ulceration in consequence of suppuration not the effect of inflammation, is extremely slow: it may remain months or even years before the parts give way.

When an abscess in consequence of inflammation is opened, it immediately proceeds towards a cure, and perhaps may have gone some steps towards a cure before the opening. As inflammation lessens, suppuration becomes still more perfect, granulations begin to form, &c. But when an abscess not preceded by the common inflammation is opened, a very different process is first to take place; the consequence is, that inflammation now takes place over the whole cavity of the abscess, which afterwards produces perfect matter, like that produced when inflammation is the original disease. However, it sometimes happens that they inflame before they are opened, in consequence of the matter distending the cavity acting like an extraneous body, not in consequence of the cause of suppuration. I have seen white swellings of the knee inflame before they were opened, then ulceration took place, and the pus was brought soon to the skin, though before it had been for months without producing the least tendency to ulceration, and of course none to inflammation; but the confinement of matter became the cause of inflammation. The inflammation and new suppuration taking place in consequence of an opening into these abscesses, is exactly similar to those inflammations and suppurations which take place in consequence of an opening made into internal cavities; and it is extraordinary that often upon opening these swellings, inflammation, fever, nay death shall follow, but if suffered to break of themselves no such effect is produced.

Of Pus.—The immediate effect of the modes of action above described is the formation of matter commonly termed pus. This matter is very different from what was discharged during the adhesive stage of inflammation, and also very different from the common secretion of internal canals; yet when these surfaces form pus it is probable they are formed by the same vessels: if so, their mode of action must be greatly altered.

In suppuration of the cellular membrane or of circumscribed cavities their vessels are but little changed at the commencement of the suppurative disposition, so that they still retain much of the form they acquired by the first stage. The discharge is at the beginning little more than coagulable lymph mixed with some serum; this is scarce different from the discharge in the adhesive stage of the inflammations: but as the inflammatory disposition subsides, a new disposition is every instant altering these vessels to the suppurative stage; the discharge is also varying constantly from a species of extravasation to the new-formed matter peculiar to suppuration. The matter removes further and further from the nature of blood, losing the yellowish or greenish hue, and becoming white, and more viscid and creamy. By the formation of this new substance, the coagulable lymph, which was extravasated in the adhesive state, and adhered to the sides of the cells, either on cut surfaces, as wounds, or on the walls of abscesses, is pushed off, and if there is a cavity, is pushed into it, so that we should find in the cavity both coagulable lymph and pus; or, if on a cut surface, it is thrown off, and is generally removed, along with extravasated blood, &c., with the dressings.

This is the process which takes place in the first formation of pus in an abscess, or from the surface of fresh wounds.

On the internal surface of canals the parts are not obliged to go through all these steps; they run into suppuration almost instantaneously.

Mode of Formation of Pus.—Pus is formed by some change, decomposition, or separation which the blood undergoes in its passage out of the vessels. To carry on this process, either a new and peculiar structure of vessels must be formed, or a new disposition or mode of action of the old must take place. This new structure of vessels, or new disposition of vessels, I shall call glandular, and consider pus as a secretion[*].

Dissolution of the living solids of an animal body into pus, and that the pus already formed has a power of occasioning their further dissolution, is an old opinion, and is still the opinion of many.

But if this idea were just, no sore which discharges matter would be exempted from continual dissolution; and I think it must appear inconsistent that matter which was probably intended for salutary purposes should be a means of destroying the very parts which produced it.

---

* [Delpech endeavoured to prove that pus was always secreted by a new membrane (*membrane puogénique*) developed by inflammation; an opinion which received some colour of support from the appearance of cysts in old abscesses. Nothing, however, is more common than to see suppuration from mucous and serous surfaces, where no trace of any such membrane is discoverable.]

The circumstance of internal circumscribed cavities, as the abdomen, thorax, &c. forming pus, and where they might often have seen pints of matter, without any breach in the solids to produce it, (which is proved beyond controversy to take place,) should have taught them better; and the prevalence of this idea certainly shows a barrenness of knowledge and observation. Such an idea might be forgiven when it was thought that the discharge in gonorrhœa arose from an ulcer; but now that it is known that there is no ulcer in the urethra, it can only continue from mere stupidity.

The moderns have been more ridiculous still: they have put dead matter into pus, and have thought that it has been formed into pus, and have thence inferred opinions similar with the former. In this case they have been putting dead and living animal matter on the same footing. But what is still further, they might have seen that extraneous matter cannot be formed into pus, by observing that in wounds, and in suppuration with extravasation, blood and pus are found separately in the same cavity, and that in extravasation of blood in sound parts no pus is produced. In abscesses from violence and erysipelas they might have seen sloughs of dead cellular membrane, hanging like wet tow, and not melting down into pus, although exposed to the action of matter for a long time. The same observation holds good with regard to dead bones, when exposed to the action of pus; besides, if, in consequence of the decomposition of these parts, some of their parts are mixed with pus, it is altered in its properties, thereby attaining a very ill smell. But if there is loss of substance in a dead piece of bone, for instance, it is produced by absorption; in proof of which we see that the loss is on that side where it unites to the sound parts, and where alone the absorbents can act.

The chemists found no difficulty in explaining the formation of pus, and this they supposed took place by fermentation. But fermentation necessarily implies that there should be something to ferment; and, according to this idea, there are three effects which contradict the notion of fermentation flatly. First, internal canals, where mucus only was formed, take on the formation of pus without previous loss of substance or previous fermentation, and they leave off the action in the same way. Secondly, internal cavities take it on without loss of substance. Thirdly, abscesses already formed leave it off. If fermentation was the cause in the first, what solids enter into the matter discharged? for the whole penis could not afford matter enough to form the matter discharged in a gonorrhœa. And how or by what power was the fermentation commenced? and how should it ever cease? for there is the same surface secreting its mucus whenever the fermentation of pus ceases? In the second case, what solids were destroyed when fermentation began? by what power is the first particle of this fluid formed in an abscess or sore, before anything exists capable of dissolving solids? And according to the third, an abscess shall form matter, become stationary, perhaps for months, and at last be absorbed; and what becomes of the ferment during the time it remained stationary?

We may safely, then, discard these notions, and say that pus is formed from the fluids alone, by the action of the living solids.

Pus appears to consist, when examined by the microscope, of globular bodies, such as compose cream*; these may be white, or not so, as we find glass appears white when powdered, though not really so. The globules swim in serum, or a fluid like serum, and most probably there is a little coagulable lymp mixed with it. The proportion that those white globules bear to the other parts depends on the health of the parts which form it; and when in larger proportion, the matter is thicker and whiter, and is called good pus, that is, the solids that produced it are in health, for these appearances in matter are no more than the consequences of certain salutary processes, which are going on in the solids, the effect of which is to produce a disposition on which both suppuration and granulation depend.

Pus has a sweetish mawkish taste, as is known when it is formed in the mouth, and it coagulates by heat. This is the same, whether from an irritated natural surface, as the membrane of the nose and other outlets and canals, or from an ulcerated surface.

These discharges from canals or outlets have been termed mucus, and not pus; and the surfaces yielding these discharges have been termed mucous membranes. A test has been recommended for distinguishing these when their appearances have been so exactly similar as to afford no visible difference, and when, as I observe, they are in fact one and the same fluid. This test was the chemical solution of the fluid in menstrua, and its precipitation therefrom, a proposal which was unphilosophical on the very face of it, and which I treated from the first

---

* [These bodies were found by Dr. Hodgkin to be irregular in size and figure, and to have no resemblance to those of the blood; from which Dr. Babington has inferred the probability that pus consists merely of lymph, in a minute state of division, suspended in serum. The existence of globules gives to this fluid an iridescent appearance when viewed between two plates of glass, which was proposed by the late Dr. Young as a test of the presence of this matter in doubtful cases, and is still considered the best which we possess. Another test, derived from the facility with which pus is diffused through water, and afterwards subsides, is applicable to a great many cases, and is much to be preferred to any of those which depend on the reaction of chemical agents. The fact however is, that pus and mucus insensibly merge in one another, which renders the distinction between them *in transitu* impossible.]

as absurd. I did conceive that all animal substances when in solution, either in acids or alkalies, were in the same state, and that the precipitation from them would be the same. But as it was so strongly asserted, and supported by experiments said to have been made, I, to satisfy myself, made several experiments with animal matter, both solid and fluid; these I dissolved in different acids, vitriolic, muriatic, &c., and made precipitates with several alkalies, both fixed and volatile, but all these precipitates appeared the same, even when examined with the microscope, exhibiting universally a flaky appearance.

The quality of the matter always depends on the nature of the part secreting it: whatever specific quality the part is affected with, the pus will possess the same; hence we have venereal matter from venereal sores, cancerous matter from cancerous sores, &c.: but though it takes on these qualities when the part yielding it is so affected, yet it does not derive these qualities from the constitution if it is so affected, unless that part is also affected. A circumstance which serves to show that the part which yields it is of the same nature with the matter produced, is that it does not prove an irritator to the surface yielding it, though it may to another; hence no suppurating surface can be kept up by its own matter. The gonorrhœa, smallpox, &c., curing themselves is a proof of this, for were not this the case we should have constant pain from the irritation and much more difficulty in the cure. We do, indeed, sometimes find that pus will irritate its own surface; but this may be the effect of some extraneous matter, as blood, &c., in the pus: the intestines will sometimes produce a discharge which stimulates them very considerably; but this may be secreted by the diseased surface, and prove an irritator to the sound part of the canal only. What I have hitherto said refers to natural pus only; but when a specific nature is added, then the secretion is altered. The first alteration is a greater quantity of serum and salts, producing a thinner discharge, called sanies; this discharge has sometimes appeared to affect the solids, and has thence been called corrosive, a property which it does not possess*, the parts only receding from the irritation; and where this is the case, perhaps, the decomposition and new combination necessary to the for-

---

* [Pus very often corrodes the external parts. There seems also the greatest reason for believing that the presence of pus is highly deleterious in several forms of inflammation, as carbuncle, diffuse cellular inflammation, erysipelas ædematodes, inflammation arising from the bite of vipers, &c. Unless free and early openings are made in these cases, the inflammation or gangrene extends, apparently from the infiltration of pus, or that diseased secretion which precedes the formation of pus into the unadherent cellular membrane. That the pus, under such circumstances, acquires a highly poisonous quality, is proved by the effects which it produces on the constitution when injected into the veins. (See p. 352, note.)

mation of pus is not perfect, in consequence of the vessels having lost that structure which is proper for the secretion of pus; and this is probably the case, as healthy granulations are not produced when such matter is secreted. By what particular organization matter is produced we can no more determine than we can the nature of any other glandular organization.

Pus appears to have a greater tendency to putrescency than the other secretions have, but I do not think this is in the degree that has been supposed. It is brought into a putrescent state by circumstances independently of the pus itself. If the air is admitted to it by a small opening in an abscess, or it is placed near the intestinal fæces, or some parts of the solids which have sloughed, then it will be fetid; or if any dead blood, as in recent sores, is mixed with it, it is fetid; but if perfectly confined in an abscess it is always sweet, and will be a long time in putrefying. In erysipelatous inflammation, however, where there is an internal inflammation, there will be putrefaction; but this is probably from the solids themselves first putrefying. Hence we find, in most cases of specific disease, that the pus is offensive, because blood is mixed with it. Where there is dead bone also pus becomes very offensive.

The final intention of this secretion of matter is not, I believe, yet understood. Some say it is carrying off humours from the constitution, or that it is a constitutional disease changed into a local one, and so discharged or thrown out of the body, either in the form of pus, or with it, as in those cases called critical abscess. Or it is presumed to carry off local complaints from other parts, by way of derivation or revulsion; hence sores or issues are made in sound parts to allow other sores to be dried up. But I am apt to believe that we are not yet well, or at all, perhaps, acquainted with its uses. We might naturally suspect that it was on the surfaces of sores to keep them moist, but this will not account for its formation on internal surfaces.

Absorption of whole parts in consequence of Disease.—The immediate effects of absorption of the body in consequence of disease may be said to be of two kinds. The first is only a wasting of a part, or the whole, without any breach in the structure or form, and this I call the interstitial absorption; the second consists of the total removal of a part, as if by art, and this is the progressive absorption. The interstitial absorption may be considered in two lights: 1st, where it leaves the part affected still a whole, though wasted; 2nd, where it entirely removes it, which latter resembles the natural process by which useless parts are removed, as the thymus gland, the membrana pupillaris, &c.

The process of removing entire parts of the body, either by the second interstitial or the progressive absorption, answers very material purposes in the machine. It is by means of the progressive that bones exfoliate and sloughs separate, that pus is brought to the skin, and that while new bones are formed old ones are removed; and although in these cases the process arises from disease, yet it is somewhat similar to the modelling process in the natural formation of bone. It is this last that removes useless parts, as the alveolar processes when the teeth drop out, or when children are shedding teeth, which allows these to drop out; and it is by these means that ulcers are formed. It is in many cases a substitute for mortification (which is another mode of loss of substance), for it is a degree of strength or vigour superior to that where mortification takes place; and in many cases it finishes what mortification has begun, by separating the mortified part.

The progressive is that absorption which begins at one side of a part to be removed, and goes on until the whole is removed, as in spreading ulcers.

These two modes, the interstitial and progressive, are generally going on at once, which may be called the mixed. This operation of absorption, like many other processes arising from disease, would often appear to be doing mischief, by destroying parts which are of service, and where no visible good appears to arise from it, as in those cases where the external covering is destroyed by ulcers or sores; but in all cases it must be reduced to necessity, for we may depend upon it that those parts have not the power of support, and it becomes a substitute for mortification. In many cases we shall see both ulceration and mortification going on, ulceration removing those parts which have power to resist death.

New-formed parts, or such as cannot be said to form a part of the original animal, admit more readily of removal than those parts originally formed: probably this arises from the principle of weakness. It is on this principle that all adventitious new matter is more readily absorbed than that matter which forms the substance of old tumours.

Remote Causes of Absorption.—The remote causes of absorption are various. The most simple appears to arise from a part's becoming useless, as the thymus gland, the ductus arteriosus, the alveoli after the teeth drop out, the crystalline lens after couching, the fat of the body in fever, either inflammatory or hectic, all which are removed by the absorbents as useless parts. Another cause is want of power in the part to support itself under certain irritations, which may be considered as the basis of every cause of removal of whole parts, as calluses, cicatrices; also of parts pressed on. From all which it would appear that parts are liable to be absorbed from five causes: first, parts pressed on; second, parts considerably irritated by an irritating substance; third, parts weak-ened; fourth, parts rendered useless; fifth, parts become dead. The two first appear to me to produce the same irritation; the third, an irritation of its own kind; and the fourth and fifth may be somewhat similar.

Immediate Causes of Absorption.—The immediate causes of absorption of the body itself must be of two kinds respecting the parts, one passive, the other active. The first of these is a consciousness in the parts to be absorbed of the unfitness or impossibility of remaining under such circumstances, the action excited by the irritation being incompatible with the natural actions and existence of the parts, whatever these are; therefore they become ready for removal, or accept of it with ease. The second is a consciousness in the absorbents of such a state of part; and both concurring to do the same thing, they fall to work. When the part to be absorbed is a dead part, or extraneous matter, the whole disposition is in the absorbents. Pressure from without rather stimulates than irritates, for we find it produces thickening of parts; but if it exceeds the stimulus of thickening, it becomes an irritator. If pressure is from within, parts rather appear to give way, and absorption takes place.

Interstitial Absorption.—This is of two kinds with respect to the effects, or, rather, has two states. The first, where it takes place only in part, as in the wasting of a limb, where disease of the joint has rendered it useless; in a broken tendon; a divided nerve going to a voluntary part; or when it takes place in the whole body in consequence of disease, as atrophy, fever, &c. The second, when entire absorption takes place, and no vestige is left; and this would seem to be of two kinds, one where it takes place only in consequence of another disease, and is a necessary and useful effect of that disease, assisting in bringing parts to the surface, &c.; but the other appears to arise from disease in the part itself, as a total decay of the alveoli without any disease in the teeth or gums, as also the wasting of the testicle. The first of our second division of absorption of entire parts is taking place in a thousand instances; it is gradually taking place in that part of the body between many encysted tumours and the surface, and is generally slow in its progress.

Progressive Absorption.—The removal of those surfaces immediately contiguous to the irritating cause, which is an absorption of necessity, is effected by progressive absorption. Absorption from pressure is the removal of the part pressed, which may either be the surface of an abscess in contact with pus, or of that part of the surface of the body in contact with some body constantly pressing, as the buttocks or hips of those who lie long on their backs.

Of the Relaxing Process.—Besides the modes of removing parts above mentioned, there is a another process, called the relaxing or elongating process, carried on between the abscess and skin. It is possible that this process may arise in some degree from the absorption of interior parts; but there is certainly some other cause, for the skin which covers an abscess is certainly looser than it would be from mere stretching; and it is very beautiful to observe how Nature goes on in her own way to produce an effect. In consequence of the pressure of pus in an abscess, Nature sets up three processes to let it out: first, progressive absorption; secondly, interstitial, by which the progressive is assisted; thirdly, the relaxing process, making the parts yield to distension. In women, the relaxation of parts is very considerable before the birth of a child; and the old women in the country know when a hen is going to lay, by the relaxation and softness of those parts. The following cases exemplify those processes of absorption.

A lady, after inflammation of some of the abdominal viscera, had the belly swell: some time after, a kind of pointing was observed in various parts of the belly, and on opening the largest a very considerable quantity of fluid (matter, I think,) was discharged; this opening was near the sternum, and the ends of the recti muscles were quite ragged. The patient died. Here was an instance of the effects of absorption, by which an exit was obtained for the matter. Suppose an abscess to go on for a long time with a smooth surface, yet if any part takes on the absorbing process the matter will be very rapid in arriving at the skin, although this process may have taken place in the thickest part. This process may be induced by an irritation in any part of the surface; thus, after opening an abscess, if matter is permitted to collect at the most depending part, it may bring on this process, whence a fresh opening will be made.

This preparation [*showing one*] represents the front of a chest, which contained an aneurism of the aorta; and here on the right side you see an instance of the elongating process, the cartilages being bent outwards, or elongated, to adapt themselves to its figure.

This is another preparation (see Pl. XVII. f. 4.),—an aneurism of the aorta. A A, ends of the aorta; B, the first sac, which contracted at C, and having proceeded to *d*, where it met with resistance from the sternum D D, it became again contracted; but having produced absorption of the sternum *d, e*, by which an opening is made externally, the sac is again expanded. Here are two other preparations, exhibiting similar appearances.

Ulceration.

Before I enter on this subject I shall make a few more general observations on absorption.

Some parts of our solids are more susceptible of being absorbed, especially by ulceration, than others under the same or similar circumstances. This is particularly the case with cellular and adipose membrane, as we often find muscles, tendons, and ligaments deprived of their connecting membrane by ulceration, as may be observed in the opening of large abscesses. The skin itself, if affected by pressure from without, is less easily absorbed than the cellular membrane; hence we may observe, that in continued pressure from without the skin will remain whole, although the parts beneath are wasted by the absorption of the cellular membrane; but sometimes the skin is more susceptible of absorption than the cellular membrane; this may proceed from the skin acting with so much more vigour, either in opposing any injury or in taking on salutary action. Although in abscesses, in tumours, and in the case of extraneous bodies, the parts all round are equally pressed, yet we find that the progressive absorption takes place only on that side nearest the skin, and arrives at the skin only on that side: a very slight degree of pressure from within will produce this effect, so slight as would from without have produced only a thickening of parts.

Bones are susceptible of a similar process. Absorption may be of two kinds,—without suppuration, or with it. The first, I believe, is universally the case with the interstitial absorption when it takes place alone, as in the absorption of callus, of the alveoli of the teeth, &c.; but the second may precede or produce suppuration where there was none before, as in old sores breaking out anew. To distinguish the second from all other modes of absorption of whole parts, I shall call that absorption ulceration which is either preceded, accompanied, or succeeded by suppuration. Absorption may be a consequence of pressure under two circumstances,—where the pressure is from diseased parts, or from extraneous substances. Of the first is that from tumours, &c.; thus, in a case of aneurism, where the coats of the artery press against the bones, the rib for instance, its coats begin to be absorbed, and, after they are absorbed, that absorption goes on in the bone, the adhesive inflammation takes place at the same time round it, and unites the circumference of the absorbed parts: another instance is where tumours make their way to the skin, without any suppuration taking place. Of this I once saw a very remarkable instance in a soldier in the Dutch service: a tumour had formed between the pia mater and dura mater, which gradually

increased to a very considerable size, and had shown itself externally
some time before the man died. Upon examination after death I discovered that the pia mater was absorbed underneath it; but the chief
absorption had taken place on the side next the skin, for on this side
the skull was absorbed, and the absorption had begun in the integuments of the scalp, which it would soon have probably ulcerated had
not the man died before Nature had finished her operations; and in this
case no matter was found either on the brain, skull, or in the integuments, owing, perhaps, to the pressure being made by a living part.
This species of absorption is attended with very little or no pain, and
its effects are as trifling on the constitution, although it may be an effect
of an alteration in the constitution, as the absorption of calluses in
scurvy, &c.

Ulceration.—I shall now take notice of that action of the absorbent
system which I call ulceration, and which is the second species of our
first division, being connected with the formation of pus, either as a
consequence or as a cause; and it is this kind which always constitutes
an ulcer.

· This process of ulceration or absorption with suppuration, is almost
constantly attended with inflammation, which led me to call it ulcerative inflammation. Ulceration is generally attended with considerable
pain, which is called soreness; but this does not attend all ulcerations,
for there are some which are of the specific kind, which give little or no
pain, as scrofula; but even in this disease, where ulceration proceeds
pretty fast, it often gives considerable pain, wherefore the pain may be
in some degree in proportion to the quickness of its operation. In those
cases where ulceration is set up to separate dead parts, as sloughs, it is
seldom attended with pain, and it is not easy to assign the cause of this.

It seldom or never affects the constitution much, although the process
is affected by the constitution.

What I have hitherto said of ulceration I shall illustrate by noticing
what occurs in an inflammation of the peritoneal coat of an intestine.
The first inflammation produced is the adhesive, which occasions an
adhesion between the inflamed part of an intestine and the peritoneum
lining the cavity, which remains, although the inflammation should stop
here; but if it does not stop here, then the suppurative takes place, and
an abscess is produced, the matter of which is collected into a regular
cavity in these adhesions, and is prevented from diffusion through the
cavity of the abdomen by the effects on the surrounding parts, by the
preceding adhesive inflammation, as well as of that which accompanies it.
This matter, by its pressure, irritates, and absorption takes place in consequence; but as none of the parts, except those between the matter and

the skin, are hardly, if at all, susceptible of this irritation, no parts are absorbed but such as are so situated : hence the abdominal muscles, cellular membrane, fat, and skin are removed in preference to the coat of the intestine. If the suppuration had at first begun in different points, the parts between are absorbed until it becomes one abscess; and when it reaches the skin we have the ulcerative inflammation. It is in the same manner that Nature acts in all abscesses of circumscribed cavities, as in common abscess, inflammation of the lung of the side next the pleura, of the pleura itself, gall-bladder, liver, &c. ; also in the case of lumbar abscesses. In the substance of the lungs we sometimes find abscesses go on in a different manner, and open into the cells, and this because the adhesive inflammation finds it difficult to connect the air-cells together; and that the air-cells do not take on the adhesive inflammation is evident from many observations. Whilst a part is under the ulcerative inflammation, irritation will increase the absorption on any part of its surface. Thus, if a large abscess forms on the thigh, opposite the great trochanter, we shall find that, from the pressure of the trochanter on the part opposite to it, ulceration will take place there likewise. An irritation we have of the same kind in milk abscesses, from the irritation of the matter in a depending part of the abscess, which shows how very easily, from the slight pressure of matter, the ulcerative process may be produced. Ulceration is, therefore, no more than a process by which parts are removed out of the way of pressure. The ulcerative process has no effect on the cuticle; but in general this is so thin as not to give any trouble, as it easily bursts. But on the fingers and hands of working people it becomes so thickened as to cause excessive pain and trouble in whitloes; and as from this cause we have so considerable a separation between the cuticle and the skin, these abscesses should be opened early. Poultices in these cases are more useful than in any other, for their moisture is absorbed by the cuticle as by a sponge, and the cuticle is rendered more dilateable. After these have been opened, or have opened of themselves, by a small orifice, the soft parts lying under are apt to push through the opening, and appear like a fungus, occasioning great pain, which is owing to the cuticle around the granulations underneath. To this escharotics have been applied; but it would appear that there is no necessity for them, as it would disappear of itself when the thickening of the parts in consequence of inflammation has gone off. But besides ulceration, the consequence of previous suppuration, which we have been hitherto describing, we have ulceration taking place where no reason can be assigned for it, except perhaps weakness be the cause, the parts not being able to support themselves. New parts are more susceptible of it than old, as cicatrices, stumps, calluses, &c. This arises from the new parts being less firm than the old original ones, as in Anson's voyage, when there was a general debility from the change of climate, &c. The appearances of ulceration are different at different times, according as the process is going on, at a stand, or the parts healing. The ulceration in the smallpox is attended with death in the parts, hence loss of substance and pitting.

Restoration of Parts.—We are now to trace the operations of Nature to bring parts back as near to their original formation as possible. These operations cannot be looked on as morbid, as they are for a salutary purpose.

Granulations.—These have, I believe, in general been supposed to be a consequence of, or an attendant on, suppuration; but the formation of granulations is not confined to a breach of the solids allowed to suppurate, as from accident, or a breach of the solids, produced in consequence of suppuration, as in abscesses; but it takes place under other circumstances, and when the first and second bond of union have failed, as in simple fractures.

I believe no internal canal can granulate in consequence of suppuration, except there have been a breach of continuity. And here I may observe, that when granulation does take place in such a canal, it is not on the proper coat of the canal, but on the surrounding cellular membrane. Few surfaces of abscesses granulate until opened, either of themselves or by art; therefore in abscesses of very long standing we seldom or never find granulations.

In most abscesses, if not in all, after they are opened, there is one surface more disposed to granulate than the others, which is the surface next to the centre of the body in which suppuration takes place, the surface next to the skin hardly ever having the disposition to granulate; on the contrary, it is sometimes ulcerating when the bottom of an abscess is granulating. Exposure is so far necessary for granulations, even in cases where there is an opening, that if the opening is only a small one, and the abscess is deeply seated, the latter will not so readily granulate, which often becomes the consequence of deep-seated abscesses not healing.

I have said that granulations are not confined to a breach of the solids attended with suppuration; for parts are capable of making new matter internally in cases where union by the first intention ought to have occurred. A case in St. George's Hospital first gave me this idea.

I was called to a man with a fractured thigh, and made use of the usual means, but without success, for no union of the fractured parts was formed in the usual time; and about the end of four weeks the man died with another complaint. Upon examination of the parts, I found that the upper end of the bone rose considerably over the under, and consequently there was a great cavity in the soft parts, the parietes of which were thickened by the adhesive inflammation, though not so much as if the parts had been better disposed for the adhesive inflammation. There was no extravasated blood, nor matter, nor coagulable lymph to be found, except a few threads, which were probably the remains of extravasated blood. Here the parts had lost two chances of being united, the one by the extravasated blood, the other by the coagulable lymph thrown out by the adhesive inflammation; and Nature had begun a third, which was that of forming granulations of new animal matter on the ends of the bone and the surface of the surrounding cavity; and adhesions, you see, had taken place between the bones and soft parts, by which the bones would have been united by a bony case. Hence we find that granulation may take place without the parts being exposed, and without suppuration*.

This mode of union by granulation is, I believe, much more extensive than has been imagined; this third bond of union taking place where the parts have missed the first and second, as just mentioned. In the exposure of cavities of abscesses we have granulations going hand in hand with, and following suppuration. As the suppurative inflammation follows injuries with exposure, it seems that this inflammation is in general necessary to granulation in these cases.

Granulations are an accretion of new animal substance on the surface of a wound, or a newly-formed surface composed of coagulable lymph exuded from the vessels, into which new substance the old vessels probably extend, and entirely new ones are formed, so that the granulations come to be very vascular, more so indeed than any other particular animal substance. The vessels pass from the original parts to the base of the granulations, and from thence to their outer surface. The surface of this new formation continues to have the same disposition for the secretion of pus as the parts on which they are formed had; therefore it is easier to suppose that the nature of these vessels does not alter by forming granulations, but they are completely changed for this purpose before granulations are begun to be formed, and that these granulations are the consequence of the change. They always also are of the same nature with the parts on which they are formed: if a dis-

---

* [The effusion of callus in this case does not seem to differ essentially from the effusion of callus in other cases. It certainly cannot be regarded as a conclusive proof of the existence of granulations without suppuration and exposure, although these do sometimes continue to form after cicatrization, as in burns and some other cases.]

eased part, they are diseased; if the disease be of any specific kind, they are of the same kind and produce similar matter. The surface of the granulations is convex, being just the reverse of an ulcerating surface, which is thus, as it were, shagreened by a great many points or small eminences : the smaller these points are, the more healthy the granulations. The colour of healthy granulations is a florid red, which would make us suspect that it is principally owing to arterial blood : when they are of a livid red they are most commonly unhealthy, and have a languid circulation in them ; however, this appearance frequently is owing to the particular position of the parts. I knew an instance of this in a young man who had a granulating wound on his leg. I was surprised to see it on some days of a healthy scarlet, and on others quite livid; but the cause of this he explained to me, by showing that if he kept it in a recumbent posture for a short time, its surface was then of a bright scarlet, but if he stood for a few minutes it would become quite livid. This appearance must have arisen from the stagnation of blood in the newly-formed vessels, and from their not possessing sufficient strength to resist the superincumbent column of blood, which sufficiently accounts for the difficulty of healing sore legs when patients are allowed to stand or walk much.

Granulations not only show the state of the part on which they are formed, but also how far the constitution is affected in many cases. The chief of those which affect granulations are the irritable and indolent habits, and, still more, fevers, which must be of such a nature as to produce universal irritation in the constitution.

Granulations have a disposition to unite with one another, which is absolutely necessary to healing ; and this is done, I suppose, in the following manner : when two granulations meet, the mouths of the opposing vessels are irritated, which causes them to embrace each other; this junction perhaps being aided by the attraction of cohesion, or they may throw out coagulable lymph, and unite in that way. I have seen granulations from the dura mater and scalp unite so closely in twenty-four hours as to be with difficulty separated, and then to bleed very freely, which shows their great disposition to unite. When the parts, and consequently the granulations, are not sound, there is not this disposition to unite, and a smooth surface is formed, which continues to secrete pus. I conceive the internal surface of a fistulous sore to be of this nature, and somewhat similar to the urethra in gleet. Ulcers of this kind are cured by exciting inflammation in them.

Granulations have less powers and shorter lives than originally-formed parts. Different animals have different periods of life, and so have granulations, and sometimes they seem to be formed with a short period of existence. They often die and slough off without any visible cause, and, coming down to the original parts, a fresh crop of granulations is formed, which in a certain time will again slough off without any apparent change in the constitution.

Many small wounds would perhaps do much better without any dressing. The blood, coagulating and drying, forms itself into a scab, which falls off and shows that Nature has completed her work under it; the same will often happen when small suppurating sores are suffered to dry. This is a circumstance not attended to, perhaps, as much as it ought: even compound fractures with a small opening, if suffered to proceed in this manner, will often give but little trouble. In blisters, where the cuticle is not removed, the process is exactly similar. It would be a great advantage to us to ascertain what sores require dressing, and what do not. I believe all cutaneous sores do best without dressing; excoriations and little pimples had best be left to themselves, for often when applications are made to any of these, a hundred little pimples will sprout up: when this is the case, I make it a general rule to desist from any application.

A young gentleman had a small pimple on his leg, to which a little ointment was applied, and in a day or two the surrounding parts were covered with similar pimples: these, being treated with similar applications, spread, until the whole leg was covered with them. When I was consulted, and asked what was to be done—"Nothing." "How is that?" "Can anything be easier?" I said; "do nothing to the leg." "Then the stocking will stick to it." "Let no stocking be worn: put the boy on a pair of trousers." The advice was taken, and the leg dried up and healed directly.

Cicatrization.—Immediately on the formation of granulations, cicatrization would seem to be in view; contraction is going on in every part, but principally from the edges to the centre, so that the sore becomes very small, without much new skin. This contraction is easiest effected on loose parts, but with difficulty when over bones, as on the scalp, shin-bone, &c., where the granulations cannot contract much. This observation should direct us, in operations on such parts, to leave as much skin as possible. This contraction continues until the whole is skinned over; but their greatest power, or at least their greatest effect, is at first. This contraction can be assisted by art, which shows there is a resistance; this is done by bandages, but these should be avoided at first, while there is inflammation, and until granulations are formed, otherwise they might prevent the granulations rising. Besides the contractile power of the granulations, there is a similar power in the surrounding edge of the cicatrized skin, which assists the power of the granulations, and is often greater than that of the granulations; this may be seen in sugar-loaf stumps, where the skin grows round and embraces the granulations like a ring, appearing to squeeze them out; but it is only in the new skin, the old being loose all round. This contractile power prevents the necessity for so much new skin, the surrounding old skin being drawn over the parts. The advantage of this is very evident, the original skin being more fit to live than the new, and less liable to ulceration. As the granulations contract, the old surrounding skin is stretched, and is probably elongated. If it is elongated, it must be so by the interstitial deposition of new matter.

Of Skinning.—When a sore begins to heal, the old skin, which had been inflamed, then becomes whitish, and especially near the edge : this is one of the first appearances of healing. The new skin is a very different substance with respect to texture from the granulations on which it is formed; but whether it is an addition of new matter, or a change in the surface of the granulations themselves, is not easily determined. We find new skin generally taking its rise from the surrounding old skin, as if elongated from it ; but that is not always the case, for in very large old ulcers, where the edges of the old skin have but little tendency to contract, new skin forms in different parts of the ulcer, standing on the surface of the granulations like little islands. These little specks show that the ulcer is healing slowly, and it seldom or never takes place the first time a part is ulcerated; but the old surrounding skin assists by shooting towards the new. The granulations may perhaps acquire a disposition to skin from their being in the neighbourhood of the old skin, but it is plain they can take on this disposition without that assistance.

Skinning is a process in which Nature is always a great œconomist. We never find that new-formed skin is so large as the sore was on which it was formed. This is brought about by the contraction of the granulations, which in some measure is in proportion to the quantity of the surrounding old skin. If a sore be in a part where the surrounding skin is loose, as the scrotum, the contractile power of the granulations being not at all prevented, very little new skin is formed; whereas if the sore is on a part where the skin is tight, as the scalp, the new skin is nearly as large as the sore.

Nature of the newly-formed Cutis.—When granulations are formed near a bone, the skin is at first fixed; but it gradually becomes loose, from elongation, by continued attempts at motion. Motion given to the part so affected must be mechanical, but it becomes a stimulus by which the parts become conscious of their not being able to exist as they are, therefore the lymphatics set to work to absorb all the adventitious substances which prevent their motion. Medicine has not as much power as we could wish in assisting this process; however, mercury seems to have nearly the same effect as motion, especially when combined with camphor, and should be used. When everything else fails, electricity may be tried, for it has restored the motion of parts after they have been fixed from inflammation after strains.

The newly-formed skin has no indentations, or lozenge-shaped marks, on it, like the old, nor has it the living principle so strong. The new cutis is at first very vascular, but afterwards becomes less so, the vessels perhaps being obliterated, or converted into absorbents, and so becoming white.

Cuticle.—That formed on the new cutis is at first horny, but afterwards shining. It is sooner restored than the cutis, and is formed at once from every part of the cutis.

Rete Mucosum.—This is much longer in forming than the cuticle, and sometimes is never recovered, as we see in wounds, blisters, &c. in Blacks, their skin in that part remaining white for ever.

EFFECTS ON THE CONSTITUTION.—I have divided diseases into local and constitutional; and when on local, I observed that they, and especially inflammation, had secondary or sympathetic affections, which were immediate or remote. The immediate were considered when on inflammation, namely, the sympathetic fever. The remote are now to be treated of.

One would suppose that the suppurative would only so far affect the constitution as by the preceding inflammation which produces it; but the contrary is sometimes the case, and the suppurative will produce worse symptoms than the inflammation itself. The condition which the constitution takes on after suppuration is sometimes productive of those diseases termed nervous, as locked-jaw, hysteria, spasm on the muscles of respiration, restlessness, debility, &c., all of which seem to arise from the suppurative action, and are not salutary effects, but harass the constitution and even produce death. The locked-jaw I shall defer for the present, and consider hectic or sympathetic fever.

Hectic fever is a remote constitutional sympathetic affection, and appears to have a very different origin from the other remote sympathizing effects, though in general the consequence of a local disease. It is the constitution affected by a local disease, or irritation, which it is conscious it cannot cure: for while the inflammation lasts, which is only preparatory to and an immediate effect of most injuries, in those parts at least which can most affect the constitution and call up her powers, there can be no hectic.

It takes its rise from a variety of causes, which I shall divide into two : 1st, From an affection of vital parts; 2nd, From an affection of parts not vital. The only differences between these is in the time of the hectic's coming on, and its rapidity and violence when it does come on. In vital parts, hectic will be produced by many complaints which will not produce it in other parts, as scirrhus of the stomach or mesenteric glands, also diseases of the lungs or liver. These also produce other symptoms, according to the nature of the part injured and of the injury : as coughs, when in the lungs; sickness and vomitings, when in the stomach; dropsies and jaundice, when in the liver.

When hectic arises from disease in a part not vital, it is generally in parts where such a quantity of mischief can take place as to make the constitution sensible of it, as the large joints. In small joints, although the same local effect takes place as in large ones, yet the constitution is not made sensible of it, so that we find scrofulous joints of the toes, &c., not affecting the constitution with hectic, and the ankle, elbow, and shoulder are much longer in affecting the constitution than the knee or hip.

Although hectic commonly arises from some incurable local disease of a vital part, or of a common part of some magnitude, yet it may be an original disease of the constitution; the constitution may fall into the same action without any local disease whatever.

Hectic may be said to be a slow mode of dissolution: the general symptoms are those of a low or slow fever, attended with weakness; but more the action of weakness than real weakness, for on the removal of the part causing the hectic there is immediately the action of strength produced. The particular symptoms are: debility; small quick sharp pulse; the blood forsakes the skin; there is loss of appetite; often vomiting; wasting; tendency to sweating, especially when in bed; constitutional purging; urine clear at one time, and at another depositing a branny brick-dust sediment; dissolution. This disease has been supposed to arise from absorption of pus; but I have long thought that the blame has been improperly laid to the absorption of pus, and the following facts will make this evident. First, hectic takes place where there is disease, and no suppuration in vital parts; also in many inflammations before actual suppuration has taken place, as in many of the large joints, called white swellings, while the same kind and quantity of inflammation and suppuration in any of the fleshy parts, and especially such of them as are near the source of the circulation, have in general no such effect. Therefore in such cases it is only an effect on the constitution, produced by a local complaint having a particular property.

I have said that with all diseases of vital parts the constitution sympathizes more readily than with many other parts; and also all diseases of vital parts are more difficult of cure than those not vital; as also diseases of bones, ligaments, tendons, affect the constitution more readily than of muscles, skin, cellular membrane, &c.; and we find these general principles hold good in universal remote sympathy with local disease of those parts and structures.

When a disease is in the vital parts, and is such as does not kill from the first constitutional effects, then the constitution becomes teazed with the complaint, which is destroying the necessary actions of health which are vital. In diseased joints there is not a proper power, or rather, perhaps, disposition to produce salutary inflammation and suppuration for their recovery; therefore the constitution is irritated with an incurable disease.

If absorption of pus always produced such symptoms, I do not see how any patient who has a large sore could escape this disease, because we have as yet no reason to suppose that any one sore has more power of absorption than another. If in those cases where there is hectic the absorption of pus is really greater than when the habit is healthy, it would be difficult to determine whether the increase of absorption is a cause or effect. If it is a cause, it must arise from a particular disposition of the sore to absorb more at one time than at another, even while in a healthy state. What reason we have to suppose that a sore in a healthy constitution has power to absorb more at one time than at another, I do not see. If this increase of absorption does not depend on the nature of the sore, it must take its rise from the constitution; if so, there is a peculiarity of the constitution; therefore the whole of the symptoms cannot arise from the absorption of pus, and the cause must be a peculiar constitution and absorption combined.

If the absorption of matter produced such violent effects as are ascribed, which are never of the inflammatory kind, but of the hectic, why does not venereal matter produce the same effects? We often know that absorption is going on by buboes taking place, yet no symptoms appear until the matter appears to produce its specific effects, and these symptoms are not very similar to those called hectic, though from reasoning we should expect that venereal matter would act with more violence than common matter from a healthy sore.

Again, as matter is often formed on the inside of veins in inflammation of those cavities, and this matter enters directly into the circulation, why have we not the hectic symptoms in these cases? We have the inflammatory, and sometimes death. We also find the matter of large abscesses which have been produced without visible inflammation, such as many of the scrofulous kind, wholly absorbed, and that in a very short time, yet no bad symptoms follow.

From all these facts and reasonings we may conclude that the absorption of pus from a sore cannot be the cause of so much mischief as has been generally supposed. If it was owing to matter in the system, I do not see how the symptoms could ever stop until suppuration ceased; yet we often do find that they get well before suppuration ceases, even when no medicine was given; and in the case of inflammation of the veins, there is reason to believe that after all the bad symptoms are gone suppuration is still going on, so that though matter is still passing into the constitution from the vein, hectic is not produced, which it must be if it was caused by matter getting into the circulation.

But I much doubt the fact of absorption going on more in one sore than another. In large abscesses hectic seldom comes on till they are opened, though they have been forming matter for months. In such cases the disposition often comes on soon after opening the abscess; in others very late; but till the stimulus for restoring the parts is given no such effect can take place. If the parts were disposed to heal, no such hectic disposition would come on. In diseased joints also, if the parts are capable of taking on salutary inflammation we shall have only the first sympathetic inflammatory fever; but as they seldom do this, the constitution is teazed by the complaint not taking on immediate and salutary steps towards a cure. Hectic, therefore, would appear in some measure to depend on the parts being stimulated to produce an effect beyond their powers, and this stimulus is sooner or later in taking place.

Treatment of Hectic.—We have as yet, I am afraid, no cure for this. I believe the cure consists in the removal of the cause, viz., the local disease. Strengtheners and antiseptics are recommended. Strengtheners are proposed on account of the debility, which has evidently taken place; and antiseptics, from the idea of absorbed pus giving the blood a tendency to putrefaction. To prevent both these effects taking place the same medicines are recommended, namely, bark and wine. Bark will in most cases only assist in supporting the constitution; I should suppose it could not cure the constitution of the disease; however it may render it less susceptible of it. When hectic comes on from some specific disease, as from venereal irritation, the bark will enable it to support it better than it otherwise would have done. Wine, I am afraid, rather does harm, as it increases the action of the machine without giving strength, a thing to be carefully avoided. However, I have not yet made up my mind about wine.

When hectic arises from the disease of such a part as the system can bear the loss of, the part should be removed. On removing the cause (as by amputation of an extremity), the pulse, from being very quick, returns to its usual state; I have likewise known the patient sleep the first night without an opiate, after having had little or no sleep for a week before, and the sweats called colliquative have been stopped; and I have known purging immediately stop. Perhaps the pain and newly excited action of the constitution may assist in the abatement of the symptoms.

Of Dissolution.—To the hectic I have joined another disease, arising from suppuration, which I have called dissolution, because few recover from it.

It may arise in long-continued suppurations, which may not be incurable in themselves, and in this it differs from hectic. Dissolution seems more the effect of the past than of the present, which is the reverse of hectic. We never find this take place in consequence of small wounds, or such as affect the constitution but little, but rather after bad compound fractures, amputations, &c. It appears more in hospitals than in private practice; more in large towns than in the country. In cases of compound fractures and amputations, we find the constitution often capable of going through the inflammatory sympathetic fever, producing suppuration and granulation, and continuing this for some time, yet sinking under them at last, and often without any apparent cause, the effect taking place more readily if the patient was in full health before the operation, than if he had been for some time accustomed to hectic symptoms.

The first symptoms are generally those of the stomach, shivering; vomiting immediately follows, if it does not accompany it; a small quick pulse; perhaps bleeding from the whole surface of the sore; often mortification and speedy dissolution. Here is a very fatal disease taking place in some almost immediately; and when everything appears to be within the powers of the animal. It therefore cannot immediately arise from the sore itself; yet the sore certainly assists, because we never see the disease take place where the sore is healed.

The removal of the local disease will not prove effectual for the cure of this as it does that of hectic, nor do I find anything that has any effect.

CHAPTER XV.

PRACTICAL ILLUSTRATIONS OF THE PRECEDING SUB-
JECTS.

*Union of a broken tendon ;—rupture of the tendo Achillis ;—principles of
treatment ;—impossibility of causing voluntary contraction of the
muscle ;—management of the injury ;—pain and inflammation trifling ;
—length of cure.—Empyema ;—varieties of contained fluid ;—symptoms differing ;—ultimate effects of contained fluid the same ;—to be
distinguished from disease of the heart.—Symptoms of the disease peculiar ;—general ;—sympathetic.—Operation.—After-treatment.—Pe-
ricarditis.—Adhesion ;—suppuration fatal.—Emphysema from fractured rib ;—operation to be avoided.—Peritonitis ;—symptoms ;—rapid
progress ;—true and erysipelatous.—Puerperal, not from inflammation
of the uterus ;—causes ;—arising after tapping.—Hernia.—Cæsarean
section.—Opening cavities of joints.—Ganglions.—Inflammations of
the eye.—Phlebitis following venesection ;—causes ;—extension ;—frequency in the horse.—Arteritis.*

Union of a broken Tendon.—The treatment of a broken tendon is very
similar to the treatment of a fractured patella, because their uses, and
in some degree their situations, are similar, namely, the giving way of
an intermediate substance between the power (that is the muscles,) and
the resistance. All come under one general principle of cure, though
the mode of treatment is somewhat different.

These intermediate parts are principally tendons, probably some ligaments, and bones. The fracture of a tendon is probably always produced by the power being in action, and the resistance counteracting
at the same time and with great velocity. We might suppose that
every tendon in the body would be liable to such accident, but I believe
there is only one that stands any chance of such effect by the natural
exertions of the body; this is the tendo Achillis *. There is also, pro-

---

* [This is a mistake: the tendons of the patella, triceps extensor cubiti, and quadriceps
extensor cruris are sometimes ruptured from a sudden and abrupt exertion of these
muscles. An example of the latter kind is at this moment in one of the wards of
St. George's Hospital. I may also mention that fractures of the collar-bone, from muscular exertion, are not very uncommon.]

bably, but one bone in the human body which can be broken in the same way, that is the patella; though there may be instances of processes of bone being torn off near their insertion, which would be somewhat similar.

The tendo Achillis seems liable to be broken by the natural actions of the body, from having at the same time to sustain the action of the power and of the resistance also. When it has only the action of the muscles to contend with, there is no danger of its rupture, because the tendon is capable of supporting a much stronger power than that of the muscles. Though the tendon is continually in this state, yet there is little danger, because when the action is voluntary all the actions tend to support one another; but in a careless unguarded action the motion is more violent and quick, and the part less prepared against it. I believe fracture of this tendon often happens when a person is fatigued and off his guard, as after dancing, &c., and after the muscles have acted spontaneously, as in the cramp; at least it happened to me after dancing, and after a violent fit of the cramp. The general principle of cure in parts displaced is the replacing them in their natural situations, which is the whole cure in some, as dislocations, and the first step to be taken in every case where the continuity of parts is broken.

When the tendon is broken it is seldom attended with pain in the parts. It commonly gives a pain, which instantly seizes the calf of the leg. The noise or snap which it produces gives no idea of the mischief done; but being at the same time attended with pain in the calf of the leg, and the patient not being able to walk as usual, he conceives that some one has struck him with a hard body on the calf, and if he is so situated as not to have been liable to a blow, he becomes puzzled to conceive what can have happened. We generally find that the muscle is thrown into a state of cramp when the tendon gives way, losing the power of relaxation by the will, or of itself. As a surgeon is seldom present when such an accident happens, it is often allowed to remain some time in that state; but the pain often leads to the right mode of cure, the patient squeezing the muscle down with his hands, which a surgeon should do if at hand. The broken ends will always at first be at some distance from each other, because they are pulled apart by opposite forces.

The parts should be allowed to remain nearly in their natural position : no inconvenience will attend a small separation of the broken ends of the tendon, namely, half an inch or so; whereas considerable disadvantage would arise if we were to push the two broken ends together by throwing back the heel (which has been the general practice). The only circumstance that would seem to forbid such practice, namely, letting the broken tendon remain without a bandage, is, that the muscle will lose half an inch of its power of contraction, which the motion of the ankle may or may not lose; but though this may be lost at first, we know muscles will acquire it again afterwards, and therefore no attention need be paid to this objection. The advantage of not throwing the heel up, and of allowing the tendon to heal nearly in its natural position is, that the patient may be enabled to walk from the very beginning of the cure, a very desirable circumstance.

However, it is not necessary to adhere rigidly to either of these modes of treatment, but to adopt a medium between the two, which will be best. The heel may, therefore, be a little raised during the time of walking only, by raising the heel of the shoe. A roller should be passed several times round the calf of the leg, and kept constantly applied, as we cannot guard against the involuntary actions of the muscles; and at night we may apply an apparatus consisting of a leathern slipper or sock, with a strap from the heel to be fixed to a belt, in order to steady the muscles.

When the tendo Achillis is broken, there is but very little inflammation attendant; but some general fullness comes on about the small of the leg and ankle, the skin looks dark from the effusion of blood, and the parts have a firm feel, from coagulable lymph being thrown out. This firmness of the cellular membrane increases near to the fracture laterally, and this assists in keeping the tendon in its place. The inflammation hardly requires any particular treatment when the foot is in a proper position.

As I would not restrain the patient from walking almost from the very beginning, (the inflammation may prevent it for the first day or two,) it is necessary to give him some directions how he is to manage the muscles under the cure, as walking cannot be performed in the usual way. I have recommended to keep the position of the foot nearly at a right angle with the leg, as in standing, but not quite so, the heel being a little raised, by some pieces of leather put into the shoe, which may be removed one by one. When he walks he must turn his toes out, and carry the inside of his foot forwards, without attempting to bend the joint of the knee; indeed, the latter precaution is unnecessary, for this motion is only necessary when the heel can be raised from the ground, which he cannot do. This foot will be for some time the leading foot in walking, for it will be an easy motion to set it forwards before the other, especially if the heel is not much raised; but it will be impossible to set the other foot forwards and leave this behind. The patient will be hardly able to mend his pace for two months, except it be by getting familiar with his present mode of walking. The ankle and foot will swell occasionally, especially in the evening; and this may continue more or less after the tendon is united, but is of no importance. Three or four weeks after the accident he may remove the roller from the calf of the leg, and about the same time leave off the slipper at night. We cannot say when he may use the muscle of this tendon; that will depend on the fitness of the tendon to be used, which can only be known by the power the patient has of putting it to use. About two months after the accident we find him gradually bringing his toes more and more forwards, until he at last walks as usual*.

It is impossible for a patient with a fracture of the tendo Achillis to act with the gastrocnemius and soleus muscles, if he were to try to do so. When the Duke of Queensberry broke his tendo Achillis he was immediately aware of what had happened, and pointed out to me the broken ends. He readily submitted to my reasoning: walked about his room as well as he could, and found it impracticable to contract the gastrocnemius muscle. Some surgeons thought the tendon could not be broken, because he was walking about his room; but in such a case the patient has no more power to contract his gastrocnemius and soleus muscles than to jump over St. Paul's.

Of simple Fractures.—A fracture is the solution of continuity of a bone, whereby more or less of a cavity or space is allowed between the broken parts. It often, if not always, happens that the surrounding soft parts are also torn by the broken ends of the bone. On the surface of this broken or torn part are the mouths of many ruptured vessels, which immediately fill the cavity with blood. This is the first stage of the bond of union. This blood, having the living principle in it, unites with the torn surfaces, in the same manner as in ingrafting the living parts of animals. An inflammation generally comes on, similar to that which produces adhesions where there is no ruptured vessel, which is of service in this case for the better union of surrounding parts, where extravasated blood cannot enter, by which means the callus becomes larger than it would otherwise be. Vessels are either continued from the old parts into this extravasated blood, or it forms new vessels in its own substance; this substance then goes through the regular stages of ossification, becoming first cartilaginous and then bony.

---

* [The period of perfect recovery is generally protracted several months before the ultimate organization of the uniting medium is effected, in consequence of the low powers of vitality which tendinous parts possess. Simple incised wounds of tendons, as in amputation, are observed to heal without difficulty; but the union of ruptured tendons is a much slower process, depending upon the slow reproductive powers of these parts. At first the union is by cellular membrane, which gradually becomes harder and tougher: very often it becomes osseous, as in Mr. Hunter's own case; but very frequently it remains a fibro-cartilaginous knot, which never assumes the tendinous character.]

Thus new parts are formed and old ones united without the occurrence of any considerable inflammation, and all owing to this circumstance of the extravasated blood being preserved, and allowed to retain its living powers. All the surgeon has to do in such cases is to put the parts as much into their natural situation as possible, and to keep them there by art in the easiest way to the patient that he can. The same idea and the same practice is extended to all unions by the first intention.

The position of the patients themselves, when the fracture is in the lower extremities, (abstracted from the nature of the fracture itself,) has been of late a consideration. It has been a question whether they should lie on their backs or on their sides. I am inclined to prefer the back; for, from the experience of one patient, who had the same thigh-bone broken twice, lying on the back was the easiest, though it was the last, method of lying; and I conceive that it is a position that can be borne longer than that on the side.

The pain arising from fracture is but little, only from the bones either tearing or wounding the soft parts. The inflammation is of course but little, if the parts have not been violently torn.

Of Compound Fractures.—If the violence of the fracture has continued the laceration through the skin, so as to have allowed part of the blood to escape, and to have exposed the remainder sufficiently long to allow it to lose its living principle, so as to become an extraneous body, unfit for the purposes of union, then the suppurative inflammation must take place, and granulations finish the union which the blood was incapable of doing. In this case the granulations become the origin and seat of formation of the callus, and go through the regular changes until they become ossified, as was the case with extravasated blood in simple fracture. In these cases considerable fever and inflammation, proportioned to the local injury, come on.

There are two cases which partake of the nature both of simple and compound fracture. The first is, where the injury was a simple fracture at first but afterwards becomes a compound, which I shall call the simple compound fracture; the other is when the fracture is a compound one at first, but the external wound so small, and the soft parts having sustained so little injury, as to require very little different treatment from what happens in the simple fracture: and this kind I call a compound simple fracture.

Of the Simple Compound Fracture.—This is owing, in some cases, to some part of the extravasated blood losing its living principle, and then acting as an extraneous body; in others it is owing to the sharp end of the bone pressing against the inside of the skin and causing it to ulcerate. In these cases we see inflammation come on, at first, as in simple fracture, with that mildness which generally attends such cases; but some days after a stimulus is given by the broken pieces of bone, or by the blood which has lost its living principle, or from the parts being beyond the power of union by the first intention, and the suppu-rative inflammation comes on.

The cases which I have seen of this kind have been much less dan-gerous than fractures that were compound from the first. The only reason I can assign for this is, that the whole of the blood produced from the lacerated parts does not lose the living principle, so that a considerable portion becomes so much a part of the living solids during the first few days as to be able to keep its ground, only a portion of it acting to produce the suppurative inflammation, which is therefore less.

The treatment of the simple compound fracture is very simple : the limb may be bound up in general as in a simple fracture, with splints and a roller, only leaving a free space for the change of dressing and to keep the parts clean.

Of the Compound Simple Fracture.—The effect of this is similar to the foregoing, though the cause is different. There are cases of com-pound fracture where the wound in the skin is but very little at first. If the broken ends of the bone have not done much mischief to the soft parts, and only made a small wound in the skin, they may be treated as simple fractures, which gives us an opportunity of retaining the uniting matter. By immediately closing up the wound with a bit of sticking-plaster, or a little lint soaked in the blood and allowed to dry on it, the greater portion of the wounded parts and broken ends of the bone will unite by the first intention, and only those parts of the solids which are exposed will suppurate. This small suppuration will oblige the surgeon to leave the wound in the skin free from bandage, in order to be enabled to look at it occasionally; though, from some accounts, it might seem that even this was not necessary. This mode of treat-ing it as a simple fracture obliges it to heal as such. This practice has been followed even when the laceration in the skin was considerable; but I have not seen a sufficient number of cases to say how far it may be extended.

Inflammation, Suppuration, and Ulceration of circumscribed Cavities.— All circumscribed cavities, as the pleura, peritoneum, &c., admit of the three inflammations. They may be formed into true and distinct ab-scesses by adhesions inclosing the matter, as in common abscess. If the inflammation does not stop at the adhesive, then suppuration fol-lows, and ulceration also becomes necessary for the exit of the matter, which is an extraneous substance. A material circumstance happens in the inflammation of cavities containing vital parts, which is, that very little sympathy exists between the surrounding part and the parts contained, whence the inflammation of the one is not always continued to the other: thus, inflammation of the peritoneal coat of the abdomen and of the intestine may exist without inflammation of the inner coat of the intestine. But this does not hold good universally, for inflammation of the tunica vaginalis spreads through the whole body of the testis.

Inflammation of the Pleura.—This membrane is more subject to inflammation than any other investing membrane. Probably this does not arise from any difference of structure, but from its situation, by which it is exposed to the operation of cold air, and from its contact with the lungs. Perhaps there is hardly one in fifty who, at the age of fifty, is without adhesion of the lungs to the pleura. We often find the lungs adhering to the whole surface of the pleura lining the thorax, and it does not seem necessary that inflammation should take place on both surfaces to produce adhesion. Abscesses may be formed here, either having the matter inclosed in a particular bag or diffused through the whole side, forming one large abscess; hence true and false empyema.

Empyema.—The cavity of the chest is subject to the two diseases of other circumscribed cavities, dropsy, and inflammation and suppuration, or empyema. These two kinds of disease will have some of their symptoms very different, though the symptoms arising from the ultimate effect, namely, the collection of fluid in the chest, will be nearly the same in both. But as this cavity has connexions with parts whose symptoms when diseased will be very different from those of this cavity simply, and as those parts will sympathize with the diseases of this cavity, we shall find that a complication of symptoms will often take place which may mislead the judgment so much as to make us suspect that the sympathizer is the seat of the disease.

This sympathizer is the heart; and as a disease of this part has produced symptoms which have been lately called angina pectoris, we find that it requires particular attention to be paid to the specific symptoms of empyema to separate them from those of the heart.

The general cavity of the chest is divided into two distinct cavities; therefore whatever disease affects one simply, cannot affect the other by its having affected this.

Water may collect in the cavity of the chest almost at once, without giving much previous notice. It may be the consequence of various causes, as cold, fever, &c. The symptoms arising from the presence of a fluid are either peculiar, common, or sympathetic, which last may or may not occur.

The first true specific or peculiar symptom arising from an extraneous fluid, in some considerable quantity, in the cavity of the chest, is difficulty of breathing, which is always an attendant, and is distinguished from difficulty of breathing from other causes by this, that the patient is always able to breathe much better in certain positions. This position will vary according to circumstances : if water is only on one side, the person can lie on that side, and on that side only ; if on both sides, he can lie on his back, not horizontally, but with the chest raised as much as possible. He feels the fluctuation of the fluid within the chest whenever he moves, especially when he raises himself up. I have heard patients often say that they could hear the fluid move. The fluid is felt pressing like a weight on the diaphragm. An anasarcous habit often takes place, and sometimes ascites. These two last symptoms would seem to arise from a universal irritable debility:

The second, or common symptoms with other diseases, of those parts are difficulty of breathing, and of expanding the chest ; great lowness and oppression ; a feeling of suffocation or of dissolution.

The third, or sympathetic, symptoms are often great irregularity of the pulse, palpitations, flutterings.

When the symptoms are known to arise from the presence of a fluid in the chest, it should in general be let out by an operation called paracentesis thoracis, which is only making an opening into the thorax and allowing the fluid to flow out. The wound should be made to unite by the first intention. The fluid to be evacuated may be of various kinds : as blood from a ruptured vessel, or wound made with a ball or cutting instrument ; or extravasated serum, as in hydrops pectoris ; or pus, the consequence of inflammation.

Whatever the fluid is which is to be discharged, I have always found suppuration take place in all the operations I have seen performed ; for when the discharge was nothing at first but serum, (as water in ascites,) yet afterwards it gradually changed into pus. This arose simply from keeping the external wound open. I am inclined to think that nothing could have saved these patients but resolution of the inflammation, and the parts falling back into their natural disposition. This, as I have mentioned, sometimes takes place in common abscesses, especially those of a scrofulous kind, and in the present cases it might the more readily take place, as there is here no change of structure or granulation of the whole surface of the pleura or lungs. However, wounds have been made into the cavity of the thorax, suppuration has taken place, and yet the patient has got well ; but how this has been brought about I cannot tell *. General Murray, to whom I have often expressed a wish to peep

---

* [There cannot be any doubt that the cure is effected in these cases by the obliteration of the cavity of the pleura, partly by coagulable lymph which is effused at the

into his chest, has been twice wounded in this way. I tried the experiment by shooting a dog; but both Nature and the dog cheated me,
for I intended to keep open the wound until the whole surface of the
pleura had taken on suppuration, when I meant to let Nature have her
way and cure the dog as she pleased, and then I intended to kill the
dog and see what she had done. But the dog would always lie on the
wounded side; and when, after death, I examined it, I found the lungs
had adhered to the wound and prevented the inflammation spreading
over the surface of the lungs. The wound, after the evacuation, therefore, should be united as quickly as possible, to prevent the whole pleura
from suppurating, which would destroy the patient in nineteen cases
out of twenty.

Inflammation of the Pericardium.—The cavity of the pericardium is
not so apt to produce universal adhesions as that of many other cavities*.
When it goes no further than adhesion the patient lives, although this
produces many disagreeable symptoms, as palpitation of the heart, irregularity of the pulse, great oppression and faintings, which in general
produce a bad state of health, a great debility, and symptoms which
have gone by the name of angina pectoris. If the inflammation approaches to suppuration, it will certainly kill.

Emphysema.—It will not be improper here to say something of the
treatment of patients affected with emphysema arising from a wound
in the lungs by a fractured rib, for if any surgical operation is necessary, great caution is required not to make the wound communicate
immediately with the cavity of the thorax, in order to avoid the mischief
above described.

If the lungs are wounded by a fractured rib, we know that the pleura
must be wounded, and that there must be a communication between the
cells of the lungs and the cavity of the thorax. There is also a communication between this cavity and the common cellular membrane of
the body by the wound in the pleura. The air escapes from the lungs

---

same time with the serum or pus, and partly by granulation; the cavity of the pleura
being precisely under the same conditions as a common abscess, and healing by the
same methods. In these cases the patient seldom regains the power of complete expansion of that side of the chest, which always remains in a more or less contracted and
flattened state.]

* [This may be accounted for by the unintermitting action of the heart, which must
present the most unfavourable conditions imaginable for the organization of the lymph.
The opposing surfaces of the pleura or peritoneum may be preserved by the patient
in the most perfect state of apposition during the progress of inflammation, by breathing only by the chest or diaphragm, according as the case may be. But the heart has
only one mode of action, which must continually tend to disturb the process of union,
just in the same manner that the continually recurrent action of the sphincter ani prevents the cure of fistulæ in that situation.]

into the cavity of the thorax, and in the act of respiration is squeezed into the cellular membrane of the body. The internal wound does not inflame so quickly as the external, because the internal depends on extravasated blood for the renewal or adhesion of parts; and the wound of the lungs, from its being in contact with the air, may be considered as an external wound, while that of the pleura is an internal one: the former will therefore probably heal sooner than the latter, whereby the air will be confined in the cavity.

The operation for the relief of this disease is making a perforation into the cavity for the relief of this disease, which operation should be religiously avoided, because it will produce the suppurative inflammation all over the internal cavities, and most probably make the wound in the lungs ulcerate. If an external opening is necessary, it should be made at some distance from the fractured rib, and never on the rib itself. If this is not attended to, it will make what was at first a simple a compound fracture, which probably would produce the same effect as an incision at once into the cavity of the thorax ; or if it did not produce this evil, would produce adhesive inflammation quickly about the fractured rib, which would prevent any future escape of air from the pleura, which should be allowed ; and for the same reason the patient should not have a roller bandage put on, as this would cause an impediment to the respiration by the other lung, and, by preventing the escape of the air, cause the whole contents of the thorax to be pressed to the other side.

Peritoneal Inflammation.—This inflammation is attended with great pain, not of the colicky kind, but a violent soreness or tenderness on external pressure. The fever, or sympathy of the constitution, arises much higher than if it arose from the inflammation of a common part, and runs through all its stages much sooner than another part. When the immediate cause of these constitutional symptoms is not known, and the effects are violent, it has been called a fever, and the chief attention has been directed to checking this fever ; but the symptoms are merely the consequence of the inflammation in a part by which the constitution is easily affected ; so that if it were possible to restore the healing disposition to the cavity of the abdomen, the other symptoms would vanish and health be restored. A diarrhœa sometimes comes on, but at other times there is costiveness, both of which I am inclined to think may be considered as sympathetic affections.

It is perhaps almost impossible at first to say what the inflammation is, whether the true inflammation or the erysipelatous, because we are only guided by the constitutional symptoms, not by the appearances. A person in seemingly tolerable health attacked at once with so violent a local disease will be at first roused, which will make it appear a truly inflammatory complaint; but if it is erysipelatous he soon sinks. Still at first the apparent indication would be bleeding, and that largely; but if it is of the erysipelatous kind we may be led by those symptoms beyond the quantity suitable to the constitution. Yet I do not know what we can do better: I should be inclined to reduce the patient to the lowest pitch rather than allow suppuration to take place, for that would certainly kill. In whatever light we consider an inflammation of the peritoneum that is capable of producing suppuration, it is one of the most dangerous diseases we can meet with. How far in such cases it might appear desirable to make an opening into the abdomen, and throw in warm water repeatedly to wash away the matter, I will not undertake at present to determine.

Peritoneal Inflammation after lying-in.—Inflammation often attacks some part or the whole of the peritoneum in women some days after childbirth, and hence has been called puerperal fever, from supposing it to be a fever peculiar to that state, and the inflammation of the peritoneum a consequence of this fever, whereas the fever is only a sympathetic symptom of the inflammation; but as this inflammation is connected with vital parts, the sympathetic fever is so much the more violent and dangerous. I believe I am the first who formed this idea of this disease.

Why such a disease should occur after so natural an operation is not easily explained. It does not arise from an inflammation of the substance of the uterus first taking place, as we might at first naturally expect; for if the uterus did inflame in consequence of delivery, there would be no more necessity for the peritoneum of that viscus to inflame than for the peritoneum of an intestine to inflame when the intestine is itself inflamed, which it seldom does; and if the peritoneum of the uterus inflamed in consequence of inflammation of the uterus, that is not a necessary cause why the whole peritoneum should inflame, excepting the inflammation was carried so far as to produce suppuration on that part of the peritoneum. But the substance of the uterus generally appears as sound as in those who have no such disease; however, although the uterus is to appearance sound, yet it may be in such a state as to give the same stimulus of imperfection as if it were entirely removed or not existing. To illustrate this we may bring forward the circumstance of two cocks' combs that were frozen and thrown off as dead sloughs, for I suppose from analogy that the frozen parts were still alive, and if so we may see that a living part may be so circumstanced as to give the stimulus of death to the parts with which it is connected. That the inflammation of the peritoneum arises from the stimulus of imperfection is also evident, because if a man is wounded in the belly with a sword which has also wounded one of the intestines, if the wound in the abdomen is closed, and unites by the first intention, the wound in the intestine will unite with some part with which it comes in contact, either by extravasated blood or the adhesive inflammation, and no further trouble will ensue, because the stimulus of imperfection has not been given. But if a man is wounded in the belly, and there is no wound of the viscera, yet if the wound is kept from healing by the first intention, the whole peritoneum becomes inflamed immediately, not from the spreading of inflammation by the continuity of surface, but the consciousness of imperfection in the membrane itself, by which the whole is brought into the same action. It is probable that the uterus suddenly contracting, the neighbouring parts, becoming sensible, as it were, of the loss of a part they have been accustomed to, inflame. Sometimes adhesion will take place, and a circumscribed abscess will be formed in the lateral and lower part of the belly, and probably the inflammation was chiefly in the round or broad ligament : first there is hardness and pain, then prominence and fluctuation, when it may be safely opened*.

Inflammation of Peritoneum after tapping.—A man whom I tapped at the hospital died the third day. I said he died of the puerperal fever. This was smiled at in the hospital, and some were pleasant in remarking on the curiosity of a man being delivered ; but a few months after-

---

* [Mr. Hunter has fallen into two errors on this subject: first, in ascribing puerperal peritonitis to an ideal cause; and secondly, in supposing that the constitutional fever invariably arises from inflammation of the peritoneum. There cannot, I should think, be the least hesitation in ascribing the inflammation of the peritoneum which ensues on childbirth to the irritation which the uterus has suffered during that process, for the inflammation is not only sometimes confined to that part of the membrane which covers the uterus, and always is most violent there, but it invariably commences from that point. The fact, however, of the same cause giving rise to inflammation of the adjacent organs is completely subversive of the imaginary cause assigned by Mr. Hunter, arising from the "consciousness of imperfection." No such imperfection can be supposed to be felt by the veins, the absorbents, or the ovaries, and yet these parts are frequently inflamed, independently of the peritoneum. Of forty-five fatal cases of puerperal fever which were examined by Dr. Lee at the British Lying-in hospital, (in all of which was found some morbid change, the effect of inflammation,) the peritoneum and uterine appendages were found inflamed in thirty-two; in twenty-four there was uterine phlebitis ; in ten there was inflammation and softening of the muscular tissue of the uterus; and in four the absorbents were filled with pus. In short, the irritation of parturition may extend to any or all the circumjacent parts within the sphere of its influence, and give rise to puerperal fever by exciting local inflammation. Local inflammation probably *always* exists, but the peritoneum is not *always* that part which the inflammation attacks.

The morbid appearances presented on dissection are extremely various, and closely resemble those which arise from inflammation of the peritoneum following the great operations of surgery, as lithotomy, hernia, &c., viz., large effusions of lymph, turbid serum, or pus separately or blended together in different proportions. Pus is not an invariable product of this inflammation, as might be inferred from the text.]

wards another having the same fate, I convinced them, by dissection, that he had died of suppuration of the peritoneum, which we must admit to happen in puerperal fever. Frequently the inflammation does not go so far as to produce suppuration, and then the patient commonly recovers; but it often runs the whole course and produces death. It seldom attacks those parts of the peritoneum that are pretty sound, or where the disease is not of long standing; but where the disease has arisen from a bad constitution or diseased viscera, it seldom fails of attacking them, especially in the second or third tapping.

Hernia.—The consideration of inflammation of internal cavities leads me to make a few remarks on hernia. We might suspect that the operation for hernia would often be the cause of universal inflammation of the peritoneum, but I believe in bubonocele and femoral hernia it is generally prevented by the sides of the skin of the abdomen being pressed together after the operation. This inflammation is met with after the operation for umbilical hernia, because the edges of the wound cannot be brought together.

In this case we should contrive that a portion of the epiploon shall remain at the bottom of the wound, and if it is not protruded I think it would be the best way to find it if possible; in this way, by adhesion taking place round the opening, the general cavity would be excluded.

Cæsarean Operation.—In this operation, and in every other instance where the lips of the wound do not come well together, assistance should be had from art to unite them as closely as possible. If it should be found necessary to use sutures, care should be taken that they do not pass through into the cavity of the abdomen, as by this they would produce effects exactly contrary to what was wished,—that of rendering the cavity perfect; for as these continue, suppuration of the wounds made by them will come on, they acting as a seton, by which the exposure of the cavity will be greater, though perhaps, from the irritation they would occasion, adhesions would be formed at the bottom of the wound before they suppurated, which might prevent the admission of air.

In a woman in whom I performed this operation, and who died, I found, thirty-six hours after death, that the intestines had adhered to the inner edge of the wound of the belly for the breadth of an inch : the uterus was entirely within the pelvis ; but the edges of the wound in the uterus had not closed at all, and a good deal of coagulated blood was found in it. I should therefore in future wait until the bleeding had nearly stopped from the uterus before I closed the external wound.

Bladder.—It may be said that the bladder being so seldom inflamed after the operation for stone, is an objection to my supposition that an opening into any circumscribed cavity, by the exposure and consciousness of imperfection induced in that cavity, is almost necessarily productive of inflammation of that cavity ; but here it must be observed that the internal surface of the bladder partakes more of the nature of an outlet than of a circumscribed cavity, admitting therefore less of the adhesive inflammation, and that it is more accustomed to and less affected by the action of extraneous matter, which must render it less susceptible of inflammation from exposure.

Cavities of Joints.—It is from the disposition that the cavities of joints have to fall into the suppurative inflammation when an opening is made into them that union by the first intention does not take place. The greatest care should be taken to put this in their power if possible, for as they do not readily run through the regular stages of inflammation, they give rise to the more violent symptoms. When they suppurate it is very tedious, and then the parts are apt to die and slough, which makes these accidents of such dangerous consequence. In cases of wounds I should think a simple bandage would be best. We should avoid making stitches, because they tend to produce inflammation, as was explained under wounds of the abdomen*.

Sacculi mucosi.—There are other cavities, besides those of the joints, which are liable to inflammation from irritation; these are the sacculi mucosi, which are in fact joints formed between tendons and tendons, tendons and bones, bones and skin. They are subject to disease, causing an increased quantity of fluid in them, not from inflammation, but from slight irritation. They are seldom attacked with suppurative inflammation; nor does the absorption of the fluid which they contain readily take place. Ganglions have been sometimes dispersed by soap plasters, and sometimes, although rarely, by electricity. A gentleman was cured of a ganglion on the wrist, which had returned after being dispersed by a blow, by the *Balsamum Canadense*, applied thick and bound on tightly. I would advise a blow to rupture the sac; but the fluid is soon reaccumulated. For a radical cure, an opening should be made, and this prevented from healing by the first intention, that it may suppurate and heal by granulations. As these are connected with joints, weakness and stiffness may be produced for a time; but this is overcome by motion.

Inflammation of the Eye.—I shall consider the eye now as a cavity.

---

* [The lighter and cooler the dressings in this sort of accidents the better. Perfect repose of the organ, an easy position, cold lotions, and a little lint dipped in blood over the wound, is probably the best, as it is also the simplest mode of treatment. If symptoms of inflammation arise, they should be combated at once by a copious venesection, which should be repeated, if necessary, until the inflammation is subdued.]

Inflammation of the eye often takes place after extraction of the crystalline lens. The lips of the cornea not adhering by the first intention,
suppuration ensues, which is followed by a shrinking of the globe. The
same effects are sometimes produced when an opening is made to discharge the accumulated aqueous humour, as also when the globe has
been suffered to burst spontaneously. This has sometimes happened
from accident, the opening into the anterior chamber not closing; but
probably these effects only take place where either the crystalline lens
or the vitreous humour have been disturbed or lost in part, but more
particularly the latter, as the adherence of the crystalline to the pro-
cessus ciliares would prevent the inflammation extending; but when separated, the posterior part of the eye becomes conscious of this, and
suppuration follows. The pus may be seen through the cornea, but no
fluctuation can be felt. It is necessary to distinguish between simple
opacity of the cornea and the accumulation of pus in the anterior chamber; they may appear similar, and both may be present at one time;
the first may be of long standing, the last must be recent : an inflammation must have very recently preceded the accumulation of pus. If
the progress of the opacity can be observed,—but it cannot always, especially in children,—we may distinguish them : if in the cornea, a dim-
ness may be seen to begin over the whole, and get white by degrees, or
it may remain in a point, and remain there only ; if pus, it will begin at
the bottom of the cornea, and its shape will be semilunar, the straight
line being uppermost, and as it advances the line will rise till it comes
to the top, and if first seen in this state it is with difficulty distinguished.

If the disease is an opacity of the cornea, reabsorption is the only cure,
and no operation is to be performed ; in the other case, the removal of
the pus is the cure. There appear to be two natural modes of cure ;
one the absorption of the pus into the constitution, which I have often
seen take place ; the other is ulceration of the cornea, as in other abscesses, and discharge of the pus. The latter is the worst mode of cure,
for the pus, by its pressure on the crystalline lens, may disease it, and
an irritation will be kept up by the distension, which should be avoided,
as the consequence will be the obliteration of the cavity of the eye, as
in any other abscess.

This, then, leads to an artificial cure, which is by removing the pus
at an early period, when we see it will not be absorbed, by an incision like that for removing the lens, by which we avoid the second or
natural cure ; but it is not always perfect, as we cannot always heal the
wound by the first intention*.

---

* [Hypopium, or the accumulation of pus in the anterior chamber of the eye, is very
often the result of inflammation of the whole internal part of the globe, which rarely

Of the Brain.—I have not seen a sufficient number of cases to determine how far inflammation attacks the pia mater when it is exposed in trepanning, but from the protrusion of brain in such cases inflammation may be inferred, as I have mentioned already. I never saw a case recover where the dura mater had been punctured*, which I attribute to inflammation of the pia mater extending to the brain below.

Inflammation of Veins.—The cavities of veins are subject to inflammation, either in consequence of inflammation of surrounding parts, or from themselves taking on the inflammatory disposition and involving the surrounding parts.

This inflammation of veins happens sometimes after bleeding, and has been attributed to a pricked tendon or nerve by some, and by others to a bad constitution; but if we consider this consequence arising from bleeding more accurately we shall find that it happens after bleeding in veins where no tendon could be wounded, and when no nerve is in the way, as often as in the others, and frequently in constitutions where there is no apparent want of health, and also where the wound, on bleeding from another part in the same person, probably with a view to cure the former, has healed readily.

The manner in which these inflammations come on shows very plainly that they arise from the wound made by the lancet not healing by the first intention, and in different arms we have also the different degrees of extension of the inflammation. In some, suppuration has only spread superficially, the veins and parts below having united, and the inflammation only seated between the vein and the skin, and then it is of little consequence; in other cases the skin shall appear united, but not close to the vein, so that a small abscess shall form between the skin and the vein. But when this imperfect union of wounded parts is carried on to the cavity of the vein, then more mischief ensues: the external wound in most cases festers or inflames, then suppurates and ulcerates; then the vein inflames from being an imperfect cavity, the inflam-

---

admits of a cure. When it proceeds from an ulcer situated on the internal part of the cornea, a cure may be expected, particularly if mercury is employed, which causes the effused pus to be absorbed. Neither of these circumstances, however, can justify the surgeon in making an opening into the cornea, unless there is at the same time an excessive accumulation of purulent fluid, giving rise to great pain and tension of the globe. In which cases relief may be afforded by letting out the pus, although little hope of saving the sight can be entertained from the operation.]

* [Wounds of the dura mater undoubtedly very much aggravate the ultimate danger arising from other accidents, but are not in themselves universally fatal. On the contrary, numerous cases are recorded of extensive penetrating wounds of the brain which have recovered without a single untoward symptom.]

mation extending both towards the heart and from it; and also, for a considerable way also, the surrounding parts join in the inflammation. We find in these cases all the different degrees of inflammation in different cases; sometimes it goes no further than the adhesive inflammation, and suppuration is prevented by adhesion being allowed to take place in this part. The veins in such cases are ever after obliterated, and may be felt, after the surrounding inflammation has subsided, like hard cords. But these slighter effects are not always all, and suppuration will unfortunately too often take place.

The suppuration has all the degrees of violence and extension. It is often so confined as only to form a small abscess near the orifice; this arises from adhesions having taken place in the vein a little above and below the orifice. In many cases the inflammation and suppuration extend further, adhesions not having taken place: sometimes a very long abscess is formed, and often there is a series of abscesses, following one another in the direction of the vein, between the orifice and the heart; but not always in this course, for we find them sometimes between the wound and the extreme parts. I have seen from a wound in the foot the saphena inflame all up the leg and thigh, nearly to the groin, and have been obliged to open a string of abscesses almost through the whole course.

I have almost always found that inflammation has taken place in the larger veins which pass through a part that has been violently inflamed. This disease often happens in horses after bleeding, for the operators do not take proper care to close the orifice in these animals. This has sometimes proved fatal; but whether from the inflammation extending to the heart, or from the matter that is secreted in the veins passing in considerable quantity into the circulation, I cannot say.

The method of preventing these ill effects is to bring the edges of the wound carefully together, when the bleeding is finished, that they may unite by the first intention. I would recommend a compress of linen in preference to plaster; for I imagine that the blood itself being applied over the orifice is a kind of bond of union which is more natural than any other application. I have seen more sore arms after bleeding where a plaster has been applied than in any other cases. I have also seen it several times where the orifice has opened a second time and bled again, and has not been properly closed.

Treatment.—If inflammation has just come on and not arrived to suppuration, a compress should be applied to produce adhesion of the sides of the vein, whereby the inflammation may be prevented from reaching the suppurative stage. If the suppuration is come on, let pressure be applied immediately above, to prevent the matter from passing to the heart, by producing adhesion there.

Inflammation of Arteries.—Arteries unite by adhesion when their sides are compressed. This we find after the division of the larger arteries after amputation. I never have seen arteries suppurate, and do not know whether they ever do suppurate, nor what would be the consequence. Perhaps it would produce mortification; but I am about to determine this by experiment.

CHAPTER XVI.

OF HYDROCELE.

*Theory of the cure simple, but in practice the operation often fails.—De-
scription of the disease;—distinguished from others.—Encysted hydrocele;—its nature;—common to all ages and constitutions;—disappears
spontaneously in children;—rarely in adults;—symptoms;—state of the
testicle to be ascertained;—hydatid;—scirrhus;—false membrane covering testes;—adhesion of testis to cicatrix after puncture;—former cicatrix to be avoided.—Palliative treatment;—hæmatocele;—diffusion of
blood into the cellular tissue;—suppuration following simple puncture.—
Radical cure;—various methods recommended;—object of all;—adhesive inflammation occasionally occurs;—obstacles to its taking place.—
Erroneous notions of the mode of cure.—Injection;—tent;—seton;—
caustic;—laying open sac;—violence of the latter method;—all severe.
—Practice of removing testicle when enlarged;—doubtful if always
required.—Causes of failure of all the above operations,—of each in
particular.—Mode of operating recommended;—after-treatment, and
consequent symptoms.—On the actions of medicines.—On diseased dispositions and actions.—Of the difference of different parts to heal.—Of
one disease curing another.*

THE disease called hydrocele is a very common one; it consists of an
undue secretion of the fluid which moistens the tunica vaginalis testis,
and admits of a cure according to the laws of inflammation, suppura-
ration, and granulation, which is the process of a common abscess.
Although the theory of the cure of a hydrocele is very simple, yet no
disease affecting the human body, and requiring an operation for its cure,
has called forth the opinions and pens of surgeons so much as this disease*. The reason of this is easily accounted for; for they have gone

---

* [This was no doubt the reason which led Mr. Hunter to enter so fully into the
consideration of the subject. " At the time," Sir Astley Cooper remarks, " I was attending Mr. Hunter's lectures, the town was divided in opinion as to the best mode of
performing the operation for hydrocele; and so great was the difference of opinion
among the students of the different hospitals, that it was quite ridiculous to observe
their warmth on this subject." The operation by injection, as recommended by Sir
James Earle, was not introduced until a few years afterwards, but has since been universally acquiesced in as one of the most simple as well as most effectual remedies
of surgery.]

so far as to find that every mode of operating but their own has failed, but have not noticed the cause of failure. It was enough for them that they could condemn. They rested contented with having recommended a method which was to them infallible; nor did the condemnation of this favourite method of theirs by others rouse them into an inquiry as to the cause of its failure.

The scrotum in man has two circumscribed serous cavities in it, which may become the reservoirs of any part of the blood that may be extravasated, but which are generally in these cases distended with water, forming an aqueous cyst. Besides this, there are other extravasations of water into the scrotum, but they are common to every part of the body as well as it.

Each of these cavities is called tunica vaginalis testis, and when either of them is filled with fluid it is called a hydrocele.

There are other cavities formed in these parts from disease, like those formed from similar diseases in other parts, and which may be called hydatids. I believe they are more common in these parts and in the ovaria in women than in most other parts, probably from their being glands of a peculiar kind.

But every distension of the scrotum with water is called a hydrocele; even water collected in the cellular membrane of the scrotum in anasarcous habits, where it has only soaked through from the parts above, or arises from irritation: this kind might be called diffused hydrocele. This collection in the cellular membrane is often so great as to be diffused into the cellular membrane of the penis, which always produces phymosis, with twisting of the skin of the body of the penis, from the frenum not being so extensible as the common skin. This often proves very troublesome, by confining the urine. The radical cure of this kind of hydrocele will be the cure of the disposition, which is commonly more constitutional than local. But this cannot always be done; and we may then give a temporary relief to the parts where the scrotum is become considerably enlarged, with much phymosis. It then becomes necessary to procure an evacuation of the water, which can easily be done by making small punctures with a lancet or needle in the most depending part of the scrotum, and also, if necessary, at the end of the prepuce. However, some attention must be paid to the state of the patient; for, if very weak and debilitated, mortification may take place at these orifices: therefore the smaller and fewer the punctures the better.

Another watery swelling, similar to the above, is described, namely, an anasarcous state of the spermatic chord. This disease I never saw*.

* [Pott and Scarpa have both described this disease, which they represent as consisting of an enlargement of the cells of the spermatic cord, which in process of time,

The encysted hydrocele is a collection of water in some cyst situated in these parts. This species of hydrocele has been divided into three kinds, according to the situation of the water: first, when it takes place in the tunica vaginalis testis; secondly, when it occurs in the body of the testicle; thirdly, when in the spermatic cord; and, indeed, by the same mode of multiplying species, I could, from my own knowledge, make a fourth and fifth, namely, hydatids at the back of the testicle, where the vessels enter, and hydatids on the body of the testicle*, within the tunica vaginalis testis; which last may be complicated with hydrocele of the tunica vaginalis, as I have seen. These two last, as also hydrocele of the cord, are only hydatids in those parts. The hydrocele in the body of the testis must also be classed with hydatids; but this I have never seen. Of those on the outside of the testis I have seen several cases. All these tumours, however, are properly only divisible into two kinds: hydrocele of the tunica vaginalis, and hydatids; for it does not alter the disease whether the hydatids be in the spermatic cord, cellular membrane, scrotum, or body of the penis: it is still hydatid, wherever placed.

As the symptoms arising from the testicle being in a state of irritation are different from those of irritation in other parts, so we shall find that the symptoms arising from, and the cure of, these encysted hydroceles will be different from those arising from hydatids in the body of the testicle; whereas these will be similar to those of the tunica vaginalis testis, because in both they have connexion with the testicle. But the symptoms arising from the cure of hydatids not connected with the body of the testicle will be similar to common inflammation in all cases of the disease.

---

particularly towards the bottom of the tumour, merge in one general cavity, divided by a number of septa more or less perfect. Essentially, therefore, it does not differ from encysted hydrocele of the cord, except in the mode of its commencement.]

* [According to Sir Benjamin Brodie, these swellings commence between the tunica vaginalis and tunica albuginea of the testicle, and not in the proper structure of the testicle as has generally been supposed; they do not therefore essentially differ from encysted hydrocele of the epididymis, except in being more strictly bound down by the tunica vaginalis, which will necessarily tend to limit their growth, and on this account to obviate the necessity of surgical interference.

Simple hydatiform cysts in the body of the testicle are referred to by Dr. Hodgkin See Med.-Chir. Trans., vol. xv. p. 289.

It will scarcely be necessary to remind the reader that the term hydatid is employed by Mr. Hunter in the old acceptation. The true hydatid has no connexion with the surrounding textures, and is probably a parasitical animal, endowed with independent vitality and a peculiar mode of propagation. These do sometimes occur in the gland of the testicle in association with malignant disease; but never, I believe, as an original and independent affection.]

The cause of the anasarcous hydrocele is very evident: it arises from a universal disposition to throw out serum; and, from the situation of the part, it becomes a universal detainer of the water as it is descending from the upper parts.

In the encysted hydrocele the cause is generally not known, especially of the hydatid kind. However, the hydrocele of the tunica vaginalis often arises from a disease of the testicle; for I have observed that many who are operated on for the radical cure show a disease in the testicle; also I have seen several hydroceles that at first were hardly anything but true hydrocele, the testicle hardly appearing diseased, yet in time (viz. a year or two) the testicle has increased gradually, and the water has been diminished so much, that hardly anything was left but a large diseased testicle, and all this time giving little or no pain.

Hydrocele of the tunica vaginalis is common to all ages; it is met with in children, in middle-aged and old men. In children they arise sometimes before communication between the tunica vaginalis and abdomen is completely cut off, so that any fluid from the abdomen can pass down and distend the bag. In appearance this somewhat resembles a rupture; for when the water is pressed upwards, it makes a swelling close up to the ring, but by squeezing, it can be made to pass up into the belly. In these cases a slight bandage or truss should be worn for some years.

Hydroceles are common to every kind of constitution; not more common to the dropsical and anasarcous person than to the healthy. which is not the case with ascites or hydrops pectoris; therefore it is probable they arise from a disease in the part, or are what may be called truly local. They are common in all countries; but they would appear to be most common in warm climates.

In general we find them go away of themselves; in young lads, therefore, in such cases, I never recommend any mode of treatment. In grown people they seldom or never go away*; I have known only two or three cases in which they have disappeared without the obliteration of the sac. I have tried several stimulants, as mercurials diluted, turpentine, &c., by way of application, but they had not the desired effect. However, I once thought that the latter, namely turpentine, checked

---

* [Many examples are on record in which old hydroceles have disappeared spontaneously; an event which is most likely to happen, according to Sir Astley Cooper, when the disease has originated in inflammation; or, according to Sir Benjamin Brodie, about once in twenty cases. However, there is no rule on this subject. As ruptures of the tunica vaginalis from external injury are not followed by a permanent cure, we have no right to suppose that slighter degrees of external violence will have this effect; although something of this kind has frequently been supposed, when spontaneous cures have taken place.]

the progress of a hydrocele. Even letting out the water simply does not prevent the accumulation again taking place, whence the term *palliative cure*.

Diagnosis.—The encysted hydrocele consists of a bag filled with water placed in the scrotum, sometimes a little higher on the spermatic cord. The principal points to be known or discovered are, whether, when a tumour appears in this part, it contains water; and, if possible, the true situation of that water as respects the testicle: for there is another disease that will imitate this so as to be with great difficulty distinguished from it, which is a diseased testicle simply.

Some ruptures put on an appearance somewhat similar to hydrocele, and when the gut contains a fluid, it often gives an obscure fluctuation; so that hydrocele is but too often confounded with rupture.

Fluids contained in a circumscribed bag are commonly easily made to pass from one side of the bag to another, unless the bag is extremely full and thick in its coats, and then there will be only a gentle receding of the fluid from the side pressed on. This is made plain to the senses by applying our hands or fingers to two different parts of the bag, and pressing those two parts alternately: this is called fluctuation. But solid bodies also, of a loose texture, inclosed in a bag, can be made to recede from pressure, and give nearly, if not wholly in many cases, the sensation of a complete undulation; a feeling which the testicle sometimes takes on in one of its diseases. Therefore, as this body sometimes conveys the feeling of fluctuation of a hydrocele, and as the latter often acquires a hardness like that of the testicle, the difference we might expect to find between the feel of water and of the testicle is in some cases wholly lost.

I think that in general a distinction is to be made in the shape; for I observe that in general when the testicle swells, it flattens on each side, having an edge forwards and backwards, and is not, like hydrocele, of a pyramidal figure, with the apex upwards, passing into the cord towards the ring of the abdominal muscles, and even in some cases passing a little way into the ring, with (in many cases) a slight contraction at the part where it does pass into the cord. But this cannot be set down as an invariable rule, for the testicle will vary in shape according to the disease and other circumstances; and hydrocele will also vary in shape according to circumstances, and if it be an hydatid, and not within the tunica vaginalis, it will have less of the pyramidal form, though even then it often retains or acquires that shape; but if flat, it may·be suspected to be the testicle. It has been recommended that we should put a light on the opposite side, and see if the tumour has a degree of transparency; but this can only take place where it must be evident from other symptoms, where, namely, the skin is not thickened, and the fluctuation is therefore perfect*.

But supposing the disease to be well ascertained to be water, we are not in all cases properly prepared for an operation until its situation with respect to the testicle is exactly ascertained, for the situation of the testicle with respect to the general tumour will vary according as the water is situated. When the water is in the tunica vaginalis, as is most common, or in an hydatid in that bag, the testicle will mostly, if not always, be placed at the posterior part of the tumour, and there is consequently but little danger of doing mischief to the testicle by any of the operations, unless adhesions between the tunica vaginalis and testicle have previously taken place, and then the testicle will be confined to the side on which the adhesions are, as well as to the posterior part. If water is contained in an exterior hydatid, then it is not at all certain in what part of the general tumour the testicle may be. Perhaps it is often not possible in such cases to distinguish the situation even by the sensations of the patient, and therefore we must always be on our guard when the situation is not ascertained. If the testicle is found on any side of the scrotum except the posterior, it is more than probable that the water is not within the tunica vaginalis, but in some cyst or hydatid placed contiguous to the testicle, or that some adhesions have taken place between the tunica vaginalis and testicle, cases of which I have seen. If an hydatid is within the tunica vaginalis, and fills up the whole tunic, it will in general be similar to the case of water within the bag itself; but it admits of a variety of complications, which may lead the surgeon into error even in the time of the operation, a case of which I think I have seen. The complication appeared to be the following: water both in the hydatid and tunica vaginalis, which led the

---

* [There is only one disease of these parts which there is much danger of being mistaken for hydrocele, and that is the medullary disease of the testicle, which it is often very difficult to distinguish from hydrocele. Besides the points of difference which have been noticed in the text, I may observe that *the oval shape* of the testicle in fungus hæmatodes is generally marked with some degree of bulging, which destroys the perfect ovality of the swelling; that the *cord* may be felt perfectly distinct for a greater extent of its course than in hydroceles of equal size; that the *feel*, although generally pulpy and elastic, is not uniformly so, but softer in some parts than it is in others; that the *weight* of the tumour is greater than that of hydrocele, and the *superficial veins* more swollen; and, finally, that the swelling commences uniformly in every part, unlike that of hydrocele, which begins at the lower part of the scrotum and gradually ascends. The test by the lighted candle ought not to be despised, especially as it conveys useful information as to the real situation of the testis, and very often gives immediate knowledge of the disease, when, from the tension of the swelling, it is scarcely possible to discern fluctuation. In doubtful cases, it is always expedient to insert a lancet or explorative needle into the tumour previously to the operation of castration.]

surgeon to remove the whole as a scirrhous testicle; for on opening the tumour and letting out the water, he found another tumour within this, which he naturally took to be the testicle itself, and which of course led to the extirpation of it. On examining the parts after removal, it was found to be simply another cyst of water, with the testicle sound within it, or rather behind it*.

There is another mode of complication which the above case gave me an idea of, and which I do conceive I once met with in a patient of my own, namely, that inflammation had taken place over the whole sac, so as for the sac to have become lined with coagulable lymph, similar to what I have seen in other cavities; that this lining at last became part of the sac; but that a part of this lining had separated from it, and the space between the two had become filled with water, as also the general cavity, so that they formed a sort of double hydrocele. This case and the anterior hydatid would, I presume, assume the same appearance.

We should naturally suppose, when the situation of the testicle is not immediately known, and where the temporary cure has been performed with success, that there could be but little doubt of the testicle being at some other part of the tumour than the part where the wound was first made; but this is not always to be trusted to, for the operation of the temporary cure often becomes the cause of adhesions of this part of the sac to the body of the testicle. This very case occurred to me when about to perform the radical cure, for after having made the first incision on the cicatrix, and cutting through the tunica vaginalis as I thought, I was cutting on the body of the testicle. In performing this part of the operation I suspected all was not right, but did not in the least expect to find the testicle, and therefore cut carefully on till I came to the tubular substance of the testicle. I of course desisted, and performed the operation in another part, at no great distance from the first, as the testicle is not a large body, and I did not require to make a second incision in the skin. There did not appear to be any additional symptoms in this case, in consequence of the wound in the testicle, which seemed to heal as readily as a wound elsewhere would do. When the testicle is in the fore part of the tumour, either from the water not being in the tunica vaginalis, or from previous adhesions there, and its situation is not known or attended to, and the operator makes an incision on the fore part where the testicle is, like that in the above-

---

* [There is reason to believe that this mistake has frequently occurred. The danger, however, of confounding hæmatocele with disease of the testicle is still greater, although the history of the case, and the suddenness with which hæmatocele commences, will never fail to point out the difference to the intelligent surgeon.]

mentioned case, and he finds he is cutting on the testicle, and determines to shift his ground, I would advise him either to go lower, or to ward one side with his future incision; but at all events not to go above the testicle, to get into the sac, for there he will most probably find the spermatic cord passing along the fore part; and by cutting through it he may cut the spermatic artery and castrate the patient, or cut the vas deferens, which will in all probability render the sore fistulous. A case of this kind I once saw, where the spermatic artery being cut, the blood escaped into the cellular membrane of the scrotum. This circumstance, of the cellular membrane of the scrotum being sometimes filled with blood in consequence of an operation, may at first mislead the surgeon to suppose it is mortification, if he is not acquainted with the cause*.

---

* [Every species of hydrocele, as Mr. Hunter has remarked, is reducible to two forms, that of hydrocele of the tunica vaginalis, and encysted hydrocele of the cord. The first, or common form of hydrocele, is a true dropsy of the tunica vaginalis, and arises from the same causes which produce dropsies in other situations. The encysted hydrocele of the cord is an adventitious production, which has no existence in the primary structure of the parts, and ought to be classed with serous cysts occurring in other parts of the body.

The varieties of common hydrocele depend on the form or structure of the sac, or the nature of its contents. The ordinary situation of the testicle in hydrocele is two thirds of the way down the tumour at the posterior part; but, as Mr. Hunter has remarked, the tunica vaginalis is liable to every possible form of adhesion, which will necessarily occasion great differences in the position of the testicle and its vessels, as well as of the external configuration of the hydrocele. When the testicle has united to the anterior part of the tunica vaginalis, at the lower part, the vessels of the cord are generally spread out over the anterior surface of the tumour, and become liable to be injured by the trocar. Sometimes the tunica vaginalis presents a honeycombed appearance on its internal surface; occasionally it is much thickened, especially in those who have resided in hot climates; or converted into cartilage, in which more or less extensive depositions of bone have taken place; at other times it is presented under the form of an hour-glass contraction, which may be either partial or complete, or may, after being partial at first, become complete afterwards. When there are no adhesions, and no thickening of the sac, the hydrocele may attain a very considerable magnitude. I have known several cases in which the apex of the tumour has advanced considerably beyond the external abdominal ring, so that no part of the spermatic cord could be distinctly identified, and the quantity of fluid exceeded from three to four pints; but a case is mentioned by Sir Benjamin Brodie which increased till it hung down to the patient's knees. The fluid of this form of hydrocele resembles that of ascites, that is, it is of a deep yellow colour, and is readily coagulated by heat. It loses its transparency, however, and becomes whitish when inflammation has been present, or becomes of a chocolate hue of various shades when from any cause the smaller vessels of the sac have been ruptured, so as to cause an effusion of blood into the cavity of the cyst: sometimes it contains a number of micaceous particles, consisting of adipocire; at other times a number of small bodies, looking like melon-seeds; and occasionally one or more loose cartilages, which exactly resemble those which are contained in the joints.

The serous cysts which are developed in the spermatic cord and epididymis, or be-

Of the temporary Cure.—I shall not say much with regard to the palliative or rather temporary cure of hydrocele, as it consists only of the evacuation of the water in the easiest and shortest way, without doing anything to prevent a recurrence of the disease, and is hardly so nice an operation as bleeding. The same care is necessary as above described to ascertain the situation of the testicle, lest the operator should puncture the body of the testicle, and, wounding, it will certainly fail in his intentions with regard to the evacuation of the water, and may be led by his failure to mistake the disease, and suppose it of more consequence than it really is; not to mention the injury which might be supposed to arise from injuring so sensible a part, though I believe this last circumstance is not of so much consequence as might be imagined, for I know a case where the water was placed in a distinct bag on the posterior part of the testicle, so that this body could not be distinguished from the general tumour by the surgeon, who therefore supposed it to be a hydrocele of the tunica vaginalis, with the testicle in its proper place; and that he might avoid wounding the testicle, he pushed his lancet into the fore and lower part, but no water came. This he repeated four times, nearly in the same place, with the same effect; and on a further knowledge of the disease it was found that all those four wounds were in the testicle; yet no bad consequence followed, nor did the patient suffer

tween the membranes of the testicle, are wholly different from the common hydrocele of the tunica vaginalis, and resemble those which are not unfrequently met with beneath the common integuments of the body, on the surface of the liver and kidneys, in the breast, the ovary, and in other situations. It is possible that they may be produced by the distension of one or more of the cells of the cellular membrane, which a partial inflammation or some other cause may have shut off from their communication with the adjoining cells; but this has not been ascertained. The secreting cyst is extremely.thin and loosely attached; and the fluid, instead of being like that of hydrocele of the tunica vaginalis, is remarkably transparent and watery, and does not coagulate by heat. The occurrence of these cysts on the body of the testicle, or epididymis, will necessarily give a lobulated and very irregular appearance to this organ, and expose it to be mistaken for malignant disease, although this mistake may easily be avoided in general, by a careful examination of the part with the fingers, or by a lighted candle. When they occur high up, they are liable to be confounded with hernia, especially as from their loose connexion with the neighbouring parts, and consequent great mobility, they may easily be pushed up towards the abdominal ring, or even through it, and in that case be protruded again whenever the patient coughs. In such cases, however, there is always a visible bulging above the situation of the ring, which cannot be entirely dispersed; besides, hydrocele in this situation may always be distinguished by pushing the tumour downwards, and then feeling for the spermatic cord above the tumour: under such circumstances, no impulse will be communicated to the finger when the patient coughs.

Hydrocele of the tunica vaginalis may coexist with encysted hydrocele of the spermatic cord, hernia, varicocele, diseases of the testicle, and hæmatocele. These complications may generally be distinguished without much difficulty, provided all the circumstances of the case are duly considered.]

more pain than afterwards, when the lancet went into the cavity of the bag where there was only water.

In such cases the best guides are the feelings of the patient, and not that of the surgeon,—a circumstance to which too little attention has been paid, for a great many diseases may be distinguished by the sensation of the part when in pain. It is well known that the pain felt on squeezing the testicle is very different from that arising from other parts; therefore if it is this organ that is swelled, the sensation arising from squeezing the tumour will be the same in every part, and will be that sensation which is peculiar to the testis; but if it is a hydrocele, or any adventitious swelling, the sensation will be different in different places, that is, when the part pressed is the testicle, the pain will be such as is usually felt on squeezing the testicle; and when the watery part of the tumour is pressed, the sensation of common pain only will be felt. From attending to this circumstance only, I have been able to distinguish a hydrocele from a pulpy testicle, when the disease was supposed by other surgeons to be the latter. However, there are cases in which I have still had my doubts about the situation, from the impossibility of pressing on it with sufficient firmness to give the true sensation when the coats are much thickened.

The operation for the temporary cure requires an incision not bigger than that made in bleeding; or it may be done with a small trocar. When the water is let out in this way, it sometimes happens that a vessel is wounded either in the skin, cellular membrane, or sac, which bleeds pretty considerably, and the blood is either diffused into the cellular membrane of the scrotum, giving the appearance of mortification, or extravasated into the sac, and fills it up probably as large as ever. Both these effects from tapping I have seen, but never saw any bad consequences arise from them, the blood being always absorbed. I could even conceive a good consequence to arise from the last, as it might be the means of forming a bond of union between the sac and the testicle by the first intention, which I have seen take place partially. This is one of the diseases called hæmatocele, described by authors; they have also described others of a different kind, but taking place from the same accident; and also some cases of hæmatocele of the spermatic cord, which I have not seen.

A blow has been known sometimes to burst the bag, by which means the water has been diffused into the cellular membrane of the scrotum, and a temporary cure has been produced in this way. The patient, and also the surgeon, have been alarmed sometimes with this case; for blood has been diffused with water into the cellular membrane, which has given the idea of mortification having taking place.

I would advise that the operation for the palliative cure should not be performed but at a time when the patient can lie by, as inflammation may come on and produce the radical cure where only the temporary was intended. A gentleman who was usually tapped every six months begged I would do it for him before he went to Paris. I objected, telling him my reasons. He was pleased with them, and postponed the operation until his return, and fortunately for himself, for it actually happened that inflammation succeeded the tapping, which proved the radical cure.

In cases where such an occurrence takes place, the wound made by the lancet or trocar has generally healed up in some measure; but inflammation has taken place in the whole sac, and suppuration has come on, and ulceration has led the matter to and through the skin. As the orifice has in many cases healed up, the cause of this inflammation is not so evident as it would be had the sac remained exposed, and the inflammation is therefore not so quick in its termination, and in many cases seems to be stationary, as if suspended between resolution and suppuration. In other cases resolution will take place when the inflammation has been very violent, and when we have been every day in expectation that suppuration would ensue. In this case I would advise you to open the sac, and complete the operation by suppuration*.

Of the radical Cure.—As various methods have been practised and recommended to effect a radical cure, it naturally leads me to make some observations on those methods, for they cannot be all equally proper in all cases; however, I mean not to be very particular in my criticisms on those different methods that have been proposed, only so far as to point out different cases where they may be attended with inconvenience, arising from particular circumstances in them; nor shall I mention these different methods further than will illustrate my own opinion. I do not even mean at present to recommend one method in preference to another, but only to show the advantages that each has, although they all proceed on the same principle, leaving to the surgeon, and in some measure to the patient, to choose for himself after he has thoroughly considered all the different circumstances of the case; while at the same time I mean to show that more depends on the mode of treatment after the operation has been performed than on the mode of operating.

The radical cure depends on the obliteration of the cavity which con-

---

* [Besides the suppuration of the sac which occasionally follows the palliative operation, particularly in West Indian patients, the sac sometimes mortifies in old people. Sir Astley Cooper has mentioned two cases of this kind, which were followed by death, from which he has judiciously enforced the propriety of keeping old persons to their beds whenever this apparently simple operation is performed.]

tains the water. There are but two natural methods in which obliteration of the sac can probably take place, namely, by our two inflammations, adhesive and suppurative; for union by the first intention can hardly take place, though I can conceive it possible in some cases where the operation for the temporary cure has been performed.

I have observed that this is a disease which never arises from the constitution, and seldom or never affects it; nor are the parts themselves much affected by the consequence of the disease, namely, the accumulation of water, especially if it is occasionally let out. It it necessary, therefore, that we should be very particular in our method of cure, for whatever danger arises rests in the mode of cure alone. We should always make a material distinction between an operation which is to cure a person of a disease which will probably kill of itself without an operation, and an operation which is performed to cure an inconvenience only, and where the danger is not in the disease but in the method of cure*.

The method of cure by adhesive inflammation is union of every part of the cavity with itself; and as the testicle makes part of the cavity, the tunica vaginalis must also unite with it. However, this method is one which I need hardly take notice of, as it is one which very rarely occurs in these cases, and as yet we have no certain method of procuring it without running a risk of the suppurative following it. It is much to be wished that such a method of cure could be put in practice with certainty and success. That it is possible for such a method to take place I know from experience, and also from the dissection of dead bodies, for we very often find the cavity of the tunica vaginalis entirely obliterated, and fixed to the tunica albuginea; but it is more than probable that in such cases there never had been water in the cavity, and therefore adhesions the more readily took place, these adhesions being a very common consequence of swelled testicle from gonorrhea. Perhaps letting out the water, and only keeping the wound open a short time, might just procure the adhesive state, and by allowing it to heal up before the suppurative took place the latter might be prevented; however, I believe the knowledge of this critical time, if there be such, is beyond the power

---

* [M. Dupuytren, in his Leçons Orales, used to remark that operations of convenience much more frequently prove fatal than others, such, for instance, as amputation of the thigh for old anchylosis of the knee, the removal or discharge of large bursæ, &c.; so much so that he was accustomed to decline operating in such cases. Surgeons occasionally allow themselves to be persuaded, by the importunities of a patient, to undertake operations against which their own judgments loudly declare: surely such conduct ought to be reprobated, as proceeding either from culpable weakness or some motive still more reprehensible.]

of human sagacity; therefore I believe it would not answer in most cases. Indeed I have seen suppuration follow simple tapping; and admitting we were masters of the degree of inflammation, yet many arguments might be brought against the probability of its success, for we might suppose it not possible for the adhesive to produce its effects universally: first, because it is next to an impossibility to evacuate the whole of the water, and that remaining would be sure to keep some parts separate; secondly, as the tunica vaginalis is much enlarged in such cases, the collapsing of the skin might prevent adhesion taking place at all; thirdly, the contact could not be so uniform as to bring all parts into apposition. I know but of two cases where this method occurred successfully.

Observations on the different methods of radical cure.—I believe I am the first who have taught that the radical cure is performed by inflammation, suppuration, and granulation; it was the general opinion, and I was always taught, that it was by adhesion; but if union took place by adhesion, without granulation, then we should not have had suppuration.

The most simple mode recommended for obliterating this cavity consists of making a small opening into the sac, and introducing an extraneous body to prevent union by the first intention in the wound, by which means universal inflammation should take place over the whole surface of the sac. This probably was not thought sufficient to raise an inflammation, therefore it was recommended to throw into the cavity by this orifice stimulating liquors, so as to increase the inflammation; they had not an idea of an imperfect cavity producing inflammation of itself. In very old cases, where suppuration is but slow in its progress, this mode may be of considerable service.

Another method was by seton, which was no more than a double tent, or two wounds instead of one.

The ideas annexed to these modes of practice were, that they produced adhesions of the sides of the sac to each other, and also to the testicle, by the first method of union. Great pains have been taken in a treatise published by Mr. Douglas to show the impossibility of the sac collapsing so readily as to unite in every part of its extent. But this is neither the effect one might naturally expect to ensue from the methods put in practice, nor what really takes place in the very cases where they were tried, as is easily known from the symptoms described by the operators themselves, which were plainly those of the suppurative inflammation, though they did not see it in that light.

... So far was this disease treated to procure adhesions of the tunica vaginalis to obliterate the sac, and perhaps it was on the same principle that a small caustic was at first applied, and which has been used with success; but in a late publication (Else's) it is recommended on principles very different from the foregoing, for it is there supposed that the whole tunica vaginalis sloughs off and passes out through the opening. But that the whole tunica vaginalis should slough away by this treatment more than when the whole cavity is laid open, is not to be conceived. It is, however, a well-known fact that the tunica vaginalis often throws off partial sloughs, and in some very old cases may slough wholly away; but it is not to be expected as a general effect. When it does slough, this is owing entirely to the diseased state in which the sac is at the time, and not to any particular virtue in the method of cure. I suspect that after caustic, more than after other methods of cure, there is an appearance very much like sloughing, so much so as very readily to deceive; this appearance is the coagulable lymph thrown into the cavity among the water from the internal surface of the sac in the time of the adhesive inflammation.

From the ignorance of the true principles of cure, and the uncertainty of success from the former methods, practitioners were led naturally into the method of opening the whole sac or bag; but most probably they were led to this practice by imitating what may be called the natural cure, in cases where the sac had burst and a radical cure ensued. It is most likely that the bursting of the sac never happened from mere distension, but from preceding inflammation and suppuration, which might arise from the distension, and in that light is only to be considered as an abscess. And here it will be proper for me to observe, that such a case might lead a surgeon to form an erroneous idea of it; for if he had not been consulted from the beginning of the disease, namely, when in the state of hydrocele, and also had not made himself master of what the disease now is, he might readily suspect it to be a diseased testicle, and might be confirmed in the opinion by the inflammation and suppuration, unless the appearance of these should cause him to suspect it not to be cancerous; but if it does not, he will be most likely led to the extirpation of the whole mass, unless by first laying open the abscess freely he should gain a knowledge of what the disease is. Even then, however, he might continue to be deceived, for the inflammation having attacked the body of the testicle, he will find it very much swelled, and to appearance diseased, especially if the abscess should not have been thoroughly opened. A case of this kind I once saw, and also the mistake above mentioned; the abscess was opened, and the testis exposed and condemned: when I saw the abscess and the testicle at the bottom, I suspected what the case was; the testicle was not removed, and the patient got rid of his hydrocele.

It is possible that a case of this kind might happen where the disease would not show itself so manifestly; for if the water had been contained in a hydatid, the testicle would not be exposed by opening the abscess, and the whole tumour might appear to be the body of the testicle. In a case of this kind the sick heavy pain and the pain of the back which attend diseased testicle would not be present, nor the pain in the small of the back; so that if these symptoms were attended to, there might still be a means of saving the testicle.

Although this natural cure might have shown the possibility of a cure being effected by inflammation and suppuration over the whole sac, and that very probably no more was necessary to produce it than making an opening into the sac, and not allowing it to heal by the first intention, yet it was certainly not understood, for it was thought necessary by some to open the whole sac, and indeed to make it still more secure by cutting off a part of the sac, or even the whole, which indeed was all that they could, unless they had dissected off the tunica albuginea from the testicle. As this method of operating is much more violent than the others, of course its consequences are more violent; it is, therefore, evidently not to be put in practice to its full extent, if a less violent and as sure a one can be devised. However, do not suppose that I mean to prefer a patient's ease during an operation to his cure.

In every one of the operations for the radical cure of hydrocele, the suppurative inflammation is an effect which is pretty violent, and therefore in many cases of thickened sac it produces an inflammation which is absolutely sufficient to kill some parts which are not able to support the actions of life, and which are thrown off in the form of sloughs.

Incision, it has been said, is to be preferred, because it gives the operator an opportunity of seeing the state of the testicle, which has been found very much diseased in such cases, so that the operator has thought himself obliged to have recourse to extirpation of it. This is a case which sometimes happens; but I suspect that, if the symptoms were particularly attended to, we might inform ourselves exactly of it before the operation was performed.

. Perhaps in most cases it would be right to perform the temporary cure first, which would show the state of the testicle at the time; and as the sac generally fills again pretty fast, there could be no danger of the testicle becoming diseased during the time of refilling: for in most cases where the testicle is diseased there is an obscurity in the feel; it will give the feel of water in some positions, and in others of more of a solid substance. However, in any of the operations, excepting that by caustic, we might judge I think of the state of the testicle as soon as the water was wholly or in part evacuated; and if the testicle is found of its natural size, there will be no reason for apprehension about it; and if very much thickened, then the surgeon is to act accordingly. But I am inclined to believe that such diseases of the testicle as are generally attendant on dropsy of its coats, and are perhaps the causes of that dropsy, seldom do much mischief.

I cannot say I ever saw a cancerous testicle that began by producing a common hydrocele, nor can I call to mind any case of common hydrocele, where the radical cure has been attempted, in which the testicle ever became cancerous afterwards. Yet I have known cases where it appeared a true hydrocele at first, and the testicle afterwards enlarged, and by degrees the water diminished, till at last the whole has been an enlarged testicle, and has been obliged to be extirpated. I have often seen the testicle diseased on opening the sac, and it has been generally thought proper in such cases to remove the whole; yet I imagine it is seldomer necessary than is thought. This disease would appear to be not sufficiently distinguished from cancer, to which I believe it has no real affinity; however, it is possible that cancer of the testicle may be attended with hydrocele. Perhaps this disease may have some connexion with scrofula, for I have seen scrofulous testicles, and have even extirpated them as cancerous. In some cases this practice is right, and it was so in those in which I did it, but it was not intentionally right; for although not cancerous, yet they often become so much diseased and so large that it is absolutely necessary to extirpate them. But still such have an advantage over cancers, as we may be pretty certain of the cure from the operation, which is not always the case where there is a cancerous disposition. If the case should appear very dubious, I should recommend an incision, that the state of the testicle may be better understood, and the patient will be equally sure of a cure.

I shall now mention the causes of failure common to every method of cure, and then the causes of failure peculiar to each.

The sac containing the water being membranous, it only can be distended by the water which it contains, and readily collapses and throws itself into folds whenever this distension is taken off; and, as every method of cure requires the evacuation of the water, the membrane will collapse, if not prevented; and this collapsing I find to be the common cause of failure in them all.

It is a principle in the animal œconomy, when any natural internal cavity is exposed, that if any two parts of the cavity are brought together they will unite, but only at the edge next to the exposed surface; beyond this, if any two parts of the surface are in contact, they will not unite, being excluded from the necessity of union by the union of the edges which are nearest to the exposure. This part that does not unite then is formed into a cavity capable of containing a fluid, and of being hereafter filled in that way: where the sac has been large and not thickened, several such cavities may be formed, each capable of carrying on the disease. Until I understood the above facts, I could not understand why we have recurrence of this disease in the same tunica vaginalis. The first time I saw that a recurrence could take place was in a patient of my own, who died of smallpox whilst under the radical cure of the hydrocele. The recurrence of the disease will follow every method which does not prevent the two sides of the sac coming into contact with one another in the time of inflammation.

Of the Causes of Failure common to the Seton, Tent, and Caustic.—In either of these three methods of treatment, if the water is evacuated immediately, or is evacuated soon after the operation, at least before suppuration has come on, it often happens that the surface of the sac surrounding the orifices shall come in contact with the body of the testicle and adhere, which will immediately exclude all the other parts of the cavity from the necessity of inflaming, suppurating, &c., so that no union of the sac is produced but at the part. I have known a seton inclosed in this way along its whole course, and lying in a canal formed for it, instead of being loose in the general cavity.

I have known the same thing happen to the parts when the caustic has been applied : the edges of the sac all round have adhered to the . testicle, so that when the slough has come away this has formed the bottom of the wound, which granulated; the wound filled up, the disease recurred, and required a second operation. I have also found sometimes, where the caustic has been used, that Nature has covered the inner surface of the eschar with new living matter, by which the inner cavity has been made perfect. A patient of mine had a hydrocele in each tunica vaginalis. I applied the caustic to each: when the sloughs came out, I observed at the bottom of each a bluish white surface, while the edges all round were red and granulating. This surface I suspected was the tunica vaginalis not affected by the caustic. I endeavoured to complete what the caustic had failed in ; but was surprised to find that I was obliged to push my lancet in half an inch before the water came, when I introduced a tent to prevent its being wholly evacuated. I made a similar attempt on the other side : I introduced my lancet half an inch, and no water came, and I then made a puncture through the sound skin, and had not to go so deep as when the eschar had fallen out.

I suppose that when a breach or waste or loss of substance is produced in the outside of any cavity (and probably in every other part) there immediately takes place an irritation suitable to this cause, and this irritation produces an extravasation of coagulable lymph on the inside, to preserve the cavity or part as entire as possible, which it had certainly effected in this case. Probably this is the common cause of failure in the immediate effect of caustic, which was not before understood.

We see the same thing take place in joints : where that part of the bone which makes part of the joint becomes dead, we find a layer of coagulable lymph laid over the dead part or end of the cartilage, which preserves the joint perfect ; otherwise the whole cavity must suppurate. In these cases of joints, as well as in the above, it has puzzled me to know how the layer of coagulable lymph was formed. If in either case death in the part did not go quite to the cavity, but leave a living surface, (no matter how thin, so as it is sufficient to produce a surface by extravasation,) we may then conceive how new matter may be laid on this surface and increase to any thickness. If we can provide one layer, we can easily make it increase. It is a curious fact, and deserves attention. It is as if Nature was making the same opposition as we should do if a neighbour was endeavouring to make a way through the wall of our house, and, as we could not prevent his endeavours on that side, we should barricade further on this side, by raising up another wall.

To avoid these failures, I have practised and recommended that the tent or seton should be as large as the opening made for the introduction of it, so as to fill up the whole wound, and to allow but little or no water to escape, until inflammation and suppuration have come on ; and in cases where the caustic has been applied I have not cut through the eschar, but allowed it to slough off, by which time the necessary inflammation has come on. This mode would seem to give the preference to the caustic ; but we find Nature taking all the steps she can to frustrate our operations whenever they are violent upon her, as described above.

In some of the cases where the sac has collapsed and united as above described, leaving a cavity beyond it loose, it has happened that the preceding inflammation has gone too far for those cavities to remain in a quiet state, and suppuration has taken place in them while under cure, forming there an abscess which either breaks through the adhesions and opens into the first sore, or makes a new passage through the scrotum, like any other abscess, and a complete cure has been effected.

I have reason to believe that from the small opening made by these three modes, old hydroceles are sometimes deprived of the full effect of exposure ; and that, though the parts inflame and suppurate, yet when the orifice has become small and taken on the closing process, the sac loses the suppurative disposition, (like the pleura when suppuration takes place,) the surface never having granulated, but simply secreted matter like the inside of a duct ; and when the exposure ceases, falls back into the natural state, and the accumulation of water recurs.

When the radical cure is to be performed, either by tent, seton, or caustic, it is more proper to do it in one part of the tumour than another. One might at first suppose that the most depending part of the tumour would be the best, as in an abscess; but in fact it is the very worst, because here the inflammation is to follow the operation, whereas in an abscess the opening follows the inflammation. Why this should be a reason for performing it in a different part may not at first sight appear; but it is to be considered that the tumefaction attendant on the inflammation which is to succeed, will not be so great in the part where the operation is performed, if the extravasated juices, which are the chief cause of the swelling, can be allowed to depend; hence the opening will be less liable to close up when made at the upper part of the bag than at the lower, where it would be in the centre of the tumefaction, and would not allow a free discharge of matter, as we really see to be the case on many occasions. To avoid this inconvenience, the opening should not be made at the lower part of the tumour; nor at the upper, for the following reason, viz., the water as it increases commonly pushes up the sac into the spermatic cord; therefore the situation of the upper part of the sac is changed immediately on the evacuation of the water; and the sac collapsing and contracting in proportion to the evacuation, its upper part moves downwards, which of course must alter the relative situation of the opening in the sac and in the skin. The opening should therefore be made in the middle of the tumour.

· *Of the Mode of performing the Operation with the Tent.*—When the bag is pretty full of water, examine the bag carefully for the testicle. The situation of this being ascertained, grasp the bag in the hand, and squeeze the water towards that side where the testicle is not. Push the lancet in until the water comes out by the side of it, and then carry it forward, and enlarge the wound to about double the breadth of the lancet. Withdraw the lancet, but keep the tumour in the same situation, that the orifices in the skin and sac may continue opposite each other, or it will be almost impossible to introduce the tent; but do not press the sac quite so hard, or all the water will come out before the tent is introduced. Introduce the tent with the right hand, and hold it till it swells, when there will be less danger of its falling out. Then put on a piece of sticking-plaster, to secure the whole.

The tent may be kept in till the edges of the wound swell, which will be in a few days, and then the tent becomes loose, after which there will be no danger of the wounds closing up, for by this time the alarm will be given to the whole cavity, and the irritation of an imperfect part will be sufficient to prevent the wound healing. I recommend a sponge tent, as it swells and keeps the orifice perfectly open, and as this swelling is greater at the two ends than between the lips of the wound, by which two disagreeable accidents are prevented: the one, the escape of the tent into the cavity of the tunica vaginalis; the other, the escape of the tent altogether from the wound.

Of the Seton.—This is to be preferred to the tent, as being more easy to perform. The most easy method is with the common seton needle: holding the scrotum as above, introduce the needle perpendicularly where we know the water is; lower the end and raise the point, and bring it through the skin about half an inch or more above the other incision. Take off the needle, and apply a piece of sticking-plaster over the wound.

A lancet and eyed probe, carrying a skein of silk, is sometimes used, but it does not answer so well.

When suppuration is established, the seton may be either left in or removed, according to circumstances.

Of the Caustic.—A small caustic applied to the tumour is commonly sufficient to produce the effect, if it acts quite through the sac. In applying it, we should attend to the feelings of the patient, to judge when the sac is deadened by the action of the caustic. The uncertainty of its acting through all the coverings of the sac has been an objection to this practice by many; and when it does fail in this way, the finishing what the caustic has not effected reduces the operation to the case of a simple puncture. I have before shown another objection also.

If the chance of the caustic not penetrating was the only objection, I should prefer the caustic to all other methods of cure for the following reasons: because it removes a small part, which gives a freer passage to the water than a simple wound; and we may produce the adhesive inflammation in the inner edge surrounding the slough before the water is evacuated, which in some degree determines the thickness of that part before the general tumefaction comes on. This gives it a considerable advantage over the puncture or seton, for they produce the general inflammation nearly as early as the local one, which proves inconvenient in many cases by thickening the scrotum at the orifice, which lengthens the passage and almost shuts it up. Besides, if the effects of caustic are produced quite through into the cavity, they excite the suppurative inflammation over the whole cavity before the water is evacuated, the presence of which more readily allows it to become universal. However, the caustic is not always a certain cure, even when its immediate effects are completely gone through, for I once saw a case where the seton had been used first, and on the recurrence of the disease the caustic was employed, yet after this there remained a small sac which required a third operation. The cause of failure in both the first was, I believe, that which I have before noticed of the edges of the opening collapsing and becoming united to the body of the testicle.

From what has been said it must appear that the great art in this operation is the prevention of the possibility of a relapse; to prevent which it is requisite that every part of the sac should be obliterated, for which purpose it is necessary that every part should be subject to suppuration.

I have now considered this disease, the precautions necessary before the operation, and the different methods of operating, with their advantages and disadvantages. I have endeavoured to show that every method hitherto recommended has in many instances failed, and I have also endeavoured to show the causes of their failure. It is proper now to consider of some method which shall not be subject to the above-mentioned inconveniences.

I have of late used the following method of cure, with a view to producing universal inflammation and suppuration of the sac.

Make an incision into the sac about three inches in length, and let the whole of the water escape; then fill it as full as possible with pretty stiff poultice, occasionally introducing your finger to direct the poultice into every corner of the bag; and, lastly, put some lint into the wound to keep the poultice in. The poultice should be made of linseed meal, and pretty stiff; if it is made into little balls it will be still more convenient. The advantages that this method has over the others are, first, that it is simpler than exposing the whole; secondly, the parts are kept universally distended by an extraneous body, so that the inflammation becomes universal; thirdly, the poultice does not become entangled in the granulations as dry lint does; fourthly, as the parts granulate and contract, the poultice is gradually squeezed out, and only requires superficial dressing during the whole time. With the same intention I have sometimes used lint dipped in oil or lard, which prevents its becoming entangled in the granulations, which without this precaution it is liable to do; so that I have known it retained in the sore for six weeks, when it was obliged to be removed to allow the sore to heal over[*].

To prevent inflammation coming on too quickly and causing unnecessary pain, I believe it is right to apply a piece of linen cloth, folded ten or twelve times, and of sufficient breadth to cover the scrotum, first dipping it in brandy and squeezing it dry. Over this apply a suspensory bandage, which should be wetted as it becomes dry.

The symptoms following the operation are those common to all

---

[*] [Mr. Hunter afterwards substituted the use of flour, which he dusted over the exposed surfaces.]

wounds, but as there is also a part in some cases concerned in this operation which has symptoms peculiar to itself, it becomes necessary to describe these: this part is the testicle. The testicle is only concerned when the collection of water is in the tunica vaginalis. The symptoms peculiar to it are in some measure those of a vital part; a dull heavy pain is felt, the stomach is sooner affected, and lassitude sooner produced, than in affections of common parts. Besides these, there is one peculiar symptom, that is, the pain in the back attending inflammation of the testicle. This is generally supposed to arise from the nerves of the testicle arising from the nerves of the loins. If this is the true solution of the case, we can only say this is peculiar to this part; therefore out of the common way of symptoms. In less than twenty-four hours the symptoms of the operation will begin; for, although the patient should have no pain, he will soon feel a lassitude, small short rigors attended with restlessness, which show that where this operation of inflammation is going on in the part, though it may not affect the senses, it is yet capable of producing considerable effects on the animal œconomy, so as very much to affect the vital principle. These symptoms increasing, the scrotum becomes sore to the touch, a greater degree of heat than common arises in the skin, the patient complains of thirst, and at last the diseased part becomes painful, swells, and throbs. The swelling is often very considerable; and, from the pain, this might be supposed to arise from the testicle, but it consists principally of the cells of the scrotum, which being composed only of cellular membrane, and that very ductile, gives way to the extravasated fluid, viz., coagulable lymph and serum. However, the testicle itself swells and inflames in hydrocele of the tunica vaginalis, especially when that body is laid bare, as might be expected, as that part, or rather its coats, inflame and suppurate. Besides, we have the symptoms which denote affection of the testicle.

The future treatment is like that of common wounds, only a suspensory is required, as it relieves the pain in the back.

After the parts are healed, the testicle, for a considerable time, appears hard and large, and the skin of the scrotum adheres to it. This gradually subsides by the contraction of the granulations, which are the chief cause of it, and by the absorption of the adventitious substance deposited by the inflammation. This natural process may be much accelerated by the use of mercurial ointment, rubbed on the scrotum, for a month or six weeks*.

---

* [There is one capital objection to all the operations above mentioned, which is their severity and danger. Many cases of death occurred, and many more of high constitu-

On the Action of Medicines.

Before I proceed to make any further observations on particular diseases and injuries, I shall say a few words on medicines, or rather of their action on the human body.

The living principle, I before observed, is susceptible of impressions which may be productive of action, either diseased or healthy, i. e., productive of restoration; each of these may be brought on by medicine. Whatever affects the animal body otherwise than mechanically must be in a state of solution. From our juices being chiefly watery, the solution of many substances can easily be conceived; but they are likewise capable of dissolving earths, metals, &c.; nay, there is, I believe, hardly any substance which is not capable of being dissolved in the human body. Earth, and even iron, is found in animal

---

tional irritation which placed the patients' lives in imminent peril. The operation which is now almost universally resorted to, and which is only cursorily alluded to by Mr. Hunter (p. 466.), is free from these inconveniences, at the same time that it very rarely indeed fails of curing the disease. It was introduced by Sir James Earle, and consists in injecting the evacuated sac with any mild stimulating liquid, such as a solution of zinc, or equal parts of port wine and water, which are allowed to remain in from five to ten minutes, according to the feelings of the patient. A moderate inflammation generally follows this operation, and in a few days the fluid re-collects: after a short time, however, the inflammation subsides, and the fluid is absorbed. The time required for the absorption of the fluid varies from one to six months. Occasionally, but very rarely indeed, the disease returns.

It was imagined that this operation effected the cure by causing an adhesion between the opposite sides of the sac. An effect which is doubtless sometimes produced, and probably in all cases to a certain extent, although later observations have proved that universal adhesion of the sac is by no means a general consequence of the operation, which cures by destroying the morbid action of the secreting vessels in some manner which has not been explained. The success of this operation is not by any means in proportion to the quantity of inflammation produced, although a certain quantity seems necessary for the effect. The inflammation arising from injection rarely exceeds the adhesive stage; although this does sometimes occur. Only three cases of this kind are mentioned by Sir Benjamin Brodie as having occurred in his experience, and these three were West Indians, in whom suppuration took place. Occasionally the scrotum sloughs. (See *note*, p. 464.)

Where the operation by injection has failed, the operation by incision may be had recourse to. In children it is generally advisable to have recourse to the seton, using a few threads of silk only, passed by a common curved needle. In encysted hydrocele of the cord the same means may be adopted; or, what is still better, the sac may be laid open, and the fore part of it cut away. If it be situated on the testicle or epididymis, and of small size, it had better not be meddled with, or it may be simply evacuated, provided it is inconvenient to the patient from its magnitude. The operation by injection does not succeed in encysted as in common hydrocele.]

substances on analysis, which must have been dissolved in the fluids, as well as essential oils, which may be detected passing off by our excretions. Taste is one proof of the power of our fluids to dissolve, for there is hardly any substance capable of stimulating but what will give a taste if applied to the tongue ; thus, almost all metals held in the mouth for a little time will give a taste : the same thing most probably takes place with substances applied to the organ of smell. The blood, from its being so heterogeneous a fluid, may have its powers of solution inferred ; and as I suppose a necessity of solution of these substances to affect the organs of smell and taste, so in like manner I suppose the necessity of solution, not only for its introduction, but for it to affect the system. Simple water possesses much less power of solution than when combined with some other substances ; thus, by the addition of fixed air it becomes capable of holding earth in solution. From some similar combination perhaps the blood and other animal fluids derive their extraordinary powers of solution.

Medicines affect the living principle by their stimulant or sedative qualities only, unless they act chemically, as caustics ; they have the effect of irritating or quieting, and these two contrary effects are generally to be found in the same substance, the difference resulting from the difference of quantity ; thus, a small quantity of heat relaxes and softens, but a larger quantity will stimulate. A stimulus is what either causes a natural action, or increases one which has already taken place, or excites an action contrary to one present, as by giving an opiate when a patient cannot sleep, &c. Medicines may either stimulate or irritate ; such as increase the natural power of acting are stimulants ; such as excite new and unnatural actions are irritants. The powers of both will be according to the medicine and the parts combined, for fixed air in the stomach increases its action ; in the lungs it destroys action*. The effects of medicine will be different according to the mode of action the parts are in at the time, that is, diseased, natural, or restorative. This is well illustrated by many diseases of the constitution, as fever, &c., curing diseases in parts which had before been incurable : if the part had not been *diseased* the effect would not have taken place, for fever deranges a healthy sore.

Actions may be, first, of healthy parts ; secondly, action produced by stimuli or irritants on healthy parts ; thirdly, action of diseased parts ;

* [Sir Humphry Davy found that when he attempted to breathe pure carbonic acid the glottis spasmodically closed, from the *stimulant* action of this gas, so as to render further inspiration impossible ; on the other hand, Foderé has remarked that a too free use of aërated waters will sometimes produce precisely the same effects as the inhalation of the dilute acid by the lungs, viz. giddiness and intoxication.]

fourthly, action of stimuli and irritants on a diseased part. Irritants may produce very different effects on a healthy part, or whilst disease already exists; thus, mercury, by its irritation, will produce diseased action in a healthy part; the venereal poison, by its irritation, will also produce diseased action in a healthy part; but from the application of mercury to a part already affected with diseased action from venereal irritation, an action results different from that which would be produced by the application of it to a healthy part; for from the conjoined action of the two, results the action of health; but if carried beyond that it may do harm, producing its own specific action. Besides this, it is to be observed that the venereal action, or in fact any other morbid action, may produce a disposition for other increased actions, which may require only the absence of the former disease to allow it to come into action. These consequences are therefore to be distinguished from the original disease, otherwise the mode of cure may be continued too long, and that which might be curative of the first disease may increase the consequent one.

In a former part of the course I mentioned susceptibility, disposition, and action. Can the same medicine have an influence on all these? Will mercury, for instance, destroy the susceptibility and the disposition for the venereal disease, when formed, as well as the action? It will certainly destroy the latter, and we have cases which would make us think it will lessen the susceptibility also; but as to its having any effect in lessening the disposition I should very much doubt; but it may perhaps retard it.

A gentleman had a chancre, for the cure of which he used a large quantity of mercury, both by friction and internally, which produced very little soreness of his mouth. The sore at last healed, and from the quantity of mercury which had been used it was thought that the constitution was preserved; but in a little time discolourations of the skin appeared: for these he drank a quart of sarsaparilla daily, without their removal; on the contrary, fresh ones appeared. I gave two grains of calomel twice a day, and he was cured. Now I suppose that a disposition for this diseased action might have existed before the mercury was first used, which disposition was by this not lessened, but only retarded, and the cure did not take place until the venereal action took place, which was then cured by the action of mercury, the first mercury not preventing the disposition from forming; and it thus appears that what will cure the action will not cure the disposition, hence lues often requires repeated courses of mercury. The ultimate effect of impressions, I have already shown, are actions; and I also showed that diseased actions were thus produced; and here is the place to observe, that in the same manner actions may be produced which are destructive of that which is diseased. But disease is not always the consequence of impression, but sometimes of imperfection of parts; thus, there may be a wasting of the body from a want of absorption of chyle from the intestines, or mesenteric obstructions. There is no impression without a counter-impression; as if one has a pain in the knee from a disease in the hip or loins; here it would be ridiculous to apply a remedy to the knee, as that is only the effect; yet this is often done*.

Medicines have visible and invisible effects. The visible may be divided into two, the constitutional and the local, the former producing the latter. The local are vomiting, purging, &c.; as an instance of the constitutional, the effects of mercury may be mentioned. Their invisible effects are commonly the specific effects, for we find that their curative do not always depend on their visible effects; and indeed their specific effects are often greater when they have no visible effect, as mercury producing salivation in the attempt to cure the venereal disease, bark in intermittents; but others cure by their visible effects.

Of Stimulants, Irritants, and Sedatives.—The two former are most commonly used by surgeons, because a want of disposition for restoration is more common than excessive wrong action; and a backwardness to heal is more apt to excite the idea of sluggishness than of excessive or wrong action, though perhaps even the latter may be the case. Medicines given slowly and continued long will produce effects very different to those produced on their sudden application, and thus it is that even stimulants and irritants may produce weakness.

On restoration of Action.—In the restoration of action of the whole body, or of diseased parts, attention should be paid to the strength of the parts, or of the whole system, for there may be too much action and too little strength, or too much strength and too little action. Strength and action should be well proportioned to produce good effects. When parts have lost their action for some time, they become weak, as we see in people recovering after drowning. If we do not attend to the degree of strength, we shall often produce irritability by hurrying on action too soon in weak parts. If a man is weak from loss of blood or from famine,

---

* [However unscientific this practice may appear, yet it is often found to relieve the pain, probably upon the simple principle of counter-irritation. If (it is argued) the knee sympathizes with the hip, why may not the hip sympathise with the knee? The principle is not very different upon which leeches are applied to the anus, and sinapisms to the feet, in affections of the head; that is, certain parts of the body sympathise with each other more readily than with other parts, and on this account are thought to afford the most favourable situations for counter-irritation; hence blisters to the knee relieve this part by first relieving the hip. The precise meaning of the term " counter-impression" in this connexion is not very apparent.]

his strength should not be tried by too much food, stimulation, &c.
When strength exceeds action, then there is room for the use of stimulants. If the effects of medicines did not extend beyond the point of
contact, their effects would be very trifling indeed; but their effects are
extended much further by sympathy. This sympathy may be either
contiguous, continuous, or remote. Such sympathies as are continuous
and similar lose their power by distance only, and medicines acting thus
may be termed local. But it is to be remembered that the remote sympathetic effect of medicines is not always the same as their effect on the
part to which they were first applied. If the continuous sympathy
was not similar, and if the effect of any medicine on any part thus affected was not continued by that same similar continuous sympathy
through that part, how trifling would be the effect of such applications;
and how could any application to the surface affect an inflammation
which extends to a great depth but by the same sympathy? It is by
sympathy that ether, applied to the forehead, relieves headache; applica-
cations to the skin of the abdomen, its contents, &c.; in short, if this
were not the case no medicine could cure without coming in contact
with every part of the diseased organ.

  On the effects of external applications.—The commonly-received opinion respecting external applications is that they enter into the pores of
the skin, and so reach the part; and on this idea practice was built.
Parts were supposed to be relaxed and moistened by the joint effects of
warmth and moisture, and on this idea warm baths were used to ruptures and dislocations. In many cases, indeed, very salutary effects
were derived from their use; but this cannot be from the cause assigned,
for the warmth of a living part is not thus increased; and a living part
may be immersed for ever in warm water without becoming moister,
except where the water is in contact. The good effects are produced
by the external parts being soothed, and by sympathy the parts beneath
lose their irritability, and the natural actions return. In suppression of
urine the warm bath is often effectual; not surely because it penetrates
from without, but because relaxation is brought on by sympathy. Volatile spirits and vapours have been used with the same idea, but it is well
known that water will often penetrate where these will not. Oils are
often used for the purpose of restoring stiff joints, perhaps from seeing
their salutary effects on rusty hinges; but rusty hinges have greatly the
advantage of the animal body, as oil will penetrate into every part of
them and wash off the rust, whereas in a stiff joint not a particle of the
oil will penetrate. The idea of their penetration has been carried so
far as to lead some to prefer animal to vegetable oil, on the supposition
that as it had come from an animal it would more easily enter an animal.

Essential oils are used as stimulants in rheumatism, &c., but I suppose their effects are only produced by sympathy.

Although I do not admit of this mechanical penetration of substances, I have no doubt of their absorption by the action of the proper absorbing vessels: thus, mercury applied to the thigh is absorbed and carried through it; but if rubbed on the bubo this can only be affected by sympathy with the skin*.

Pressure and Friction.—The ultimate effect of these seems to be similar, namely, stimulating, but from different causes. If pressure is used as a stimulant, it must be gentle; if violent, it will irritate, and produce vesication, as we see in bedridden people. Pressure produces increase of action, by first impeding action, the impediment acting as a stimulus on the part. Friction is more powerful, more active and immediate than pressure, and may be applied to larger surfaces; it does not impede action as pressure does at first, but rouses the parts into action, and excites a warmth in them. Stimulating or irritating medicines render friction more powerful in torpid parts. Fibres, by frequent rubbing, are stretched, and lengthen.

Heat, cold, and electricity produce effects not only at the part to which they are applied, but much deeper also. Water, as it conducts quicker, is a better vehicle for the application of heat than air. Cold, when applied to the skin, has great and immediate effects. We have two opposite effects from cold-bathing, according to the mode of application and the state of the constitution at the time. By its quick and sudden application the power which the body possesses of forming heat is called up and exerted, and a glow of heat is soon felt on the surface; this is what takes place in a strong constitution; but if it is too often repeated in the same day, or the constitution is weak, instead of being refreshed, the person is more languid, is chilly through the whole day, the constitution not having sufficient power to restore the heat so suddenly abstracted.

Heat would seem to be produced in the vital parts; and it is to be observed that both birds and beasts have warmer clothing over their vital organs than their extremities, which abound more with oil, even in the bones. Action from the application of cold may be diseased, being sometimes the action of weakness; it may also act by sympathy, as cold applied to the back will stop a bleeding from the nose. Applied to the skin it will produce pain in the intestines, and a relaxation of the bladder. In a sprain it is common to pump cold water on the part, as it is

---

* [Later observations have shown that many of the phenomena of absorption are referrible to imbibition. See "Absorption by Veins" in Vol. IV.]

supposed to produce action in old sprains. I believe it is not so plainly indicated, except where the constitution is sluggish.

Heat pervades all matter: the quality made evident to our senses is here meant; for the matter of heat is to be found more in some bodies than in others, though their sensible heat may be the same. Heat may be native or foreign: the latter I mean to consider here. Heat may be either stimulant, irritative, or sedative. It tends directly to increase action; cold, to lessen it. A case explaining my idea of the necessity of adapting action to the strength may be introduced here.

A child, with fever of the putrid kind and sloughs in her throat, was very low and weak; she had taken bark, and had been blistered. I was called on account of a large slough appearing on the blister, to which I applied poultices, with opium. It was proposed to apply stimulating applications, which I objected to, on the idea that action had been already beyond the proportion which it ought to keep with the powers of the patient. The warm bath was likewise proposed, and on the same ground objected to; but it was tried, and my opinion confirmed, by the ill effects it produced. In fact, in such a case as this I should be careful of not increasing action too far; for as it is spared, so must the powers and the strength be preserved.

Heat is either applied in a dry or moist state; the first can only convey absolute heat to the part: water or bran in a bladder are the best dry applications. Electricity is the only application, perhaps, which can be said to penetrate, and its influence is very extensive.

On Diseased Dispositions and Actions.—I have formerly compared the dispositions of the body with the dispositions of the mind, and observed that dispositions were cured by actions taking place.

In some cases the action entirely destroys the disposition; in others it destroys it only for a time, but the disposition is renewed; in others the whole action never destroys the disposition, or if it does, the action goes on without the disposition, as if from habit, till stopped by some unnatural power, as medicine.

In the first case, where the action destroys the disposition, it is the action of restoration, as suppuration after inflammation. In the second case the disposition is destroyed for a time, or its power of continuing the action is destroyed for a time, but recurs again, because the original cause, whatever it is, continues to exist, and is capable of renewing the disposition again, which again renews the diseased action. This is the case with all periodical diseases, as agues, &c., and even some natural actions, as the menses. But whenever the constitution or part is capable of forming the full action of the disease, then that constitution or part is perfectly master of the disease, and it will seldom if ever prove dangerous, excepting it should produce some local effects in a vital part, as sometimes is the case with the gout. Let us take an ague as an example: it consists of three actions, which complete the whole, namely, the cold fit, hot fit, and sweat. If it stops in the cold fit, debility is either the cause, or it takes place; if it stops at the hot fit, strong action takes place, which will probably prove a continued fever; if it goes through the third, then it is completed. It often happens that it is not able to form the hot fit, and, as it were, passes over it with sweat, which is cold and clammy, as if the discharge were not common sweat. But such cases approach to dissolution, for the sweat appears not to be the termination of diseased action, but the termination of all action. Fits of all kinds, as epilepsies, are the same; they are a full action of the disposition; for such people shall be ill for days before the fit comes on, and after the fit they shall recover perfectly, only feeling a little weak from the exertion.

Of the third we have an instance in the lues venerea; for it appears, from experience, that it goes on increasing, till it is either cured or destroys the patient. (See *note*, p. 300.) Cancer the same, and probably many other diseases.

Of the first class there are many more diseases than we might at first imagine. Vomiting would appear to produce the cure of sickness; for sickness is the disposition; and the action, which we must suppose to be the ultimate effect, destroys the disease. Causes may produce a disposition, and that may bring on action at some distance of time, although health may intervene.

A young man applied a strong solution of corrosive sublimate for the cure of an itching of the pubis; by this application a violent inflammation was produced. I ordered a wash of lime-water, to decompose any part of the sublimate still adhering, and a poultice of oatmeal and lime-water to cover the parts, with tinctura thebaica sprinkled over it, which gave him much relief. This was continued two days, when I ordered him the bark, to diminish irritability; but the apothecary chose to give him an emetic first, which brought up a great deal of blood from the stomach, for which Dr. Heberden, who was called in, ordered tincture of roses; but this proved ineffectual. Seeing the patient dying, and well knowing the good effects of turpentine in stopping bleeding externally, I gave him two spoonfuls every two hours of an emulsion made with Chio turpentine; cold water clysters being also used. He continued for some time very low, and had scarcely any pulse, having lost so much blood; but he recovered, and got strong and fat. He now became dropsical, but recovered from this by the use, first of emetics, and then of squills and turpentine. Here the loss of blood produced not only debility but a disposition to dropsy, which disposition was not at first brought into action, and the patient got fat and well; but the disposition being at length brought into action he became dropsical.

It is on the same principle that many acute diseases cure chronic, the disposition being removed by a full action taking place. Should we not therefore attempt to induce this action for a permanent cure ?

This practice is attempted in some obstructions to the full actions of natural operations, as in the menses ; the period of attempt being when the natural effort is made, which is judicious. In intermittents, when there is not full action, perhaps giving a glass of brandy in the hot fit, and sudorifics to complete the termination, might be proper. At present this is only conjecture ; but it shall be tried.

On the greater or less Disposition of different Parts to Heal.—Some parts of the body have a stronger disposition to heal in consequence of common inflammation than others. Those parts which have the greatest powers sympathize most and inflame most, as the muscles, skin, and cellular membrane ; but we must also observe that these parts have different powers in different parts of the body. Other parts have but little powers of healing, which may be owing to their natural want of powers, as tendons, ligaments, bones, &c. These parts often lose their living principle, and are sloughed off, which is often salutary. The cellular membrane is common to different parts, and partakes of the power of such parts ; thus, that connecting tendon to tendon has much less power than that of muscle. The sensation of those parts which are backward to heal is very different from that of the muscles and skin, as we should find on pricking them.

There is a difference in the power of healing, according to the age.—The diseases peculiar to different ages we have observed, some of which are specific. Those diseases which are common to all are less difficult to heal in youth than in old age. In youth the healing powers are much stronger than when that period is passed ; and this is still more the case with regard to the powers of restoration than in the cure of diseases. Ages I divide into growth, rest, and decline. The powers of restoration may be ranged in the same order, and may be supposed greater in a child of two years old than in one which is younger, because it now has strength adding to its powers of growth, the increase of strength being in proportion to its growth up to a certain period.

One Disease often cures another.—We have observed that there may be universal sympathy with local affection : now this principle is capable of being reversed. One local disease often cures another, as hernia humoralis a gonorrhœa ; and we have a local complaint curing a constitutional, but this local complaint is probably caused by the constitutional, the whole disease centering in one part, as gout, which I have called an act of the constitution. It is on this principle that blisters, setons, and issues are ordered : the former are useful, but from the latter two I have seen but little advantage. Constitutional diseases may cure local ones ; the reason is, no part escapes the constitutional disease. I have seen fevers cure old ulcers, noli me tangere, &c., which is done by destroying morbid action in the part : the local diseased action and the constitutional producing the third act, or health. Constitutional diseases sometimes cure themselves without taking on the complete action or crisis. When a local disease cures another, (which is often the case,) it must be by contiguous or remote sympathy, as headache by blistering the arm, gonorrhœa by swelled testicle, &c. ; but I have seldom seen the second affection cured by bringing back the former. Local may be cured by constitutional, but may have reflected back on it the same disposition as that from which the constitutional action proceeds.

Of the Mode of Recovery.—As there is no disease but what has a peculiar mode of cure of its own, and every particular part a particular mode of curing its own diseases, it is necessary to see how far in this case Nature imitates natural principles. We shall first give the original or natural ones, and then show that Nature is always uniform in her operations, and when she deviates is still regular in her deviations. We may observe that a disposition is given at first to particular parts, and that that disposition continues in restoring their own properties, as cartilage grows cartilage, bone bone, &c. ; but sometimes she changes the disposition, as the parts become adapted for different purposes, as where a joint is created at the end of an unreduced dislocation. Nature's adherence to her original principle may be exemplified by observing that in the regeneration of bone which was originally cartilage, as the long bones, there when a fracture takes place she begins by forming cartilage, but in the head, where the bone was at first membrane, there membrane is formed.

CHAPTER XVII.

INJURIES OF THE HEAD*.

Injuries of the head;—of four kinds;—concussion;—compression;—wounds;—want of due support.—Three first to be treated of;—symptoms attending all three.—Concussion.—Compression, from internal or external causes.—Wounds, and loss of substance.—Want of compression from loss of blood.—General remarks on fractures of the skull;—mode of examining them;—complications;—treatment.

INJURIES of the brain may be said to be of two kinds: one where the imagination is diseased, as madness, which probably arises from many different causes, which we have nothing to do with at present; the other, where it has suffered from some external or internal injury, which is mechanical. This mode of injury may be of four kinds: first, concussion; secondly, compression; thirdly, wounds, and loss of substance; fourthly, want of due compression, which last does not come within our present subject. To these may be added a consequent, namely, inflammation; but as this may arise from other causes, and is not always the consequence, it only requires to be mentioned. The first may be simple, that is, existing alone, or it may be complicated with one of the others. The first three kinds of injury will produce symptoms similar to each other, but very different from the fourth, as also from what may be called the fifth, or inflammation.

The symptoms of an injury done to the brain can, I think, be but two, viz., an increase of imagination, or a diminution. The first is least frequent, and I should suspect arises from a slight cause rather than from a violent one, namely, such derangement as takes place in common madness, fevers, inflammations of the brain, &c., and which may arise from very slight compression.

The three first injuries will generally give the appearance of too much repletion. The muscles about the mouth and throat become flaccid, hence laborious respiration; and as respiration must go on, a kind of

---

* [It may be observed that the lectures on gun-shot wounds have been omitted, in consequence of their great similarity, both in substance and arrangement, to Mr. Hunter's published opinions on the same subject. It was considered useless to repeat them under these circumstances, especially as they are less perfect in several particulars.]

rattling in the throat is produced, which often works up the saliva into a froth. But all these symptoms will be in proportion to the injury done, and perhaps many other circumstances. The fourth will produce an insensibility, attended with restlessness similar to convulsions or fainting; and I suspect that the fifth produces a delirium, if but in a slight degree. In all cases of affection of the brain, sympathy takes place in the stomach, which produces vomiting; but I believe that in order that this symptom should take place it is necessary that the senses be not entirely gone, for those who are struck perfectly insensible, I believe, do not begin to vomit till they begin to recover in some degree their senses.

Sometimes erysipelatous inflammation of the head arises, and then the patient often feels violent headaches, sometimes approaching to delirium, rigors, &c. In these I suspect that the brain is in some degree affected with the same inflammation, therefore the symptoms are not to be attributed to the immediate effect of the blow.

Concussion is always from some considerable violence. It may arise from some degree of displacement or alteration of the texture of some part of the brain, so as to destroy the arrangement on which health, sensation, &c., depend.

Compression may arise from accident, or from many other diseases. Those arising from accident may be either immediate or secondary. Immediate, as when a piece of the skull is beaten in upon the brain, or a blood-vessel ruptured, producing apoplexy. The secondary is from slow extravasation, as from inflammation, or the formation of pus. Compressions arising from disease will always be the immediate effect of that disease. They may be said to arise from eight causes; two of which may be called external, the other six internal. The two external are, when the brain is compressed either by the skull being beaten in, or from the thickening of the bone by disease. The six internal causes are: first, distension of the ventricles by water; secondly, distension of the blood-vessels of the brain; thirdly, inflammation; fourthly, formation of pus; fifthly, extravasated blood, as in apoplexy; sixthly, tumours in the substance of or on the brain.

Wounds or loss of substance are somewhat similar. When the substance of the brain is broken in upon, loss of substance may or may not be the immediate effect of the violence. It is the immediate effect, when part of the substance is carried off by the violence; but the consequence, when a part is lost in consequence of an opening being made to take off any fluid that is pressing.

The fourth species, where there is want of due compression, arises from large bleeding, or where the water is let out which the brain has been accustomed to bear, as in hydrocephalus or spina bifida, which are rare, and which are out of the power of surgery*.

Whichever of the three first species of injury takes place, the effects are nearly the same, if the degrees are the same; and whatever are the causes of compression, the symptoms are the same.

If we only know that symptoms have arisen in consequence of violence, then it is necessary to know the date of the violence, that we may know whether the symptoms are the immediate or the secondary effects, or both; for they are often attendants on one another.

The symptoms of concussion, if slight, are always the immediate effect, that is, a more or less immediate loss of sense, &c., which is proportioned to the violence done. Under certain circumstances, the effects of concussion will be more violent than what belongs to the injury itself; for a man who is drunk may get a blow on the head which, joined with the effects of the liquor, will produce violent symptoms, and may lead the surgeon to do more than is necessary. Therefore it is better to wait until the drunken state is gone off, and the effects of concussion left pure.

When there is depression of bone or extravasation, the symptoms of concussion are lost, though it may be at the bottom of all. If the symptoms of concussion have kept up eight or ten days, we may expect extravasation has taken place; if three or four weeks, suppuration. We may know whether the symptoms are caused by blood or pus, by their going off entirely and then reappearing. If they come on soon after, it is blood; if not for a week or so, it is probably pus.

A gentleman for two years after receiving a blow on the skull was delirious. I felt a little depression, and applied the trepan, and took out a piece of bone which had been depressed all this time, part of the internal table of which was absorbed, and pus was lying on the dura mater†.

---

* [Modern experience has shown that both these diseases are capable of relief from surgery. The operation of drawing off the water, when performed under favourable circumstances and with proper precautions, holds out a reasonable hope of success, and has effected a cure in several cases.]

† [The great importance of injuries of the brain may justify a few observations in this place, for the purpose more especially of pointing out the distinction between the symptoms of concussion, compression, and lacerations of the brain, which is a part of the subject which has been only slightly adverted to in the text. Indeed, Mr. Hunter has said that these " three kinds of injury will produce symptoms similar to each other."

I. *Concussion.*—When a severe injury is inflicted on the head, the patient is instantaneously deprived of volition and the power of voluntary motion; the pulse becomes feeble and intermittent, and the whole system labours under a remarkable depression, approaching to a state of syncope. After a few minutes, or perhaps several hours, the patient recovers his consciousness; the action of the heart is re-established; the sick-

General Observations on Fractures of the Skull.—Fractures of the skull may be divided into three kinds, and these are sometimes com-

---

ness, with which he was at first affected, passes off, and nothing remains but a severe headache, which may last for several days as a solitary symptom, or else recur at different intervals, upon any occasional excitement.

These effects of concussion may of course be variously complicated with wounds of the scalp and brain, compression of the brain, and fractures of the cranium; but very often these complications do not exist; and yet after death no perceptible lesion of the affected organ can be detected, except perhaps a separation of the dura mater from the internal table of the skull, or the extravasation of blood in minute specks in the substance of the brain. In the severer forms of concussion, indeed, the brain is generally lacerated in one or more parts, from whence it is reasonable to suppose that disorganization of a less palpable and extensive kind is also produced in the slighter forms, although it is not capable of being detected by the eye.

Now it is observable, that although one of the first effects of severe concussion is complete insensibility, yet this state is soon followed by one in which the sensibility is only impaired, so that it is not difficult to rouse the patient by any sudden and strong impression. Upon being roused, his manner is generally peevish, obtuse, and incoherent, and he instantly relapses into his former state of tranquil lethargy, as soon as he is left undisturbed. There are no indications of paralysis: the pupils contract on exposure to light; the pulse, which at first was exceedingly feeble, now rallies and rises above the natural standard; the circulation is easily accelerated upon the slightest exertion, and there is very generally an intense headache, which becomes proportionably more severe as the reaction of the circulation takes place and the sensibility returns.

The dangers attending this species of injury are twofold. The first arises from the state of collapse immediately following the injury, which may be so considerable that the constitution is not able to make any effectual effort to rally from it. The second arises from the inflammation which may afterwards ensue. Cases of the first description are of rare occurrence and only require that the surgeon should bear in mind the possibility of such an event, in order to guard against it by the administration of cordials whenever the necessities of the case seem to demand these aids to reaction. The danger of inflammation is much more formidable, and will be in general in proportion to the severity of the first symptoms and the rapidity and violence of the reaction. Other circumstances, however, will exercise an important influence on this event, as, for example, the separation of the dura mater from the cranium; the existence of disorganization or rupture of the minute structure of the brain; the denudation of the pericranium from the bone; or the patient's being in a state of intoxication at the time of the accident. These circumstances will greatly increase the dangers of his situation, and require a more vigorous adoption of such measures as are calculated to avert inflammation. At first, when the reaction of the heart has taken place, the patient should lose a considerable quantity of blood, so as completely to subdue the force of the circulation; afterwards, for the most part, it is only an occasional bloodletting which is required, and that to a moderate extent. These measures should be assisted by perfect repose of body and mind; depleting and cooling medicines; cold applications to the head; a spare diet, and a raised position of the head and shoulders, which should be persisted in more or less for several weeks, even although all apparent effects of the injury have disappeared. It is unnecessary to observe, that the old practice of applying the trephine in such cases is in the highest degree pernicious, and cannot possibly answer any good object.

The occurrence of secondary inflammation, at the end of four or five days to as many weeks, should be jealously watched for, and instantly combated by the most vigorous

plicated with one another: first, when the external table is beaten in;
secondly, fissures; thirdly, when the bone is broken off into a loose

---

depletion. Such cases generally terminate unfavourably; but happily they are of less
frequent occurrence than they were formerly, in consequence, it may be presumed, of
the steady antiphlogistic measures which are now almost universally resorted to in the
first instance. When, however, these symptoms arise, followed by rigors and the evidences
of compression, attended at the same time with a puffiness in some point of the scalp,
or a glassy unhealthy state of the wound, if there happens to be one, then the application
of the trephine, to let out the matter which is collected between the dura mater and the
skull, is justifiable, and ought not to be delayed. Still it must be evident that this
operation will be unavailing when the matter is effused on the interior of the dura
mater, which very frequently happens in such cases.

2. *Compression.*—The enumeration of the causes of compression by Mr. Hunter will
probably be found to include every possible variety; yet it is to be observed that compression produces different effects, according as it is gradual or sudden; in the substance
or on the exterior of the brain; in one spot or diffused over a large surface; or as it is
situated at the inferior or superior part of this organ. The slow encroachment of a
tumour on the brain does not so suddenly rob the patient of his faculties, as a portion of
the cranium suddenly depressed by accidental violence; neither is it of common occurrence for sanguineous effusions on the surface of the brain to produce hemiplegia,
although this is one of the most frequent symptoms of apoplexy arising from spontaneous effusions into the substance of this organ. " There is reason," Sir Benjamin Brodie
observes, " to believe that pressure is on the whole more dangerous when it affects the
lower part of the brain than when it affects the upper part; and it has appeared to me
that more urgent symptoms are produced by a given quantity of blood when it is effused
into the cells between the tunica arachnoides and pia mater than when it is collected in
one mass so as to produce a less general pressure." In speaking, therefore, of the effects
of compression, I would wish to be understood as confining myself to that form of the
affection which arises from accidental violence.

It should never be forgotten that the blow which occasions a fracture and depression
of the cranium or an extravasation of blood is likely to produce concussion also, although,
as Mr. Hunter has remarked, the symptoms of concussion in such cases will be propor-
tionally less severe as the cranium has yielded more readily to the cause of fracture.

The leading symptom of compression of the brain is insensibility, which is generally
much more complete than that which arises from concussion, and more nearly allied to
that of apoplexy, with which in other respects the symptoms of this accident closely
correspond. The pulse is oppressed and slow; the pupils are dilated and immoveable; the respiration is slow and stertorous; and the voluntary muscles are paralysed. Sickness and vomiting do not usually occur, at least in the worst cases, until
the cerebral symptoms have undergone some mitigation, and it is observable that the
symptoms all disappear the moment the compressing cause is removed, which explains
why a copious venesection shall frequently produce a temporary but fallacious amendment. When these symptoms arise from depression of bone, they show themselves
immediately after the infliction of the injury; but when they depend on an extravasation of blood, a longer or shorter interval elapses before they come on, depending on the
rapidity of the effusion, which will in general be greater in proportion to the celerity
and violence of the reaction from the first impression of the accident. Not unfrequently,
therefore, the first insensibility is produced by concussion, then the patient recovers, and
then relapses again upon the effusion taking place. In other cases, the insensibility,
which was only partial at first, gradually terminates in complete stupor, corresponding

piece. I have also been told of a case where the symptoms of an injured brain arose, but the skull showed no fracture or fissure; and on remov-

to the gradual manner of the effusion; in other cases, again, the patient does not recover from his insensibility until inflammation has set in, and then the two sets of symptoms are confounded together. In short, the symptoms of compression not only vary in degree, but as they happen to be complicated with those of other injuries of the brain; and it is worthy of remark that the same amount of compression gives rise to symptoms of very different degrees of severity in different cases; while of two individuals in whom the early symptoms appear to be equally urgent, one may die in the course of three or four hours, and the other may survive for several days; in one the symptoms may wholly subside in the course of a day or two, and in the other continue, at least some remains of them, for several months or even years. Sir Astley Cooper, for example, has related an extraordinary case, in which a total loss of volition and voluntary motion continued for upwards of thirteen months, on which Mr. Cline afterwards operated successfully by removing a depressed portion of bone, which restored the young man to the perfect possession of his intellect in the course of four days.

But compression may give rise to other symptoms besides those which have been mentioned, as, for example, pain in the head, general convulsions, furious delirium, partial paralysis of particular muscles or sets of muscles, and various states of the pupil. The pupils, as I have already mentioned, generally remain permanently dilated; sometimes, however, they remain permanently contracted, or contract and dilate as usual, although in other respects the patient may be in a complete state of insensibility. Dr. Hennen has related a case in which the admission and withdrawal of light operated differently to what it usually does; and Sir Benjamin Brodie has referred to cases in which the two pupils were in opposite states, or in which they dilated and contracted independently of light and darkness. The loss of one entire class of sensations, as of speech, smell, taste, hearing, or sight, is not very uncommon; or the affection may be even still more partial, as, for example, a ptosis of one eye, a paralysis of one arm or one side of the face, the destruction of the sexual powers, or the loss of memory, which may be either of recent or of remote events. In some of these cases dissection has disclosed some local cause of pressure, while in others the removal of a depressed portion of bone has immediately removed the symptom, so as to leave no doubt on the mind as to the real cause which produced it. In many instances, however, it is only possible to offer a conjecture, derived from general analogy and the particular circumstances of the case, guided by the knowledge which we possess of the functions of the different parts of the brain, from all which it would appear probable that these partial lesions are sometimes due to disorganization of, or pressure on, certain districts of the cerebrum, from whence the nerves to the paralysed parts are specially derived. However, as Sir Benjamin Brodie has remarked, "it is difficult to conceive that pressure on the brain should exist in so great a degree as completely to destroy a complete class of sensations, and at the same time be so partial as not to affect any other function of the nervous system. On the other hand, it is also difficult to regard these as the effects of concussion of the brain, since it is one of the characteristics of concussion to produce no more than a diminution of sensibility, and that diminution, instead of continuing for months or years, is completely relieved in the course of a few days, and probably in a much shorter space of time."

The most common situation in which blood is effused in accidents of the head is between the dura mater and tunica arachnoides, especially towards the base of the brain. It may occur, however, between this last-mentioned membrane and the pia mater, or between the pia mater and the brain, or in the substance of the brain itself. It may also occur between the dura mater and the cranium, whenever the connexion between

ing a portion with the trephine, the inner table was found beaten in, the
external table being perfectly sound.   I have seen several instances

---

these parts has been destroyed by the violence of the injury. It is, however, to be observed that considerable effusions of blood rarely occur in this last situation, except
when the cranium has been fractured in the direction of the middle meningeal artery,
and the artery has been ruptured in consequence.

The treatment of compression arising from depression of bone will be spoken of in a
future note; but where compression arises from extravasation of blood, the same general
principles must be followed as in cases of concussion, both to prevent any further effusion
and to obviate the danger of inflammation. The question however arises, whether any
operation can be beneficial for the purpose of giving an exit to the effused blood? In answer to which it may be replied, that as a general rule no operation can be beneficial
in these cases, both on account of the difficulty of ascertaining the precise seat of the
effusion, and the impossibility in the great majority of cases of reaching it when it is
discovered. When, however, a blow has been inflicted over the meningeal artery, and
the symptoms of compression are not only not relieved by venesection, but gradually
become more urgent, it will be extremely proper to give the patient the chance of the
operation, which will also be proper in other cases where the seat of the injury is well
marked and the stupor is hourly becoming more alarming. Unquestionably it would
be unwise and unwarrantable to resort to an operation too hastily, but under the circumstances which are supposed an operation will scarcely be supposed to add much to
the danger of the case, at least the operation of dividing the scalp in order to ascertain
whether the bone bleeds freely, or whether there be any fracture. If the bone does not
bleed so freely as it ought, or if there be a fracture, these are justifiable grounds for
perforating the cranium; and the surgeon will be further justified in puncturing the
dura mater if he finds an accumulation of blood beneath that membrane pressing on the
brain. It ought, however, to be remarked, that it will always be expedient to remove
the cranium extensively whenever the trephine is resorted to for this purpose, or for affording an escape to pus, as without this is done only half the benefits of the operation
will be obtained.

3. *Wounds of the Brain and Membranes.*—The peculiar danger of wounds of the brain
and its membranes arises, in the great majority of instances, not so much from the immediate effects of the injury as from the extensive and intractable inflammation which
afterwards follows, giving rise to effusions of pus, disorganization of the substance of the
brain, and hernia cerebri. When the head receives a severe concussion, the brain is
liable to be lacerated, particularly towards the base, in consequence of the inequalities
of the cranium at that part; and the symptoms in such cases will necessarily be complicated with those of concussion as well as with those of compression: but when the brain
has been simply incised or punctured, very often no symptoms whatever arise to indicate that the bodily or mental functions are in the least degree impaired; indeed this
absence of symptoms is sometimes very remarkable, and extends to cases in which considerable portions of the brain have been lost, or foreign bodies been lodged in it.
Wounds of the brain, however, are always dangerous, and it is not to be supposed that
there can be an extensive destruction of a part so important as the brain without immediate death, or death in the course of very a few hours. A confusion of intellect beyond
that which simple concussion usually produces, and twitches of the muscles of the extremities, are diagnostic marks by which (as Sir Benjamin Brodie has observed,) these
cases may sometimes be distinguished. The same author also observes: " I have not been
able to discover, among all the works which I have consulted, a single instance of recovery from a wound of the posterior lobes of the cerebrum, of the cerebellum, or me-

where the external table was beaten in, and the inner table not hurt*. Depression of the external table may be complicated with extravasation or concussion, and may become the cause of extravasation or of the formation of pus. Fracture may be complicated with fissure, that is, fissures often run from the fracture a very considerable way along the skull. Where the external table only is beaten in, it is owing to the meditullium being thick and spongy, and allowing the external plate to sink into it. This is generally done by a small instrument with a good deal of velocity, as the edge of a horse's shoe. Every violence that can produce complete fracture must cause more or less depression, though it may not be very visible; and sometimes, if the force has not been very great, the piece may be returned again into its position immediately. Besides, the inner piece is always broader than the point where the violence has been applied on the external. All fractures of the skull may be called compound; for if not so naturally, they are made so by the removal of the scalp. They differ widely from fractures in general in other parts, as healing the parts is only necessary in fractures of other bones, but here we have to prevent the mischief arising from the broken bone to parts essential to life.

Fractures of the skull of themselves produce no symptoms respecting the brain, only those of a broken bone; but when they are complicated with other effects, then symptoms arise accordingly, more or less according as the fracture is greater or less. There may be bleeding at the nose and ears when the fractures must be running over these parts, but

---

dulla oblongata; and in the great majority of cases in which a cure has taken place, the injury has been confined to the frontal bone, and that part of the brain which is covered and defended by it."

It is unnecessary to observe that the general principles of treatment which have been already pointed out are equally applicable to wounds of the brain, and must be persevered in with the most watchful assiduity. The local treatment resolves itself into the management of fracture, which will be considered in an ensuing note. I shall only, therefore, further observe, that the most judicious surgeons of the present day unitedly concur in the wisdom of forbearance, and in not attempting to extract foreign bodies, unless this can be done with the most perfect facility.]

* [Dr. Hennen has given an account of a case in which the internal table of the skull was splintered, and at one part driven more than half an inch into the membranes of the brain, although there was not even a fissure of the external table. Cases of a similar kind are preserved in almost every museum, and are easily accounted for by the greater brittleness of the internal table. Of course the same cause will produce similar effects in ordinary cases, so as to render it impossible to ascertain the actual amount of pressure which exists in any given case from mere inspection of the external fracture. In children the bones generally are more tenacious than in adults, in consequence of containing less earthy matter. Hence the cranium may be depressed or indented in them without being fractured, just as a tough or green bough will yield to a force in a very different manner from a dry stick.]

they may occur without a fracture of these parts, and there are symptoms of other injury besides fracture. When complicated with concussion, the symptoms of this will be less according as the fracture is greater, for it is from the bones not giving way easily that the head is violently and quickly moved so as to produce concussion. These effects will be according to the weight and velocity. When the weight is great and the velocity small, we shall have more concussion than with a small weight and great velocity: hence from gun-shot wounds we seldom have any concussion.

In cases of fissure only it may admit of a dispute whether we are always to trepan. If there is no symptom of an injured brain, certainly it will not be necessary. It may not be necessary even when attended with symptoms of an injured brain, for the injury may only be from the concussion, and we never trepan in a concussion. However, as we cannot tell for certain at the time whether the symptoms arise from concussion, compression, or from extravasation of blood, it may be more adviseable to trepan, as the operation can do no harm. In cases of depression of the outer table it would also be unnecessary to trepan; but it will be impossible to say that it is certainly a case of this kind: for, though there may be no symptoms of an injured brain, there may be depression of the inner table, which may do mischief afterwards. In young people there may be fracture with depression which may cause no bad symptom at the time, but as the patient grows up bad symptoms may arise, probably from this cause, that there is not sufficient room for the natural growth of the brain.

In all cases of violence attended with compression, either from fracture or not, the trepan is absolutely necessary; but we cannot always promise relief from the operation, nor can we always apply it where it is necessary. When compression is by bone, and its situation known, and the situation is a proper one for trepanning, there is no difficulty; but when the compression is by blood or pus, and there are no external marks of violence, then it is more puzzling. However, rather than let the person die, one would trepan somewhere or other; and if this did not answer, one would not stop here: for I have seen a collection of matter on the opposite side to that on which the blow was inflicted; yet this is a case where one would promise but little encouragement, there being but little chance of success.

Even when we have external marks of violence to guide us, and do trepan, yet this is often not sufficient to free the patient from the compression, for these fluids are often formed between the dura mater and the brain when none is found between the skull and dura mater. The dura mater must not, however, be perforated without good grounds;

we should be as certain that there is fluid contained under the dura mater as we were certain of the necessity of applying the trepan in the first instance. In all cases where I have seen the dura mater wounded, it was by a crucial incision, and the patients have all died. When it is necessary to open the dura mater, I would recommend making a simple incision, for this would be more likely to heal by the first intention, and we could then move the edges to one side, and see if there were any injury below. Whenever I have seen the dura mater opened, the brain has worked through the opening, and the patients have died*. This was the case with a Mr. Cooper, whose dura mater I opened with a crucial incision on account of the state of parts beneath : he died, and I think it is probable I killed him, by opening the dura mater. Patients, under these circumstances, might probably have died, independently of the opening, but this I think would certainly kill them.

Fractures very rarely run through the base of the skull where operations cannot be performed; but if the bones of the base of the skull are only fissured, it will be of sufficient service to trepan on the fissure as low as we can follow it. I have trepanned once below the insertion of the muscles of the neck, and with success.

Trepanning on sinuses has been condemned, but it can do neither harm nor good if the blood is between the dura mater and pia mater; if there is only a depression on them it can only obstruct the sinuses, and not affect the brain.

An incision is sufficient to examine for a fracture if made sufficiently long; and if a fracture is found, it is to be followed to its full extent: but where it is found necessary to trepan, it will be proper to remove the scalp, and do it freely, for an operation should have no incumbrance which we can prevent. We should scalp carefully, lest there should

---

* [As hernia cerebri may occur simply from the support of the cranium being removed, it will à fortiori be more likely to occur when the dura mater is removed also. I should remark, however, that hernia cerebri does not necessarily ensue under these circumstances.

It may be proper to observe, that the treatment of this disease consists in the judicious application of pressure until the fungus is repressed below the level of the dura mater, which then heals over it and prevents its reproduction. This plan generally succeeds, although the old method, consisting in the removal of the surrounding bone, or of the fungus itself, almost invariably failed.

The danger of hernia cerebri being formed when the cranium is removed may justly be urged as an argument for not having recourse to the operation of trephine without the most satisfactory reasons, to which may be added, the still more alarming risk of inflammation and sloughing of the dura mater from accidental violence inflicted by the trephine, or from the mere effects of simple exposure. The fact also of a portion of the cranium being left undefended after the recovery of the patient, should not be neglected in estimating the dangers of this operation, which unquestionably are very considerable.]

be some loose pieces of bone underneath which we cannot see, by which otherwise we might plunge into the brain ; and yet I own I cannot always call to mind this caution at all times when operating*.

It has been recommended lately, after trepanning, to put the scalp down again, and unite it by the first intention ; but I doubt whether we should be able to bring the angles perfectly together ; and if not, part of the dura mater must be exposed, and must suppurate.

A fungus is very apt to arise from the dura mater. Why this should be more than from any other part I cannot say

A poultice is the best application after either scalping or trepanning, because it always admits of immediate removal, and keeps parts in an easy agreeable state†.

---

* [It is impossible to help being struck with this confession, so characteristic of the love of truth and candour which Hunter possessed. Indeed, the same remark appears to me to apply to all the preceding observations, in which may be traced a hesitation and forbearance of judgment uncommon to the author, as if he had not fully approved of the existing rules of treatment, although he had not yet gone to the extent of substituting others in their stead.]

† [No part of surgical treatment (with the exception perhaps of aneurism,) has undergone such important amelioration as that which relates to injuries of the head. Whoever will look into the writings of the period when these lectures were delivered will be astonished at the officiousness of surgeons in counteracting the restorative efforts of Nature by their rude interference, and converting into complicated wounds what were simple in their origin. Hunter was unquestionably less infected with this evil than most of his contemporaries, but still we cannot but observe the influence of this spirit in the directions which he has laid down for the treatment of fractures of the cranium, for which reason it will be necessary to guard the reader against drawing false conclusions on this important subject.

The propriety of these observations will be apparent from considering the cases in which Hunter thought the application of the trephine was justifiable, viz. 1, in young children in whom there was depression without symptoms ; 2, in cases of depression of the outer table only ; 3, "in cases of fissure only it may be more advisable to trepan, as the operation can do no harm"; 4, "in all cases of violence attended with compression, either from fracture or not, the trepan is absolutely necessary," and if blood is not found on one side, to trepan on the other ; and lastly, in fractures of the base of the cranium.

Now it is to be observed that there is as much, if not a much greater, difference between simple and compound fractures of the cranium as there is between simple and compound fractures of the thigh ; consequently, nothing can be more unadvisable and rash than to convert a simple fracture into a compound one, unless the urgency of the symptoms is such as imperatively to demand interference.

In regard, therefore, to simple fractures of the cranium, it may be laid down as the general rule of practice, never to interfere without the strongest reasons for so doing, nor even then until a reasonable time has been allowed for the symptoms (which may depend on concussion,) to subside, and depleting measures been freely employed. Under such treatment the symptoms will often disappear after a short time, and the dangers of subsequent inflammation be infinitely lessened. Nothing surely can be worse than the attempt to anticipate the symptoms of compression by resorting to the trephine.

And in regard to compound fractures of the cranium the same rule is to be observed. If there are no symptoms, the surgeon should desist from any interference, and endeavour, to the utmost of his power, to procure union by the first intention. If, indeed, the depression is very considerable, it may be advisable to elevate it, although there are no symptoms at the time; but if there are symptoms, it will be right and proper to do so in all cases. The same principle should guide the surgeon in the extraction of splinters of bone and foreign bodies, and restrain him from making the attempt unless his object can be accomplished without adding to the irritation of the injury. It is scarcely possible to imagine a case in which an operation so near the basis of the cranium as the author has described can answer any useful object.]

CHAPTER XVIII.

OF THE DISEASES OF BONES AND JOINTS; OF FRAC-
TURES, DISLOCATIONS, &c.

*Bones liable to all the diseases of soft parts.—Death of bone.—Caries.—
Diseased actions;—ulceration;—induration.—General treatment of diseased bones.—Accidents to bones;—simple fracture;—principles of
treatment;—period and mode of union;—false joints.—Inflammation of
bones;—treatment.—Suppuration of bones.—Compound fractures;—
treatment;—communicating with joints.—Question of amputation.—
Fracture of patella, olecranon, and outer ankle.—Suppuration in bones;—
spina ventosa;—necrosis;—treatment.—Of the contraction of diseased
joints.—Sprains;—treatment.—Dislocations;—observations on their
reduction.—Formation of new joints.—Accidents and inflammation of
joints.—Loose cartilages.—Anchylosis.—Diseases of joints.—Wasting
of muscles.—Exfoliations and necrosis;—treatment, by actual cautery.
—Extraction of sequestra.—Rickets.—Mollities ossium;—treatment.
—Exostosis;—treatment.—Exfoliations of cartilage.*

Bones have been very much considered separately from other parts
in their growth, structure, and diseases. Bones being less subject to
changes after death than the soft parts, are therefore more favourable
for the explanation of their diseases after death, such as ulceration, tumours, &c.; and diseased bones of all kinds may be picked up in
churchyards.

The bones, in their causes of disease, in many of their diseases, in
the terminations of these, and in their restoration, are similar to the
soft parts. They are susceptible of the different inflammations and
their consequences, but they are more backward to heal, forming fistulas; in their specific diseases also they resemble the soft parts. But,
unluckily for bones, they can hardly swell; nor can their coverings
swell without its being immediately suspected as venereal, so that
mercury is often given to the detriment of the patient. Nor can they
require a different treatment, as regards their vital power, from the
soft parts, though they may in the mechanical part; but it will be
found that they require a different mechanical treatment only in consequence of their solidity. The hardest bones are most liable to venereal

affections; the softer to scrofula; but the surrounding parts very often partake of their diseases for very wise purposes. Their diseases do not so readily recover as those of soft parts, as the restoring powers are much more weak and tedious in their operations. This slowness is probably owing to an indolent disposition and weak powers. This may, in some measure, arise from the earth in them being a part not possessed of the living principle; yet we find that the hardest bones are cured the soonest; but this is when there is exfoliation, which shows they are more ready to die, and, consequently, to exfoliate.

Their diseases are often very serious, in consequence of our ignorance of the extent of disease, as well as of its nature; for though, from an increase of size or a fistulous opening, we may know the bone to be diseased, still we obtain very little information as to its nature.

Death of Bone.—Bones often lose their life from becoming detached, and their surface being either exposed to the air, or to matter surrounding it. The reason of this is, that bones receive most of their nourishment from the surrounding parts, as from the periosteum; therefore it is natural to suppose that the surface at least will become dead when this part is removed. This may be observed on the projecting end of a stump. The harder the bone, the more ready it is to lose its vital principle by exposure. Sometimes the external surface dies easier on being laid bare than the internal: this is the case in the skull; the external will often exfoliate without the internal*.

Caries.—Death of the exposed surface makes a material difference in the appearance of ulcers of the bone, and they have been classed accordingly. In one case surgeons found the surface of the bone dry; in others moist, and covered with matter; hence the distinction of dry and moist caries; but this arose from ignorance of the disease. When the bone is entirely dead, then there is dry caries; but in the moist the bone is inflamed and ulcerated, and furnishes a discharge, not being dead. When it was perceived that the dry caries only exfoliated, the actual cautery used to be applied on the idea of drying the moist caries; but this was done without knowing the principle on which it was done, viz. that of entirely destroying the life of the bone. By caries I should understand a rotten bone, and by a rotten bone a dead bone. But the distinction between a diseased bone and a dead bone has not been sufficiently attended to, for the term caries has been commonly applied to a bone in the state of an ulcer, and also to a dead bone. Now a disease must always be in a living part, whether soft or hard; but the same

---

* [The reason of this is that these two layers are nourished by two different sets of essels.]

term applied to the two different states of bones can give no just ideas of the disease which it is intended to designate, for that which is commonly called caries is, strictly speaking, an ulcer in the bones ; but ulcers of the bones are as different from the death of these parts as ulcers in soft parts are different from common mortification.

Diseased Actions of Bone.—Bones are very susceptible of diseased actions and dispositions, and sometimes a very slight accident will convert a disposition into an action, as in scrofula ; and this may again be increased by the part of the bone which is injured ; thus, in the case just related the effect is most considerable when it happens at the end of a bone forming part of a joint. The situation, with respect to the body, is also a cause of retardation in healing, as it is in the soft parts.

Ulceration.—Ulcers of a bone are exactly the same in their immediate causes as those of a soft part, and in some of their effects also, the difference not being that of the disease but of the structure. Bones admit of every mode of absorption that the soft parts do. The most common cause of absorption in them is pressure ; whatever makes an unnatural pressure gives a stimulus for the removal of the bone. Bones admit of being absorbed from debility, or want of power to support themselves ; but this I believe only takes place in newly formed bones.

Induration.—It does not appear that ossific inflammation takes place in the parts pressed, so as to make them firmer and harder, as in the soft parts. If bones were rendered harder they would have less power, and therefore would be more liable to death. However, there is often a thickening or running up of the bone all round, as in old dislocations, so that a new joint will be formed. Diseased bones communicate their disease to contiguous parts ; most commonly to the nearest, as the periosteum ; when near to the joints, to the ligaments or cartilages.

General treatment of diseased Bones.—This I shall refer, as much as possible, to the treatment required in soft parts, which is very similar, though the slow action in bones renders it more tedious, and requires a somewhat different method of cure.

If an abscess is seated in the soft parts, and also in the bones, that in the soft parts will readily be recognised, from the difference in its appearance and feel from any of the surrounding parts ; and it will in general approach the skin very soon, which, however, will depend very much on the nature of the disease and of the soft parts. The abscess in the soft parts will generally make a passage for itself, without the necessity of an artificial opening. But this is not so in bone ; if a spontaneous opening takes place, it is not sufficient for a cure ; therefore the trephine is often necessary ; or it may be necessary to destroy the living principle in the bone, and then the actual cautery will be necessary.

To kill the soft parts the caustic is sufficient; but the actual cautery is required for bones.

Of Accidents to Bones.—The effects of accidents which hurt a sound bone are never to be reckoned as disease while it retains the actions of restoration natural to the animal body.

Injuries done to bones are of two kinds: one, simple injury without exposure; the other, injury with exposure. One simple injury is a bruise; another simple injury is a loss of continuity, as in a simple fracture. The union of the bone in simple fracture is exactly similar to the healing of a wound in the soft parts by the first intention; but here adhesive inflammation is unnecessary, though it generally happens from the irritation, and then adhesive inflammation is substituted for union by the first intention.

Simple Fractures.—A simple fracture is a solution of continuity, generally with laceration of the surrounding parts, attended often with splinters of bone attached to the soft parts, or loose. The space between the broken surfaces of the bone and other parts are first filled with extravasated blood from the ruptured vessels. This blood coagulates, and in time becomes vascular, as in the same mode of union in soft parts, forming a callus*. Then the arteries and absorbents, by their action,

---

* [I have already observed, when speaking of the mode of union by adhesion in soft parts, that this is always accomplished by the effusion of coagulable lymph, which afterwards becomes vascular, and not by the organisation of coagulated blood. The only difference in regard to bone consists in the time required for the ultimate organisation of the new-formed structure. It is probable that there is no difference in the quality of the lymph (as it is first poured out,) from any of the structures of the living animal body, because the organic elements which enter into the composition of these structures are essentially the same, whether of bone or any other parts, viz. cellular membrane, nerves, blood-vessels, and absorbents. When a bone is fractured, the periosteum and surrounding cellular membrane concur with the broken surfaces and lining membrane of the bone to pour out a mass of lymph (*callus*), which gradually undergoes successive transformations of structure, until the new-formed part closely assimilates in all respects to the old structure. For the first week or ten days it is observed to consist of a soft vascular granular-looking mass, which gradually assumes, toward the twentieth day, a white and cartilaginous aspect, and at the same time diminishes in bulk: from this period to the fortieth or fiftieth day the diminution of the callus still proceeds, and the process of ossification is now observed to have converted the greater part of it into true bone, although towards the centre of the mass a portion may still remain, which is not fully converted into bone before the expiration of the fourth or sixth month. If at the end of this period the bone be examined, it will be found to be thick and irregular at the point of fracture; the medullary cavity will be found to be obliterated, and the new bone to possess the hardness of ivory. Ulterior changes, therefore, still go on for two or three years, which at last end in the complete restoration of the external form of the bone, as well as of the internal medullary cavity and reticulated structure. Dupuytren has called the external callus, which embraces the broken extremities of the bone like

model the part, and form it into a cellular substance, in which the arteries deposit calcareous earth. It is first formed into cartilage, and then into bone. Adhesion of the detached splinters also takes place, interstitial absorption making them softer, and less pointed; and this takes place not only in those which are attached to the soft parts, but even in such as are entirely loose. (This was shown in a thigh-bone, in which one of the splinters had been turned quite round on its axis, and adhered by its outer surface to the bone.) Therefore these pieces must retain the living principle, and probably only this, while those that remain attached have more. I never examined a compound fracture without finding some of these loose pieces, which shows they must be common. Their union must be similar to that in the transplanting of teeth.

Callus.—The modelling of the callus to the parts in the neighbourhood is very evident in ribs that have been fractured, for on that side next the lungs the inequality is very inconsiderable. Whether the modelling in these cases is purely from the mechanical pressure of the lungs, or whether it is from absorption in consequence of that pressure, I cannot pretend to say: probably both may act. The increased solidity of the new substance is either from the deposit of new matter, mixed with the first, or from absorption of the first, and deposit of new matter instead. I think the last the most likely.

Ossification of the Callus.—The ossific substance is first deposited at the extremity of the bones themselves, and then extends to the callus; at the same time several points in the callus are forming ossific matter. Young people seem to have a greater disposition to form ossific matter than old, but there is a difference even in those of the same age. This new substance is similar to the original bone, and on this account probably is stronger than that from granulation; however, it is not so durable as the original bones are. This process must necessarily be more tedious than in the soft parts, in consequence of the second process which is required; sometimes no union takes place for a length of time after the accident, and the variety of callus is great.

Treatment in simple Fractures.—Parts to be united by the first intention are first to be placed in their habitual position; but this cannot possibly be effected in all cases, nor is it always necessary in soft parts and when there is no external wound. In those parts which are for the support of the body, the fractured parts must if possible be brought into

---

a bulky ferrule until the union is consolidated, the *cal provisionel.* There is not, however, as it appears to me, anything peculiar in this process to require the application of a new name, for the surrounding induration which attends the union of soft parts is precisely a similar phenomenon.]

their original and natural position, before they are retained by bandage, &c. ; but in some of these it is impossible, as in the ribs, clavicle, neck of the femur, &c., especially in fat lusty people. In such it is very difficult to say what the case is, or how the parts are situated. In the extremities there is more room for the exercise of art, but not in all equally.

Simple fractures seldom affect the constitution except the soft parts are much lacerated ; then there is generally constitutional affection in proportion to the degree of inflammation. Rest of the part is necessary : in most cases, therefore, splints and bandages are used ; and when there is much inflammation expected, a folded compress, moistened with some cooling lotion, is applied until the inflammation subsides, and then rollers and splints are applied, which should be tightened as the limb subsides. Spasms often arise from the splinters pricking the soft parts : I should think that a solution of opium would be the best application to remove this symptom. The position for the patient to lie in was formerly on the back ; but the side is now generally adopted. However, I think its whole advantage is that it has the appearance of novelty, and is not a real improvement ; but time will establish the truth. I prefer the back position, with the knee bent, as the patient will support this for the greatest length of time, and it is always the position of debility. In this position the limb will be kept more steady, and will be less liable to be moved by moving the body*.

Period of Union, and manner in which this effect takes place.—The time in which the bone will be united will depend on circumstances. In the soft parts union will often take place in forty-eight hours ; but it will require a much longer time in bones. In the first place they cannot be brought so closely into contact, therefore a larger quantity of new matter must become vascular ; secondly, there is the second or ossific process to be effected ; thirdly, there is laceration of the soft parts ; fourthly, the state of the constitution and restorative powers may be weakened ; fifthly, age. The situation too of the bone will cause a variation ; the lower requiring a longer time than the upper extremities. In the middle-aged, and of a good constitution, union will take place in three weeks, so as not to admit of perceptible motion. If much longer in uniting, it

---

* [The use of fracture-boxes, consisting of two inclined planes, the angle of which is regulated by a rack-work, has led to the almost universal adoption of the position on the back in fractures of the lower extremities. These boxes are of various construction, but most of them combine the double advantage, first, of an easy position, resulting from the semi-relaxed posture of the principal muscles, and, secondly, of admitting of the application of fresh bandages and dressings without being required to disturb the fractured member. Mr. Earle and Mr. Amesbury have contrived beds on the same principle, which effectually combine these advantages, and must be considered as most important acquisitions in the treatment of compound fractures.]

will be very uncertain at what time this will take place: I have known it months, and yet unite at last. This slowness seems to be from imperfection in the two first bonds of union, the adhesive and the cartilaginous; sometimes from a want of disposition to ossification*.

These two, union by the first intention and that by adhesion, constitute the two first modes of union of bone; the third is where these two have failed, and here the union is effected by means of granulations from the broken ends of the bone and from the soft parts, which granulations become converted into bone (see *note*, p. 427.) It is difficult to account for the failure of the first two: often it depends neither on the constitution nor the part; for the constitution has often been good, as is seen by it bringing on new inflammation on exposure.

I have seen a simple fracture where the two first processes, namely, the conversion of the blood into a vascular substance and the deposition of cartilage, had taken place, and the third had failed; and then, on allowing the parts a little motion, they got firmer, and at last perfectly strong.

False Joints.—Sometimes simple fractures will not unite at all. This is a worse consequence than any of the foregoing, there being no soft union even, or, if there ever was, that being absorbed. Here the surrounding parts thicken and form a kind of capsular ligament, and the extremities of the bone rub against each other at each motion of the limb, by which stimulus the broken parts are absorbed, and the extremities become smooth, and in time are covered with something similar to cartilage, and at length the cavity between them becomes filled with a fluid very much resembling synovia. In this case it is necessary to lay open the new cavity and irritate the ends of the bones, and then, by

---

* [It may be observed that this want of disposition is particularly manifested during the periods of pregnancy and lactation, which would seem to divert the powers of the constitution from the reparation of the injury to the more important object of nourishing the offspring. The same effect will be produced by excessive depletion, or constant motion of the fractured extremities of the bones. By the former the naturally weak reproductive powers of bone are still further reduced, and by the latter the ossific process is arrested, and a new disposition created for the formation of a bursal structure, similar to what takes place in other parts of the body when friction is employed. It should be observed that constant motion of a fractured bone will inevitably lead to the formation of a false joint; but this will be differently formed in different cases. If the process of union has been interrupted from the commencement, the broken extremities will be found rounded off and covered with hard enamelled surfaces, inclosed by an adventitious synovial bursa; but if the interruption has taken place during the ossification of the callus, then the extremities of the bone will be united by a cellular or fibro-ligamentous structure. I am not aware that true cartilage is ever reproduced when removed from the surfaces of joints by ulceration, or ever found as a new formation on the extremities of bones forming a false joint.]

keeping them in position, bony union will often take place. It has been recommended to saw off the ends of the bones; but all that seems necessary is to irritate them sufficiently to excite a fresh inflammation*.

Inflammation of Bones.—Bones are subject to the adhesive, suppurative, and ulcerative inflammation, as the soft parts are.

The adhesive inflammation of bones is attended with this peculiar circumstance, namely, the formation of new bony matter in the inflamed parts, and therefore may be called ossific inflammation. Soft bones and the soft parts of hard bones are the most liable to inflammation and suppuration. Whether this arises from the structure of the bones or from some other cause, I cannot say.

The suppurative and ulcerative inflammation is the same in the bones as in soft parts, as is also the granulation and cicatrization.

When an injury is done to a bone sufficient to cause inflammation, or if inflammation arises spontaneously in a bone, then, some time after, there appears a swelling. This state is similar to the adhesive inflammation in soft parts. But pain appears to be the first symptom of inflammation in bones, and to precede the swelling a considerable time, whilst in soft parts they appear together. From this slowness in swelling it would appear to be a different operation, and it is difficult to understand how a bone can swell from extravasated lymph or calcareous matter, yet it is impossible to conceive that it is from any other causes. A swelled bone is true bone, and nearly as hard as any other bone†; it is easily distinguished from the sound bone and from swelling of the surrounding parts. A cylindrical bone seems most liable and ready to swell at its extremity or softest part, which is the last-formed part; and this is agreeable to what I have before said, that the latest-formed parts

---

* [It has not been found that any plan uniformly succeeds. Among the least severe methods adopted in these cases may be mentioned blisters over the seat of fracture, or lateral or longitudinal pressure (according to the circumstances of the case) of the broken ends of the bone, so as to excite inflammation. Thus, Sir Everard Home procured a fractured femur to unite by encircling the limb with a stiff leathern belt, and making the patient walk. A seton passed between the ends of the bones has succeeded in a few cases; but the excision of the fractured extremities is much more effectual, although it is attended with the great inconvenience of shortening the limb. Mr. Hunter's is certainly a less severe method, and may be applicable to those cases, such as fractures of the tibia, where the bursal sac can easily be exposed; although I should mention that it has lately failed in two cases in St. George's Hospital. I believe, however, that time and a well-adjusted apparatus will succeed in the great majority of cases, without having recourse to any other method.]

† [There is great difference in this respect in different cases. Bones, in general, become spongy and light from inflammation; but there are other cases in which they acquire a hardness and denseness of structure little inferior to that of ivory.]

are weakest and least able to resist disease. But in the bones of the skull the swelling is generally in the centre.

Pain in inflammation of bones is more violent than in other parts. Whether this arises from the nerves being more compressed, or from the nature of the nerves themselves, is not easy to determine. This is rather a heavy depressing pain than an acute one, and is similar to that of rheumatism, generally more violent at night when warm in bed. This symptom is common to all inflammations of the bones and periosteum, though it has been supposed to be peculiar to venereal affections.

In this stage the constitution is not much affected, except from the long-continued pain, which may be so continued and violent that the patient may in the end become considerably affected by it. We cannot divide the bones, like the soft parts, into vital and non-vital; therefore we have not two species of symptoms. We have oftener, however, hectic from inflammation of the bones than from that of the soft parts.

The parts surrounding the bone generally, if not always, sympathize with the ossific inflammation; first producing simply adhesive inflammation of the periosteum, then of the muscles and cellular membrane. When considerable, this adds much to the swelling: the periosteum becomes fixed to the bone itself, so that this seems more swelled than in reality it is.

The soft parts contiguous to the bone, besides sympathizing with the inflammation, receive the ossific disposition. The cells which contain the marrow are subject to be affected, so that the cavity is filled up, and the bone increased in size. The ossific disposition takes place in the surrounding parts much oftener than either the swelling of the bone or the ossific disposition of the cavity; therefore it seems an easier operation to Nature. This ossific disposition in the soft parts assists in the union of fractures and in the formation of anchylosis.

Here are bones [*exhibiting them*] where the ossific or adhesive inflammation had taken place in the substance of the bone, producing thickening of that substance; others where inflammation has taken place on the surface of the bone; and here, similar to the exudation of coagulable lymph on the soft parts, a coat of adventitious bony matter is laid on the surface of the bones by ossific inflammation. This in some, you may perceive, is laid on so close and so thin as to appear like ossification of the periosteum; in others it is loose, and capable of being shelled off. In this bone of a lion it is laid on in places nearly half an inch thick, adhering closely to the bone; and in this it appears, from the little connexion it had with the bone, that the bony matter had grown from the surrounding soft parts.

From this preparation of one of the bones of the lion, which had been injected and steeped in acid, it appears that this newly-added bone was vascular, and had only lost its earth·by this steeping, its form still remaining; it therefore must be as much an animal substance as the original bone. This appearance on the surface of bones, some years ago, before I gave these lectures, would have been supposed to have arisen from caries. If a bone is bent, broken, or hurt, &c., the consequent inflammation produces an addition of adventitious matter, which will strengthen the part even beyond what it originally was. In disease of the bone, when the ossific disposition does not exist, we may observe that the periosteum is very slightly attached to the bone, being as easily raised from it as the cuticle may from the skin.

Treatment.—The swelling of a bone, if of no specific nature, requires little chirurgical treatment, but will most probably require internal and external medicines before it can be reduced to its original size.

If a bone be only in a state of adhesive inflammation, every method is to be used that is used in inflammation of other parts, as bleeding, rest, &c.; and if in the lower extremities, a horizontal position will add greatly to the cure. Fomentations will give ease, especially when near the skin. However, this treatment is sometimes ineffectual, and suppuration comes on.

Suppuration, however, is not always the consequence; for in some cases the bone becomes indolent, and remains swelled for years. I believe bones are more likely to take on the indolent habit than other parts. The adventitious bone may always be considered as in a weak state, not being an originally-formed part, and as it is often in parts where it becomes an incumbrance, must be considered as a disease; and if it could be removed it would be of service; but in most cases this could not be done without producing worse effects.

When bones take on this indolent habit, it will be necessary to rouse the diseased part to action. For this purpose mercury may be used internally, and pursued for a considerable time in a middle dose between what would be used in a venereal affection and what would be given as an alterative.

Mezereon has been much recommended in indolent swellings. The decoction recommended by Dr. Russell is to be made as follows. Fresh mezereon root one ounce, pure water a gallon and a half. Boil it in a copper vessel tinned, over a moderate fire, down to a gallon. Towards the end of the boiling, add an ounce of liquorice-root, sliced. Half a pint is to be taken three times a day, which is more than most can drink. This does not increase any of the secretions, excepting being a laxative in a very few cases. It has been tried with double the quantity of mezereon, but was then too pungent for the stomach. Patients using this decoction are not confined to any regimen. The medicine has been strongly recommended in the Medical Observations by Dr. Russell. The cases he has described I should not call venereal, though they were treated as such, but scrofulous; therefore we may find mezereon a good remedy in scrofula. It cannot be considered as a specific in syphilis, as it is only useful when the bones are affected.

Of the Suppurative Inflammation in Bones.—When the ossific inflammation is not cured, suppuration takes place. There is no visible difference between suppuration in bones and in the soft parts; for as bones are composed of animal matter with calcareous earth, there is no reason why they should not go through the same process. Suppuration does not indeed take place so readily in bones, the inflammation often not reaching so far. Whether this proceeds from an indolent disposition stamped on them from the first, or from their structure, I do not know; but whenever suppuration takes place in them it is a serious piece of business. The periosteum and surrounding parts are more ready to take on suppuration than the bone itself, yet it may originate in the substance of the bone. The consequence of suppuration is ulceration, which may also originate from pressure, or blood lying on the bone. There is, I believe, no difference between the ulceration of soft parts and of bone, the adhesive going on with the suppurative in the soft parts; so in the bone we have the ossific going on with the suppurative. To repair the loss that has been made, Nature sets herself to work to repair the loss with granulations. The intention of these is, to fill up abscesses; to repair compound fractures; to restore the part lost by trepanning, &c. Nature sets about to repair these injuries of bones by the same original principles by which bone was first formed: thus, if a cylindrical bone is to be restored which was originally formed on cartilage, the first step to its reproduction will be the formation of cartilage; if a bone in the skull, it will be of membrane. But we sometimes have too great a disposition to ossification in the granulations, so as to make the new part bulky and inconvenient. A difference is observable in the newly-formed substance which arises from ossific inflammation and that which is formed from granulations in consequence of ulceration. The former has a smooth fibrous appearance, very different from the latter, the surface of which is granulated, as if the bone had grown from the centre to the circumference, the grain being of a sandy texture.

Compound Fractures.—These differ from simple fractures in the first and second modes of union being lost; and therefore the third, by granulation, takes place. The granulations between the ends of the bone and on the lacerated surfaces take on an ossific disposition, and the suppuration is always more or less surrounded by the adhesive inflammation, so that it extends pretty far, and consequently the callus is large. Hence these fractures are so tedious and dangerous, especially when in the lower extremity, which is their usual situation. There are no bounds to the mischief done by a compound fracture: the loss of the uniting substance by the wound, and the loss of the living principle to what remains by the exposure, are causes of the failure of the first process; and, besides, the ends of the bones are sometimes so locked together as to require to be sawed off, or so denuded of their investing membrane as to lose their living principle and to exfoliate, as the dead part must be thrown off before the wound can heal. This sometimes takes six or eight months, and is so extensive as to be very dangerous. The inflammation too which follows the accident is commonly very considerable, and may proceed to mortification.

Treatment.—The only peculiarity in compound fracture by which it differs from other lacerated wounds is the breach of continuity of the bone, which admits of motion in the part where none was intended. This singularity it is which requires a peculiarity in the treatment, as this motion and the operations of Nature are in contradiction to each other. A variety of inventions have been employed to prevent this motion; but the dressing of the wound every day counteracts the effect of every invention that has been thought of, and it is perhaps impossible to dress the sore without motion. (see *note*, p. 508.) At first the part is generally put into a poultice, but changing this must give considerable movement. Instead of a poultice, I would lay the leg or arm in cloths, doubled several times, and wetted with goulard, and lap them over so as to come into contact. These should be wetted occasionally, and continued until the inflammation is over and the suppuration takes place. When the wound is on the back of the leg we shall be obliged to raise the leg every day to apply the cloths. A bit of oil-cloth should be put under the leg, and wiped clean every day.

The time of union of a compound fracture is necessarily much longer than that of a simple fracture, from the processes they have to go through, and is very uncertain; but the union of the bones is generally effected long before the external wound is healed up, for whatever retards the cure of the bone retards also the cure of the sore. When granulations have been formed and bony union is late in taking place, and the wound is healed up or nearly so, it should be treated like a simple fracture in the same circumstances, and gentle pressure is of use, as walking, with a machine to take off the weight of the body: here necessity acts as a stimulus for bony union to form.

Compound fractures do not always take on the bony union; but there

is never a want of soft union, as there is at times in simple fractures;
and therefore new joints are never formed, as they are sometimes when
simple fractures do not unite by the first or second modes of union.

Compound Fractures communicating with Joints.—Joints do not so
readily go through the suppurative and granulating inflammation when
wounded as other parts; and it would be improper for them to do so, as
it would produce anchylosis. If, in a compound fracture, the fracture
extends to a joint, the question arises, What shall we do ? The injury
may be viewed in one of three lights: first, as a compound fracture;
secondly, as a laceration of a joint; thirdly, as a compound of both. If
it is such a fracture as seems impossible to recover, it is not necessary
to consider the joint at all, but amputation must be performed. If the
laceration into the joint be such that, although the fracture may not be
considerable, inflammation and suppuration of the whole joint must come
on, then it is probable that amputation must also be its fate. But if the
fracture appears to be such as may unite, and the laceration in the joint
be such as can unite by the first intention; if the fracture be such a one
as we think would do well when restored to its situation, if not complicated with a wound in the joint, it becomes dubious what ought to be
done. If the wound in the joint will admit of being kept from exposure,
then we may consider the case as one of compound fracture only. This
sort of injury most often happens at the ankle-joint, the tibia being very
liable to fracture at its lower extremity. All wounds of the joints should
be healed by the first intention, if possible*.

Of Fracture of the Patella, Olecranon, and outer Ankle.—The peculiarity attending these fractures is, that they make the lateral part of a
joint so exposed that the fracture communicates with the cavity of the
joint which gives an exit to the immediate bond of union. The treatment of the patella and the olecranon will be very similar, because they
not only make the lateral parts of joints, but they have inserted into

---

* [The question of amputation in cases of compound fractures, is one which depends
on many circumstances: as, for example, the implication of the great joints; the degree
in which the soft parts are bruised and injured and the bone comminuted; the injury
of the principal vessels or nerves of the fractured limb, as well as the age, previous
habits, and present conveniences of the patient. Without, however, going into the subject further, it may be sufficient to mention that surgeons are now more in the habit of
trusting to the efforts of Nature than used formerly to be the case; so that cases which
would certainly have been condemned by Pott and Hunter are frequently saved in the
present day. Where youth and a sound constitution exist, the surgeon should be especially careful not hastily to condemn a fractured limb because the joint happens to be
implicated, or on account of any other simple circumstance; but should reflect how
extensive the resources of Nature are, and that an attempt to save the limb in the first
instance will not necessarily preclude his having recourse to the remedy of amputation
in a later period of the case.]

them the tendons of considerable muscles. Hence the fractured ends are separated from each other, instead of riding over one another as in common fracture, and a different treatment is consequently necessary.

As the fractured patella is commonly produced by a contraction of its muscles, especially when opposed by a resistance of other muscles, the fracture is then transverse, and then the muscles are at liberty to contract to their full extent, and consequently the broken part of the bone above is drawn up the thigh with them, for the rectus muscle has more than a simple power of extending the leg, namely that of bending the thigh on the pelvis.

Treatment.—When the ends of the fractured bones are pretty soon brought tolerably close together, I can conceive that union may take place as in simple fracture. Before the year 1750 it was the practice to endeavour to bring the broken ends of the bones as near together as possible, with little or no motion allowed; but after that a fashion arose (for we have fashions in surgery as in everything else, arising perhaps from a person happening to do well who had not been treated in the old way,) of letting the parts separate, and of not forbidding motion so strictly; but now caprice has I believe had its day, and we are taught by reason and experience that the parts should be, when cured, as nearly as possible in their natural situation. To effect this, the upper portion of the patella should be brought down as much as we can, and the common bandage be applied. It may be imagined that in the treatment it is not only necessary to extend the leg, but to lay the thigh at right angles with the body; but from a complete knowledge of all the circumstances, it will appear that this practice is not at all necessary; for as the rectus has a greater power of contraction than extending the leg, so it must also be granted that it has a greater power of relaxation; therefore it is not necessary to place the leg at right angles with the body.

Fracture of the patella seems to be cured by Nature, in the manner of the simple fracture, by granulation, because the first and second bonds of union have escaped into the cavity of the joint and have been absorbed. But, perhaps, if the ends were brought together earlier, they might be united by the same means as the common simple fracture, especially as we sometimes see a luxuriance round their edges, which is probably owing to the ossific disposition having taken place in the coagulum. But if the first and second modes fail, I conceive the third, by granulation takes place: the ends of the bones and ligaments exuding coagulating lymph, which coagulates immediately, and, taking vessels as in other granulations, becomes not bone, but a kind of tendinous or ligamentous substance; which seems a wise provision of Nature, because if they were united by bone, this might be of such a length as would prevent the motion of the joint, except with the leg at right angles with the femur.

When union is formed it would be proper to give some passive motion; but voluntary motion is always better, because the will is always sensible how far the powers of a part extend, and will attempt no more; but if force is used to extend a part, all the muscles of which have not their due power, it may be thrown into such a situation as to give an improper action to a weak muscle : the will alone is proper to perform those actions she has determined on herself.

The method of cure by ligament only is very tedious; but there are other things to be done after this union has taken place. First, the accommodation of the muscles to their new situation, where less length is necessary, from the patella having become longer; secondly, the new contraction in this new situation; thirdly, acquiring sufficient strength in it.

We have reason to believe that the greatest contraction in a muscle is somewhat greater than the joint will allow of; for we find them firm when the limb is stretched as if the power was greater; and when the part is deprived of this firm band we find the muscles draw the bone up higher than they should. Thus the upper part of the patella is always drawn up when the bone is broken. While the union is taking place, the muscles are accommodating themselves to the great length of the bones. After this it will be necessary to bend the limb and keep it so, in order that the muscles may be thus enabled to admit of an elongation equal to the flexure of the limb, by which means the patient will be enabled easily to bend the limb. Extension will not be so easy; but still by perseverance it may be acquired, as the following case will show.

I called with a friend to pass a day or two with a family in the country. The lady of the house had had her knee fractured, and had been treated according to the maxims the surgeon had learned while attending the London hospitals, which at that time were to leave the whole unconfined, and take no measures to bring the portions of bone together. She recovered from the accident, but was totally unable to use the limb, and had to be wheeled about in a chair. Her leg was made to swing backwards and forwards, as she sat on a high table or chair, but still she had no power of contracting the rectus muscle, and as soon as the force that gave the motion ceased, the motion ceased with it. It was not until several years after the accident that I saw her; and, having spent a whole night in considering the probable cause of her loss of power, it appeared to me that the space between the two attachments of the rectus being much shortened, while the muscle continued of the same length, the utmost degree of its contraction would scarcely be able to straighten itself, much less move the patella and leg also. I advised her to sit as before, but instead of having her leg moved, to move it herself. This she could not in the least effect at first. I considered, however, that the power of contraction which the muscles possess beyond that necessary for the mere purpose of extending and flexing the limb, as mentioned above, is probably obtained by the mind's influence on the muscle; and that, in this case, if the influence of the mind was frequently exerted on the muscle, it would gain this power of contraction, in which it would probably be aided by the interstitial absorption taking place, and actually shortening the muscle and suiting its length to the office it was to perform. I therefore advised her ladyship to repeat her exercise, as often as she could, every day for a month, assuring her that if at the end of the month she had obtained the least power of motion, I had not a doubt that she would again be enabled to walk by a regular exercise of the muscle. The event proved as fortunate as I could wish: the lady, at the end of three or four months, being able to walk, although she had not walked for years.

Fracture of the Olecranon.—The olecranon may be considered as a fixed patella, the inserting-point of a considerable muscle, and when broken is drawn up as the patella. The immediate treatment is the same; but the consequences are often different, as it should always be united by bony union. The arm should be extended, and kept so; and the upper portion brought down, if up, and retained by a bandage, which will be somewhat similar to those used after bleeding. When soft union has taken place, and bony is beginning, passive motion of the joint should be made. As the union gets stronger, the motion should be increased, but should not be very great, till bony union is completed, as before this it will bend the olecranon over the lower end of the os humeri, and occasion it to make a smaller curve than it should do, even an angle; by which the full extension will be prevented. This, by proper attention, may be avoided.

Fracture of the Ankle Bones.—It is possible for these to unite in general, like simple fractures, as the displacement can hardly be very considerable, unless great injury has been done, here being no muscle fixed to them, the contraction of which would draw up the parts; so that the extravasated blood and juices may be sufficient to unite them by the first intention.

Suppuration in Bones.—I shall first consider that on the surface of bones, or on the periosteum; secondly, in the substance; thirdly, in the medullary parts; fourthly, may be reckoned that in the joints, which is similar to that of a bone; but, as it is attended with consequences peculiar to the nature of the part, I shall treat of them after.

When inflammation attacks the surface of a bone, the first effects are adhesive; and when suppuration takes place, the periosteum is separated as far as the suppuration extends, making underneath a cavity for the matter. As the adhesive state takes place some way round the abscess, there is in many cases a circle of adventitious bone formed in the periosteum round the abscess. This will be more or less, according to the rapidity of the suppuration: if it takes place soon, there will not be time for the ossific inflammation; if slowly, a ridge will be formed, as is often the case in the cranium, giving the appearance of bone being wanting under the muscles. As soon as ever it is known that suppuration has taken place, it should be freely opened, to prevent as much as possible the separation of periosteum*; granulations will form, and in proportion to them will the ossific disposition follow, which ossific disposition is often not confined to the granulations, but exists in the surrounding cellular membrane, &c.; so that, around the bone, ossific matter is deposited which increases it very much in thickness: this is seldom the case when the granulations are healthy, but almost always when unhealthy. The oftener bones have undergone inflammation and ulceration the thicker they become, and also much more subject to it, as we evidently see in working-people's legs, &c. Often, from the separation of the periosteum, part of the bone dies, and must exfoliate.

The second Species.—This is of greater consequence, as more of the bone becomes diseased. When inflammation attacks the substance of the bone, it is seldom that the whole diameter of the bone swells, generally only on one side, where the suppuration is. This must at first be much confined, from the solid parts around, and ulcerative inflammation is obliged to take place early; and accordingly, as in common abscesses, the ulceration goes on towards the soft parts, and until it arrives there it is impossible to tell whether there is abscess in the bone or not†. It will burst, as usual in abscesses; but this probably does not so quickly

---

* [The propriety of this direction cannot be questioned as regards those cases where collections of matter between the periosteum and bone give considerable pain, or where, suppuration not yet having taken place, the suffering from the periosteal inflammation cannot be subdued by the ordinary antiphlogistic and mercurial treatment. It should be recollected, however, that considerable collections of pus, arising from a venereal cause, are frequently dispersed by an appropriate treatment directed to the cure of the original disease; especially when such collections are situated on the frontal bone.]

† [Notwithstanding the great obscurity which involves the early existence of these cases, yet it is not always impossible to discover their true nature. In the clinical lectures delivered by Sir Benjamin Brodie, that gentleman has related several cases in which he has detected and given exit to circumscribed abscesses in the heads of bones entering into the composition of the large joints. Such cases are marked by a fixed deep-seated pain in some determinate spot, unattended by any considerable swelling of the parts, or disease of the neighbouring joints.]

take place here as in soft parts. When near the external surface, and so near the periosteum as to give it the stimulus of adhesion, then the adventitious substance is formed on the external part of the bone, while its substance is gradually lessening internally by absorption; but the addition externally is not in proportion to the internal loss, and therefore it bursts externally. [*Preparations of this were shown where suppuration and ulceration had taken place in cylindrical bones, as in the tibia, &c.*] This used to be called spina ventosa.

The third Species.—Inflammation in the medullary part is still more serious in its consequence than the last. The body of the bone thickens from the adhesive disposition, and also the ossific disposition takes place in some degree in the periosteum all round, so that the external parts are much increased in bulk: this only takes place in the bones of the extremities, where strength is necessary, and never in the scalp, &c. The ossific disposition in the medullary parts takes place at all points of the abscess; and by this the other part of the marrow is saved. When suppuration takes place, there being no vent obliges the ulcerative inflammation to take place: on all sides and on the outside additional matter is deposited, Nature intending to keep up the strength which it is losing internally; the newly-formed bone is itself disposed to the ossific inflammation, by which it in many parts becomes much thickened, so that the remaining shell is often entirely new. Where the two opposite processes do not bear a proportion to each other, the bone becomes often so very thick as to resemble a compound fracture. In the two last mentioned we have often exfoliations, as well as in the first; but they are less favourable, from their situation being different, and are called internal exfoliations. The head of the tibia is more subject to abscess than any bone in the body. The medullary arteries and membrane, which furnish nourishment for the internal laminæ of the bones and marrow, is the seat of the inflammation producing it. [*A preparation was shown where it was very large, but only a mere shell remaining.*]

Treatment.—When the adhesive or ossific inflammation does not stop, but goes on to suppuration, it must be treated as inflammation in soft parts. When the suppuration is superficial, so that the bone only makes one of the sides of the abscess, the matter will come immediately to the surface.

All the soft parts are to be laid freely open, or entirely removed. This is necessary *in all* wounds, where healing does not take place from the bottom, to expose them and bring on inflammation; and when there is exfoliation, the opening is more necessary, as it cannot heal until this is removed, and it will sooner be removed and healed by exposure. It will often be necessary to remove a part; but when the skin and bone are very near, then it must be only a simple opening, without removing the skin, as in such cases the skin is fixed very much to the bone, and should not be lost; and again, here the granulations have less power to contract than in deeper and more fleshy parts, and there is less danger of sinuses or fistulous openings: but when deep-seated, simple and free openings are insufficient, and some parts must be removed, otherwise the external opening will close, and fistulous openings will remain till the bone has recovered. Bones are very apt to fall into an indolent inactive state, which should be discovered, and stimulating dressings applied. Oily dressings have been objected to; but oil has neither a power of promoting nor retarding granulations, though the former has been imagined to be the case. By this means they are often cured, but are afterwards very liable to new inflammation; and this is generally attended with ulceration, which begins in the skin. This is owing to weakness in the part, and is most frequent in the lower extremities.

In some cases it will be necessary to apply the actual or potential cautery to the bone.

The treatment of these cases is various, and the cure is generally very difficult. They are seldom understood: at first they may appear as a common abscess, and are often opened and dressed as such, which, proving generally ineffectual, leads the surgeon to a more particular examination, and he easily discovers a diseased bone, if the opening has been free. As the bone cannot be dilated by a cutting instrument, it must be killed either by the potential or actual cautery, or sometimes the trepan will be useful. After exfoliation is finished, the same dressing as in caries is required; but in many cases it will be necessary to do something more. The cavity of the abscess in some requires to be exposed, by removing surrounding parts, as is sometimes done in abscesses of the soft parts before they will heal.

Of the Matter in Diseased Bone.—The matter discharged from a sore where there is diseased bone is seldom good matter, especially if it become fistulous. The diseased bone that is bare is often producing mechanical effects, such as rubbing the soft granulations, so that there is a small quantity of blood mixed with the matter, which gives it a bad colour. Such matter generally blackens or in part corrodes silver probes. This probably arises from the hepatic air (sulphuretted hydrogen gas) which Mr. Kirwan has discovered to be produced by the putrefaction of animal matter.

Of the Shortening of Muscles of Diseased Joints.—Joints when diseased naturally get into a middle state between flexion and extension; and, as the joints are passive, this must be performed by the muscles, and either by their voluntary or involuntary action. This stiffness of the joint depends on the involuntary contraction of the muscles, and is in consequence of the muscles sympathizing with the joint. But this involuntary contraction is not like tetanus : the muscles in this state feel like strong cords, and, if straightening the joint be attempted, it seems to the patient as if these cords were breaking. As the joint loses its power of motion by the disease, in that proportion the muscles are altered ; they adapting themselves to the quantity of motion the joint will admit.

In the artificial extension of a joint which has been contracted, the muscles which are contracted should never be called into action, because the parts which ought to lengthen will thus be shortened. To illustrate this, let us suppose the gastrocnemius and solœus muscles to be contracted, and to draw up the heel, so that the patient rests on his toes, his foot being in a line with his leg : in walking he will involuntarily use these muscles to give firmness to his leg. In this case we should give support to the heel in a degree. By this means the patient, convinced of his ability to bring his heel as low as the support requires, will cease voluntarily to contract the gastrocnemius and solœus muscles, and they by degrees will acquire the property of relaxing themselves ; which, if the heel was entirely supported at first, they would have no occasion for, and while altogether unsupported they never could.

Of Sprains.—In sprains the ligaments are probably often torn ; for in most sprains there is a considerable extravasation in the surrounding cellular membrane.

Considerable pain is felt, at the time of the accident, of the heavy dull kind, which often produces sickness, and the blood leaves the skin of the body generally. Considerable swelling takes place, and this is almost instantaneous. The swelling arises from two causes : the surrounding cellular membrane being loaded, and the increased secretion of synovia into the joint. This will be more visible in the joints where the capsular ligament is loose, as in the joint of the knee above the patella.

These symptoms are succeeded by inflammation, which produces great pain and sensibility on motion. These parts are very insensible in a sound state, but they easily move from a state of insensibility to one of sensibility. Nature does not seem to have bestowed so much pains on these parts as on others, for they have very weak powers of restoration, which produces tediousness of cure.

Treatment.—In the first place, rest should be employed, with topical bleeding. Pumping on, or long immersion in cold water, and friction with vinegar, lees of wine, spirits of wine, &c. on the part have been recommended. Whether these last remedies serve any useful purpose or not I am undetermined; but we know that sprains are at last seldom perfectly cured. I have known the effects of a strain continue through life (above fifty years), always swelling and becoming painful on the least violence. Where there is a perfect cure obtained, I suspect the ligaments only have been injured, and not the cartilage, which is extremely slow to restoration. 'Though the mechanical strength is recovered, yet a weakness is often found to remain, which may sometimes be removed by some application which has not been before applied, as a pitch plaster, opodeldoc, &c., which gets the credit and the name of a specific : but these often fail. The same applications are often recommended in the second stage as in the first, but to use it in the same way must be improper. In the second stage cold water should be applied no longer than to excite heat. Sprains often remain very painful after the original symptoms have been removed : this pain is often removed by giving the part motion, as if some part was moved into its place by that motion; but it is most probably by the motion's giving the parts an opportunity of adapting themselves to each other's action.

On Dislocation.—This term generally is applied to bones, and probably might also be applied to cartilages, when any two bones forming a joint are displaced. Probably the articulating substance or ligament is torn; but this circumstance is not yet well ascertained. In many joints a lateral motion must be applied to produce it, the muscles being at right angles with the bone that they move, &c. When the head of the bone has moved beyond a certain point, then the antagonist muscle is unable to bring it back, and then it requires some passive motion to bring the bone so far back that the antagonist muscle can replace it. A lady had the tibia brought too much below the os femoris, by too great flexion : the surgeon attempted to replace it, by bringing the foot forward, and so to replace it by the extensor muscles : but I thought the tibia was got beyond the centre of motion ; therefore I conceived that the above means would make it worse : he then, by my direction, raised the head of the tibia a little upwards, by placing the hand in the ham, and the reduction of it was then finished by the extensor muscles.

General observations on the Reduction of Dislocations.—As joints are composed of two parts, one more moveable and the other more fixed, the more fixed might be called the reactor, and the moveable part the actor. When a violence has been applied to the actor there is a deformity occasioned, as if this was out of its place, yet both are equally so. In dislocations the powers are generally applied to the actor, and though in most cases the reactor does its office spontaneously, yet it often requires assistance. In most joints of the body the reactor can be made more fixed, as, e.g., the body in dislocated hip, but in the shoulder there wants a counter resistance, or reactor, the scapula being so very moveable, and hardly to be fixed by art: hence extension is obliged to be more on the muscles, as the latissimus dorsi, pectoralis, &c., than on the ligament where it should be; therefore, to reduce it it is necessary to make the scapula a fixed point, to do which often requires much labour and some art. When you stretch the shoulder as far as it can, the scapula is brought forwards as much as possible, but the latissimus dorsi and pectoralis major prevent the os humeri from being extended on the scapula beyond a certain point, which is much against you in the reduction.

In reducing a dislocation the bone should be returned exactly in a retrograde motion, overcoming that effect first which was produced last, and then a lateral motion is to be made in a contrary direction to that motion which occasioned the dislocation; in doing this the most immoveable part is to be the fixed point if possible, and the moveable is that which is to be extended. This is to be done as soon as possible after the dislocation, as afterwards the parts will become adapted to their new situations, and render the reduction more difficult, and sometimes impracticable.

New Joints produced in consequence of Dislocations.—We have sometimes new joints produced in consequence of dislocations when the bones are not reduced, which brings the parts into somewhat of the condition of simple fracture; and there is the same disposition between the two surfaces in contact as in simple fractures which do not unite by the soft continuity of parts. But this can only be when the dislocated bone comes in contact with another bone, as the thigh-bone with the ilium. When the two bones rub and press on one another absorption of the external surface takes place, the adhesive ossific inflammation goes on around the edges, a fluid is secreted in the cavity, and thus we have the new joint. These joints of necessity oftenest take place in the thigh-bone than elsewhere, but sometimes between the os humeri and the scapula.

The effects of Accidents and Inflammation of Joints.—They being circumscribed cavities, are subject to the same diseases as other circumscribed cavities, as inflammation, &c., but their peculiar structure sometimes renders their consequences different. Nature is very little disposed to take on the adhesive inflammation, because the necessary consequence would be loss of motion in a part originally intended for motion. This makes inflammation in joints so much worse than in any other circumscribed cavities, for, as before observed, if adhesive inflammation does not come on, the inflammation and consequent suppuration must spread through the whole cavity.

The joints are mechanically strong; yet this is not that sort of power which resists disease; but they have sometimes a greater disposition than other parts to disease; and sometimes they become diseased from the violence of accidents. They are slower of cure, from their composition, than other circumscribed cavities are; besides, they are also subject to specific diseases, from the materials which they are composed of, and more backward in their cure. Inflammation in joints is generally of more serious consequence than in other parts; even when resolved it is disagreeable; yet this is always to be wished for. Inflammation from accidents often does well without any adhesion, but not when it arises from other causes. In all inflammations of joints there is a swelling, from extravasation, into the cellular membrane and cavities, as in the knee above the patella, where there is a sacculus mucosus. In inflammation from accidents the treatment must be similar to that in other parts, but here suppuration is particularly to be prevented if possible. Rest, topical bleeding by leeches and cupping, fomentations, blisters, purgatives, &c., are here to be particularly employed; but as joints are very apt to become scrofulous, the patient should go to the sea when the swelling becomes chronic and appears to be at all stationary. Another cause of accidents here, besides strains, is extravasation of blood.

Of loose Substances found in Joints.—These are ligamentous, cartilaginous, or bony. Though there are often extravasations into joints, yet they seldom produce adhesions, although sometimes there are appearances as if blood extravasated into the cavity of a joint had become vascular. To explain this we must have recourse to the living principle of the blood. This I suppose, when it is extravasated into a cavity, adheres to the cavity, and is not absorbed, nor loses its living principle, but becomes vascular, and afterwards membranous, cartilaginous, or bony, according to circumstances. Its attachment being rendered small by motion, it becomes easily broken off. The treatment of these cases we have before mentioned when the joint was sound; sometimes there is more than one of these substances. I know a gentleman who has four; therefore if an operation was to be performed we must take care to manage it so as to extract all of them at once.

They may often occasion lameness in other joints where they are not discoverable; but they are most liable to form in the knee-joint, from its greater size, and other joints might not so readily show their existance. These loose-bodies can only be removed by making an opening into the joint, and this should only be done when they are evident. On the inside of the upper end of the patella is the best place; the loose pieces should be squeezed to that part, and then carefully surrounded by three or four fingers of an assistant: the incision should be longitudinal, and in length proportionate to the size of the loose bodies. The wound should be closed immediately by adhesive plaster and the uniting circular bandage, and the patient kept in bed for some days to procure the first mode of union if possible, the leg being kept quiet and extended, and the occurrence of inflammation carefully watched.

Anchylosis.—This is an union of bone with bone which ought not to be united, and is of two kinds,—one by soft parts, the other by bone. In inflammations of joints we often have adhesions by a soft medium. Very considerable inflammation is necessary to produce anchylosis in joints, and much time is necessary for their perfection, as we see in white swellings. The adhesions are sometimes partial, sometimes universal. The soft is from two modes, viz. adhesion and granulation. The soft only can take place when there is naturally no intermediate substance, and the joint is surrounded by capsular ligament.

Bony Anchylosis.—I shall divide bony anchylosis into five kinds, four of which are in the surrounding parts, by ossific inflammation, the other by an entirely new substance, betwixt the extremities of a bone. Distinct and separate bones are naturally united, either mediately or immediately; that between rib and rib, between tibia and fibula, and radius and ulna, is lateral attachment. The second is when there is an appendage for the union of two bones, as in joints in general; this is of two kinds, viz. 1st, when the whole surface is united by soft parts, or ligament, as vertebræ to vertebræ; the other, when only round the extremities by capsular ligament. These will have different effects. When there is no continuity of soft substance, but only the bones, then the inflammation is obliged to shift the ligaments for bone.

Of the first, from lateral attachment where there is no joint.—This generally takes place only when the bones are so near as to partake of the ossific inflammation between them, as in the tibia and fibula. This anchylosis is of little inconvenience, except between the ulna and radius, when their motions will be rendered imperfect. [*A preparation was exhibited which showed the union of a tibia and fibula, by the ossification of the interosseous ligament; another, the union between two ribs; and another, the union between two of the metatarsal bones.*]

The second, or in surrounding parts.—This often takes place in bones united by their whole surface, as between vertebræ and vertebræ, and

I have seen it between sacrum and iliam; it often occurs in the human species, but much oftener in horses. The ossific inflammation would appear in such to arise from the bone, as it is found to be in different degrees. Sometimes the ossific inflammation attacks the periosteum around the connecting substance, leaving this as free from bone as ever. In a horse the vertebræ unite, not by ossification of the intermediate substance, but by the periosteum covering them becoming ossified. The same also occasionally happens in the human vertebræ, the intermediate substance not being at all ossified.

Of the third, or between bone and bone.—Within joints, but with a continuity of substance, anchylosis often takes place in the vertebræ, by ossific inflammation having existed in the intermediate substance. These specimens [*exhibiting them*] show the intermediate substance ossified, while the external parts are little or not all affected. In the spine of a lion both are affected.

The fourth, by capsular ligament.—This is much worse than the former, here the bones having a considerable motion, and this motion very necessary; but in some of these joints there is more inconvenience from anchylosis than in others: it is from the capsular ligaments taking on the ossific disposition, after strains and other injuries; however, this is much less frequent than the others, and very long in coming about throughout and all round the ligament, though a partial anchylosis may take place which will render the joint stiff. [*A preparation of the os ilium, anchylosed in part with the glenoid cavity, by the surrounding capsular ligament becoming in part bony, was shown. In the elbow another was shown, of this species of anchylosis.*]

The fifth, by the whole substance of the articulation.—This is of two kinds, and these kinds are the only ones which can admit of the soft anchylosis. It is somewhat similar to the union which takes place in soft parts; it arises from two causes, viz. 1st, from inflammation of the parts themselves; 2ndly, from the inflammation of the surrounding parts, the parts themselves partaking of it. Sometimes the cartilages are ossified, and a new substance is formed on them, which I rather think arises from granulations without suppuration. Joints have lost their motion from inflammation in surrounding parts. A lady had an inflammation come on from the opening of a sacculus mucosus on her elbow, which inflammation was very violent, and extended to the joint, soon after which she lay in, and died of puerperal fever. On opening the joint, soft union was found to have taken place, which, if she had lived, would probably have become bony, and the joint would have been anchylosed, merely from adhesive inflammation.

Of Suppuration in Joints producing Anchylosis.—This is of two kinds, viz. truly inflammatory and scrofulous; the former we shall now treat of principally. If the inflammation is carried on, an abscess is formed in the cavity, as in any other part; and the suppuration is more universal in the cavity than in other parts, being diffused through the whole. This continues to approach nearer and nearer the external surface, and either breaks or may be opened: so far as they are connected with bone they are similar to compound fractures; but the suppuration is slow, and takes place with difficulty, and then generally falls into the natural scrofulous disposition, which renders it tedious. The suppuration is then imperfect, appearing to partake of both the adhesive and suppurative. The ulcerative disposition is slow in bringing the matter to the skin, which arises from the indolence of the prior suppurative disposition and inflammation. The ulcerative inflammation sometimes goes on, so as entirely to alter the joint, that is, the receiving cavity becomes larger, and the received part less; this is often the case in the hip joint. These cases then become very tedious, and generally very uncertain in their cure. Before they are opened they are generally become so indolent that opening has very little effect; and often when scrofulous such a disagreeable inflammation comes on as to destroy the patient, and therefore amputation had better be performed at once if this disagreeable inflammation does not take place immediately after opening; yet a fistulous opening is generally the consequence.

Soft Anchylosis from Granulations.—A joint so healed has no cavity left, the surfaces uniting. A joint coming to suppuration from not being resolved in the first mode, but forming granulations, is more tedious than in the soft parts. The granulations cannot contract here, as they do in the soft parts, and the powers of restoration in them are very weak.

Bony anchylosis takes place when the granulations ossify, so that the two bones are united into one exactly similar to a compound fracture. [*Preparations were shown; one, of the thigh united to the acetabulum; another, of the ulna to the os humeri; and another, of the metatarsal bones.*] But when the suppuration is healthy the joints sometimes recover: in such cases the matter is sooner discharged, and the parts are more disposed to return into their original state.

The modes of cure.—The first attempt should be to resolve the suppuration without opening. In some the cartilages have been destroyed (which may be known by the bones rubbing against each other), and replaced. This I have seen in the knee. When a healthy process is going on, the joint should be attended to. Rest should be prescribed, both before and after it has taken place; when it is recovered pretty well, a little motion, and gently repeated, should be allowed; thus a cartilage will gradually form on the parts moved.

The second mode of cure is the formation of granulations, which makes anchylosis complete by their union.

Of Muscles loosing their Action from injuries done to Joints, Tendons, and Ligaments.—It is remarkable that an injury done to tendons, ligaments, fasciæ, &c., especially of the strain kind, impair the muscles more than when the muscles themselves are injured, so that these muscles appear to sympathize with those parts of little action, and become wasted and weakened in consequence. I think this arises from sympathy, or a consciousness of the parts being unable to answer to the action of the muscles, and it comes nearest to human reason of any thing in the body. If the affection be temporary, as in common inflammation, the muscles do not waste, being then conscious that the parts will recover. If one tendon is materially weakened, the muscle will also; and then, if the motion of the joint depends on that muscle, lameness will be occasioned, and the other muscles will become also affected. If a joint recovers, the powers of the muscles begin to recover in proportion. This is the case after injuries of the joints, as fractures, or ruptured tendons; and the first intelligence of recovery in a joint will be the enlargement of the muscles. This is the case in paralytic parts, from the cutting of a nerve; the wasting is not occasioned by the deprivation of the nerve depriving it of nutriment, but from the muscles losing their power of exertion. If the hip is affected, the muscles of the leg or knee will waste, whilst those of the foot will not be altered, which would be the case was their wasting owing to want of nutriment from the nerves. If the elbow is affected, the muscles of the arm surrounding it will waste, whilst those of the hand will not be affected. When the muscles waste, in consequence of a disease in the joint, the surgeon will often say it is from want of action; but if he will only observe the other leg, he will find the muscles nearly of their full size, though they have had no more motion than the muscles of the diseased leg. The mind, likewise, loses its power over the muscles, for the will has never any power over muscles while the parts they move are unfit for motion, even although the muscles are not wasted.

The effects which a disease of a part has on distant parts.—Many diseases of this class produce diseases of debility, as, for example, involuntary contractions of muscles, œdema, inflammation, and sometimes mortification in parts beyond them; thus, in a disease of the loins some of these effects follow in the lower extremities. Though they only arise while a disease is present, and is in its height, yet the disease may be cured, and the inability in the joint remain, as is the case in anchylosis.

But here I may observe, concerning the contraction of muscles just mentioned, that it may take place together with these diseases, as in white swellings of the knee. But then it is very different from these diseases, the contraction proceeding from an endeavour of the muscles to adapt themselves to the state of the joint, whilst these are only like symptoms of beginning dissolution in the parts. This debility is not like common paralysis; the latter is a wasting of power in the muscles, from a want of stimulus; but this is a real disease from irritation. It is perhaps reducible to a species of sympathy similar to general hectic, from a local disease, and it may be called local hectic; but it sometimes goes beyond hectic, even to mortification.

Effects of Local Diseases on Joints.—Joints that have a secondary motion with the diseased part, from having muscles common with it, may be included. These joints gradually creep into the middle state of motion, but sometimes beyond this, so as to be more bent. Thus, the thigh is often bent forward, and also drawn more inward, so as to be immoveable, from diseased loins or hip. The knee also is frequently affected, even as if it was itself diseased. The limb first wastes; next is œdematous; and afterwards often inflames and suppurates, which is sometimes very extensive. From continuation of one position, and want of action in the antagonist muscles, the joints, from necessity, become unfit for motion, and are afterwards often very imperfectly restored.

Exfoliation.—This is the separation of a dead bone from the living, and is not generally understood. By the term we should be led to suppose that only the common separation of scales from a bone was meant, for the other exfoliations are not answerable to the term. We have many opinions of this process from different authors, but all are very imperfect. The bone that separates cannot come away by rotting, for it is only dead, and not in the least putrefied. Bone is composed of two parts,—an animal substance, and an earthy substance intermixed with the animal. Hard bones, and the hard part of bones, have a larger proportion of earth than the soft or spongy bones; they have also fewer vessels.

When a piece of bone becomes absolutely dead, it is then to the animal machine as any other extraneous body, and adheres only by the attraction of cohesion to the machine. The first business of the machine, therefore, is to get rid of this cohesion and discharge it. For effecting this separation there are several natural and successive operations going on.

The first effect of the stimulus is on the surface of the living bone, which becomes inflamed; whether new vessels are formed, or the old ones become larger, is undetermined; but by injecting the surface of the part it appears evidently much more vascular than the other parts.

The surrounding parts also inflame, as the periosteum and cellular membrane, and often take on ossific inflammation. This produces another process : first, absorption of the earthy matter, and all the surface between the living and dead parts of the bone become as soft as if steeped in acid, while the dead part remains as hard as ever. To complete the separation, the absorbents continue their office, and absorb the living parts also, and the first process is in a small degree attended with the second. The operation of separation does not take place equally; it begins at the circumference, and continues on to the centre; and before the centre has begun the absorption of the earth, the circumference has begun the second. This progressive process in the suppuration causes the exfoliation to be tedious, so that the centre is the last place that separates. In pretty broad exfoliations, long before the centre has gone through the operation, the living parts perform their office, in producing granulations from the surface, and continue, in proportion to the waste, to fill up the space. When the dead part is wholly loose, it is, like all extraneous bodies, pushed up to the surface. It often happens that the granulations ossifying, the exfoliation is locked in at the edges, thus giving it the appearance of internal exfoliation. Thus, while Nature is busied in getting rid of that part of the bone which is dead, she is laying on additional bone on the outside, the intention of which seems to be that of keeping up the strength of the bone, which would, without this addition, be lessened by the loss of substance. This opinion is, I think, supported by this circumstance seldom occurring in this manner in any bones but those of the lower extremity, which support the animal. If this is true, it is a curious process, by which Nature endeavours to support the strength of these bones during a loss of substance, by throwing on the outside bone in proportion to the loss of substance within. Nor is the process by which this adventitious bone is afterwards removed less curious, and the piece of dead bone set at liberty ; for from all that living bone adjacent to the dead piece, granulations arise, which push up the dead piece against the upper sides of the cavity ; and in consequence of this pressure against the newly formed bone, the absorbents are set to work to remove it, and in proportion as this is absorbed the piece is pushed out, the granulations filling the space behind it. That in the separation of a dead piece a part is absorbed, I think is very evident; and that there is a loss of substance at the time of separation is obvious from this circumstance, that if a circular piece is taken out of the skull, and the circular edge of the remaining bone has its life destroyed by the actual cautery, to any distance, this deadened part will separate and come away, which it might not be able to do without a loss of substance between the living and dead bone.

Another proof of the loss of substance in this supposed case is, that the side of the circular piece which is separated.will retain its spiculæ, while the edges of the remaining bone, so far from corresponding with them, are quite smooth. Now, as there is room in this circular hole to allow the ring of bone to come out, its regularity cannot be the effect of new matter added between the spiculæ, but is in consequence of the absorption of those spiculæ. It appears from this last-supposed case that it is my opinion that the absorption is of the surface of the living bone; but I by no means wish to be understood that no absorption of the dead piece can take place; for, on the contrary, I believe that Nature sometimes finds it necessary to the completion of her process: it generally takes place when the separation is slow, and the granulating process is quick. This absorption of the dead bone takes place in the fangs of the shedding-teeth. [See *note*, p. 255.]

The first appearance of separation is an alteration in the part round the exfoliating piece. This alteration is first a sponginess; next, its becoming fuller of little holes; then a small groove is produced, a kind of worm-eaten canal about the thickness of a shilling, becoming gradually deeper and deeper; and the depth is irregular, according to the extent of the original cause. The small holes appear at first in the surrounding parts, and these appear more vascular, the more so the nearer the diseased bone. Sometimes parts become dead without any change of colour, dying almost suddenly, perhaps by exposure or a blow; and the surrounding part becomes spongy: the dead portion then looks the soundest; but when killed by previous diseases it is black. It is astonishing to see what little curiosity people have to observe the operations of Nature, and how very curious they are about the operations of Art.

After exfoliation, the living surface still continues soft until bone is formed. If it be a cylindrical bone, it has the appearance of a fœtus's bone deprived of its epiphysis: it is hollow, but fills like a growing bone, in every respect, by bony matter deposited. Hard bones exfoliate quicker than soft, and the harder parts of soft bones sooner than the soft; the bones of full-grown people sooner than those of the young*. If you lay a hard bone bare to any extent, it always dies; but not always if the soft ones. Situation has the same effects as in other diseases: in the foot or leg it is slower than in other parts less removed from the

---

* [The great attention which Mr. Hunter bestowed on all matters connected with diseases of the bones entitle his opinions to the greatest respect. Believing, however, that the bones afford no exception to the general principle, that the actions of parts are vigorous and rapid in proportion to their vascularity, I am compelled to dissent from the fact expressed in this paragraph.]

centre. In exfoliations we often find considerable pulsations in the matter, lying in a hole which communicates with the granulations, which are formed under the exfoliating bone : sometimes it is hardly perceptible ; this will depend much on the state of the granulations, their health, fullness, &c.; if all these are joined, the pulsation is very considerable ; also according to the proportion which the size of the hole bears to the granulations underneath. After trepanning, the whole expansion of the arteries of the brain becomes visible, by being seen at one point : so it is with granulations, when the quantity is considerable in proportion to the hole. This depends on mechanical principles : so it is with mercury in a·thermometer ; we see it rise when in the stem, while in the ball it would be invisible.

Exfoliation from accidents,—as from a blow, which is often of sufficient force to kill a sound portion of a bone, as in compound fractures, gun-shot wounds, at the ends of bones after amputations, &c., all of which do better than when it arises from diseased parts, the common processes of separation being carried on more vigorously.

Exfoliation from Disease, as Caries.—Disease is often carried so far as to produce death in a part of a bone, and exfoliation is often very salutary, but not always so. Surgeons have endeavoured to cure a diseased bone by killing it ; but this is often not so salutary as when it is spontaneous ; for in the latter the whole diseased part generally dies ; but it is often the contrary, or partial, when it is produced by art. The actual and potential cautery have been used for this purpose, and the practice probably arose from an idea that all diseased bones were disposed to separate by exfoliation, and that this would hasten it ; but exfoliation is not, as has been supposed, a necessary consequence of disease in a bone, but it is the death of the bone which makes exfoliation necessary, to separate the dead piece. Now caustics neither hasten the process of separation either here or in soft parts ; but the actual cautery, indeed, often has the power of inflaming the living surrounding parts, which invigorates and stimulates them to what they were before incapable of, its use in this, and its superiority to the potential cautery not being commonly known. When the actual cautery can deaden the whole diseased part, a cure may be expected ; when art is to be used it is uncertain, as the quantity of disease in a bone can seldom be known ; however, at times it may guessed at, and, as the seat and thickness of the bone vary, the cautery must be varied also. If the bone is diseased deeply, the cautery should be much heated, and very thick, so as to retain its heat longer : but these means are often insufficient, and the disease goes on teazing the part a long time, particularly in the lower extremities. In cauterizing, it is better to burn beyond the diseased part than not enough. But its frequent failure has occasioned the use of it to be much laid aside.

Situations of Exfoliations.—There can only be two species of exfoliations, viz. external and internal; but they are often mixed, and then admit of a third kind, which I call the inclosed exfoliation. The external arises from internal causes, and is in many parts a simple operation, meeting with no obstructions, as in the head, ribs, &c. But in the extremities it is often complicated, and becomes inclosed, and then appears as an internal exfoliation.

Internal Exfoliation.—These less frequently arise from accidents than the former; but may arise from the two last suppurations of bones. The part which is to be exfoliated loses its life, and ulceration goes on in the internal surface of the surrounding living bone, to make room for the exfoliation.

In internal exfoliations a part of the centre of the bone becomes dead, while the enlargement of the cavity lessens the substance of the surrounding part, and consequently weakens that part. But Nature wishes to furnish a substitute; for the stimulus of weakness being felt, the surrounding parts become affected, and undergo the ossific inflammation, by which the bone is thickened; and this continues in proportion, and as long, as the internal part is unremoved, or not cast off.

Mixed Cases of Exfoliation.—The first is when an external one appears to be internal; the second is an exfoliation of the whole thickness of the bone in one part; the third of the whole bone. These I call inclosed, or incased exfoliations, generally occurring in the lower extremities. These three being different at first, are not very easily conceived.

First species of Inclosed.—Sometimes when the surface of a bone becomes dead, before the separation of the piece of bone takes place, the ossific inflammation comes on, and entirely covers the exfoliating piece, leaving only a little hole for the discharge of matter. This takes place, first, when the periosteum is inflamed, and the granulations from the edges of the exfoliated pieces also ossify; but the process for freeing the portion of bone has been described already.

The second species is when a piece of any given length becomes dead throughout; the appearance of internal exfoliation is here still stronger than in the last case. Exfoliation or separation begins on the living surfaces of contact, at the two ends of the dead bone or piece, and ossific inflammation comes on in the surrounding parts, so that it becomes incased. This rarely happens, but when it does, the separation of the exfoliated piece is very tedious, as the stimulus is given to all surrounding parts.

The third species is where the ossific disposition takes place in the soft parts, from end to end, and the whole becomes inclosed in a case of bone. The difficulty lies in conceiving how it becomes inclosed at the ends where the joints are constituted; but probably it is from these ends being alive, and exuding coagulable lymph from their surfaces, or else from lymph being exuded from the surrounding ligaments, and that becoming a basis, so as to keep the joint complete.

Of extracting Exfoliated Bones.—As it is uncommon for parts to heal before the exfoliated pieces are extracted, or if they do heal, not to break out again, their extraction becomes proper, if practicable; but this is often difficult in many cases, from the situation, as also from the obscurity respecting the real circumstances, of the exfoliated piece: but in internal and in the incased kinds it becomes still more difficult, even though all the circumstances attending the exfoliated piece were known perfectly. The surrounding soft parts render many things respecting bones obscure; but wherever the bones are found loose and bare, attempts should be made to remove them.

The pressure of a probe on a piece of bone will generally satisfactorily inform you if the part is detached, by its mobility. If detached, we may often gain time by removing it, and in general this is proper and the best practice. If it does not allow of a removal from its extent, it is best to break the exfoliated part into pieces; though it may be often difficult to ascertain this, as the edges are often covered with surrounding soft parts. The internal exfoliations, and also all the mixed species, may be often assisted; but the difficulty lies in ascertaining the state of the incased piece, without which little can be done, nor should much be attempted. In the internal and mixed, which are not only covered by soft parts but also living bone, it will be difficult to ascertain. In mixed cases it may be evident that exfoliation has taken place, and is incased by bone; and for such, a dilatation must in order to expose some of the living bone. The next thing is to separate the dead bones: probably some of the living bone must be sawed through, (the best saw for which purpose will be one in form of an *axe*,) to allow of the extracting the dead pieces and such living parts as are broken off, which often happens; or the dead must be broken into many pieces. Both these I have done, as I will illustrate by a case.

A young gentleman had an abscess form about the middle of the arm; when this was opened, the bone was found bare. It was opened in two places: first, on the outside of the arm above, and next on the inside below. The openings did not heal, and the bone could plainly be felt at both. He had been in this way some years, when he came to London. On examining the parts I could plainly feel the bone with a probe, and move it upwards and downwards a little, but at the extent of each motion it seemed to be fast. It was plain that the bone should be removed, if possible; but how was it to be done? I chose to expose the bone at the upper and outer orifice, this being less engaged with the nerves, vessels, &c., and also being more convenient to operate upon. An incision was made on the bone downwards and forwards on the outside of the biceps flexor: the end of the exfoliation was exposed, as also the upper part of the bony case. I followed this downwards and obliquely inwards, and when I had exposed the whole, I sawed it, in the direction of the exfoliated bone, to the exfoliation itself; but as this did not open so as to allow the disengagement of the bone, I put in the spatula to force it open, but could not; however, I did it in part, so as to get a wedge of wood into the opening, which kept its position. The next time I forced it open a little more, and pushed in a thicker wedge, and in two or three trials more I was able to bring out the exfoliated bone. It was a piece of the middle of the os humeri, about three inches long, and of its whole thickness.

Of Rickets, or the Constitutional Defects of Bones.—This complaint would appear either to be a fault in the general constitution, or in the principle of the formation of bones themselves; but as it is peculiar to one class of constitutions, which are all weak ones, it might be thought to arise from weakness. If weakness is necessary to produce this disease, it must be one attended with a peculiar disposition. And this is probably the case; for we can hardly suppose that such a disposition in the bones could produce this species of constitutional weakness. However, as it is a weakness attended with a disposition of a particular kind, it is possible it may arise from this fault in the bones, so far as the constitution sympathises with the state of the bones. It is of a particular kind, as all weak people are not affected with it. This peculiarity of disposition, I suspect, is somewhat of a scrofulous nature, at least the two effects are often found in the same subject, whether the causes are the same or not. It would appear to be a want of power in the bones, or of disposition in their vessels, to form calcareous earth and animal matter, but less of the last than of the other. It is most common in young subjects, and is generally attended with enlargements, and the bones often bend from the incumbent weight. From the increase of size in growing subjects, it would appear that the proper quantity of earth is the cause of the limitation of size of bones, or that the bone has a greater freedom of growth when not checked by a due quantity of earth or its own solidity. This is more perceptible in the joints, as they are there softer than in other parts, and hence these parts are most subject to this disease. It is only in young and growing bones that this increase of size from the deposition of the two substances can take place, it being only an effect; but a full-grown person may be rickety without any increase of size, their bones not admitting of it. The definition of rickets, then, is a deficiency of earthy matter in growing or full-grown bones. In the adult we see the bones bent by the action of the muscles.

But the cause in the adult is different, it being a disposition to remove what is already formed and deposited by absorption; however, a disposition to absorb would appear very different to a want of disposition to deposit, and may probably arise from a very different remote cause; for though the effect is similar, yet I can conceive both to have the same original cause. If a softening of the bone is to be the disease, it is only taking place by two different means; for as there is probably a constant replacement of the earthy matter, this disease may arise in adults from a want of power or disposition to supply the place of that which the absorbents remove.

Of Rickets in Adults [mollities ossium*].—The disposition to absorb the hard substance of a bone, or the disproportion between the process of deposition and absorption, which produces rickets in adults, is often in a much greater degree than in young subjects; for in the most rickety child I have always observed some earth in the bones, but in adults I have seen the bones become as flexible as a tendon almost. In different parts of the bone we find different dispositions; but the disposition of absorption gets the better of the ossific disposition in other parts of the bone, or of the disposition to deposit earth.

Of the Effects of Mechanical Pressure and Muscular Contraction on

---

* [Mollities ossium differs from rickets in respect of the age at which it occurs, being a disease of adult age affecting the whole of the bones, whereas rickets is a disease of childhood which is principally manifested in the bones of the lower extremities and spine, and but rarely in the bones of the pelvis or upper extremities. They agree, however, in this, that when a section is made, the bone is found to be more cellular than usual, the cortical part is reduced to a mere shell, the cells are filled with a bloody or gelatinous-looking substance, and the deficiency of earthy matter is such that the bone is easily divided with a common knife. Dr. Bostock found in some instances of mollities ossium that the quantity of earthy matter was not more than one fifth, instead of being two thirds of the weight of the bone. It may further be observed that the disposition to mollities ossium is rarely overcome when once formed, but the disposition to rickets is generally worn out as children grow up; and, in proportion as this happens, the long bones at the seat of curvature are found to be flattened laterally and strengthened on the concave side, where the support is required. Fragilitas ossium, depending on the superabundance of the phosphate of lime in old people, accompanied with a disposition to ossific deposits in the different structures of the body, may be considered as a vice of nutrition of the opposite kind. A remarkable case of this sort of ossific transformation of the muscles and other structures is preserved in the Hunterian Museum, in which the movements of the patient must have been as effectually manacled as by the enchanted wand of Comus.]

Rickety Bones.—The bones are often bent by mechanical pressure of the body, and by muscular actions, into very peculiar forms, and often impede the actions of other parts. The joint forms a more acute angle than it would in health, and then the muscles get a greater power of action. It is most frequent in the back-bone, pelvis, and thigh-bones, in the angle made by the cervix femoris, knee, tibia, &c. In these it is most frequent, from the two powers acting (viz. weight and muscular action). The ribs are made straight, or rather bent inwards, by the pressure of the atmosphere, so that the child can hardly breathe; a bad formation of the skull will affect the senses; crooked spine will affect the health from an alteration in many of the viscera. In the female pelvis many dreadful consequences occur in delivery. When a bone has admitted of a bias, a disposition takes place on the side unnaturally pressed, for a deposition of bone, so that we find a bony substance formed there which acts as a prop.

In the leg the bone is bent forward from the muscular action behind. We have seldom these bends in the upper extremities, as only one of the powers is acting, viz. that of the muscles; however, they are sometimes bent, as an example of which an os humeri was shown. In the thigh the curve is generally forwards and towards the upper part, as was seen in an os femoris in which Nature had deposited a quantity of earth on the concave part. Rickety people are generally knock-kneed, from one condyle being less than the other; it always is somewhat less, unless in bow-legged people. Bow-legged people are in fact straightest with respect to the bones, the femur and tibia in them being in a straight line.

Of the Cure.—The cure is not yet discovered, nor is the preventative of absorption in the adult yet known. The original cause being the same in both, the treatment should be the same. The indication is to give strength and tone to the system by bark, sea-bathing, &c.; but these only seem to give general health. However, I have the greatest opinion of sea-bathing, bark, and chalybeates.

Of Exostosis.—This is in a great measure peculiar to youth. It is an increase of bony matter in particular parts of bones. It is of two species: one is local, and may be supposed to be similar to many tumours growing in the flesh, and probably may occur in any constitution; the other requires particular constitutions, and seems to be constitutionally interwoven with the formation of bones in such people. They are principally connected with the soft parts of bones, appearing generally at their extremities. When universal, the whole soft parts of the bone are affected. It sometimes appears suddenly, and is of various figures, sizes, &c.; but sometimes it comes on gradually and increases gradually.

These protuberances often swell to a considerable thickness beyond their origin or attachment, by which means a small neck is formed. Sometimes they have a power of growth within themselves, and do not in all cases continue to grow from their origin. Sometimes it affects only one bone, at other times almost every bone in the body. It is a shooting out of bone from a bone, as the horns of a buck's head. It is not the effect of ossific inflammation. The substance of the bones in these constitutions is often enlarged in the soft parts, as in rickets, which leads me to suppose the same original cause is common to the two diseases.

When near the joints it often produces lameness, and disturbs the action of the muscle so as to alter the motion of the joint. The cases of a gentleman and lady were mentioned who were subject to the former of these processes, which was very troublesome; the lady was evidently scrofulous.

Cure of Exostosis.—As it appears to be more connected with the natural formation of bone than with disease, it is of more difficult cure than if it arose from disease; for disease is always producing action tending towards a cure. It is hardly ever to be cured by medicines either external or internal; but as it is sometimes spontaneously removed, we should endeavour to promote the absorption of it, by rousing up this power. If, however, we are not masters of this power, and we know of no such, they may be removed by art, if this can be done with safety. The situation first should be well understood, and the parts covering it well known. The instrument must be adapted to the kind of exostosis and to the situation; the common ones are a saw, cutting pincers, and chisel. First lay the part bare, either by removing a part of the integuments, or by making the incision somewhat longer than the tumour, so as to make more room, after the separation of the lips, for its removal. If anything more than skin covers the exostosis, as muscle, it should be only divided, not removed. When there is a hard root, and deeply situated, a cutting pincers or chisel is necessary; but if superficial, as on the tibia, it may be sawn off. I have removed them from under the deltoid muscle, and also from the tibia. The immediate dressings must be suited either for healing by the first intention or by granulations from the bottom of the bone. If the first, exfoliation may take place; but this is of little consequence, therefore it should generally be attempted, as it frequently will succeed; and if not, suppuration ensues, and it is easily and speedily thrown off.

Diseased Exfoliations of Cartilages.—Cartilage is a particular animal substance, and composed wholly of animal substances, coming nearer to horn than any other structure. I divide them into two kinds: first, such as constantly change into bone at a certain age; secondly, such as do not change into bone, as that of the nose, ears, &c. They appear to have but weak powers.

When there is a fracture, the union is bony by ossific inflammation in the cartilages, which change into bone; but in the permanent cartilage there is a renewal of its own substance. Sometimes the inflammation goes on to suppuration; but they seem to have insufficient power to admit of ulceration: yet they may be absorbed by the absorbents of other parts; as in white swellings, when suppurated, the cartilaginous ends are removed by the absorbents on the surface of the ends of the bones that the cartilage covers. It may be ulcerated in this manner in other joints also: in the knee we find all the different stages of absorption of cartilage; granulations will shoot from under, through the cartilage, and sometimes, when there is not much matter in the joint, these granulations will inosculate and form a bony union. [*Preparations of cartilage were shown peeling off the ends of bones.*]

Changes of Cartilages of Joints by exposure.—The only effect seems to be that they become softer, which is occasioned by interstitial absorption, which sometimes proceeds so far as to remove the whole and leave the bone bare; a case of which was given in the finger after amputation. When the cartilage is exposed, the surrounding parts granulate and surround the cartilage like a purse, not adhering to it for some time after the wound is healed, for cartilages will never heal by the first intention. A woman had her arm amputated at the shoulder-joint, with a flap, by Mr. Bromfield; and in two years afterwards she died of a fever in St. George's Hospital. Upon examination, I found that the cartilage had not adhered to the flap, which in that part had a smooth surface; nor had any granulations arisen from the surface, which appeared unaltered.

Exfoliation of Cartilages.—The separation of a dead part is called exfoliation, for there can be no ulceration of cartilage. However, this is very uncommon, as the absorbing powers are very deficient in cartilages to remove dead parts. I have never seen it. I have seen them black and dead, but then the whole cartilage came away, together with the end of the bone; therefore it could not be called exfoliation of cartilage from cartilage, but of bone from bone. But the cartilages are capable of being absorbed, from the granulations formed under them on the surface of bones. The permanent cartilages are just similar in their separation, &c. I have seen them separated in sores of the part, as the nasal cartilages.

CHAPTER XIX.

OF HÆMORRHAGES AND ANEURISM.

Causes of hæmorrhage.—Hæmorrhage: 1st, natural; 2nd, diseased;—arising from irritation;—stimulating styptics to be avoided;—occurring on membranous surfaces;—3rd, from wounds;—checked by contraction of arteries;—artificial modes of checking hæmorrhage;—oil of turpentine.—Coagulation of blood;—stretching of arteries;—ligature;—modes of applying it.—Secondary hæmorrhage.

Of aneurisms;—true and spurious;—different kinds of each according to authors;—divisions fanciful;—definition of an aneurism.—Cause of aneurism;—experiments on coats of arteries.—Situation of aneurisms.—Action of heart not the only cause of aneurism;—local disease in the artery; and want of equable support round the vessel.—Natural cure of aneurism from obstruction of the artery;—œdema of the limb;—sloughing of the skin over an aneurism.—Treatment of aneurism.—Objections of Pott and Bromfield to operations for aneurism.—Strictures of the latter on Mr. Hunter's operation.—Necessity for early operation;—improper practice of waiting for the dilatation of collateral channels.—Mr. Hunter satisfied of the propriety of his operation;—arteries on which it might be practised.—Mode of operating where a tourniquet cannot be applied;—when it can.

From what we have said of the blood, it must appear to be of great consequence that it should be distributed to every part of the body in its due proportions; but in disease a much nicer proportion is necessary than in health.

Effusions of blood arise from three causes: 1st, from natural causes; 2ndly, from disease; and 3rdly, from violence. Of the first species is the menstrual discharge. The second kind arises from many diseases both constitutional and local: those from the constitution are numerous, as bleeding at the nose, &c., which often appears to be a species of derivation, or the effect of a diseased action on this part, as is sometimes the case in piles, where they may be considered as produced by the constitution; those from local causes may be called spontaneous, as bloody flux, bleeding from piles, vomiting or spitting of blood, diseased menses, &c. The third proceeds from violence, destroying the continuity of the vessels, among which must be classed aneurism.

Of Hæmorrhage from Disease.—At present I shall only speak of the second and third hæmorrhages, from disease : these I have divided into constitutional and local. The constitutional should in general be encouraged rather than checked; but the local are next to our present purpose. The local arise from two causes : 1st, from a peculiar irritation, which can be cured only by quieting the irritation; or, secondly, from a species of relaxation, or want of power or action, in the vessels of the part. The first I have seen in many operations, when a new irritation had taken place; as when the divided vessels had contracted and checked the bleeding, they have opened again on the application of a cautery near them. The intention of this would appear to be the removal of the extraneous body; it also occurs in many wounds and sores which do not secrete good pus, but pus mixed with blood.

For the cure of this species, instead of styptics, we should apply sedatives, the best of which is opium; and sometimes, probably, solutions of lead. The effect of these will be according to the peculiar irritation. A boy, for instance, had a bloody sore on his shin from an accident, for which he first used a common poultice; but as it still continued to bleed and not to heal, I ordered a poultice made with poppy-head decoction, under which it went on well, and soon healed. Nothing affects the system more than too great a loss of blood : the body becomes languid and cold, and the heart seems disposed to suspend its action, as if a natural method was instituting to stop the bleeding, and also to keep the actions of the machine proportionate to its power. But I know not what the cold sweating is to do. An animal cannot subsist long in this state but the constitution will begin to rouse up its actions again; there will be a full pulse and seeming strength : but if the weakness is very great, this apparent action or reaction of the system does not long continue. When the pulse is strong and the body warm, it would appear an indication for bleeding; but this is improper, and the loss of a small quantity of blood at this time would probably kill the patient*. The rising of the pulse in hæmorrhage is often an effort of Nature to live, and cannot be reduced, although it still further increases the irritability of the system.

Hæmorrhage from the second cause always exists in the small vessels, and commonly in the membranes of some outlet or excretory duct, and also in sores which have become in some measure like those secreting surfaces. It probably arises from a want of disposition to contract.

---

* [Dr. M. Hall has amplified on this observation in an able paper in the seventeenth volume of the Medico-Chirurgical Transactions, in which he has pointed out the dangerous consequences which may arise from mistaking the reaction consequent on repeated losses of blood for an indication for further depletion.]

The cure is the same as that from violence, viz. the application of powdered resins, oleum terebinthinae, and other styptics.

Of Hæmorrhage from Violence.—All wounds do not admit of union by the first intention, as when a large vessel is wounded, when the second mode of union is necessary. But large vessels are sometimes wounded without much harm, which either depends on the mode of division, or their situation with respect to surrounding parts. The bleeding from vessels has in many cases a good effect, as in fractures, and is then in small quantity; but when copious it hinders this salutary effect, as is sometimes the case in simple fractures, and commonly in compound.

The suppression of Hæmorrhage is effected by three modes, viz. the natural, the accidental, and the artificial.

The first is from the contraction of the muscular coats of the arteries: this power is one of the natural ones, and the accident is the cause of this contraction by its stimulus. It is most powerful in the small vessels, as the blood's motion is less in them; but even in large vessels it is considerable. I am of opinion that an amputation below the knee in most cases would not kill by its hæmorrhage, even if left to itself; but this experiment can only be ascertained by accident. The artery in the thigh of a bear stopped bleeding before the animal was at all weakened, and the carotid artery of an ass also stopped bleeding after being divided; but I believe that the arteries of most animals have more of this power than those of man. It sometimes appears as if this contraction was not permanent, but relaxed and contracted at intervals; but when vessels repeatedly bleed there is probably a want of contractile disposition, for then the whole surface is bloody, and the patient becomes very weak from the loss of blood, and often dies. This contraction of the vessels can be increased or diminished according to circumstances. The first cause of increased contraction is exposure, which is very evident in operations; for when the wound is dressed it will bleed again, and again cease when exposed, so that here the contraction must be from exposure. I conceive that leeches occasion a free discharge of blood by their having a specific power or acting as a poison on the vessels, so as to weaken them and prevent their contraction thereby.

The assistance which may be given to the natural contraction is by means of stimulants, which, however, can only affect the small vessels: their action is simply stimulating them to contraction. Whatever stimulants are used, they will be assisted by the power of the vessels and their sympathy with each other. A dossil of lint dipped in oil of turpentine, after having first wiped the wound clean, in order that it may reach the vessel, is the best, and may be renewed pretty often. I have seen it immediately stop vomiting of blood from the stomach after all other means had failed, [see p. 488] given internally with white of egg as often as the stomach would bear it. In external hæmorrhages where it had not the desired effect applied externally, I would give it internally: it is the best, if not the only true styptic; thus, in a case of nasal hæmorrhage which nothing would stop, I gave ten drops of oil of turpentine in a draught, and repeated it every two or three hours, which entirely stopped the bleeding in less than twenty-four hours, and it never returned*.

The second, or accidental, mode is of two kinds: first, the coagulation of the blood as it flows, not within the mouths of the arteries, as has been always described by authors, but around them. This can only take place when the arteries can contract a little into the surrounding cellular membrane by which the blood is divided, and this assists its coagulation; and the pressure of it on the mouths of the bleeding vessels assists in stopping the hæmorrhage. This disposition can be increased by spongy bodies applied to the mouths of the vessels; in some cases lint is sufficient, and flour will assist the lint; cobwebs also are useful on the same principle, and the process of coagulation will also be increased by agaric, from its increasing the surface of coagulation, as well as by its pressure on the vessels; but these can only be useful in wounds of small vessels, where the circulation is slow, so that the blood can coagulate, and are improper in wounds of the larger vessels. The tourniquet may be applied here, but it should not be twisted too hastily.

Another mode arises out of the natural, and may be considered in some degree as natural. It is a property in flexible bodies to have their diameters contracted as they are lengthened: in arteries this might be carried to a great degree when permanent effects are to be produced. It is necessary that they should be lengthened so much as to destroy the contractile power; for this is the way Nature takes to stop the bleeding of ruptured vessels. Thus we see that arteries which are lacerated

---

* [It is scarcely necessary to observe, in the present day, that this eulogium on the oil of turpentine is unmerited. Of external styptics, (if any really deserve that name,) a saturated solution of alum is much to be preferred; and certainly no internal medicine has equally acquired the general confidence of medical men as the superacetate of lead conjoined with opium.

The arrest of hæmorrhage is attended by the following circumstances: 1st, the retraction of the artery within its sheath; 2nd, its diametrical contraction; 3rd, the effusion of blood into the cellular spaces between the vessel and its sheath; 4th, the formation of a coagulum or plug within and around the vessel; 5th, the effusion of lymph; and, lastly, the contraction and obliteration of the cavity of the vessel to the next principal branch, and its final degeneracy into a ligamentous cord.]

will more readily stop bleeding than if cut with a sharp instrument, as was proved in the case of the miller related by Cheselden; and this is the way Nature takes to stop the bleeding of the navel-string in beasts. Surgeons do not take advantage of this; but farriers and gelders do, as their practice of tearing the artery through in gelding animals shows[*].

Of lateral Wounds in Arteries.—The lateral wounds in arteries are commonly, though improperly, called false aneurisms, on account of the formation of a tumour with pulsation; it having been supposed that only the external coat of the artery had been wounded, and that the internal had given way in consequence of having lost the support of the external coat; but the fact is that the blood escapes into the cellular membrane, and, coagulating there, forms a kind of sac, cutting off all communication with the other cellular membrane, and, assisted by external pressure, may stop the bleeding for the present; nay, the wound may heal up by the first intention; but by constant and increasing pressure, the surrounding cellular substance, containing the blood, by degrees gives way and forms a perfect cyst. These may be divided into two stages: first, while the case is yet recent; secondly, when the cyst is formed.

The first of these will either kill or come to the second, if not operated upon; after which, if the operation is not performed, the patient must die: therefore it is best to perform the operation as soon as possible, as the second will also kill if not operated on. In the first stage then, if possible, the artery should be taken up. The operation is very simple: first apply the tourniquet, then lay the artery sufficiently bare, and tie it above and below the wounded part; the part included between the ligatures will, when it becomes dead, slough off, therefore does not require

---

[*] [The principle of *torsion*, as practised by several of the French surgeons, is precisely the same as that which is here laid down in respect of lacerated arteries; that is, the extremity of the artery is drawn to a point, and does not return to its original calibre, in consequence of the destruction of its elasticity. We may also further add, that the rupture of the internal and middle tunics, which generally happens on these occasions, will tend to occlude the mouths of the vessels still more completely by entangling the blood among the lacerated fibres and promoting its coagulation. But how far the first of these effects, or the obliteration of the calibre of the vessel, depends on the destruction of any vital property, as of muscular contractility, may well be questioned, since the same effect takes place on dead arteries when similarly treated.

A preference is given by some surgeons to this means of arresting hæmorrhage, in as much as it obviates the necessity for ligatures, and does away therefore with one cause of obstruction to union by the first intention. Torsion, however, is objectionable: 1st, because it cannot generally be depended on where large arteries are concerned; and 2ndly, because it requires a considerable isolation of the vessel from the surrounding parts, and sometimes leads to a sloughing of the extremity of the artery, which must operate as a much more dangerous foreign body in the wound than a simple ligature.]

to be cut out. The ligature should be first made on that side of the artery next the heart, and the tourniquet then slackened a little, to satisfy the surgeon of its safety; afterwards the whole should be dressed as a recent wound.

Of the artificial Means of stopping Hæmorrhage.—The method is to stop the mouths of the bleeding vessels; but this is often very difficult, on account of the vessels being hid by being deeply-seated, and is made more so by the continuation of the bleeding, especially in a part where a tourniquet cannot be applied. I shall consider the artificial means employed for this purpose under two heads: 1st, chemical; 2nd, mechanical. The first acts by destroying the natural texture, and of course the life, of the mouth of the vessel. The most powerful of these is heat, viz. the actual cautery, which should not be too hot, nor should it indeed be used at all unless other means fail. It acts by drying and co-agulating the blood, and destroying the life of the part to which it is applied*. The iron should be thick, not too short, as large as the part will admit of, of a reddish heat or approaching to it. Concentrated acids have been applied with success, and whatever assists in coagulating the fluids, as ext. saturni; and I have sometimes thought of trying boiling water.

The mechanical method of stopping bleeding is by compression, and is the most secure: we therefore have recourse to it when every other means has failed. It consists in inclosing the vessel in a ligature. The spasms and convulsions which appear after operations, have been attributed to the nerve being inclosed with the artery in the ligature; but this seems false, it being only in particular habits that such symptoms occur, patients more generally recovering after the use of the ligature with no bad symptom than otherwise. I have sometimes tied nerves on purpose along with the artery, particularly along with the radial artery in amputations of the fore-arm, and never observed that any bad symptom succeeded†.

---

* [Besides this, the actual cautery corrugates and shrinks the animal textures, by which the bleeding orifice is obliterated. A similar but less powerful effect is produced by the mineral acids.]

† [It can scarcely, I imagine, be necessary to warn the reader against so slovenly a practice, which may be attended with the most painful and dangerous consequences. In every case it is desirable to secure the extremity of the vessel as distinct from the surrounding parts as possible, which will not only lessen the irritation, but be the best security against the occurrence of secondary hæmorrhages.

The ligature should be of as small a size as possible consistent with strength, and be drawn with sufficient strength to cut through the internal tunics, which will then heal as incised wounds in other situations: but an artery which is diseased or inflamed becomes brittle, and will not bear the same strain as a healthy vessel.]

There are two methods of applying the ligature, viz. the needle and the tenaculum : the last cannot be employed on all occasions, only under particular circumstances. But the needle admits of application on almost all occasions. It has been objected to as taking up surrounding parts; but this is essentially necessary in old persons, where the arteries have lost their elasticity. An artery in the centre of a muscle should be taken up by the needle. The tenaculum should only be employed where we have sound arteries to deal with, and when these are situated in the interstices of muscles. If the artery is in the substance of a muscle, the tenaculum would take in more of the surrounding parts than a needle would do, and the ligature will be less secure. I think the ligature should be larger than it generally is made.: the proper tightness is not easily ascertained; but it should be drawn more tight in proportion to the bulk of the parts inclosed. The degree of force used in this case would cut through the artery alone. The size, consistence, and round-ness of the artery, and quantity of surrounding flesh, must direct us in the force which is necessary to make the ligature. The thicker the ligatures, the greater surface they compress. In small arteries the liga-ture need not be tight, slight compression answering the purpose.

Of secondary Hæmorrhage after Operations.—This happens more par-ticularly to the large vessels, and generally occurs a few days after the operation, owing to some circumstance or accident therein : the liga-ture not having been made tight enough, or else too tight; or from much surrounding parts being included, and some of these ulcerating, the liga-ture gives way. If there is not a loose tourniquet about the limb, the patient may soon bleed to death, or the bleeding lays the foundation of future disease, as lingering weakness or dropsy. This secondary bleed-ing is very difficult to be stopped, especially when granulations are formed, as the artery at the bleeding part cannot be seen. However, an anatomical surgeon will not be at a loss to know the situation of the vessels; but admitting this, even then, the taking up an artery far above the surface of the wound will be a considerable operation. It will be right however, especially if the extremity of the artery be sup-posed to be diseased, to lay it bare above the diseased part, and then take it up where it is sound.

A. B. came into St. George's with a white swelling, for which it was thought necessary to remove the limb. Instead of granulations ulceration came on : the artery bled at times; but before any one could come to his assistance it would stop : at length, however, the bleeding was so great that he was considerably weakened, and soon died. Upon examining the limb the artery appeared sound, till we got within an inch of the stump, when it appeared black, and seemed to have lost its elasticity; the circumstance of the bleeding stopping, and returning again, I am inclined to attribute to the patient's being low and faint at the time he was losing the blood, but returning again on the recovery of his strength. In these cases a diseased artery should be suspected; and I think it would be best to dissect for the vessels, and see whether it be so or not, and if found diseased, to take it up in a sound part. It is recommended by some surgeons to make a strong compression on the stump, which may be done by means of a thick pad, covered over with tin, and applied to a screw tourniquet, to prevent bleeding; but I would observe that the long pressure of the tourniquet is painful and inconvenient. Exposing the stump to cold air will at times stop the bleeding. These secondary bleedings, as far as my observation goes, happen oftener to the radial and ulnar arteries than any other. The artery not healing by the first intention may be attributed to various circumstances, as ossification, extreme weakness, or the neighbourhood of a considerable branch.

OF ANEURISMS.

The injuries and diseases of arteries, called aneurisms by authors, are so various as to render it impossible to give a definition of them. They have been divided into true, and false or spurious aneurisms. The true, by Le Dran, are divided into three kinds, and Heister multiplies the division greatly. Le Dran's first is a regular dilatation of the coats of an artery; 2nd, where one coat has given way, and the other coat, unable to sustain the force of the circulation, allows itself to be dilated; the third is a mixture of these two. The false are numerously divided by Heister and others: one is a true aneurism burst; another is a wound in an artery, which will produce various effects according to the treatment, all of which are called so many aneurisms; but I do not consider a wound in an artery an aneurism, even if in an aneurism itself. Heister gives us the size of aneurisms as described by authors, which is only showing us the ignorance of those authors in allowing them to come to such a size before the operation was performed; but I wish never to see one that can be made the subject of an operation larger than a walnut before it is operated on. I have already shown that a wound into an artery is not an aneurism; so that I conceive there is only one disease which is properly to be called an aneurism, viz. the first, or true: nor is this divisible into different kinds; the second kind is only ideal; and the third is the consequence of one part of the sac giving way sooner than another.

By an aneurism, then, I understand the dilatation of the coats of an artery, arising probably either from disease or accident, producing weakness, which becomes the remote cause, while the force of the circulation is the immediate cause. It probably may also arise, however, from a disproportion in the blood's motion, and then the disproportion between the force of the circulation and strength of the artery is both the remote and the immediate cause; but this is probably only in the larger arteries, where the force is greatest. However, whatever may have been either the remote or immediate cause, it must in fact in all cases arise from a disproportion between the force of the blood and the strength of the artery, the coats being weakened so as not to be able to support the force of the blood in its passage along its canal, which therefore gives way. This weakness of the coats of the artery would appear, in most cases, to depend on disease; for accidents, *cæteris paribus*, have generally the powers of recovery. As a proof of this, I will relate an experiment made to ascertain the truth of the existence of the mixed kind, which was supposed to arise from a partial destruction of the coats of an artery, and that the remaining coat being too weak to sustain the force of the circulation, gave way, and distended. That the artery might have the full force of the blood's motion, I chose the carotid artery, as being near the heart.

One of the carotid arteries of a dog, for an inch in length, was laid bare, and its coats removed, layer after layer, until the blood was seen through the remaining transparent coat, and I had gone as far as I dared; I then left the artery alone for three weeks, when I killed the dog, expecting to find a dilatation of the artery, as had been asserted; but to my surprise the sides of the wound had closed on the artery, and the whole was consolidated to and over it, forming a strong bond of union, so that the whole was stronger than ever.

Mr. Cruickshank has, I think, produced an experiment in opposition to mine, where, after the artery was denuded and thinned, the parts surrounding it were kept from uniting with it, and an aneurism formed: but this experiment does not apply here; for in what instance could such an alteration be made in the artery, and the surrounding parts not unite to it? So that the blood's motion was insufficient to produce the proposed effect. The force of the heart, however, has some power in operating as a remote or first cause of aneurisms. Aneurisms are most frequent in the larger arteries, as at the arch of the aorta; and more frequent in the second order of arteries than in the third; but they are sometimes found even in the fourth or fifth. I have seen an aneurism of the arteria pudica where it was passing out of the pelvis, and in which we must suppose a previous disease of the artery, as the force of the heart is small. The nature of the artery contributes likewise, the structure of the large arteries being chiefly of elastic matter, and not near so muscular as the small ones, which have therefore greater powers of resistance. It would appear that there must be a specific disease of the artery in most cases, for dilatation is too local for so general a cause as the force of the heart.

As aneurisms have hitherto been allowed to go on till they have either destroyed the use of the part, or killed, little has been known with regard to their nature or manner of appearance at first. Instances discovered in dissection have given us the only insight into their original appearance. In several which I have seen there was a pretty regular dilatation of the coats of the artery ; but in many there was great reason to believe it began at one side. If we were to form our ideas of the first formation from the appearance of those of long standing, we should suppose the dilatation always began on one side ; for when we open an aneurism that is very large, and examine the internal surface, we find that the coats of the artery are commonly still remaining on one side of the sac and not on the other ; but I suspect that the appearance arises from the dilatation going on faster on one side than on the other after the artery has been considerably distended, which may arise from the vessel being not equally diseased all round, or being more exposed to the force of the heart on one side than another, or less supported by surrounding parts.

From the knowledge of the greatest force of the heart in the different arteries, and from the knowledge of those arteries which are not equally supported on every side, let us see if we could not, à priori, say where the swell would be, if such and such arteries were diseased on every side equally, and became considerably dilated. First, in those arising from the force of the blood's motion ; for instance, when an aneurism takes place at the curve of the aorta the dilatation is upwards, because it is there that the blood pushes with most force, passing in a straight line when in the ascending aorta at the fore part, and when in the beginning of the descending at the back part. When in the carotids, the swell is outwards and forwards, because there is less resistance ; in the subclavian, forwards ; in the axilla, downwards ; in the abdomen and thigh, forwards ; in the ham, backwards ; but in the leg, on which the pressure on the artery is equal on all sides, it is difficult to say on what side the swell would be, and hence it is that the bones of the leg are so often diseased when aneurisms happen there, caries or ulceration ensuing when the dilatation increases to a considerable size. Even in the last-mentioned situation the force of the heart directs, in some degree, the swell of the tumour ; but that is not until the sac is a good deal enlarged. The force of the blood against the most distant part of the sac endeavours to carry it on further in the direction of the motion of the blood, which in time makes a pouch; therefore it is elongated in the direction of the sound artery. The sac often, by its increase, presses on the sound part of the artery, and becomes the cause of its obliteration, as I have seen more than once. Hence the blood becomes irregular in its motion, and has time to coagulate, till the sac becomes filled with coagulum, which is strongest and densest on its external surface. The coagulation takes place at the most distant parts from the direct current of the blood; the firmness and colour of the laminæ in different parts of the tumour are such that it is easy to distinguish an old coagulum from a new one; the external laminæ are of a dusty brown colour, and these laminæ grow gradually redder as we advance inwards towards the current of the blood. As the dilatation increases, the coats of the artery are either thickened by the thickening process, or the cellular membrane already thickened becomes firm, and adheres from a consciousness of weakness. When the aneurism proceeds to this state it generally gives way to the circulation.

It must be observed that the force of the blood on the sides of the sac diminishes in an inverse ratio to the increase of its sides*, which therefore are longer in dilating than might be imagined; but after proceeding to a certain length the adventitious coat gives way, and the blood is effused into the surrounding cellular membrane, producing distension; and when the artery is a considerable one, there is an obstruction to the blood's motion in the collateral branches, producing mortification. When the artery opens externally, it is always on that side where the artery gives way most. The ultimate effect of such events will vary somewhat, according to the situation of the aneurism; thus, if it be of the carotid artery the effusion on its bursting will soon occasion suffocation, &c. When an aneurism is in an artery whose dilatation brings it to the skin, the coagulum comes first, and obstructs the circulation in the skin: the skin inflames and mortifies, forming a black slough, which dries and adheres to the coagulum. As the slough separates, there is an oozing of blood at the edges, which becomes more and more, till at last in a large artery, as the aorta, the plug may be wholly pushed off, and the patient die instantly. If in a smaller artery, death will be more gradual.

---

* [The author does not seem to have been acquainted with the hydrostatical law of equal pressure contained in the following words; viz., that when a quantity of fluid contained in a vessel is submitted to compression, the whole mass of the fluid and the whole surface of the vessel, however large, is similarly and equally affected: consequently the enlargement of the sac can make no difference as to the quantity of pressure which any given portion of that sac has to sustain. See Arnott's Physics, vol. i., p. 242, 4th edit.]

Of the Method of Treatment, with the Opinions of Messrs. Bromfield and Pott.—This disease, if not attended to, is as dangerous as any that can affect the human body, because it is such as must always, even in the smallest arteries, kill; for as it arises from disease, the artery has neither the disposition nor power to relieve itself. Death must therefore be the consequence, either from the bleeding, or the consequences arising in the parts into which the blood is effused. Nor does it appear that the artery, either above or below the swelling, where it is sound, takes the alarm, or is stimulated to action; so that there is no resource, and death is the consequence. However, this disease is often capable of removal. When increased to a large size it is a very difficult operation; but I should wish it to be performed when the tumour is small. Messrs. Bromfield and Pott having written on this operation, and their opinions being different from mine, it is necessary that I should defend those opinions which I have adopted, and which I have spread abroad.

Mr. Bromfield objects to every operation, either amputation, or for the aneurism; this would be just if what he asserts was true, viz. that the whole of the arterial system is in general diseased, which however is certainly not the case. He says, too, " that the injecting of parts in dead bodies having shown that in particular subjects the branches sent off have now and then formed anastomoses with other branches given off lower down, has led to very extravagant notions of the smaller branches being always able to carry on the circulation; and an extravagant proposition has been suggested by some people to tie up the principal trunk of an artery in the extremities. I once saw an attempt of this kind in a true aneurism of the ham, in which I shall only remark that the patient died; and I do believe that the embarrassments which occurred, as well as the event of the operation, will deter the gentleman" (meaning me) "who performed it from making a second attempt in a similar case." Now, unfortunately either for Mr. Bromfield or myself, this is the very case from which I have formed favourable ideas of the success of future operations of a similar nature. Mr. Pott, after describing the disease in its last and most violent stage, just preceding dissolution, and when it has done all the mischief it can do without destroying the life of the patient, says, " If a man was to be asked how the disease was to be treated, he would answer, from theory, that the artery should be tied above and below the tumour, and the coagulated blood be evacuated; but that the artery is generally diseased some way above the dilatation, especially the popliteal." He also observes, " that the want of collateral branches of sufficient size to carry on the circulation is another powerful impediment to the operation."

2 N 2

When the aneurism has arrived at the stage which Mr. Pott describes, perhaps the only thing is to amputate above the dilated part of the artery ; but Mr. Pott should have considered, that before these threatening symptoms there is a stage when all the surrounding parts are sound. If this be true, would any man allow a disease in a part to go on till the surrounding parts are diseased and past cure?

The events of all diseases are of two kinds : first, where the termination is certain ; 2nd, where it is dubious. The aneurism is of the first kind ; its event is certain. Now I do aver, then, that there is a stage of the disease in which the operation is safe. I do not, certainly, know how to judge of this state from the external appearance, but from what I have seen of aneurisms, I believe it will allow of considerable latitude. My opinion is, that the operation should be performed, 1st, when the disease has done no mischief to the surrounding parts ; 2nd, where it is distinct and circumscribed, not connected with parts which may not be curable when exposed, as bones ; 3rdly, when there is a distinct pulsation. How early the operation may be performed I do not certainly know, but my opinion is that it may be done as soon as the aneurism is known to exist. By some it has been recommended to permit the disease to exist some time first, because, say they, as the circulation becomes obstructed, a freer communication will take place between the branches above and below ; but this would not be until the obstruction had subsisted some time, and I would not wait for this, for fear of the consequences described by Mr. Pott.

When the disease is in an advanced stage, I agree with Mr. Pott in thinking amputation necessary and preferable, but not under the circumstances above mentioned. The earlier, therefore, the operation for the aneurism is performed the better, not waiting with the expectation that an increased size of the aneurism will produce an increased size of the collateral branches. That the popliteal artery, according to Mr. Pott, is oftener diseased above the aneurism than other arteries, I cannot well determine, but can see no reason why it should be so. If the artery, however, cannot be tied above the aneurism in the operation, where can it be tied if the limb be amputated ? *Why not tie it up higher in the sound parts, where it is tied in amputation, and preserve the limb ?*

The circumstances to be regarded chiefly turn upon the collateral branches being sufficient to carry on the circulation. The only arteries which admit of this question are the popliteal, femoral, and brachial ; the other arteries either having a very free anastomosis, or being out of the way of any operation.

In this account it may be supposed that I carry my notions too far ;

but it is to be understood that I only give my own feelings upon this subject, and I go no further in theory than I would perform in practice, if patients, being acquainted with the consequences of the disease, would submit to, or rather desire, the operation; nor do I go further than I now think I would have performed on myself were I in the same situation. Not that I would have it supposed that I would recommend this at large: I would have no one perform an operation that he is not clear about the propriety of himself, especially when it requires more anatomical skill than falls to the share of most practitioners.

. *Of those Arteries which admit the Operation.*—These are, first, the carotids above the sternum; 2nd, any of the branches of the external carotids; 3rd, the subclavian (after having passed the scaleni muscles), and of course its trunk and branches down the arm; 4th, the crural, immediately after having passed Poupart's ligament, and given off the large muscular artery. How far it would admit of an operation above the giving off of that artery I do not know, but I have seen one instance of that branch and the vessel itself being obliterated by an aneurism, and yet the limb was supplied with blood.

Some of the branches of some of these arteries which I have mentioned will be very difficult of access; therefore, if not in parts that will admit of amputation, the patient will be likely to die. It will be very difficult to take up the anterior and posterior tibial and interosseous arteries, and it will be often necessary to amputate, from the difficulty attending taking them up, besides that the bone will often be diseased before we discover the disease, and this will make amputation necessary.

If an aneurism should take place in the axilla, I should doubt of the propriety of taking up the artery above the clavicle, because I should doubt of its being sound. The same with the femoral artery, where it passes from under Poupart's ligament; unless the aneurism was lower down, and I might expect to find the artery sound.

In dissecting tumours from the neck I have frequently laid bare the carotid artery; now, if by any accident during the operation the artery had been wounded, I should certainly have taken it up with a ligature; or if the tumour had been so engaged with the artery that I could not disengage it, I should have tied it above and below the tumour, with every hope of success.

The operation will be easiest, both to surgeon and patient, while the disease is in its infancy. Although I would perform the operation on all the arteries I have mentioned, and if I laboured under them myself would have them performed on me, yet I would wish every person to judge for himself, and not attempt an operation if he is fearful.

General Observations on the Operation*.—In performing this operation the first attention should be paid to preventing the flowing of blood during its performance, which alone leads to two methods of performing it: 1st, where the tourniquet can be applied; 2ndly, where it cannot.

Where the tourniquet can be applied, this should be first done. In the next place make a longitudinal incision in the course of the tumour, of greater extent than the tumour; cut gradually into this, scoop out the coagulated blood, and sponge the inside of the sac; we should then slit up the sac, to discover the openings of the arteries into it. The inferior orifice will be most readily discovered, as it will throw out some little blood of a venous appearance. To discover the superior orifice the tourniquet must be slackened; the artery then should be tied, at least an inch from the sac, at the superior part; but it is not necessary to observe this rule with the inferior part.

When a tourniquet cannot be applied between the heart and aneurism, as in the carotids, an incision is to be made through the integuments; the sac is to be laid bare, but not opened; the artery is to be searched for, and tied above and below on the sound part. The sac is then to be opened, and the coagulum scooped out; and after being cleansed and spunged, the sac may be left to slough, and the wound dressed as other fresh wounds.

The blood which comes from the lower orifice has become dark by stagnation, or slow motion; hence also the dark colour of blood when an artery is wounded below, while the tourniquet is applied, the blood not being venous, as some have thought, but arterial, which has taken a retrograde course. I believe we should not be anxious about the collateral branches; I have lost several advantages from this mis-

---

* [It will be observed that the operation Hunter here describes is not the one which goes by his name, but that which was usually practised previously to the general adoption of the Hunterian operation. The first case in which Mr. H. operated according to the latter method occurred in December 1785, rather more than a twelvemonth before the delivery of this lecture; and he did not as yet feel sufficiently sure of its superiority to the generally received method to recommend it strongly to his pupils for their adoption.

I gladly avail myself of this opportunity of referring to Mr. Guthrie's able and elaborate exposition of this department of surgery, in his work " *On the Diseases and Injuries of Arteries*," in which the extent and accuracy of Mr. Hunter's labours are set forth with great judgment. The Hunterian operation for aneurism was not the result of fortuitous discovery, but of accurate and minute knowledge, derived from a laborious investigation of the morbid anatomy of the arteries, and of just reasoning upon the data which he thence derived. The preparations and drawings relating to this subject contained in the museum of the Royal College of Surgeons, convincingly show that Mr. Hunter anticipated the greater number of modern discoveries, at the same time that they evince the indefatigable zeal with which he pursued his researches on professional subjects. By referring to the valuable work above mentioned, I shall save myself and the reader a great deal of trouble in these notes; and I am very happy in having the opportunity of expressing my acknowledgements to the worthy author. I also beg leave to refer the reader to Sir Everard Home's paper on the same subject in the third volume of this work, and to the remarks in " *the Life*," p. 97, et seq.

taken delicacy. I believe the circulation will always go on after the femoral artery is secured by ligature.

Cases of Aneurisms.—1st, a young man had for two years a pain in the calf of his leg, similar to cramp; at length he received a blow in the ham, and a swelling, with pulsation, appeared soon after. I gave it as my opinion that the operation should be performed, and if it did not succeed, then to amputate. The operation was performed, and the patient apparently was going on well, till the fifth day, when the ligature giving way, the artery burst above, either from its being tied too tight or too loose. I was now obliged to dilate the wound still higher, and take up the artery higher up; but, apparently from the loss of blood before the tourniquet could be applied, the patient died a day or two after. The leg and thigh were both found to be putrid and emphysematous, and that was the case even above the aneurism. When I saw this man dying from the loss of blood, it struck me as a proper case for transfusion, and if I had been in his situation I would have had the blood of a sheep or hog transfused into my vessels. I do not know exactly how to account for the failure of this operation, whether from the unsoundness of the vessel, or the tightness or the smallness of the ligature; but from the appearance of the limb before the bursting of the artery, and the injection of the vessels after death, all seemed favourable for the operation. The artery also was sound above the part where the first ligature was applied. From these considerations, I should certainly be encouraged to perform the operation again, though this was the case which led Mr. Bromfield to condemn the operation. The second was a case of femoral aneurism in the middle of the thigh, in which the operation was performed by Mr. Bromfield, jun., in presence of Mr. B., sen., after his publication. The tumour was oblong, and extended five or six inches in length, and the operation was performed in a short time, and with success. In the third, where the operation was performed by Mr. Martin for the popliteal aneurism, the patient soon got well, and was able to dance. The fourth was an aneurism in the gluteus muscle. In cases where the arteries in several parts had the disposition to this disease, or, in other words, where many aneurisms were formed, the operation would not be adviseable.

In December 1785 I performed the operation at St. George's Hospital, in a case of popliteal aneurism, in a manner different from that ordinarily practised, and with success. The particulars of this case are given in the London Medical Journal. I would only observe, that in future I would advise only tying the artery in one part, and not to endeavour to unite the wound by the first intention. In that case four ligatures were applied upon the artery.

CHAPTER XX.

OF SPECIFIC DISEASES, TUMOURS, HYDATIDS, &c.

Of Ulcers and the causes which retard their cure.—Abscesses.—Specific diseases.—Irritable and indolent dispositions.—Hypertrophy of parts from chronic inflammation.—Varicose veins.—Corns.—Chilblains.— Of the unnatural growth of parts.—Preternatural accumulations of fat. Elephantiasis.—Observations on the cure of indolent dispositions.— Tumours.—Encysted Tumours.—Tubercles.—Solid tumours.—Warts. —Polypi.—Tumours in the cellular membrane.—The removal of tumours. —Tumours of bones ;—their varieties.—Encysted Tumours.—Hydatids. —Cuticular tumours.—Of the inflammation of adventitious substances. —Fistulæ.—Fistula lachrymalis.—Fistulæ of the buccal glands.— Fistulæ of Cowper's glands.—Fistula of the parotid gland.—Fistula in ano.—Fistula in perineo.—Cure of Fistulæ.—Of the treatment of contracted joints.—Of tetanus.

I come now to speak of what I call specific diseases, but before doing so I shall notice the causes which retard the cure of ulcers in sound parts.

These often arise from circumstances not at all connected with the soundness of the parts, as their situation, depth, nearness to tendons, or vicinity with respect to the heart. The situation may make it tedious, though the parts are otherwise strongly disposed to heal, which is often the case in deep-seated abscesses ; the nature of the parts may retard the cure, as when abscesses are situated in parts endued with slow or weak living powers, as bones, ligaments, or tendons. In such cases the matter goes a considerable way before it reaches the skin, while the superficial parts are more disposed to heal than the originally diseased deep-seated parts, so that abscesses soon become fistulous.

The cure depends on removing the obstacle of depth by free opening, exposing, as much as the nature of the part will admit of, the bottom of the wound, and preventing the healing up of the superficial parts ; but this must not be done unless or until the deep-seated parts are as much disposed to heal as the superficial, so far as respects their natural power, as in cases of exfoliation. Many are slower in healing from the nature of the parts themselves, as bones ; but the treatment in such indolent dispositions is very different from that of acquired indolence ;

for in these there is a disposition to act, whilst in indolence, which is natural, this is wanting. Hence it is dangerous to rouse these parts much, and accordingly we find that the mildest treatment is generally the best, often employing sedatives to lessen the consciousness of danger, as opium, which has often the best effect on parts naturally slow or indolent in disposition, as tendons.

Many sores which go on well at first take on afterwards a quality contrary to health. All kinds of sores are subject to this change; but in specific and poisonous ones, the poison must first be destroyed before a good disposition can take place. The causes of this change of disposition are many, but few of them are visible. The most visible is their situation in the body, as in the legs, which are far removed from the heart, and where the healing is prevented by much walking. The slowness often arises from exercise and intemperance, which are first to be attended to in the cure. A horizontal posture, with temperance, should be the first thing advised in sore legs in general, as removing the accidental impediments to healing.

When sores do not heal, after having removed the above causes, some other cause must be remaining, as either an indolent or irritable disposition, or some specific quality, which is frequently to be discovered by experiment. If irritable, sedatives are to be used; if indolent, stimulants; but if it is not known which of the two exists, first try one, and then the other; if neither of these is effectual, a variety must be tried till you find that which agrees best. Sometimes one of these does good for some time and then loses its efficacy, the sores becoming stationary, when we must change the application. When sores are indolent in healing, there is a surrounding thickening, but this is seldom the case when healthy granulations arise; in such, compression is proper; and if walking cannot be avoided, then light bandages, and sometimes a thin plate of lead, which is also often useful when the granulations are loose and there is a disposition to thickening. But these sores are very apt to return, which points out some particular remote cause, which I will presently describe. The sores of poor people are often in a bad condition from bad living, much exercise, or cold, and are often mended by rest, a horizontal position, fresh provisions, and warmth in hospitals, and the change is generally very speedy. If they do not soon improve I always suspect that something more is operating, as irritability or indolence, when I try experimentally different remedies till I pitch on one that is serviceable.

The surface of the sore will easily discover if there is disease beneath, as of the bones or periosteum. If the granulations are broader than the disease underneath, the granulations over the diseased part are unhealthy, whilst those not so are healthy, and heal so that the sore becomes smaller and smaller by the gradual contraction of the granulations.

Sores are often forced, as it were, to cicatrize, but the cuticle is not good, and the part removes it, and removes it again and again, till sometimes at last it becomes a good one; at other times the cuticle becomes very thick, and irritating the cutis underneath, which is very tender, it is then thrown off like a scab, and leaves the skin underneath ulcerated. These cases must be treated as they were before they were cicatrized; that is, they must be kept moist, and any cuticle which is unnecessary and thick must be scraped off. The medicines that first healed the sore, combined with water, should be applied to the sore; as, when tar agrees, tar-water should be applied.

Abscesses.—In all abscesses we should consider, in the first place, whether their seat is on or in the part at which they appear, for often they are abscesses of parts that are distant from that in which they appear. Thus, the external appearance of lumbar abscess is in the thigh, the loins, or between the ilium and sacrum. Abscesses of the liver also make their appearance externally; likewise spurious empyema and abscesses of the kidneys, which last often resemble lumbar abscesses, although their seat has been ascertained by the extraction of a urinary calculus. All these generally pass through and between some bands, as tendons, ligaments, or bones, and their first passage is small; but the abscess, getting into the cellular membrane, spreads, and gives the appearance of a large abscess of that part. None of these, however, penetrate so far as the lumbar abscess, owing to the position of the body, and the disposition of the inflammation having no tendency to set bounds to the spread of the matter.

Treatment.—Little can be done for these cases; they should be opened slightly or not at all. In the lumbar abscess opening is often productive of hectic fever, much sooner than if left to itself, and consequently death takes place much sooner. But when internal abscesses, whether pointing at a distance from the seat of disease or not, are likely to heal, as those of the liver, they should be opened as freely as possible, in order to know the extent of the disease. If they cannot be traced to the bottom, injections may be used, as they are apt to become indolent. I have used stimulating solutions of caustic, infusion of myrrh, lime-water, and injections of decoction of bark.

OF SPECIFIC DISEASES.

I am now to treat of dispositions and actions which are not productive of restorative actions; those which we have hitherto treated of, where a salutary disposition is put on, in consequence of violence done to a part, I do not call disease. This is the most complicated part of surgery, as it requires a knowledge of sores and of every local action that can be in a part: it is the physiology of surgery, as a knowledge of the constitution is of medicine. The diseased sores alluded to will admit of being divided into local and local constitutional; but none are entirely constitutional. The first includes many diseases, as cancer, chancre, mortifications, and many others, which have simply some specific quality. The second, all the poisons and some mortifications. All uncommon actions, commonly called diseases, are divided into common and specific. The common I have treated of. The irritable and indolent may be thought improper to be placed among the following, which are the specific, because either of them may attend all specific diseases; but almost all uncommon actions are in some measure specific, all arising from a specific tendency, or susceptibility, brought into action by some leading cause, and therefore not taking on the restorative process as they ought to do.

Every specific disease must have some peculiar action distinct from another. A true specific disease is that which has only one peculiar action. Some have many causes, as gout, yet have only one specific mode of action; others, as the morbid poisons, have only one specific cause. The first is divided into two: regular and irregular. The regular are truly specific, as agues; of the irregular there are many which show disturbed modes of action, as inflammation in scrofulous habits; but these always are very imperfect, from the specific action hindering them from going on properly. These are the opposite to the salutary dispositions for restoration.

Unsound dispositions may be divided into two classes: such as have too much action, and such as have too little action; or better, perhaps, into irritable and indolent. The remote causes are many, but the immediate cause may be the same in both: few of the remote causes are known. Irritable and indolent might be classed amongst the common diseases, and not with the specific, as every specific disease may be accompanied with them, and all specific diseases are generally attended with one of them; but some specific diseases are more irritable or indolent than others, and are also different in different constitutions.

Of the Irritable Disposition.—Irritability is that disposition which cannot remain at rest under an injury either in a part or the whole, nor can it set about a restorative action. This depends on some peculiarity both of the nerves and living principle, for there is often much sensibility as well as irritability in a part; or, on the contrary, it may be confined to one only. The one would show that there is an affinity or connexion between these two principles; the other, that this is not absolutely necessary.

Irritability is of various kinds, but generally may be called passive: as even in the most irritable constitution there must be some other disease or some violence to bring this disposition into action. Thus, convulsions are induced by tickling the skin. Many constitutions are thrown into violent actions from injuries, producing irritable inflammation. But all inflammations are not to be called irritable; those which are exactly sufficient for restoration cannot with propriety be called irritable.

Irritability is most commonly constitutional, but not evidently so altogether, as one part is often irritable, while other parts are not: for example, a lady had a vesication on her shoulder, which all throughout its action gave amazing pain; yet at the same time she had one in the arm which gave very little inconvenience. And we find disease producing irritability in parts which were not irritable before; therefore it cannot be said to be constitutional altogether.

Irritable inflammation most frequently arises from injuries done to an irritable habit. A local disease may produce irritability in a part, whilst the constitution is not irritable at all; it is then entirely local. But the constitution may be rendered irritable from a local cause, as in bubo. An irritable disposition is generally known by a disposition to inflammation, and that inflammation not terminating in any crisis. It would appear to be a mixture of the suppurative and erysipelatous, at least the erysipelatous seems to attack irritable constitutions most frequently; but probably the erysipelatous attacks when there is weakness, and erysipelatous goes off as soon as in other habits. The effusion and extravasation in irritable inflammation is more watery, so that the swelling is rather œdematous and more diffused; the continued sympathy is very strong, so that it spreads often to a very great extent, and sometimes becomes universal. In many of the irritable inflammations of the skin, excoriation takes place, and the water exudes like a blister. When it is local it is very circumscribed, terminating all at once; in many cases it cannot be distinguished from common inflammation terminating soon, but here the irritability is slight. These often terminate in the indolent, as those arising from cold.

Of the Cure by Resolution.—To cure irritability is extremely difficult, as lessening sensibility is more difficult than exciting parts when indolent. Whilst the parts are only inflamed, we should first avoid every thing which would irritate or hasten suppuration. A cataplasm of bread and milk is the most simple resolutive application, and the best till we know how further to proceed. But when from any accident there is too much irritability, something to lessen susceptibility should be used, as opium in the poultice, a fomentation of poppy-heads, or the preparations of lead. However, I think preparations of lead may do harm, as they lessen the restorative power as well as the irritability.

If suppuration takes place, it should be suffered to go on to the true suppuration. Cutting is very disagreeable to these irritable parts, for the irritability still remains, and they will not heal kindly. Caustics are much better adapted for opening abscesses in such constitutions, and should always be preferred, and more especially if opium is joined to them, as either with or without opium they irritate much less than cutting. The matter is generally of a consistence little more viscid than serum. There is often coagulable lymph on the sore, in which case there is little discharge of pus, which is also often the case in the indolent.

The milder the after-dressings are the better; none is preferable to the opium poultice, as they are apt to ulcerate and spread, which opium prevents better than any other dressing. When they begin to have a healing disposition, a mild cerate is preferable to dry lint. Bark internally, as lessening irritability and giving strength to the system, is of considerable service, together with the exhibition of opium; but in some we find a treatment directly opposite necessary, the mildest dressings giving the greatest pain, whilst warm dressings, as oleum terebinthinæ, give agreeable ease, although at first they give great pain in such sores. There is some peculiarity in the part which is removed by these stimulants; but unfortunately all these fail at other times, and we do not possess a sufficient number for the variety of constitutions we meet with.

Of Indolent Dispositions and Actions.—Local diseases attended with indolence produce generally the following effects, viz. an increase of the parts diseased, which is of three kinds : 1st, increase of growth of the natural parts; 2nd, a thickening of the diseased parts; 3rdly, an entirely new-formed substance.

The first has no variety; the second is occasioned by adventitious matter extravasated and effused into the cells, which I call interstitial increase, which will produce two different effects : either general swelling, which I call the diffused interstitial; or circumscribed increase, which I call the circumscribed interstitial. But the last has two causes, and is of two kinds; therefore the first owes its figure to the part being circumscribed, the other is from the nature of the disease. The third is always circumscribed, which I call the circumscribed adventitious. They are often spontaneous in their origin.

Indolent dispositions may be either with or without inflammation, and also suppuration; they arise from either a disposition of the constitution or part. This is more rare than the irritable, and is seldom carried so far.

Few constitutions are so quiet as not to call forth their powers when a part has received any injury. But specific affections may sometimes prevent them, and then the common powers have no effect; for in lues and scrofula thickened sores are very frequent.

There may be indolence without any known specific cause; yet I suspect that there must be something specific concealed, which arises from peculiar constitutions in different complaints, as when tumours that are indolent are formed in glands. All constitutions, however indolent, are susceptible of inflammation, and very few diseased parts are exempt from it; yet sometimes indolent sores are not inflamed by the common causes of inflammation, as exposure; sometimes, in the irritable, sloughs are formed, which is a cure by the disease itself. After indolent parts are once inflamed, they are very apt to become indolent again, when the inflammation is removed. When indolence is in a diseased part it cannot be totally constitutional, but sometimes local, as in cancer and scrofula. When this indolence takes place in a part, the cause often steals on gradually, so that the part is not roused by it. Indolence is natural to tendons, ligaments, and bone, and when all these causes cooperate, the disease is worse; but indolence may take place in other parts, from some visible cause, as in muscles, and skin producing thickening.

Many thickenings are owing to specific causes, as the induration of cancer, venereal diseased glands, sometimes affections of gout and rheumatism, and bone is subject to the same disease as in exostosis. Thickenings of parts are either from visible or invisible causes: the first arise from some external inflammation; the second from some diseased action in the part. The remote cause may be predisposition, climate, or way of life.

Local indolent diseases are generally confined, yet they sometimes spread; but here the cause must be more diffused. They spread but little, because indolence is but a small cause of sympathy; the sympathy is more continued when the sympathizer is of the same indolent disposition as the diseased part. Indolence in local diseases is attended with an increase of the part, sometimes similar to that produced by adhesive inflammation: this effect attends many unnatural actions of parts as well as inflammation. The parts swell more in this disposition than in the others; for in this there is neither any disposition to suppuration or resolution, and therefore there is an increase in the thickening disposition.

The division of this thickening is of three kinds, as before observed. The first is most visible in the adipose membrane; the second, as before; the third, adventitious, and which forms a tumour. The immediate causes are : 1st, a preternatural increase of the part itself; 2ndly, interstitial increase; 3rdly, the formation of an entirely new part. The first consists in an increase in the figure of a part, as of a gland, a cell, any whole limb, or other whole part : the second is often circumscribed in cellular membrane, appearing to be newly formed; but it is not so, but interstitial, as scirrhus in a glandular or cellular part, which becomes loaded with cancerous coagulable lymph formed by inflammation : the third is an original circumscribed swelling, arising in common cellular membrane, skin, bones, &c., and which should be called true tumour. In some of these diseased parts another disposition or mode of action, viz. ossification, arises; whether from a peculiar disposition arising from this disposition, or to increase the strength of the part, I am uncertain. The first is most probable, as strength is unnecessary where it is generally formed, viz. on the edges, &c. I shall lay it down as an axiom that all thickened parts are to be accounted new-formed parts, although they may be in original parts. The idea of their being all new parts shows why they should be disposed to form calcareous earth.

Thickening, which is generally the first symptom of indolent complaints, often gives little or no pain; so that the sensibility is often not observed till some time after. The thickening gives so little pain as hardly to be communicated to the sensorium; but the heavy dull kind of pain afterwards often becomes very disagreeable, producing sickness, which is more peculiar to some parts than others. The colour is of no particular kind, which shows a languor of the blood in them. The hardness is sometimes so great as to become cartilaginous.

The causes of this thickening are with difficulty assigned. In common inflammations there is increased action, and this is probably the case in indolent inflammation; but this increased action is of a peculiar kind, which may be called indolent inflammation, which is a peculiar mode of inflammation. The immediate causes are various; but what the final intention is in most cases is very obvious. In common inflammation it is to form adhesions and limit the disease, but in the indolent it is to give strength.

The visible causes of indolent disposition are various. 1st, The thickening may depend on a diseased part being accustomed to an irritation, till this irritation, losing its power, leaves the part in an indolent state and incapable of a recovery. Probably all may be first ranked under the irritable. 2ndly, From effects being produced by a disease not indolent in itself, but violent at first, as the gout. 3rdly, From a slow alteration in structure taking place, in consequence of gentle irritation, as gentle pressure, which will take place in every part. 4thly, A long application of cold, which produces weakness. 5thly, Peculiarities in climate ; as bronchocele in Derbyshire, and swelled legs in Barbadoes. These, and especially the four first, have no connexion with the constitution, yet may be assisted by a constitutional predisposition. They are seldom very diffusive, from their confined sympathy. The first of the first division are most frequent in the lower extremities, these parts being most frequently interrupted in their salutary actions. The second, arising from a disease in itself violent, as the gout, are apt to be very indolent. The third cause is mechanical and very extensive, even universal, and seems to be the consequence of a stimulus, as if increase of strength was wanted, as in the tunica vaginalis, from the increased quantity of water in hydrocele, cysts of hydatids, &c. Veins from this cause become varicose, and the cuticle is often thickened by this in working people; but this is frequently carried too far, and produces corns, or it may produce ulceration if the pressure exists in a still greater degree.

Varicose Veins appear to arise from pressure. A long column of blood presses along the inside of the veins of the lower extremities, and the veins being weak are stimulated, which increases their thickness and strength to resist this distension : sometimes they are so much thickened as to obliterate the whole cavity. The smaller veins are more or less affected, probably in the same manner as the large ones are in the legs, and hence the whole leg is indolent : they often suppurate, when it is almost impossible to heal them. This disease is in general too extensive for extirpation, although when it can be done this practice is very proper.

Corns.—The cuticle admits of being thickened from pressure in all parts of the body : hence we find that on the soles of the feet of those who walk much the cuticle becomes very thick; also on the hands of labouring men. We find this wherever there is pressure, as on the elbow, upper part of the little toe, ball of the great toe, &c. The immediate and first cause of this thickening would appear to be the stimulus of necessity given to the cutis by this pressure, the effect of which is an increase of the cuticle to defend the cutis underneath. Not only the cuticle thickens, but the parts underneath, and a sacculus is often formed at the root of the great toe, between the cutis and ligaments of the joints, arising from the same cause, to guard the ligaments below. Sometimes, when the pressure is uncommonly great, inflammation takes place in this part, especially if there are corns, the sacculus suppurates and opens externally, and this forms what I believe is called a bunion. The sacculus then closes again, and leaves the parts much as they were before.

The cuticle is not only thickened from pressure for salutary purposes, but it is also carried to disease. A corn is a thickened cuticle arising from external pressure, which is preternatural and continued. Uncommon or preternatural pressure on the surface must always affect the cutis more or less, producing a disposition in it to guard itself; but pressure is capable of producing another effect, which is according to the amount of pressure : when applied in a moderate degree, it gives a disposition to the cutis to continue the growth of the cuticle, forming layer upon layer. By this continuation of growth the cuticle becomes thicker; but if the pressure is too violent, then a diseased increase of the cuticle takes place, commonly in a very small portion of the part pressed, often in a point. This thickened part being pressed from without, commonly sinks its own thickness into the cutis, which is the cause of the pain and troublesome symptoms. The cuticle being formed in layers peels off in layers, and if inflammation attacks the cutis underneath, this takes place ; and hence the term 'onion', which has been applied to these corns.

There is often a sort of joint formed by a sacculus mucosus under the cutis, allowing of motion in the corn : if this inflames and suppurates, a cure is often effected.

When corns are of long standing and run pretty deep, they generally produce a degree of indolence in the healthy actions of the parts pressed on, which makes the cure tedious.

The cure of corns is of three kinds, viz. natural, palliative, and radical. The first is by removing the primary cause, or pressure, which is done by leaving off shoes, or by introducing a soft substance, as plaster, between the corn and shoe. Two plasters are necessary, one with a hole opposite the corn, and another to be applied over this ; and these should be continued as long as the cause is continued. Leaving off the pressure is the best mode, and then the effects are easily removed. The palliative consists in removing as much as possible the external surface, which relieves the pressure. This is done by holding the corn half an hour in warm water, when it swells, and then paring off as much as possible of it. It is difficult to remove the whole without injuring the surrounding cutis, which is often of bad consequence in old people, where fatal inflammation and mortification have been caused by it. The radical cure consists in removing the whole corn or thickened cutis. The cuticle may be raised here, as it is in every other part, by blisters : but its thickness prevents this effect taking place so early. Warm stimulating plasters will in general be sufficient. The causes of corns when carried too far often produce inflammation and suppuration, and whichever way the suppuration is produced, it is liable, if not attended to, to become very tedious; for the skin having a greater disposition to heal than the parts underneath, produces a fistula : so that such sores should be dressed to the bottom, and if they are indolent at the bottom should be stimulated by appropriate dressings.

Indolence from Cold.—Cold is a powerful obstructor of the natural animal powers, whilst at the same time it is exciting action, producing irritable inflammation and death. It is a true cause of mortification. Indolent swellings from cold arise from two different modes of action : 1st, when so gradually applied as not to excite irritable inflammation, but a gradual sluggishness; 2nd, when it produces irritable inflammation from the parts being weakened. Cold does not immediately obstruct the natural actions of the whole or part, but excites the whole or part to another action, viz. the production of heat. The extremities, from their great distance from the seat of the living power, and from being smaller, are most liable to this. Thus these parts become first irritable and then inflamed; but it is an increased disposition to act, with lessened powers. Hence the effects of cold are greater or less, according to the constitution. The weakly, the fair, and the delicate have the least power of generating heat.

Chilblains are the common effects of these causes, and from the foregoing effects of cold we are led to a rational cure : first, to remove the cause, then to apply warmth, or rather to keep the parts temperate. Chilblains commonly get well in summer. The cure, perhaps, should be divided according to the two stages of the disease, viz. the irritable and indolent ; but how far the treatment should correspond in this way I cannot say. They have been cured when they looked purple and livid by gentle stimulants, as oleum terebinthinæ, or camphorated spirits of wine. Such applications bring on the florid red of inflammation, which generally terminates well, for they seem to counteract the stimulus or irritation of cold. Steeping the parts in warm vinegar has done much good ; when they ulcerate, the same exciting mode seems best. But they are sometimes so irritable as to require quieting; for which' purpose a poultice or decoction of poppyheads is equal to anything. When the itching begins, rubbing the feet over with powdered chalk will be effectual to prevent it : the rubbing is useful, and the chalk keeps the feet warm by being a bad conductor of heat.

The invisible causes of indolent dispositions are also various. The 1st of the spontaneous is a diseased increase of growth; 2nd, interstitial swelling; 3rd, new-formed substance. This division, according to the mode of increase, is into three kinds, viz. increase of natural parts, the interstitial, and the tumour. All these are liable to happen in every part of the body. These increases are either known by the sight or by the feel.

Of the unnatural Growth of Parts.—These often form what may be called a species of monstrosity of parts, either diffused or circumscribed. They are generally situated in the cellular membrane, and feel doughy and soft, and are usually superficial, extending to the skin till it hangs as if by its own weight, sometimes having a broad base, but often hanging by a small neck : they appear to be in the cellular membrane what exostosis is in bone. These parts are less ductile than the natural parts. I have seen the double chin become one of these ; I have seen them on the belly. Perhaps they produce absorption in the parts on which they press ; for the bones underneath have been sometimes found deficient.

Preternatural accumulations of fat take place in the same manner ; not depending on a deposit of interstitial substance, nor being adventitious, but a preternatural growth ; and are common to every part of the body, not excepting the internal parts. People have died of fat on the pericardium, and sometimes it is found in the bellies of cattle, as sheep. In the human subject these accumulations acquire an immense size, being composed of very solid fat, and in some degree moveable, being in separate parts, or lobulated, when between the skin and muscles. They may in general be distinguished by the former being of a regular uniform softness, whilst the latter appear to be composed of solid pieces of fat, having a surface irregular to the feel.

The interstitial or diffused thickening of a part arises from the interstitial deposition of matter in the cells of the part, and is of three kinds.

Elephantiasis.—The first, or diffused, is very slow in increase, forming gradually. A whole leg will become stiff and feel tight by a loaded cellular membrane. It is most frequent in the legs, and almost peculiar to some countries and to some peculiar constitutions. A similar increase occurs in the thyroid gland : but this is of the second kind. The diffused is very common in the legs of Barbadoes' people ; I have also seen it in this country, but very rarely. The legs of young people I have seen so swelled as to be all of a size. It arises from an extravasation of coagulable lymph equally diffused ; the parts become firm and similar to dropsy, only there is no pitting : it may be a kind of dropsy, for dropsical swellings often degenerate into this kind of swelling ; yet the cause of the two may be very dissimilar : it is most frequent in young people. From its being so diffused and general, and in the legs, and most at the lower parts, I should think one of its immediate causes was a depending situation, with a weakened action of the system in general, as a simple bandage to support these parts often prevents it. [*A preparation was shown, in which a thickening of the leg put on the appearance of brawn.*] There is no fixed cure. In the case I saw I recommended mercurial ointment to be rubbed into the parts, and a slight bandage. The ointment was omitted; but the patient got perfectly well in a few months. If these had failed, I should have sent him to bathe in the sea. Pressure hinders the extravasation of more fluid, and we see that tight boots make the legs thinner.

The second kind is an original disease, though it may be attended with pain and inflammation. It is not circumscribed, though confined to a spot, but gradually lost in the surrounding parts. It spreads in proportion to the power of continued sympathy. A node is similar in appearance to what this is of the soft parts, and perhaps is of the same kind.

The pain of indolent swellings is very little or none at first, which is owing to the slow increase of the part not arousing the sensibility; but afterwards they have a heavy dull pain, producing sickness. This is often from the size, as well as from the tumour itself pressing on some other parts; for sometimes there is more pain in the surrounding parts than in the tumour itself. I may also observe that they seldom or ever inflame, but continue increasing till they press on surrounding parts, and raise inflammation in these parts and not in themselves; they are then often broken down into a curdly substance, but appear not to be dead, as they do not give the stimulus of extraneous matter: though the surrounding parts become thickened, yet they cannot properly be called encysted. If it appears to be scrofulous, the cicuta, sea-bathing, sal sodæ, sea-water poultices, &c. are to be tried; but these are sometimes useless, and extirpation becomes necessary; or sometimes cutting into them is sufficient. They sometimes suppurate, and then the sores are very difficult to heal.

The third kind consists in the interstitial increase of a circumscribed part. This is it when the swelling keeps to the original part, that part being circumscribed, as lymphatic glands, and also tumours or enlargements of the liver or spleen. They seldom affect the cellular membrane till they suppurate, and often not then at first, which shows they have something specific in them; for if merely indolent the surrounding parts would sympathise with them, as is often the case in the mixed cases. Although these diseases are interstitial increases, yet they often become similar to a tumour, and are understood as such.

Observations on the Cure of Indolent Dispositions in Diseases.—We must first inquire whether they are wholly constitutional, partially so, or merely local, as upon this rests our treatment. We must not be satisfied with the present symptoms, but inquire into the constitution, whether it is indolent or irritable. Such as arise from the constitution are generally more diffused, and are often in many parts; and such constitutions as produce local complaints show something wrong in them; however, the symptoms are not always satisfactory. I suspect these indolent dispositions of the constitution require a specific stimulus, having something specific in their nature. They do not spontaneously take on steps of cure, as inflammation does; and if they suppurate, they do not suppurate kindly; and a variety of things are required to assist them. The first thing to be done is to remove the cause, if practicable, which it often is not, as changing the country and situation. In all, resolution should be preferred, if possible, by absorption; for suppuration will do much harm. To procure suppuration in such, a particular mode is required, for we are not to lessen the living powers, as in adhesive inflammation that is healthy, but to increase them. The earlier the treatment is pursued the better, before the habit has suffered, or the surrounding parts have sympathised: sometimes a constant application of mercury to the part, which produces a kind of irritation short of inflammation, is advantageous; if this is insufficient, fumigations with cinnabar, or with plants which have essential oil in them, may prove serviceable. If these fail, we must remove the indolent disposition by exciting an action which they are incapable of taking on themselves. Salutary inflammation in surrounding parts will produce other good effects in indolent diseases, for indolence arises from a want of predisposition to healthy action; thus, blistering the parts, and giving cordials internally, are often of use; but the more violent the inflammation, the more effectually is the indolence of the part removed, if it can bear it. Many indolent swellings are content with their own natural actions, as natural parts are with theirs; but this is not so always; but they take on an inflammatory action, not salutary, but leading to a bad kind of suppuration. The means of restoring the thickened parts is healthy inflammation, which, as it goes off, does not leave them in their former state, but occasions an absorption of the extravasated matter; nevertheless the part, after healing, often retains somewhat of the original disposition.. This treatment will not do either in cancer or scrofula.

Of the Suppuration of Indolent Parts.—Resolution cannot always be effected, and suppuration will take place, which suppuration seems to arise from defective animal powers, and not from exerted powers. The matter is glairy, and the superficial parts are so little susceptible of this that the matter is long in coming to the skin; so that stimulating medicines must be applied to bring on, if possible, good suppuration, which can seldom, however, be done. Quick ulceration is best effected by exciting and hastening the inflammation: this is necessary in sound abscesses even, but much more necessary in indolent ones. The next thing is opening them, which should not be done too early, as the matter which remains in may increase the inflammation, which is necessary to the cure. When an opening is made, it should be as large as possible; and even crucial incisions are frequently necessary: in many cases scarifying the sides of the abscess is proper, to excite quick inflammation, and if there are any sinuses these should be traced to their full extent: the parts then feel a greater necessity of action. But this is not always sufficient, for after good granulations are formed, the indolent state often returns, the granulations becoming dark-coloured, and the matter thin and glairy, according to the specific nature of the indolence; this is the case often in old sores which have become habitual from bad treatment. In old indolent parts and encysted tumours the sac is often thickened, and even ossified, and the inflammation then is sometimes so violent as to threaten mortification. But these parts often become insensible to the common causes of inflammation, and when inflammation does arise it is sluggish. In such, nothing can cure but dissecting out the parts. Many abscesses, if out of the reach of surgery, or ill-treated, run into an indolent state. Many means are necessary in treating them, but we know of few useful ones: balsams and warm dressings are commonly used; sometimes they do good, at other times they have no effect; and when they agree they lose their powers by continuance, when it becomes necessary to change them, or increase their power. These balsams should often be mixed with red precipitate. Tincture of myrrh also is often very useful in indolent sores, requiring to be applied often, as it soon loses its efficacy: solutions of alum, tincture of bark, solution of lunar caustic, aqua camphorata, &c., are often useful, and require to be applied as often as three times a day, or oftener if the disease is considerable.

Of Tumours.

By this term is generally understood a circumscribed enlargement in a part from disease, not strictly a disease of a natural circumscribed part, as a thickened diseased gland.

Of circumscribed interstitial enlargements in common parts.—These seem to depend on an accumulation of extravasated coagulable lymph, either in the adipose or cellular membrane, or both. They are of two kinds; one is probably scrofulous, and not so circumscribed as the other.

The wen is commonly found in the cellular membrane of every part, but how formed it is difficult to explain; perhaps there is an absorption of the natural original parts underneath. The increase of cancer is much in the same way; a good deal of the cancerous matter appears to mix with the natural parts; but these natural parts appear to be lost as the cancerous matter increases. The specific quality of wens is not yet known*. They retain their living properties, and sometimes swell to an enormous size; sometimes they remain stationary, and sometimes they become solid throughout, so as even to be as hard as cartilage: when cut into they look like a lemon, but not so regular: they seem to have no leading cause, constitutional or local. Calcareous earth is often deposited in them. The first mode of preventing them, if we had any, would be by resolution, both by topical and internal applications; but we have none of much power in this respect. For those which are external, as in the cellular membrane, such remedies as were recommended in the diffused are proper; but these are more difficultly removed than the diffused, and, being circumscribed, are less capable of sympathy, and more indolent: perhaps mercury is the best resolvent for them; electricity is not so much to be depended on as mercury: suppuration of them, by cutting, or any other mode, will do no good. They produce a sore which it is impossible to heal, and which often becomes cancerous; therefore suppuration should be avoided, as it diffuses the cancerous disposition. Extirpation is the only remedy, so that the earlier this is acceded to the better. Their situation makes caution necessary, in the avoiding to wound surrounding parts. I have laid bare the carotid in the necks of women, also the temporals for two inches, and often have laid the trachea bare. By care and attention these operations are very easy and safe. The jugular vein I have also laid bare; but I would tie its two ends, as it is afterwards very apt to slough.

Tubercles may be classed under the head of spurious tumours: they are most frequent in the viscera. They are mostly of the lymphatic kind,

---

* [Sir Astley Cooper has described a species of encysted tumour or wen of the common integuments, which evidently depends on an obstruction of the follicular ducts of the skin, in consequence of which the sebaceous follicles become distended by the accumulation of morbid secretion. Ranula, and the enlargement of the labial glands, are analogous cases, and it is extremely probable that many other forms of tumour, such, for instance, as the serous cysts which are developed in the viscera, and the solid tubercles which occur in similar situations, owe their origin to a like cause, that is, to an obstruction in the primary branches of the excretory ducts. In general, however, the origin of adventitious growths (see note, p. 367), and the distinction of their specific natures, is involved in much obscurity, so that every attempt which has yet been made to classify them according to their natures has failed. The truth of this observation respecting the classification of tumours has been generally felt, and will be perceived in the ensuing observations of the author.]

and are often formed in the lungs of young people, and sometimes grow
to a considerable size : they are often on and in the liver, the spleen,
the uterus, the coats of the intestines, the peritoneum, and sometimes
on the epiploon : the lungs are frequently full of them, and they are the
cause of most consumptions. How they are formed, and whether glandular or not, I cannot determine ; but I think they arise from scrofulous
dispositions taking place in the lungs : their texture is often smooth.

Solid Tumours.—Tumours may be divided into solid and encysted,
which are very different diseases. Solid tumours differ from wens in
being an entirely new-formed substance, and of new structure. Their
situations are three : 1st, on the skin, forming warts, which are also
sometimes seen on the mouth, lips, and œsophagus ; 2nd, in the inside
of membranes, or canals, which are termed polypi ; 3rd, in the cellular
membrane of every part of the body. They commonly arise from one
fixed point, as a root, and then spread out in all directions, if the surrounding parts allow of it. These tumours, formed in solid substances,
are perfectly circumscribed ; they are generally more detached from the
cellular membrane than the lymphatic glands.

1st. *Warts* are external or superficial : they also form on the inside of
the lips, beginning of the vagina, and prepuce. Warts differ, according as
the cutis and the cuticle differ, in different parts : when these parts are
firm, the warts are hard, as on the hands ; but if soft, the warts are soft,
as on the mouth or lips. They appear to arise from the true skin of
the parts, and generally arise from, and are fixed on, a small extent of
surface, projecting considerably, so as sometimes to be even pendulous,
with a narrow neck. In hard parts they arise only to a small height,
and appear to split into many parts, and often by accident become
painful, bleed, and inflame. Those on the penis sometimes have a broad
basis, and rise not so high, and divide into points. On the inside of the
labia pudendi they often grow very large. It is difficult to assign their
cause, but sometimes we see an immediate cause, as the venereal disease
in the genitals.

2nd. *Polypi* arise on the canals, or passages, each of which seems to
produce a kind peculiar to itself, as the nose, vagina, uterus, &c.* ; they

---

* [It is questioned by some pathologists whether polypi, analogous to those which
arise from other mucous membranes, are ever found in the uterus; at all events, those
tumours which are usually called polypi of the uterus are ascertained to be of a different kind. These latter are in fact precisely similar in structure to the fibrous or fleshy
tubercles so frequently found imbedded in the tissue of that organ, which vary in their
appearance according to their situation, which allows them sometimes to assume the
pedunculated form. This I think is rendered quite certain, from the fact that they occur
-on the outside of the uterus as well as on the inside, and in that case hang into the
cavity of the pelvis, just as in other cases they do into the cavity of the uterus.]

are supposed also to arise in the urethra, and I have seen them in the rectum in men. They have generally small necks, and require extirpation : those from the Sehneiderean membrane are generally in a cluster, numbers arising from the same root ; internally they consist of a reticular membrane, whose insterstices are filled with a watery fluid, and, besides this, an external covering, both of which coats are vascular, but more particularly the external. They are inconvenient according to their size, often causing a tickling in the nose, which excites sneezing : when large, they are evident to the eye, either externally or internally, appearing to be semitransparent bodies within the nostrils ; but when protruded so low as to be exposed to the air, they become opake, &c., and are then sometimes supposed to be cancerous ; and, indeed, we should be cautious in extirpating them, as cancerous tumours are sometimes found in the nose. The best mode of removing them is with a forceps, but seldom more than one can be removed at the same time. If the polypus is forward, it must be extracted anteriorly by the nostril, the patient blowing the nostril as much as possible, to bring it forward. When the operation is simple, it is merely necessary to twist it off by a rotatory motion of the forceps.

3rd. *Of the third species.*—This is an entirely new substance in the cellular membrane, often irregular, attached by loose cellular membrane to the surrounding parts; we have also often such in bones which have been diseased : they seem to occasion the absorption of natural parts. Pressure often hinders their growth, and sometimes even occasions their removal by absorption ; but this is not always efficacious, and then extirpation is the only remedy. When in soft parts, we use the *knife*, and each incision may go as close to the tumour as possible, the surrounding parts not at all sympathising ; but if there is a root, then a little deeper : if the root goes to the surface of the bone, we cauterise it. On the bone, pressure will keep them down, or even make them lower than the common surface of the surrounding bone. Tumours often arise and shoot out from the alveolar processes, and the alveolar process often takes on the ossific disposition along with them : sometimes, but not always, they have bony matter in them.

On the Removal of Tumours.—We should first consider the kind of tumour and part ; if a simple body, the knife is the best mode of removing it. The first difficulty in the mode of opening it is, at first setting out, to know whether one or two incisions should be made in the skin. One incision is often sufficient, and two are often necessary ; one is sufficient where the tumour is small, or very loosely attached to surrounding parts ; but two are necessary when the tumour is large, or where the skin is diseased over it, so as to confine it much, even if small, as on the head, or sole of the foot. A simple incision is sufficient in fatty tumours, except when very large. In the dissection of common tumours we need not be at all nice about the tumour, nor in removing any of the surrounding parts; but in scirrhus, or cancer, the incision must be extended to surrounding parts, and this is not for convenience, but for the success of the operation.

For these wounds there are two modes of treatment; some heal by the first intention, others by suppuration. The first, when the skin will cover the whole sore, bringing the ligatures out at the under angle, when any are required to secure the vessels; but when the sides cannot be brought perfectly in contact, or when sloughing is expected, suppuration must take place; but in many such cases some part may still be healed by the first intention.

Of Tumours in Bones.—Besides ossific inflammation, as before mentioned, we have sometimes tumours, arising from extravasation of blood or scrofulous inflammation.

1st. Those from extravasated blood appear sometimes to arise from the surface of the bone, or else from its substance. The bone becomes lost in proportion to the size of the tumour; which arises from an unnatural accumulation of matter pressing on the part, occasioning absorption: this is most remarkable when the tumour is on the inside of the bone, which then appears as if scooped out; and as the cavity enlarges by absorption, the body is in proportion accumulated. This kind of tumour, arising from disease, differs from that arising from accident, as from fractures, these not exciting ossific inflammation in the surrounding parts; except, indeed, when in the leg and thigh, where, strength and support being needed, Nature forms new bone to supply the deficiency of the old. I can hardly tell whether the extravasation of blood is a cause or effect. Bones will break from this kind of tumour by very slight causes, such as by turning in bed; for before the whole cavity of the bone is absorbed, the bone generally gives way, and is fractured by a very slight cause: after the bone gives way, the extravasation increases from the continued disease and new-ruptured vessels. This kind of fracture happened to the Archbishop of Canterbury. Mr. Grindle has many examples of this in different bones in his possession.

2nd. The second of these diseases in the bone which have the same appearance, is an accumulation of curdly substance; probably it is coagulable lymph, and may be reckoned among the encysted tumours. The ossific inflammation often goes on here, till the bone acquires great size, but in these the outer ossific accumulation is not in proportion to the absorption, and therefore, being only a thin shell, it gives way; this is most common in the head of the tibia, and is called spina ventosa. Scrofula, attacking bones, makes them soft, and also thick, although their structure often remains; however, sometimes it is altered, scrofulous matter being deposited, and then the natural matter is removed, till at length all the matter which forms the bone becomes scrofulous. Such cases in a bone generally increase so much as to approach the skin, which inflames, ulcerates, and exposes the parts; and this increases the internal disease, which neither nature nor art can possibly cure; and then a hectic, sooner or later, according to the habit of the patient, seizes and destroys him. These two different causes, perhaps, have some connexion, yet the last is most scrofulous. In the treatment, we ought first to prevent the extravasation, &c.; but we neither know the disease, nor how to effect this intention. If known early, perhaps exposure and sea-bathing would be the best cure.

3rd. These tumours are of two kinds: 1st, tumours simply, which are often scrofulous to appearance; 2nd, the cancerous, which at present I defer. The first kind I have often seen, and most frequently in the lower jaw, and upper part of the tibia. The latter is probably a species of spina ventosa. If the disease seems to be true scrofula, then sea-bathing may cure it, but this is more difficultly known than in soft parts. When of the soft kind and convenient, pressure should be tried, which often is of great service, as in Mr. Squire's case; but when this fails, electricity, or the mercurial ointment and camphor should be used; and when this also fails, an operation often becomes necessary; an incision should be made upon it, and it should then be dissected out as in scalping, as close to its root as possible, with a little of the surrounding parts with it. If from bone, it is impossible to remove any of it by the knife, and it becomes necessary to cauterize it. Sometimes a saw or pincers are necessary for its removal, and cauterization of the cavity afterwards.

Encysted Tumours.—These commonly consist of a bag, or cyst, filled with a substance softer and different from the surrounding parts, though not necessarily so. The cysts are of two kinds, viz. natural and acquired. Natural, as the tunica vaginalis containing a fluid morbid in quality or quantity; fallopian tubes; the uterus or oviducts of animals; when, for instance, their foetus or eggs are preternaturally retained; these parts then taking on the nature of the coat of an encysted tumour. Sometimes they arise from an obstruction of the duct of some gland, which forms a tumour: I have seen them on the inside of the lip from this cause. The second, or acquired, are in consequence of disease in solid parts, and have much the feel of common tumours. It might be supposed they were common tumours suppurated; but they are original specific diseases. They contain varieties of matter; and hence they are divisible into several kinds: as, 1st, hydatid, from their contents being watery; 2nd, various matters of different consistency; 3rd, a curdly substance. The thickened cellular membrane, condensed by pressure, forms the coats of the first and second; but I know not how the third coat is formed: some of them probably are scrofulous; and if so they are no more than very indolent abscesses in those parts, having acquired a strong coat, which I think is sometimes the case.

1st. Hydatids vary in kind, from the variety of their situation. All accumulations of water in cavities are properly hydatids. (See *note*, p. 456.) The water may be either in a natural cyst, as the tunica vaginalis, pericardium, &c., or in a cyst formed by disease. This second division is of two kinds, but both occur in the cellular membrane. The first is filled with serum, and therefore similar to the above: the second is lined with a peculiar substance. Those of the first kind are most frequent in those parts which have an enveloping membrane, as the abdomen and thorax; and are more common to some of these than to others, though it does not arise from their having a cavity, but from a peculiar disposition of these parts: these hydatids project into the cavity. Those in the cellular membrane are very uncertain in their situation. The first kind, or simply watery, are often in women's necks, or in the thyroid gland. I once saw a large cluster in the neck of a woman. As they increase in size their coats increase in thickness: those in the cellular membrane thicken soonest; for the lining membranes, or cysts, only thicken by a species of adhesive inflammation. The second differ from the former, and are made up of two parts: the strong external coat is lined by another, of a dusky white colour, much like the retina of the eye, and gelatinous; this coat is generally as thick as thin pasteboard, and as strong as thick wet paper. In many hydatids there is an additional or third coat on the inside of this, which is less opake; and sometimes a fourth, and so on, till at last nothing is seen but coats; none of which, except the external one, is vascular. It is easy to account for the formation of the external coat; but difficult for the internal ones. Whether the external is the first, and the parent of the others, or the consequence, is not easily determined; but the last is most probably the case, as when formed, they stimulate so as to produce a vascular coat; but whichever is formed first, we must suppose that it is capable of continuance. I suppose the first formed is the nucleus, and so on; similar to a nest of pill-boxes, one within another. There is another somewhat similar, but more irregular; the external vascular coat being full of small ones, as shown in this preparation [*exhibiting it*]. Does this last species proceed from indolence? Many animals die of them in the liver, in cold climates, especially sheep: it is in them called the rot. Hydatids cause little sensation, and are seldom known till of a considerable size.

Hydatids of the Uterus.—Those of the uterus and ovaries are generally circumscribed bags *, and generally are numerous, especially in the ovaries, and appear somewhat similar to those of the scrotum; forming a species of hydrocele of the part. At first they are thin, containing a transparent fluid; but afterwards they become thicker, and the fluid is bloody, or like a jelly. They have when small but little attachment, but afterwards get to adhere to each other, when they grow often very large, and increase the size of the belly, forming ovarian dropsy. The history and progress only of the case can in general distinguish it from ascites; at first there is a partial, moveable swelling, rolling from side to side in bed. Afterwards they become fixed, but even then, in thin people, inequalities may be felt: when large, they become fixed to the parietes of the abdomen; and if the person is not very fat, a fluctuation may be felt. The health is but little affected by them. Hence the cause is very different from ascites, where the health is first injured. Tapping is only a palliative cure, and a large trocar is required, as the fluid is generally gelatinous, and then only one cell is opened. If taken in the incipient stage, they might be taken out, as they generally render life disagreeable for a year or two, and kill in the end. There is no reason why women should not bear spaying as well as other animals; It would be simply opening the cavity of the abdomen, which we often do without inconvenience in healthy constitutions†.

Hydatids in the Kidneys.—They are of the first species, of the adventitious, and are generally situated between the first and second laminæ of the external coat; but they are certainly often in the internal substance of the kidney. Sometimes there are a great number. Those

---

* [The hydatid which forms in the uterus is peculiar to that organ, at least in the generality of cases, being of a pedunculated form, and generally grouped together like a bunch of grapes. Hydatids in this situation often attain a great size in the aggregate, and are expelled by a parturient effort. There is reason for suspecting that this form of hydatids most frequently arises from impregnation, in which case the destruction of the ovum is almost universally the consequence.]

† [This recommendation has been adopted in several cases, but the success has not been found to warrant its repetition. The difficulty of ascertaining whether one or both ovaries is affected, as well as the obscurity in which the disease is involved in its earliest stages, are insurmountable objections to the operation; for I do not suppose that any one would be so bold as to propose it after the cyst has attained any considerable magnitude. Besides, it sometimes happens that the disease remains stationary for many years; and in other cases a cure is effected by the suppuration of the cyst consequent on tapping, the danger of which is scarcely greater than that which would attend the operation of extirpation.]

in the coats are never detached or pendulous; the coats are thin, and look like a red grape; they give no symptoms of any kind, nor do they require or admit of any remedy. Sometimes those about the kidneys burst into its pelvis, and come away by the urethra. A gentleman had a considerable swelling on the left side of his belly which had been a long time collecting, and evidently contained a fluid; on a sudden a considerable quantity of fluid was discharged from the bladder through the urethra, and along with it a large number of hydatids; some whole, others burst; but the swelling of his abdomen subsided and he got well: however, he afterwards filled again; but he again emptied them by the ureters, and he is now perfectly well.

Hydatids of the Liver.—The liver may be said to have none but those of the second species of the adventitious; they are generally, but not always, on the exterior substance of this viscus. In some rare cases they have produced ascites by their coats bursting internally; and sometimes they have been discharged externally by their coats adhering to the peritoneum, and inflammation and suppuration coming on. When known to be a bag containing fluid it may be opened, but I would not be in a hurry to do this.

Hydatids of the Lungs.—These are of two kinds: first, a collection of water simply in one or more cells; the second, of the adventitious kind, either external to, or in the substance of, the lungs. Some open into the trachea, and are coughed up in abundance; sometimes they produce spurious empyema, when they should be opened pretty early, to prevent their affecting the substance of the lungs by pressure.

Hydatids of the Brain.—These I have never seen increase so far as to cause inconvenience. In some animals they are common when young, and are successfully taken out. They are very frequent in the plexus choroides.

Hydatids of the Thyroid Gland.—Sometimes these are very large, and produce difficult respiration and deglutition.

Hydatids of the Cellular Membrane.—These are generally of the first species of the second division of the adventitious, containing a transparent fluid. Some parts, and more especially women's necks, are more subject to them than others. They are also pretty common on the inside of the lips of men.

2nd. The second kind of encysted tumour contains matter of various kinds, and are very similar to hydatids, often containing in part a watery fluid. In the ovaries, fatty, cuticular, and hairy tumours are sometimes formed.

The treatment for the two first is the same. From their situation we may divide their cure into two kinds; one admitting of external applications, the other not; but I know no medicine which will cause their absorption. When external, therefore, the only means is opening them, when they will inflame, suppurate, and may be managed as in common hydrocele; but so much nicety is not here required, as the sac, being generally thick, will not collapse. In some a free opening is only necessary; sometimes they inflame spontaneously, but rarely, and even then a free opening is necessary, on account of their indolence. If the sac is much thickened, the exposure by opening will generally kill it, and cause sloughing; yet exposure is not always sufficient, but the whole sac will require dissecting out, and especially when we consider that there is sometimes in these a cancerous disposition.

Of the Cuticular*.—The adhering cellular membrane forming the sac, takes on the disposition of the cutis, or more properly is changed into cutis, and is capable of generating an external one when exposed; it is lined, indeed, with a cuticle. These cysts often have so much the disposition of the external part, as to have hair grow in them, which is the same as that which covers the animal, as, for instance, wool in the case of sheep. Every part of the body is subject to them, but some parts particularly so. The ovum is subject to all kinds of encysted tumours, and to these more than other parts; and they probably throw off the cuticle every year, or oftener, the cuticle being filled with hair. They are also filled with various matters; sometimes with a caseous substance, in others with oil, fat, bones, &c.: they occur also in the eyelids, in the skin near the eyes, and in the lips, and all grow to a large size.

There are two methods of cure, one dissecting out the tumour, the other opening it freely, or taking off the projecting part and leaving the basis: on the eyelids, when very superficial, they often burst, matter is discharged, and they get well. On the head they are opened and get well. I have seen the external skin only taken off, which gave rise to an inflammation round its edge, which suppurated and granulated, and healed over, producing a cure.

A gentleman had a large encysted tumour on the muscles of the abdomen; this was opened by taking out a circular piece of the integuments, comprising the fore part of the sac. The wound of the integuments suppurated; but the internal surface of the sac, which was now fully exposed, never suppurated the least, so that the wounds of the integuments granulated and healed, tucking down the integuments to

---

* [The reader is referred to Cooper and Travers's "Surgical Essays," p. 215, for an account of encysted tumours forming on the scalp and face. These strictly come under the designation cuticular, and have been adverted to in a previous note, p. 567.]

the thin surface of the sac. The patient has remained well ever since; but has a large cicatrix, part of which is composed of what was the internal surface of the sac. The surface of the internal coats of these tumours has a skin somewhat like that which covers the glans penis, different in some respects from that with which the rest of the body is furnished, but not of such a nature as to suppurate on exposure.

3rd. Encysted tumours in a part depending on an indolent disposition or suppuration are commonly deep-seated, and their progress is very slow at first; they appear as an abscess, and might be suspected to be encysted, from their giving no pain. I have seen sometimes a chain of them leading from the skin; that nearest the skin appeared to be the original of them. These often deceive the surgeon, who is either satisfied by opening or dissecting them out, suspecting no more of them; and I know no characteristic mark of their presence when the original one is deep-seated: when external, the examination after the removal of the first may distinguish them.

Of the Inflammation, Suppuration, and Ulceration of new-formed parts or substances.—We shall find these parts more liable to dissolve than the natural parts are, having weaker powers of action. In proportion, therefore, to the quantity of new matter, is the part weaker; and these parts go through their diseases much quicker than original ones. When new-formed parts are under the necessity of inflammation, a very slight cause is sufficient; and the inflammation goes on more rapidly than in original ones; and it requires more attention and care to stop its progress. They are both more ready to mortify and suppurate. If in the adipose membrane or skin, and the inflammation is beyond resolution, then no suppuration, but ulceration, takes place, and mortification rapidly ensues; but it will be confined to the new-formed part, except in very bad constitutions. When suppuration has taken place, or mortification, there must be also ulceration, which is very rapid; so that an abscess in parts where an abscess had been before, will be much quicker than before in pointing, or than in other sound parts: if mortification takes place, the separation will be almost immediate. Hence it appears that it is a deposit of matter originally from the constitution, and she lays a claim to it in removing it and repairing it again at pleasure. Simple fractures sometimes disunite, though stronger than by granulations; in these cases no inflammation is produced, at least not so much as to produce suppuration. Union of parts by granulations often disunite, both in soft and hard parts, hence old sores and old fractures disunite. This disposition of fractures to disunite is most frequent in the lower extremities; the substance appears to be shorter lived than the original part was, as in old sores, which so frequently break out again.

In parts united by simple extravasation, and adhesive inflammation, which again ulcerate, there is no suppurative inflammation, but there will be in parts united by granulations and suppuration. Ulceration, though frequent after compound fractures, is seldom so considerable as to destroy the new-formed bone wholly, though often in part: these are the causes of bad ulcers, and of what are called foul bones. It most commonly occurs from a fault in the general system, as scurvy; and upon this principle, sloughs take place soonest in new-formed parts, the separation depending on ulceration.

For the cure of these cases we must first examine into the causes: if from scurvy, when the patient is at sea; or if from their depending position and too much exercise, when the ulceration is in the legs; in which case rest and a horizontal posture are to be used: but there is something very peculiar in the lower extremities; they will become better and yet again slough.

Of Fistulæ in general.—The term fistula gives a very inadequate notion of the disease, the fistulous canal being only the sign of the disease, —the means of conveying a fluid or extraneous matter to the surface.

A fistula is the consequence of the powers of a part not being able to remove the original cause, so that the original cause and some of its effects remain.

The causes of fistula are various, but may be divided into two classes: first, the obstruction of the passage of some natural secretion, as fistula of the parotid gland; or of the canal for the passage of extraneous matter, as the intestines being strangulated so as to mortify, or being wounded; but all obliterations of the ducts where the fluids make a new passage will not be termed fistulæ: secondly, the formation of pus or extraneous matter in a part requiring a passage, as in fistula in ano, fistula in the joints, and fistula from diseased bone.

We shall first consider the first cause of fistulæ.

1st. The obliteration of ducts, or canals, is the first cause. This arises from obstruction of the natural passages, in consequence of which a new one is formed for the passage of the natural secretion. These obliterations often arise from a thickening of the sides of the ducts, as in the urethra, nasal duct, &c., from inflammation; sometimes from the venereal disease or scrofula; and sometimes from accident, as in the parotid duct. These obliterations are often very troublesome, obstructing the evacuation of the natural secretions, which is very teazing to the part, and when complete is very serious in its consequences. In most there is a new passage when complete, which is made by inflammation and ulceration; these new passages are called fistulous: the discharge is the natural secretion, mixed with the pus from the inflamed vessels of the sides of the passage. If this new passage answers all the purposes of the original one, it cannot well be called fistulous; when from a mortified or wounded intestine, it is called an artificial anus; when in the perinæum, it is for the passage of the urine. There are often accumulations of secreted juices besides the above, arising from the same causes, and producing the same consequences, yet not called fistulous.

Of the Fistula Lachrymalis.—This arises from an obstruction taking place in the passage of the tears from the lachrymal sac into the nose. The causes are often foreign to the nature of the parts themselves, as the smallpox or measles. This I suppose not to originate, as has been supposed, from a pustule at the end or mouth of the duct, but from inflammation running along the duct and causing the sides of it to adhere; it also may arise from ulceration of the duct from a venereal or scrofulous disposition in the part; but most frequently from obliteration of the canal from inflammation. The tears not passing, the inner surface of the sac becomes stimulated by pressure and distension, and the salts of the tears, which have little or no effect while the sac is natural, when diseased irritate it and produce inflammation. The sac swells, suppurates, and opens externally, and discharges the tears by this opening till the natural passage opens or a new one is made. If the os unguis had been susceptible of the stimulus and had ulcerated, it would have been fortunate, but it only thickens to defend itself from the disease; for we find Nature has made internal parts less susceptible of such stimuli, the ulceration only taking place next the skin, so that it would perhaps be better for us if Nature would sometimes vary from her usual course. This internal thickening is sometimes so great as to unite the external part of the nose to the septum, and render the operation of perforating the os unguis less successful. Opening the old passage seldom succeeds, as it is very liable to become diseased again, as in strictures in the urethra, which are so apt to recur; and here bougies cannot be had recourse to, occasionally, as in the urethra. The operation, however, should not be done precipitately, as the duct often clears of itself and the patient gets well.

Of the Obliteration of the Ducts of the Glands of the Lip.—These glands lie immediately under the skin of the lips, and when there is an obliteration of any of these ducts, a tumour is formed, which sometimes bursts of itself. As the secretion goes on, the new opening cannot heal, and it is then, though improperly, called fistulous, as it does the office of the natural passage, and yet is often stopped again: sometimes they do not burst, and I have dissected them out; for although they occasion little pain they are very troublesome.

Obliteration of the Ducts of Cowper's Glands in the Female.—This may be the case in the male, and probably would occasion fistula in perinæo.

An accumulation of slimy matter takes place, and the ducts swell just under the skin, on the inside of the labia, near the carunculæ myrtiformes. They increase in size, and sometimes are mistaken for hernia: they should be opened before becoming very large, by a crucial incision : and to prevent their union by adhesion after opening, they should be touched with lunar caustic : perhaps a round hole made by the lapis septicus would answer better than an incision. They first appear like a little encysted tumour, which increasing, becomes so troublesome as to prevent the person sitting. A lady had a very large one, which was taken for a hernia of the foramen ovale. She went to Paris, where it was thought an abscess and opened.

Obliteration of the Duct of the Parotid Gland.—The parotid gland, from its superficial situation as it passes over the masseter muscle, is very liable to be wounded. Such a wound will afterwards become the orifice of the duct, and will heal in part, to a fistulous size : the duct itself going to the mouth probably closes, as the saliva must then be lost; and as its flowing here is very inconvenient, it is necessary to direct it to the mouth, which may be done with a needle, threaded with a round thread passed to the bottom of the fistula, then directing it to the mouth and feeling for the point internally, pushing it to the finger and drawing it through, leaving the thread in ; and perhaps it will be necessary to bring the thread out of the corner of the mouth and to tie the two ends externally. The thread should be left in till the new duct has lost its healing disposition, and then heal the external one; but it may perhaps be necessary to make it a new surface before it will heal by making the fresh surfaces adhere by placing them in contact.

2nd. The second species of fistula, or that from disease, arises from the disproportion in the disposition to heal of different parts, viz. the internal and the external ; the skin healing, while the deeper-seated parts, or seat of the disease, have no disposition for it. It may arise from two causes : 1st, from any extraneous substance in the inner parts ; 2ndly, from a diseased state of the original part, when the disease formed. The first happens in large deep-seated abscesses, which are prevented healing at the bottom by the pressure of the matter. The second has two causes, the first from the part being naturally indolent, as tendons ; the second from a disease in parts naturally ready to heal, but the disease being deep-seated, the skin is more ready to heal than the bottom of the fistula, and thus obstructs the necessary free discharge.

Fistula in Ano.—Generally originates two or three inches up the side of the rectum. The first process is inflammation, and the formation of an abscess ; then the matter comes down by the side of the gut, and, opens on the buttock. Sometimes the gut is so diseased as to give way, and then we have an opening into it, which being the easiest and readiest way for the matter, it is thus discharged, and then we may have no external opening; but if there has been one, it does not heal. The cellular membrane about the anus is sometimes the seat of encysted tumours, which are mistaken for fistula, although they do not proceed from inflammation. The treatment differs in these two very considerably: the tumour is often opened or breaks, but the inner surfaces of the two are very different. The abscess only requires opening, and then cures itself; but the encysted tumour, when opened externally, generally becomes fistulous, and opening into the gut will often not succeed, if attention is not paid to make them heal from the bottom; therefore it is necessary to keep them well open by dressing, or the two divided parts will unite at the edges after opening. When a fistula in ano has both an external opening and an opening into the gut, surgeons are in general satisfied with opening from one to the other; but the fistula sometimes runs higher up by the side of the gut than the inner opening, and then we should not attend to this opening, but get to the bottom of the sinus.

Fistula in Perinæo.—In whatever part of the urethra the seat of the disease is, whether the prostate gland, or the membranous or bulbous part; the external opening seldom heals as long as the seat of the disease has no disposition to heal. This, I apprehend, arises in most cases from sympathy with a disease in deeper-seated parts; or, in other words, a deep-seated disease is capable of stimulating superficial parts, so as to prevent the natural action for healing. Let us compare this disease with the state of parts after lithotomy. If the incision is made in sound parts, and the whole injury be a stone, which is extracted, the parts readily heal, in spite of the urine passing through that channel. This, then, shows that there is another cause of their not healing. Now if the parts higher up are unsound, as the prostate, &c., though the incision was made in sound parts, it does not heal: if perchance it does, the disease still continuing, you will have probably two or three fistulæ. If the parts are unsound beyond the fistulæ, you will be continually plagued with a return of them. Bougies should not be kept in too long, as they sometimes make fresh fistulæ in perinæo. Several fistulæ may arise from one disease. A diseased bottom may have many fistulous sores leading to it both in the perinæum and anus; and if one of these be laid freely open, so as to expose the diseased part, the rest will heal.

When the disease is in one fixed part, there is a canal leading to it, which I have called a fistula; but if more than one, these different ones are called sinuses. A fistulous orifice is generally a small opening in the skin, having no sore surface in view, and is easily distinguished from other sores: if the diseased part is deep and of long standing, the external skin will be thickened more or less near the orifice, from the contraction of granulations within the canal, so that sometimes there is a protuberance even by the contraction. But this appearance is also common to all diseased parts some way under the skin, when the skin does not partake of the disease; when it does, this appearance is less considerable. If near a bone, this is suspected to be affected. When the seat of disease is near the skin, as when on the tibia, then we may be certain the diseased cavity below is not large.

The *cure of fistulæ* consists in first removing the immediate cause; for frequently they get well by simply removing the obstruction. In fistula lachrymalis, a new opening, or the restoration of the old one, is the cure. A fistula in perinæo will often be cured by stretching and dilating the canal of the urethra by bougies, which removes the obstruction. The cause of our first division of fistulæ, arising from confined matter, is sometimes easily removed, but not always, by opening the suppurated part in the most depending situation, when, if the parts are readily disposed to heal, a cure takes place. The second, from a diseased state, must have the disease removed or extirpated if possible; but this is often impracticable. A perfect exposure is the next object; but the case will not often admit of it, and then becoming incurable it sometimes produces hectic, as in lumbar abscesses, and abscesses of the liver which open externally but cannot be exposed. The constitution in such cases is to be most attended to, and everything done to lessen the irritation; but in most cases life is miserable, and we only protract it a little longer by our best efforts. Fistulas in the lungs and liver in consequence of abscess, and in the intestines from old obstruction, can only have their orifice kept open for the discharge of the matter. Fistulas in ano are generally easily come at, and are then of easy cure. At first it is simply an abscess from disease on the outside of the rectum; if not, it becomes so by inflammation and suppuration. This is proved by the cure, which is not simply a free opening where the abscess points, but opening the abscess from its original seat is necessary for the cure: slitting up the gut to the origin of the abscess is necessary in all cases of fistula in ano*.

Of the attention necessary in diseased and wounded Joints respecting their motion.—I shall now speak of the preservation and acquirement of motion in joints when diseased, and after disease. We must consider

---

* [The reason of this necessity is the constant action of the sphincter muscle, which is divided in the operation.]

.in both the necessity of removing the first cause of the disease, or we
·shall be increasing it by endeavouring to preserve or to acquire the lost
·motion: nothing can promote contraction of the joint so much as mo-
·tion before the disease is removed. In healing wounds in general, and
especially those connected with joints, great attention should be paid
·to the motion of the joint: when all inflammation is gone off, and healing has begun, a little motion, and frequently repeated, is necessary to
prevent their healing in one position. Wherever there has been an
inflammation, a stiffness will remain; but the parts will stretch, and the
motion again become free, by gradual motion and friction. But in healing of wounds by granulations there will be more rigidity. When there
has been loss of substance, from mortification and gun-shot wounds, there
will be still greater rigidity, and consequently more attention is requisite. In violent inflammation there is a union, by a broad surface and
close contact, and then motion is sometimes altogether irrecoverable.
The parts may often be made to stretch by degrees: this is either by
active or passive motion. The active or muscular motion is insufficient,
.if the disease has existed long, as the muscles often lose the power of
acting. The passive or foreign power may be of three kinds: 1st, the
hands of another person; 2ndly, the addition of matter to the moving ·
part, so as to increase its momentum; 3rdly, putting the moving part
into such a position as to increase its gravity, which will produce the
same effect as the two former; but yet the assistance of the muscles
.are necessary also. The position is either the middle state of action,
which is natural in disease, or it is in consequence of gravity. The arm
in diseases of the shoulder, if in bed, lies a little out; but if up, it hangs
by the side naturally. Joints are of two kinds, some with flexors and extensors, with a given power; the other have not only the above, but a given
support, which support acts generally in the centre of gravity. This division makes a material difference in the position of joints. If in the former of these there is a disease, the part naturally falls into a half-bent
state, and will heal so if not prevented; but it is different in the other
kind, for in whatever position they are placed, when there is a weight, the
weight becomes the object of the mind, and not the motion; and the
joint must be kept wholly in this position, which is a position rather
contrary to that which it was meant to be kept in. This is most remarkable in the ankle-joint, because the point of support will not be the
natural one: the foot will be hanging in a straight line with the leg, which
is just the contrary to that which arises from the elongation of the
muscles of the ankle. Suppose the elbow contracted, and I want to
put the flexor muscles into an elongated state, neither the muscles nor
mind being able to do this; the hand, apparently, is not heavy enough;

but suppose I should then put a little weight into the hand, in order to assist a little, then the mind will be fixed on the weight to support it, the flexors will support it, being influenced by the mind; and thus we shall do harm by increasing the power of the flexors. But if the mind is fixed on the extensors, and not at all on the support of the weight, then the weight will be serviceable by extending the flexors while contracting the extensors.

In the endeavour to elongate the muscles in any part of the body, they should never be allowed to contract, which would counteract the elongating powers. In contractions of the gastrocnemius muscle, the heel should be always supported, to take off the mind from the support of the body; the body should be supported by art, by supporting the heel, but this should be incomplete, and gradually made more so. When the knee is bent, the above method will assist when the person is obliged to walk; for when sitting, throwing and swinging the limb about will assist most, and sometimes attaching a weight to the limb. I would advise lying on the face, and with such a position of the knee that the foot should touch the plane on which the body was, and then raising the foot more by bending the knee more. When the contraction is in the thigh, we cannot have all these auxiliaries. With respect to the shoulder it will be much the worst, as it will scarcely be possible to assist its position by any auxiliary. I have thought a pulley might be contrived to raise the arm, with a weight fixed to the end of the cord; or the patient might be requested to lay on that side, having his arm through a tube and hanging out the other side. Every possible method should be tried: if a man could walk on his hands awhile, the arm would then by its own weight come to a right position with the body, which would be sufficient.

TETANUS.

The symptoms of this disease are involuntary contractions of the voluntary muscles of the body, and sometimes of the involuntary, which makes it fatal. This affection is sometimes only partial, and at other times general. When on the muscles of the jaw, it is called locked jaw; when on the fore part of the body, as the pectoral and anterior muscles of the neck, emprosthotonos; when on the muscles of the back, drawing the head backwards, opisthotonos. Tetanus should first be properly arranged as to class and species. It may be properly classed with every unnatural contraction of muscles which may be called spasm, of which there are many species, most of which have some specific difference. It is of the same genus as spasmus cynicus, cramp, wry neck, subsultus tendinum, &c. It may be also classed with St. Vitus's dance, and it seems to have great affinity with ague, as this disease sometimes attends it; but the ague is only the predisposent, or immediate cause. It also seems to be allied to catalepsy and epilepsy : these arise from affections of the brain and nerves, but they may arise from different causes. Most of the above diseases are acted upon by affections of the mind, and this is sometimes the case with tetanus. This disease sometimes occurs in animals, as horses, cows, sheep, &c., from which it might be supposed that these animals were subject to it from their way of life being somewhat similar to man's. I had a stag which died from locked jaw, from a compound fractured leg.

Some muscles are more liable to it than others; those of the lower jaw are the most so; but as the disease increases, another order of muscles is affected, which I think arises from a species of sympathy : other involuntary actions have also their predisposed parts, as the cramp, which is mostly in the lower extremities. The muscles of the neck are most liable to that species of permanent contractions which constitutes the wry neck.

Of the Causes of Tetanus.—The principal inquiries which have hitherto been made have been on the cure, and not on the nature of the disease, or its similarity to others. This part of the subject I shall now consider, and also in what climates it is most frequent. Irritation from an injury done to a nerve, ligament, or tendon is generally supposed to be the cause, as it generally occurs from wounds of tendinous or ligamentous parts. This at first would seem reasonable ; but we must determine first what is irritation. That is called irritation which excites inflammation, and a patient is said to be irritable when a part or the whole constitution is easily affected by any slight cause. But everything relative to locked jaw does not arise from irritation of the wound itself, neither from inflammation or symptomatic fever; for in such states the constitution is not disposed to it. It arises from an irritable habit, which may be increased or produced by irritation, but not such as is capable of producing inflammation. When there is inflammation, the locked jaw arises only when that is subdued. When from causes incapable of exciting inflammation, the irritation may be considered the immediate, but not the remote cause; for there must be a disposition for the disease, such a cause being insufficient for producing such effects : thus also madness is produced from the slightest causes when the mind is predisposed; so it is in agues and fevers, the constitution being particularly predisposed at the time to such diseases. If it were from inflammation, the locked jaw would come on at first, or when the inflammation is most violent; but then the constitution is strong, which is a state unfavourable to the disease. It is perhaps impossible to say what are-all the remote causes which produce this effect; probably many combined; and it would be impossible to give all the immediate, but I shall give as many of both as I have observed.

Constitutions most susceptible of the Disease.—First, there is a disposition of the nerves, and that principally of the nerves of the voluntary muscles and sensation, rendering sensibility more acute in such, so that they can scarcely bear to be touched. This appears to be from irritability of the nerves, and not from irritability of the living principle. To produce the disease only a slight immediate cause is necessary, which is the case also in most irregular actions of the nervous system, as we see in tickling, which will produce convulsions, though these would not be produced by a bruise in the same part. Those most susceptible of the disease are of weakly delicate frames and of suspicious minds, and not of strong and robust ones. It is common to have involuntary actions of the muscles in weakly constitutions, as we see in pregnant women, who are subject to cramps, fits, &c., although the living principle is acting at the same time vigorously: this was also the case with myself, at a time when weak. I threw a stone at a deer, and over-exercised the muscles of the arm, which produced cramp and extravasation in my arm, and loss of the use of the muscles: this produced sickness and paleness, and after a little time cramp came on in my leg; but at last this and the other symptoms went gradually off: if the irritation had continued, a locked jaw might have come on. Now here, from the irritation, a spasmodic affection was produced in a person in health. This species of irritation is very different from irritation of the living principle causing inflammation.

Climate seems the first of the predisposing causes, and that which can probably produce it without other causes: the second is the consequence of considerable local inflammation: the third is irritation. The immediate cause is often a small wound of a part possessing but little living powers. In warm climates it is most frequent, and consequently it is seldom found in cold weather. In the West Indies and in the Mediterranean, besides tetanus, we also find the diseases with which I have classed it very frequent. Sweden, Denmark, and other cold climates are not subject to it. The cramp is most frequent in warm climates, and also in bed; fits also are most frequent in bed, for warmth seems to have a peculiar effect in producing a particular disposition in the nerves; and when there is an immediate slight cause, such diseases readily take place; nay, some are disposed to such actions without any immediate cause, which probably arises from climate, joined with a strong natural predisposition. The cases which I have seen from wounds were those of the tendons, for these parts heal less readily, and the

constitution is much weakened by wounds of such parts, so that sometimes a limb will waste from such a cause,—wounds being much more
irritable here than in other parts, and particularly when attended with
loss of blood. Nothing produces irritability more than a great loss of
blood, especially when accompanied with a wound, and with this disposition of constitution. The wounds producing it are either considerable
or slight: the first is a predisponent, the second an immediate cause.
When I have seen it from the first, it was after the inflammatory stage,
and when good suppuration was come on; in some where it had nearly
healed, and the patient was considered healthy, under the disease as
well as before. Some have had locked jaw after the healing was completed. In such I have supposed the inflammation was the predisponent
cause, rendering the nervous system irritable as soon as it was removed.
When it comes on in horses, as after docking, it is after the wound has
suppurated, and begun to heal. A young man burnt his face with gunpowder: in a fortnight after he was nearly well; but a short time after
a locked jaw came on and continued for two months, and then recovered;
but before that time his wounds were perfectly healed. It arises from
slight wounds, before either inflammation or suppuration comes on. A
man had a locked jaw about a fortnight after a nail entered the sole
of his foot, which he did not at the time regard as of any consequence,
the wound not being larger than that from bleeding, and not attended
with any pain, inflammation, or hardness: he died; and after death I
found a black line continued to a hard body under the skin, which could
be dissected out almost like a lymphatic gland, and was found to be a
bit of leather, surrounded by coagulable lymph: the black line was the
mark of the nail. Here was no pain which could be the cause, and
little, if any, inflammation, and the suppuration had not begun; hence
it appears that the spasm arose from the slight irritation. Would producing a greater irritation have prevented or cured in this case? or
would dissecting out the extraneous body have done this?* These two
kinds of wounds appear very dissimilar; I consider that the inflammation
is the predisponent cause in the large ones, and that in the case of slight
wounds there must already exist a predisposition, which only requires
an immediate cause to bring it into action. The disease oftener arises
from slight wounds than large ones, which may partly, but not entirely,
arise from such being most frequent. Locked jaw arises from other
weakening causes; it sometimes arises at the termination of a fever,

---

* [We should probably answer this question in the negative, considering that the
progress of the symptoms is not in any degree checked by the *entire* removal of the
irritation by amputation of the injured part. The fatal result, on the contrary, is generally precipitated by this means.]

and also at the termination of a flux, which is one of the most weakening diseases we have. It is singular that it should begin in the muscles of the lower jaw, and extend from these as a centre; but this is not a general rule, as it has been known to begin in the muscles of the neck. When it is confined to the muscles first attacked it may then be considered as mild.

Tetanus appears to have a dangerous period, in which it is most liable to attack vital parts, which period seems to be before the constitution has become much accustomed to it; when of longer continuance, not having attacked vital parts, its liability to attack them seems lessened, which is generally in a fortnight, as the constitution has then become accustomed to the spasms, and can better bear them: I have never seen one die where it had existed three weeks, and after this it often continues, sometimes for several months. Sometimes they may recover in three days, which is generally the most fatal period; but sometimes they may go on three weeks, and afterwards recover. If violent, it kills about the third or fourth day from the attack.

As it appears to attack parts not necessary to life, it seems strange how it kills; and, seemingly, the patient is in good health at the time, without inflammation, and with a good appetite; and yet, though not starved to death, from the difficulty of deglutition, it kills: however, it is sometimes combined with other diseases, and then it is difficult to say which disease kills; but when it is alone, the following seems to be the case: the disposition increases, and the effect, spreading to vital parts, affects the muscles of respiration, as the diaphragm and intercostal and abdominal muscles, as we see in gout when it attacks a vital part.

The first symptom is a stiffness in the muscles of the lower jaw, or neck; but before the patient is sensible of it, its progress is generally gone some length, not having had occasion to open the mouth wide, for when it is perceived it is probably only by accident: this stiffness makes the articulation imperfect. When the spasm is perceived, a hardness may be felt in the temporal and masseter muscles, and most of the muscles of the face become contracted: if it extends, the muscles posteriorly on the neck become stiff, consequently the head is erect, and generally drawn backwards; the spasm extending to the muscles of the back, it becomes one concave arch, preventing the patient from lying on his back, and a heavy pain is felt at the lower part of the sternum, from the spasm probably of the diaphragm: from this and the abdominal muscles being contracted, respiration is almost suspended, and the pain is similar to that of the cramp. By this pain, and the dyspnœa, we judge of the muscles of respiration and the diaphragm being affected. General spasms next come on, as subsultus tendinum, cold sweats, and death; and it is remarkable that the patient generally, if not always, retains his reasoning faculties during the whole progress.

Of the Treatment.—All the antispasmodics have been given, but without apparent success; opium has kept its ground the longest, but with little reason, as it only quiets; but from some patients having got well under its use, its name has been raised : I have tried it, both in large and small doses, though always unsuccessfully. I think medicines have no power without they produce some visible effect : opium never removes the cause, though it will prevent the effects; it cures spasms, and removes pain, but it does not remove the cause. It often does good, by not allowing the symptoms to do harm to the constitution. The first appearance of a cure is a recovery of strength, as weakness is a predisposing cause; and the first indication should be to strengthen the system. I should recommend everything to produce extreme external cold, as cold applications, consisting of snow with salt, to the part, and that the patient should be put into an ice-house or sent to a cold climate as soon as possible*. I know of no internal medicine. The pain is somewhat relieved by counteracting the violent contraction of the muscles : opening the mouth by force has eased it; but this has also killed, by causing a translation of the disease : keeping the back bent has also given ease; but these have relieved only in the incipient state. Electricity has a temporary effect, in relaxing the muscles, and in partial affections has cured, by rendering the contractions gradually less violent.

A man fractured his arm, and about a fortnight after had symptoms of a locked jaw. I found several pieces of bone in the wound, which I supposed produced irritation; these I extracted, and gave two grains of opium every two hours, dressed the wound with tinctura thebaica, and over all applied a poultice : he continued as bad as before. The next day I directed bark and opium: on the fourth day he was better; on the fifth much more so, and his pulse good; he was bled, which was repeated on the sixth, immediately after which he fell into a fit, and died in half an hour. This sudden change could not be from the loss of blood, though assisted by it, and by his natural aversion to bleeding : he was of a nervous constitution, and his spirits were easily affected. It was probable that this affection of the nerves was transferred to the

---

* [A remarkable case of tetanus, which was cured by an accidental exposure to cold and inclement weather for upwards of sixteen hours, is related by Sir James Macgrigor in the 6th vol. of the Medico-Chirurgical Transactions, p. 450. Dr. Elliotson has also alluded to a case of tetanus in a horse, which recovered under nearly similar circumstances. Med. Gaz., vol. xi., p. 474. It is needless, however, to say that not any remedy has yet been discovered which is uniformly, or even generally, successful in controling the symptoms of this disease.]

heart and brain, and probably the mind had something to do in this business. In another case of locked jaw I gave three grains of opium every quarter of an hour, but the patient died; the opium had no effect, and the muscles were not relaxed by death. On opening him, no pre-ternatural appearances were found. In one case I tried saccharum Saturni, because lead produces paralysis, and as I conceived the locked jaw a disease directly opposite to paralysis; I gave it in pills, and it produced costiveness, and a peculiar sensation: a glyster relieved him, and he was better, and they omitted the pills because he supposed they made him costive, and would not be persuaded to take any more. He was at last seized in the night with a difficulty of breathing, and spasms on the abdominal muscles, which killed him. In this case I lamented that the lead could not be continued. The ol. animale has been tried, unsuccessfully.

I attended another patient in England, with Sir N. Thomas. Assafœtida and opium were given without effect; these were left off, and bark given in large quantities. Dr. Warren being called in, advised, among other things, a bath prepared of milk and water. After this he seemed better, but died soon after.

I discovered, to my amazement, the different modes of different physicians. Sir N. Thomas had read much, and knew all the antispasmodics from the days of Hippocrates downwards. Dr. Warren having just cured his son of locked jaw, implicitly followed the same practice in this case, being unable to alter his rules of practice in the smallest degree, as occasion might require.

CHAPTER XXI.

OF SCROFULA.

Symptoms well marked, and usually easily distinguished;—a specific disease, but without a morbid poison;—appears to have a sedative quality;—not confined to man ; —certain constitutions most susceptible of it ;—certain parts most liable to its attacks ;—certain ages also ;—not proved to be hereditary ;—climate a predisposing cause;—and season ;—immediate causes numerous.—Inflammation of scrofula ;—suppuration ;—pus ;—ulceration ;—cicatrization ;—difference according to the nature of parts. —Disease of the hip.—Lumbar abscess.—White swelling.—Consumption.—Scrofulous testicle ;—scrofulous breast ;—distinguished from cancerous testicle and breast.—Cure of scrofula ;—warm climate ;—medicine ; — sea-bathing ;—regimen ;—local applications ; — surgical treatment.

Scrofula is so well marked, and has so many characteristics, that few can mistake it; yet I suspect there are three diseases which have a great affinity to it, viz. spina ventosa, exostosis, and rickets. The first seems to be a pure case of scrofulous suppuration in bones ; the two last to be only varieties of scrofula. Scrofula is to be classed as a specific disease, but not as a poisonous one. It has, in a degree, the power of making neighbouring parts sympathise, by continued sympathy. It seems to have resident in it a sedative quality, as the disease goes on without any increased action, and from there being no adhesive inflammation. The pus which is formed passes along the interstices of the muscles, and is there even incapable of irritating.

Other animals, besides the human subject, are liable to it, and probably from the same causes ; thus, we find a disease very similar to it in young turkeys, and also in monkeys, and I had once a young boar which died of a similar disease; that is, it had swelled lymphatic glands almost everywhere, and thickenings of the joints, like white swellings : but every constitution is not equally susceptible of it, although probably every constitution is more or less susceptible of it. In some there is peculiar susceptibility, so as to have it produced by a slight immediate cause ; but this susceptibility is lost by age. So, likewise, some parts are more susceptible of it than others. Those most susceptible of scrofula are the delicate, who cannot bear much fatigue or cold without being affected, who are very irritable, and cannot bear strong impressions, as of mercury, who are of irritable minds, light-haired, and of fair complexions. In fair people there is a more languid circulation than in dark, and they would appear to have less red blood. When it attacks after the age of puberty it seems not so much confined to colour. When it attacks dark people I think they have a thin skin. Every part has in some degree its specific disease, and this disease has its parts. Some parts are even disposed to it without the above causes, even by the slightest accident. 1st. The lymphatic glands, particularly the superficial, and those most exposed, as those of the neck and lungs, which last may be reckoned external. As the office of these glands seems to be for giving passage to the absorbents, with their contents, it might be supposed it was only dependent on absorption; but as this is a specific disease, and not confined to these parts, we must look for another cause, and then too the lymphatic vessels might be supposed subject to it; which they are not; hence these glands must have some specific properties rendering them liable to it. Joints also are particularly liable to it, and especially those of the feet and hands, from their having so many joints, with ligaments and tendons. The elbow and knee come in next, and sometimes the hip and shoulder, and frequently the vertebræ. In short, every part is subject to it, but no part more than another, except the above mentioned. The skin has less disposition to it than any other part, for the skin will resist the neighbouring disease for a long time.

Although all ages under the above circumstances are in some degree subject to it, yet youth is more particularly so, for beyond the age of fifteen the disease is less frequent, although it will occur from that period up to forty; few cases, however, occur above forty-six. In youth it principally attacks the lymphatic glands; at a later period, the testicle; and the same thing happens in other animals.

I do not think that scrofula can be proved to be hereditary, for if we compare the number of scrofulous subjects who have, and who have not scrofulous parents, we shall find them pretty nearly equal. I have known many families where it has arisen spontaneously, the parents or predecessors having never been subject to it; and on the other hand, I have known parents who have had it, and their children have perfectly escaped. It certainly often runs in families, but only when the natural predisposition and immediate causes are present: fair delicate children will probably have it by the influence of climate. An hereditary disease should act universally; it should pass to all the descendants of a diseased parent; to the dark as well the fair complexioned; to the old and young, and in all countries and climates alike. The children may have the predisposition, but this does not come up to the meaning of hereditary disease. It is only the predisposing cause which can be hereditary. It is hereditary for people to be born with lymphatic glands, but it is not necessary for people to be born with them diseased. Probably a susceptibility of peculiar irritations may be hereditary, as we see in families with regard to smallpox, &c.; but this is an infectious disease. The weak and delicate are incapable of supporting the changes of temperate climates : the most delicate go into this disease, and the parts most subject to it are those which are the most delicate. Climate may be considered both as an immediate and a predisponent cause ; the different kinds of weather, as damp and cold, seem to be the great disposers to the disease; however, in cold climates, where there is most constant dryness, it is less frequent. That irregularity of cold and moisture is one of the greatest disposers to it, is evident, from its never happening in warm climates; but the inhabitants of warm climates coming into cold ones often become affected with it. Some parts of the same country are more subject to it than others, which is also the case in other diseases, as agues, consumption, &c. The animals of warm climates often die of indurated lymphatic glands when brought to cold ones, as turkeys, the joints of their toes being first affected, in a similar manner to white swellings. The disease which is called the pip in fowls is also the scrofula.

The seasons likewise have considerable effect; for, indeed, they may be said to form temporary climates in some parts of the earth. Thus, in summer the disease is less frequent than in winter, and often that which is produced in winter is carried off by summer. But the regular cold of winter does not affect these people so much as spring, for the spring disturbs the constitution, and rouses parts disposed to scrofulous action similarly to a slight fever. The autumn has the same effect as the spring, but not so powerful. Every unnatural affection of the constitution has the power, in some degree, of calling forth scrofula; but the disease is never an act of the constitution. Though there is constantly a constitutional susceptibility, its effects are always local. It is a constitutional local susceptibility.

Scrofula appears spontaneously to arise up every day, the susceptibility in some being so strong that by the simple continuance of the immediate predisposing circumstance (climate) they fall into it, without any other immediate cause. The immediate causes are many. Everything capable of producing unnatural actions in a part is capable of exciting scrofulous action where the susceptibility exists : thus, the fevers of smallpox, measles, and chickenpox often produce it. The lues produces scrofulous buboes; the irritation of mercury in curing the lues produces nodes; cold also produces it, principally in the glands of the lungs or neck; and strains, gout, and rheumatism often leave the affected parts in a scrofulous state. These causes are more violent than that of climate, and produce the disease usually from a pretty considerable irritation, attended with the inflammation arising from the accident, combined with that of the specific kind; but the swelling soon becomes indolent, so that it does not soon get well, and if opened, the sore is still not healable. We should therefore avoid opening it as long as possible. The true scrofula seems attended with little or no inflammation; or if it is so, its sedative quality prevents it from producing pain; but when there is less of the true scrofula, it may give pain; however, it is attended with many of the effects of inflammation, as extravasation of coagulable lymph, producing swelling and also adhesion of the cellular membrane, or of the sides of circumscribed cavities. I have seen the whole of the intestines adhering to the peritoneum, seemingly from a scrofulous cause, and having scrofulous tumours and suppurations in them also: the symptoms were tightness in the belly, without pain, and costiveness; at other times purging. The adhesions in the lungs of consumptive people are probably of this kind. Their indolence and want of pain led me to suspect that scrofula has sedative qualities which it gives to the matter, which does not irritate the parts unconnected with the disease. Where the inflammation is visible its colour is of a purplish red, which is a proof of a languid circulation.

The progress of scrofula is commonly very slow, but sometimes the lymphatic glands swell considerably in one night; but then there is a quick and immediate exciting cause, such as cold or fever, in which case there is common inflammation joined with the specific, which soon leads to suppuration, although after the phlegmonous inflammation is gone off it becomes truly scrofulous. The swelling at first is interstitial, but after some time there appears to be a change of structure, as in the lymphatic glands, the testis, and more particularly the bones, the whole bony structure of which is absorbed, so as to leave nothing but a true scrofulous deposit, similar in appearance to a scrofulous gland. When in the extremities of the joints, the part in view is thickened, with little pain; this is principally seated in the ligaments; the joint looses its motion, and the whole limb becomes weak and wastes away.

Scrofulous suppuration is very imperfect if it is truly of this kind, and there is often none at all. The extreme parts may lose their life entirely; yet they do not mortify, but form a curdly matter, similar to that in encysted tumours. This want or loss of life, if there was no specific action, would cause inflammation, as other dead parts would; but scrofulous parts are incapable of this stimulus. Many scrofulous tumours suppurate and ulcerate, especially when near the skin; but this is not entirely the suppuration of the original disease, but from the inflammation of the neighbouring parts. The matter, like common matter, is often a mixture of pus with coagulable lymph, which last is often most in quantity; it is a kind of glairy and often a curdly matter, being a mixture of the solid parts which are dead with the vitiated secretion. The ulceration is generally very slow, and when near the skin is often stationary, even after the appearance of redness; sometimes it will remain in this state for several months, with a broad surface, not coming to a point, the skin assuming a shining purplish hue; but there is no absorption of the matter, as is generally supposed, from the scrofulous indolence. It seldom happens that granulations form, the sore remaining months, and sometimes years, without any. When formed, they look transparent, as if loaded with water, and have little power of contraction. The cicatrization is as slow as the other processes, from the essential and leading steps to it being backward. The skin around loses its natural elasticity, and so does not give to the contiguous granulations a skinning disposition.

To describe the appearance of scrofulous tumours and sores is impossible, but we can easily distinguish them by sight. A scrofulous swelling generally begins in one of three ways: first, by a circumscribed tumour; secondly, by a more diffused tumefaction; thirdly, by suppuration, without any tumefaction. These all frequently appear in the same person at once. The first is seated in the lymphatic glands, and assumes this form from the part being circumscribed, and also because the parts do not give the stimulus by contiguous sympathy to the adjoining dissimilar parts; but there are some which seem scrofulous, and yet are not in the lymphatic glands. These I have called tumours; as, for example, those in the uterus, the breasts, &c. Of the second kind are scrofulous joints, and the diffused swellings on the skin, toes, fingers, hands, and also on the testicle; although, when the whole testicle is affected, it is generally circumscribed. Of the third kind are certain loose bags of matter, without any tumefaction to distinguish them, although near the skin; these are often pretty deep, and therefore are adapted to the parts they are in. There is no true adhesive inflammation in these cases, when they occur in true scrofulous habits. In the breasts it begins like a scirrhus, and is sometimes taken for one; but it has no pain, and is so gradual in its growth that it produces no tumour in the axilla, so that it may be safely removed. In the testicles it often goes off and returns again. The second kind, when near the skin, often ulcerates, and hollows the skin by the cellular membrane, giving way more readily than the skin; so that when suppuration comes on, the swelling does not subside, as in other cases. When in a bone, it is generally very slow, and the matter consists of a curdly substance. If the bone is dead, exfoliation is very slow, and in such cases the bone is eaten away by the exfoliations, as we mentioned when on the subject of exfoliations; that is, the absorbents of the surrounding granulations take it up.

The different appearances in scrofula will vary according to the nature of the part, and to these we have given different names: scrofula in the joints we have called white swelling; in the loins, lumbar abscess; in the lungs, consumption; in the hip, hip-case. Some of these are not suspected to be scrofulous. When it attacks particular parts, it produces symptoms peculiar to the part; but in some parts which are not very necessary to health, it is not easily discovered. If the extremities are attacked, we find a lameness; and if a joint, a wasting of the limb. When it attacks visible joints, it is in general easily known; when it attacks the knee, it has commonly true inflammation conjoined with it, probably from its being frequently excited by accidents.

Disease of the Hip.—In most cases of lameness, or wasting of the lower extremities, the affected limb appears longer than the other, in consequence of the patient pressing most on the sound limb, and putting the diseased one further out from the pelvis, so as to raise the ilium. This is particularly the case in diseases of the hip, although the leg is not found to be longer than the other, if the patient is laid on the back. It arises from the centre of motion in the pelvis being rather altered by habit, which is removed if laid on the back. But sometimes, when the muscles are much wasted, the limb is shorter, which I cannot account for, nor why the limb is sometimes drawn up more, and sometimes put out further than the other. Mr. Cline says the limb is actually longer and shorter in different stages of the disease, and accounts for it thus: in the first instance, inflammation takes place in the ligaments of the joints, occasioning the parts to swell, and a larger quantity of synovia to be accumulated in the joint, which displaces and pushes out the head of the femur, thus occasioning a lengthening of the limb; but as the disease advances, absorption takes place, not only of the accumulated synovia, but also of the bone itself, with the surrounding ligaments; and the head of the bone being drawn into the new enlarged cavity, by the action of the gluteus and other muscles, occasions a shortening of the limb; and this lengthening and shortening of the limb is peculiarly evident on laying the patient on the belly. The glands in the groin of the affected limb become enlarged, from absorption of the matter. The first appearance of scrofula in the hip is announced by a weakness in the limb, followed by a wasting; but sometimes there is a thickening of the surrounding parts before suppuration comes. It is

sometimes difficult to distinguish it from lumbar abscess, which I shall
next proceed to speak of.

Lumbar Abscesses.—The mode of their coming on evidently proves
them to be scrofulous: lumbar abscess comes on almost insensibly, but
sometimes the patient can remember a pain in the part, a pain on the
knee, or a pain on the outside of the thigh, leading to the foot. These
are often called growing pains, which shows that the disease is affecting
other parts; which symptoms, arising from sympathy, are often more
severe than the original disease. The progress is often so slow, that
the weakness is frequently not apparent even when matter is approaching the surface, as on the thigh or loins. It often arises or is caused by
injuries, as strains; in which case it is attended with more than usual
sensibility and weakness. Its occasional removal by sea-bathing proves
it to be scrofulous. It seldom occurs after thirty years of age, except
from accident, so that it is most frequently met with in young subjects,
who have other symptoms of scrofula.

White Swelling, in its beginning and progress, is generally similar to
other scrofulous cases; stealing, as it were, upon the part, and occasioning stiffness. There is sometimes a fluctuation with pain, but then
it is not truly scrofulous; the pain is sometimes scarcely perceivable,
but at other times it is considerable. These cases are of two kinds,
one of which is truly scrofulous, the other is only common inflammation, mixed with more or less of scrofula; the latter terminates in adhesion or suppuration. In scrofulous sores on the fingers of children,
the pieces of bone are often destroyed, and come away insensibly, the
finger becoming shorter and alarming the friends, to whom it is necessary that we should explain the circumstance.

Of Consumption.—Most consumptions are of a scrofulous nature,
which is evident from the attending circumstances and cure. They are
very frequent, in this and other scrofulous climates, in the fair and
delicate, and in the young and middle-aged. They come on generally in a true scrofulous way by catching cold. By this the glands in
the neck are enlarged, at the same time that tubercles form in the lungs,
which afford a scrofulous secretion, or are converted into a curdly substance, which in the end ulcerates and opens into the bronchi. Sometimes they occasion pain, and generally a cough, difficult respiration, and
expectoration. The pain is considerable if the immediate cause is violent, as great cold; and the dyspnœa and cough will be according to the
degree of inflammation. The spitting varies according to the inflammation, being at first mucous, but after ulceration is formed purulent.
The patients generally die; but as all consumptions are not scrofulous,
we should distinguish them. The diagnosis may be formed by the vio-

lence or mildness of the attack; by the slow or rapid progress of the disease; by the degree of pain in some one part, and by the hardness and quickness of the pulse, &c. Spitting of blood, which is sometimes violent, at other times trifling, is not always followed by a consumption. Does this bleeding arise from a disease in the lungs, or from a small vessel giving way ? I cannot answer this question; but this I know, that such symptoms often precede a consumption. If the lungs are affected, the symptoms will arise from the functions of the part being impeded, as difficult respiration. When we examine consumptive people after death, we generally find a true scrofulous appearance; and as it is clearly scrofulous, it admits only of one mode of cure, which strengthens the opinion of its being scrofulous. The physicians here keep their patients as long as they can, and then send them away to Bristol and other places to die. But, if we see the symptoms pretty early, and consider it as scrofula fallen on parts which are essential to life, we should not trifle with it as with a finger; we should send them to a warm climate at once, or near to the sea-side; for bathing and short voyages tend much to cure scrofula, and consequently to cure consumption. Bleeding, however, is often necessary, to proportionate the quantity of blood to the quantity the lungs are able to circulate; otherwise bleeding is very injurious, as tending to produce greater weakness, when already great delicacy exists.

Of the Scrofulous Testicle.—The testicle is the next part in order of susceptibility for the disease, and when so affected has been often supposed to be cancerous. Scrofulous testicles begin without any visible cause, are slow in progress, and are often cured by sea-bathing; when they suppurate, the suppuration is scrofulous. I have seen them in lads of sixteen years of age, but never sooner; from whence we might think that they are not scrofulous. They are seldom seen in old people; for as the action of the testicle before and after puberty differs, its diseases probably differ also.

Of the Scrofulous Breast.—I have only seen one truly scrofulous breast, which came on at the age of twenty-six, and increased gradually to thirty-eight. It was sixteen or eighteen pounds in weight. In this case there was no disease leading to the axilla, as in cancer; so that I dissected it out, and it healed kindly, although the patient had other scrofulous appearances at the time. It was perfectly circumscribed, which is never the case with cancer, when of any size. Cancer may be so at first, when small and loose in the cellular membrane; but when as large as a large egg, it affects the surrounding parts, and is more diffused. True scrofula, however, if attended with inflammation, will also adhere, and diffuse and lose itself in the surrounding parts, so as to put on a cancerous appearance.

Diagnosis between Scrofula and Cancer in the Testicles and Breasts.— A cancerous testicle affects the absorbents going from the testicle and the spermatic cord; but I do not think that this is universal, since we sometimes find the cord unaffected, but in scrofula it is never enlarged or affected at all. The distinction, however, in some cases, is very difficult. As we operate in cancerous cases because the cord is sound, so we must often do so in scrofulous cases which have no cancerous disposition. In the scrofulous breast we have no thickening leading to the axilla, or in the axillary glands, but in cancer they are thickened from continued sympathy; and this is, perhaps, the best criterion.

From the circumstance of the cancerous disposition spreading by what I call continued sympathy, the surrounding parts being contaminated and taken in with the original disease, the skin in all these parts takes on the same disease with the cancer; but in scrofula it does not do so strongly : therefore when a cancer breaks it spreads, but in scrofula the skin seems rather to have a disposition to heal.

Of the Cure of Scrofula.—The remedies must be directed both to the constitution and to the part affected ; but if we had a specific medicine, then attacking the constitution alone would be sufficient, as it is in the venereal disease. As to external parts, the only certain cure is extirpation, and this is very confined and is often improper, because the parts frequently get well of themselves; still we are often obliged to have recourse to this means. Internal medicines have very little power: they cannot alter the constitution of fair people, or prevent the effects of climate, or change the disposition of parts ; neither can they make young people old. They can only lessen the susceptibility of the constitution, but do not reach the cause; hence there will soon be a relapse, if they are discontinued, climate being often of itself an immediate cause of the disease.

We can sometimes affect the constitution by changing the climate; but changing the climate will not always effect a cure, for when vital parts are affected it is seldom done till too late. Change of climate is equally necessary in other cases as in tubercles of the lungs, these all depending on the same constitutional disease. Scrofulous patients should go towards the south, or near the sea-side, or take short voyages. Sea-bathing in consumption appears tremendous, but it should be adopted in a warm climate. When these means cannot be complied with, strengthening remedies are useful, as bark and cicuta, with cold bathing ; but these have no specific effects. Mezereon seems to have great power in the cure of this disease: a man with a very large swelled elbow, which appeared to be scrofulous, (although he had more pain than is usual in scrofula,) had been under a course of mercury for a venereal affection when the swelling came on; he rubbed it with a liniment composed of acetum scillæ, but with no advantage: he was then directed the mezereon decoction, and soon recovered the motion and natural figure of the arm. The cure was completed in twelve days, without any sensible effects from the medicine or the liniment, which he continued to use. A woman with enlarged lymphatic glands of the neck, which did not subside as usual with warm weather, I cured by mezereon. I gave it in the following manner: mezereon root, one ounce; water, six quarts; liquorice root, half an ounce. Boil down to four quarts. Half a pint to be taken twice a day, or as much as the stomach will bear.

Sea-bathing seems to have the greatest specific power. In general it is used in summer; but the disease requires it most in winter. It is to be considered in two lights: first, as a simple bath; secondly, as to its specific quality. Baths are of three kinds: cold, warm, and tepid; the specific effect being the same, whatever may be the temperature. When other diseases attend scrofula, for which baths of certain temperatures would do harm, the sea-bath should be regulated accordingly. In some constitutions a different degree of warmth is suitable from what is suitable in others. In some cases two good purposes may be answered, for in some the cold and specific are both wanted, and in others the tepid and specific. The directions for sea-bathing are in general insufficient, but they should be particularly attended to, as with some the cold bath will disagree, independently of all disease; some will be rendered cold all day by it, though they will recover by its specific effect, which is always the same in all constitutions. I do not think that the sea-bath lessens permanently the susceptibility to the disease, but that it is a temporary cure for the present diseased action, and prevents the effect of immediate exciting causes; but after leaving it off, the susceptibility returns, and the disease often returns in winter after a summer course of bathing. Next to sea-bathing and mezereon, hemlock seems to have the greatest specific power. Burnt sponge has been recommended, but I am in doubt of its specific powers. Mineral alkali is serviceable, but its specific powers are very weak.

Warm clothing, and that next the skin, is most proper, because it keeps the warmth constantly the same. This is Nature's method in the cure of animals, and it should be particularly attended to in children: the outward clothing may be according to people's fancy. Children of this disposition should never expose their naked feet to cold and wet, as is frequently the case. The exercise should be gentle, and the diet principally of a vegetable kind; but I consider this of little service, as the disease is frequent in those countries where little else but vegetable diet is eaten.

From the indolence of scrofula we might *a priori* think that many local applications would be serviceable, especially those of a stimulating kind; but these all prove injurious, as mercury, copperas, balsams, &c.: indeed, few applications are of any service. I have myself only found benefit from cicuta and sea-water. The juice of hemlock made into a poultice is serviceable after suppuration has come on; and poultices made with sea-water have done good, when the cicuta has failed, especially in white swellings, before suppuration has taken place; and I may also mention that this water, as a lotion, applied to sores, often gives them a healing disposition.

The best surgical treatment for those cases which will not admit of removal, is to do nothing. Where suppuration is superficial, openings into the abscess should not be made, as they are often absorbed spontaneously, and when they break of themselves they heal the soonest; but exceptions may arise, as when an opening is required to extract an exfoliated bone; otherwise openings only add to the causes which produce such diseases. Those parts which cannot be removed, as lumbar abscesses, are generally incurable; and the question is, are they to be opened or not? The only answer I can give is, that before opening them patients are generally pretty well, but immediately after opening them they become unhealthy and hectic, which continues till death. Hence the practice of opening them shortens life; but sometimes they get well by this practice, that is, perhaps, about one in a hundred: and it may be thought right to treat all as if they were curable, as we cannot distinguish: this must be left to the surgeon and the particular circumstances of the case.

The common effects of surgical treatment will not be found to arise in cases of scrofula: cutting always does harm. In common indolent abscesses, free openings is the best remedy, and the production of as much violence as we can; but this will not do in scrofula and cancer. In scrofula, irritable inflammation frequently supervenes, or erysipelas extending to the cellular membrane, and producing sloughing; for we find that no violence can increase the restorative action without also increasing the original disease. We find few actually die from the disease, although the vital parts are attacked. When the lungs are affected, it is the difficulty of the respiration which kills; when the mesenteric glands are affected, death happens from the want of nourishment; when there is lumbar abscess, the constitution is worn out by long-continued discharge and teasing complaints; but when superficial parts only are affected they generally get well. Accident produces many visible causes of cure, as fevers, &c.; and probably many invisible ones too. Climate is often a cure as well as a cause of the disease. Children are most favourably situated for a cure, from the daily variation of their constitutions. Puberty often produces a cure, which may be called the natural, and is most manifest in women. When the disease begins at a later period it has not these resources, but is more tedious.

CHAPTER XXII.

OF MORTIFICATION AND CARBUNCLE.

Mortification ;—death of parts ;—accompanied by pain :—with or without inflammation ;—treatment.—Caustics and cauteries.—Carbuncle ;—peculiarity of situation ;—often numerous ;—attacks free livers ;—appearance, progress ;—constitutional and local treatment.

THE effects of life are preservation and action : death is the loss of both. Life may exist in the whole, or only in a part ; but it must always be in a vital part. Other parts may be dead, without affecting materially the machine. The immediate cause of death in a part would appear to be a loss of circulation : this may arise in various ways, but it must be the effect of some cause. Mortification is very different from universal death : the loss of natural life arises from some universal action having taken place, the same structure still remaining ; but it is altered in mortified parts, all is blended in one mass of animal matter, and cannot possibly be injected.

Partial Death, or Mortification, arises from various causes, yet there is probably in all of them some cause which may be called specific. There are many others which may be considered as immediate and remote causes, as happens in gout, which may be produced by many causes, yet the specific cause has a peculiar mode of action in this as it has in other diseases. Mortification is commonly attended with great pain, characterised by burning, and, if it is in view, the stagnation of blood in the vessels always produces a livid colour. The same burning sensation takes place from pressure, if carried sufficiently far to produce mortification, and is familiar in people's heels after lying long in bed. There are two kinds of mortification, one without the other with inflammation. The first arises from causes less visible than the other ; that is, there is no increased action, or sensible heat, although the burning pain is considerable. What the predisponent cause is I cannot tell* : I have suspected something like a spasm of the small vessels, but I cannot be certain : we know spasm will sometimes threaten mortification, as we

* [Later observations have rendered it highly probable that dry gangrene always depends on a more or less complete obliteration of the great vessels : either the arteries or veins, but particularly the latter.]

see in priapism, by which I have seen mortification produced in a dog. When the disposition is present, the action goes on; as we see in sores, some parts being of a purplish hue, and going on in this way, while health is in the other parts. In some of these cases, a part withers and dies, and does not stimulate the living parts, so as to produce separation, for a long time; but I have seen too few of these cases to judge of them accurately. The second kind seems to arise from a change taking place before death. Inflammation seems to be the immediate cause; but this inflammation has two remote causes, of which one is weakness, which is the commonest cause of mortification; but the other, or that which produces carbuncle, is not well known.

Inflammation sometimes depends upon an increased action with increased power of the vessels; but in mortification it must depend on an increased action with diminished power; in all cases where this kind of mortification takes place, we have evidently a deficiency of the animal powers. In young people, mortification is generally preceded by fever; in old by debility; and the weakest parts generally give way first, as the toes. But debility alone does not produce mortification, if there happens to be strength in the part sufficient for the action which is induced: debility, therefore, is only a predisposing cause. We see this in scarifying anasarcous legs, in weakness from accident in weakened parts, in bruises, in frost-bitten parts, or wherever action is produced beyond what the powers of the part or system are able to sustain. But the increased action is not necessarily inflammation; it may be a salutary endeavour of the part to restore itself; which salutary action the powers of the part cannot support, and hence it gives way and dies. When frost-bitten parts are exposed to heat, the debility is increased by the necessary action, which action the strength of the part cannot bear. Heat is congenial to life; but it should be proportioned to the degree of life, otherwise it will increase the debility. On this principle it is that cold air is so serviceable to people weakened by disease. In frost-bitten parts, for example, the living principle is much diminished by the previous cold, and heat must be gradually applied, in proportion to the quantity of life which remains; but as the manifestations of life increase, so should the heat be increased also, otherwise by applying a degree of heat, at once, too great in proportion to the life, the part will mortify, which is invariably the case in man and all other animals; for warmth induces a more than ordinary exertion of the living powers, which may even be so considerable as to destroy the powers themselves. This proportion of power and action should be attended to in many common diseases: as appears from a case which I have already described.

Parts which have been weakened seem much disposed to take on the continued sympathy; and the parts, finding this disposition, become irritable, and are easily inflamed, which inflammation produces death oftener than any specific inflammation. Mortification, however, is neither peculiar to weakened habits nor to accidents; but is often consequent on common inflammation, as in compound fractures. In a state of health the powers are much greater than the action; but when this state does not exist, either the powers or the action must be predominant. Thus in mortification the powers are too weak for the action; but this weakened power is produced by various causes, such as old age, accidents, or erysipelas. The skin of such as take on this irritable action is generally opake, and looks withered even in the young subject.

Of the Cure.—If our principles are just, it will be easy to lay down a rational practice. Practitioners have been conscious of the predisposing cause, which is debility, but not of the immediate one, which is increased action. Hence bark, cordials, wine, &c. have been given, by which an artificial or temporary action has been excited; but this practice produces an increased action, without producing increased powers, and afterwards the debility is greater. Antiseptic substances have also been employed, such, for instance, as preserve dead flesh; but this is very absurd. The local treatment has been equally so: consisting in the application of warm dressings in the wounds made by scarifications; thus stimulating parts, the actions of which were already too violent. This practice might be suitable enough in the first kind of mortification, where death comes on without any increased action or effort. Will anything lessen action, and increase also the powers? Wine will not; bark is the only remedy of this kind we have: other medicines may be given on this principle, but none of them are so efficacious; opium for instance is useful, from lessening the action, but it does not increase the strength: it is, as I have ascertained by experiment, more especially useful when applied to the part than when given internally.

Of Caustics and Cauteries.—The death of a part may be produced by a deficiency or privation of the living principle, and is then called mortification; but it may also be produced by mechanical and chemical causes, as bruises, the actual cautery, or caustics. Too much action will also arise from a violent stimulus, as arsenic, and kill a part, and in proportion to the deficiency of the living principle, the sooner will death be induced: as happens in bruises, in which the cellular membrane sloughs before the skin, though the skin is the part which is most injured. The more vascular a part is the greater is the power of life; hence muscles, glands, skin, &c. difficultly part with their life; whilst bones and tendons soon die by exposure, from want of living power to support the necessary inflammation. The actual cautery coagulates the juices, in consequence of which the living principle cannot exist. When caustic alkali is combined with animal or vegetable substance, the compound forms a kind of soap which is soluble in water. The operation of a caustic is not immediately on the living principle, but chemical; but its effects are retarded in some measure by the living principle, so that it acts more rapidly on some parts than it does on others. As no substance acts chemically till in solution, the caustic must first be dissolved, which is slowly effected by the perspiration on the skin. By the application of a caustic, a blister is raised, and serum accumulated, which dissolves a greater quantity of the caustic; and this effusion is the consequence of all irritations, and is intended to get rid of the cause of irritation. Alkalis are in many cases to be preferred, although from their ready solubility they are disused in some cases. Their action is so very expeditious that the presence of the surgeon is required: they ought, therefore, only to be used in superficial abscesses, as they give much pain and spread, and would take up too much of the surgeon's time when the parts to be destroyed are deeply seated.

The caustic alkali, or lapis infernalis, should have its end wetted with water previously to its being applied to the living part; as soon as it is through the cuticle, the cutis effuses serum, which should not be allowed to extend beyond the intended slough, but should be wiped off with an armed probe. It is impossible to say what time will be necessary for this effect, as it will depend on the thickness or depth of the part; but when a very long time is necessary, we may scarify the upper part so as to quicken its effects; and this I may observe is a very ready way of opening superficial abscesses, when near the skin. When we make an issue in this way, we should go as low as the cellular membrane. The common caustic consists of caustic alkali and quick lime, which should be mixed with soft soap, or with liquid caustic alkali, if its powers require to be increased; the concentrated acids are likewise employed, as for example the vitriolic and nitric, which should be applied, like the caustic alkali, by means of a piece of glass, or some other substance which will not be acted upon. The metallic salts are chiefly employed to destroy luxuriant granulations, as blue vitriol, lunar caustic, &c.; but if they are used to produce a deep slough, they must be used in powder, mixed with some soft substance. These last substances only coagulate the parts, but do not chemically combine with them, as the alkalis do. Arsenic seems to have both a chemical and a poisonous effect upon the living textures.

Now as most parts are capable of communicating their sensations to the brain, the gradual destruction which caustic occasions produces considerable pain. This may be alleviated by mixing opium, or extrac-

tum thebaicæ with the caustic, or by the application of an opiate plaster
an hour or two before the caustic, which will have a very good effect,
especially in women and children, who cannot well bear the caustic long
enough to produce its proper effects without these alleviations*. A
long while generally elapses before we can bring a cut issue to a proper
degree of suppuration, as the means which are employed for keeping it
open prevent a good suppuration, by keeping up inflammation; but
caustic seems to answer better, by destroying a certain quantity of substance, which separates in the form of an eschar, and leaves an open
sore that will generally suppurate freely. In some the eschar is slow
in separating; in others it will be thrown off in about ten days; but in
others it will require three weeks, the separation being always more
rapid when the caustic goes fairly into the cellular membrane, which
has less life than the cutis.

The separation of a dead part from a living is performed by the absorbents, which take into the circulation the edges of the sound parts
which adjoin to the dead, and thus the dead part being set at liberty
drops off. But in order to effect this, inflammation is first produced, and
then ulceration or absorption follows. The separation takes place sooner
or later, in proportion to the life of the part; hence the skin, muscles,
and parts which are nearest the heart, slough readily; tendons and bones
slowly; and cellular membrane less readily than the skin. Life in a
part is in proportion to the number of vessels it has for its simple support, the vessels for other purposes not adding to its powers of life, considered in itself. In new-formed parts, however, the separation is not
so slow as in original parts, although they are disposed to slough
more readily; but this depends on a different principle, viz. on weakness,
which is consistent with what has been already observed. How far the
brain is capable of sloughing I cannot determine, but I should imagine
that people would never live long enough for this process to take place.
In vegetables we find dead parts rot; but they are not separated as the
dead parts of animals, because they have no absorbents; but if they separate, they do so by a process of putrefaction.

Soft parts, when about to slough, first become darker coloured, and
if exposed to the air become dry and hard. The separation always begins at the external edge, forming a groove between the living and dead
parts; this groove becomes gradually deeper, till at last it is quite

---

* [Nothing is so effectual for alleviating the pain occasioned by potassa fusa as the
application of common vinegar, which immediately combines with the alkali to form a
neutral salt. It possesses also another advantage, in restraining the operation of the
caustic, which in some instances is very apt to spread beyond the assigned limits.]

through, and the slough drops off. Why the separation should begin at the surface I do not know, except that the external parts are more ready to take the alarm, or that the skin goes through its operations and separates more rapidly than the cellular membrane; but as we find in bones that the exfoliation always begins at the external edges, I cannot offer the above as an explanation. Its beginning from the edge makes the separation at first only from the circumference, but sometimes it is from the centre, as when matter is formed underneath.

The separation of which I have been treating is of two kinds; first, where the cause is constitutional, as in mortifications; secondly, where it is local, as by caustic. To the first kind of separation much attention is to be paid, as the mortifying disposition must cease before the part already mortified can be removed. When the separation is begun, if the parts are small, they may be allowed to go on their own way; but where it is a whole limb, it is necessary to remove it, as the length of time required for the separation would often wear out the patient's constitution. The when and the where this is to be done is a matter of great importance. We should certainly remove the bulk of the mortified limb; but as there is danger of inflammation and fresh mortification being brought on, from cutting the living parts, even though the mortification should be stopped, from the constitution being mended, we must wait till we see a healthy line of separation, and, by the appearance of the granulations, judge of the propriety of amputation. I would recommend removing the part in mortifications of the leg, by cutting into the dead parts near to the living; and after a time, if it be necessary (which can only happen in the legs), the irregularities can be removed. In sloughs from caustic, practitioners used to cut out the eschar; but as a part remains which requires the same length of time to separate as the whole, nothing is gained by this proceeding.

Carbuncle, or *Anthrax*, is an inflammation of a specific kind, which is shown by its regular termination. It may in some measure be reckoned a cutaneous disease, commonly beginning in the skin. The mortification which takes place in the parts succeeds inflammation; yet it does not always arise from inflammation, attended with general debility; nor does it always take place in the weakest parts, as the foot, but commonly near the source of circulation. That there is some peculiarity in the constitution, is perfectly evident, from the patient being apparently otherwise well, with a good pulse. It seems to be a specific effect of this inflammation to produce death in the part. It most frequently appears on the back or the neck, and seldom in the fore part of the body, which is very singular. Carbuncles seldom come alone; but seldom more than one begins at the same time, but in succession: I have seen them extend over the whole back. .Another peculiarity is, that they seldom attack any but those who have lived above par, especially in eating; in which respect they resemble gout,. as well as in the circumstance that they are generally inclined to occur in fat people. I suspect that any irritation, applied to those in whom there is this peculiarity of constitution, brings them on ; therefore to an elderly man of this disposition I am cautious of applying blisters. The inflammation is in the cellular membrane, and though very similar to the erysipelatous, is yet very different. It does not produce adhesive inflammation, but runs into mortification, as the. erysipelatous does ; neither does it produce true suppuration. At first it appears like a pimple or smallpox pustule, in the cutis, the matter of which would seem to penetrate to the cellular membrane, and affect it; but perhaps the disease itself extends to the cellular membrane in the first place, although the first idea is most probable, as there is no adhesive inflammation to prevent that being the case. The tumefaction is considerable, but flat: the cells being filled with pus, mixed with coagulable lymph. The matter approaches to the skin by ulceration ; or if very tight, it mortifies. The matter oozes from several openings, like water out of a sponge. ' At last, in most cases, the cellular membrane dies, and the ulceration in the skin extends. Sometimes the whole sloughs off together,·leaving a wide chasm, with inflamed lips. When suppuration takes place, there is continued sympathy in the surrounding contiguous parts, and then the inflammation becomes more of the adhesive kind. The local peculiarities are as follow : 1st, it begins like a pimple ; 2ndly, the inflammation spreads a little, giving it the appearance of a boil; 3rdly, the inflammation spreads under the skin, and a doughiness takes place, the skin itself not being much affected, the tumour having a defined edge, and being six or seven inches perhaps in diameter. The skin now becomes affected, beginning at the first point of the disease, and spreading throughout; little pimples are frequently formed upon it, which often communicate with the cellular membrane beneath. Bounds are at last set to it by the surrounding adhesive inflammation. The practice should be to open it as soon as it begins to form a base, to prevent its spreading further. When it has gone through all its stages the process of cure begins, and it heals as soon as other sores, and one is often healing while others are forming.

Boils, I suspect, are all of the carbuncular species, but less in size, with more of the adhesive inflammation, which prevents their spreading. Boils have another distinction, which is, that they seldom produce suppuration equal to their inflammation ; and, as in carbuncle, there is produced a visible slough, so there is a core in boils which answers to the slough. When boils are very large the constitution is in fault, but not so when few and small; they are then supposed to be salutary. Boils are most frequent in youth, carbuncles in age; yet we find boils in old people; but carbuncles are seldom in people below the middle age.

Treatment of Carbuncle.—As carbuncles begin with a species of inflammation, which terminates in mortification, the patient being generally of a full habit and in apparent health, it might be asked if the constitution should not be treated by evacuants. I would treat it always according to circumstances; but in the latter stage I have always found evacuations improper. Evacuations never answer in constitutional specific inflammations, as they do in common inflammations. Bleeding in gout and erysipelas is often very injurious, yet it is occasionally necessary: neither in inflammation from poisons has it a good effect, unless where the constitution is ready to run into violent common inflammation, in addition to that produced by the specific power of the poison; hence, in smallpox, gonorrhœa, &c., bleeding is sometimes useful: but evacuations and bleeding never agree so well with those who have lived above par as in the temperate; hence they are more useful in acute rheumatism than in acute gout. Cordials and bark, and warm medicines, are commonly given, and made more stimulating by the addition of tinctures; and these are given for two reasons; first, because the part is dead; and secondly, because the patient often becomes much debilitated. But such medicines can only keep up the strength and the action depending upon strength, but cannot overcome the specific nature of the disease; therefore we should give others, that we may at last find out a specific; yet, if we had a specific, these remedies would be often also necessary, as they are in lues. I have, however, tried other means, but with little success.

A gentleman, ætat. 70, who had lived well, and had had a universal dropsy, which he appeared to be cured of, was attacked with inflammation on the left shoulder, which turned out to be true carbuncle, which, as soon as it was opened, was followed by several more near the spot. The person under whose care he was gave him one drachm of powder of bark with ten drops of tinct. thebaica every hour, which rather purged him: he also took calomel and opium, the former of which was increased, to see if mercury would do good; but it had no effect; neither did it prevent more from forming. One was very large, and there were several smaller ones in different parts of the back; one was opened pretty early, which seemed to stop its increase, and I opened another at its orifice, with caustic, which discharged the matter, and seemed to stop its progress. The first during this time was healing. When the first appeared he seemed to be in good health, but afterwards he gradually lost it, his appetite became bad, his pulse quick and small, and his ankles a little swelled. As neither bark nor calomel and opium had been of any use, I said to Dr. David Pitcairn, "Now do not let us permit this patient to be lost, whilst we are only using such means as experience shows to be of little or no effect; let us try something new; for, David, this is a case more belonging to my province than yours, and I, being an older man, have seen more of them than you have, and can tell you what perhaps you did not know, that we have no powers in this case that are known." Now David is a truly sensible man, and not governed by form; he therefore agreed, but wanted to know where we were to begin. "Why, with the first letter of the alphabet, and go through the catalogue of the materia medica, so as we do not stop too long on the letter B (Bark), as is generally done." As cicuta was a medicine of considerable powers, and then not thoroughly known, we began with that, of which the patient took half a drachm in the day, but without effect. I then tried sarsaparilla, both in powder and decoction: the powder was made into bread and pudding, to eat through the day, but with no good effect. Dr. Pitcairn now proposed decoction of elm bark, from having seen it of use in erysipelatous inflammation, there appearing an affinity between this disease and erysipelas; this I assented to, but from a thought which had struck me, I wished to try the fossil caustic alkali (soda); so they were given together, and we thought they were of service, as it was during this course that the patient recovered, though it must be confessed it was very slowly; but some fresh ones which had shown themselves disappeared again. I have given fossil alkali to several since with good effect. I was myself always troubled with boils, until I took forty drops of this lixivium night and morning in milk for two months, when all my boils disappeared, and I have since had no return of them. Another gentleman asked my advice on whom two or three carbuncles had begun to appear, and he was perfectly cured by this treatment.

The topical treatment consists in the free dilatation of the skin which covers the sloughing cellular membrane; but as this comes after all the mischief is done, I think it a bad practice at the latter stage, although applications to the part are useless until the slough is separated. Small openings at the beginning, to prevent the increase, is all we should do, and not make any openings afterwards*.

---

* [The practice of modern surgeons is to make free openings in all stages of the disease, for which the best reasons may be given. An escape is thus afforded to the diseased sloughs and secretions, and an opportunity given to apply appropriate dressings to the sore; but the propriety of this treatment chiefly arises from the indisposition of the skin to ulcerate sufficiently extensively to allow the sloughs to come out. See *note*, p. 418.]

CHAPTER XXIII

OF POISONS.

General considerations respecting poisons ;—definition of a poison.—Mine-ral poisons.—Animal poisons, natural and morbid.—Morbid poisons;—their origin ;—effects local, constitutional, or mixed.—Of local diseases.—Itch;—nature ;—cure.—Cancer, definition of ;—origin and progress ;—effects only local ;—does not affect the constitution ;—reasons for this opinion ;—extension of the disease by three modes ;—absorption of the poison ;—does not produce specific fever ;—no proof of poisonous disease of the constitution.—Local effects of cancer ;—predisposing causes.—First appearance and symptoms of cancer ;—progress towards suppu-ration ;—treatment ;—destruction of cancer ;—extirpation ;—mode of effecting it, and cautions to be observed.—Cancerous testicle.—Fungated sores.—So-called cancer of the penis.

No unexceptionable definition of a poison can be absolutely given, for almost everything capable of injuring in a healthy or unhealthy state may be considered as a poison. They are such as destroy either the structure or the functions of an animal. The last may be similar to the weather, which often affects the mind, and may be called a poison of the mind. But there are many substances which, when applied to a healthy state of the body, may injure, as poisons ; yet when applied to an unhealthy state they will counteract that state, and keep up health as long as they have the power of irritation. The healthy action, then, being a *tertium quid* of the unhealthy and poisonous, these are to be con-sidered as medicines which have different effects at different times, and under different circumstances, as food ; sometimes they are capable of cur-ing one diseased state and not another, even of the same specific disease ; indeed, each disease has its own peculiar specific. Many substances act as poisons in some constitutions and not in others ; as muscles, &c. thrown into some stomachs poison them ; also strawberries and cider in some persons cause flushing and erysipelatous inflammation. Whatever our idea of a poison may be, we must generally exclude the idea of quantity, for even the most innocent substances may become poisonous by quantity, as common food. Some cannot eat meat of any kind without being af-fected, but can eat fish or fowl without harm. If we do not pay regard to quantity we cannot distinguish poisons from medicines, as many of our medicines may even be given so as to poison or to produce no effect at all. So vague are our ideas of poison that we do not give the name of poison to all the actions of the same substance when it is formed to act in two different ways, though it may kill in both ways. A man killed by swallowing a piece of glass could not be said to be killed by a poison, because we know its effects; but powdered glass swallowed would irritate the coats of the stomach, and kill, and would hence be called a poison. Many other things might be called poisons, as cold water drunk when a person is hot, producing fever, erysipelatous inflammation, the eruption called a surfeit, &c.

Poison is not only what is taken in by the stomach, but also by the lungs, as mephitic air, which kills immediately, and has no cure; so likewise many applications administered externally are called poisons. Our present idea is that they act in three ways, viz. mechanically, chemically, or on the living principle. The two first always act locally, but the third either on the whole or on a part. We do not call everything a poison which acts mechanically, as swallowing a knife; but we suspect a different mode of action from powdered glass or hair, and therefore call them mechanical poisons, imputing the effects to some hidden power, which is in some measure right, it being their irritating effects on the living principle of the coats of the stomach, not simply cutting and lacerating mechanically as the knife does. These ought not therefore properly to be called mechanical poisons. Melted lead or boiling water will kill chemically, yet cannot properly be said to be poisons. Some only irritate the part, the substance being too weak to have any chemical effect. Nor is everything which acts on the living principle to be called a poison; but we should distinguish between poisons of this kind and medicines; yet we find "a slow poison" is a common saying, as brandy. Arsenic kills by inflaming the stomach, and not by a peculiar action, therefore it is not a poison; nor is anything else which kills by common inflammation or common effects. I would define poison to be a substance which has a peculiar mode of irritating, a peculiar mode of affecting the living principle, and which produces its effects more or less in any quantity, however small. Of this kind are most of the morbid poisons; but smallpox falls short of the definition, in not keeping up its effects after having once affected the same person.

Of the different ways in which Animals may be affected by Poisons.— There are three ways of their acting, and also a mixed way. The *first* is where the poison affects only the part in contact with it, and no part of the general system, except from the local injury. This includes the three kinds of poisons, viz. mechanical, chemical, and those acting on the living principle. Examples of these are glass acting mechanically, sublimate of mercury acting chemically, and the matter of cancer, which acts only on the living principle. The *second* is when the poison affects the constitution, which constitutes it a morbid poison entirely, as, for instance, the jail distemper; but how it gets to the constitution is unknown. The *third* is when the whole nervous system is affected, as by poisoned arrows, honey, muscles, nux vomica, and probably also the bite of a mad dog, which produces no visible effects on the injured part. The *mixed*, or compound, is of two kinds : first, when it produces inflammation of the part, as was observed of cancer and itch, and at the same time affects the whole constitution, as the venereal disease, which the cancer and itch do not. The second is that which has three different modes of contaminating a part, like the third class, viz. 1st, locally, as in the itch; 2nd, like the jail fever, which acts first on the constitution; and 3rd, like the first of the compound, producing local inflammation; of this kind is the smallpox, &c. We might make a fourth out of those in which the poison might be taken into the constitution without producing local effects in the first place, as in jail fever, natural smallpox, &c.; but these are then received by contact, and not by insertion. In some the constitution is unaffected till ulceration has taken place, from knowing which we can often prevent their general effects. How a poison lies inactive so long is with difficulty explained, but it is a principle belonging to each, each having also its own specific latent period before it affects the constitution.

Mineral Poisons.—The mineral poisons are mostly metals, the poisonous qualities of which depend on their solution in our juices; their virulence is often increased by their combination with acids, as, for instance, mercury with the muriatic acid; but they can poison either by affecting the living power, or by acting chemically; chemically when strong, and by irritating when diluted. Minerals are capable of acting in the three different ways; when mechanically, it might be supposed to be by altering the composition or arrangement of the animal fibre, so as to injure without destroying the living principle: but such cannot properly be called poisons. They may act chemically by combining with animal substances, as the vitriolic and other acids, and caustics. When they act on the living principle without seeming to alter the part to which they are applied, they are probably absorbed, and excite universal irritation, as, for instance, lead and mercury, which, when given too largely, seem to have this property; but each of these will kill by their action on the stomach. I know of no mineral poison that produces universal sympathy when locally applied, except it is applied to the stomach.

Most of them produce peculiar complaints, as we see from lead, mercury, arsenic, opium, &c.

The Vegetable Poisons appear to be of three kinds : first, the natural juice of plants without having undergone any secretion ; secondly, the secretions of plants, as honey and the essential oils ; thirdly, those which have undergone a change by a chemical process, as the oil of tobacco. These produce their effects in two different ways, similar to the mineral, viz. chemically, and on the living principle. Their power on the living principle is much more extensive than that of the mineral, and their effects are peculiar and different from those of any other disease, so that they are generally well characterized.

The Animal Poisons act principally on the living principle. Nothing shows the variety of animal matter more than the poisons. The blood may be considered as the fluid animal, because it contains all the parts which compose the animal, and the whole body is composed out of it. The solids which exist already must have the power of decomposing this fluid according to the stimulus of each part, and on that the natural and morbid secretions depend. I shall consider these under the heads of natural and morbid poisons.

1st, *Natural Poisons.*—Many of these first affect the stomach, as some kinds of fish ; others consist of animal secretions, which are produced by particularly formed organs, provided with an appropriate apparatus and ducts, for the especial purpose of secreting and inserting the poison in the bodies of other animals. These secretions do not affect the parts which contain them, although they would probably poison the animal itself if inserted into any other parts than those which naturally contain them, as, for instance, in scorpions, which poison each other, although the Abbé Fontana denies this as to the viper. The second species produce their effects in two ways, by contact or by insertion. Those which affect the skin by simple touch are various, as sea insects, the ant, &c. ; but before the others can possibly operate they must be conveyed into a wound, which brings them to the living principle, on which they will always act under these circumstances, but not when the cuticle is entire ; hence all these animals make a wound before they can act. This second species are all of them very active, producing immediate effects, both locally and constitutionally, otherwise they would not answer their intended purpose, which is the defence of the animal. According to the quantity, they would appear to be more or less violent in their effects, as in small animals the effect is the same in kind, but not in degree, as in a large one ; thus a large one kills, while a small one does not ; the rattlesnake being longer and larger than the common viper, kills much sooner.

Those which poison by the touch, first produce a soreness, and some swelling and inflammation, which latter is of the adhesive kind, although the swelling is generally œdematous. Those which act externally and locally do not occasion swelling at any distance, so that the continued sympathy is not great, as that from the ant. These all appear to have their peculiar distance, unless the effects are increased by rubbing, itching being generally their consequence. Those which become constitutional have also local effects, which, however, are not so fixed as those from the other sort; for in these a kind of continued sympathy exists, and a dissolution of the parts comes on, which produces extravasation of blood, and consequently a dark colour. The first symptom is pain, and if the poison is absorbed there is also a sore red streak, extending to the lymphatic glands, situated between the injured parts and the thoracic duct. The glands also, which are principally in the bend of the great joints, swell, and become painful, showing either absorption of the poison, or that the lymphatic system sympathises. A cold fit often follows, and sometimes convulsions and death in a short time. The injured parts likewise swell, and become dark and livid, from vessels carrying red blood which did not originally do so; but the continuance of the local effects does not arise from the constitution, otherwise similar effects would manifest themselves in other parts of the body. Suppuration of the part to which the poison is applied rarely happens; but by absorption this may sometimes happen, as in common buboes. Effects such as we have been describing are seen in the viper, scorpion, &c. Some insects poison in the act of sucking their food, as the gnat and bug, and these seem to produce specific diseases; that is, they appear not to suck the common red blood from the vessels, but to produce an inflammation, and afterwards suck the extravasated blood from the inflammation which they have occasioned.

2nd, *Of Morbid Poisons.*—These probably arise from a diseased state of the body or part, which originated either spontaneously, or from the application of similar matter from another animal. This is proved by the late origin of all of them. We have many daily arising spontaneously, and which continue their excitement. The cancer is a proof of this, and I once thought the same of hydrophobia; but Mr. Meynell tells me he never had a hound mad but what had been bitten. Some of the morbid poisons are lost, and others are losing ground every day for want of frequent communication: some of these act in a fluid state, and others in a state of vapour. The venereal poison requires contact, and possesses itself of those parts which are most frequently in contact: some affect the secretions so as to make them poisonous, as the saliva in the mad dog. It may perhaps in time happen that the human race shall be extirpated by poisons alone ; but it is more probable that many poisons are extirpated, and that new ones arise in their stead every day. Morbid poisons differ from the natural in requiring a morbid action in the body to produce them, as cancer, which is either the produce of a similar disease, or arises spontaneously. These produce greater variety of effects than the natural, some of which are local, and others both local and constitutional.

Some affect the whole system rapidly, as the variolous matter ; but not so the venereal. Many of them are not content with simply poisoning those people who come within their influence, but communicate it to others, who in their turn are capable of affecting others. Every part of the body is more or less susceptible of being poisoned. The effects of some poisons seem confined to peculiar animals ; as cancer, which occurs only in the human species. Others affect various animals ; as hydrophobia, which attacks horses, cows, dogs, cats, geese, fowls, &c., when they are bit. Others only affect animals of the same species, as the variola. Some appear to choose peculiar ages ; as the cancer, which never occurs in young people. Many choose a peculiar sex, or peculiar parts only are affected by them, some parts being more susceptible of some actions than others : as, for instance, the breast, of cancer ; the skin, of smallpox ; and the salivary glands, of hydrophobia. Both the great and small effects of morbid poisons depend less on quantity than those of the natural do. Some poisons perform their own cure, as in those cases where the constitution is only capable of being affected by them once ; which, as we have no artificial cure, is a happy circumstance. But others seldom or never affect the system in such a manner as to oblige it to discharge the poison. Some perform their own cure, when the mode of their action is on a peculiar part, as gonorrhœa.

Of the Modes of receiving morbid Poisons.—If morbid poisons are applied in a solid state, they must become fluid, by the moisture of the part, before they can act. The manner of receiving them and being affected by them is in three ways : 1st, when the effects are always local and never reach the constitution, as in cancer ; 2nd, when the constitution only is affected, as in jail distemper ; the 3rd, or compound, is when the poison can affect one only or both at the same time, as the lues and smallpox. The first is of two kinds : first, when the patient contracts a poisonous disease, either from known causes, or from violence committed on parts which are capable of running into diseased action and of communicating the same to others, as cancer and lues ; the second is where the disorder is external and local, so as to affect only the cutis, as the itch. The manner of receiving the second, or entirely constitutional, may be either by effluvia or contact. The first, or that by

effluvia, is owing to the air being impregnated with poisonous vapours
arising from the animal body; but how the poison is received into the
constitution is unknown, there being no traces of it before it shows itself by the fever, as in the jail-distemper and hooping-cough. The second of this division of constitutional poisons is the plague, which is
caught by contact; but whether it could or could not be produced by
inoculation is unascertained. The mode of receiving the third, or compound kind, is twofold: first, it differs from merely local poisons, because it seldom acts locally at first, as the variola; for we receive this
disease naturally without knowing it until the constitution is affected.
Secondly, it can affect both the constitution and the part, as the above;
but generally there is local inflammation, and sometimes ulceration,
previously to the constitution being affected, as in lues.

Of the Itch.—This is one of our first class of the first division of morbid poisons, which affect by simple contact and are always confined to
the parts to which they are applied. Scabies never affects the constitution; from which I conclude that it is never absorbed. However it
originated, it is now become a common poison. It produces small ulcerations, which are generally much confined; but when the disease is of
long standing they are as large as a sixpence, and covered with a scab.
First there is a small vesicle, which discharges a kind of matter, which
gradually thickens until genuine suppuration takes place : the matter
which is thus formed produces ulcers of the same specific kind, although its powers of contaminating are evidently weak, as cleanliness
prevents contamination. The irritation of it is scarcely sufficient to produce inflammation, and continued sympathy hardly ever takes place in
it. It gives no pain, but occasions a sense of itching. It is generally
caught by shaking hands, or from lying together, as the lower orders of
people commonly do, who are most subject to this disease. Unclean-
liness aids this effect; therefore washing the hands, even after the matter is on them, prevents the disease from taking place. When it arises
from lying in an infected bed, or from a nurse, it is generally communicated to every part of the body; a fact which gave rise to an opinion
that its origin was derived from nastiness. The disease has been said
to arise from animalculæ; but these, if present, are, I am sure, unnecessary for the existence of the disease, as I have often examined the matter and found no animals in it; yet they may sometimes be in the matter. I forget who was telling me lately that Dr. Teigh had shown them
to be, not in the pustule, but in the skin near it, as little black specks.
It is capable of affecting the cutis when covered by cuticle, but not
where the cuticle is thick. It affects parts thinly covered with cuticle
most, as between the fingers, but often no part escapes, making the cure

very troublesome; for as the cure is effected by local applications, it then becomes necessary that they should be extended over every part of the body.

Although a specific disease and a poison, yet it has several cures, which act in various ways; but all must have powers to remove the irritation of the disease. Mercury often cures and often fails; yet a girdle often will cure when the unguent will not. Solution of sublimate of mercury sometimes cures, as does a decoction of hellebore. A sulphureous unguent is most efficacious; but it is volatilized by the heat of the body, and is disagreeable. If mixed with water, the smell is somewhat prevented; but it is then less efficacious. Sulphur given internally reaches the skin, and produces a smell thereupon, and will then cure; but to produce this effect it must be given so largely that it is apt to prove purgative: opium therefore should be conjoined with it. Sulphur, however, is the only certain remedy; and when properly used, it may be depended on.

Of Cancer.—The diseases commonly classed under this name are in appearance very different, and probably are very different in their nature; they should not, therefore, be called by the same name. I would call that cancer which produces the following effects; viz. a circumscribed tumefaction with much hardness, and a drawing in of the skin covering it, as if the cellular membrane underneath was destroyed: then a species of suppuration takes place in the centre, and ulceration of the external surface. This is its most frequent appearance. It most commonly attacks the conglomerate glands, and first the female breast; also the uterus, the lips, the external nose, the pancreas, and the pylorus; besides which the testicle is very subject to it, though that is not to be classed among the conglomerate glands. So that when I speak of cancer, I mean a peculiar disease in some of the above parts. There is another disease which is also called cancer, which I have called fungated ulcer. The frequency of a disease in any one part is apt to lead us to suspect that this one disease is peculiar to that particular part; but scrofula attacks these parts also, in the form of a tumour, and a distinction between them would be a great advantage, although this probably can only be made in the breast, which is subject to both diseases. When small, they probably cannot be distinguished; but as they increase, the distinction is more easy. If cancer, it will vary its appearance by becoming less circumscribed, not having so determined an outline, from the cellular membrane around becoming diseased; the skin will be less moveable, the nipple more or less retracted, and the lymphatic glands going to the axilla will swell. But in scrofula there will be no surrounding disease, no affection of the nipple or axillary glands, no adhesion, even though the tumour be large; I have seen one loose, when it weighed eighteen pounds; the veins become also enlarged. When scrofulous tumours are large, and become slightly inflamed, they get more diffused, and put on a greater resemblance to cancer; but in cancer the inflammation comes on earlier, and goes on with the disease. In cancer, the surrounding parts that are affected by continued sympathy also become cancerous near the skin, that is, all the parts become blended in one mass; but in scrofula, although the surrounding parts are in action, yet that action is not so scrofulous as the part itself; so that the skin will sometimes heal over the scrofulous tumour, as I have seen in the testicle when suppuration had taken place, by which I determined the disease was not cancerous. The tumefaction is from interstitial extravasation of coagulable lymph, and the tumour is more ready to inflame than in the scrofula. Cancer is one of the first class of our first division of poisons, viz. that which only produces local effects, though it has been supposed to contaminate the constitution; which would be terrible indeed, as we have no specific nor even a palliative for it.

The reasons for this opinion are the following. When a cancerous tumour has been removed often, the sore does not heal, or breaks out again. Sometimes it breaks out again in another part of the body; which has been thought a proof of its arising from the constitution. This last circumstance as often arises where there has been no operation as where there has been one; it does not therefore depend on that circumstance as a cause. However, the operation having or not having been performed does not affect their argument, unless they could prove that cancer is an act of the constitution, and acts as a drain or concentration of the cancerous poison, and that by stopping this it must go somewhere else. But the proportion of those who have it break out in two different parts of the body, compared with those who have it only in one, is about half what the latter bear to those who have not the disease at all, or about five hundred to one. I never saw it in two different parts of the same person; but I have seen it in more than two distinct points of the same part. It often arises in distinct points of the same breast, but seldom at the same period; and some of these may be so much in their infancy when the operation is performed as not to be observable, but afterwards increase and require a second operation.

The surrounding substance of the breast has often little tumours, sometimes containing a blackish fluid; these may be called cancerous hydatids. It is therefore best to extirpate the breast completely at once, to remove the whole complaint. It must further be proved that the continuance of the disease, or contamination of other parts, is not owing to the healing or not healing of the sores. The above reasons for believing it constitutional would satisfy any one not of the profession; but for surgeons to be influenced by them shows an ignorance of the first principles of the animal œconomy. They should recollect that though it affects the neighbouring parts, and the parts through which the poison passes, by sympathy, producing a similar disease, it does not affect distant parts, like those which really affect the constitution. A scirrhus or cancer appears to have three modes of contaminating : 1st, by continued sympathy, which is common to other diseases; 2ndly, by remote sympathy, which is peculiar to itself; 3rdly, by contact, or communication of its matter to other parts by contamination. I have called these consequent cancers, in opposition to the original. Absorption would appear to arise during both stages of the disease : first, by the absorption of the tumour in a scirrhous state, that is, the coagulable lymph, which possesses the cancerous property ; secondly, by the absorption of matter produced by suppuration. Both appear capable of contaminating the absorbents through which they pass, and so far agree with local morbid poisons ; but it may be a compound poison, so as to affect other parts, as smallpox does. Whether it is a compound poison I will leave you to judge from the following remarks on the effects of poisons on the constitution.

Whether a poison be a compound one or entirely constitutional, it first produces a fever that is universal, a specific general irritation ; and, if compound, local irritation also, which local irritation produces a discharge, as in smallpox and measles, the discharge being similar to the original in these, but not so in the venereal disease.

Let us now see how far cancer agrees with these : if it does agree, it must be a compound; if it does not, it must be entirely local. A cancer in the breast or testicle is similar to the inflammation and ulceration after inoculation, or to a chancre, only differing in specific properties. The matter of lues and variola may be absorbed and cause inflammation of the absorbents, and the cancerous matter is also capable of absorption and of contaminating the parts as it goes along, so as to form buboes, or what I call consequent cancers ; so far therefore these diseases are similar. But the above diseases are very quick in their effects, while the cancer is very slow ; and so far their cases are dissimilar. The variolous poison occasions fever and an eruption similar to the original one ; but the venereal poison does not do this, its effects being merely local, consisting of blotches on the skin, &c. ; neither does the cancerous poison when in the constitution produce fever, nor is there any local effect which arises strictly from the constitution. Does cancer then produce any effect on the constitution ?

When it has existed a long time we find slight fever and hectic; but this is no more than the effect of all long-continued irritations, or sores which are not disposed to heal, but no peculiar effect is produced from this affection on the constitution. The effect which has been mentioned is produced even by the venereal poison when of long standing, but it is different from the specific. I have seen locked jaw and difficult respiration produced from a cancer in the breast; but these were occasioned by the irritation of a non-healing sore: smallpox does not produce this hectic. It has been said that cancers are produced by ill health, as rheumatisms are; but this arises from the age of cancer being the age of such complaints, and being thus the predisposing cause of both, but not particularly of the cancerous disposition. Let us compare the cure of cancer with that of the venereal disease, when the latter can be extirpated externally. If we remove entirely a chancre, the sore heals readily and does not return, and if this is done before any absorption has taken place, then there will be no future disease; but if after absorption has taken place, and after a bubo has formed, then, although the sore will heal, the bubo will go on, and the constitution will be affected. So likewise, if we remove a cancer, and no absorption has taken place, the sore will heal and the constitution will not suffer; but then the whole must be removed, as in the local venereal disease, otherwise it will return. If removed, and there has been absorption, the parts heal, though the consequent cancer goes on; but if the whole cancerous parts are removed, the constitution is free: here it differs from the venereal; for there, when absorption has taken place, sores break out in other parts, but this is not the case in cancer. The general opinion has been the reverse of this. This shows that a cure is the consequence of a total removal of the parts, notwithstanding absorption has taken place, if all the diseased parts are removed.

The only powers of contamination of this poison are: 1st, when it spreads from the centre, thus producing a disposition to the disease in the surrounding parts, and an extravasation of interstitial matter; 2nd, when the disease extends to distant parts, as when little tumours form under the skin at some distance, not in the line of absorbents; and 3rd, when it produces the same disease in the absorbents and glands. This last is easily conceived, from its being a poison; but the affection of a part that seems to have no connexion whatever with the diseased part is not so easily accounted for.

When scirrhus is entirely let alone, it is commonly very slow. A small lump in the breast may sometimes continue for many years; but whenever inflammation takes place, its progress is accelerated, in as much as inflammation is an increased action of the part itself, as well as of the surrounding parts; so that if we remove the tumour in this condition, the glands in the breast will probably inflame and sometimes suppurate, although often these effects are not cancerous. When inflamed, the tumour increases very fast, but the sympathy is very slow, which is common in many diseases. When distant parts, not in the line of the absorbents, are affected, it would appear that such parts are very slow in taking on the diseased action, although the disposition has been formed, for we frequently see that they do not take on an active form for some years after. In those cases where there is absorption of coagulable lymph, it becomes a question whether the lymph is cancerous, or whether the affection is only sympathetic: most probably it is the last. The last two forms of the disease are generally very slow, which circumstance makes them dangerous, as it cannot be ascertained when parts are really affected with the disease, which often necessitates a second operation, it being necessary to remove all the parts which have undergone the disposition, although the inflammation or tumour itself is circumscribed.

The predisposing Causes of Cancer are three in number, viz. age, parts, and hereditary disposition; perhaps climate also has considerable effect, though not itself a predisposing cause. The cancerous age is from forty to sixty in both sexes, though it may occur sooner or later in certain cases. The testicle, for instance, often becomes cancerous at twenty or thirty; but then not from the disposition of the parts alone, but from accident*. Cancer has been supposed to be in young people's eyes; therefore it is most probable that the breast is less subject to it at this age, and other parts are not so much confined to age in this disease. We often see tumours in the breast at thirty, and probably some of them are cancerous, although scrofula is more to be suspected. When cancer occurs in the breast of women under forty, it is more rapid in its progress than when the patient is older, and also more extensive; remote sympathy likewise takes place more readily in them than in the old, so that the operation succeeds better in the latter on this account. However, we seldom find it in the young or very old; although of the two it is most frequent in the latter. When it occurs in the young, does it not show a very strong disposition for the disease, and therefore more danger, from a greater likelihood of its returning?

* [The distinction between the various forms of medullary disease and cancer was not well understood in the time of Hunter, and consequently he has classed together several diseases which modern pathologists have very properly separated. It is unquestionably true that cancer may exhibit itself before the age of forty, and fungus hæmatodes after that period: still, as a general rule this does not happen, nor is there any individual fact more characteristic of the difference of these diseases than the different periods of life at which they respectively occur.]

The parts most disposed to Cancer are those peculiar to the sexes, as the breasts and uterus in women and the testicles in men. Cancers are more frequent in women than in men, in the proportion of three to two; owing, perhaps, to the more frequent changes taking place in these parts in the former. It is that change which renders them unfit for conception and changes the whole system, which is particularly obnoxious. Thus, the three disposing causes are: 1st, a peculiar part; 2nd, the age of the patient; and 3rd, the peculiarities of the part at this age. The parts next in order of frequency, and which are common to both sexes, are the conglomerate glands about the lips, nose, throat, tongue, pancreas, stomach, especially the pylorus; intestines, especially the rectum. Besides these, we have it in the eyes and glans penis. The disease also appears in other parts of the body; but, as most other parts are similar in structure, it does not attack one more than another. It sometimes falls on the bones from contamination, but on no one in particular.

Whether Hereditary.—Some suppose cancers to be hereditary; but this I can only admit according to my principles of hereditary right; that is, supposing a person to possess a strong disposition or susceptibility for a particular disease, the children may also; but I have not yet ascertained the generality of this fact. In many persons it would appear that some of the predisposing causes are sufficient to become the immediate ones; as when the diseased action takes place at a certain stated time, without any immediate cause. Are they more frequent in one country than another? I have heard they are very rare in the West Indies; and they do not seem to be frequent in the Friendly Islands, where the women fight for prizes, and aim chiefly at the breast; so, most probably, climate has some power, both in disposing to the disease and in preventing it.

Symptoms.—On the first appearance of a cancer it is a hard tumour, and being specific it is circumscribed, having its specific distance, when it is called scirrhus, which is a cancer not yet ulcerated. Sometimes the first symptom of a cancer in the breast is a bleeding from the nipple, which must come from the ducts of the lactiferous tubes; and this I have seen in men. In the testicle it sometimes begins by forming a hard knot, but is generally more universal. When in the lip, there is a thickening of some part of it, and this increases till ulceration takes place: it comes on similarly in the nose. There is one peculiarity in cancers, which is, that when the skin is affected there is a wrinkling or tucking in of it, which appearance always leads to suspicion of cancer. It often begins in the antrum, and distends the whole face; but I rather suspect this to be of the fungated kind. In the bones it begins by a soft swelling, which I also suspect to be fungated, from its forming such luxuriant fungoid granulations when ulcerated. In the testicle sometimes a softness and even an obscure fluctuation may be felt, although I suspect this not to be cancerous. The pain at first is so trifling as scarcely to be noticed; but when there is a disposition to suppuration and ulceration, a shooting lancinating pain is felt, and also a dead heavy one, which pain increases more in proportion than the disease appears to do. It is more violent in some parts than in others, depending in some degree on the sensibility of the part; thus, it is more violent in the breast and testicle than in less sensible parts. Cancer, however, produces no symptoms peculiar to itself; they are only such as would arise from any injury to the part capable of producing the above effects, independently of any specific quality. Cancer of the lip,.of the nose, or of any other part, will produce no peculiar symptoms; but in the testicle, symptoms peculiar to that part will be occasioned, as, for example, pain in the loins and sickness, with suppression of the secretion of semen; in the bladder, the symptoms will be like those of stone; in the rectum, purging and tenesmus; in the stomach, sickness and vomiting; within the skull, headache and coma. Cancer appears to give rise to no constitutional symptoms, except such as would arise in other diseases from the long-continued wearing pain and perpetual discharge.

The progress towards suppuration is of two kinds: one by external ulceration, the other by the scirrhus becoming encysted. The first happens when the tumour reaches the skin and affects that part with disease, when the skin first becomes shining and then ulcerates and forms a sore which is called a cancer. While this is taking place, inflammation is beginning from internal exposure, and the exposure increases the inflammation. The other mode depends on a change in the substance of the tumour itself akin to suppuration, but which is very different from any other kind of suppuration. The cavity contains a fluid, which fluid appears of various kinds, and in some cases begins very early. In some breasts, where such an encysted tumour has been removed, many small knots are found during the operation, by either cutting through or against them: they often suppurate without any inflammation, therefore there is seldom any inflammation until there has first been exposure. When the matter has been evacuated, common inflammation and suppuration take place, and the disease then proceeds rapidly.

Cancerous matter may be reckoned of two kinds: first, that in the tumour, which is various; in some serum, in some blood, and in others coagulable lymph, or else a yellow curdly matter. The second is of a bad quality, and proceeds from the internal cavity, which is similar in all respects to that formed externally by ulceration. The fluid from a cancerous ulcer is most commonly of a purplish red, which makes the skin of that colour; the absorption here seems to be of the intermediate substance between the skin and cyst. When near to the skin, it inflames and ulcerates as in other ulcerations.

Of the Treatment.—No cure has yet been found; for what I call a cure is an alteration of the disposition and the effect of that disposition, and not the destruction of the cancerous parts. But as we have no such medicine, we are often obliged to remove cancerous parts; which extirpation, however, will often cure as well as we could do by changing the disposition and action. Arsenic seems to have some power of this kind, and its effects might be increased, by being used internally and externally; but its use is very dangerous, and I am afraid insufficient for the disease. This is a remedy which enters into the empirical nostrums which are in vogue for curing cancer; and among which Plunkett's holds the highest rank. But this is no new discovery, for Sennertus, who lived the Lord knows how long ago, mentions a Roderiguez and Flusius, who obtained considerable fame and fortune by such a composition. I was desired to meet Mr. Plunkett, to decide on the propriety of using his medicine in a particular case: I have no objection to meet anybody: it was the young one; the old one is dead, and might have died himself of a cancer for aught I know. I asked him what he intended to do with his medicine. He said, "To cure the patient." "Let me know what you mean by that: do you mean to alter the diseased state of the parts? or do you mean by your medicine to remove the parts diseased?" "I mean to destroy them," he replied. "Well then, that is nothing more than I or any other surgeon can do with less pain to the patient." Poor Woollett the engraver died under one of these cancer-curers: he was under my care when this person took him in hand. He had been a life-guardsman, I think, and had got a never-failing receipt. I continued to call on Woollett as a friend, and received great accounts of the good effects; upon hearing which, I said if the man would give me leave to watch regularly the appearance of the cancer, and see myself the good effects, and should be satisfied of its curing only that cancer, (mind, not by destroying it,) I would exert all my power to make him the richest man in the kingdom. But he would have nothing to do with me, and tortured poor Woollett for some time; till at last I heard the sound testicle was gone, and at length he died.

Arsenic may be given internally with safety. If applied externally to a large surface, it will often affect the constitution, though to a small one it may be safe and efficacious; as, for example, a grain of arsenic to four ounces of water, applied in a poultice twice a day: this will often destroy the cancerous disposition and render the sore more healthy. Sometimes the quantity of arsenic must be increased; and when it gets better, less must be used. When the cancerous disposition is too strong to be removed by this means, we must destroy the parts; and for this there are two modes: 1st, by destroying the life of it; 2ndly, by an operation. The destruction of all the cancerous parts is the intention in both: in destroying locally any specific disease which has the power of its own increase, the whole must be destroyed. That first method I divide into two: 1st, the power which life has of destroying itself, by producing an action it cannot support; 2ndly, by chemical effects. The second method is by an operation; but the first method is not so extensive as the second, for with the knife we can go where the other cannot reach; so that the first can only be employed where the disease is exposed and circumscribed. When lying on a nerve or artery, the deadening method has the recommendation of safety.

The first mode produces too much action, as would appear from the effect of arsenic, which does not act chemically, but produces inflammation, and probably weakness also; so that the diseased parts will be destroyed by it, while the sound parts will remain alive: and this makes it preferable to caustic, which is not only too violent but deadens the sound parts as well as the unsound. Plunkett's medicine is made as follows: crowsfoot, 3 drachms and 2 scruples; dogfennel dried, 1 drachm; crude sulphur, 2 drachms and a half; white arsenic, 5 drachms: beat in a mortar, and form into a powder: one or two drachms of which are to be mixed with the yolk of an egg, and being spread on a piece of bladder to be applied so as to cover the sore*. Arsenic alone would produce too violent an inflammation, and destroy the sound parts by mortification. The second, or chemical mode, is by caustics, by which life is destroyed by the combination of the caustic with the parts it comes in contact with, making but little distinction between those which are sound and those which are unsound; but these cannot be used very extensively, for obvious reasons.

The second mode, or Extirpation.—In considering the propriety of this we must often be more careful than in the above modes; and as the knife may be extended further, so the diseases may be more complicated than in the other modes. We should first consider if the whole disease can be safely extirpated, and if so, the operation is proper. Some cannot be extirpated safely, as when in the extremities; but in such cases the whole limb may be safely removed, which should in doubtful cases

---

* [Any preparation containing so much arsenic must be exceedingly unsafe and dangerous.]

always be done. But sometimes in the breast it is so fixed to the ribs as not to be entirely removeable. Now, to know if a cancer is proper for operation, two things should be considered, viz. the cancer itself, and its consequences. Great attention should be paid to the tumour, whether it is moveable or not; for as the disease is further extended, so the parts are more united to the tumour. If it reaches a part which cannot be removed, as the hips, or parts which cannot wholly be removed by amputation, then nothing can be done; but if the tumour is not only moveable, but the part naturally so, then there is no impropriety in removing it, with regard to the tumour itself; but before removing it, or a limb, we must consider if there are any consequences. We should examine, for example, the glands in the groin or axilla, to ascertain if they are thickened or swoln, and also the course of the absorbents; for if these are sound and moveable, then the disease may be safely removed. But if any are so deep or fixed as not to admit of removal, then we must consider whether the whole limb can be removed, above the consequent tumours; and if not, we ought to do nothing. All the above circumstances being considered, and no objections existing, the breast may be safely removed; and if any consequent cancers easy of extirpation are found, they may be safely removed also. But it requires very great caution to know if any of these consequent tumours are within proper reach, for we are apt to be deceived in regard to the lymphatic glands, which often appear moveable, when, on extirpation, a chain of them is found to run far beyond out of our reach, which renders the operation unsuccessful. As this is not easily known, I would, in most cases, where the lymphatic glands are considerably enlarged, advise that the case should be let alone. We cannot be too nice in our examination, nor often too rough-handed in the operation. In cases where the original and consequent tumours are circumscribed, and sufficiently moveable, the operation has generally been successful, being nothing more than a common wound. But the parts may have acquired the diseased action, and thus render the operation unsuccessful, although that action was invisible. Whenever there are such appearances the parts should be removed as soon as possible: on the contrary, when the disease has not been entirely removed by the knife, from its not having been carried into the sound parts, the operation is unsuccessful; and these are the circumstances which gave the idea of the disease being constitutional: but let us observe what part of the sore does not heal, and what part breaks out again after the operation. This is either in the cicatrix, or in the lymphatic glands. Now, if the whole disease is not removed, the sore either does not heal, or if it does, the cicatrix breaks out again; so likewise, if the surrounding contaminated parts are not removed, although the whole original disease is, then, some months after, there will be a new ulceration there ; and so with regard to the glands also, if any of these are so far diseased as to require extirpation, but too high up for the knife. I have sometimes seen, after the operation, the glands under the clavicle swell, and push out the clavicle on the lower part of the neck; it has also happened, that after removing the glands in the axilla the absorbents between them and the original disease have become contaminated, in which case they should be removed as soon as possible. The contamination extends in other instances on the inside of the sternum, in the course of the internal mammary artery. Sometimes these consequent cancers appear long after the operation, even years, when they should be immediately removed. After the visible disease is removed, we should minutely examine the sore, so as to feel and press every part, and if anything is hard or irregular, remove it. After operating in the axilla, we should introduce the finger into it, in order to discover if any of the other glands are affected ; and before the part is dressed the tumour itself should be inspected, to see if there are any corresponding appearances, so as to lead to the supposition of a part being left; but this can only be done in those from the breast, those only being circumscribed. Having once had the misfortune to leave a part, I let it go on for a few days, when the sore granulated healthily all over, except at that part, which had a blueish appearance, and discharged a dark-coloured matter. I then dissected that bit only, and the patient recovered. If a contaminated part is left, it comes into action in a few months after the operation ; and if two or more are left, they all appear about the same time, and should be removed if they can as soon as possible, before they have contaminated other parts, when, in general, it will succeed, as far as I have seen. If these are not removed, other parts will be contaminated, and kill in the end; but if parts contaminated do not come into action at the same time, after the original is removed, we shall not succeed. It is surprising to see how a young man, if he catches an idea which has any novelty, will write away on it and tell you wonders. Thus, Mr. Fearen has lately recommended healing by the first intention in this disease, which is the last thing to be thought of, as we have here only in view the total removal of the disease, and not the healing of the wounds. But no man should write a book without taking every circumstance of the disease into consideration; he should not write from a single idea, which many circumstances may render futile. I have used this plan in small circumscribed cases in the breast, where there was very much skin, although I have been very liberal of my removal at the same time.

Of the effects of Cancer in the Breast when incurable.—When the glands become indurated the fluids are not absorbed, in consequence of which there is a stagnation and extravasation of serum, causing œdema of the parts around. The arm, and the integuments of the chest below, swell, and the fingers are sometimes rendered immoveable, and very painful. The inflammation about the diseased parts spreads, and causes a tightness around, which occasions dyspnœa, and in this stage sympathetic cancerous tumours often arise at a distance, and hectic fever comes on. We must now give large doses of opium, which yet do not often relieve the pain. I have seen the œdema of the arm before there was any tumefaction of the lymphatic glands; but when œdema occurs, which is not the consequence of absorption, there may nevertheless be afterwards hardness of the glands from this cause : however, the œdema above mentioned puzzled me, having never before seen it without the glands being enlarged, and I have never seen another case.

Of the Cancerous Testicle.—The same observations are here applicable as in the breast, with respect to the propriety or impropriety of an operation. If the cord is thickened the operation is doubtful, the consequence going often further than at first appears. If it has not extended so high as the ring, I would advise extirpation, it being the only resource left. When the testicle has affected the scrotum there may be absorption to the glands of the groin, as in lues ; of this I have seen one case, where, half a year after the operation for the removal of the testicle and scrotum, the glands in the groin ulcerated, and killed the patient. In this case the testicle had become adherent to the scrotum. I cannot say how far it would have been proper to have removed these glands at first, but from the adhesion the scrotum was necessarily removed. I was at first puzzled to account for the appearance of cancer in the groin, as we know the testicle receives its vessels, &c. from the loins, and therefore the glands in the loins become affected by the disease extending along the course of the cord ; but when I recollected that the scrotum was affected, I knew it to be owing to the lymphatics of the scrotum, which pass through the groin. In cancerous diseases the surrounding parts become contaminated, and these again contaminate others ; but in scrofulous suppuration the surrounding parts, although affected, are not scrofulous, because this is not a poisonous disease. Before suppuration breaks out we can form little idea of the state of the part as to its malignancy : but after it breaks out we can, for if healthy it will recover itself, and granulate healthily ; but if the contrary, it will not ; hence, in the suppuration of the testicle, we cannot say whether it is scrofulous or cancerous till it is ulcerated, when the mode of healing informs us of the disease.

Of Cancer of the Lip.—If small, the operation for the hare lip should be preferred, and it is right in this case to have the cure in view as soon as the operation is done, although we should be sure to remove the whole disease. These principles attended to will be sufficient to guide us in the management of cancers in other parts of the body.

Of Fungated Sores.—These are commonly called cancers, and are similar to them in being incurable, although they differ in other respects. The cancer eats, as it were, away parts, though there is still an increase of growth or tumefaction; but in fungated sores there is a spongy fungus which cannot be kept down. It is, in fact, a specific well-marked disease, which appears common to every part, which I believe the cancer is not. I have seen it in the antrum, the tibia, the eye, the testicle, and the rectum. Its beginning, I believe, is in the form of a tumour, both of the encysted and solid kind; for I have seen an encysted tumour opened which threw out this fungus, which is very soft, spongy, and pulpy, of a dirty black colour, very easily torn, and very apt to bleed: the matter does not seem to be poisonous, for the glands and absorbents never appear to be diseased by it. Here [*exhibiting it*] is a preparation to show the disease on the sole of the foot, and here another, of the tunica vaginalis, in which the fungus was very extensive, as was also this fungus on the penis. A woman had a large one on the upper part of the foot, for which I amputated the leg, and in this case the glands in the groin were not affected, and she recovered, which shows there was no poison to contaminate by absorption. A man had a swelled testicle, which was not very painful, and the cord was not affected, which led me to think that it was scrofulous: the scrotum became affected by local sympathy, and adhered to the testicle. I removed the testicle, but not entirely the adhering skin, and after some time a fungus arose from the skin, and his health became impaired by the repeated hæmorrhage. I tried arsenic made into troches with flour, which were stuck into the fungus, but still these did not destroy it sufficiently, and the man afterwards died. If this had been cancerous the progress would have been different, for the skin would have become cancerous from contamination, and the cord would probably have been affected in the same way. On dissection of this fungus from the cicatrix of the old skin the glands above were found sound. This species of fungus is pretty regular in structure; it is striated, and radiated, and its external surface is larger than that of the surface of contact. Nothing is left for it but to remove it, no natural cure being known; but we should be careful to remove the whole of the diseased parts that have the disposition, as they will otherwise soon take on the action. It kills without appearing to have done much mischief, whereas cancer does much local mischief, and so do the consequent ones, before death. The first case of fungated ulcer from accident which I ever saw was one from a blow on the arm, which was afterwards obliged to be amputated.

Cancerous Diseases of the Penis are somewhat similar to the former, consisting of a fungus, which begins on the glans, and increases till the whole becomes an excrescence, which resembles the fungated sore when cut or torn, except that it is much slower in its progress : sometimes it attains a large size, and appears like a cauliflower; and sometimes it is in the form of a tumour, covered with skin, and ulcerated at some parts only. These tumours may, I think, be classed with the true tumours, which consist of a new-formed substance; but I do not think they ever arise from the venereal disease, as has been supposed. Extirpation, in my judgement, is the only surgical resource; and if so, it should be done as early and as effectually as possible.

The Hæmatocele Specifica Testis takes its name from the nature of the contents, which are blood, serum, or often a firm coagulated blood, the extravasation arising from a diseased action, or a peculiar mode of secretion, and not immediately from accident, as is the case with one species, which leads me to call this hæmatocele specifica testis. It is often taken for a cancerous testicle, and removed for such, and the fluid blood is then mistaken for cancerous extravasation, though it is common extravasated blood in the tunica vaginalis; although I will not deny that there may be new cysts occasionally found that may contain blood, as other new cysts do matter. Those which I have seen have felt like an obscure hydrocele, or something between hydrocele and scirrhous testicle. (See *note*, p. 460.) As it is so uncertain what is the true case, I have always advised tapping in the first place. In some there is much serum, and this in the centre of the coagulum, which adheres to the sides of the sac, the whole feeling like a thickened sac ; and often the sac is really much thickened. In some the testicle has been so pressed as to burst, and to fill the cavity of the tunica vaginalis ; but whether this is a specific disease or not, or a cancer similar to that in the breast, I do not know. I rather think it is specific ; but if not specific, the treatment of hydrocele would be proper ; but it must be distinguished from sarcocele, as in that a different treatment is necessary. But we find it will not admit of the same cure as hydrocele. The coagulum adhering to the sac keeps off the stimulus of imperfection, and prevents a cure, so that in many cases it would be perhaps best to dissect out the whole tunica vaginalis. Perhaps in some the blood may become part of the solids, by becoming vascular, as was shown in a preparation. A gentleman in China had, he thought, a swelled testicle, for which he used mercurial ointment. On coming to England, I could not determine the case, but rather thought it a hydrocele. I tapped him ; but no fluid was discharged, although the lancet was pushed in an inch deep. Mr. Pott was called in, who thought it a scirrhous testicle, and the operation was performed. On examining it, a bloody serum was found in it, and the coats of the sac (which was the tunica vaginalis,) were extremely thick, and the testicle was much squeezed by it. I should think it was a mixed case, and might have been cured as hydrocele; but am not certain.

In a case of true hæmatocele there was first an uneasy sensation, and the testicle was painful to the touch afterwards; the swelling increased, and was mistaken by a surgeon for hydrocele; then the hardness increased, and the pain became acute; several punctures were now made, which brought on much inflammation, which required that an opening should be made, in order to examine the parts, which were found to consist of grumous blood and a thickened coat. It was advised that all should be removed, together with some of the skin; but I think not enough, for although the parts healed readily, yet some months afterwards a swelling in the abdomen reappeared, and destroyed him. On dissection, there was found a set of tumours extending to the diaphragm, on the epiploon, together with some others in the liver, respecting which it was a question whether they were scrofulous or cancerous; they went along the loins, in the course of the absorbents, showing them to be cancerous; but the tumours in the epiploon, which is a part not in the course of the absorbents, staggered me in that opinion, and other circumstances puzzled me still further. At present I know not where to class this disease, but I find it has not the powers of recovery when put in the way of it by exposure.

ANALYTICAL TABLE OF CONTENTS

TO THE

SURGICAL LECTURES.

CHAP. XV.—Practical Illustrations of the preceding
Subjects.

CHAP. XX.—Of Specific Diseases, Tumours, Hydatids, and
Tetanus.

CHAP. XXI.—Of Scrofula.

CHAP. XXII.—Of Mortification and Carbuncle.

CHAP. XXIII.—Of Poisons.

ERRATA.

Page   8, 3rd line from bottom, and page 9, 7th line from top, *for* Moraud *lege* Morand
—— 189, 4th line from bottom, *for* 1792 *lege* 1782
—— 201, 2nd line from top, *for* Nathaniel Rumsey *lege* Henry Rumsey
—— 229, 6th line from bottom, *for* Bourdon *lege* Bordeu
—— 243, 5th line from bottom, *for* Journ. des Mag. des Sciences Méd. vol. viii. *lege*
        Journ. des Prog. des Sciences Méd., tom. viii.
—— 353, 5th line from top, *for* Rostau *lege* Rostan
—— 418, 7th line from bottom, *for.* ædematodos *lege* œdematodes

NOTICE.

THE "WORKS OF JOHN HUNTER" will be comprised in Four Volumes 8vo, illustrated by 63 Plates, in a Separate Volume, in quarto. The remaining volumes will appear at intervals of two months, price 17s. 6d. each, accompanied with a Fasciculus of Plates.

For the convenience of Students, the first three volumes, comprising the "SURGICAL WORKS" of the Author, have been constituted a separate work, with separate title-pages, indexes, and preface, price 17s. 6d. each: leaving it to the option of the purchaser to add the fourth volume, containing Mr. Hunter's papers on comparative anatomy, if he shall think proper, afterwards. The plates to this portion of the work will be bound up with the volumes.

Volume II. will be published on April 14th, and will contain the Treatises on the Teeth and Venereal Disease, with Notes by

THOMAS BELL, F.R.S., F.L.S., F.G.S., Lecturer on the Teeth and on Comparative Anatomy, at Guy's Hospital. And

G. G. BABINGTON, Surgeon to St. George's Hospital, and formerly Surgeon to the Lock Hospital.

LONDON:
PRINTED BY RICHARD TAYLOR,
RED LION COURT, FLEET STREET.

CPSIA information can be obtained at www.ICGtesting.com
Printed in the USA
LVOW041859141112

307335LV00010B/4/P

9 781166 118099